China
and Glass
in America
1880–1980

China and Glass in America 1880–1980

From Tabletop to TV Tray

Charles L. Venable

Ellen P. Denker

Katherine C. Grier

Stephen G. Harrison

Photography by Tom Jenkins

Dallas Museum of Art

Distributed by
Harry N. Abrams, Inc., Publishers

China and Glass in America 1880–1980: From Tabletop to TV Tray
was organized by the Dallas Museum of Art.

The exhibition and publication were underwritten by the Tri Delta Charity Antiques Show, an anonymous donor, the Frederick and Mildred Mayer Foundation, Laser Tech Color, Inc., the Bressler Foundation, the Cummings Ceramic Research Foundation, the Robert F. Venable Memorial Fund, and Robert C. Floyd.

Exhibition Itinerary

The Newark Museum
March 15–June 18, 2000

Dallas Museum of Art
July 23, 2000–January 7, 2001

Dallas Museum of Art

Managing Editor: Debra Wittrup

Publications Assistant: Catherine A. Proctor

Marcus Curatorial Intern: Susan Green

Rights and Reproductions: Jeanne Lil Chvosta

Visual Resources Manager: Rita Lasater

Project editor: Patricia Draher

Manuscript editor: Jennifer Harris with assistance by Pamela Zytnicki

Index by Bonny McLaughlin

Designed by John Hubbard

Typeset by Marie Weiler in Quadraat and Rockwell with selected heads in Bellevue

Produced by Marquand Books, Inc., Seattle

 Color separations by Laser Tech Color, Inc.

Case: Cover, *Pottery, Glass and Brass Salesman,* 1930

Frontispiece: *Our America* chop plate, Vernon Kilns, ca. 1937 (detail, cat. 172)

Page 6: *Fiesta* pitcher, Homer Laughlin China Company, 1935 (detail, cat. 28)

Page 10: Punch bowl, Libbey Glass Company, ca. 1905 (detail, cat. 70)

Printed and bound by CS Graphics Pte., Ltd., Singapore

Distributed by Harry N. Abrams, Incorporated, New York

ABRAMS
Harry N. Abrams, Inc.
100 Fifth Avenue
New York, N.Y. 10011
www.abramsbooks.com

Library of Congress Cataloging-in-Publication Data

China and glass in America, 1880–1980 : from tabletop to TV tray / Charles L. Venable . . . [et al.]; photography by Tom Jenkins.
 p. cm.
 Catalog of an exhibition held at the Newark Museum, Mar. 15–June 18, 2000 and the Dallas Museum of Art, July 23, 2000–Jan. 7, 2001.
 Includes bibliographical references and index.
 ISBN 0-8109-6692-1 (alk. paper)
 1. Ceramic tableware—United States—History—19th century—Exhibitions. 2. Ceramic tableware—United States—History—20th century—Exhibitions. 3. Ceramic tableware—Social aspects—United States—History—19th century—Exhibitions. 4. Ceramic tableware—Social aspects—United States—History—20th century—Exhibitions. 5. Glassware—United States—History—19th century—Exhibitions. 6. Glassware—United States—History—20th century—Exhibitions. 7. Glassware—Social aspects—United States—History—19th century—Exhibitions. 8. Glassware—Social aspects—United States—History—20th century—Exhibitions.
I. Venable, Charles L. (Charles Lane), 1960– II. Jenkins, Tom, 1953– III. Dallas Museum of Art. IV. Newark Museum.

NK4695.T33 C58 2000
738'.074'7642812—dc21   99-59422

The paper used in this publication meets the minimum requirements of the American National Standard for Information Sciences—Permanence of Paper for Printed Library Materials, ANSI Z39.48-1984.

Contents

Director's Foreword   7

Lenders and Donors   9

Acknowledgments   11

Preface   13

Chapter 1
**Dishes and More Dishes:
Tableware in the Home**   17

Chapter 2
**Getting a Piece of the Pie:
American Tableware Makers**   103

Chapter 3
**Foreigners at Our Table:
Imported China and Glass**   185

Chapter 4
**From Warehouse to Your House:
Tableware Marketing**   285

Chapter 5
Design, Industry, and the Consumer   325

Afterword   417

Catalogue Documentation   420

References   471

Figure Credits   480

Index   483

Director's Foreword

China and Glass in America, 1880–1980: From Tabletop to TV Tray presents a comprehensive look at a century of changes in American design, culture, and industry as seen through the medium of tableware. The exhibition and book bridge the gap between scholarly and popular interest in the decorative arts by juxtaposing the critically acclaimed avant-garde objects desired by museums and collectors of modernist design with more artistically conservative but commercially successful wares loved by many consumers. By approaching the subject as a study in material culture in which design, production, marketing, and consumption are all examined, *China and Glass in America* explores the revealing forms of the objects in the context of the daily lives and traditions central to the heritage of a great many Americans. In so doing, it offers a unique and accessible look at continuity and change in American culture over the span of one hundred years of tableware production and use.

This project was thoughtfully conceived and laudably realized by Dr. Charles L. Venable, curator of decorative arts at the Dallas Museum of Art as well as the museum's chief curator and deputy director. It follows in the tradition of his acclaimed *Silver in America, 1840–1940: A Century of Splendor*, mounted by the museum in 1994. In this new effort, he was excellently seconded by Stephen G. Harrison, assistant curator of decorative arts. We thank them both for this accomplishment and appreciate the remarkable enrichment of the museum's collection of china and glass of the period, a happy dividend of their research. Amassing such a holding was made possible only by the generosity of donors across the country. Especially important has been the commitment of Elizabeth and Duncan Boeckman and Jessie and Charles Price, Dallas patrons of the decorative arts who contributed significantly to the museum's 20th-Century Design Fund, the source for many acquisitions.

For their contributions to the publication we thank our colleagues Ellen Paul Denker and Dr. Katherine C. Grier, who joined Venable and Harrison in this scholarly enterprise. Unlike most multiauthor publications, this volume does not consist of separate related essays; rather, the scholarly team worked in concert to produce a unified text written in a single voice. Venable served as project director and general editor. He also authored all of chapter 4 and the majority of chapters 3 and 5 as well as the preface and afterword. Grier wrote chapter 1, with the exception of Harrison's vignette, or extended sidebar, on specialty wares. Denker was responsible for chapter 2, while Venable authored the vignette on plastics in that chapter. Harrison contributed the section in chapter 3 on English exports to the United States and the two accompanying vignettes, and he authored the concluding section of chapter 5. The great majority of the object entries in the catalogue documentation were written by Venable and Harrison, with Denker contributing entries on several early items and all of those made by Lenox China.

Members of the Dallas Museum of Art's staff who have made special contributions to this undertaking include photographer Tom Jenkins; Susan Green, Marcus curatorial intern; Debra Wittrup, head of exhibitions and managing editor;

Catherine Proctor, collections and exhibitions assistant; Gabriela Truly, head registrar; Jeanne Chvosta, associate registrar, rights and reproductions and collection records; Angela Leonard, associate registrar for exhibitions; Douglas Hawes, former assistant curator of decorative arts; and the museum's education and library staff.

Margaret Kaplan at Harry N. Abrams believed in the project from concept to fruition, and editor Patricia Draher very ably dealt with the challenge of a manuscript written by four distinctly different individuals. The staff of Marquand Books—notably Ed Marquand, designer John Hubbard, Marta Vinnedge, and Marie Weiler—produced the lavish volume that accompanies the exhibition.

One of the nation's distinguished collections of American fine and decorative arts is possessed by the Newark Museum, and we are extremely pleased that *China and Glass in America* will be seen first in those highly appropriate surroundings. Mary Sue Sweeney Price, director, and Ulysses Grant Dietz, curator of decorative arts, have been very good friends of this project, and we offer them especially warm expressions of appreciation, both for sharing in the presentation of the exhibition with the Dallas Museum of Art and for lending important objects to it.

We are beholden to all the lenders who have generously made their works available to the exhibition. The Dallas Museum of Art is deeply grateful to the sizable number of collectors who donated works from their collections to the museum's permanent holdings as a result of their enthusiasm for this groundbreaking project. With our thanks, individual acknowledgments appear in the list of lenders and donors.

In addition we extend heartfelt gratitude to the project's numerous benefactors, which include the Tri Delta Charity Antiques Show, an anonymous donor, the Frederick and Mildred Mayer Foundation, Laser Tech Color, Inc., the Bressler Foundation, and the Cummings Ceramic Research Foundation.

John R. Lane
The Eugene McDermott Director
Dallas Museum of Art

Lenders and Donors

Lenders

Mr. and Mrs. Duncan E. Boeckman
Dallas Museum of Art
Dr. and Mrs. L. M. Harrison, Jr.
Brian and Edith Heath
Heidi B. Hollomon
Andrew Krauss and Ted McDermott
William Swann and William Leazer Collection
Lenox Archives
The Newark Museum

Mr. and Mrs. William Pasley
Charles A. Robinson
Drs. Martin and Judith Schwartz
Carole Stupell, Ltd.
William Swann and William Leazer
Alice G. Venable
Sara Margaret White
Anonymous lenders

Donors

Rozwell Sam Adams
Betty Bell
Greg and Teresa Benkert
Arthur and Marie Berger by exchange
Mr. and Mrs. Duncan E. Boeckman
Mrs. Alfred L. Bromberg
Faith P. Bybee
Marie and John Houser Chiles
Dallas Antiques and Fine Arts Society
Dallas Glass Club
Dallas Symposium
Kenn Darity and Ed Murchison
Bert and Ellen Paul Denker
Estate of Freda Diamond
Eason Eige
W. C. and Sally Estes
The Arthur A. Everts Company by exchange
Robert C. Floyd
Friends of the Decorative Arts
Gerald Gulotta
Mr. and Mrs. Jeremy L. Halbreich
Stephen G. Harrison
Hattie Higginbotham Hartman
Mrs. G. W. Hayes
Edith Kiertener Heath
Heidi B. Hollomon
Ronald S. Kane
Belle Kogan
Laguna
Glenn Lane

Mrs. Wallis H. Lee
Stanley Marcus
Charles R. Masling and John E. Furen
Noritake Company, Inc.
Margaret E. (Peg) O'Neill
Alvin and Lucy Owsley Foundation
David T. Owsley
Michael E. Pratt
Eugenia Reedy
Wendy Reves
Mrs. Russell Remhert
Mr. and Mrs. John Rogers
George Roland
Michael L. Rosenberg
Mr. and Mrs. William Rubin
Mr. and Mrs. Viktor Schreckengost
Carole Stupell, Ltd.
William Swann and William Leazer
Estate of Kathleen Bass Tewes
Margaret H. Tremblay
Mrs. Estelle Underwood
Mrs. L. A. Vaughn, Jr.
Dr. Charles L. Venable
Mr. and Mrs. Robert F. Venable
Dr. Sylvia M. Venable
Mr. and Mrs. Nelson Waggener
Waterford Crystal, Inc.
Barbara Boyd and Hensleigh C. Wedgwood
Gary D. Wooley and R. Gene Lewis
Anonymous donors

Acknowledgments

Projects as complicated as *China and Glass in America, 1880–1980: From Tabletop to TV Tray* cannot be accomplished without the encouragement of numerous individuals. During the past five years scores of people have assisted with various aspects of this book and exhibition. I am most grateful for their help, and thank them on behalf of the Dallas Museum of Art as well.

From this large group certain institutions and individuals have been exceptionally supportive, sharing their time and information freely. The staffs at the National Heisey Museum in Newark, Ohio; the Museum of Ceramics in East Liverpool, Ohio; and the Corning Museum of Glass in Corning, New York, deserve special mention in this regard. So too do individuals at several other museums, archives, and companies. In Staffordshire, England, we thank Kathy Niblett and Miranda Goodby at the Potteries Museum; Sir Arthur Bryan, Gaye Blake Roberts, and Sharon Gater at the Wedgwood Museum and Archives; Paul Wood, Robert Copeland, and Stella McIntyre at Royal Worcester-Spode; and Joan Jones and Alexander Clement at Minton/Royal Doulton. At Waterford Crystal in Ireland Jim O'Leary, Terry Murphy, and John Connolly were particularly helpful. Those who provided invaluable assistance in the United States include Neville Thompson at the H. F. du Pont Winterthur Library, Stephen Short of Fondron Library at Southern Methodist University, Rodris Roth at the Smithsonian Institution, Anne Madarasz and Ellen Rosenthal at the Historical Society of Western Pennsylvania, Louise Polan at the Huntington Museum of Art, Cleota Reed at Syracuse China, John G. Sayle at Hall China, Charles Gifford and Osamu Tsutsui at Noritake, and the staff of Lenox Brands. Maj. Gen. Jeffery D. Kahla (Ret.) and Fred Blum of the headquarters of the Army and Air Force Exchange Services were keen to answer our questions.

In the wholesale and retail world we are indebted to Robert C. Block, Robert C. Floyd, Joseph Giarrocco, Roger S. Horchow, Stanley Marcus, Keith Stupell, George E. Thompson, and Barbara Boyd Wedgwood. Designers who graciously permitted us to interview them include Winslow Anderson, Freda Diamond, Gerald Gulotta, Miroslav Havel, Edith Heath, Dale Hodges, Harold Holdway, Belle Kogan, Eve Midwinter, Jack Prince, David Queensberry, Donald Schreckengost, Viktor Schreckengost, and Eva Zeisel.

Of the many collectors, dealers, and researchers consulted, the following went beyond the call of duty to share information: Bernard A. Banet, Regina Blaszczyk, Harry Bradley, Biff Brigman, Jo Cunningham, Eason Eige, Neil Ewins, Cheryl Goyda, Michael Kaplan, Michael Lindsey, Bob Page, Michael E. Pratt, Jaime Robinson, and Judith Schwartz. Also the staff of Laser Tech Color, Inc., was most generous; Kimberlee C. Davis and Russell Scott Brazell were especially helpful to this effort.

At the Dallas Museum of Art this project was fortunate to be supported by many talented people. A core group of staff contributed enormous time and energy to this project: Jeanne Chvosta, Tom Jenkins, Angela Leonard, Catherine Proctor, Gabriela Truly, Debra Wittrup, and former staff member Douglas Hawes. Marcus curatorial intern Susan Green deserves special mention in recognition of the excellent job she did on this project while at the museum. Numerous other colleagues also helped this effort succeed, including Jacqui Allen, Carolyn Bess, Lawrence Bruton, Giselle Castro-Brightenburg, Alex Contreras, Randy Daugherty, Natalie Davis, Gail Davitt, Shelly Foster, Carol Griffin, Bob Guill, Carl Hardin, Cheryl Hartup, Kay Johnson, Vince Jones, Jim Landman, Rita Lasater, Mary Leonard, Martha Lopez, Rick McWilliams, Ron Moody, Melissa Nelson, Kevin Parmer, Dan Reaka, Chad Redmon, Barbara Scott, Russell Sublette, Doug Velek, Kathy Walsh-Piper, Jeff Williams, Gary Wooley, and Cathy Zisk. In addition former director Jay Gates and the museum's new director, John R. Lane, must be thanked for the support they have shown this endeavor.

Several personal thank-yous from the coauthors are also in order. Katherine C. Grier is indebted to research assistant Lu Ann Snyder and to her mother, Anna Foster Grier, for the valuable insights she provided in her interview. Stephen G. Harrison thanks his parents for their support, and is especially grateful to his mother, Glenda Lee Harrison, for sharing her many stories about dishes and dining in the south. Ellen Paul Denker appreciates the encouragement of her husband, Bert Denker. I owe thanks to Sylvia M. Venable for the many hours she spent transcribing hours of recorded interviews, as well as to my daughter, Alexandra, and Martin Webb for being supportive and patient while I sat before my computer screen, caught up in a world of dishes.

Finally, I want my coauthors to know how much I appreciate their efforts. Without the hard work and keen insights of Kasey Grier, Ellen Denker, and Stephen Harrison my efforts to chronicle this history of American tableware would have been for naught. The dual goal we established at our first meeting was to produce a scholarly book that would interest the general public and manage to remain friends in the process. I know we have accomplished the latter and hope we have done the former.

Charles L. Venable
Deputy Director and Chief Curator
Dallas Museum of Art

For thousands of years artisans have shaped wet clay and molten glass into vessels. From crude, low-fired pots and cast glass to extraordinarily thin-walled porcelains and brilliantly blown crystal, humans have transformed these materials into objects of infinite variety and quality. Produced the world over in enormous quantities, ceramic and glass cups, bowls, plates, pots, jugs, and jars are omnipresent in our society and play important roles in numerous public and private rituals. As in ancient cultures, tableware physically surrounds our food, the sustenance of life. Used daily by millions to store, prepare, and serve food, clay and glass utensils are so highly valued that they are hoarded in great quantities.

But despite the central role of tableware in numerous cultures over centuries, most art museums do not seriously collect *dishes*. Plates and teapots certainly do grace many galleries in this country and abroad, but most are examples that have been made worthy by the patina of time or rarity. In the applied art world older is definitely better; rare is more desirable than plentiful; handmade surpasses industrially produced; and decorative is more worthy than utilitarian. If given a choice, private collectors and museum curators usually will choose vases and figures over soup bowls and gravy boats.

The factors of age, rarity, means of production, and function have worked against the collection and study of modern tablewares. Because age is so highly valued, material made over the last one hundred years is often dismissed as uninteresting. The situation is further complicated by the fact that the making of plates, bowls, and glasses typically dominated the production of most commercial potteries and glasshouses. Therefore, tableware survives in large quantities and thus often cannot claim the distinction of being rare. In contrast, vases, except in the case of specialized factories, were generally produced as a sideline, as "artware." As a result, such pieces are inherently rarer than the millions of plates and glasses that poured from factories both at home and abroad. Furthermore, factory production is not easily romanticized, unlike the operations of a small-scale shop.

Since the turn of the century, when the apostles of the Arts and Crafts movement railed against the evils of factory production as devaluing the role of the artisan, decorative art collectors and in some cases consumers have placed a premium on objects made by hand. While some hand labor is still employed in many potteries and glass factories, the industrial goal is to produce as much product of the highest quality possible at the lowest price. Thus the designer of dishes cannot be an artist in the true sense of the word. Unlike the studio potter or glassblower, an industrial designer is constrained by the limitations of manufacturing processes and the marketplace. For some, these realities render industrially produced tableware unworthy of collecting and studying.

The perceived superiority of modernism in twentieth-century design history has also been detrimental to the study of most tableware. The legacy of the Bauhaus and New York's Museum of Modern Art has dominated scholarly discourse in the field of design and the applied arts since the 1940s. These institutions, and the academic and museum prophets that disseminate their precepts, have at the close of the twentieth century deemed irrelevant any taste that did not seek to be avant-garde. Trivialized were designs that sought to evoke warmth and comfort as opposed to the coldly functional. Shapes and patterns that incorporated references to an idealized past were devalued in favor of ones that boldly embraced the future. Perhaps more than anything else, it is the almost complete adoption of the modernist canon by scholars and museum curators that has so compromised both public and private collections of twentieth-century design. In almost every case the proponents of simple, functional forms attract the attention of the art and academic establishments.

In the United States, for example, brilliant modernist designers like Russel Wright and Eva Zeisel gain the spotlight, and have been honored with monographic exhibitions of their work. However, as this volume demonstrates, the classic modernist vision was not the only one at work during the past century. In fact, it can be argued that in the domestic sphere modernism was not the dominant force. Even today it is the rare consumer who adopts a modernist aesthetic at home. Highly successful in the workplace, where chrome, glass, and steel somehow seemed appropriate, modernism was and still is dwarfed by conservatism in the private sphere. At home, revival styles still hold sway along with an ever increasing desire for comfort that results in overupholstered furniture and wall-to-wall carpeting. On the table, plates and glasses of articulated shape and colorful pattern typically triumph over pristine white.

The scholarly result of all these factors is the general neglect of industrially produced tablewares. Certainly some fine work has been done on the ceramics and glass industries. But unfortunately most studies are disseminated through academic channels and thus are not widely read by the public. In the case of art museum publications directed toward wider audiences, projects have tended to focus on the work of a small group of avant-garde modernists, a few select companies, and older objects. Numerous books exist on eighteenth- and nineteenth-century china and glass, Arts and Crafts pottery, the studio movement of the mid-twentieth century, and contemporary crafts.

The one genre of publication that has explored the complicated world of tableware during the century between 1880 and 1980 has been the so-called collector's book. During the past twenty years, this type of book has become plentiful in the marketplace and garnered a huge following among the general public. Typically eschewed by scholars and curators, these publications are oriented toward purchasing tablewares rather than pursuing serious scholarly research. The authors are most concerned with telling collectors what patterns were made by a specific company, which patterns and objects are the rarest, and what they are worth on the market. In recent years, however, some authors have attempted to move beyond the fine points of collecting to take a more intellectual approach, chronicling specific factories with respect to their designers and products in worthwhile ways.

This study builds on the work of numerous individuals with many perspectives. Because I felt what was lacking with respect to tableware was an in-depth overview, I found two works particularly inspiring. The first is *From Kiln to Kitchen: American Design in Tableware* (1980), by Susan E. Pickle; the second is *Ceramics: Twentieth Century Design* (1986), by Frances Hannah. Both of these brief texts succeeded at organizing a large quantity of useful information into highly readable prose.

As will be apparent from the pages that follow, this book and the exhibition that it accompanies are almost entirely based on the collection of the Dallas

Museum of Art. Beyond resolving simply to build a significant collection of tableware in the mid-1990s, we further decided to create a collection with a particular focus. Since the museum already had good holdings in American decorative arts, especially nineteenth- and twentieth-century silver, acquisition efforts concentrated on wares that were sold in this country. America was the world's foremost market for domestic tableware during the twentieth century; thus, focusing on the United States as an international marketplace allows one to put American-made objects in a world context. To that end, Dallas's collection includes not only work by many seminal designers and a host of anonymous ones but also objects made in many of the great ceramics and glass centers of Europe, Asia, and the United States. Furthermore, it contains examples of virtually all major forms, shapes, and styles of decoration. However, the collection and this book primarily chronicle objects made for home use. While tablewares made for hotels, restaurants, railways, and other institutional entities can often be beautiful and fascinating, their story is an allied, but different one.

We have tried to apply the highest artistic and technical standards expected of an art museum while attempting to represent a wide range of goods produced for private consumers of various economic levels and different strata of society. In researching what the museum has acquired and those items generously loaned from private and public collections, the scholars assembled to complete this project diligently sought to contextualize the objects so that readers and viewers may gain insight into the extremely complex and fascinating realm of the American domestic tabletop. *China and Glass in America, 1880–1980: From Tabletop to TV Tray* is the culmination of these efforts.

Charles L. Venable

Note to the Reader

For specific designs, the names of shapes, patterns, glazes, and body types are italicized. Names of lines in roman typeface designate broad categories of products that encompass multiple shapes. The names of many firms changed over time; the current form at the particular time discussed is used. Catalogue objects are identified from left to right unless otherwise indicated. Complete entries for the object photographs appear in the catalogue documentation section.

Dishes and More Dishes: Tableware in the Home

*I hope you will always remember that you do not just replace things,
you replace memories, faces and times long past but not forgotten.*

—MERRY K. ANDERSON, thanking Replacements,
Ltd., for locating her grandmother's china pattern,
August 3, 1991

A walk through any antique mall or flea market will reveal a striking number and variety of dishes offered for sale. Battered cardboard boxes and old dish drainers pressed into service as display racks contain the remnants of well-used sets of everyday dishes—chipped *Fiesta*, variations on the *Willow* pattern, or abstracted floral or folk-art designs. Sometimes a tabletop will be stacked with an almost complete set of fragile-looking bone china, the pieces ornamented with flower sprigs or undulating borders with gold rims. These were somebody's "good china," temporarily homeless because a household is broken up or an estate settled. But so many pieces survive—almost a set for twelve! No one buys a set that big these days. Glassware is less abundant, which is not surprising given how appallingly easy it is to break glass of all kinds. But here the odds and ends of sets range from very expensive delicate "crystal" goblets to rectilinear art deco "refrigerator sets." What did people *do* with all those dishes?

Many Americans have had a lifelong love affair with tablewares. All the authors of this book plead guilty to this minor vice. In their homes cupboards bulge with treasures purchased from junk stores, outlet mall dish stores, gourmet-cooking shops, department stores, antique stores, and even crafts fairs. Some vessels are souvenirs of travel, while other pieces were wedding, birthday, and Christmas gifts. Not only are the authors confirmed "dishaholics," but they are also the recipients of legacies of family dishes. In the case of Ellen Paul Denker (b. 1947) that legacy is actually a memory. Denker and her sisters as adults have had to buy replacement sets of Universal Potteries' *Ballerina* in gray to satisfy their collective yearning for the dishes of their childhood in Saint Louis (cat. 1). The original set was considered the best in the house for many years after their parents' marriage in 1947. But the decision to use the dishes every day was ultimately disastrous for their survival.

The other three coauthors will receive ceramics of various ages and types that their mothers have been "curating" for decades. For Katherine "Kasey" Grier (b. 1953) there is a large set of rose-sprigged Bavarian china edged in gold that was the "good" china of her Pennsylvania-German great-great-aunt, Alice Hassinger, who died in the 1930s. What will come to Charles Venable (b. 1960) is a large set of Franciscan Ware in the *Woodside* pattern. His grandmother Nannie Lane, known to her grandchildren as "Nana," bought the first pieces herself, but the set was mostly assembled in the mid-1940s by her family. Venable's mother, Alice, and his aunt Charline saved their allowance so that they could purchase pieces and give them to their mother as birthday, Mother's Day, and Christmas gifts.

Finally, Stephen Harrison (b. 1965) along with his two brothers will receive from his mother, Glenda, all that remains of a set of green and white Limoges porcelain (cat. 2). The original set was acquired by Harrison's great-grandmother Mary Anna Fly on the occasion of her marriage in 1891. Mary Anna and her husband, Anthony Fly, lived in the tiny Mississippi town of Summitt, south of Natchez, so it is likely that the porcelain was purchased either in Natchez or New Orleans, where Anthony Fly, a pharmacist, would have gone regularly on business.

Most people do not serve many dinners for company that would require the use of such sets of china, but they would not part with them, either, for those dishes are remembered from family celebrations and holidays long past. Such "good" things did not come out as often by the 1960s because they could not be put in the new dishwasher, and they were too nice to use for meals in the kitchen, where most families ate. There are stories that go with china and glass: "Those belonged to Aunt Alice Hassinger, who married Milton Hassinger from the Hassinger Lumber Company. She was a famous hostess, always had such nice things and set such a pretty table. . . ." Perhaps a hostess the likes of Aunt Alice Hassinger will never be seen again, but when her great-great-niece sets the Christmas dinner table with those pink-and-white dishes and breaks out her own holiday recipes—a first course of stuffed mushrooms, turkey with artichoke-heart stuffing, garlic mashed potatoes, green beans with almonds, and two kinds of pie for dessert—she will be doing what women in her family have done for decades, taking time for a ceremonious meal and marking it as exceptional through the use of special objects like dishes.

This chapter looks at the tablewares made and used in the United States between 1880 and 1980 from the perspective of social life at home. It explores what American women (for in the past, dishes, especially the good china, almost always "belonged" to women) did with all those dishes. The story begins with the moment they brought their selections home from general stores, china and glass shops, department stores, and five-and-dimes; or they received a barrel of dishes from a mail-order company at the railroad station or, once free rural delivery began in 1913, at their own doorstep; or they opened the boxes containing wedding gifts that symbolized their new,

Cat. 1 Curvaceous solid color tablewares were in vogue around 1950. The gray coffeepot is an example of *Ballerina*.

Cat. 2 Frilly Limoges porcelain was popular at the turn of the century.

independent households and their ability to entertain their social peers with a more formal hospitality. Changes in the dining utensils with which American women set their tables, the aesthetics of the settings they created for serving and eating the meals prepared in their kitchens, the changing occasions for sharing food, the locations where eating took place, and the contents of all those serving bowls and platters can tell us much about broader changes in everyday life between 1880 and 1980. They also demonstrate some surprising continuities.

Because this is a short overview of a complex subject, it is not possible to do justice to regional differences in either food or social life. However, perhaps the most significant thread in the story of changing American patterns of entertaining at home in those hundred years is the appearance and wide adoption of a national set of middle-class meal preparation and service conventions, including, in the early twentieth century, widespread use of nationally marketed processed foods that became the basis of a distinctive, if not always lovely, middle-class cuisine. While reading this chapter and those

that follow, readers should compare their own experiences, and those known from family stories and traditions, to the ones outlined here. Similarities and differences will of course exist, and the individual characteristics of each reader's own history of dining at home will offer nuance to this broader account.

Abundance and Display

In 1880 middle-class Americans were enjoying the full flowering of the culture that we call Victorianism in America. Victorian culture was preoccupied with civilized progress and found in the leisurely domestic rituals of dining comfortable reassurance that social life was advancing in step with technology, science, and the arts.[1] Dining was also a useful tool for social gatekeeping. Some acquaintances merited only a cup of tea and piece of cake, while intimates might be admitted to a Sunday evening family supper. But the most elaborate, portentous, and rare social occasion was the formal dinner party. By the 1880s the middle-class hostess expected to possess the equipage of such a meal even if it was used only once or twice

a year. Etiquette books, one of the most popular genres of advice books in the nineteenth century, always devoted space to negotiating a formal meal's potential traps.

One should not forget the food that was the core of all those social rituals, either. In the 1880s cooking involved considerable labor in processing raw materials—an uncut quarter of beef, a bushel of potatoes still covered with dirt, a peck of unshelled peas—into finished dishes. Except in the wealthiest households, even the few women who could afford full-time household help were involved in kitchen work. Although big city markets were beginning to feature out-of-season foods thanks to the railroads, the relative expense of many foodstuffs compared to today's prices, along with seasonal scarcity of fresh vegetables and even such basic commodities as eggs and milk, sometimes made setting a social table a challenge. Even with these very real limitations, cooking was one way that middle-class housewives could express their creativity as well as their care for their families. (When someone asks where the work of many nineteenth-century women artists is, remember to reply that a lot of it was eaten!) Women's considerable cooking skills were at the heart of most social life, from candy pulls to church socials to formal dinner parties.

Following feasting traditions hundreds of years old, food for special occasions in Victorian America was marked by several characteristics. First, it had to be abundant to the point of waste. This was especially important for items that had been historically rare and expensive, even if they were less so at the time. Good examples are fresh meats, "rich" cooking loaded with butter and cream, desserts made with commodities such as white flour, cane sugar, and even tea, one of the first foods to merit the creation of a distinctively middle-class social ritual in the eighteenth century.[2] Second, at least part of the menu presented socially had to display the art (in the original sense of "artifice") of the cook. Artifice could be displayed through such techniques as molding foods into complicated shapes. Baked goods in which the original components were utterly changed as if by magic, and garnishes in which plain dishes were transformed through decoration with other edibles, also displayed artifice well. Finally, the meal had to be distinguished by its presentation prior to eating. Presentation involved designated spaces such as a dining room; particular table settings with fancy linens and other decorations; vessels that enhanced the look of the food such as a large platter, a soup tureen, or even a picnic basket; and special utensils for consumption such as an orange spoon or demitasse cup.

These three principles of feasting—abundance, artifice, and special presentation—held throughout the century. Their relative importance in social dining varied over time and by occasion. The ladies' luncheon of the early twentieth century, for example, stressed artifice and presentation over abundance. It must be remembered, however, that all three principles were always in dialogue with one another in social meals, from the formal dinners of the 1880s to 1950s cookouts. If readers analyze their own social consumption of food, including time spent in restaurants, they will find that the dialogue continues.

The tools used for social dining changed dramatically over time, reflecting both changes in social life and the development of a tableware "fashion system." The manufacturers and marketers of china and glass wanted to sell more goods; the authors and publishers of books on entertaining sought to sell more copies; and the editors of tastemaking magazines pursued greater circulation and advertising revenues. They made table setting a distinctive fashion system of its own. Between 1880 and 1980, these three tastemaking enterprises supported continuous innovation and novelty. And consumers found tableware novelties desirable because they suggested that their owners had special social skill and knowledge. Objects helped set the tone of new kinds of entertaining. Think of the chip-and-dip sets stored in boxes in the garage or attic; think of the characteristic occasions for using those sets— cocktail parties, cookouts, and buffets. These events would have been unrecognizable to a Victorian hostess.

Underlying the meaning of all forms of feasting is the reality of its ephemeral nature. Much labor—historically, largely women's labor—was expended on table settings and on time-consuming dishes that were destroyed the minute guests unfolded their napkins, leaving behind only an unpleasant gooey residue on the dishes and containers filled with shapeless leftovers. The meal left behind memories as well. The transitory nature of the experience makes elaborate dining all the more culturally valuable because it almost immediately becomes gossip or, in rare occasions of particular excellence or awfulness, myth.

By the 1920s several decades of professional intervention by home economists and the rise of the American processed-food industry changed what many, perhaps most, Americans ate routinely—and also changed the way women cooked. Women who could afford a housekeeper often could not find one to hire, and even those who had always done their own work experienced changing personal priorities and new boundaries in their roles as housekeeper, wife, and mother. Influenced by national advertising in women's magazines and home economics course work in American high schools and universities, housewives offered their families novel kinds of dishes, reflecting a new preoccupation with both convenience and revolutionary ideas about nutrition, including the discovery of vitamins in the 1920s. This modern cuisine relied on canned and boxed foods; transformation and artifice in cooking now often consisted of creating a surprising melange of these prepared foodstuffs in concert with more traditional raw materials. While regional differences in cooking did not disappear by any means, middle-class people in particular participated in the development of a new national, commercialized cuisine based on nationally distributed brand-name foodstuffs.

The ways entertaining was conducted at home changed as well. Women's continuing (even perhaps increasing) importance as the principal hostesses for each other over the first half of the twentieth century is apparent in the increasing variety of new hospitable occasions directed toward other women and toward children in the first decades of the twentieth century. Margaret Visser points out, "We eat whenever life becomes dramatic: at weddings, funerals, at parting and welcoming home, or at any moment which a group decides is worthy of remark."[3] True, but what does it mean when old kinds of social eating decline or change dramatically, and when we make new kinds of dramas? Here one must look at changes outside the household to explain the broad shift from Victorian formalism to consciously "casual" dining and entertaining in ordinary households in the 1920s and 1930s, including competition from a new world of commercialized leisure in the early twentieth century.

The decades after World War II consolidated these changes in food and social life. They added some unexpected twists, including the increasing importance of restaurant dining for American families and further challenges to established eating patterns brought by new household appliances. From the 1950s on, the television, a new "hearth" in American living rooms, promoted snacking and dining in front of it on individual "TV trays" as an alternative approach to family meals. The microwave oven, which arrived in the 1970s, made it possible for even children to feed themselves thanks to the appearance of a wide array of packaged food intended specifically for microwave-oven use.

Such forces inspired worries about the fate of the family dinner. (In fact, people had expressed concern about it periodically over the entire century in question.) The defenders of family togetherness at mealtimes recognized that sharing the same fare at the same table represented a symbol of collective identity, even if family dinners were sometimes fraught with stresses that challenged the ideal. Just as everyday food became "convenient" to the point of being a satire of itself, the late 1960s and 1970s saw a revival of interest in complicated, skilled cooking at home: a new national appreciation was born for the regional dishes that had been largely ignored by

both the scientific cooks and the proponents of what was called fine dining. In addition, middle-class men began to cook for company, venturing beyond the slabs of meat they had scorched standing over 1950s barbecues. While in 1980 women were still primarily responsible for family meals, men played a larger role in preparing food for social occasions.

Theatrical Social Life, 1880–1920

One fact about which scholars of the Victorian era are in universal agreement is that by the 1880s increasing numbers of Americans were unabashedly materialistic and expanded their consumption of goods to communicate their identities as refined, respectable folk. While many Americans were still too poor or too far away from cities with big shopping districts to actively participate in this new world of goods, probably half of the American population could afford at least some of the middle-class "decencies" and "luxuries" that brought new types of comfort and pleasure to their daily lives.

In 1890 families with an annual income above $800 (a sum that could support a comfortable lifestyle in small-town America) had a more limited range of consumer choices than a comparable family today. They could not buy cars or home computers and other electronics; instead, families with extra money to spend, even relatively small amounts, often directed their hard-won dollars toward careful selections of household furnishings. Some of the most important expenditures—the subject of considerable debate in the burgeoning advice literature directed to middle-class consumers—were objects that represented the social identity of the family to household visitors. These typically included the furnishings of the front hall (where first impressions would be formed), the parlor, and the dining room.[4] A householder demonstrated gentility by displaying good taste in the selection and arrangement of furnishings for the home's social rooms, and by showing personal cultivation through graceful use of possessions as props for entertaining.

GENTILITY AND THE HOME

Gentility was a set of ideals for personal excellence that had been in place among Anglo-American elites since the eighteenth century.[5] Throughout the nineteenth century, this ideal trait constituted a social standard that respectable people emulated. Its standards for personal conduct and self-presentation were subject to periodic debate. (Was, for example, gentility compatible with republican politics? Or was it an expression of old aristocratic tendencies?) Even so, the ideal dominated proper social life well into the twentieth century.[6] Ordinary folks seemed to enjoy creating and participating in ceremonial, even theatrical, social gatherings more than they seem to at the end of the twentieth century. Dining provides an excellent case study of the ways this preference for domestic ceremony shaped the material culture of Victorian America. A proliferating array of tablewares, as discussed below, was necessary not only for the theatrical ceremony of the formal dinner party, but for the small daily rituals of family meals in the late nineteenth century.

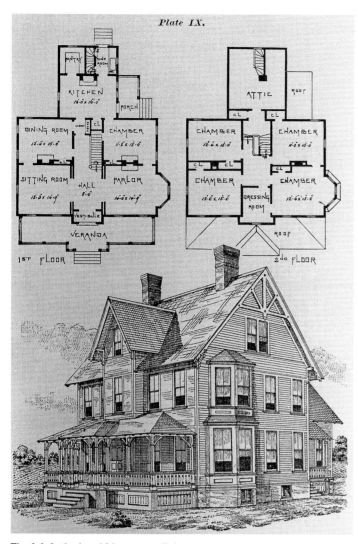

Plate IX.

1ST FLOOR   2ND FLOOR

Fig. 1.1 In the late 19th century dining rooms were quite large (upper left plan).

This ceremonial activity needed a special space, of course. According to Clifford E. Clark Jr., in the second half of the nineteenth century, "Ownership of a house with a separate dining room had become one of the prime symbols of the achievement of middle-class status." Dining rooms, called dining parlors, had sometimes appeared in elite houses in colonial America, but it took a century for the room to become common among the middle class. By the 1870s plan books employed a "generally accepted set of conventions" for placement and decor of dining rooms (fig. 1.1).[7] For many, however, dining rooms doubled as family sitting rooms, while the parlor was preserved for more ceremonial occasions. Dining rooms thus contained a miscellany of furnishings, including the expected table and chairs and some kind of china cabinet or sideboard, but also other seating—a lounge or small sofa, a rocking chair or two. Having the space to set aside a room exclusively for dining could represent a real triumph. In her memoir *Home Grown*, author Della Thompson Lutes recalled that when her family moved from a farm to the town of Jackson, Michigan, their more modern house had a parlor, a sitting room, and a separate dining room. The latter especially pleased her mother, "whose latent social instincts had of necessity been kept in check" by the smaller, older farmhouse.[8]

By the second half of the nineteenth century the decor of American dining rooms had developed certain distinctive qualities that further distinguished it from the furnishings of the other social spaces in houses.[9] Women had come to have principal responsibility for interior decorating decisions, and they seem generally to have followed a set of conventions that interpreted some rooms as feminine and others as masculine. Parlors were feminine spaces with curvaceous French-style furniture, lace curtains, paintings or prints of uplifting subjects, étagères containing bric-a-brac, and representations of female accomplishments, from needlework cushions to a piano or parlor organ stocked with sheet music for amateurs. Through most of the nineteenth century dining rooms were often one of two consciously "manly" spaces in middle-class houses, the other being a library when space permitted.

Dining rooms needed tables and chairs, of course. The ideal was an expansion table, with leaves that could be added to accommodate a crowd. The expansion type first appeared in the 1830s and quickly replaced the old drop-leaf table or pairs of tables that had to be pulled together to form one large surface. A set of identical chairs had been a prized component of household furnishing since the seventeenth century, representing both economic means and new visual standards that prized uniformity in interior decor. Victorian sets of dining chairs were sometimes quite large—twelve or more—even in middle-class households. Authors of furnishing advice recommended dining-room chairs have either cane, rush, hair cloth, or leather seats so that food spills could be cleaned up easily. Surviving dining-room sets suggest that shoppers often followed this practice.

Other rooms had tables and chairs, too, but Victorian dining rooms featured one form of furniture that was unique—the sideboard, used for storage, the display of prized pieces of family silver such as tea sets, and as a service table for extra food or tablewares at mealtimes (fig. 1.2). The sideboard was the descendant of a medieval furniture form, the "cup board," a rough set of wooden shelves (boards), covered with fine textiles. The cup board was used in great halls to display the wealth of lords in the form of silver and gold items, such as chalices or cups, servers, and other objects that were impressive but portable and easy to melt down in times of financial crisis.

The modern "side board," a closed furniture form with doors and shelves and display space on top for ornamental knife boxes and family silver, was an eighteenth-century rethinking of the old cup board. By the mid-nineteenth century, the sideboard took the form it would retain until well into the twentieth century, when it was often replaced by a simpler low server and a china closet (one or both). It had a cabinet, with doors and drawers below, a broad top for serving, and an upper structure with open shelves for displaying examples of the owner's best china, glass, or silver (fig. 1.3). Some nineteenth-century sideboards had mirrors in their upper sections that not only reflected light around the room but also visually multiplied the family treasures on display.

The masculine character of Victorian dining rooms was

Fig. 1.2 New England dining room with trophy images and sideboards, ca. 1900.

Fig. 1.3 With surfaces for food, cabinets for storage, and shelves for display, sideboards were integral to the 19th-century dining room.

made abundantly clear through the display of trophy images (fig. 1.2). These included braces of dead rabbits, game birds, or fish, often depicted fully life-size, and narrative prints of hunters in the field or of their living prey, such as deer or quail feeding or alert to a nearby human presence (the viewer). Sometimes sideboards bore expensive carved reliefs of dead game, including wooden trophy heads of stags and fully rendered hunting dogs. More common, however, were earthenware serving dishes featuring dead game and seafood (cats. 3, 83).

By the 1870s hunting imagery usually turned up in pictures, whether oil paintings in well-to-do households or pairs of chromolithographic prints that the picture trade called dining room pictures. These were sold in furniture stores well into the twentieth century. In the 1870s and 1880s it was also common for taxidermists to offer "trophy mounts" of real birds. The creatures were not necessarily the prizes of hunting vacations—many were probably purchased at city meat markets—but their presence implied that they had been killed by the man of the house. Mounted deer heads, the souvenirs of guided trips in the Adirondack Mountains or the west, also appeared on dining-room walls. While fainthearted customers could instead buy dining-room pictures depicting abundant displays of the fruits of agriculture, the most popular subjects seem to have been still lifes of small game. Dining-room pictures celebrated the idea that the master of the house was able to bring home the bacon, or the canvasback duck, as the case may be. Hunting skill, and the suggestion of economic life as a competition between hunter and game, were heroic metaphors for middle-class patriarchs who increasingly competed only in the world of pencil and paper.[10]

In well-to-do households of the late nineteenth century, most dining equipage was normally hidden from view, with the exception of the sideboard display. Larger houses had pantries located between kitchens and dining rooms that not only muffled the mundane sounds of food preparation and service but made it easier to maintain a large inventory of china and glassware. As such houses were fully plumbed, these pantries sometimes had their own sinks, which segregated fragile treasures from the bustle of the kitchen.

In contrast, for more modest households that were just beginning to acquire large matching sets of fancy dishes, concealing this wealth of "best china" was unacceptable, even if a room or closet was available for its storage. Too much sweat and desire had gone into its acquisition. Hence the introduction of the china cupboard or cabinet, a piece of furniture that aroused controversy among the advocates of simplified decor in the 1920s. China cabinets first appeared in trade catalogues in the 1880s and were in common use by 1900 (fig. 1.4). Because the point of the china cabinet was frank display, it generally consisted of an ornamental frame of wood holding together expanses of glass. A memoir by Ethel Spencer of her family's everyday life in turn-of-the-century Pittsburgh recalled that her family did not have a sideboard. Rather, the dining room held not one but two golden oak china "closets" where "the best glass and china rested undisturbed for most of the year."[11] Sidney Morse, whose advice manual *Household Discoveries* (1908) was clearly directed to a rural or small-town audience, pronounced the china cabinet "a useful and beautiful article of furniture" that gave a modest dining room "character and beauty."[12] The ability to display tablewares was so important that if a family could not afford a china cabinet and had a closet in the dining room, he recommended taking the door off its hinges, equipping the space

Fig. 1.4 The Dr. Newton J. Phenix family in their dining room before a Japanese theme party, Colorado City, Texas, ca. 1895.

with shelves, and covering the opening with a curtain that could be opened when the room was in use. Constantly looking at the dishes saved for special events reminded family and visitors of what might occur when the occasion was right.

THE SOCIAL MEANING OF FOOD

Although food in its raw state was abundantly present on dining-room walls and sometimes on dishes themselves, nineteenth-century cooking and eating were ironically predicated on a complete taming of nature. That is so because food, especially raw food, is symbolically charged. Although the average person does not often stop and reflect dispassionately about what he or she ingests, it is worth pausing to introduce

several pertinent ideas about food from the discipline of anthropology.[13] Human beings use their bodies as a measure of reality. Through metaphors we make culturally shaped comparisons between things in order to understand the world. Sometimes we describe the body of a highly trained athlete as a "well-oiled machine," for example, suggesting both its strength, the care lavished on it, and its predictable level of high performance. This comparison would make no sense in a culture that does not use complex machines routinely, and it also says something about faith in technology and in the ability to control the human body, keeping it from "breaking down."

People think metaphorically about their bodies and use them as ways to communicate without words. We do this every day through dress and what has been called body language, but also by small or great acts of physical incorporation —eating. Sharing food is a significant way of communicating through the body, for food is the only cultural artifact that routinely crosses the boundary between the self and the outside world. By incorporating food into ourselves, we incorporate its cultural meanings as well. Think, for example, of anorexics, who use their ability to control food intake and their bodies to the extent of starvation as a metaphor for self-control in a scary world. Through the act of eating together, we allow others to see us engage in a potentially embarrassing animal act; when the mouth is open, the teeth are exposed and the body's insides can be glimpsed. Sharing a meal is an act of fellowship but also of vulnerability, and humans are intuitively

Cat. 3 Victorians loved multicolored majolica featuring geometric patterns, flowers, fruit, and dead game.

Fig. 1.5 Norman Rockwell painted an idealized Thanksgiving meal in *Freedom from Want,* 1943.

reluctant to eat full meals with people they do not like or know very well.

Alone or in groups, the body also represents what anthropologists call the "social body." Think, for example, of Thanksgiving (fig. 1.5). Americans believe so strongly that Thanksgiving dinners across the country should be uniform in their core constituents of turkey (an indigenous American bird), stuffing, and cranberry sauce that they go out of their way to make sure homeless people under the nearby railroad bridge receive dinners like those of other citizens. No matter how marginal such people seem to the community the rest of the year, Americans make the gesture of including them in this annual ritual feast. When they sit down to Thanksgiving dinner, be it at a relative's house, a restaurant, or even a Salvation Army soup kitchen, Americans declare their national oneness (or have it declared for them); they symbolically constitute a single national social body through the act of eating.

Sharing food may create group identity, but food itself is ambiguous. Food is "natural" in that it originates in the wild realm of nature that humans can control only imperfectly, even if they pretend otherwise. Vegetables come out of dirt, for example, a fact that supermarket displays of carefully washed and bagged carrots and spinach leaves try hard to disguise. In the case of meat, food is even dangerous—if people are willing to eat the muscle, sinew, and blood of a chicken, who says they are not willing to take a bite out of their dinner partners? One way to explore the fundamental concerns of a past society is to look at the attitudes and practices associated with gathering and preparing meals, food preferences, and a

society's mediation of the act of eating through codified behaviors (table manners, dress codes) and specialized implements and settings.

ETIQUETTE AND EQUIPAGE

Food must also be seen as a source of ritual. Americans have always used food and feasting to mark the annual cycle and life's important events. The harvest feast that schoolchildren learn to call the First Thanksgiving was a transplanted rural English tradition put into practice as soon as circumstances permitted. The ideals of gentility percolating through Euro-American society in the eighteenth and nineteenth centuries introduced the concept of dining as an important form of individual self-expression as well as communal identity. Dining involved consuming costly food using special equipment in a setting created for the purpose, and it also entailed performing a set of behaviors, or manners, that choreographed ingestion and interaction with other eaters in new ways.

The shared belief that dining was a vital form of cultural communication and performance in the nineteenth century reached its apogee in the Victorian formal dinner party. What John Kasson has called "that great institution of the late nineteenth century . . . loomed before the socially insecure as an excruciating ordeal by fork, the 'great trial' on which one's social reputation depended."[14] Dinner-party manners, at least as articulated by the plentiful etiquette books of the late nineteenth century, emphasized effortless self-control, even to the appearance of disinterest in the multiple courses of elaborate dishes served. This attitude reflected the recognition that the process of eating had the potential to reveal the animality, the uncontrolled appetites of the diner. Thus one etiquette book warned, "Eating is so entirely a sensual, animal gratification, that unless it is conducted with much delicacy, it becomes unpleasant to others."[15]

The implements used in the formal dinner were crucial to this social performance. A little historical background will be helpful for understanding developments after 1880: by the seventeenth century, one sees among the noble classes of Europe an increasing interest in each person having completely separate tools for dining. This trend moved slowly down through the social ranks; most ordinary people in the seventeenth century, including the Puritans in Massachusetts, still shared a communal eating vessel and ate mainly with their fingers. The proliferation of individual place settings, even very simple ones such as a bowl and spoon, throughout the social hierarchy did not simply bespeak increasing prosperity. It is clear that some well-to-do folk ate without utensils. Rather, the "one man, one spoon" movement suggested an increasing sense of the separateness, and on some level the privacy, of the individual person. By the mid-nineteenth century, only the most poverty-stricken or isolated people would have shared a vessel for eating, and flatware, at least sets of knives and spoons, was almost universal.[16]

While individual place settings differentiated people, matching sets of tablewares also were increasingly valued in the seventeenth century. Sets of chairs, of plates, or of flatware accomplished two things: First, they made statements about the financial means of the owners and their aesthetics or sense of style. Second, using a set of objects reinforced the idea that the participants around the table were a community of social peers. After the 1760s, when English potteries introduced new methods of industrialized production of ceramics, sets of virtually identical dishes in a widening range of forms became available to fashion-conscious households. By the mid-nineteenth century, families with relatively modest incomes could afford some quantity of matching ceramics, glass, and flatware, although few could have sprung for the full complement suggested by the popular domestic advice author Catharine Beecher in her 1858 *Domestic Receipt Book*: one dozen each of forks, silver spoons, dessert forks, dessert knives, dessert spoons, and glass tumblers for water; two dozen each of wineglasses and large knives; three dozen dessert plates; and four dozen dinner plates.[17]

The increasing number of vessels and implements available to ordinary persons at the table over the course of the nineteenth century made a telling statement about the advancement of food and civilization. The containers in which individual dishes were served grew more refined and elaborate. Tops helped keep dishes warm, and lifting the elaborate covers on vegetable dishes and tureens was like opening a present. Faceted cut glass caused preserves and pickles to shine like jewels. The decorative rims of individual plates and bowls framed their contents, while the light colors of many wares offered visual contrast. Furthermore, the implements of dining separated the diner's body from the food served in more and more elaborate ways. Some etiquette books even advised women attending formal dinners in the late nineteenth century to wear gloves throughout the meal so their skin would not even come in contact with the silver, china, or crystal. The underlying idea was that, in the most civilized kind of dining, food was doubly subjugated to the hand of mankind—first cooked and then manipulated by complicated tools, which reinforced how human beings differed from animals and animalistic, "primitive" people. The more tools, the more civilized the diner. Exceptions proved the rule, as in the case of picnics. In late-nineteenth-century America picnics were a kind of play on the rituals of dining, possible only because picnickers could assume that they would be returning to the world of sophisticated implements. Hence the choice to abandon tools and eat "finger foods" was more pleasurable. This same sense of play was associated with certain types of food, such as corn on the cob or fried chicken, which made it acceptable to eat with the hands (fig. 1.6).

Just as the rituals of dining could reinforce a sense of community among peers, they could unmask the parvenu who did not know how to use the range of specialized tablewares that proliferated in the late nineteenth century, particularly silver and silver-plated flatware (fig. 1.7).[18] Until late in the century, sterling silver had been too expensive for most consumers, and at the time of Catharine Beecher's advice on equipping a dining room, middle-class households used a mix of steel knives and forks with bone handles and spoons of pewter or silver plate.[19] Thanks to electroplating technology that was introduced in the 1840s and 1850s and the falling price of silver bullion during the second half of the century, more families acquired silver-plated and solid silver flatware and serving dishes. In general, late-nineteenth-century culture loved specialization. On the one hand, specialization represented in everyday life the extreme desire to classify things that was so prevalent in natural history circles at the time; on the other hand, it revealed to Victorians the increasing complexity of their advancing civilization. In 1905 the bride who received newly patented *Vintage* pattern silver-plated flatware theoretically could spend the rest of her days acquiring every one of the 101 different implements available by 1916.[20]

Another danger awaiting attendees at formal dinner parties was the food itself. Not only did food have to be "tamed," but writers of late-nineteenth-century cookbooks worried frequently about dishes being "digestible." This concern reflected both the realities of frequent dyspepsia (indigestion) from bad or greasy food and a metaphorical understanding of the problem of incorporating natural matter into bodies that were seen for the most part as cultural creations rather than physical ones. That is, the more civilized a person was, the greater the difficulty of digesting incompletely civilized food. Long cooking of vegetables and meats and multistep preparation made food more digestible, or civilized.

Abundance and apparent waste, expense, and artifice in food preparation and presentation also guided dinner-party cooking. Formal dinner menus involved multiple courses rather than the simple display of abundance that typically

Fig. 1.6 American middle-class family eating corn on the cob, 1888.

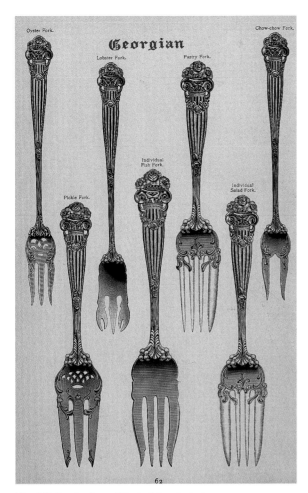

Fig. 1.7 A selection of Towle Manufacturing Company's *Georgian* forks show the highly specialized nature of flatware at the turn of the century.

MENUS FOR FULL COURSE DINNERS.

Blue Points.
Consommé à la Royal.
Olives. Celery. Salted Almonds.
Swedish Timbales with Chicken and Mushrooms.
Fried Smelts. Sauce Tartare. Dressed Cucumbers.
Saddle of Mutton. Currant Jelly Sauce.
Potatoes Brabant. Brussels Sprouts.
Suprême of Chicken.
Mushrooms à la Sabine.
Canton Sherbet.
Canvasback Duck. Olive Sauce.
Farina Cakes with Jelly.
Celery Salad.
Apricot and Wine Jelly.
Nesselrode Pudding. Rolled Wafers. Parisian Sweets.
Crackers. Cheese.
Café Noir.

Little Neck Clams.
Consommé au Parmesan.
Olives. Salted Pecans.
Bouchées.
Fillets of Halibut à la Poulette with Mayonnaise.
Tomatoes. Delmonico Potatoes. String Beans.
Larded Fillet of Beef with Horseradish Sauce.
Glazed Sweetbreads.
Artichokes with Béchamel Sauce.
Sorbet.
Broiled Quail with Lettuce and Celery Salad.
Bananas. Cantaloupes.
Sultana Roll with Claret Sauce.
Cinnamon Bars. Lady Fingers. Bonbons.
Crackers. Cheese.
Café Noir.

Fig. 1.8 Multicourse dinner menu from Fannie Merritt Farmers' *Boston Cooking-School Cook Book* (1896).

marked the traditional informal "suppers" of old-fashioned community social life such as dancing parties. The *Boston Cooking-School Cook Book* (1896) by Fannie Merritt Farmer explained that a proper "full course dinner" had twelve courses and offered sample menus (fig. 1.8). Mrs. John A. Logan's *The Home Manual: Everybody's Guide in Social, Domestic, and Business Life* (1889), a one-volume compendium sold door-to-door to individuals with social aspirations, informed its readers that dinner parties had a first course of raw oysters, a soup course, a fish course followed by one or two entrees, a roast, a game course, salad with cheese and bread and butter, dessert and ices, a fruit course, and bonbons followed by coffee in the drawing room "when the courses have not occupied too much time."[21] Diners who attended a dinner with most of those courses had to carefully control their appetite so that each dish could be sampled. The tight, long corsets that virtually all women wore to social events in the late nineteenth century must have made formal dinners even more difficult to negotiate. Men and certainly women likely left a lot on their plates—individual expressions of the rule of abundance and waste.

As can be seen from Fannie Farmer's menu, meat—many kinds of meat—was crucial to the dinner party. When the menu included turtle, fish, and fowl, both tame and wild, it represented not only waste but the rightful dominion of humans over animals. Medieval and Renaissance feasting had often made a point of presenting the animal's body whole so that the source of the meat and the relative choiceness of the piece offered were perfectly clear. Dinner-party menus in the 1880s and 1890s were much less likely to feature whole animals, with the exception of the occasional suckling pig or turkey or goose. Nevertheless, we have seen that diners were surrounded by decor reminding them where meat came from. "Game sets" and other serving dishes frequently depicted living animals, and ingenious cooks often molded at least one flesh course into the form of an animal's body. While today's consumers are much too squeamish for such frank acknowledgment of the link between death (the animal's) and life (the human's), vestiges of this practice survive in the form of turkey platters and fish dishes, as well as the occasional salmon mousse molded into the shape of its former self (cats. 4–6).

The amount of labor it took to support the apparatus of formal dining of course meant that the fully elaborated ritual was confined to households with servants. Hostesses who did not normally employ more than one or two servants probably brought in additional temporary help. By the 1880s the most fashionable plan for multicourse dinners was *service à la russe* (Russian service; fig. 1.9). In this form of service the table was left free for the display of decorative china, glass, silver, and food, while serving dishes were carried to the sideboard or

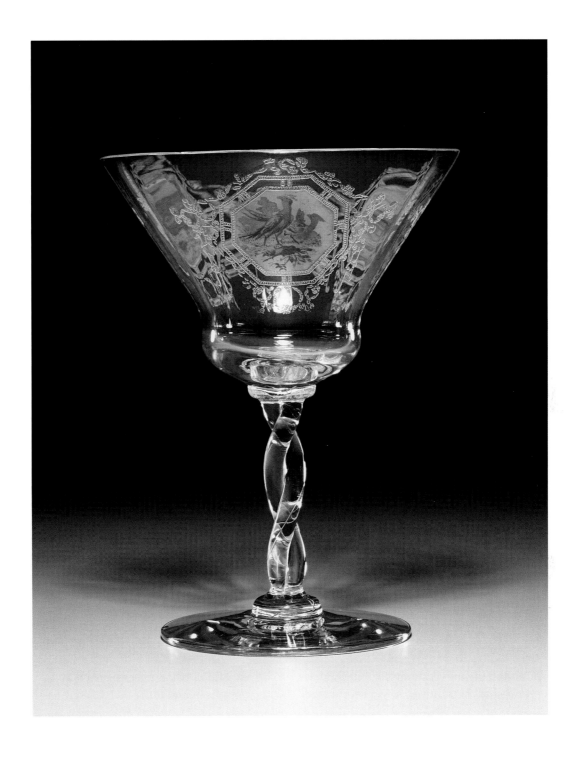

OPPOSITE:
Cat. 4 Johnson Brothers' fish platter added lively color to a seafood course in the 1950s.

Cat. 5 Bright red crustaceans made in Czechoslovakia spiced up the table in the 1930s.

Cat. 6 Realistic images of game birds on this glass are a late example of a 19th-century taste.

dishes and more dishes: tableware in the home |

serving tables where servants prepared each plate before setting it before a guest. And of course somebody had to deal with the mountains of dishes and table scraps behind the scenes. Yet, fewer people than expected had servants. In the 1870 U.S. Census, one woman listed herself as a domestic servant for every 8.4 families. There were 188 servants for every 1,000 households in New York in 1880, 141 in 1900. If many of the truly well-to-do households with servants had more than one, the number of respectable women who did their own work with the help of their daughters—or who used part-time help like a laundress or seamstress and hired a local "girl" to help with parties—was probably quite large.[22]

The irony of the formal dinner party was that its lavish display of food and the sensual qualities of the rich cooking and copious meats seemed to be a kind of gustatory call to physical pleasure. Yet the structure of the courses, and the delicacy and elaboration of the tools for serving and eating, suggested that sensual abandonment was not part of the menu. This double-mindedness about the pleasures of food certainly did not affect all diners equally, but the ambivalence expressed by the etiquette book quoted above was congruent with a similar cultural ambivalence about other kinds of physicality, including sex and sport.[23] And the contradictory messages of the formal dinner enjoyed a strange kind of resonance with another, simultaneous discussion about food associated with diet reform and the domestic science movement discussed below.

By the last quarter of the nineteenth century families of relatively modest means were able to participate in a modified but recognizable version of the formal dining ritual. For one thing, whether or not they served multiple courses for company, they could purchase an assortment of specialized food service vessels and tools that were intended to enhance the experience of dining precisely because they were so special. Routine became ritual when the consumption of pickles and butter, for example, was ceremonialized with ruby-glass containers in silver stands and footed dishes. Arranging whitened celery on the table became almost a form of floral display, given the urn-shaped glasses or colored "canoes" in which it was served (cats. 7, 140).

The new technology of canning and improvements in food transportation, including refrigerated railroad cars, meant that middle-class consumers in search of variety, especially from the monotonous diets of winter months, indulged in what one would now describe as food fads. These inspired potteries, glasshouses, and silver manufacturers to provide novelties for serving and eating such luxurious treats as fresh asparagus (tongs and dishes), oranges shipped from Florida (pointed orange spoons and round citrus glasses), raw or canned oysters from Chesapeake Bay or the Gulf Coast (trident-shaped oyster forks and special plates), ice cream (ice-cream forks and dishes), lemons (sets of lemonade pitchers, glasses and "sipper" spoons with hollow handles), and hothouse grapes (grape shears and baskets). While oysters could be served on any plate in a pinch, one etiquette book noted, "More elegance is expressed by the use of plates designed expressly for them" (cat. 83).[24]

The full complement of tablewares needed for formal dining was costly enough that it was often a once-in-a-lifetime acquisition, to be expanded by individual serving pieces and specialized sets (see pp. 35–37). In fact, the timing for expanded middle-class participation in formal dining is coincidental with changes in the celebration of weddings, including a much-expanded practice of giving wedding gifts (fig. 1.10). (This expanded wedding-gift giving is in turn coincidental with a similar "gift inflation" related to the celebration of Christmas.) The equipage associated with dining formed the core of this new wedding gifting. The 1884 premium list for the *Ladies' Home Journal* recommended that a club of thirty subscribers use the silver flatware premium as "a serviceable present for a young housekeeper."[25]

Advice on wedding gifts repeatedly listed table linens, extra sets of silver spoons and forks, and nut-picks and fruit knives; cut-glass serving pieces, tumblers, sherbet dishes; and breakfast sets, odd sets of plates, and chocolate or lemonade

Fig. 1.10 A turn-of-the-century bride proudly poses with her wedding gifts.

sets. A common practice in jewelry stores was to package individual service pieces and three-piece sets of table knife, fork, and teaspoon boxed in velvet for gift giving; the mail-order firm Montgomery Ward & Co. also used this type of packaging. New York-based Higgins & Seiter Company, a china and glass business that offered a catalogue for "those wishing to purchase '¼ less than elsewhere'" advised that "the best Wedding Present is something useful as well as ornamental, and of service to both contracting parties. Fine China and Rich Cut Glass possess these qualities to a greater extent than any household article."[26] One author noted in 1912 that gift givers could take comfort because "the selection is endless, for this is another province where a woman never knows when she has had enough."[27]

Once a family was established, the ability to offer hospitality at home clearly revolved around food between 1880 and 1915. Accounts of the more typical experiences of sharing food suggest that people adapted both the established rules of formal presentation and the longstanding tenets of feasting —abundance and waste, artifice, and special presentation— according to the limitations of their own circumstances. A pair of small engravings printed in *Hill's Manual of Social and Business Forms* (1884), a popular one-volume "cyclopedia," makes it clear that genteel dining was ideally not family dining; it belonged to the world of adults (figs. 1.11, 1.12). Yet children were participants in the important social occasions, and middle-class girls learned the rules of entertaining by being present and helping. Some remembered the beauties of the dining table and its bounties with pleasure.

Della Thompson Lutes's *Home Grown* (1937), a remarkable memoir of growing up in southern Michigan in the 1880s and 1890s that centers on food and social life, offers several examples of formal and informal feasting as adapted by a relatively prosperous rural community. Daughter of a cabinet-maker and carpenter turned farmer, Lutes recalled several different kinds of social "suppers" from her childhood, the most elaborate being a monthly oyster supper. Shucked oysters came in "square-shouldered, sharp-angled cans" and

Fig. 1.11 "Bad Manners at the Table" (1884).

Fig. 1.12 "Gentility in the Dining-Room" (1884).

were a prized delicacy even a thousand miles inland. Her Uncle Matt and Aunt Martha participated in monthly "oyster suppers given by the Glass Ball Shoot to which Uncle Matt belonged. . . . Country dances, sociables, candy pulls, and parties of different kinds were frequent and gay, but the Shooting Club was somewhat exclusive and a little more opulent in its aspect."

The oyster supper was, in effect, the formal dinner for this particular community, hosted by the owners of the largest and "most comfortably equipped" house in the community. Lutes's account of the meal is so vivid that it is worthy of lengthy quotation:

> The pen that would picture to the eye that never
> saw . . . a table so bespread with lavish provender
> as was that set for an Oyster Supper at the Fowler
> farmhouse . . . must justly poise in reflective mood
> above the page. With what poor words shall it
> describe the fragrance, first of the opening cans,
> then of the heating broth as it steals through the
> kitchen door to the anterooms . . . ? How portray
> the long, wide table extending the length of the
> large dining room, duplicated by a second in the
> room beyond, each seating at least twelve people,
> the thick satiny folds of their cloths hanging al-
> most to the floor—for this was in the days when a
> housewife prided herself upon the size, quantity,
> and quality of her table linen. . . . In the centre of
> each table stood a stately silver caster with cruets
> of sparkling glass, each bottle handsomely etched
> and stoppered in heavy excellence of cut and pat-
> tern. Flanking these were huge bowls of slaw. . . .
> And beyond these at one end a high cylindrical
> glass dish holding celery, and at the other one
> somewhat similar swinging in its silver frame
> and filled with long spikes of cucumber pickles,
> slightly tart and strong of dill. . . . At each place
> was a large white china plate with gold band
> around the edge, and threadlike circle of gold in
> the centre. Silver flanked the sides: knife, soup
> spoon, oyster fork, to the right; dessert fork, din-
> ner fork, to the left, and a goblet for water just
> above the plate alongside a tiny butter dish—
> the same sometimes used to hold the cup when
> tea or coffee was poured into the saucer to cool.
> Mrs. Fowler's goblets were of the thumbprint
> pattern, not so handsome as my mother's bell-
> flowers, but catching every reflected beam from the
> hanging lamp overhead with its many prisms. The
> large linen napkin, folded snugly square, lay
> at the left.[28]

While the house had a serving girl and an "extra woman" had come to assist with preparations, some food was placed family-style on the table, and the women doubled as wait-resses for the men and children. Guests helped each other to the courses of shucked raw oysters served in saucers, oyster stew, and scalloped oysters made in milk pans wrapped in white towels "to disguise their plebeian nature, and make them easy to handle."[29]

A close look at the oyster supper menu shows that the range of supporting dishes was limited, reflecting the realities of a winter food supply in a cold climate (plenty of cabbage) and the traditional art of pickling. Oysters were the centerpiece, but fresh celery was a winter treat and received its own vases. Finally, the artifice and abundance of feasting were well represented in the dessert course, especially by the layer cakes that demonstrated considerable cooking skill and the significant expenditure of up to a dozen egg whites when precious eggs were out of season. Lutes reported that some of the women she knew from her childhood "made cakes as some paint pictures, weave tapestries, or create images in stone."[30]

Family celebrations that called into service all the fragile treasures of the dining room also created strong memories. Ethel Spencer's memoir of upper-middle-class life in turn-of-the-century Pittsburgh remarked at length on the great annual event that saw the use of all the good china, her parents' annual wedding anniversary party for seventeen or eighteen family members. Because of the size of their family, the Spencers took all meals in the dining room, but they usually ate with silver-plated utensils. For this occasion the sterling silver and the dishes that normally rested in the two dining-room china closets "came out of retirement to have the year's accumulation of dirt washed away":

> The dining room table was pulled out to its fullest
> extent and the extra boards that spent the rest of
> the year in the cupboard under the front stairs were
> put in place. The table was so elongated that it had
> to be placed diagonally across the room, one end
> in the bay window and the other edging the door
> into the hall. An enormously long white damask
> tablecloth, designed for just such occasions, came
> out of hiding to grace the table, and the best nap-
> kins along with it. When the table was set with the
> freshly polished silver, its glitter was dazzling. I
> specially liked the little silver butter plates, washed
> with gold, that had been one of Mother's wedding
> presents.[31]

Taking all three meals in the dining room was a middle-class nicety that many advice writers presented as the standard for their readers until well into the 1940s. Etiquette books urged middle-class families "to conduct their daily meals as an unceasing rehearsal for company." The basic requirements for respectable dining at home were that family members be appropriately dressed, each family member have his or her own equipage for dining, and the table be well set and orderly, a metaphor for what should take place on its spotlessly clean surface. Kasson argues that "From infancy on, in the manner in which one ate, one gradually imbibed the lessons of modern civilization: to discipline the cravings of the stomach and the 'lower' body by force of intellect, will, and habit."[32]

Fig. 1.13 Even breakfast could be an elaborate multicourse affair.

Fig. 1.14 With father at the office, lunch moved into the kitchen around the turn of the century.

Most turn-of-the-century cookbooks and household manuals promoted the ideal of dining-room family meals, but they seem largely to have been directed to women who could afford the services of at least one full-time servant. Since perhaps only 15 percent of households had that level of help, there is a decided air of unreality to this advice, which might best be understood as a collective representation of middle-class ideals. What conscientious wife and mother would not have wanted to offer her family the three-course breakfast depicted in *Mrs. Rorer's New Cook Book* (1902; fig. 1.13)? In the northern states even middle-class Americans probably ate many of their wintertime meals in the kitchen as a matter of convenience and comfort, since kitchens were the warmest rooms in houses without central heat.[33] They may have moved back into a combined dining and sitting room for the warm months to escape the coal or wood range that always radiated heat. Southerners who could afford to build larger houses and hire servants followed somewhat different patterns, since kitchens were stiflingly hot most of the year.

The choice of the dining room or kitchen as the site for eating was not simply a matter of class but of comfort and practicality as well. Even prosperous rural folk who shared many urban middle-class patterns of consumption, like the Lutes family, ate in the kitchen so that the "menfolk" did not have to change out of their work clothes. And as middle-class dining patterns changed, especially in the expanding suburbs of the late nineteenth century, a new rhythm of meals was established. Increasingly the "breakfast, dinner, supper" routine—where a large midday meal was shared with a father who worked nearby and could walk or ride home—was replaced by the "breakfast, lunch, dinner" pattern followed today: women prepared a simpler, lighter midday meal for themselves and their children (fig. 1.14); lunch was more likely consumed in the kitchen, while the evening meal took place in the dining room.

Begun in Chicago in 1872, Montgomery Ward & Co. pioneered mail-order catalogues by printing a single page of dry-good items for sale. It was the first American mail-order firm to sell general merchandise. Sears, Roebuck & Co., which eventually became Montgomery Ward's great rival, was not established until 1886 and did not mail out a general merchandise catalogue until the mid-1890s. Although both firms were known in the mid-twentieth century as much for their department stores as for their catalogues, their respective chains of department stores were not begun until the 1920s. Montgomery Ward opened its first store in 1926, more than fifty years after the company's founding.

Mail-order catalogues are a valuable source for historical research on everyday life. Not only did they offer rural and small-town residents access to consumer goods otherwise available only in urban specialty stores, but they also provided a useful overview of the advances of taste and technology with extensive commentary for their customers. The captions and images of catalogues introduced readers to new kinds of goods, explained the distinctions among the different price levels of goods, and gave advice on being a modern consumer. A careful reading of mail-order catalogues from a store like Montgomery Ward reveals the real preferences of the customers as well as their desire to be progressive—or their inclination to be conservative—in what they bought.

A close examination of the crockery and glassware departments in Montgomery Ward's *Catalogue No. 57, Spring and Summer 1895,* along with its selection of silver and silver plate, offers an interesting perspective on the uneven movement of the ideal of civilized dining down the social scale. The "Crockery Department," as it was called, promised prospective purchasers that its eighteen patterns were "all very desirable wares of the best English, French, German, and American manufacture" (fig. 1.15). Some customers clearly resisted the proliferation of dishes taking place in many middle-class and elite households. The text reassured them: "You do not have to take the large, expensive, and sometimes superfluous dishes that come in regular made [dinner] sets, as all of our dinner ware is open stock."

Open stock was a marketing strategy by which customers could purchase small groups of dishes, and eventually single pieces, rather than entire sets all at once (see chapter 4). This method of acquisition was important to customers who were buying one good set of dishes that they intended to keep for life. So was the popularity of the pattern itself. In the catalogue buyers were steered toward conservative choices so that they could later find replacements for broken pieces more easily. Advice books agreed that it was wise to select "a stock pattern . . . in a standard design . . . as the well-known willow or onion pattern . . . so that broken pieces can be replaced over a long period of time."[1]

While the small wood engravings illustrating Montgomery Ward's tablewares lack fine detail, the written descriptions make clear just how conservative consumers were assumed to be. Seventeen of the twenty-five patterns offered were decorated with floral designs, mostly using monochromatic brown or blue transfer-prints. Five patterns were plain white, with or without gold edges; eight had scalloped edges. The cheapest open stock was a brown-and-white pattern of pansies called *Ravenna* by the English firm J. H. Weatherby & Sons; a dozen 8-inch plates cost $1.17. The most expensive, *Carnot* pattern "French china," one of two Haviland & Co. contributions, was "hand decorated with delicate sprays of cornflowers" in pink and blue and had "clouded" gold handles. It cost $4.41 for the same dozen plates (for similar examples, see cat. 2). The selection of forms available in Montgomery Ward's catalogue of open stock included separate tea and coffee cups, four sizes of plates, soup and sauce plates designed with a center well, deeper bowls often labeled for oatmeal or oysters, side dishes for vegetables or soft desserts called nappies, individual butter pats and bone dishes, and several sizes of individual baking dishes, along with a wide array of serving pieces including platters of varying sizes, covered tureens and dishes, butter dishes, sauce boats, creamers and sugar bowls, pickle dishes, pitchers in several sizes, casseroles, and cake plates. All were priced by the dozen.

Montgomery Ward did continue to offer six of its patterns as sets, which eliminated the problem of choice for some customers. The company's own *Coral* pattern was offered as a fifty-six-piece "tea set" (really a starter set that could be used for everyday meals) for $5.10; a ninety-eight-piece set for $7.75; or with four more large serving pieces for $11.00. Although the catalogue stated that it was "intended for an every day set," *Coral* was nevertheless highly decorative. Its sturdy graniteware body featured scalloped and "gold-lined" edges, decorated with "leaves and sprays of a natural gay tint and wild blossoms in delicate blue."

The glassware selection included an array of plain and pattern-pressed tumblers for as little as $.30 a dozen and one patterned goblet for as little as $.45 a dozen, but their glory was an array of "Genuine Rich Cut Glass" and fancy pressed and engraved glassware in both clear and ruby glass (fig. 1.16). Intended to augment incomplete china services, four-piece table sets, which included a spoon holder, creamer, sugar bowl, and butter dish, or larger sets with matching water pitchers, cake stands, berry bowls, salt and pepper shakers, and other pieces were for everyday use or were modest substitutes for the silver serving pieces that customers would have preferred. Special water or lemonade

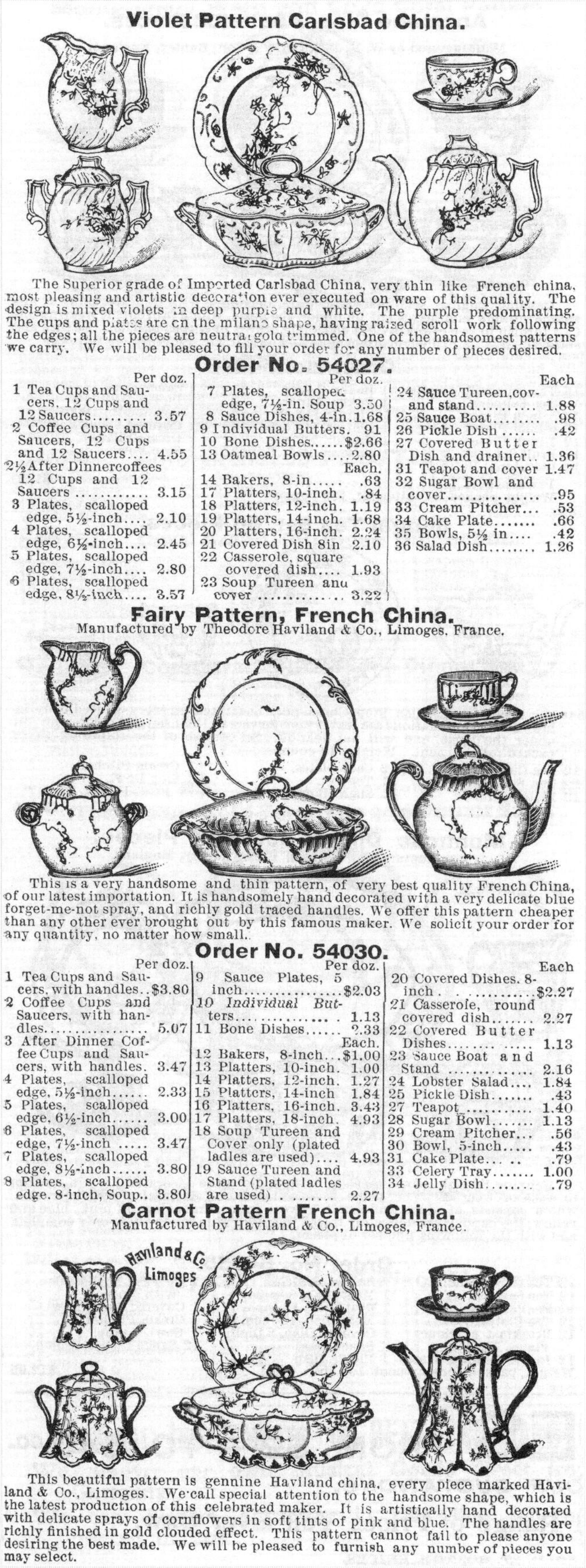

Violet Pattern Carlsbad China.

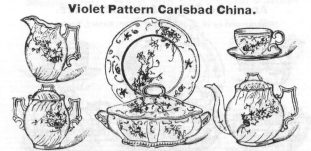

The Superior grade of Imported Carlsbad China, very thin like French china, most pleasing and artistic decoration ever executed on ware of this quality. The design is mixed violets in deep purple and white. The purple predominating. The cups and plates are on the milano shape, having raised scroll work following the edges; all the pieces are neutral gold trimmed. One of the handsomest patterns we carry. We will be pleased to fill your order for any number of pieces desired.

Order No. 54027.

	Per doz.		Per doz.		Each
1 Tea Cups and Saucers, 12 Cups and 12 Saucers	3.57	7 Plates, scalloped edge, 7¼-in. Soup	3.50	24 Sauce Tureen, cover and stand	1.88
2 Coffee Cups and Saucers, 12 Cups and 12 Saucers	4.55	8 Sauce Dishes, 4-in.	1.68	25 Sauce Boat	.98
		9 Individual Butters	.91	26 Pickle Dish	.42
2½ After Dinner coffees 12 Cups and 12 Saucers	3.15	10 Bone Dishes	$2.66	27 Covered Butter Dish and drainer	1.36
		13 Oatmeal Bowls	2.80	31 Teapot and cover	1.47
3 Plates, scalloped edge, 5½-inch	2.10		Each.	32 Sugar Bowl and cover	.95
		14 Bakers, 8-in	.63	33 Cream Pitcher	.53
4 Plates, scalloped edge, 6½-inch	2.45	17 Platters, 10-inch	.84	34 Cake Plate	.66
		18 Platters, 12-inch	1.19	35 Bowls, 5½ in	.42
5 Plates, scalloped edge, 7½-inch	2.80	19 Platters, 14-inch	1.68	36 Salad Dish	1.26
		20 Platters, 16-inch	2.24		
6 Plates, scalloped edge, 8¼-inch	3.57	21 Covered Dish 8 in	2.10		
		22 Casserole, square covered dish	1.93		
		23 Soup Tureen and cover	3.22		

Fairy Pattern, French China.
Manufactured by Theodore Haviland & Co., Limoges, France.

This is a very handsome and thin pattern, of very best quality French China, of our latest importation. It is handsomely hand decorated with a very delicate blue forget-me-not spray, and richly gold traced handles. We offer this pattern cheaper than any other ever brought out by this famous maker. We solicit your order for any quantity, no matter how small.

Order No. 54030.

	Per doz.		Per doz.		Each
1 Tea Cups and Saucers, with handles	$3.80	9 Sauce Plates, 5 inch	$2.03	20 Covered Dishes. 8-inch	$2.27
2 Coffee Cups and Saucers, with handles	5.07	10 Individual Butters	1.13	21 Casserole, round covered dish	2.27
3 After Dinner Coffee Cups and Saucers, with handles	3.47	11 Bone Dishes	2.33	22 Covered Butter Dishes	1.13
			Each.	23 Sauce Boat and Stand	2.16
4 Plates, scalloped edge, 5½-inch	2.33	12 Bakers, 8-inch	$1.00	24 Lobster Salad	1.84
		13 Platters, 10-inch	1.00	25 Pickle Dish	.43
5 Plates, scalloped edge, 6½-inch	3.00	14 Platters, 12-inch	1.27	27 Teapot	1.40
		15 Platters, 14-inch	1.84	28 Sugar Bowl	1.13
6 Plates, scalloped edge, 7½-inch	3.47	16 Platters, 16-inch	3.43	29 Cream Pitcher	.56
		17 Platters, 18-inch	4.93	30 Bowl, 5-inch	.43
7 Plates, scalloped edge, 8½-inch	3.80	18 Soup Tureen and Cover only (plated ladles are used)	4.93	31 Cake Plate	.79
8 Plates, scalloped edge, 8-inch, Soup	3.80	19 Sauce Tureen and Stand (plated ladles are used)	2.27	33 Celery Tray	1.00
				34 Jelly Dish	.79

Carnot Pattern French China.
Manufactured by Haviland & Co., Limoges, France.

This beautiful pattern is genuine Haviland china, every piece marked Haviland & Co., Limoges. We call special attention to the handsome shape, which is the latest production of this celebrated maker. It is artistically hand decorated with delicate sprays of cornflowers in soft tints of pink and blue. The handles are richly finished in gold clouded effect. This pattern cannot fail to please anyone desiring the best made. We will be pleased to furnish any number of pieces you may select.

Fig. 1.15 Offering of china from the Montgomery Ward & Co. catalogue, 1895.

Glassware—Continued.

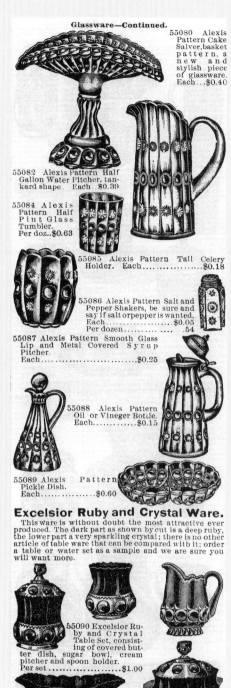

55080 Alexis Pattern Cake Salver, basket pattern, a new and stylish piece of glassware. Each...$0.40

55082 Alexis Pattern Half Gallon Water Pitcher, tankard shape. Each. $0.39

55084 Alexis Pattern Half Pint Glass Tumbler. Per doz..$0.63

55085 Alexis Pattern Tall Celery Holder. Each.................$0.18

55086 Alexis Pattern Salt and Pepper Shakers, be sure and say if salt or pepper is wanted. Each....................$0.05 Per dozen....................54

55087 Alexis Pattern Smooth Glass Lip and Metal Covered Syrup Pitcher. Each....................$0.25

55088 Alexis Pattern Oil or Vinegar Bottle. Each............$0.15

55089 Alexis Pattern Pickle Dish. Each.................$0.60

Excelsior Ruby and Crystal Ware.

This ware is without doubt the most attractive ever produced. The dark part as shown by cut is a deep ruby, the lower part a very sparkling crystal; there is no other article of table ware that can be compared with it; order a table or water set as a sample and we are sure you will want more.

55090 Excelsior Ruby and Crystal Table Set, consisting of covered butter dish, sugar bowl, cream pitcher and spoon holder. Per set....................$1.00

55091 Excelsior Ruby and Crystal Berry Set, consisting of one 8-inch dish and six 4-inch dishes. Price...$1.10

55094 Excelsior Ruby and Crystal Berry Set, consisting of one 8-inch dish and twelve 4-inch dishes.....$1.65

55096 Excelsior Ruby and Crystal Half-gallon Pitcher, the prettiest jug made. Price....................$1.00

55097 Excelsior Ruby and Crystal Tumblers to match pitcher. Per dozen.....................1.50

55098 Excelsior Ruby and Crystal Celery holder. .50

Fig. 1.16 Selection of pressed glass from the Montgomery Ward & Co. catalogue, 1895.

sets were attractive for women's entertainments or for temperance households, where the two beverages were offered as healthful alternatives to wine or beer at meals.[2]

In the late nineteenth century, interest in artistic decor encouraged the proliferation of special sets of dishes intended to embellish single courses. Since the seventeenth century the most important aesthetic standard for home furnishings of all kinds had been that they match completely. People of means decorated rooms with single styles of furniture and in one color only. The same standard had previously applied to tablewares. But the craze for artistic decoration that started around 1880 meant that good taste now included the ability to mix and match different styles and colors of objects. The anonymous author of *Good Manners,* published when the desire for artistic decor was at its height, advised:

> Not very long ago sets of china sufficient for the entire service of a dinner were considered essentials of even simple housekeeping. . . . Now the same number of pieces are rarely seen in uniform color of pattern, except in the closets of a house whose mistress has numbered them among her possessions for a long time. For each separate course of a dinner there is an appropriate service of ware which may be . . . obtainable for a very small sum. Fish sets, game sets, meat sets, oyster sets, sour sets, etc. are fashionable in widely differing styles, varieties of ware and coloring.[3]

What a relief this must have been for women who had not received as gifts, nor been able to purchase, all the dishes they felt they needed when they married. What once would have been "making do" became "aesthetic," and mixing and matching "harmonious" patterns seems to have remained a standard practice ever after.

The 1895 Montgomery Ward catalogue clearly reflected this trend in its tableware novelties. Along with the glass and silver pieces described above, the crockery department also offered small sets of teawares and individual cups and saucers. Salad bowls, celery dishes, bone dishes, and butter pats filled out table services, while cake and fruit plates, berry sets, and ice-cream bowls made dessert special. "Tom and Jerry" sets for alcohol punches were the only overt nod to the social lives of men.

How accessible were Montgomery Ward's tablewares? Interpreting these prices in modern terms is difficult, but historians calculate that $1.00 in 1895 can be compared to $16.00 in 1991.[4] Thus, a young family of modest means could have outfitted itself with the fifty-six-piece tea set of *Coral* for the equivalent of about $82.00 and a dozen simple glass tumblers for under $5.00. Silverware, even plated or white metal, represented the largest investment—a dozen white metal teaspoons priced at $1.10 in 1895 dollars would be almost $18.00 in today's terms. Cheaper options existed, but Montgomery Ward did not aim at that audience. The relatively high cost of nice things, and the way that the mail-order house offered them as open stock suggests that aspiring families built collections of decorative tablewares over time. The Montgomery Ward catalogues enticed rural and small-town consumers with new and wonderful things, as well as items with which to augment possessions that they already had, like tableware. The fact that catalogues arrived in the mail several times a year ensured that additions would almost certainly be made.

Notes

1. Morse [1908], 73.

2. W. J. Rorabaugh, cited in Grover 1987, 24–46.

3. *Good Manners* 1888, 120.

4. McCusker 1992, table A-2, "Consumer Price Indexes, United States, 1700–1991."

Domestic Science and "Dainty" Eating

The rise of "domestic science," or "home economics," at the turn of the century not only changed patterns of entertaining but promoted, and to some extent succeeded in bringing, changes in the American diet.[34] The discipline was an effort to subject the largely private routines of housekeeping to the same kinds of rational planning that marked the rise of the modern corporation and the professionalization that reshaped such fields as law and medicine and created new ones such as social work. Domestic science was invented by women themselves who attempted to dignify and expand through education the traditional gender roles they were unable to or did not want to challenge more broadly.

Female advocates of the new scientific approach to food did benefit from research on the nutritional characteristics of its components, but they also shared some eccentricities with pre–Civil War food reformers such as Sylvester Graham (whose legacy lives on, in what he would consider a highly adulterated form, in the modern graham cracker). Graham, Orson Fowler, and other diet reformers argued that much American food, especially the large quantities of meat consumed everywhere, overstimulated the body, shortened the life span, and even worse, made men subject to animal passions that advancing civilization needed to control and suppress. A good diet—most supported a diet largely of whole grains, vegetables, and fruits with carefully controlled amounts of meat or none at all, no alcohol, and few spices—stimulated the body only moderately and encouraged the higher intellectual and spiritual faculties.[35] In other words, it was antisensual.

Domestic scientists represented a second and more influential wave in the debate over the impact of diet on both health and morals, but they appropriated certain antisensual assumptions. "A great change in the methods of living has taken place in America during the last few years," applauded Sarah Tyson Rorer, the principal of the Philadelphia Cooking School. "There was a time in the memory of teachers yet quite young when schools of cookery were places where persons were taught to make all sorts of fancy, oft and occasionally used [rarely served] dishes. In fact, to succeed with these elaborate dyspeptic-producing concoctions was the highest ambition." The modern teacher or cookbook, which she praised as "an ever present teacher," now rejected "elaborate cooking to please the palate and appetite, and the general habits of people." Such individuals were "still in the palate stage of existence," believing, poor things, that the most important aspect of food was that it taste good. "Strive to reach a higher plane of thought—eat to live," Rorer urged. She even linked what she considered "food debauchery" with drunkenness. "Is the headache that follows a food debauchery more pleasant or pardonable or less injurious than that which follows drink? Results of intemperance are identical. Simple living and high thinking have the approval of learned men and women."[36]

What did this scientific approach to food bring to the American table? The new cooking promoted by Fannie Farmer, Sarah Rorer, and other stars of the new domestic science was largely, although not by any means exclusively, what would have been termed "plain cooking" to differentiate it from the "rich" delicacies of formal dining. With its reliance on lard and butter and sauces, some of this food seems quite rich today from the present cholesterol-conscious perspective, but much plain cooking did in fact rely on simply roasting and boiling ingredients. And in fact the majority of people ate rather plain food most of the time anyway. In her wonderful book *Perfection Salad*, Laura Shapiro argues that scientific cooking led to "a persistent, irreconcilable standoff between the functions of cooking and eating." Because scientific cooking disdained "the proof of the palate," its processes "emphasized every aspect of food except the notion of taste; and, similarly, the only procedure of kitchen or dining room that nearly always passed without mention was the act of eating."[37]

SETTING THE TABLE

One of the stranger subfields to grow out of domestic science was an entire literature on scientific table setting in which the food in question was simply a substance to be distributed smoothly from "factory" (kitchen) to "consumer" (diner). In the mid-nineteenth century, etiquette books and ladies' magazines had sometimes offered directions on new methods of table service, such as the *service à la russe*. Now, however, table setting and service were part of the curriculum of cooking schools, and books like Lucy G. Allen's *Table Service* (first edition, 1915) not only reflected professional training for "waitresses," a new genre of female occupation, and the vanishing species "domestic servant," but directed advice to scientifically minded young housekeepers as well. Allen taught "table-service courses" at Fannie Farmer's School of Cookery in Boston, and her little volume received Farmer's blessing "with the hope that it may help those who are striving for the beauty of a well-ordered house and of gracious service."[38]

Table Service is indeed a technical manual, and its publishing history suggests that it was a popular one. After the first edition, the book was reprinted thirty-five times until 1949, and revised in 1924, 1933, and 1940. Chapter after mind-numbing chapter is devoted to such topics as "Laying Table for a Home Dinner and Serving in Detail." Allen was utterly serious about the "detail" part. Serving a four-course dinner of clam chowder, roast beef with potatoes and canned corn with bread, dressed lettuce and graham bread sandwiches, and blanc mange with crackers and cheese is laid out in thirty-five separate steps. The main course was to be served as follows:

VI. Place platter of beef and Franconia potatoes (napkin).

VII. While host carves, place dish for canned corn at left of each plate. Take dishes from serving-table, one in each hand. Place the one in left hand at left, change the one in right hand to left hand, and place; return to serving table and repeat till all are placed.

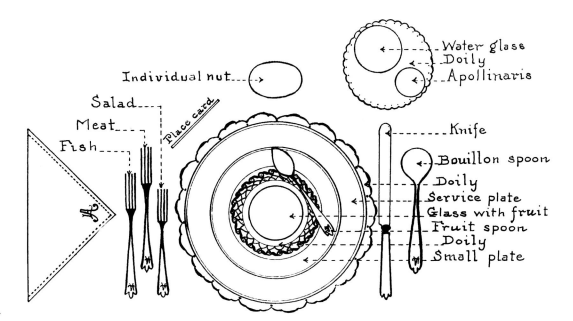

Individual nut
Salad
Meat
Fish
Place card
Water glass
Doily
Apollinaris
Knife
Bouillon spoon
Doily
Service plate
Glass with fruit
Fruit spoon
Doily
Small plate

Fig. 1.17 Table-setting diagrams put everything in its proper place.

VIII. Take filled plate from host (left hand), and place heated plate, the extra one for serving (right hand).

IX. Place filled plate before person to be served (left hand), removing heated plate (right hand), take to carver, and proceed as before.

X. Pass the gravy, ladle in dish (napkin).

XI. Pass canned corn, spoon in dish (napkin).

XII. Pass bread (napkin).

XIII. Remove roast with carving set and spoon on platter.

XIV. Remove carving cloth.[39]

Throughout the book carefully labeled diagrams also demonstrated such topics as "Luncheon Cover in Detail," emphasizing a rigid geometry in the arrangement of the tabletop (fig. 1.17).

This approach to table setting and service was an offshoot of Taylorism, the study of scientific time management that sought "one best way" to do any job efficiently. The women who found this approach to table service seductive probably adhered to the "business model" of the scientific housekeeper articulated in so much of the literature: "The home is the woman's 'job' and the table is one of the most important details of that job. If it appeals to her 'customers' (the family) the other departments of her 'business' seem to run more smoothly."[40]

Books like *Table Service* make clear just how complex and class-bound the Victorian vision of even middle-class family dining could be. It was a view that assumed and required the presence of surplus, cheap, female labor, both paid and unpaid.[41] With six diners, even that four-course family dinner required twelve service dishes, a coffeepot, sugar and creamer, ten pieces of service flatware, thirteen pieces of china and glassware per person and eight pieces of flatware per person

for a total of 151 objects needing washing and storing following the meal (not counting the pots and pans)!

The literature of table service developed a second, longer-lived offshoot that emphasized style in table setting and that even developed a small cult of celebrity associated with famous hosts and hostesses and with tableware manufacturers and retailers considered especially fashionable, such as Lenox China and Tiffany & Co. Tabletop style books seem to have appeared around the turn of the century. One of the first examples was a pamphlet offered by post "to all except the merely curious" by the china and glass retailer Higgins & Seiter in 1903. Called "Serving a Dinner," it was authored by "the famous expert OSCAR of the Waldorf Astoria."[42] Sarah Rorer, whose commentary on civilized progress and cooking has been discussed, became another food celebrity as "the nation's instructress in cookery" for the *Ladies' Home Journal*. Her name appeared on an early celebrity table-setting book in 1905. *How to Set a Table* was distributed by the flatware manufacturers R. Wallace and Sons for 4 cents in postage.[43] This literature, along with associated in-store marketing events such as contests, expanded dramatically in the 1930s and 1940s (see chapter 4).

THE LADIES' LUNCHEON

The domestic science movement was coincidental with, and perhaps contributed to, the proliferation of feminized occasions for household entertaining. If some housewives came to believe in the business model of housekeeping (which was certainly different from the "sacred calling" metaphor that shaped their grandmothers' perceptions of housework), they might also have accepted the necessity of rest and recreation that was part of the new rhetoric of business success in the early twentieth century. The expanded world of domestic social life included a revival of the tea party and the emergence of the ladies' luncheon as an important occasion until its decline in the 1960s and 1970s.

After the Civil War increasing numbers of American men had joined fraternal orders, from the Masons to the

Fig. 1.18 Peggy Wood, star of *I Remember Mama,* with tableware maven Carole Stupell (right) setting a luncheon table in Stupell's New York shop, 1954.

Woodmen. There they created a highly theatrical social life for themselves that, it has been argued, helped them cope with the rapid changes in business and work life in the great era of American industrialization. Men's boosterish service clubs for businessmen such as Rotary, with its lunchtime meetings featuring sing-alongs, came into prominence in the 1920s. With few exceptions, women were not part of that social life, which took place in buildings they often were not even allowed to enter. But for middle-class women at least, their impulses to join with other women found an outlet in women's clubs. The clubs about which the most is known today—such as the Women's Christian Temperance Union (founded 1873–74), the General Federation of Women's Clubs (founded 1890), and the National Association of Colored Women (founded 1896)—were settings where women received information on the latest ideas in domestic science or on reform efforts benefiting women and children. It seems clear, however, that there was considerably more local club activity among middle-class women. In this expanded social life—which included book clubs, literary societies, garden clubs, and card clubs—women consciously created entertainments for their peers in such traditional female meeting places as churches and private houses.

The organized formal tea party flourished anew under these conditions. The first set of truly special-use ceramics in many American households of the eighteenth and first half of the nineteenth centuries had been for serving tea—teapot, hot water kettle, waste bowl, sugar bowl and creamer, and matching cups and saucers. Tea drinking was often the only expression of "formal" sociability available to people who could not assemble enough equipment for a dinner party, and it was one of the signal rituals of eighteenth-century gentility. Although men attended formal teas on occasion, the tea party was also the first largely female dining ritual. (In this country, until the

1820s, the dinner party seems to have been largely a male event, as was all sociality driven by alcoholic beverages.)[44] In the late nineteenth century the old ritual of the tea party received a boost partly as a phenomenon of the colonial revival, especially with the Martha Washington Tea, a kind of combination tea and costume party where women dressed in "colonial" garb. Although tea itself was no longer an expensive treat, and coffee came to be added to the menu, teas organized by social clubs, alumnae associations, and as part of neighborhood social life continued to be popular well into the third quarter of the twentieth century. Such events provided the perfect opportunity to display collections of teacups, a ceramic form that many American women collected until the 1960s, as well as one's culinary skill in the form of miniature food, such as sweets and finger sandwiches cut into decorative shapes. These delicacies were often served on special glass or pottery "snack sets" that allowed the user to stand while nibbling and drinking tea (cat. 9).

Teas remained popular female entertainments into the 1960s because of the relative simplicity of tea food—and the opportunity teas presented for using wedding-gift or heirloom silver that otherwise gathered dust, as well as china, glass, and linens (cat. 8). One writer opined, "There is no wiser way of fulfilling one's social obligations" and pointed out that, for the infamous "woman without servants," a tea party was one of the only instances where one could feel free to ask friends to assist in pouring while the hostess greeted guests.[45]

The ladies' luncheon was especially beloved by the domestic science establishment and received a lot of attention from table-setting advisors, cookbook writers, and women's magazines for decades. Because women were not expected to want a hearty meal at midday, the table decor's "daintiness and feminine charm" were at least as important as the food presented: "Perhaps it is a formal affair for a visiting guest, for your favorite committee, or that all-important moment when you break the news that you are a bride-to-be. Whatever it is, the setting brings out all your originality. In detail and atmosphere it is the complete expression of your talents as a hostess."[46] Originality in the ladies' luncheon was more important than for family dinners, since the audience was a woman's true peers.

The ladies' luncheon in the first half of the twentieth century brought to the ephemeral art of domestic table decor a new level of elaboration (fig. 1.18). The old-fashioned display recalled by Della Lutes and Ethel Spencer of dishes and silver on spotlessly white linens, perhaps ornamented by condiment dishes and a centerpiece of garden flowers or fruit, was no longer adequate. Rather, luncheon tables might be criss-crossed with chains of real daisies on a green cloth, or draped with fishnet embellished with an armada of miniature boats or drifts of seashells from a vacation at the ocean, while swags or balls of flowers or ferns swung from the lamp above the table. Crepe paper decorations were a particular craze in early 1900s, and tabletops were littered with giant flowers and butterflies, palm trees, valentines, and figures of colonial ladies. Colorful napkins of crepe paper were introduced at the same time and were probably the first use of disposables for at-home entertaining. Published plans for such parties often included novelties in tablewares, such as inexpensive colored glass luncheon sets or pieces painted by the lady of the house herself. By emphasizing the short-lived and replaceable in tabletop settings, the ladies' luncheon and its associated forms moved these activities firmly into the fashion system. Dishes were no longer an investment but a seasonal whim, like a new hat (fig. 1.19).

During most of the twentieth century manufacturers who diligently sought to convince women that tableware was indeed a replaceable item of fashion developed new designs and forms specifically for the ladies' luncheon while promoting old ones for this setting. Clear and colored glass plates and serving pieces, for example, never seem to have really caught on for dinner, but they were extremely popular at lunchtime (cats. 10, 75). Since women were not supposed to drink liquor, punch bowls were sold to help quench the female thirst when they gathered (cat. 11). The snack sets mentioned above were also heavily promoted for ladies' lunching, as were some of the more avant-garde tableware lines. Because women put such emphasis on fashion and creativity at luncheons, the tableware could be much more imaginative, even controversial, compared to the conservative ware used at formal dinners. When marketed as a luncheon service, a line like Eva Zeisel's exuberant *Town and Country* (1946) for Red Wing Pottery was more acceptable to women who were not particularly interested in contemporary design (cat. 12).

The feminine social occasions that magazines, books, and manufacturers encouraged featured a special gendered cuisine designated as "dainty." As an expression of the feasting tradition, dainty cooking still relied on the profound transformation of the raw materials but is notable for its single-minded emphasis on the visual characteristics of food—and its rejection of gross abundance. Proponents of the new scientific cooking believed that attractive presentation was important, especially for family meals, not for the simple delight it fostered but because it activated critical digestive processes such as salivation. Since dainty cooking was intended for the feminine cognoscenti, there was no need to worry about stimulating appetites, which were supposed to be thoroughly in check.

Dainty cooking, reflecting the increasingly visual culture of late-nineteenth- and early-twentieth-century America, created decorative food with dollops of color and elaborate garnishes, and gave rise to table settings that matched the food. Color-theme meals, where all the dishes were dyed pink with beet juice or rendered white with liberal applications of white sauces, were essential for the success of thematic get-togethers such as Valentine's Day luncheons. Aesthetics were clearly more important than "nutritive value" or anything else in the recipes presented in Janet McKenzie Hill's *Salads, Sandwiches and Chafing-Dish Dainties* (1899). An entire book of dainty food, Hill's little volume featured fifty extraordinary photographic illustrations of various unlikely combinations (fig. 1.20). Edna Sibley Tipton's *Table Service for the Hostess* (1926) suggested that thematic meals be tied to the seasons; she offered a menu for August, "the seashore month," in which rather inexpensive ingredients were transformed by a shell theme:

Sardine and Hard-Boiled Egg Hors d'œuvre (in oyster shell)

Chicken Salad Sandwich (made with whole wheat bread and cut in the shape of an oyster shell)

Olives (served in eggshells)

Peas (in their own shells)

Tomato Slices

Ice Cream on Meringue Shells

Nuts in their Shells

Bonbons (served in large sea shells masquerading as bonbon dishes)[47]

Meals like this were one long culinary pun or puzzle. Sylvia Lovegren's marvelous cookbook and food history, *Fashionable Foods: Seven Decades of Food Fads* (1995), noted that in ladies' luncheon menus of the 1930s dishes such as the infamous "surprise" sandwich loaves (which survived into the 1960s) were all "garnished, masked, encased, or made to look like something else."[48]

OVERLEAF:
Cat. 8 Tea and coffee services like this one by Franciscan were used primarily for women's social occasions by the mid-20th century.

Cat. 10 Duncan & Miller Glass Company's *Terrace* is an example of the type of glass tableware that became popular in the 1930s.

Cat. 11 This *Caribbean* punch set (1935) would have seen service upon festive occasions.

OPPOSITE:
Cat. 9 In the postwar years, speckles, stripes, and grid patterns were all the rage on inexpensive dishes including snack sets (left).

Cat. 12 Unusually shaped dishes like Red Wing Pottery's *Town and Country* were popular for lunch but were generally deemed too informal for dinner.

Fig. 1.19 Glass plates were especially popular at ladies' luncheons starting in the 1920s.

Fig. 1.20 Presentation was everything when serving dainty food.

The Onset of "Casual Dining," 1920–1945

The early-twentieth-century vision of an orderly household where scientifically prepared and graciously served meals provided moral and physical sustenance to high-minded family members (without overstimulating their senses) was seriously challenged by new options for middle-class living in the years following World War I. One of the most concise and thoughtful summaries of the effects of rapid social change, *Middletown*, by Robert S. and Helen Merrill Lynd, appeared in 1929. The couple and their team of researchers in the 1920s intensively studied Muncie, Indiana (called Middletown in the book), using the methods of social anthropology to determine how the lives of ordinary Americans in smaller urban centers had changed since the 1890s.

By the 1920s Middletown's men and women increasingly embraced social gatherings that got them out of the house; in fact, sometimes it seems that they could not wait to leave the domestic shrines that had dominated social life in the previous generation. In the new "country clubs," for example, members of the community's elite class could mingle over newly popular sports such as golf or tennis or meet as couples over dinner. The Lynds noted that the business class (their useful term for the expanded world of white-collar and professional workers and local elites) often gave parties "in some public or semi-public buildings outside of the home; a woman may entertain a table of guests for luncheon as part of a large Country Club luncheon; or two women may hold a bridge party or reception in the ball room of a hotel or the parlors of the Elks' Club elaborately transformed for the occasion into a Japanese garden; or four wives and husbands may jointly entertain a dozen mutual friends at dinner at a hotel or the Elks' Club and then repair to one of their homes for an evening of bridge."[49]

The etiquette books of the 1920s validated this change, which entailed an expanded conception of women as actors in public and embraced settings that had not even existed thirty years earlier. The author of *American Etiquette* (1926) gushed, "Today a large part of formal entertaining in cities is no longer *at home*. Elaborate dinners, teas, and luncheons are given at one's club, or at *cafés*, exclusive 'tea rooms,' and in the elegantly appointed private dining-rooms now provided by the best hotels" (fig. 1.21; cats. 13, 14).[50]

Although home entertaining had not disappeared in Middletown, it now took a more organizational form. According to the Lynds, Middletown was also "dotted with social clubs, chiefly women's clubs, but in a limited number of cases they included husbands as well: the Kill Kare Club, Jolly Eight, Best of All Club, Happy Twelve, Bitter Sweet Club, and so on. Here cards, games among the working class, music, or dancing, and always 'refreshments' offer Middletown an alternative from routine duties of life."[51] The popularity of card clubs, especially "mixed" ones, in Middletown was something rather new. The middle-class couples' bridge club, for example, reflected new ideas about what was called companionate marriage, where husbands and wives were supposed to be each other's friends as well as partners in the serious business of life.[52] Women's card clubs of the 1920s frankly eschewed cultural or social uplift, the justification for the earlier women's club movement. That women had time for afternoon card parties also reflected changes in housekeeping routines for wives whose dwellings were equipped with electricity, cooking gas, central heat, and full plumbing.

OPPOSITE:
Cat. 13 Dishes like these brightly colored and boldly patterned Czech wares were favored in tea rooms and at breakfast.

Cat. 14 *Pyramid* and *Tea Room* (right) were made for commercial and domestic use in the mid-1920s.

Fig. 1.21 The Green Teapot Tea Room, New York, 1906.

Time-consuming daily chores like filling and cleaning lamps and stoking and cleaning a coal range had disappeared from middle-class households; while women who did not work outside the home were certainly busy running their homes, they had greater flexibility in their daily schedules.

Canny tableware producers and marketers capitalized on this new kind of social life with novelties in ceramics, glass, and table linens (cats. 15, 16, 153; see pp. 54–56). Although ware especially designed for games such as mah-jongg existed, equipage for entertaining while playing bridge was by far the most common. These "bridge sets" consisted of special plates, glasses, and serving pieces, often with a theme of the four suits. Many hostesses served light snacks right at the table during breaks in play. Table-linen sets of a cloth and four napkins could also be purchased for use on card tables. During the depression, *Crockery and Glass Journal* advised struggling retailers on "Using Bridge Sessions to Stimulate Sales." The article discussed display tables at James McCreery & Co., New York, which were set for a "bridge tea," "bridge salad," and "bridge luncheon." These featured twelve-piece "bridge service" sets along with other "'bridge conceits' . . . to make your party successful, because we understand bridge psychology."[53]

OPPOSITE:

Cat. 15 Hostesses at mah-jongg parties served refreshments on Noritake porcelain designed for the occasion.

Cat. 16 The popularity of card playing provided commercial opportunities for Limoges China Company at midcentury.

The eclectic taste of nineteenth-century American consumers prompted tableware manufacturers, especially silverware producers, to offer novelty dining accessories ranging from asparagus tongs to oyster plates (cat. 7). While the twentieth century saw a decline of specialty items in silverware, clever pottery- and glass-makers continued to satisfy the insatiable American appetite for dishes by providing specialized ware for every occasion and every type of food. Fish and game services consisting of a single large platter and twelve plates, each elaborately decorated with a different type of fish or fowl, remained popular with middle-class consumers as a means of attaching special significance to these foods as a main course (cat. 4). Less formally the chop plate served the same purpose, turning a large round platter of meat into a presentation focal point for hungry eyes.

Other types of ware were developed to accompany specialized entertaining. The creation of the "ladies' luncheon" and the resurgence of card playing in the 1920s led to the appearance of the first snack plates—asymmetrical dishes for finger food with a well for a coffee cup that were small enough to sit on the corner of a card table (cats. 9, 15, 175). Larger sets were also designed for use at more elaborate functions that included luncheon. Often decorated with images of cards, dominoes, or mah-jongg game pieces, these colorful accompaniments mirrored the lively conversation and spirited competition that marked such club events (cat. 16).

If card parties were the favorite social pastime of the afternoon, the cocktail party became the Jazz Age's mark of sophisticated evening entertaining. Glassware makers responded with stylish shaker sets, decanters, and glasses specially designed for every potent concoction imaginable, from martinis to highballs (cats. 17, 37, 75, 177).

The 1930s heralded the introduction of other notable novelty sets for special meals. "Spaghetti sets" first appeared in 1933, when a trade reporter announced that the Philadelphia importing firm of Fisher, Bruce & Co. had available "one of the cleverest ideas that has been brought out for some time." This spaghetti set, appropriately, was made of Italian earthenware. The set consisted of a large covered

bowl, six 9-inch coupe-shaped dishes, and a smaller bowl for cheese. Noting that these sets were intended for informal suppers, the reporter reassured readers that spaghetti sets could also be used for other treats such as "clam chowder, chow mein, and the like."[1]

Corn sets were also introduced around this time, featuring individual cob-shaped dishes as colorful and realistically decorated as nineteenth-century majolica (cat. 34).[2] There were egg plates as well, in both ceramic and glass. Round dishes with individual wells to hold deviled eggs, these serving plates were the perfect complement to informal gatherings around the barbecue or buffet table.[3] With dishes like these and promotions geared toward annual holi-

day events, tableware manufacturers sought to convince American consumers that a specialized dish was all it took to turn a meal into an occasion.

Ever since the pilgrims paused to give thanks for their harvest, Americans have gathered around the table to celebrate holidays with a special meal. This practice is not unique to the United States, but with the close proximity of Thanksgiving to Christmas, no other country has such a sustained holiday shopping season, providing tableware makers with ample opportunity for creative production. Perhaps the most famous example of specialty holiday ware is Spode's enduring Yuletide design, *Christmas Tree,* created in 1938 (cat. 18). The pattern itself emerged quite randomly

OPPOSITE:
Cat. 17 A. H. Heisey & Co. ushered in the repeal of Prohibition with barware appropriately named *New Era* in 1934.

ABOVE:
Cat. 18 Spode's *Christmas Tree* pattern launched a wave of holiday novelty ware.

Fig. 1.22 This early artificial Christmas tree of 1939 is reminiscent of Spode's design.

from the collaboration between Spode's agent in North America, Sidney E. Thompson, of the firm Copeland & Thompson in New York, and a young staff designer named Harold Holdway at the Spode works in Stoke-upon-Trent, Staffordshire, England.

About twice a year Thompson would travel to Staffordshire and stay several weeks working on new designs aimed at the American consumer. The young Holdway had been with W. T. Copeland & Sons (the maker of Spode) only for about four years, so he was still the most junior member of the design team when the art director, Thomas Hassell, called him to the front office and introduced him to Thompson.[4] The American agent was a formidable presence whenever he came to the Copeland factory. By then the North American market had become the most important priority for design, and everyone's job depended on the success or failure of patterns designed for sale there. Holdway was therefore somewhat anxious when Thompson told him that he "wanted something for Christmas" to fit on a line of plates, cups, and saucers. What should it look like? Except for a few decorative gift plates, there had never been any special dinnerware for the Christmas season.

Holdway went back to the studio and emerged a short time later with a watercolor drawing on a plate. In the center was one large Christmas tree, its branches laden with gifts and ornaments. Hassell thought the single large tree dominating the plate was ghastly.[5] Thompson took to it, however, remarking, "I think you've got something there Sonny, but there is one thing wrong—in America we put all the presents under the tree at the base, and the next morning we open them."[6] Young Holdway went back to his desk and returned with a design showing the presents, all boxed and tied with bows, sitting under the tree. Thompson was pleased, but this time Holdway thought the whole layout was a bit too symmetrical, and he suggested adding a sprig of mistletoe at the upper right. Painted rims of either green or mulberry red were added, and in the space of an hour the most popular pattern ever sold by Spode was born.

At first only a dinner plate and a cup and saucer were produced because no one could predict the reaction to the new pattern. The response was immediate: every New York buyer that Thompson showed it to loved the design and placed an order. *Christmas Tree* was an instant success, prompting countless copies and knockoffs. To guard against the market considering the pattern a one-time novelty, Thompson ordered the motto "Wishing You a Happy Christmas 1938" removed from the backstamp after the first run. He did not want any date or the word "Christmas" on the plate, even though the association with the holiday was quite obvious. Thompson planned that the consumer would buy the set as a regular pattern to be used annually from Thanksgiving to New Year's, and believed he could sell more Christmas dinnerware than Thanksgiving turkey platters, which were considered a novelty accessory.

After World War II, when the Copeland factory almost closed because of the changing taste of its consumers, the mulberry border was dropped and more pieces were added to the line to increase sales. *Christmas Tree* became so successful that it kept Spode in business, and the pattern is still in production at the end of the century—a testament to the enduring American taste for specialty ware on the tabletop.

Notes
1. "Five and Ten Cent Glass Dinnerware Business," *CGJ* 112:1 (Jan. 1933): 17.

2. *CGJ* 127:1 (June 1940): 24.

3. *CGJ* 140:4 (Apr. 1947): 2.

4. Holdway interview 1997.

5. Copeland interview 1997.

6. Holdway interview 1997.

PROCESSED FOODS AND THE COMING OF THE CASSEROLE

The increase in organized social life affected family eating patterns as well. While the authors of *Middletown* still insisted that "the dining-room table is the family's General Headquarters," they acknowledged that the family meal was "under the decentralizing pull of a more highly diversified and organized leisure—in which Hi-Y, basket-ball games, high school clubs, pedro and bridge clubs, civic clubs, and Men's League dinners each drain off their appropriate members from the family group."[54] The Lynds noted that Middletowners worried about this trend, although no one seemed to have a solution—and no one wanted to give up the new social whirl.

If meals were less important, so too was cooking for the family. Middletown's residents themselves had noticed that "cooking occupies a less important place today" in both "business class" and working-class families, and that even in home entertainments "the trend is away from the earlier attention to elaborate food."[55] In Middletown the shift toward processed foods, which had begun across the United States decades earlier with the national marketing of branded groceries, was firmly in place by the 1920s. A local butcher commented on a recent preference for cuts of meat that could be cooked quickly: "Folks today want to eat in a hurry and get out in the car." Bread making had disappeared from most Middletown houses. The increased use of commercial canned vegetables, fruits, and soups was actually considered a blessing because not only did it mean "less time spent in home canning but a marked spread in the variety and healthfulness of the diet of medium- and low-income families throughout the bulk of the year when fresh garden products are expensive."[56]

Middletown women spent less time cooking, and their decisions about what to cook also were mediated in new ways. The Lynds recognized that changes in diet were "facilitated by the development of the modern women's magazine," which was very popular among Middletown's women:

> Under the old rule of thumb, mother-to-daughter method of passing down the traditional domestic economy . . . the home tended to resist the intrusion of new habits. There were practically no housekeeping magazines bringing knowledge of new skills and different methods. . . . Through these periodicals, as well as through the daily press, billboards, and other channels, modern advertising pounds away at the habits of the Middletown housewife. Whole industries mobilize to impress a new dietary habit upon her.[57]

Not only were the editors of women's magazines apparently in cahoots with the processed-food corporations, even the school system promoted a new kind of cooking in the day- and night-school home economics courses that served a reported 1,500 girls and women from the 9,200 homes of the city.

While Middletowners had grabbed a firm hold on the new ways of postwar America, the researchers noticed some ambivalence about changing food habits. Large quantities of meat remained the centerpiece of dining. Families with modest incomes or traditional tastes still "put up" tomatoes and fruits, especially jellies. And the Lynds noted, "One of the federated women's clubs recently gave over a program to a debate of the question, 'Shall a Conscientious Housewife Use Canned Foods?'"[58] The answer was a resounding Yes! Packaged foods had become staples in American pantries only during the previous generation, but women embraced them rapidly—boxed crackers such as Uneeda Biscuits, canned soups from Campbell Soup Company, canned vegetables and fruits sold under the labels of the new grocery chains such as the Kroger Company and the Great Atlantic and Pacific Tea Company, condiments from H. J. Heinz Company, and a large assortment of cold breakfast cereals from the Kellogg Toasted Corn Flake Company and its competitors.[59]

Since professional domestic scientists were employed by the new "test kitchens" of companies like Campbell Soup Company to help expand the market for their products, they developed a new genre of recipe that was widely distributed through giveaway cookbooks, magazine advertising, and the editorial content of women's magazines and newspapers, which relied on income from the ads purchased by processed-food companies. These new recipes always included the company's processed-food products as key ingredients. Already seasoned with salt and sugar, canned soups and bottled condiments became the sauces that bound together fresh ingredients such as ground meat or potatoes; canned beans could be spiffed up by adding cut-up frankfurters; or symphonies of convenience foods could be created by mixing cans together.

The late 1930s and 1940s mark the point in American culinary history when the "casserole" truly became a staple of everyday cooking. Practitioners of scientific cookery had long recommended baking ingredients together in a sauce *"en casserole"* to cope with leftovers, especially meat that was too precious to waste (the other dainty preference had been the croquette, a technique of food preparation that has virtually disappeared from both home cooking and restaurant menus). Books like Marion Harris Neil's *How to Cook in Casserole Dishes* (1912) introduced casseroles as acceptable social food. Processed foods changed the formula, however. In 1916 Campbell Soup Company published *Helps for the Hostess,* the breakthrough book that promoted using soups instead of struggling with lumpy, curdling homemade sauces. The title is significant. Soup cookery was company food right from the start. And in 1934 Campbell introduced the revolutionary soup-sauce—cream of mushroom.[60] By 1939 the *Better Homes and Gardens Cookbook* included an extensive section on casserole cooking, and the 1946 edition of *The Joy of Cooking* (first edition, 1931) by Irma S. Rombauer featured four "quick casserole dishes" consisting of canned fish, a starch of some kind (including canned potatoes), canned soup, and canned vegetables. Rombauer's tuna, noodle, and mushroom soup casserole—"an excellent emergency dish"—began to appear regularly on American tables.[61]

To accommodate the proliferation of casseroles and to boost profits, tableware makers added a new form, the

Cat. 19 Replete with curls and swirls, Charles Murphy's casserole designs for Red Wing Pottery were among the most playful in the early 1950s.

Fig. 1.23 Casseroles were the centerpieces of many a meal in the 1950s.

casserole dish, to their product lines or simply renamed the traditional covered vegetable dish during the interwar period. By midcentury the casserole dish was perhaps second only to plates, cups, and saucers in importance. These dishes came in both glass and pottery. Corning Glass Works made them from its new "miracle" glass, Pyrex, and employed teams of home economists to convince women to use its product rather than traditional metal and ceramic baking dishes. Big and showy, and thus more expensive than most tablewares, casserole dishes were embraced by potteries, which turned them out in a dizzying array of shapes and colors during the second and third quarters of the twentieth century (fig. 1.23; cats. 19, 22, 78, 88).

Beyond encouraging cooks to concoct casseroles with their ingredients, food processors invited them to simply stop doing certain kinds of skilled tasks—making soup stocks from bones, pickling vegetables and fruits to provide variety to winter diets, and mastering sauces and gravies. Companies acknowledged and answered the guilty little voice in the back of women's minds by appropriating the adjective "home-made" as a brand descriptor. A full-page advertisement by H. J. Heinz in the November 1933 issue of *Ladies' Home Journal* suggested, "Why not go Completely Puritan with your Thanksgiving Feast but prepare it in one-tenth the time that Priscilla spent," thanks to Heinz "home-made" canned soups, pickles and condiments, mincemeat pie filling, and even Heinz plum, fig, or date puddings.[62]

THE HOME TRANSFORMED

By the late 1920s the elements of a self-conscious kitchen decor and tablewares intended to bring style to kitchen dining appeared in both dime and department stores (fig. 1.24; cat. 20). The Victorian kitchen had been a food factory, designed for processing large quantities of raw materials into edible forms and dealing with the enormous amount of waste, from carrot tops to chicken feet, generated during the process. Many families took their meals at the kitchen table, and domestic advisers repeatedly told women they should make their primary work spaces "cheerful" and comfortable with rocking chairs, houseplants, and cages of singing canaries. But kitchen work and kitchen dining were not graciously informal; they were simply practical.

Changes in domestic architecture helped to make living, and eventually entertaining, in the kitchen an acceptable middle-class alternative. Many Americans adopted smaller but more convenient and fully modern living places, including flats in apartment blocks, bungalows, and little houses in a host of retrospective styles—from English Tudor to American colonial (fig. 1.25). Because of the expense of being fully electrified, plumbed, and centrally heated, these dwellings had to enclose fewer square feet if they were to be within reach of middle-class budgets. It is telling that as Americans opted enthusiastically for modern domestic systems, the formal parlor was the room that disappeared and the dining room shrank in size considerably.

The dining room was typically a rear ell of the main living room in bungalow floor plans; it could easily serve as "a combination sitting-sewing-library-dining-room" and, in a pinch, be separated from the front room with portieres.[63] In houses with narrow galley kitchens, the dining room was the only space for eating, but many kitchen plans now included cozy "dining nooks." Although they still argued for family dinners as dining-room occasions, the authors of the *Modern Priscilla Home Furnishing Book* (1925) applauded kitchen meals as part of a new emphasis on less formal living:

> For a good many years we have turned up our noses at eating in the kitchen, partly because we did not take special care to have the kitchen one of the most attractive rooms in the house. Since we have begun the healthy habit of making it so, we are resuming the wholesome and labor-saving fashion of having breakfasts and sometimes lunches in the same room where they are cooked. . . . Most modern kitchens are now built with a breakfast nook either in the kitchen or closely adjoining it.[64]

The Victorian sideboard, symbol of family wealth and hospitality, was also a victim of shrinking household space and the move to simplify furnishing schemes in American houses of the early twentieth century. To accommodate the smaller dining rooms of bungalows, the sideboard became smaller and often lost its ample upper display spaces and

Fig. 1.24 Colorful kitchen cabinets were fashionable in the 1920s.

Fig. 1.25 Smaller houses meant smaller dining rooms by the 1920s.

mirror. Edward Stratton Holloway, author of *The Practical Book of Furnishing the Small House and Apartment* (1922) praised a bungalow dining room where the sideboard was "pleasantly free from the bar-room display of glassware and the like, only too frequent in American homes."[65] He recommended that a practical storage alternative was a simple chest of drawers or a side table "as in Chippendale's time." Emily Post felt that the sideboard was unnecessary to a small dining room; a serving table would suffice.[66]

With the changes in household entertaining charted by the Lynds in the 1920s, the trends toward compactness and convenience in architecture, and the coming of economic depression, the formal dinner party limped into the 1930s in a much simplified form. Menus featured a smaller number of courses and less ostentatious food, although the published instructions for hosting a formal dinner still suggested that the experience was reserved for the couple whose means permitted hiring at least temporary help and whose house met other criteria. "Of course, one does not give a highly ceremonious dinner, or a formal, elaborate luncheon, in a house that is not well organized and well appointed—or if one does not

OPPOSITE:
Cat. 20 Homer Laughlin China's *Colonial Kitchen* was part of the movement toward warm, cozy kitchens.

have the skill, the service, the furnishings, the tact essential to such functions," sniffed Lillian Eichler, author of *The New Book of Etiquette*. This, despite the fact that "dinner-giving, even formal dinner-giving, is very much simpler than it was before the war. The dinner table that groaned under the load of ten or twelve courses has vanished, and modern menus are not only much simpler but very much lighter. . . . Places are no longer marked with gilt-edged cards, nor do guests always march into the dining room in stiff procession. Many of the old elaborate customs have been dropped."[67]

NEW TYPES OF ENTERTAINING

Under the regime of the new simplicity the "well-set table" displayed "the least number of pieces possible. The overburdened table, cluttered with all sorts of appointments, is in poor taste, as is the table made gaudy with unnecessary decorations. . . . At no time should there be more than three forks and two knives at any one cover [place setting]." It seems clear, however, that class distinction survived in other ways. Although the old standards of genteel etiquette, which had pressed the ideal of effortless self-control of highly artificial behaviors, no longer held sway, the new simplicity demanded another kind of effortlessness, even from a hostess with no help of any kind. This was the new order of "personality" and "charm," the code words for describing the successful

Cat. 21 Rimless and stackable, this plate from Universal Potteries' Melody Series of 1952 was perfect for buffets.

Cat. 22 Saving time with oven-to-table wares became increasingly important to women early in the 20th century.

modern hostess of the 1920s, 1930s, and beyond. The "frankly simple and informal" dinner actually required extremely careful planning so that the hostess did not have to leave the table repeatedly, including the use of a serving cart, a recent innovation in dining-room furnishings, for collecting dirty dishes and holding the second course in readiness. A single trip to the kitchen following the second course and filling the cart with the main course, dessert, and the coffee service were all that was necessary.[68] Informality was a style, not simply a reflection of thoughtlessness or lack of planning. By 1941 Helen Sprackling, whose articles on entertaining and interior decor were well known from magazines such as *Women's Home Companion* and *Better Homes and Gardens*, declared that "Even the most ultra of dinner menus today seldom has more than five courses. . . . Generally speaking, there are only four courses." The fish course had finally gone the way of the dodo.[69]

Late "suppers" at which guests chose their own refreshments from an array of dishes had been part of household entertainments such as evening dance balls in the nineteenth century, where large numbers and limited space made seated formality impossible. However, the serve-yourself supper received a makeover in the early twentieth century with the introduction of the fashionable "buffet": guests served themselves from a table laid with the entire meal and ate while sitting on the living-room furniture or at tables set only with cloths. The buffet notion appeared in advice books by around 1915 and was treated as something new (table-setting maven Lucy G. Allen felt compelled to define the term for her readership that year). It gradually provided a useful and popular formula for middle-class informality, and some even suggested that buffet service had actually become "smart" during the depression: "The buffet party was the social pattern of the hour. It demanded little in social skill but it had one definite virtue: it was honest."[70]

As buffet-style service became the norm for most home entertaining through the twentieth century, it changed party food and tablewares (cat. 21). Buffet food had to be easily handled because guests needed to serve themselves a portion or be served by the hosts or a helper with relative ease. This necessity made casserole hot dishes and food in tidbit form increasingly popular. Specialized buffet wares, used for cooking and presenting food and for keeping it warm, also proliferated. Helen Sprackling praised the "fascinating casseroles and baking dishes, which can go straight from the oven to the table" and the new selection of "electric serving appliances, perfected to keep an entire meal warm or to do the actual cooking at the table" (cats. 22, 23).[71] Buffet service also encouraged the use of serving-dish novelties, since the only

Cat. 23 A blend of science and art, *Moderne* carafes kept coffee piping hot at the table.

setting the hostess could use to impress guests with her originality was the service table itself. Dishes used for buffet service needed to be sturdy and stackable—or disposable by the 1950s. Hence the creation of the coupe-shaped plate. Russel Wright popularized this easy-to-stack rimless form in his highly successful *American Modern* dinnerware (introduced 1939; cat. 24). The shape made its debut in American fine china as part of Eva Zeisel's *Museum* line in 1946 (cat. 188).

At the turn of the century another novelty in entertaining, the chafing-dish supper, was introduced to middle-class cooks. The chafing dish, a shallow pan on a stand that used an alcohol lamp as its source of heat, apparently was at first a fad embraced by fashionable society at the Waldorf-Astoria Hotel in New York (fig. 1.26).[72] It quickly became part of the wedding-gift repertoire, but college students and middle-class working women also adopted it as a medium for cheap entertaining. The "most characteristic and novel feature" of supper made in a chafing dish was that cooking actually took place in front of the guests on the dining table. "This is what lends fascination to the process," wrote one cookbook author.[73] Chafing-dish cuisine was necessarily simple—

omelets, scrambled-egg mixtures, tidbits of precooked meat and fish reheated in sauces made on the spot, or cheese rarebit served with toast were especially popular. Advice authors recommended chafing-dish cooking for late or Sunday-evening suppers, "merry little after-theater parties," and luncheons. The problem with chafing-dish cookery was that the earthy process of cooking had to appear as effortless as company manners were supposed to be, as the ingredients for each dish were "daintily placed forth in pitchers or plates" and assembled while the cook talked and laughed with her company.[74] The serving style required a lot of confidence (and probably a number of rehearsals) because planning and timing had to be perfect. Nevertheless, the chafing dish was another step toward the demystification of the cook's feminine art, and toward the studied informality in entertaining that blossomed between the world wars.

THE SEA OF DISHES RECEDES

What did smaller living spaces and the new kinds of informal entertaining mean in terms of sets of dishes? When possible, Victorian housewives had kept two sets of dishes, a set of

Cat. 24 Strong and compact, and boasting innovative colors and shapes, *American Modern* appealed to millions following its introduction in 1939.

"everyday"—something relatively simple and sturdy like plain white stoneware—and a more fragile, often larger set, perhaps German or French porcelain, that was reserved "for good" (cats. 2, 79). One can tell from the 1895 Montgomery Ward catalogue that both everyday and "good" china represented long-term investments for families of modest means, to be augmented by a handful of novelties and periodically replenished from open stock if possible. The most popular everyday dishes seem to have been plain white, usually with a scalloped edge, or a monochromatic transfer-printed motif on a white ground. These preferences reflected the visual aesthetic of good housewifery, one that emphasized whiteness as a widely understood sign for cleanliness and womanly competence. White bedsheets and tablecloths, white napkins and towels, and spotlessly white ceramics (improper washing would have been instantly visible) were both sanitary and difficult to achieve.

Between the wars women still tried to keep both good and everyday sets of dishes. The results of a 1942 survey of newly married women conducted "to discover which of their wedding presents had been the most successful" demonstrated that the Victorian ideal of silver, china, and glassware selected to become family heirlooms still held sway.[75] This enduring ideal encouraged conservative taste, as the endless variations on colonial revival patterns demonstrate (cat. 25). However, even good sets continued to shrink in size. Editors of *Crockery and Glass Journal* in 1927 commented on new demand for "short sets" of forty-two pieces (settings for six and serving pieces): "Various reasons have been advanced as to why the demand for short sets will continue, and it does seem that the main reason is that little room exists in the modern apartment house for the old fashioned dinner service" of one hundred or more pieces.[76]

Shrinking household space was really only one factor, however. New kinds of entertaining were promoted by a food "fashion system" of processed-food companies and tableware

manufacturers, as well as home economists, magazine editors, and cookbook authors who had professional relationships with these industries. The Lynds had already noticed the impact of these interests on Middletown diets in the mid-1920s. Their impact only increased as the decades passed. A speeded-up cycle of fashionable novelty also encouraged consumption of smaller sets of tablewares that could be more easily purchased and replaced without guilt as new ideas about tabletop fashion were introduced. Staying on top of changes in style seems to have been increasingly important for consumers of tablewares. For example, even the modern hostess of the American hinterlands who purchased Montgomery Ward's New Art china in 1930 for $8.29 to $10.25 per set (approximately $69 to $84 in 1991 dollars) had to be assured that the designs had been recently introduced, and that "except through our catalogue these dishes will probably not reach the smaller cities of America before 1931."[77] The implication was that these designs were as ephemeral as the social occasions they graced or the dress of the hostess—and that was just fine.

The look of many of the sets used both every day and in the new ways of entertaining also changed in response to the food fashion system. Women snapped up brightly colored glassware and pottery in department stores and five-and-dime stores alike (cats. 72, 166). The five-and-dimes became increasingly important outlets for modern tablewares as the depression lingered. In 1933 *Ceramics and Glass Journal* pointed out that the economic crisis, "coupled with machine process, has driven a good deal of department store business into chain stores. . . . Kitchen glass, glass dinnerware, stemware, tumblers and decorative glass pieces may be purchased in great variety at 5¢, 10¢ or 20¢."[78] Two years after the 1936 launch of the ever popular *Fiesta* ware, which was sold in department stores, the Homer Laughlin China Company introduced *Harlequin*, a very similar but less expensive line sold by F. W. Woolworth & Co. for several decades (cats. 26, 28).

Tastemakers suggested that smart homemakers needed multiple sets of tablewares for everyday use. Stores sold tea sets and luncheon sets, but breakfast sets seem to have been a particularly popular special-use category. One gathers that not just a good meal but a cheerful, sometimes even zany breakfast table was somehow critical to the success of family life: "A gaily printed cloth, inexpensive colored pottery, an amusing pair of salts and peppers, a bowl of oranges or a red geranium for the decoration and you are off to a good start. You can find it all at the '5-and-10' if you have to" (cats. 27, 29, 151).[79]

The new kinds of informal pottery produced by American companies between the wars looked different from the everyday dishes of 1880 in ways that were intended to characterize trends in family and social life as the designers and manufacturers perceived them. "Casual" or "modern" tablewares reflected several distinct design concepts. Radical modernism based on avant-garde European art movements was rejected in the marketplace (cats. 162, 163), and thus many of the new wares of the 1920s and early 1930s were really only reinterpretations of long-standing preferences. Their brightly colored decal patterns descended from the popular transfer-printed floral patterns of the previous century, although the flowers were sometimes grafted onto streamlined shapes. However, tableware manufacturers increasingly offered consciously modern-style designs and colors in great variety in the 1930s and 1940s (fig. 1.27). No longer were most everyday dishes spotlessly white: contemporary tablewares were often glazed with vivid colors that did not always complement the food served on their surfaces; their edges were ornamented with speed lines, and their handles with semi-abstract whirls and wing shapes; their salt and pepper shakers and water pitchers were futuristic.

The new designs seemed especially appropriate for the only space in most houses that unabashedly celebrated modern technological progress—the kitchen. Kitchenwares of all kinds, from toasters to teapots, were more likely to show the

Cat. 25 Lenox China evoked romantic images of America's colonial past during the 1910s and 1920s with the names *Washington Wakefield, The Virginian,* and *The Mt. Vernon.*

rounded corners and other elements of streamlined design than other furnishings in houses (cats. 30, 31). The kitchen was often the only room in the house where machinery was openly displayed and celebrated—bright chrome percolators and waffle irons, compressor refrigerators, gas or electric stoves, irons and other gadgets. Next door in the living room, the family radio, the first of the new "electronic hearths," was still often encased in a colonial-style cabinet. Streamlined tablewares seemed to celebrate the kitchen and its work as a technological domestic utopia, where families ate in plain sight of some modern labor-saving wonders and actually ingested others, such as canned soup and "fruit cocktail."

As the United States was drawn into World War II, the relative simplicity of ration-coupon meals taken in the kitchens of households where nearly every adult, male or female, was either in the service or working in a mobilized industry, probably felt appropriate. Still, not everyone was pleased by the return of middle-class dining in the kitchen. In 1944 the *Boston Sunday Herald* published an editorial on the subject, whose author looked ahead with some distress on a world where new housing would be missing formal dining rooms:

This prospect can hardly be contemplated without mixed emotions. . . . It wasn't so long ago that probably the majority of American families ate in the kitchen. For that matter, it was scarce two generations ago when a great number of American families not twenty miles from [Boston] bathed in the kitchen too, in winter—on Saturday nights. . . . Dining rooms, no less than bathrooms, came as a step-up in urbane living. You put on your coat in the dining room and the meal became a kind of domestic ceremony, not just a stoking of the human boiler. There were pictures on the wall, and on the table pretty crockery or china, nice glassware and napkins. To eat in the kitchen was the slump back into sloppier ways of life.[80]

The writer wistfully concluded, "If there was no maid, the children were taught to set the table, and to mind their manners, too."

The most important contribution of the war years to changing patterns of entertaining at home may have been the

Cat. 26 Inspired by *Fiesta*, Homer Laughlin China's *Harlequin* was cheaper and more fragile.

Cat. 27 Homer Laughlin China's low-priced *Swing* line was contemporary with the Big Band era.

Cat. 29 In 1931 the Jeannette Glass Company added *Sierra* to the stream of inexpensive colored pressed glass that poured from depression-era glass factories.

"progressive dinner," in which neighborhood households pooled their ration coupons and traveled from house to house for each course of a meal. A 1943 article by the relentlessly cheerful food writer of the *Ladies' Home Journal* offered an example of how to make a big occasion out of modest fare: "Soup with Bill and Babs . . . a chicken avocado affair" created with condensed soup, a "frosted meat loaf" by "Nell and Madge," "salad at the Bob Pattons," and "divinely thin sugar cooky shells with cherry ice cream" and coffee at a fourth house. The formal dinner party had been thoroughly disassembled and parceled out.[81]

Socializing in the Atomic Age, 1945–1960

After World War II ordinary people returned to the business of everyday life that had been postponed or thwarted for so long both by economic circumstances and the war effort. The

OPPOSITE:
Cat. 28 Streamlined and spray glazed, *Fiesta* is one of the most successful dinnerwares in the history of the United States.

choices they made about where and how to live fostered distinctive patterns in social life that amplified the trend toward casual entertaining of the interwar years. Aided by the G.I. Bill, more men received college educations and moved into white-collar work that had been beyond their fathers' reach. The expansion of middle management in corporations and the relatively high wages enjoyed by skilled workers meant that more Americans than ever before could, and did, consider themselves part of a large, somewhat amorphous, middle class. The Veterans Administration loan program encouraged house ownership, and young families occupied new starter suburbs (the most famous being the Levittown developments in New York and Pennsylvania) and created distinctive social circles for themselves.[82] The busy social life of 1950s suburbs was orchestrated largely by women, many of whom had either gone to college or worked at demanding jobs during the war years and afterward supported husbands attending school. Finished with these phases of their lives, such women returned to full-time, and increasingly child-centered, housekeeping.

Fig. 1.27 As seen in this ad, making it match was important by 1932.

Fig. 1.28 Electrical refrigeration in the home caught on quickly in the late 1920s.

LIFE IN SUBURBIA

While suburban families considered themselves part of the great American middle class, they often had to economize to support a veteran husband's continuing education, to purchase and furnish a house (consumer spending rose dramatically in the decade after the war), and to begin the process of having and rearing children. Simultaneously, home entertaining received a boost because of a renewed nostalgic emphasis on life at home caused by lingering insecurities stemming from World War II. When books and women's magazines showered hostesses with advice on giving charming, informal buffet suppers and thrifty progressive dinners, and on making the kitchen the heart of social life, it seems they were expanding the norms of middle-class dining by embracing, without saying so, the kinds of social life that had never been abandoned by people further down the socioeconomic ladder. Working-class, ethnic social life had centered around the kitchen table by necessity and choice, but now advertisers in *Ladies' Home Journal* declared that "kitchen parties are fun . . . especially with a Chromcraft plastic top dinette. It's so gay and pretty you don't need decorations! But best of all, the gang can raise plenty of rumpus without staining or scratching the furniture."[83]

The kitchen had become a decorative, attractive, and even technologically utopian space in the interwar years, but the decade following World War II furthered the change with what one author called "the socialized kitchen":

There efficiency and a hospitable atmosphere are combined to give great family satisfaction. The dining room and kitchen can be converted into one large kitchen-dining unit for family use as a general work and playroom. If meals must be kept warm, and at the same time the children's study supervised, and perhaps a piece of sewing completed; all three activities may be accomplished comfortably, and the family group be held together. Such a social kitchen can be the most attractive room in the house.[84]

Think back for a moment. No proper nineteenth-century housewife would have allowed any but the closest friends, relatives, or workers to spend time in the kitchen—it was her "shop floor," the behind-the-scenes space where the mysteries and arts of her craft were practiced. But the new kitchen was a social space with nothing to hide, and modern cooking, which relied more and more on processed foods, was much less arduous and messy (figs. 1.28, 1.29).

By the 1950s the so-called ranch house was the popular new design that replaced the bungalow and various colonial-style cottages as the most expressive architectural form for middle-class ideals of family life. Although no vernacular western house had a floor plan quite like it, the name of the ranch house suggested the all-American origins of the one-story form. The ranch plan allowed the principal living

Cat. 30 Since many of these vessels by Hall China were made to survive crowded refrigerators, they were potted with extremely thick walls.

Fig. 1.29 Gas appliance manufacturers urged American women to cook with gas, ca. 1950.

spaces—living room, dining room, and kitchen—to flow together with wide, doorless portals. The path from the front door often led directly into the kitchen, while the living room was to one side. And the dining room and kitchen were often integrated by a pass-through counter rather than a full wall between the spaces.

Distinctive dining-room decor did not disappear in these more vestigial spaces. In fact, the sideboard enjoyed a modest revival in the postwar era with the appearance of what people termed a "breakfront" or "buffet." Included in the matching sets of colonial revival or blonde Scandinavian modern dining-room furniture that populated these new dwellings, these sideboards, not unlike their ancestors, typically had doors for storage below and a set of open shelves above, secured by sliding glass doors. In the bottom section stacks of dishes and serving pieces quietly awaited their turn at exhibition above. In many families women organized, even curated, the display of tableware on the sideboard and throughout the dining room. Sometimes assortments of antique dishes received prominence; at holidays the shelves held Thanksgiving, Christmas, or Easter decorations. But even though the adorned dining-room table was only a few steps from the pass-through, many if not most families always ate in the kitchen. The dining room was now reserved for holiday meals and company occasions. Children were allowed to do school projects or jigsaw puzzles on the opened dining table because they could be left undisturbed there overnight.

By now the established formula for the largest sets of dishes had become place settings for eight. Thanks to advancements in glass-pressing technology, firms like Macbeth-Evans Glass Company and Anchor Hocking Glass Corporation could sell sets of glass tableware cheaply (cat. 32). The latter firm offered its "miracle-glass" dinnerware, Jadeite, in sets of fifty-three pieces for $6.95 (approximately $33 in 1991 dollars), pronouncing the greenish glass "both charming and practical for your dining room, breakfast nook, camp, lodge or summer retreat."[85] The largest set of Harmony House brand earthenware offered in the *Diamond Jubilee Sears, Roebuck Catalog* for 1961 included in each of its eight place settings dinner plates, salad/dessert plates, cups and saucers, soup plates, small sauce dishes, as well as a handful of serving dishes (cat. 33). Open stock choices added a few other forms along with a wider range of serving dishes, but the multiplicity of bowl and plate sizes, along with small specialty forms (such as butter pats) that had represented the apex of dining specialization eighty years earlier had long since disappeared.[86] Furthermore, the most popular way to buy pottery may have been the sixteen- or twenty-piece starter set. In reality manufacturers did not make much profit on such small quantities of ware, but they hoped that newlyweds or single people who purchased starter sets would eventually augment their pattern with more expensive open stock serving pieces like coffeepots and casserole dishes.

The days of the celery glass and caster set might have been gone, but manufacturers continued their established practice

Fig. 1.30 Free-flowing spaces characterized the ranch-style house in the 1950s and 1960s.

OPPOSITE:
Cat. 31 *Stratoware* had no protruding handles to break, but its thinness shortened the ware's lifespan.

Cat. 32 Using innovative technology, Macbeth-Evans Glass Company made *Petalware* by the ton in the 1930s.

Cat. 33 Salem China Company's *Constellation*
was distributed by Sears, Roebuck & Co. under
its Harmony House brand name.

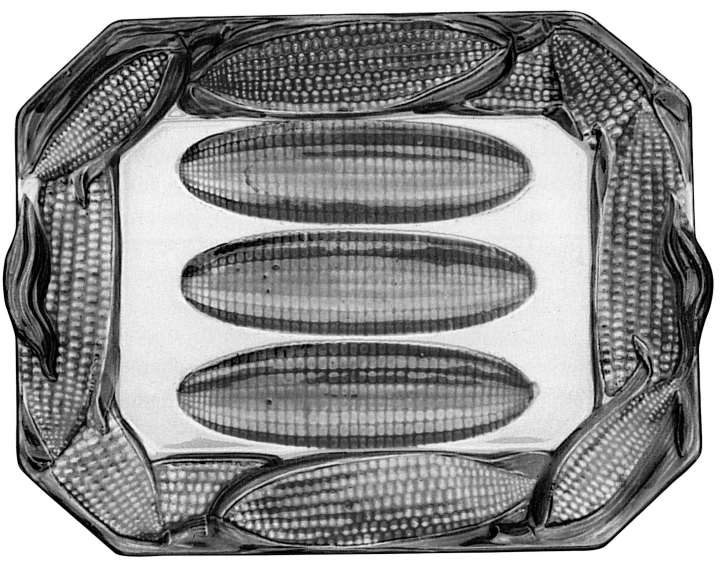

Cat. 34 Although the Japanese did not eat corn on the cob, they catered to Americans' fondness for the New World plant with specialized pottery.

Fig. 1.31 Cocktail parties were "inescapable" by the 1950s.

of creating new genres of serving pieces to reflect food fads and changing modes of entertaining. In 1948, for example, A. H. Heisey & Co. announced to retailers the "hostess helper," an early form of the chip-and-dip set that became ubiquitous in the 1950s. "Its uses are almost limitless—for casual luncheons, buffet suppers, midnight snacks—for all occasions calling for quick, tempting food displays." The idea was new enough that the ad had to explicate possible uses: "For sea food snacks, For cheese spread and potato chips, For tossed or molded salads, For a floral centerpiece, For mayonnaise service."[87] While the Victorian oyster plate disappeared, the corn-on-the-cob set, deviled-egg serving plate, and artichoke plate that had first appeared in the 1930s proliferated in the postwar era (cat. 34; see pp. 54–56).[88]

Characteristic ways of entertaining in the middle-class suburbs perpetuated certain older forms—including the card club and the buffet supper. Anna Foster Grier, part owner of a new ranch house in the early 1960s (and mother of coauthor Kasey Grier), fondly recalls progressive dinners in her suburban neighborhood as an inexpensive, fancy, and entertaining evening out. Four houses served as the sites for cocktails, salad, the main dish, and dessert and nightcaps; each hostess used her best china, glass, and silver so that her course was an occasion in itself.[89] The cocktail party and the cookout, which had been present on some social calendars before the war, took on new popularity. And a third, completely original kind of entertaining came into being—viewing television with invited guests. In retrospect, these three were the signal forms of socializing from the late 1940s through the 1960s.

COCKTAILS AND CANAPÉS

While urbane American men had been drinking cocktails in hotel bars and the nicer taverns in the 1880s, drinking hard liquor in what was termed "mixed company" was rare until the 1920s. Cosmopolitan men and women took up social drinking at home, imbibing mixtures of hard liquor, fruit juices, seltzer, and various garnishes despite Prohibition. Many Americans did not drink before Prohibition or after its repeal in 1933, but cocktail parties became a popular form of entertaining even among teetotalers, who had at their disposal multiple recipes for elaborate nonalcoholic "mixed drinks." Still, cocktail parties are usually associated with the 1950s and the suburbs, where they had become an "inescapable way of entertaining."[90] These events required a wide range of specialized equipment and had considerable impact on both social life and fashions in food (see pp. 83–88).

Because of the amounts of liquor involved, cocktail parties were not cheap, but they were easy to stage. Usually scheduled just before the dinner hour, cocktail parties allowed guests to come and go at will, so that even a small house could accommodate a crowd. The greatest challenge for the hostess was figuring out how much liquor to stock. Advice authors offered various formulae based on assumptions about how much people would drink; three cocktails per guest seems to have been typical, so party goers were "well-oiled" by the time they left the premises. Martinis and Manhattan cocktails could be mixed ahead of time in quantity and stored in the refrigerator in sealed containers. This practice not only saved ice, but could supply leftovers for a future cocktail hour.[91]

Cocktail party food consisted of assortments of hors d'oeuvres and canapés. These bite-size morsels had to be negotiated with one hand while the other clutched a drink; even so, the food needed to follow the feasting rule of abundance, as did the liquor. Large platters or cheese boards featuring multilayered arrangements of tidbits fit the bill. In the twilight of her career, Lucy G. Allen, the author of *Table Service*,

Fig. 1.32 Skewered and garnished hors d'oeuvres were classic cocktail party fare.

published *A Book of Hors d'Oeuvre* (1941) to introduce the subject and offer advice. She explained that "the custom of serving these relishes is a foreign one," but assured her readers that they could easily become experts at this new kind of miniature cuisine: "Never hesitate to assemble a platter of odds and ends, for if attractively arranged they will have the appeal of assorted hors d'oeuvre. . . . The very first requisite for making successful appetizers is imagination, plus whatever happens to be on the shelves or the pantry." In a decisive break from dainty food, Allen insisted that successful canapés, especially those served with cocktails, had to be "highly seasoned and flavored," and some of her recipes included such daring ingredients as cayenne pepper and multiple garlic cloves.[92] Of course, all those salty and savory cocktail puffs and anchovy–cream cheese pastes on toast, and the gluey party dips, which guests ate by shoving a cracker or potato chip directly into the communal bowl (a breathtaking departure from longstanding rules of middle-class dining decorum), meant that guests needed to drink more.

Cocktail snacks helped start Americans down the slippery slope toward their late-twentieth-century habit of snacking rather than eating real meals. Cookbooks of nothing but snacks, food intended to be eaten either between meals or as a substitute for formal meals, appeared in the 1940s. One such book published in 1949 was *500 Snacks*, an inexpensive example of the many publications promoting the idea of the Scandinavian smorgasbord, a modified buffet consisting of a hearty spread of canapés, hot and cold dishes, salads, and sweets served all at once. The attraction of the smorgasbord was "the opportunity our hostess gives us to enjoy our own choice from the enticing selections. . . . We help ourselves to the dishes we want, returning to the board again and again."[93]

The world of the hors d'oeuvre also introduced American diners to what Allen called pierced savories—that is, spiky little arrangements of foods on skewers or toothpicks. These rapidly became a convention of cocktail party and snack food because they looked fancy but could be assembled easily and without cooking (fig. 1.32). By 1947 a "wonderful party" could be had on nothing but "tantalizing, provocative *canapés*, 'partified' salads, and delicious as well as substantial sandwiches."[94] And by 1968, the author of a Campbell Soup Company cookbook could proclaim snacks "the most often eaten meal in American homes."[95]

Cocktails and Drinking in the Home

Americans have long communally partaken of alcoholic beverages to celebrate and cement social bonds, from the Communion cup to the glass raised in casual fellowship at the bar. How the realm of drink is organized—who can drink where, what behaviors are acceptable, and which kinds of alcohol are popular—reveals much about the changes in American social life over time. This evolution is particularly clear in the case of the cocktail, a type of alcohol consumption that developed distinct subcultures from its inception. Originally a manly morning "eye-opener," the cocktail attracted a cult following among middle-class men in the mid-nineteenth century. At the turn of the century it became the slightly risqué drink of choice for the "new woman," and by the end of national Prohibition in 1933 the cocktail was widely associated with a new kind of drinking: respectable yet trend-conscious men and women together, at home, imbibed drinks made with hard liquor involving an elaborate equipage of glasses, shakers, swizzle sticks, and other gizmos—and had a new kind of middle-class fun as their social inhibitions melted away.

Alcoholic drinks were a ubiquitous and relatively uncontroversial part of home life until the end of the eighteenth century. The colonial goodwife routinely brewed "small beer" and tended barrels of fermenting cider for herself, her husband, and her children to drink. Hard cider, which contained about 7 percent alcohol, and small beer, having only a tiny amount, were considered nutritious and healthful family drinks, and they laid the groundwork for a lifetime of communal tippling at home, on the job, and in the taverns that served as informal community centers. Imported spirits such as brandy and rum were more expensive and less likely to be consumed in quantity daily, although the well-to-do routinely drank them with meals. Such beverages were also more likely to be consumed in the quasi-public space of the tavern, a setting almost entirely occupied by men (with the exception of the tavernkeepers' wives and daughters, occasional female travelers, and local women of dubious virtue). Thus the world of social drinking not only was divided into private and public, but was also organized by gender. Women tended to drink at home, and rarely in the company of strangers.

While the colonists were heavy drinkers, relatively few seem to have been considered problem drinkers, and it is clear that community values emphasized moderation in consumption, including relatively mild punishment for public drunkenness. That was the case until the end of the eighteenth century, when the male citizens of the new American republic seem to have upped their consumption of hard liquor exponentially, due in no small part to dramatic increases in local production of corn-based whisky. Concern about heavier drinking inspired the most famous early critique, *An Inquiry into the Effects of Ardent Spirits on the Human Mind and Body,* by Dr. Benjamin Rush. The tract, published in 1784, did not demand that Americans set aside all the old forms of alcoholic beverages; rather, Rush argued that wine and beer were healthful in moderate amounts. He maintained, however, that chronic drunkenness fueled by craving for distilled liquor not only had implications for individual health but, if widespread enough, could lead to the downfall of the American experiment in republican government.

Rush's tract was the first widely regarded action in a complicated (and still ongoing) "culture war" about the place of alcohol in social life in the United States. The temperance movement, which coalesced in the 1820s and gathered steam in the next two decades, was the single most popular social reform movement in American history—and the one most likely to involve women as active participants. American women interested in controlling alcohol were not simply killjoys. Consumption in America was so excessive it had evolved into the deeper problems Benjamin Rush had feared. Women and children were endangered both economically and physically by the inebriation of their husbands and fathers, and the very political process was soaked in booze. Election day, when men's votes were courted with vats of hard-liquor punch, presented a particularly horrific display. So did the neighborhoods of workers and immigrants, where whisky-and-beer taverns were the settings for blood sports such as bare-knuckle boxing and cockfighting.[1]

By the second half of the nineteenth century, many middle-class households had adopted a temperance approach of total abstinence. In this stance, even formal entertainments such as dinners were "dry." Just as drinking households ceremonially served wine, abstainers made a ritual of offering lemonade, ice water, or imported mineral waters such as Apollinaris, using special plated pitchers and goblets that would otherwise have served for a nice sauterne. Even when temperance sentiments were at their strongest, however, many middle-class families continued to integrate alcohol into important social occasions; they still believed in moderate, controlled drinking. Women no longer made small beer, but they brewed fruit cordials for home consumption and cooked with spirits. The occasional formal dinner party continued to be graced with wine, although probably fewer kinds were offered than the most demanding domestic advisors suggested (cat. 35). Dances and other evening socials featured milk-based or wine punches that stretched and weakened the expensive ingredients while still providing that indefinable zest to social interaction.

In Victorian households, cordials and wine, and wine punches of various kinds, were considered appropriately feminine beverages, while the cocktail belonged to the potentially dangerous and controversial world of masculine

public drinking. Scholars agree that the origins of the cocktail are mysterious; many claim it as a peculiarly American contribution to the history of alcoholic beverages. The anonymous author of the *The Savoy Cocktail Book* (1930) stated that the first published definition and recipe dated from 1806: "a stimulating liquor, composed of spirits of any kind, sugar, water, and bitters."[2] While most denizens of taverns seem to have taken their whisky straight, cocktails became an important feature of the bars in first-class hotels that opened before the Civil War. In addition to being a businessman's eye-opener, they were bottled for consumption during hunting and fishing trips, according to the author of the first bartending manual, "Professor" Jerry Thomas.

Inventive barmen like Thomas offered their clientele other kinds of mixed alcoholic beverages as well—fizzes (made with that "health beverage" of the nineteenth century, soda water), flips (rum with beaten egg and sugar), and cups (wine and liqueurs mixed with fruit), among others. With the exception of alcoholic punches—mélanges of wine, hard liquor, liqueurs, and sometimes soda and fruits, which still appear at holiday parties—all of these are now grouped under the general rubric "cocktail." Thomas's manual, *How to Mix Drinks, or, The Bon Vivant's Companion* (1862), kicked off a whole literature of barmen's guides, and it seems Thomas can also be credited with introducing a highly theatrical sensibility to the drinks he mixed at saloons from San Francisco to New York. Not only did he own a set of solid silver bar utensils, valued at $4,000, but he invented drinks such as the blue blazer—boiling hot water and whisky were ignited and poured from beaker to beaker before the flames were doused and the concoction presented to the customer.[3]

Between the Civil War and the imposition of national Prohibition following passage of the Eighteenth Amendment to the Constitution in 1919, Americans who imbibed increasingly drank lager beer rather than the distilled "hard" or "spirituous" liquors that were the basis for cocktails. Introduced by German immigrant brewmasters in the 1840s, lager beer was brewed from hops, malt, and water and was aged for a mellow flavor. The 893,000 German immigrants who arrived in this country between the 1830s and 1860s not only brought their superior beer, but also introduced a new style of drinking—in public with their families, at pleasure gardens run by ethnic associations. Lager beer drinkers did not as a rule drink to get drunk; both men and women consumed beer, and their children were often sent to fill the household beer pail for their mothers or fathers at the local tavern.

By the turn of the century increasing numbers of Italians, who drank wine at home (the least popular of the three major alcoholic beverage types in America until the 1970s), added a new wrinkle to drinking patterns that were already highly pluralistic, varying by region, ethnicity and class, religion, and political conviction.[4] The behavior of the Germans and the Italians reinforced the idea that consuming alcohol at home was not necessarily dysfunctional, and that women and men could drink together socially, even in the presence of children, who were introduced to moderate consumption of alcohol by adult example.

After years of being a footnote in the national history of strong drink, a genuine craze for cocktails appeared in the 1920s, right under the nose of the law. Prohibition did not punish the consumption of previously owned stocks of alcohol in private households; nor did it affect homemade wine and beer. (Although the latter was illegal, little effort was made to enforce this portion of the law). As passage of the Eighteenth Amendment grew certain, some Americans planned for their comfort by accumulating large stocks of liquor, and they continued to enjoy their cocktails, albeit quietly. Less prosperous and foresighted citizens soon turned to purveyors of bootleg alcohol, but it was expensive, and even drinkers who were willing to wink at the law seem to have reduced their consumption significantly.

While prosperous citizens could go on drinking cocktails, although perhaps in smaller quantities, poorer Americans were forced to significantly reduce their intake of any kind of alcohol—and it is important to remember that many citizens stopped drinking because it was illegal. Prohibition enjoyed wide support among the millions of Americans who did not drink and who still associated alcohol with a variety of social ills. After the repeal of Prohibition, many adult Americans remained abstainers, even as the cocktail party became one of the most popular forms of entertaining in the 1940s and 1950s.[5] Alternative "social drinks," like coffee and tea and especially "soft drinks" such as Coca-Cola, saw dramatic expansion in sales between 1919 and 1930.[6] Coca-Cola's blanket advertising campaigns suggested that a carefree social life was a necessary outcome of drinking the potion—something soft drink advertisers still suggest routinely. At the same time, because distilled liquor was more economical for bootleggers to make and distribute than beer, some Americans might have been pushed into drinking hard liquor and thus into trying a new array of cocktails that incorporated bottled soda waters and fruit-juice mixers to mask the terrible taste of bootleg "hooch."

The coincidence of Prohibition with changes in other standards of behavior for middle-class women by the 1920s brought respectable men and women together as social drinkers in greater numbers—in the speakeasies that flourished in the 1920s, in parties in hotel rooms rented for the

purpose, and in private houses where men and women increasingly drank cocktails together. Although in the late nineteenth century some adventurous hostesses had served drinks before guests adjourned to the dining room, Victorian propriety had generally frowned upon women imbibing hard, "male" liquors such as whisky and gin. By the 1910s, modern young women were sipping cocktails at the new cabaret nightclubs or the euphemistically named "tea dances" put on by fashionable hotels, to the horror of some of their elders. When Prohibition forced more drinking back into the private household, the respectable women who had always partaken of wine and punches, and their daughters who were now used to sipping cocktails in public places, for the first time joined their fathers, brothers, and boyfriends in "cocktailing" at home.[7]

Full repeal of Prohibition did not take effect until December 1933, but the makers of glassware and drinking equipment, from stainless-steel shakers to cut-glass decanters, anticipated a marketing bonanza the whole year. In the pages of the April 1933 *Crockery and Glass Journal,* representatives of the Brewing Trades Institute suggested that "few industries will be more favorably affected than the glass and crockery industry" by the needs of newly reopened neighborhood taverns and the private hostess who "more than her pre-prohibition sister, wishes to have proper accessories for each drink. . . . Mugs, steins, goblets, and glasses will be sold as never before."[8] Fashionable New York department and specialty stores by then were already highlighting collections of barwares; special displays recreated bars in elegant saloons and demonstrated how a couple might set up a "rumpus room" as a kind of private tavern, equipped with a fully plumbed bar featuring a foot rail and stools (cat. 17; fig. 1.33).[9]

In October 1933 *Crockery and Glass Journal* advised "What to Drink—How to Serve It," explaining in a concise table the kinds of wines associated with the courses of a formal dinner and the necessary stemware, even though that genre of entertaining at home was declining rapidly.[10] By November the trade journal warned its readers, "Repeal is due in less than a month! And millions of Americans don't know a pousse-café from a Roemer. So the great campaign of educating people in the niceties of drinking and the correct use of glassware is now going full blast. It is expected to multiply the demand for stemware." The journal praised the educational advertising by the New York department store B. Altman & Co. in which the forms of various specialty glasses were illustrated and their proper names and uses outlined (cat. 71).[11]

Fig. 1.33 Fostoria Glass Company brochures helped teach Americans to drink in the early 1930s.

Vessels associated with social drinking had long included novelties and jokes. The seventeenth century had its "fuddling cup," and the Victorian era its "Tom and Jerry" set, a punch bowl and cups inscribed with the names and used to serve a particularly potent rum-and-brandy concoction (credited to Professor Jerry Thomas, dubbed "the greatest Bartender of the Past" by *The Savoy Cocktail Book*).[12] The design of barwares of the 1920s and repeal period tended to be either elegant or hokey (cat. 37). Both types reflected a self-conscious camaraderie, by turns silly and serious, that also turned up in drink names. Proliferating cocktail recipes reflected the popular culture of the era and its interpretation of sophisticated, modern living. Drinks were named after the fashionable hotel bars where they had been invented (the Monte Carlo Imperial, the Hoffman House, the Savoy), after fashionable resorts (the Havana), exclusive clubs (the Racquet Club), steamships (the *Queen Elizabeth*), and movie stars (the Mary Pickford). Some were given humorous names associated with their putative effects (thunder and lightning, nose-dive, Mississippi mule, Satan's whiskers).

Nothing epitomizes the self-conscious cocktail culture better than the cult of the martini, however (cat. 36). The martini apparently began life as the "Martinez"; the first known recipe appeared in an 1884 bartender's guide that described it as "a Manhattan made with gin instead of

Cat. 37 Images of revelers and temptresses made drinking in the home stylish at midcentury.

cocktail, like all its kin, declined in popularity in the 1970s and 1980s. Middle-class Americans rediscovered boutique-winery vintages and custom-brewed beer as adjuncts to the new gourmet cooking, and they worried about the deleterious health effects of hard liquor (fig. 1.39). But the drink has returned, as Generation X drinkers have adopted and adapted their grandparents' cocktail culture. If the martini is back, can the pink squirrel and the maiden's blush be far behind?

whisky."[13] The recipe evolved, gradually becoming "less sweet and more dry," and by the 1910s the drink enjoyed its own distinctive glass and was headed to a fame that cannot be explained rationally. Adopted and celebrated by literary and artistic patrons, the martini became "an American modernist masterpiece."[14]

By the 1950s, the unisex martini had been masculinized. It became the power drink of the postwar corporate culture, the subject of tireless (and tiresome) debate as recipes moved toward the "very dry" martini (as close to 100 percent gin as bartenders wielding eyedroppers of vermouth could make it). The distinctive image of the martini glass adorned neckties, record-album covers—even tables with glass tops were shaped like giant martinis. The

Notes

1. For an influential account of the whisky glut in the early republic and the resulting national drinking binge that launched the temperance movement, see Rorabaugh 1979, 61–146.

2. *Savoy* 1930, 13. A case can be made that the mint julep was the first American cocktail; it certainly fostered a cult associated with its preparation comparable only to the obsession with the martini in the mid-twentieth century.

3. The authoritative account of Jerry Thomas's life remains Asbury 1927, 421–30.

4. For a discussion of American drinking patterns as a reflection of cultural pluralism, see Lender and Martin 1987.

5. Ibid., 136–46.

6. Ibid., 147.

7. This passage relies on the provocative explanation of changes in women's drinking patterns in America, including the relationship

of middle-class women's evolving attitudes toward alcohol in the context of suffrage, found in Murdock 1998.

8. "Prosits Equals Profit," *CGJ* 112:4 (Apr. 1933): 15.

9. Photograph with extended caption in "Rumpus Room at Roos Brothers," *CGJ* 112:4 (Apr. 1933): 16.

10. "What to Drink—How to Serve It," *CGJ* 113:4 (Oct. 1933): 43–44.

11. "Here's How Stores Tell the . . . World What Glassware to Use," *CGJ* 113:5 (Nov. 1933): 16–17.

12. *Savoy* 1930, 4, 162.

13. For the history of the martini, see Rudin 1997: 32–36ff.; and Tamony 1967: 124–27.

14. Rudin 1997, 40.

COOKING OUT

While Americans had enjoyed picnicking since the nineteenth century, the cookout, the iconic contribution of post–World War II suburban living to American social life, was not simply a direct descendent of this tradition of open-air dining. Its central feature, meat cooked over an open flame by a male cook, belonged to the ideal of camp life promoted by adherents of strenuous exercise and character-building male sociality such as the Boy Scouts (founded 1907). While camping had once been the inevitable consequence of a life spent working in the outdoors, from driving cattle to laying railroad track, in the 1870s and 1880s health reformers had promoted the camping vacation as a wilderness respite for middle-class "brain workers." Camp cuisine—pan-fried fresh-caught fish or roasted game, pans of beans, potatoes and corn on the cob cooked in the coals—eaten on tin plates without tablecloth, napkin, or multiple forks and spoons was an indispensable part of the experience.

Influenced by the powerful image of casual social life in California, middle-class domestic architecture of the 1920s and 1930s all over the country often included screened or glassed-in summer rooms and paved terraces that could be furnished with a new genre of metal, wooden, or wicker

Cat. 38 Tableware decorated with longhorns, rifles, and wagon wheels became popular as Americans ate red meat in increasing quantities.

outdoor furniture. By the 1930s tableware makers in California and elsewhere actively promoted outdoor dining and marketed an array of casual dishes sometimes featuring Southwestern motifs and colors as appropriate vessels for entertaining outside (cat. 169).[96] The fad for outdoor living was probably slowed by the depression and World War II, but it came into its own as part of the postwar suburban lifestyle, which was family and neighborhood centered.

Books like Harold Wallis Steck's *Right in Your Own Backyard* (1942) and magazines with strong do-it-yourself components such as *Better Homes and Gardens* printed plans for "patios" (a Spanish word with strong associations of old California) and their accoutrements. Steck's small book pointed out that a barbecue could be as simple as three stones with chicken wire across them, but he provided plans for an "outdoor kitchen" with storage cupboards for wood and utensils and a grated cooking surface as large as a stove top, along with a "wheelbarrow hostess" that could trundle dishes, bar supplies, and ice for eight people.[97] Most people settled for portable grills by the 1950s, which displayed a plethora of forms and features including wheels, broilers with revolving spits, warming drawers, hoods, and tile work surfaces (fig. 1.34). Special sets of barbecue tools—forks, tongs, turners, and spits that looked like primitive weaponry—were oversized not only to protect the cook from a fire but to emphasize their manly character.

Fig. 1.34 Barbecuing in the 1950s, the quintessential American male ritual.

The cookout and its special equipment turned cooking into a masculine social performance in front of a mixed crowd including women. (Camp cooking with the Boy Scouts had been strictly a male activity.) Not that this was the first time cooking in front of the guests had been a fad; recall the chafing-dish suppers of the previous generation. But in the two decades after 1945, cooking out became the ultimate expression of casual entertaining, with a theatrical quality and an aesthetic every bit as complex as the formal dinner party of 1880. "Food tastes better with a little showmanship, you know," a 1946 article on barbecue equipment pointed out.[98] The cookout allowed an almost tongue-in-cheek performance of gender roles around the preparation and service of meat, not unrelated to the iconography of hunting and meat that characterized the Victorian dining room. And indeed "the hunter" cooked the product of the "hunt"—be it hot dogs, slabs of beef, or pork ribs—over an open flame, while individual guests could choose the individual piece they wanted cooked from the raw meat displayed. The preparation of most cookout food was actually done by women. Anna Grier recalls that "women worked hard behind the scenes so that the men could perform."[99] The companionate relationship of the husband and wife could be demonstrated through special dress such as "his-and-hers" barbecue aprons with hokey pictures of cowboys, cavemen, or Polynesian beauties or captions like "Big Daddy" printed on the front.[100]

While cookout service was really just another kind of buffet supper, the aesthetics of cookout tablewares were distinctive. Salt and pepper shakers were oversized and humorous, made from carved wood or shaped like ears of corn, chefs' heads, or pigs. Giant wooden salad bowls on legs, oversized carving boards, and wooden "trees" holding pickles and other condiments added to the rustic-primitive theme, as did linens, pottery, and glassware featuring rural or western motifs and names like *Country Modern*, *Winchester '73*, and *Wagon Wheel* (cat. 38). By the 1940s paper plates and cups were available for the most informal get-together, but the new plastic melamine dinnerwares of the early 1950s offered another popular, unbreakable alternative (see chapter 2).[101]

THE TV DINNER

The third distinctive social occasion of the postwar era after the cocktail party and the cookout was the television-viewing party. The rapidity of television's acceptance into households was unparalleled by any other technological marvel of the twentieth century. The first sets had been offered to the public only in 1946, but by 1955, 65 percent of American homes had a television; the figure was considerably higher in the middle-class suburbs and lower in rural America, where reception was poor.[102] Not only did the television require people to rearrange their living rooms so that everyone could see the flickering screen clearly, but it engendered new kinds of furniture intended to support other activities in front of the set, particularly eating. TV-tray tables, soon essential to furnishing first homes, appeared in advertising in 1952. Manufacturers tried to develop a variety of portable furniture that

Fig. 1.35 TV dinner dining, 1968.

could be moved into positions around the set—dinettes on wheels, serving carts with electric outlets so that hostesses could make simple dishes in front of the set, and even a small rolling refrigerator.[103]

Advice books quickly picked up on the craze for television parties. Writers compared the etiquette of such events to group radio listening or do-it-yourself programs of recorded music with the host serving as the announcer. Small groups of "a few friends of the same mind" worked best, as did parties organized around sports events that featured snacks. However, Charlotte Adams, an editor of *Charm* magazine who published a sensible and relaxed text on party giving in 1950, noted one major difference with television parties: "When people come to see television, or when you turn it on at the request of guests, there is less likely to be conversation."[104]

Television also had a distinctive impact on family dining at home. Even if the middle-class family had retreated to the kitchen for its meals, its members still sat around a table facing one another. But television watching during dinner became a handy way for families to avoid dinnertime bickering, and it offered novel content for people who had run out of conversation topics.

Table-setting books offered advice on creating pretty

settings for TV trays, but the idea seemed ludicrous (fig. 1.35). Eating in front of the television deconstructed both social dining and the family dinner even further, and it encouraged enthusiastic use of convenience foods—particularly that recent innovation, the "TV dinner." Growing out of wartime technologies, as so many household inventions of the 1950s had, the frozen dinner was the ultimate convenience food. When Swanson & Sons introduced the TV dinner in 1954, it cleverly paraphrased the typical American holiday meal, a turkey dinner. Besides such associations, the choice of turkey allowed the food company to use 52,000 pounds of unsold turkeys it had on hand in ten refrigerated railroad cars. The selection was instantly successful, and Swanson sold ten million dinners the first year. Today, three million Swanson TV dinners are consumed each week. The favorite varieties from the 1950s are still the most popular at the end of the century—turkey, fried chicken, and Salisbury steak.[105]

Escaping the Kitchen

For Victorian women, cooking was a craft; for women influenced by turn-of-the-century domestic science, it was a calling, but by the mid-twentieth century women were willing to admit that the daily round of meal getting was a bore. It is clear that by the end of World War II, many young women neither knew how to cook nor were terribly interested in the process; they had, after all, been busy doing other things, and increasing numbers had to or chose to work. Cookbooks complained about this: the *Cookbook for Brides* (1947) stated that "at the time of marriage, only two out of ten brides know how to cook," a "sad indictment of our sense of values."[106] This lack of skill, however, presented food processors and their cohorts at women's magazines with an irresistible opportunity to promote cooking instructions for the ever-widening assortment of convenience foods. In 1950 came the publication of *Betty Crocker's Picture Cookbook*, a ring-bound text that demonstrated cooking techniques with photographic narratives and which included such instructions for the inept as "assemble ingredients" and "preheat oven" at the beginning of each recipe. Written in the voice of a friend rather than an impatient mother or a snobby expert, the *Picture Cookbook* sold a million copies in its first year alone.[107]

In 1960 frank distaste for kitchen labor led to that runaway bestseller, Peg Bracken's *The I Hate to Cook Book*, a volume dedicated to women who would rather "fold our big dishwater hands around a dry Martini instead of a wet flounder, at the end of a long day." She announced that color spreads in women's magazines in which the food matched the china depressed her, and she named "childbearing, paying taxes, and cooking" as experiences that remained painful despite repetition. With wonderful chapter headings such as "Spuds and Other Starches, or, Ballast Is a Girl's Best Friend," Bracken's book featured recipes that sometimes made use of several different cans of soup at once and relied on inspired additions such as a cup of red wine to make the resulting agglomerations tasty. Taking a swipe at the test kitchens of the food processors and women's magazines, she announced that her

recipes "have not been tested by experts. That is why they are valuable."[108]

Thanks to the food fashion system, the 1950s and 1960s became the golden age of a new kind of artifice in the form of convenience-food "gourmet cooking," epitomized by the Campbell Soup Company cookbooks of the 1960s. The 1968 edition promised, "You only need to spend an average of 90 minutes a day in the kitchen as compared with the 5 hours your mother used, thanks to convenience foods and better packaging. A recent study by the Drexel Institute of Technology showed that meals made with convenience foods can save you a total of 10 hours a week, compared to 'cook-it-yourself' foods."[109] Cooking needed to be easy or women would not do it; yet it had to produce dramatic, tasty results—hence the popularity of dishes like continental beef stroganoff made with cream of mushroom soup. Sometimes a dish needed to be all these things and cheap to boot—hence frankfurter crown casserole, which required only a half pound of wieners (cut in half and then lengthwise), a can of cream of mushroom, and some vegetables to produce a one-dish dinner for four (fig. 1.36). Women augmented canned soups with vegetables, spices, and meat to showcase their creativity and skill (and perhaps assuage their guilt).[110] Anna Grier recalls that the stay-at-home mothers of her suburban neighborhood devoted considerable competitive energy, if not lots of time, to creating customized cakes from box mixes, sometimes blending two or more kinds along with adding new ingredients.[111] These enhanced cake-mix recipes appeared on the backs of boxes, in magazine advertisements, and in the editorial content of women's magazines. The resulting "supercakes" had a tendency to turn up at social events such as birthday parties, church banquets, and school occasions for which mothers provided food.

No discussion of convenience-food gourmet cooking would be complete without at least a brief mention of the gelatin salad, which represents for many "the good, the bad, and the ugly" in the genre (fig. 1.37). Before the arrival of sheet gelatin in the 1870s, a by-product of industrialized slaughterhouses, a cook who wanted to prepare a "jellied" dish faced the unpleasant task of creating homemade calf's foot jelly unless she could find isinglass (made from the air bladders of fish). Some jellied dishes were rare and special treats for feasting occasions; others were prepared for invalids.[112] Even gelatin sheets required extensive preparation, including straining, before the finished product was rendered clear. After the 1890s, when unflavored gelatin in small boxes could be purchased, molded salads and gelatin desserts gradually entered the repertoire of home cooks.

Another important addition to the various processed foods of the early twentieth century was Jell-O, although it was not a universal success until cooks had easy access to refrigeration beginning in the 1920s. Gelatin salads (the line between the molded salad and what are now considered desserts was a wiggly one) were the perfect place to trap and disguise the vegetables that family members needed to eat in balanced meals but eyed suspiciously. Made with ginger ale, canned

Fig. 1.36 A creative dish of the times: frankfurter crown casserole, 1968.

Fig. 1.37 Recipes for molded foods took a playful attitude: "cool-as-a-cucumber salad circling a mayonnaise basket."

fruit, nuts, and whipped cream, these quivering dishes were fabulous dainty food for women's luncheons. Suspending bits of meat or seafood in tomato aspic or lemon gelatin, molded salads were perfect for buffets because they could be so easily sliced, although they were always in danger of escaping the serving plate and slithering to the floor. Molded gelatin seems to have been valued as much for its jiggly good looks on serving tables as for its flavors, and as a segment of Americans began to object to the cooking advice of the processed food industry in the 1960s, gelatin salads went out of style in some quarters.[113] However, they still survive—even thrive—in cookbooks published by churches, hospitals, clubs, and other volunteer organizations and at the potluck social dinners still given by such groups.

THE TABLETOP AT MIDCENTURY

In the postwar period china and glass simultaneously reflected the continuing preoccupation with casual entertaining and an expansive, almost theatrical sensibility in the shapes of tablewares and their decorative motifs. Food writers for women's magazines trumpeted the code words "charming" and "romantic" to describe the best dinner parties, which were also "a perfect balance of good food and gracious service with no detail left to last-minute inspiration."[114] That is, dinner parties still required quasi-military precision from the woman of the house, although they were supposed to look as casual as the sweater thrown over her shoulders. One important design genre was the peasant look, which featured primitively painted floral and fruit motifs (cat. 39; see chapter 5). Some designs featured a pop-culture sense of Americana,

from barnyard roosters to displays of red, white, and blue; others played with exotic "oriental" themes such as bamboo (cats. 41, 109). The most deliberately modern wares in the 1950s and 1960s included lines reflecting the influential new Scandinavian design. Some featured cheerfully conventionalized flowers and sunbursts that resembled folk-art stenciling; others were rough stoneware reminiscent of handmade pottery (cat. 203). These new lines were so decisively different from formal dinnerwares produced at the same time that they suggested a real bifurcation between modes of social life. And casual was clearly better. Pottery dinnerwares of the 1950s and 1960s were playful, even exuberant to the point of zaniness, like the experimental, processed-food gourmet meals they contained (cats. 40, 198).

Formal tablewares did not disappear, of course. In the 1950s women's magazines were awash in advertisements each spring for Lenox "fine china," Fostoria crystal "reflecting your good taste," silver-plated flatware and holloware of "timeless beauty," and Quaker Lace tablecloths that cast "a web of enchantment over your party table."[115] These advertisements were all aimed at the bridal market, and many of the patterns they featured, such as Lenox China's *Kingsley* or *Rutledge*, were simplified reinterpretations of patterns that had been popular for formal dining since the nineteenth century: plain rims with colored bands or scalloped edges with floral motifs (cat. 60).

New practical requirements that middle-class households had for tableware also affected what people owned. Family cooks needed to keep dinner plates warm in the oven for commuting husbands and children detained by after-

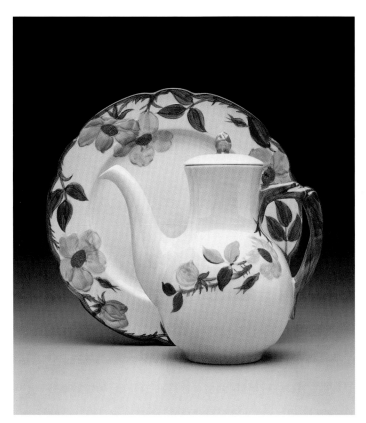

Cat. 39 With rose-covered borders and branch-shaped handles, *Desert Rose* by Franciscan was an instant success from its introduction in 1941.

Cat. 40 Dorothy Thorpe's tablewares with spherical handles (here with a teapot by Sascha Brastoff) are among the most playful ever designed in the United States.

school activities. Householders also wanted to be able to put those plates in their brand new dishwashers. This requirement affected the market for fancy china, since gold rims and translucent teacups could not be cleaned in early models of dishwashers, which used harsh detergents. Melamine tableware, popular in the 1950s and early 1960s, could go in the dishwasher, but it melted at oven temperatures and scratched easily.

For these reasons women kept using ceramics, finding in heavy earthenwares and stonewares the sturdiness and utility they needed (cats. 42, 43). They also were attracted to new materials, such as the austerely simple, white *Centura* tableware introduced by Corning in the late 1960s (fig. 1.38). Corning's campaign for this line made from a new ceramic material, trademarked *Pyroceram*, suggested to consumers that they really only needed one set of dinnerware, elegant enough for social occasions yet sturdy enough for the "bumps and bruises" inflicted by their automatic dishwashers and "those that happen in the hands of your not-so-automatic dishwasher called 'Honey.'"[116] The company may have been right, but what fun was that? Most brides still wanted to pick out a pattern even if the dishes, like the white-with-gold-rim china of seventy years earlier recalled so vividly by young Ethel Spencer, saw use only once or twice a year.

When the microwave oven appeared in the 1970s, it too had an impact on the market for dinnerwares. A 1976 article on microwave ovens in the trade paper *Gift and Tableware Reporter* warned store owners that "unit shipments on micro-

wave ovens this year totaled 1,383,000, pushing sales up 63% over last year's figures." The article noted growing use of the label "suitable for microwave ovens" and the appearance of new single-serving cooking vessels intended exclusively for microwave use. It mentioned that the Worcester Royal Porcelain Company was adapting its patterns for microwave use by leaving off the gold rim, while Heller Designs was promoting a line of "microwave/oven to table glass bakeware."[117]

The microwave oven changed some kinds of cooking (it certainly affected preparation of the baked potato), and it completed the decentralization of the family dinner begun in the 1950s by the television. Even small children could "nuke" popcorn, leftovers, or frozen meals for themselves. Some American families had given up eating together completely by the late 1970s—except occasionally for Sundays after church and major holidays. During the week, many people relied on their stomachs to say when it was time to eat; the family freezer was full of frozen entrees, and the cupboards loaded with snacks that could be heated in a minute or two in the new microwave.

The Cooking Revival, 1960–1980

While most middle-class families seemed to embrace the ever-expanding universe of convenience foods in the 1960s, two countercurrents led some women—and increasing numbers of men as well—to turn to their kitchens for a new kind of leisure pursuit: cooking. In the early 1960s, Julia Child's television program, *Mastering the Art of French Cooking*, along with the accompanying book "enchanted viewers and assured them that if this seemingly average American woman could cook, then so could they."

And because of Julia Child's popularity, cooking schools and cooking equipment stores blossomed almost overnight. Fish poachers, charlotte molds, chefs' knives, and copper beating bowls became best-sellers. Wire whisks sold out in Pittsburgh after one of her shows. A butcher who usually sold seven geese a year reported selling sixty-five after Julia cooked a goose on television. Everyone seemed to be in the kitchen with Julia.[118]

Although not everybody really was in the kitchen with Julia, the formal dinner party did return as a wave of gourmet culture swept the country. But the reincarnated formal dinner stood in marked contrast to the self-imposed austerity in the face of abundance seen in the Victorian formal dinner party. The new middle-class dinner party featured the food as a source of both exuberant pleasure and conversation as guests compared recipes and sources of hard-to-find ingredients, tried new wines, and shared war stories about personal cooking disasters and triumphs. Some couples found in gourmet cooking a novel shared hobby. Inspired by the magazine *Gourmet* (first published 1941) and by the increasingly sophisticated food and entertaining sections of *House and Garden* (American edition first published 1901), the earliest participants in this movement began patronizing better restaurants and learning about wine. By the 1970s some couples were taking cooking classes and attending wine tastings together (fig. 1.39). Coffee-table-sized cookbooks heavily illustrated with color images of native and international cuisine were especially inspirational.

Miami hostess Jewel Stern recalls how influential Time-Life's *Picture Cook Book* (1958) was and how she, her husband, and her like-minded friends pored over every detail and tried to re-create the pictured delicacies exactly. Furthermore, they traveled both in the United States and abroad, visiting many of the great restaurants listed in the book's "Dining Out" section. Stern was so immersed in the gourmet movement in the 1960s and 1970s that she kept meticulous records of each dinner party she and her husband hosted in their home (fig. 1.40). Preserved on index cards, these documents helped Stern recall who had been invited to what parties, what had been served, and what linen and tableware had been used. Keeping track was important so that the next event would be an exciting experience for the cognoscenti of food and food display. Taken as historical documents, Stern's notations of past parties record both profound and subtle changes in diet and nomenclature. "White wine" was elevated to a Pouilly-Fuissé in 1960; "spaghetti" became "pasta" a decade later.[119]

Two other strands appeared at about the same time as this rediscovery of cooking and food. One was the rebirth of interest in regional American foods, marked for many by the publication of Jean Hewitt's the *New York Times Heritage Cook-*

Fig. 1.38 Thin as porcelain and tough as nails, *Centura* glass dishes proved popular in the 1960s.

Fig. 1.39 As part of the larger culinary revival, wine consumption rose dramatically in the 1970s.

Cat. 42 Franciscan's *Shalimar* of 1972 had an exceptionally sturdy clay body that could survive the rough ride of a modern dishwasher.

book (1972). Kasey Grier received it for Christmas from her parents in 1973 while still in college. Hewitt turned heirloom recipes—"America's culinary heritage"—into formulae with accurate measurements. Grier was fascinated by the game recipes and instructions like "how to prepare a snapping turtle for soup," an appalling process that involved bleeding the headless body for a full twenty-four hours before the carcass could be butchered and cooked with celery, carrots, onions, and bay leaves (she never tried it). Hewitt's book was just one of scores of books that brought authentic regional cooking to a national audience and was accompanied by the rise of gourmet restaurants featuring regional, often "poor-folks," food enhanced by young trained chefs who could not resist putting a personal stamp on old favorites.

The second strand of culinary change was alternative "whole foods" cooking, inspired by a new generation of health reformers and the environmental movement, which urged Americans to eat lower on the food chain for political and ecological reasons. Anna Thomas's *The Vegetarian Epicure* (1972) represented this new gourmet health food to many. College students and other environmentally concerned cooks

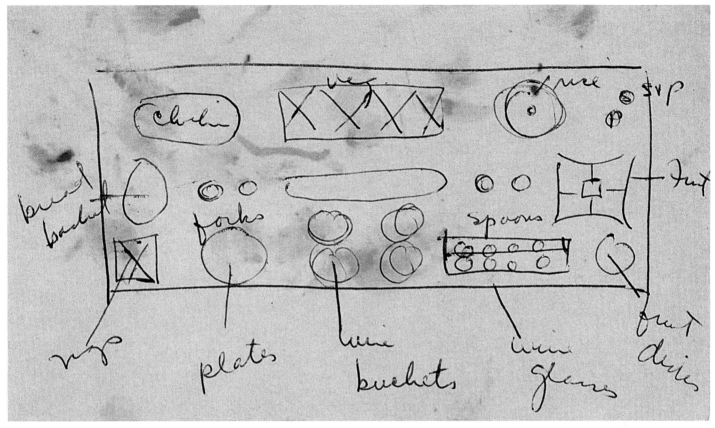

Fig. 1.40 Hostess Jewel Stern's buffet table diagram for a party given June 12, 1964.

purchased the book and struggled to master its complex, multistep recipes, which contained no meat but under no circumstances could be considered low fat. Grier recalls a particular adventure with an elaborate casserole she planned to serve for a dinner party. By the time she mastered the béchamel sauce and the multistep preparation of the eggplant and vegetables required for the dish, every pot and pan in her kitchen was dirty. The smallish pottery casserole that resulted tasted good, but all the labor behind the finished product was invisible, and the food seemed to disappear awfully quickly.

The tablewares accompanying this mix of alternative cuisine ranged from *haute* to down-home. Some Americans turned to contemporary craft potters for dinnerware sets and serving pieces and told their mothers that they did not want grandmother's dishes. Some even chose handmade or handmade-looking pottery as their bridal pattern (cat. 121). In 1971 the president of Hall's Department Store, the well-known specialty store in Kansas City, noted that many "brides have moved away from fine china, crystal and silver, which represented the bulk of our business. While we are not going out of the fine china business, we are seeing a change in emphasis."[120] This sea change was toward casual pottery, informal glassware, and stainless steel.

Other women still desired formal dining paraphernalia. Although many of their peers no longer felt the need for such things, more than half of the brides patronizing Hall's did register for sterling, fine china, and crystal in 1970.[121] Rather than purchase tableware, some young women selected from the sizable stock of formal china, glass, and silver that their mothers had faithfully curated. Most of the mothers might have tried hard to liberate themselves from the "drudgery" of complex cooking and formal dinners, and rejected dishes that had to be washed by hand and silver that had to be polished; but some of their daughters, and increasingly their sons, chose such wares for themselves.

By 1980 these new middle-class cooking hobbyists made use of convenience foods, especially on weekdays in families with two parents working full-time, and their daily dinners took place in the kitchen, if they existed at all. Although the earlier tradition of the genteel family dinner in the dining room did not reemerge, formal dining with friends utilizing complex food and food display had returned as a leisure pursuit. By the late 1980s an art-oriented firm like Rosenthal Porzellan beckoned these young American gourmets with exciting avant-garde designs that appealed to their sense of eating as entertainment (cat. 44). A sales brochure for the wildly patterned *Flash* line stated:

> The "Flash" Ceramics Programme is a complete series of tableware for the individualist who is always seeking new horizons—a kind of "Science fiction à la carte." Table settings can be composed exactly to one's own individual taste . . . and your choice will very much depend on how daring or imaginative you are! Thus, every buffet becomes a stage setting, every brunch a "lightning start" in your quest for new culinary adventures!"[122]

Cat. 44 Decorated with lightning bolts and checker-boards, Rosenthal's *Flash* epitomized tableware as fashion.

By the 1980s some Americans had returned to the formal dinner party, where tableware was a stage set but eating was a frankly sensual experience rather than an exercise in self-discipline and civilization. However, for every gourmet there were many more for whom dining in style was indeed a thing of the past. These Americans led lives in which processed foods, utilitarian dishes, and microwaves reigned supreme. In the area of the tabletop, as with so much in this country, America had become a land of diversity, not conformity.

OPPOSITE:
Cat. 43 The late 1950s lines *Taylorton* (tray) and *Informal* (pitcher) were promoted as oven-to-table wares.

Notes

1. A useful overview for the general reader of the expansion and consolidation of middle-class culture after 1880 can be found in Schlereth 1991.

2. On abundance in feasting traditions, particularly meat, see Visser 1991, 27–37; and Elias 1978, 117–22. On white sugar, see Mintz 1985.

3. Visser 1991, 22.

4. Ames 1992; Schlereth 1991; Clark 1986.

5. Bushman 1992, 30–99.

6. For the meaning of the act of furnishing and a discussion of the impact on gentility in Victorian America, see Grier 1997.

7. Clifford E. Clark Jr., in Grover 1987, 146, 152.

8. Lutes 1937, 206.

9. This account of nineteenth-century dining-room furnishing conventions is derived from Williams 1985; Ames 1992; Garrett 1990. For the early history of the cupboard, see Eames 1977, 55–72.

10. In her research on everyday life Katherine Grier has never found a complaint about eating dinner surrounded by pictures of dead game, although it is notable that no dining room pictures of dead chickens or veal calves were produced. A whiff of romance apparently made the difference.

11. Spencer 1983, 19.

12. Morse [1908], 73.

13. The comments here were shaped by readings of Douglas 1973; Douglas 1972, 61–81; Mintz 1985, xv–xxx, 1–18; Elias 1978; Goody 1982.

14. Kasson 1990, 197.

15. Ibid., 199.

16. In her study of dining in Washington, D.C., in the early nineteenth century, Barbara G. Carson studied 224 probate inventories dating between 1818 and 1826 for information on dining patterns. Twenty percent of her sample still apparently ate with their fingers, and another nineteen percent were still without forks, see Carson 1990, 30–31.

17. Beecher 1858, 237; cited in Williams 1985, 81.

18. For an in-depth discussion of the rise of the silver industry in the second half of the nineteenth century, see Venable 1994.

19. Steel knives remained a separate item to be purchased because they were sharper than silver or silver-plated ones and better for cutting roasted meat. Nowadays silverware drawers are often equipped with a separate set of steak knives for this same reason.

20. Hogan 1980, 94–97.

21. Logan 1889, 5–6; see also Kasson 1990.

22. Strasser 1982, 163; and Cowan 1997, 198.

23. For a discussion of attitudes toward sexuality and the body, see Bederman 1995. For a useful discussion of attitudes toward diet and exercise, see Green 1986.

24. *Good Manners* 1888, 121.

25. Supplement, *LHJ* (Aug. 1884): 1.

26. Advertisement for Higgins & Seiter, *LHJ* (June 1898): 23.

27. Elizabeth Warburton, "Selecting the Right Wedding Present," *LHJ* (Oct. 1912): 75.

28. Lutes 1937, 216–17.

29. Ibid., 219.

30. Ibid., 221.

31. Spencer 1983, 102–3.

32. Kasson 1990, 193, 194.

33. This statement is qualified with "probably" because, in fact, it is not known for certain if most families ate in the kitchen in winter.

34. The best account of the impact of domestic science on both women's roles and the American diet remains Shapiro 1986. This brief summary draws heavily from her research.

35. Green 1986, 30–53, 327–30.

36. Rorer 1902, 3–4.

37. Shapiro 1986, 71–72.

38. Allen 1919, Introduction, n.p.

39. Ibid., 57.

40. Tipton 1926, v.

41. According to Cowan 1997, 196: "Despite the many changes in the work processes of housework occurring between 1870 and 1920, the maintenance of a fairly comfortable domestic standard of living required the labor of at least two adult women. As late as 1925, Americans still believed that a middle-class standard of living could not be achieved without employing at least one full-time household servant."

42. Advertisement for Higgins & Seiter, *LHJ* (May 1903).

43. Advertisement for Wallace and Sons Manufacturing Company, *LHJ* (Jan. 1905). For an interesting account of Mrs. Rorer's career as a cooking celebrity, see Weigley 1980, 195–207.

44. Carson 1990.

45. Jenkins 1946, 54.

46. Sprackling 1941, 163–64.

47. Tipton 1926, 50–51.

48. Lovegren 1995, 66.

49. Lynd and Lynd 1957, 281.

50. Schubert 1926, 114.

51. Lynd and Lynd 1957, 286–87.

52. On the rise of the companionate marriage, see Lystra 1989 and Mintz and Kellogg 1988, especially chap. 6.

53. "Using Bridge Sessions to Stimulate Sales," *CGJ* 107:3 (Mar. 1929): 74.

54. Lynd and Lynd 1957, 53.

55. Ibid., 154.

56. Ibid., 154, 155–56.

57. Ibid., 157–58.

58. Ibid., 156.

59. Strasser 1982.

60. Anderson 1997, 142–69.

61. Rombauer 1946, 120–21.

62. Advertisement for H. J. Heinz Company, *LHJ* (Nov. 1933): 120.

63. Holloway 1922, 128.

64. *Modern Priscilla* 1925, 150.

65. Holloway 1922, 129.

66. Post 1939, 361.

67. Eichler 1937, 197–99.

68. Ibid., 199–200, 204.

69. Sprackling 1941, 194.

70. Ibid., 4.

71. Ibid., 177.

72. Lovegren 1995, 206.

73. Neil 1916, 14.

74. Ibid., 15–16.

75. "What Brides Think about Wedding Presents," *HB* 34 (May 1942): 62–63.

76. "Will Demand for 'Old Time' Sets Return," *CGJ* 104:2 (13 Jan. 1927): 14.

77. Advertisement from the 1930–31 Montgomery Ward & Co. catalogue, reproduced in Cunningham 1982, 178.

78. Jack Olsen, "Five and Ten Cent Glass Dinnerware Business" *CGJ* 112:1 (Jan. 1933): 17.

79. Sprackling 1941, 168–69.

80. "Eating in the Kitchen," *Boston Sunday Herald*, 3 Dec. 1944; cited in *CGJ* 136:4 (Apr. 1945): 29.

81. Ann Batchelder, *LHJ* (Jan. 1943): 38–39.

82. For a detailed discussion of family life in this era, see May 1988.

83. Advertisement for Chromcraft dinettes, American Fixture & Manufacturing Company, Saint Louis, *LHJ* (Mar. 1948): n.p.

84. Jones 1946, 17.

85. *LHJ* (June 1948).

86. Sears 1961, 1251–257.

87. Advertisement for A. H. Heisey & Company, "Heisey's 'Hostess Helper,'" *CGJ* 143:3 (Sept. 1948): back cover.

88. *CGJ* 127:1 (June 1940): 24; 140:4 (Apr. 1947): 2.

89. Grier interview 1998.

90. Lovegren 1995, 207.

91. For a discussion of cocktail mixing in bulk and liquor estimates, see Adams 1950, 74–81.

92. Allen 1941, 4–6.

93. Berolzheimer 1949, 2.

94. Malone 1947, 205.

95. Campbell Soup 1968, 13.

96. *CGJ* 120:5 (May 1937): n.p.; "'Eating in the Back Yard' Theme Sells Pottery," 121:3 (Sept. 1937): 22.

97. Steck 1942, 28.

98. Younkin 1946, 46.

99. Grier interview 1998.

100. For images of barbecue accessories, see Bosker 1996.

101. Probably the first announcement of disposable paper tablewares dates from 1885, when the *Ladies' Home Journal* breathlessly announced the use of papier-mâché plates for bread and cake by a "daring landlord in Berlin." "The landlord liked them because they were so cheap they could be thrown away after once using. . . . Housewives will cordially welcome the introduction of this sort of table furniture into America." "Paper Plates," *LHJ* (Feb. 1885).

102. Spigel 1992, 31–32.

103. Marling 1994, 188–92.

104. Adams 1950, 167–68.

105. "Recognition Heats Up for Inventor of 3-Compartment TV Dinner Plate," *Dallas Morning News* (5 Oct. 1999): 174, 24A.

106. Malone 1947, Foreword.

107. Marling 1994, 204–5.

108. Bracken 1960, vii, ix.

109. Campbell Soup 1968, 5.

110. Ibid., 22–34.

111. Grier interview 1998. For a hilarious discussion of the meaning of cakes in 1950s cooking, see Marling 1994, 223–28.

112. For a typical selection of jelly recipes, including arrowroot and tapioca "jelly," intended for invalids, see Child 1832, 31–32. Child also offers a jellied "blanc-manger" and "cranberry jelly," intended as desserts, 118–19.

113. Lovegren 1995, 7–8.

114. Ruth Mills Teague, "Conversation Piece," *LHJ* (June 1948): 204, 207.

115. *LHJ* 70:4 (Apr. 1953): cover, 142, 158; 70:5 (May 1983): 12–13.

116. *LHJ* 85:5 (May 1968): 102.

117. "Latch onto 'Micro'—The Word for '77," *GTR* (Dec. 1976): 1, 28.

118. Lovegren 1995, 227.

119. Stern interview 1999.

120. "Brides Flip Veil, Sales Pattern," *GTR* (June 1971): 1.

121. Ibid. Of those who registered for flatware, 64 percent chose sterling; for dishes, 53 percent chose fine china; for stemware, 60 percent chose crystal.

122. Rosenthal Porzellan. "'Flash' Rosenthal Studio-Line" (sales brochure). Selb, Germany, 1994.

Getting a Piece of the Pie: American Tableware Makers

Chapter 2

The truth is, and it is vain to disguise it, that we are a sort of independent colony of England—politically free, commercially slaves.

—HENRY CLAY, 1820

Every kind of ceramic and glass object on the worldwide market was available in America from the earliest days of European settlement. Because the American market for tableware was by the twentieth century the largest in the world, ceramics and glass manufacturers with dreams of selling beyond their own shores lusted for even a small share of the profits. This situation made it difficult for American potters and glassmakers to prosper in the manufacture of fine tableware. Mundane products like window glass, bottles, bricks, drainage tile, and kitchenware offered comfortable market niches for American pottery and glass makers, but profiting from the finer wares—delicate china dinnerware and splendid cut crystal—was extremely difficult. When foreign manufacturers cut prices below cost to attract more buyers, American makers simply shifted to products with higher profit margins. In spite of brief periods of effective protective tariffs, American ceramics and glass manufacturers before the late 1870s largely shied away from competition at the high end of the market.

American Pottery before 1880

Despite its colonial status, the North American continent hosted a large number of lively outposts where a European style of life continued with little interruption. There were Spanish garrisons in the southeast and southwest, English and French forts in the north, and Swedish and Dutch settlements in between. Soldiers, immigrants, fur traders, and merchants brought favorite items on the voyage or had them shipped as precious cargo along with other necessities. Dining and washing, the activities most closely associated with objects of ceramic and glass, continued to be accomplished in much the same way as they had in the old country. Spanish and Dutch majolica, English sgraffito ware, and Chinese porcelain have all been found in North American archaeological sites of the seventeenth century.[1]

As new wares were introduced into the international marketplace of the eighteenth century, American colonists could add them to their cupboards as soon as their households could afford them. English salt-glazed stoneware, creamware, and pearlware, as well as English porcelain, could be purchased in the colonies shortly after they became available in England (fig. 2.1). In July 1780 New York merchant Frederick Rhinelander ordered nine crates of "blue painted Ware . . . to be fine white (and not Cream Coulour) painted we believe it is called pearl blue."[2]

Fig. 2.1 Hard and durable, English salt-glazed stoneware was used by the American colonial elite in the mid-18th century.

Josiah Wedgwood & Sons had introduced pearl white (today called pearlware) to the English market only a year earlier in June 1779.

Chinese porcelain was represented in American china closets from the beginning of European settlement. Prior to the American Revolution this ware usually passed through merchants in England or Holland before being shipped to American ports (fig. 2.2). But in 1784, a year after the Treaty of Paris was signed, the American ship *Empress of China* set sail for Canton, returning with the first load of porcelain for the American market.[3] Although Chinese export porcelain was among the most expensive of the fine wares in the seventeenth- and eighteenth-century market, it became more affordable by the early nineteenth century. Indeed, most antebellum homes contained some blue-painted Canton china. Wealthier householders purchased the florid *Rose Medallion*, *Rose Mandarin*, and *Bird and Butterfly* wares during the middle years of the century. But by the late nineteenth century Chinese porcelain was common, having degenerated into a heavy, coarse ware with cursory painted decoration. By 1900 Japanese porcelain had entered the American market, and French and German china set the benchmark for design, quality, and price in tableware.

French porcelain became fashionable during the early years of the new republic (fig. 2.3). Virtually all the china bought for the White House during the nineteenth century was imported from France.[4] White hard-paste porcelain made in Paris with chased gold, colorful floral motifs, and bold em-

blematic decoration set the fine china standard for the second quarter of the nineteenth century. Although many small factories in Paris supplied ware to America during the first quarter of the nineteenth century, the center for porcelain making shifted to Limoges after 1830. Large deposits of kaolin had been discovered there in 1768. When the rail network was sufficient to support shipments of china from the distant village into the French capital, the number of factories located in Limoges increased rapidly.[5]

Most Americans associate the name Haviland with Limoges, especially when describing their grandmother's or even great-grandmother's table service. The Haviland family, however, was not French but American, having immigrated to the colonies from England in the mid-seventeenth century.[6] The Havilands established potteries and decorating shops in Limoges to make French porcelain that they brought into America through their own import house in New York (see chapter 3). By the late nineteenth century the family was selling so much frilly French china decorated with delicate flowers that potteries in Germany and the Austro-Hungarian Empire began to vie for their American customers. Successfully competing with the Havilands and other French producers, factories in Thuringia, Bavaria, and Bohemia were providing substantial quantities of French-style china dinnerware for middling American tables by 1900.

EARLIEST EFFORTS

Throughout the first three centuries of European occupation North American potteries struggled to find the right niche. Potteries in most early settlements made bricks and roofing tiles, which were too heavy for colonists to import. Utilitarian redware for use in kitchens, dairies, and taverns was also made in small potteries staffed by the owner/potter, members of his family, and perhaps a journeyman or apprentice.[7] Colonial wares from these potteries followed European models so closely that it is difficult today to identify their sources of production without technically analyzing the body of each example.[8] At least two majolica potteries are known from archaeological or documentary evidence, including the pottery on Governor William Berkeley's Green Spring Plantation in Virginia (after 1660) and the Coxe-DeWilde pottery in Burlington, New Jersey (1688–92). Wares were made for local distribution and export as well; for example, "white and Chiney ware" (probably tin-glazed earthenware) from the Coxe-DeWilde pottery was sold to markets as far away as Barbados and Jamaica.[9]

During the eighteenth century more potteries were established to keep pace with the growing population. Since the populace was still largely rural, most of these potteries were scattered across the countryside, established wherever the local resources and market would support the enterprise. Some urban areas also witnessed the embryonic growth of the American pottery industry. The village of Charlestown, Massachusetts, near Boston, for example, by the mid-eighteenth century was home to some forty potters who shipped their handiwork well beyond the immediate vicinity, supplying

Fig. 2.2 American colonists imported Chinese porcelain beginning in the first days of settlement.

wares to many New England coastal towns.[10] Clusters of large potteries sprang up around New York Bay, within easy shipping distance of one of the country's fastest growing markets. Potteries from Norwalk, Connecticut, to Rahway, New Jersey, made a variety of redware and stoneware forms for food service, processing, storage, and home sanitation.[11] Farther south, Philadelphia was the hub for the manufacture and distribution of vessels along the mid-Atlantic coast.

Some evidence exists that more delicate earthenware made of refined clay was produced in eighteenth-century America. Little came of these early efforts, however, because the market was so saturated with English ware that there was no room for, and indeed no interest in, the American product. English-style creamware is noted in a 1769 Boston newspaper, although no examples have been identified with certainty. John Bartlam made creamware in Cain Hoy, South Carolina, from 1763 to 1770, and William Ellis produced it in Salem, North Carolina, beginning in 1773.[12] Archaeological evidence indicates that refined earthenware might also have been made in Philadelphia during the second quarter of the eighteenth

century, although the dominance of English wares in the market and the disruption of the Revolution stemmed production.

The American arrangement of small, scattered inland potteries and larger urban, coastal ones continued well into the nineteenth century. As the production of stoneware (a high-fired, nonporous, but generally heavy type of pottery) expanded, the potteries tended to cluster near big cities and along the major transportation networks being built. A vigorous tradition of stoneware vessel production was established along the upper Hudson River and the Erie Canal after it was completed in 1825. Stoneware clays from the Raritan Formation in northeastern New Jersey were shipped up the river and through the canal, while finished goods went into the countryside or retraced the path the clay had traveled.

It should come as no surprise that the first fully industrial pottery in America was established in Jersey City, New Jersey, across the Hudson River from America's fastest growing city—New York. Begun as a porcelain factory in 1824, the Jersey Porcelain and Earthenware Company was bought in 1828 by Scotsmen David and James Henderson, who proceeded to

Fig. 2.3 Parisian porcelain was the pinnacle of fashion in mid-19th-century America.

make press-molded stoneware beverage vessels and transfer-printed pearlware with up to eighty workers by 1835.[13] The success of the industrial methods of press molding and transfer printing, and the distinct division of factory labor at the Hendersons' pottery, led to the establishment of other sizable potteries in the region that contributed to the American ceramics industry. Frenchmen Michel Lefoulon and Henri DeCasse started the Salamander Works in Woodbridge, New Jersey, in 1836.[14] Americans Christopher Webber Fenton and Decius Clark established what was to become the United States Pottery Company in Bennington, Vermont, in 1846.

Although most of the potters at these companies were trained in England, Scotland, and Europe, their work reflected subtle changes in the marketplace, as the style of tableware—still dominated by English and French sources—began to take on distinctly American characteristics. The *Cascade* pitcher in parian ware (a matte-finished porcelain) by English modeler Daniel Greatbach for the United States Pottery Company, for example, draws on the fondness for naturalism evidenced in Western decorative arts in this period, yet the pitcher's design is rooted in the turbulent landscape of the American wilderness rather than the tamed berry patches of staid English gardens (fig. 2.4).

In addition to the pearlware plates in the *Canova* pattern made at Jersey City, transfer-printed pearlware dishes were produced in Indiana during this period. In 1837 English potter James Clews and two men from Louisville, Kentucky, potter Jacob Lewis and importer Samuel Casseday, established the Indiana Pottery Company in Troy, near Louisville. Clays suitable for making whiteware and coal for fuel were located nearby. Clews had immigrated to Indiana from Staffordshire, England, the previous year and was followed by thirty-six potters he recruited from Europe. Several more English potters, such as James Bennett, who were already working in American potteries joined the Indiana workforce.[15] Clews undoubtedly planned to make blue transfer-printed pearlware tableware, which he had produced with his brother Ralph in England, but there is little evidence that such wares were made in Troy. Snuff jars are what remain today. The staff began to leave over the next several years as production was cut back, and Clews sold his shares back to the company in 1842.

During this same period the nascent American porcelain industry began to take shape. Modest beginnings in the eighteenth century had borne little fruit.[16] The little American China Manufactory of Gousse Bonnin and George Morris, which operated in the Southwark section of Philadelphia from 1770 to 1772, turned out enough work for at least a dozen pieces to survive more than two centuries. Drawing heavily on the expertise of English potters, Bonnin and Morris made porcelain tableware decorated in underglaze blue that closely mimicked the wares imported from Bow, Liverpool, and Lowestoft, England. High production costs in America, variable results, and Morris's untimely death led to the quick demise of the enterprise.[17] Yet during its brief life, this factory helped sow the seeds for further investment in native industry among Philadelphia's wealthy Quakers. When in 1826

Fig. 2.4 The United States Pottery Company's *Cascade* pitcher was one of the few original designs made in America during the mid-19th century.

William Ellis Tucker embarked upon making porcelain tableware decorated in the French taste, he had capital at hand to build the pottery and staff it with workers and raw materials.

Tucker's American China Manufactory remained in business until 1838, in spite of the death of its founder in 1832 and the need to scramble for investors on a regular basis. William Tucker's brother Thomas continued the operation, and Judge Joseph Hemphill was a stalwart investor in the later years. The pottery closed after Judge Hemphill sold his interest in 1837 and the unstable economy of the period (with no protective tariff) undercut Thomas Tucker's valiant efforts. This ambitious operation made a wide variety of tablewares, beverage vessels, and ornamental shapes. All were decorated by hand with the elegant gold bands and flourishes and polychrome flowers of the Empire taste, but also with American eagles and flags, portraits of Washington and Lafayette, and scenes in and around Philadelphia.[18]

Several early china makers based themselves in Philadelphia partly because of the ready availability of white kaolin clay deposits nearby. Creating a successful porcelain manufactory in the greater New York area was more of a struggle. Dr. Henry Mead was among the first to venture into this territory of high production costs and low or no return on investment. Only one vase remains from the experiments he carried out in New York. Frenchmen Louis François DeCasse and Nicholas Chanou took over Mead's little pottery in New York about 1825, while Mead's experiments were resumed by George Dummer and William Shirley in Jersey City beginning in December of the same year. There Dummer built a relatively large pottery building next door to his glass factory and reportedly hired as many as one hundred workers, some of them French.[19]

A highly successful china and glass merchant in New York in the early era of protective tariffs, Dummer reasoned that he could provide stylish luxury goods for his shop with a minimum investment in shipping (across the Hudson River rather than the Atlantic Ocean) and no middleman to pay. The glass factory built in 1824 proved to be successful and continued in business until 1862, but porcelain production was much more difficult. Although the pottery took a silver medal in 1826 at the Franklin Institute in Philadelphia, which held an annual fair to encourage native manufacturers, the factory was closed by 1828. Only one small bowl, decorated in the French taste with a simple gold band at the rim, has been attributed to this pottery, although the owners submitted sauceboats, custard cups, serving dishes, and plates as well as teawares and small figurines to the competition in Philadelphia. According to an observer who interviewed Dummer at the time, investors had spent $50,000 developing the product and facilities before finally abandoning the effort.[20]

Although all of these early-nineteenth-century porcelain factories in New York, Jersey City, and Philadelphia decorated their wares in the French taste with solid gold bands and colorful bouquets of bright flowers, the shapes came primarily from the English lexicon.

A succession of factories in the Greenpoint section of Brooklyn, New York, proved to be heartier. By 1844 German brothers William, Francis, and Anthony Boch established the city's first porcelain factory, William Boch and Brothers. By the time the pottery exhibited wares at the Crystal Palace Exhibition of the Industry of All Nations, held in New York in 1853, it was making a wide variety of "house, lock, & furniture trimmings; porcelain pitchers, mugs, vases, and other fancy wares," including figurines and "grave-yard monuments."[21] The trimmings included many familiar household bits—stair rods, doorplates, key escutcheons, and knobs for shutters, doors and drawers.

Tableware is noticeably absent from this list of mundane trimmings, beverage vessels, and ornaments. The Boch brothers evidently saw the folly in trying to compete with imported English and French tableware. So too did their rival Charles Cartlidge. The Englishman Cartlidge arrived in New York as the agent for William Ridgway's Staffordshire potteries. When Ridgway went out of business in 1848, Cartlidge set up a pottery in Greenpoint. Cartlidge's first products included porcelain buttons (then replacing the mother-of-pearl variety), signs for doors and rooms, number plates for church pews, keyhole escutcheons, furniture casters, and a variety of knobs similar to those made by Boch. Cartlidge, however, was perhaps more creative in finding a market niche: he also made

a variety of specialized forms, including inkstands, paperweights, handles for cutlery, parasols and canes, shawl pins, candlesticks, smokers' paraphernalia, cuspidors, tableware, and pitchers. China painters working at the two Greenpoint factories added gold trim and brightly colored flowers in the rococo revival taste that was popular at the time.

TRENTON AND EAST LIVERPOOL: CENTERS OF INDUSTRY

As the U.S. population grew during the second quarter of the nineteenth century, the development of cheap and effective transportation systems and the availability of abundant natural resources began to have a significant effect on the regional concentration of the ceramics industry. Despite the early dinnerware potteries in Philadelphia and Brooklyn, these large cities were not destined to harbor the growing American ceramics industry, which would ultimately be centered in two smaller industrial cities. By the time of the Civil War, Trenton, New Jersey, and East Liverpool, Ohio, were favored as regional pottery centers. In Trenton an extensive canal system, in place by the mid-1830s, could deliver coal from the enormous deposits in northeastern Pennsylvania and raw materials from various places to the city.[22] After processing these resources into ceramic vessels, the potteries could ship the wares, in some cases along the same pathways, to the burgeoning markets in Philadelphia and New York. East Liverpool's advantages were nearby essential natural resources—clay and coal—and a location on the Ohio River, by which finished goods could be delivered east to Pittsburgh and south to Cincinnati and New Orleans and places in between.[23]

Simple earthenware pottery was already a staple product in Ohio when East Liverpool began its rise as a pottery center. Before 1840, however, the state's potteries were small and scattered across the countryside. A total of 99 potteries employing 200 people are listed in Ohio's 1840 census. By 1850 there were 120 potteries in the state employing 556 persons. The 6 potteries in East Liverpool counted 153 employees, meaning that they represented 5 percent of the total potteries in the state and 28 percent of the pottery workforce.[24]

James Bennett, who arrived in 1839, is identified as the first potter to set up shop in what was a sleepy Ohio river town. Although East Liverpool had been laid out in 1816 (over a previous town, Saint Clair, founded in 1802), little manufacturing had taken place there. Bennett, an English potter lured to Indiana by the failed Clews enterprise, was on his way back east when he heard about the clay and coal reserves near East Liverpool. Bennett's three brothers came to help in 1841, but by 1844 they had moved upriver to Pittsburgh to take advantage of rail services and fuel there.

Although the pottery industry began slowly in East Liverpool, it grew substantially by the end of the century, aided materially by the completion of the Cleveland and Pittsburgh Railroad through the city in 1855. The later rail connections from Chicago to New Orleans ensured rapid and distant distribution of the city's ceramics. For many years production consisted primarily of coarse yellowware and Rockingham (mottled brown) ware typically used in food preparation rather than formal food service. But in 1872 the East Liverpool potteries began making a relatively nonporous off-white ware called whiteware, graniteware, or white ironstone for the kitchen, dining room, and bath. Of the twenty-three potteries in the city in 1877, nine were making whiteware. In that same year Knowles, Taylor and Knowles used local natural gas to fire a kiln for the first time. Use of this new fuel, which was cleaner, cheaper, and faster than coal, gave East Liverpool a competitive edge over Trenton, its eastern rival, which had no natural gas at hand and was even slower to develop combustible producer gas for fuel. By 1895 East Liverpool had become the largest production center of ceramic table- and toilet-wares in the United States.[25]

Trenton was slightly later than East Liverpool in establishing its ceramics industry, but the city's location on the East Coast gave it a great advantage. Although simple hand-crafted pottery had been made in Trenton since the late eighteenth century, the first industrial pottery was produced there in 1852. By 1854 a little factory owned by the Englishman William Young was turning out tableware for exhibition (and prizes) at the Franklin Institute. Lured to Trenton from Charles Cartlidge's porcelain factory in East Liverpool by Charles Hattersley's persuasion and capital, Young and his three sons set up a sizable operation making yellowware and Rockingham kitchenware; white ironstone tableware; and porcelain pitchers, hardware, and harness trimmings. Likewise, James Taylor and Henry Speeler abandoned their little pottery in East Liverpool to relocate in Trenton at the same time as Young. An Englishman who had immigrated first to Jersey City to work for the Hendersons and then moved westward, Taylor thought East Liverpool held promise as a prime location to make pottery for the western trade. But after several years of struggle in Ohio, he saw that East Liverpool needed more time to mature. Trenton looked like it would blossom sooner—and so it did.

Unlike East Liverpool's potters, who depended for so long on their local clay resources, Trenton's industrial potters began making whiteware as soon as they settled in the city. In 1856 Taylor and Speeler won a first class premium at the Franklin Institute for "China, Granite and Earthen Ware." The record for this exhibition notes, "The china . . . is fully equal to the best heretofore exhibited; the granite is the best we have seen of American production, the body equal to standard manufacturers abroad . . . the whole . . . being manufactured by anthracite coal."[26] Trenton's potters went on to deserve this praise; they made substantial amounts of tableware for the American market even before the Civil War, first white with low-relief decoration and later printed and painted.

Whether working from Trenton or East Liverpool, American potters had to overcome the market's pronounced prejudice against their wares. So strong was the American attachment to foreign ceramics at this time that buyers were reluctant to admit that American craftsmen could produce comparable ware. Many potters used backstamps and makers' marks that mimicked English marks so that consumers could not tell where the dishes had been produced. The practice might well have been suggested by urban wholesalers anxious to distribute American ware with lower transportation costs. No matter how the custom started, it was late in the nineteenth century before a concerted effort was made to inform the buying public about the country of origin.

When the United States Potters' Association was created in January 1875, members agreed to come out from under the domination of foreign design:

> We should not in the future as we have been doing in the past, copy all or nearly all of our patterns from foreign manufacturers. We have sufficient talent in this country to originate new designs, more elegant and more suitable for the wants of the American people. By securing this object, we can sooner give to our products the stamp of a national character, and show to the consumers that they are and have been using large quantities of American goods sold to them as of English manufacture.[27]

In 1877 the Homer Laughlin China Company went a step further and began using a backstamp depicting the American eagle viciously attacking the English lion.[28]

In her 1878 book *The Ceramic Art: A Compendium of the History and Manufacture of Pottery and Porcelain*, historian Jennie J. Young complained that "French art is to a Frenchman the finest and best the world ever saw. Englishmen support English art because it is their own. . . . American art may be good, even equal to the best, but unfortunately it is American. Receiving no notice, the artist loses even the benefit of criticism, and concludes that his own people compliment themselves by believing that no work of art can be produced among them." She then described the practice of putting pseudo-English backstamps on American whiteware:

> Inquiry among the dealers brings out the whole truth. Their customers look for the English mark, and finding it, are satisfied. After this we need not inquire if the English granite-ware is superior to the American. There is no question of superiority or inferiority, but only one of the potency of a name. . . . No objection is ever made to its appearance, its finish, purity, durability, or decoration, only it has the misfortune to be American, and its parentage must be concealed at all hazards.[29]

Despite having to overcome a wide variety of technical problems and the domination of the tableware market by English and French makers, American potters began to claim a growing share of certain markets. When the East Liverpool potters started making whiteware in 1872, their contribution to the market added substantially to the whitewares already being made by potters in Trenton, Baltimore, New York, and Boston. This effect can be seen in the records of the U.S. Customs Office, which tracked the number of "packages" of ceramics imported from Staffordshire. By 1866 imported packages reached a peak of 119,782, but the domestic makers of whiteware entering the market in greater numbers after the Civil War began to erode this enormous importation. By 1874 the number of imported packages had been reduced to 45,378.[30] Finally the American industry was successfully competing with England.

American Glass before 1880

The marketplace for glass in America before 1880 shared many similarities with that of ceramics. Early and long-standing dominance of English ware led the nascent American glass industry to concentrate on utilitarian glassware. Many of the earliest glassmakers prospered by offering window glass and bottles as their main products, much as makers of bricks and utilitarian stoneware found their niches in the American ceramics market. The historical record shows, however, that American makers of table glass prospered sooner than those who made table china. Perhaps because so little nineteenth-century glass is marked, the issue of country of origin never arose. Instead of judging acceptability by a backstamp, as American consumers did with ceramics, they assessed quality in glass by its overall appearance and design. Another factor could be that U.S. glass manufacturers greatly increased their market in the nineteenth century through inventions that allowed an increasing number of consumers to own glass. Using technological inventions associated with pressing, glassmakers were able to make more glass faster and cheaper as the century progressed.

FOUNDING FATHERS

Every type of glass available in England and Europe in the seventeenth and eighteenth centuries has been associated with the North American market from the earliest days of its development, either through archaeological retrieval or from clear histories of ownership (fig. 2.5). Even elaborate Italian drinking vessels have been found in American sites.[31] Glass manufacture was encouraged from an early date. European investors were principally interested in using distant lands as reservoirs of raw materials to supply home industries. With glass, however, investors saw the value in using native woodland resources to make glass in the colonies for export. Two early-seventeenth-century glasshouses failed quickly because a large capital investment was required before there was much return. Conditions had improved greatly by the early eighteenth century: nearly twenty glasshouses were established between 1732 and 1780, and while most concentrated on the staples of window glass and bottles, at least three were ambitious enterprises that focused on producing quantities of table glass.[32]

Caspar Wistar started his business in Salem County, New Jersey, in 1738 with four German glassblowers and a large financial investment. The vast forests of southern New Jersey, high-quality sand available along the Jersey shore, and a ready market in burgeoning Philadelphia, the most important colonial American city, promised fair profits. And indeed the glasshouse prospered until the Revolution. The staple prod-

ucts were window glass and bottles, but a small amount of tableware was probably distributed through the Wistar store and Wistar family.[33]

William Henry Stiegel opened his first glasshouse in Manheim, Pennsylvania, in 1764. Like Wistar, Stiegel made window glass and bottles, but he was anxious to meet colonial needs for fine table glass as well. By 1769 he advertised an extensive line of beverage service forms, including tumblers, wineglasses, water glasses, decanters, and water bottles as well as cruets for serving condiments. The enterprise was short-lived. By 1774 Stiegel was in financial straits after an overly enthusiastic business expansion.[34]

John Frederick Amelung's operation in Maryland was perhaps the most successful of the eighteenth-century start-ups. In 1784 he brought equipment and workers from Germany to Frederick, near Baltimore, and was advertising both window glass and table glass for sale from his New Bremen "Glassmanufactory." By 1789 many diverse forms were available, including "all kinds of Flint-Glass, such as Decanters, and Wine Glasses, Tumblers of all Sizes and any other Sort of Table Glass." He noted also that he engraved "Devices, Cyphers, Coats of Arms, or any other Fancy Figure on Glass."[35] Despite a fair success, Amelung's enterprise faltered after catastrophic winds and fire damaged the manufactory. His stroke in 1794 further impeded the company's profitably, although his son continued the business for several years. Amelung had petitioned the U.S. Congress on several occasions for capital to expand his operation. Although he was never able to secure any congressional loans, his proposition that duties be raised on imported glass was executed by Congress in installments between 1790 and 1794.

Despite the market freedom offered by the success of the Revolution, American glassmakers found it easier to profit by producing mundane products than by competing with British imports. Glasshouses built to serve the growing populations west of the Allegheny Mountains, and those long established in the forested areas of New Jersey, upstate New York, and New England continued to manufacture the standard products. In contrast, glass factories specializing in fine tableware tended to be located in or near cities that offered ready markets close enough to preclude major losses from shipping overland. The native glass industry was boosted first by the market disruptions caused by the Napoleonic Wars and the War of 1812 and later by the Tariff Act of 1824.

Pittsburgh was the site of the first successful maker of lead-glass tableware. The Englishman Benjamin Bakewell, a Pittsburgh merchant, founded Bakewell & Co. in 1809. Many partnerships followed until the company closed in 1882. Although Bakewell's company is best known today as a maker of quality lead, or "flint," table glass, the firm made a wide variety of domestic and commercial products, including window glass, chemical ware, bottles, and lamps. President James Monroe's 1818 order for cut glass for the White House

from Bakewell provided the imprimatur necessary for rapid expansion of his operation. But Bakewell's company was deeply in debt by 1818 due to the lack of tariffs sufficient to protect young industries. In that year the firm owed $50,552 and carried another $37,960 in unpromising accounts.[36]

By the end of 1819, the value of glass being made in Pittsburgh had fallen from $235,000 to $35,000. Under the "American System," promoted by Henry Clay and passed finally by the U.S. Congress in 1824, high tariffs protected U.S. manufacturers and allowed the national economy to develop high wages for workers and ready markets for agricultural commodities. Such levies became habitual in both the glass and ceramics industries in the United States, and radical changes to importation fees during the nineteenth century periodically sent these sectors into panic and decline.

French and English craftsmen were recruited to work for Bakewell and his various companies, but his workshops also became the training ground for many boys who apprenticed with these craftsmen and later founded their own firms. James Bryce, for example, born in Scotland in 1812, had arrived in Pittsburgh by 1819. In 1827, when fifteen years old, he was indentured to Bakewell, Page & Bakewell. Although Bryce briefly worked in the grocery business after the economic panic of the late 1830s, he returned to glassblowing in 1845 and founded Bryce, McKee and Company in 1850 with his brothers Robert and John and the brothers Frederick and James McKee. The company was the first of many partnerships and the beginning of a long history of Bryce family companies (cat. 46).[37]

Encouraged by the successful ventures in Pittsburgh, enterprising businessmen started glasshouses elsewhere to serve other regions, taking advantage of the tariff protection that would greatly expand the economy. In eastern New England important glasshouses were established in South Boston, East Cambridge, and Sandwich, Massachusetts. The Phoenix Glass Works was founded about 1820 by Englishman Thomas Cains, who immigrated to America in 1812 at the age of thirty-two, fully a master craftsman and eager to seize his opportunities in a new land. Cains worked first at the newly created South Boston Flint Glass Works, a subsidiary factory to the Boston Crown Glass Manufactory. The parent company specialized in window glass, while the South Boston furnace managed by Cains produced tableware, chemical apparatus, bottles and flasks, lighting goods, and apothecary supplies.[38] The South Boston Flint Glass Works closed its doors in 1827; Cains's Phoenix Glass Works prospered until 1869, when it entered receivership, and finally closed in 1870. Phoenix's table glass output embraced the whole range of glassmaking techniques of the period, including free-blown, mold-blown, cut and engraved, and pressed glass.

By 1855 South Boston had become a major production center, employing 586 men in three glasshouses producing $1,190,000 worth of glass in one year.[39] The Mount Washington Glass Company was another South Boston glasshouse. Although its fame today derives from the creative art wares made under the direction of Frederick Shirley later in the

Cat. 46 The Bryce family was known for the high quality of its pressed glass by the 1880s.

century, the firm contributed substantially to the table glass market from its inception in 1837. Founded by Deming Jarves and later briefly run by his son George, the company came into the hands of William L. Libbey, formerly its bookkeeper, in 1861. Libbey astutely moved the operation in 1869 from its dilapidated facilities in South Boston to the modern factory of the failed New Bedford Glass Company in New Bedford, Massachusetts, but then left the firm in 1872 to become agent for the New England Glass Company. When Shirley joined the Mount Washington staff in 1874, their work moved steadily toward greater quality and ornamentation.[40]

Glasshouses in East Cambridge also contributed a critical supply of table glass for the American market during this period. The New England Glass Company opened in 1818 in the old works of the Boston Porcelain and Glass Manufacturing Company. The group of investors included merchants Amos Binney, Edmund Munroe, and Daniel Hastings and their associates along with Deming Jarves, who managed the enterprise. The company became one of the largest manufacturers of glass tableware in the United States. "Experienced European Glass Cutters, of the first character for workmanship in their profession" were put to work immediately in a newly erected wing for glass cutting powered by steam.[41] The founders decided to produce their own red lead for flint glass, and made so much that they sold it to other glasshouses. By 1820 eighty men and sixteen boys and girls were making $65,000 worth of "fine, plain, mould, and rich cut" glass annually.[42] In 1855 five hundred workers had an annual output of $500,000. William Libbey leased the works in 1878 and brought his son Edward into the company in 1880. William died in 1883, and Edward took over management of the firm. But erratic business conditions and strikes undermined the company's prosperity in the 1880s. Libbey closed the works in 1888 during a strike and took many workers and managers with him to set up a new factory in Toledo.[43]

The New England Glass Company made every kind of stylish glassware demanded by the market during its long history. Always of exceptional quality in design and finish, its output frequently won awards at fairs and expositions. The company introduced a wide variety of decorative techniques over the years, including such novelties as silvered glass, commonly known today as mercury glass, first shown at the New York World's Fair of 1853, and many of the firm's craftsmen produced distinguished work. Louis Vaupel, for example, emigrated from Germany in 1850 and quickly became foreman of the engraving department. His great skill was lavished on elaborate scenic engraving and passed on to a number of American-born engravers.[44]

Yet the firm's most important contribution to glassmaking in America may well be its role as the factory where glass-pressing technology was first perfected. Blowing and cutting lead glass was costly, requiring a large retinue of workers. Amelung's Maryland operation, for example, employed as many as three hundred to five hundred workers in the late eighteenth century. The technique for mold-blown glass, blowing the vessel into a metal mold, was in use in European and American factories by the early nineteenth century. In this process the vessel is formed and decorated at the same time (fig. 2.6).

Further experiments by American glassmakers yielded even more impressive results in the 1820s. Although the practice of pressing glass into molds can be traced to ancient Rome, methods of enhancing the process by machine were perfected in several American glasshouses. Recent scholarship has identified Henry Whitney and Enoch Robinson of the New England Glass Company as holding the first significant patent (granted November 4, 1826) for this technology.[45] Glassmakers in Jersey City, Pittsburgh, and elsewhere, however, were also experimenting with new mechanical pressing devices and patenting them in the late 1820s and early 1830s. Furniture knobs were the principal product at the beginning of the pressed-glass era, but brightly patterned tableware followed quickly.

Although the early wares from these methods tended to mimic the standard British cut patterns, new shapes and styles of glass eventually emerged, lending a fresh liveliness to the design of glass tableware in this period. The acanthus leaves, Gothic arches, and scrolls typical of late Empire design gave way to elaborate lacy pastiches of multiple motifs, from hearts and scrolls to thistles and proverbs. The Boston and Sandwich Glass Company made a wide variety of these patterned products in its facilities on the Cape Cod peninsula of Massachusetts.[46] The company is credited with such extensive production of lacy pressed glass that the ware is referred to generically today as Sandwich glass, although a fair amount of it was made elsewhere (fig. 2.7). Along with its main rival, the New England Glass Company, the Boston and Sandwich Glass Company dominated the market for domestic glass tableware in New England.

The company was created by Deming Jarves, who left the New England Glass Company in 1825 and founded the Sandwich Manufacturing Company in July of that year. By early 1826 he needed investors to help him through financial difficulties, and so the Boston and Sandwich Glass Company was born officially in February 1826. Jarves next founded the Mount Washington Glass Company in South Boston around 1837. The ever-active Jarves then established the Cape Cod Glass Works in 1858. These firms made the wide variety of glass for general domestic use that the market demanded.

The new technology for producing pressed glass meant that skilled foreign craftsmen had little advantage over native-born workers. The fact that local workers could quickly learn the new skills necessary for pressing is borne out by statistics. In 1832, for example, the *Barnstable Journal* reported that nearly two hundred men and boys were "constantly employed" at the factory. Two-thirds of this number were Americans "and nearly one half of them born in Sandwich or its immediate vicinity." Indeed, the enterprise employed and supported "over one quarter of the population of Sandwich."[47]

In the New York area, three important glass factories made high-quality rich cut tablewares during the second quarter of the nineteenth century: Richard and John Fisher's

Bloomingdale Flint Glass Works in Manhattan, John Gilliland's Brooklyn Glass Works, and the Jersey Glass Company in Jersey City, directly across the Hudson River from lower Manhattan.[48] Established by New York china and glass merchant George Dummer and two partners, the Jersey City enterprise eliminated the English glass exporters' markup and transatlantic shipping from Dummer's costs, thereby allowing him to keep a greater portion of the difference between manufacturing expenses and consumer prices. Glass craftsmen from Europe were recruited to this then-small town, where the firm built housing for its workers and operated a company store. In its prime during the 1840s, the company employed 150 workers. A wide range of "CUT Plain & Moulded GLASS of all descriptions" for domestic use was advertised, including many table forms, lamps, and knobs.[49] Little of the ware was marked, however, making it difficult to recognize. To add to the confusion of identification today, cutting shops that used blanks (unornamented glassware) from domestic and foreign makers flourished in the New York market.

Eastern Pennsylvania became another important center for fine table glass during this period. The Union Flint Glass Company was started in the Kensington section of Philadelphia in 1820 by workers from the New England Glass Company and was winning exhibition awards by 1827 for its cut wares. William Gillinder founded the Franklin Flint Glass Works in 1861 in Philadelphia. After his death in 1871, his sons continued production under the name Gillinder Brothers. Their exhibition factory at the Philadelphia Centennial Exposition in 1876 attracted a great deal of attention and fed the early interest in cut-glass tableware by showing consumers how it was made and decorated. Christian Dorflinger's glassworks and cutting shop opened in 1865 in White Mills, Pennsylvania, and spawned numerous cutting shops in nearby Honesdale during the late 1800s.[50]

As the century progressed, a new formula for cheaper pressed nonlead glass was developed. At the same time growing western markets and cheaper coal and natural gas shifted the centers of production from the East Coast to the Midwest. While glasshouses in the east catered to the luxury trade, producing elaborate cut glass and high-priced decorative novelties, factories farther west in Ohio and West Virginia serviced a broader market. The villages of Cambridge, Fostoria, Bellaire, and Findlay in Ohio and Morgantown and Wheeling in West Virginia became the new centers for the production of pressed patterned glass. Some older companies, like the New England Glass Company, shifted away from pressing and resumed making costly table glass for its regional market rather

Fig. 2.6 Three examples of glassware made by blowing glass into metal molds, an important technological innovation.

than repeatedly lowering prices to compete with the western glasshouses. In addition general prosperity in the country was increasing. With more people making more money, higher prices could be demanded for quality products. Heavy blown glass with brilliant cutting became a necessity in the homes of the upwardly mobile. At the same time elaborate copperwheel engraving became fashionable. Highly skilled engravers from the German and Bohemian industries supplied the American market with fancy floral patterns, intricate plant and animal motifs, and views of American scenery and enterprise. Demand became so intense that even native talent was trained to supply ware for this market.

While art glass was still to come after 1880, the desire for glass of all kinds in the domestic sphere was already well established among consumers by this time. In the industry itself

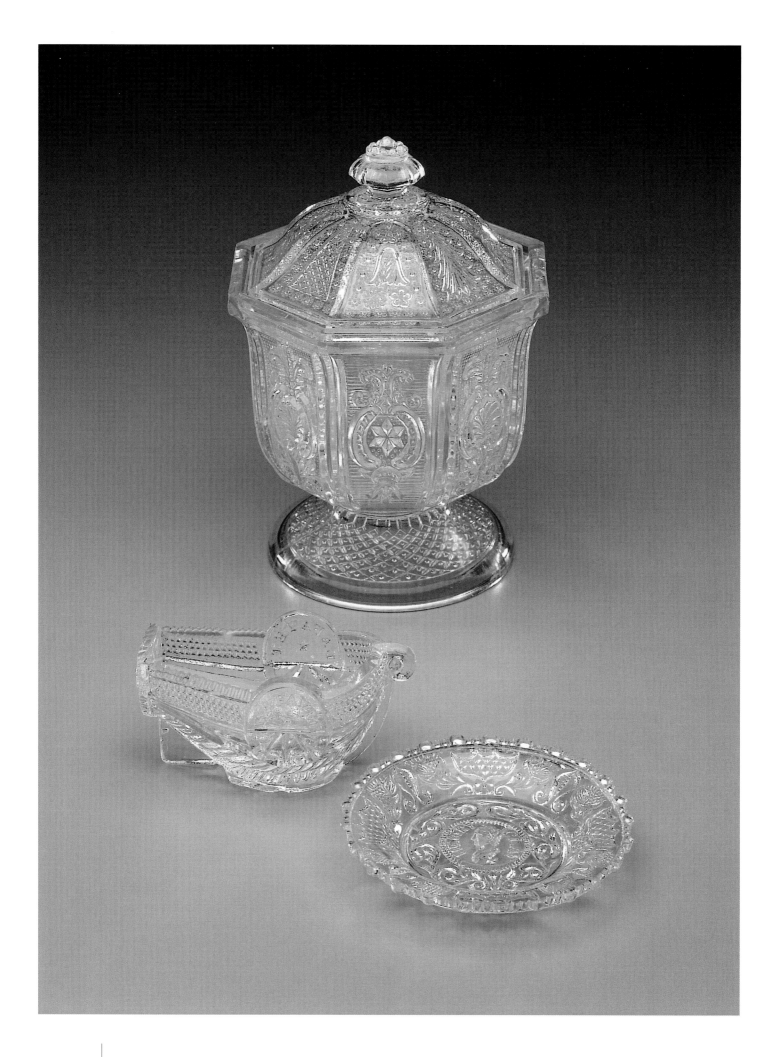

consolidation and regionalization were well underway with large companies emerging in New England; the mid-Atlantic region, particularly in southern New Jersey and eastern Pennsylvania; and the Midwest, especially in western Pennsylvania, West Virginia, and southeastern Ohio. Although many mechanisms that defined and shaped the ceramics industry also greatly influenced the glass industry—particularly the development of population centers, the exploitation of natural and man-made transportation systems, and the use of natural gas—the glass industry was relatively profitable in 1880, and its future was assured by a growing population that desired glass objects for practical and ornamental purposes. Whereas the ceramics industry struggled to meet the prices of cheap pottery imports, the glass industry provided the U.S. market with a broad range of products from the very finest cut and engraved table glass to the most mundane fruit jar.

Potting Becomes an Industry: Ceramics after 1880

American potters were well on their way to establishing a viable ceramics industry by the mid-1870s. The English imports that had dominated the market through most of the eighteenth and nineteenth centuries were declining in the face of the growing number of U.S. whiteware makers. In 1870 consumption of English pottery peaked at 42 percent by value of all ceramic tableware purchased in the United States and then began to decline.[51] Nevertheless, the relatively small American potteries were still struggling with tariffs that favored importers rather than manufacturers, with a workforce that was accustomed to high wages and low productivity, and with unyielding competition among themselves for the same market. Although the growing number of whiteware potteries was forcing English imports out of the market, the discovery and increasing use of natural gas as a fuel in Ohio threatened the industry in New Jersey. Firing kilns with gas was substantially cheaper than using coal, giving potteries in Ohio a distinct advantage.

THE TURNING POINT

At a meeting in 1874 Trenton's potters proposed the creation of a trade organization to represent the industry. In December of that year, three of them—John Hart Brewer, John F. Thompson, and C. Hilson—circulated a letter among the whiteware and yellowware potteries of the United States calling for the establishment of a national association of "earthenware manufacturers for the purpose of promoting their general interest and welfare."[52] On January 13, 1875, at a convention in Philadelphia, the United States Potters' Association (USPA) was formed. John Moses of Trenton's Glasgow Pottery became the first president. His executive committee included M. Tempest from Cincinnati, James Carr from New York, and Basil Simms from East Liverpool. Brewer was named secretary, and Thomas Carll Smith of New York was named treasurer. In electing these men, the USPA recognized the leaders of the industry. By the 1870s Brewer, Moses, Carr, and Smith had been running vital potteries in their respective cities for some time. All had entered the pottery business in the United States during the 1850s and 1860s. They were, therefore, intimately familiar with the major problems facing the industry.

Chief among their concerns was tariff rates. Indeed, the tariff rate was a paramount concern for all USPA members, and one of the organization's major activities was to show a united front in lobbying Congress to set and maintain high protective tariffs. In this regard the makers were in direct opposition to the buyers and retailers on whom they depended for business. Low tariffs favored the retail end of the business, in which lower wholesale prices paid for goods translated into higher profits for the storekeepers, as well as for importers.

Potters, on the other hand, wanted high tariffs so that they could keep their own prices up. Low tariffs squeezed their profits between meeting the foreign competition and paying high wages to workers. This situation had been exacerbated in 1872 when the U.S. government cut duties on imported pottery by 10 percent. Although rates were raised in 1883 to over 50 percent of value, the fact that America still had the highest paid workforce in the world allowed foreign countries that paid potters far less to undercut domestic products. In the minutes of the 1883 USPA annual meeting, the potters noted that American workers were paid four times more than their English and Continental counterparts: "This difference in the condition of American and foreign labor illustrates the difference between labor free, honorable and remunerative, and labor poorly paid, disfranchised and consequently debased. Nothing but a suitable protective Tariff can protect this labor, but by suitably protecting the manufacturing industries of our country."[53]

The first USPA officers elected in 1875 no doubt all felt that the American ceramics industry had existed for too long in the shadow of the English (cat. 47). "We should not in the future, as we have been doing in the past, copy all or nearly all of our patterns from foreign manufacturers," declared members of the newly formed organization. "We have sufficient talent in this country to originate new designs, more elegant and more suitable for the wants of the American people." They hoped American potters would give to their products "the stamp of a national character, and show to the consumers that they are and have been using large quantities of American goods sold to them as of English manufacture."[54] Some potters dispensed with the standard backstamp of the pseudo-English type and started using their own names to identify the origins of the ware. Others broke away from standard English whiteware or stoneware designs and introduced new shapes to the market. The new officers of the USPA were true leaders in such respects.

James Carr immigrated to the United States from Staffordshire, England, in 1844, working first for the American Pottery Company in Jersey City. Like English potters before him, Carr saw great contrasts between the way English and American potteries were run. In these disparities, he also

OPPOSITE:
Fig. 2.7 Mechanically pressed glass was an American invention.

getting a piece of the pie: american tableware makers | *117* saw how to make a place for himself and his talents. Although he struggled for years, trying to survive by making Rockingham ware and yellowware primarily in potteries in South Amboy, New Jersey, Carr's situation changed in 1856 when he organized the New York City Pottery with investor Alexander Morrison.

In 1858 Carr switched to white vitrified stoneware table and toilet articles as his main products, and over the years added parian statuary and majolica artware. "As to bone china," he recalled many years later, "when I got ready to make it and had all my shapes and materials on hand I found that a large firm down town was selling English china made in Longton [England], much cheaper than I could make it, so I used up the material and stopped."[55] Jennie Young, author of *The Ceramic Art* (1878), reported that Carr was using "six or seven different bodies, all composed of American materials. The staple product of the factory is stone china, which is largely sought in biscuit by decorators. Dinner services are decorated with all the care usually reserved for porcelain."[56] Carr retired from his pottery in 1888, and by the turn of the century at the age of eighty, he was considered to be the oldest living American potter and "one of the fathers of the pottery industry in this country."[57]

Businessman Thomas Carll Smith joined the Boch brothers in their Brooklyn pottery as an investor about 1861. Soon thereafter he bought the pottery works. Smith's Union Porcelain Works thrived on many of the same types of products that the Bochs had made, including porcelain house trimmings (key escutcheons, doorknobs, and the like), molded pitchers, cuspidors, cups and saucers, shaving mugs, toddy sticks, lemon squeezers, and a wide variety of other specialty table items (fig. 2.8). Sets of dinnerware in strong serviceable shapes decorated simply with wide colored borders and small scattered floral and ornamental motifs were also made by the company, which closed just after the turn of the century. Young, who surveyed the company's work for her book, described the tableware as "household porcelain . . . [with paste] of good quality." She complained that the painting lacked skill but stated that Smith had overcome the problem "and now employs a number of decorators whose work augurs well for the continued prosperity of the establishment."[58]

John Moses emigrated from Ireland in 1850, working first in Philadelphia as a dry goods clerk and after 1855 in Trenton as a bookkeeper. In 1864 he and several investors founded the Glasgow Pottery and a year later hired the potter Isaac Davis to oversee the factory. Within a decade the establishment was doing well. When the new periodical *Crockery Journal* (later

Cat. 47 English high-fired whiteware and stoneware were particularly popular with Americans during the second half of the 19th century.

Crockery and Glass Journal) profiled the pottery in January 1875, the company was said to have "the largest manufacturing capacity, besides being one of the best appointed potteries in this country, containing all the latest and best machinery adopted to the manufacture of crockery."[59] Two hundred workers produced enough vitrified whiteware for six kilns. In 1874 the company logged $175,000 in sales. At the time they were most famous for their Boston Tea Party teacups, distributed nationally for use at tea parties that celebrated the centennial of the Revolutionary-era event. Despite the pottery's success, however, little else is known about the Glasgow Pottery. After Moses's death in 1902, the family sold the buildings to a neighboring pottery.[60]

John Hart Brewer was drawn into the pottery business in 1865 by his uncle, Joseph Ott, an investor who had signed on with William Bloor in 1863. Bloor, an English potter, migrated back and forth between East Liverpool and Trenton beginning in the late 1840s. In 1848 he made doorknobs in East Liverpool in partnership with William Brunt. By 1854 Bloor was back in Trenton as a member of the Taylor and Speeler firm. When Taylor, Speeler, and Bloor exhibited at the Franklin Institute in 1856, their display included Rockingham-glazed earthenware, vitrified whiteware, and china. In March 1861 Bloor drew his first kiln of wares for his East Liverpool Porcelain Works (also known as the United States Porcelain Works). His price list of whiteware, porcelain, and parian ware shows a variety of table- and toilet-wares, including plates, dishes, baking dishes, coffee and tea sets, ice cream dishes, tureens, compotes, pickle dishes, basins and ewers, chamber candlesticks, and fancy articles in parian.[61]

When he returned to Trenton by 1863, Bloor formed a partnership with Joseph Ott and Thomas Booth (both Trenton investors) to create the Etruria Works in a new building on Clinton Street. Booth's minor interest in the firm was sold to Garret Burroughs in 1864, who in turn sold the interest to John Hart Brewer, Ott's nephew, in 1865. When Bloor left the company in 1871, his interest was bought by his partners, and the firm became Ott & Brewer. Although Brewer was presumably ignorant of pottery operations when he bought into the firm at the age of twenty-one, he had learned a great deal during the six years of his association with Bloor. When Bloor left, Brewer took over direction of the pottery.

In time Brewer became an important figure in the pottery industry in general. A founder of the USPA in 1875, he served in many of its offices, including as president, in subsequent years. Brewer also worked hard to promote the pottery industry in political circles as a state legislator and later as a U.S. congressman for two terms. In Congress he helped create a tariff policy favorable to the pottery industry. Following his death in 1900 his fellow potters adopted a resolution recognizing the "genius" he had shown at late-nineteenth-century fair exhibits, where he had "revealed to our people the possibilities of our industry, in the halls of Congress [where] he championed our cause, as Assistant Appraiser at the Port of New York [through which] he protected our interests, and as president of [the USPA] and chairman of many important

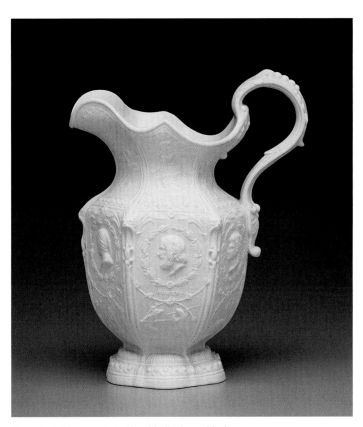

Fig. 2.8 As demonstrated by this finely molded pitcher, the quality of American-made ceramics had greatly improved by the 1870s.

committees [through which] he led our association to success at great and irreparable loss to himself."[62]

Brewer's material genius shows today most clearly through spectacular art porcelains and a few extraordinary table services produced by his pottery between 1876 and its close in 1892 (cat. 48). However, the factory was also well known in the industry for its sturdy and fashionable table and toilet articles of white granite and opaque china. Year after year, his staff of some three hundred workers routinely turned out these more mundane products to fill the shelves of china shops and country stores with serviceable crockery. Early dinner services were mostly white with relief-molded decoration, but a decorating department was added in the 1870s. Here, the plain ware was embellished with transfer-printed decorations, usually floral, which were further enhanced with color painted on by hand (cat. 49). Beginning in fall 1881 the development and design of these patterns was under the direction of Walter Scott Lenox. At the time Lenox was a young Trenton designer who had previously been in partnership with engraver Charles Ulrich to supply polychrome printed decorations to area potteries for use on dinner, tea, and dessert services.[63]

The addition of decorating departments to the whiteware factories was a decisive new movement for American potteries. Before the late 1870s any necessary decorating was added by independent decorators who operated large and small workshops near the potteries or in big cities. Decorations were ordered by china merchants to be applied to the specific shapes of individual potteries. Sometimes these orders came

into the decorators' workshops directly from the merchants, but they could be passed on to the decorator through the potteries. However, as customers routinely began asking for more and more embellished tableware, the large whiteware potteries added their own decorating departments. These divisions were complete with printing facilities and legions of decorators who hand painted color onto wares, applied transfer-printed ornament, and later, added decal decorations to pottery (cat. 50). Transfer printing and filling the prints with colored enamels became a popular technique in the early 1880s. Decalcomania was introduced in the 1890s and had replaced transfer printing by about 1905. In this process colored lithographic "decals" were cut from printed sheets and applied to a vessel's surface, and the ornament was made permanent through firing in a kiln. Although several decorators and potters in the United States (such as Lenox) experimented with this technology, it was actually perfected abroad, and the

Cat. 49 Made by English and American firms in
the late 1800s, these plates feature decoration
inspired by Japanese art.

Cat. 50 Decorated whiteware from Ohio and New Jersey competed with English imports by the 1870s and 1880s.

earliest regularly successful decals came from German and English printers.[64]

One of the first activities of the USPA was to organize U.S. potters to exhibit at the Philadelphia Centennial Exposition in 1876. John Moses, as president, called for "great exertions to bring such displays of ware to the Centennial Exhibition as would convince Americans that foreign articles should no longer be regarded as superior to those of American manufacture."[65] This effort proved less successful than Moses and others had hoped. The exhibitors were primarily from the mid-Atlantic region. However, Edwin Bennett of Baltimore did not exhibit; nor did the large Ohio potteries. Only the newly created Laughlin Brothers pottery of East Liverpool contributed to the USPA exhibit. As former china dealers in New York, Homer and Shakespeare Laughlin understood the marketing value of a world's fair, and their efforts were rewarded with a medal for whiteware.

Carr's New York City Pottery, Ott & Brewer, and Smith's Union Porcelain Works attracted notice for their sculptural work from models produced by three sculptor-modelers: W. H. Edge for Carr's pottery, Isaac Broome for Ott & Brewer, and Karl L. H. Müller for Smith's pottery. As contemporary descriptions and images of these displays reveal, the ceramic

artware and sculpture created by these talented modelers were indeed impressive (fig. 2.9).[66] Edge, Müller, and Broome brought artistic talent into pottery workshops that were otherwise staffed with modelers trained in the industry rather than in schools of art and design. Although the efforts of Carr, Smith, and Brewer to introduce artistic concepts to the industry did not take hold immediately, their accomplishments were not lost on their colleagues. The annual reports of the USPA following the Philadelphia Centennial Exposition frequently mentioned the need to establish schools of design intended specifically for the pottery industry.

The sculptural work of these potteries served to draw attention to each firm's more common wares. For example, Ott & Brewer also exhibited whiteware and cream-colored dinner and toilet articles noted "for their solidity and beauty of tint."[67] The whitewares were based largely on popular English patterns, specifically John Maddock's *Cable* and T. Furnival & Sons' *Cambridge* patterns. The decorations on the toilet items were described in detail by the trade reporter covering the fair, and included a wide range of decorative types from elaborate and colorful flower painting to chased gold ornament in the Grecian revival taste.

The Philadelphia Centennial Exposition captured a fleeting moment in the history of the American ceramics industry. At the exhibition U.S. potters proved their ability to compete artistically with imported ware. Although this feat eluded the notice of art commentators, retailers understood how American potters had met the challenge of the market for better design. Unfortunately, this artistic success was short-lived. The potteries in New York, Trenton, Philadelphia, and Baltimore remained prominent for another decade or two, but their influence began to wane as the Ohio factories came of age in the decades around the turn of the century.

The Laughlin Brothers' medal for whiteware was in reality more important than the critical acclaim given to the sculptural artwares displayed at the centennial fair. By 1900 or shortly thereafter Carr's, Brewer's, Smith's and Moses's potteries would all close. Certainly these establishments sorely felt the loss of leadership as their owners passed away, but more important, the firms were victims of the marketplace. By 1900 enormous quantities of decorated china were flowing into the country from rival potteries in France, Germany, Austria, England, and later Japan. Even Homer Laughlin left the pottery business in 1899, turning over the operation to W. Edwin Wells, an astute businessman rather than a sentimental potter of the old school. Despite its improving quality, thick earthenware with little or no decoration went out of fashion and was replaced by thin, hand-decorated foreign-made china. Only a few potteries invested in the development of new clay bodies during this period. And the few that did primarily chose to make heavier institutional ware, since they could not compete with the low price of foreign ceramics made specifically for the American table.

Fig. 2.9 James Carr's New York City Pottery exhibit at the Centennial Exposition, Philadelphia, 1876.

ADVANCES AT THE TURN OF THE CENTURY

Despite the potential contribution of these potteries to domestic dinnerware, the battle for the American market continued unabated. The level of protective tariffs fluctuated, while domestic potters periodically united against the interests of importers and retailers of foreign goods. "Permit me to say that an emergency is always upon us," warned John Hart Brewer at the 1883 USPA meeting, "and especially so when Congress is in session."[68] Keeping an eye on how the tariff was raised and lowered and whether it was figured on the manufacturer's prices to the importers or the fair market value of the ware was like watching a tennis match. Even as late as 1937 the USPA's president complained that the latest tariffs were figured on foreign valuation of the ware. "One thousand percent of nothing is still *nothing*," he observed bitterly.[69]

Perhaps the most dramatic results of tariff changes can be seen in the 1890s when the effects were exacerbated by a serious economic depression in the United States and a damaging potters' strike. In 1893 American potteries produced $20 million worth of ware. The very next year, however, Congress passed the Wilson-Gorman Tariff Act that cut levies on imported ceramics nearly in half. As a result pottery production in the United States dropped to $12 million in 1895 and then sank to $10 million the following year. Fortunately for U.S. producers, drastic cuts in import duties were reversed in 1897, and the industry soon returned to a production level of $20 million.

The tariff, as well as the high price of American labor, was an unquestionably important issue, but such matters were not the only points of concern. Successful potteries grappled with many other aspects of the business: the overall quality of their products, the needs of special markets, more efficient manufacturing, the cost of materials and labor, and favorable shipping rates from the railroads. These were areas over which potters had some control even when the tariff was working against them. "The increase of importation," reported the USPA secretary to the 1894 meeting, "seems chiefly in decorated goods, and there is a growing demand for more expensive goods, and the American manufacturer must keep up with the artistic development."[70]

The comparative figures presented at the 1894 meeting, based on reports from the U.S. Treasury Department, showed that the value of imports had nearly doubled between 1884 and 1893 from nearly $5 million to $9.5 million. Increases within these larger numbers were telling. While imports from Great Britain increased 60 percent, imports from France increased 85 percent, those from Japan rose 166 percent, and those from Germany and Austria (Bohemia) combined grew 210 percent. More significant, however, was the increase in importation of "Decorated and Ornamental Ware" from a mere $655,000 in 1875 to nearly $7 million in 1893, an increase of 1,000 percent.[71] American potteries were then supplying approximately 50 percent of the American market but servicing only its middle and lower ranges with brown Rockingham ware and yellowware for kitchen use and whiteware for the table. They had succeeded in facing down competition from the English ironstone makers but had not, for the most part, counted on the new challenge presented by the decorated-china makers in Europe and Japan.

The Greenwood Pottery Company in Trenton was founded during this early period but continued well into the twentieth century, buttressed by sturdy institutional products. Established in 1862 as Stephens, Tams & Co., the pottery was operated by William Tams, a Staffordshire potter who worked first for William Young and Company in Trenton and then created his own firm with money from James P. Stephens and Charles Brearley. Tams's son James took over the operation when William died in spring 1866. In 1868 the pottery was incorporated as the Greenwood Pottery Company with at least five kilns in operation, making it one of the larger operations in Trenton at the time. The firm's sturdy whitewares were a market mainstay for many years. Later the pottery developed a vitreous china, made thin for domestic use and thicker for institutional use, that was perhaps the first of the American china bodies to form the basis of the American institutional dinnerware industry at the end of the nineteenth century.

Ambitious potters understood that the American industry would have to move toward a reliable and hard, but more refined, ceramic body to compete with established French imports and the growing threat from German makers, both of which produced porcelain (a high-fired and refined pottery made primarily from white kaolin clay). Jennie Young notes in *The Ceramic Art* that five Trenton potteries were working on the development of better ware at that time: "Within the past two or three years all have been turning their attention to work of a more or less artistic character, some directing their efforts more particularly to decorating, and others to the perfecting of a body which shall enable them to compete with the manufacturers of porcelain. In this latter respect the Greenwood Company has met with gratifying success, and has given their ware the name of 'American china.'"[72] In the nineteenth and early twentieth centuries, as today, "china" was a term that could be used to describe dishes in general, but could also refer to the finest, most refined wares made from porcelain or similar types of bodies.

James Tams of the Greenwood Pottery Company and James Pass, manager of the Onondaga Pottery Company in Syracuse, New York, were perhaps the two most aggressive potters with regard to development of this new china. Whiteware table and toilet items were the earliest products made at Onondaga following its establishment in 1871.[73] In 1885 it introduced a semivitreous high-fired and nonabsorbent ware that was guaranteed against crazing. Although this was not truly porcelain, the next body type was a fully vitreous china very similar to porcelain. Named Imperial Geddo and introduced in 1891, this new body was used for tableware designed in the French Limoges style and artware decorated in the English taste. Within four years the firm confidently was calling its ware Syracuse China. In a paper delivered to a British audience in 1930, Pass's son Richard and Charles Fergus Binns noted that several firms had been searching for the right formula:

> It is not possible to assign credit for the first success of American china to any one person or factory. The Greenwood and Maddock potteries in Trenton, the Knowles, Taylor and Knowles Company and the Sebring family in Ohio, and the Onondaga Pottery Company in Syracuse, New York, competed closely in the quality of the ware, but the last named . . . succeeded, under the direction of the late James Pass, in manufacturing a thin, translucent china decorated with underglaze colors.[74]

Although Onondaga Pottery called its china body American China and claimed to be the first to manufacture a fully vitreous china for domestic use, Greenwood Pottery might also have made that declaration. The company placed an advertisement in an 1879 issue of *Crockery and Glass Journal* announcing its "New American China" in "Thick, Half-thick, and Thin China Ware."[75] The ware was offered in "New Rome and Haviland's Cable Shapes." "Dinner sets in Thin China" included twelve-place settings for domestic use with dinner, breakfast, and tea. Beyond the basic pieces, standard place settings at this time included separate bowls for soup and fruit, individual bread and butter plates and cups and saucers. To complete the service various platters, covered dishes, casseroles, ramekins, tureens, covered butter dish, sauceboat and stand, tea and coffee cups and saucers, teapot, sugar bowl, cream jug, slop bowl, pitcher, and miscellaneous serving dishes were required. Although more research needs to be carried out, the description of Greenwood's American China in an earlier issue of *Crockery and Glass Journal* suggests that the company may have been producing a very fashionable ware more than ten years before Onondaga's product.[76] A contemporary observer noted:

> The American porcelain of this manufacture [Greenwood Pottery] can to-day be found in use in many of the leading hotels and restaurants in New York City and Philadelphia, as well as among private families. . . . The thin china goods in this ware are especially beautiful, being, if anything, more transparent than the French, and of a purer color. This is not what is called "semi" or "stone" porcelain, but is the real article itself, having a perfect vitreous and translucent body. This porcelain possesses unusual strength, and is made *entirely of American material.*[77]

Although the manufacture of dinnerware for domestic consumption had declined in Trenton by the turn of the century, vitreous institutional china manufacture became a specialty of the city's potteries. The Greenwood Pottery Company grew and prospered under the Tams family's management, increasing in size by expanding its building and absorbing nearby potteries. The pottery finally succumbed to the Great Depression and closed in 1933 after seventy years in business. James Tams also had an interest in the Trenton China Company, organized in 1880. This venture, however, was relatively short-lived. In 1892 Thomas Maddock & Sons bought the plant and set up a corporation separate from their renowned sanitary pottery, which produced bathroom fixtures. The Lamberton Works of the Maddock Pottery Company made both thick and thin vitreous china (cat. 51). The thick type was called Trenton China; the thin type, Lamberton China. The Maddock Pottery operated this company until 1923, when the works were leased to the Scammell brothers. The Scammell China Company continued making the same products under the Lamberton and Trenton names until 1953. The wares from these potteries, generically known as hotel ware, were ubiquitous. Anyone who ate in a restaurant, diner, school or hospital cafeteria, or on a train or steamship might see their food on plates and in bowls made in Trenton.

Yet even with such widespread distribution Trenton's hotel ware potteries had competition. If the market for serviceable whiteware had ended on the home front, it was replaced with a demand for vitreous china made for institutional tables. The Onondaga Pottery Company, Buffalo Pottery, and Iroquois China Company made New York State a significant center of hotel ware production. Mayer China and Shenango Pottery Company were located in Pennsylvania, while in Ohio was Sterling China (cat. 52). Beyond those listed here, many other potteries survived for long periods by manufacturing institutional china. Some, including Syracuse China and Buffalo Pottery, are still in business today.

Potteries that continued to produce whiteware found new ways to market their tableware to the growing number of Americans who could afford, and therefore demanded, dishes decorated to their taste. Consumers traditionally would have bought ceramics and glass from specialty china and glass dealers in cities and general merchants in rural areas (see chapter 4). However, during the late nineteenth century, department and chain stores, mail-order houses, and

companies that gave premiums with purchases (soap, cereal, tea) offered new ways of attracting customers, reaching consumers who were increasingly able to add beauty to their everyday lives.

Before the advent of department stores in the 1870s, dry goods like furniture, china and glass, silver, carpets, draperies, hats, and clothing were sold in cities for the most part at specialty stores, while country merchants carried a general line of merchandise. In the late nineteenth century department stores offered a new and exciting shopping experience. Cheaper merchandise was sold through five-and-dime or variety stores, and mass merchandisers developed chain stores—F. W. Woolworth & Co., S. S. Kresge Company, J. C. Penney Company, and J. J. Newberry & Co. to name a very few. Urban department stores were usually owned and operated by local merchants, whereas chain stores were built in large and small cities throughout the country, their stock managed from a single central office. Chain store buyers arranged prices with manufacturers and let local operators choose from a limited range the merchandise that they could sell locally. These mass merchandisers and variety store owners bought china and glass cheaply and sold the goods quickly on close margin to make fast profits.

The potteries and glasshouses of the Ohio River valley were perfectly suited to supply these new consumers. Cheap fuel and easy access to western markets were essential for the growing U.S. economy. The region had aggressive Ohio potteries, like Homer Laughlin China Company, that put themselves in a position to take advantage of the resources of fuel and location in order to cater to the needs of mass retailers (see pp. 131–33). Chain stores like Woolworth's demanded low prices, high volume, timely delivery, and fresh designs from their suppliers. And as these merchants consolidated their business during the early twentieth century, these four issues became ever more important. Woolworth's, for example, had 189 stores in 1908 and more than six hundred stores in 1912 after buying up a number of competitors in the United States, Canada, and England. By 1916 the Woolworth's account represented 40 percent of Homer Laughlin's gross sales. In 1927 Woolworth's was selling Homer Laughlin tableware in a far-flung empire of 1,581 stores. For an important customer like this five-and-dime giant, the Ohio pottery could ship orders in four to six days because it kept large inventories of the chain's most popular patterns. For small accounts, however, ware was decorated to order and took six weeks to four months for shipment.[78]

Some merchandisers found it more convenient and profitable to own their own pottery. S. S. Kresge Company, for example, bought the Mount Clemens Pottery Company in Mount Clemens, Michigan, in 1920 and manufactured exclusively for its own stores until 1965. Much of the ware for Kresge's, including the most innocuous and ubiquitous of its patterns, *Petal*, was identified simply with the mark USA or was unmarked entirely. Similarly, John D. Larkin of the Larkin Soap Company of Buffalo, New York, was anxious to have on hand plenty of premiums to be given away in exchange for Sweet Home Soap wrappers or as prizes in boxes of Boraxine. In 1901 he established the Buffalo Pottery, which made a variety of earthenware, some for premiums and others, like the *Deldare* line, for sale through retail outlets (cat. 53). A vitreous body was developed in 1915, and during World War I the firm's entire output was sold to the U.S. government. After the war the pottery's focus was changed. Larkin Soap Company began importing premiums and turned its pottery production to institutional ware, which is still made there.

Many companies used premiums as a way to attract buyers, recognizing that Americans love to get something for nothing. Including items in the packaging and rewarding brand loyalty with premium programs were common practices. Decorated American-made earthenware was one of many types of premiums that these companies could buy cheaply. Tea companies, grocers, and manufacturers of soap, cereal, and baking powder are just a few of the businesses that used American pottery premiums. Of these, perhaps Jewel Tea Company's *Autumn Leaf* had the broadest distribution. The Hall China Company made a majority of this pattern between 1933 and 1976. Other makers as well supplied the Jewel Tea Company with the pottery premiums. Once a pattern was established for a premium, the company ordering the ware was free to make deals with any supplier that it felt confident could provide the merchandise when it was needed, and at a price that fit the premium budget. If one pottery made negotiations difficult or failed to provide adequate ware in a timely fashion, the buyer simply went to a competitor. As some premiums became more popular, coordinating items were made in other media—for example, glassware and kitchen canisters were also available in the *Autumn Leaf* pattern.

In addition, American potteries were major suppliers for mail-order catalogues that tempted rural housewives to spend their extra money on fashionable home furnishings. As with premium distributors, catalogue companies often sold wares under house brand names even though the wares were supplied by different potteries. Sears, Roebuck & Co.'s Harmony House pottery brand is an example of this practice. Wares made by Hall China, Homer Laughlin, Laurel Potteries, Universal Potteries, and Salem China Company were sold under the Harmony House label (cat. 33).

At the turn of the century pottery owners sought to stabilize their costs by building better labor relations.[79] The traditional industrial practice of potteries paying for ware that was "good from kiln" had created a wide range of abuses in England. Each station or skilled area was staffed by master artisans who hired, managed, and paid their own helpers. Often these assistants were family members, thus making a factory a series of independent but interrelated workshops for clay preparation, molding, sticking and handling, clay finishing, dipping, decorating, and so forth. In Great Britain this system was in part responsible for the oversupply of labor that resulted in very low wages and the immigration of large numbers of British craftsmen to the United States during the second half of the nineteenth century.

To a great extent the American ceramic industry was built

Cat. 52 American potteries supplied sturdy ware for restaurants and railways from coast to coast.

on British tradition. The fact that so many pottery owners and workers had been trained in the English system, however, accentuated its negative aspects. Thus belligerent attitudes of workers and continued abuses by owners characterized much of the development of the industry in Trenton and East Liverpool during the late 1800s. Pottery owners ultimately came to understand that there had to be a better way to manage labor. Periodic walk-outs and lock-outs and speed-ups and slow-downs by workers put regular production in serious jeopardy. Receiving payment for only the "good from kiln" pieces created antagonisms in the workforce rather than cohesion. And the workshop system, with its emphasis on quotas, allowed workers to come and go on their own schedules as long as their share of the work was finished. This practice destabilized and demoralized the factory floor. Alcoholism was a serious problem, and many Mondays were missed.

Furthermore, there were major differences between the workforces in Trenton and East Liverpool. Trenton, where the industry had first developed, retained many traditional craft practices and definitions of work from the old system, whereas East Liverpool began to adapt to changing industrial standards much earlier. In an attempt to stabilize the market and keep the two cities from bitter rivalry, the pottery owners through the United States Potters' Association continued the English practice of price fixing by using a price list. But dumping of underpriced ware on the American market by foreign manufacturers and liquidated American companies threw the list into chaos.

After 1880 owners sought to save money by hiring large numbers of women and children, paid at much lower rates than men (figs. 2.10, 2.12–.14). This practice was especially true in the decorating shops that were added during this period where the women worked as "fillers-in," painting enamel colors into the black outlines of transfer-printed patterns.

Mechanical improvements also occurred during the second half of the nineteenth century. Steam became available for running the wheels and lathes. A long lag time passed, however, before the method was adopted industry-wide because

Cat. 53 John D. Larkin, soap king, founded the Buffalo Pottery, which made these colorful dishes before World War I.

Fig. 2.10 Girls worked in decorating shops, performing tasks such as cutting ornament from a printed sheet, 1886.

artisans were required to pay the owner for steam and many opted to have children provide motive power at little or no cost. Mechanical shaping presses called pull-downs were introduced for the wheels that "jiggered" or shaped plates, but for many years these were useful only for small-diameter ware. The uneven application of such new technology gave rise to arguments between workers and owners over what constituted skill: handwork versus machine operating. When ornamental decals were introduced in the 1890s, there was much consternation over the decline of decorating skills. Artisans who had learned the exacting skill of hand decorating saw operatives adding colorful embellishment to ware instantly with the flick of a decal.

Most of all it was the dependence on lower-priced goods, given away as premiums and sold through five-and-dime stores and mail-order houses, that set the East Liverpool potters apart from their Trenton brethren. An observer for the U.S. government commented at the turn of the century that "there is comparatively little migration from the Trenton potteries to those of East Liverpool, no matter how scarce help may be in the latter district. The reason is that the Eastern workmen can not or will not rush at the pace set in East Liverpool plants."[80]

While the history of the ceramic trade union movement in America is best gleaned from other sources, the most critical event for the purposes of this study was the attempt in 1897 by the USPA to get the National Brotherhood of Operative Potters (NBOP), made up primarily of East Liverpool operatives, and Trenton's Potters' National Union (PNU) to standardize piece rates.[81] At the heart of the matter were arguments between the two unions as to their regional differences and whether mechanical jiggers would be put to work in Trenton shops. Although no agreements were reached at this stage, the groundwork was laid for cooperation among the two unions and the USPA. Both operatives and owners recognized that a stable market would grow through standardizing

Fig. 2.11 Unloading a traditional bottle kiln, a hot and strenuous job.

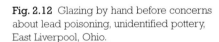

Fig. 2.12 Glazing by hand before concerns about lead poisoning, unidentified pottery, East Liverpool, Ohio.

Fig. 2.13 The dusty and laborious task of cleaning and sorting unglazed ware, Edwin M. Knowles China Company, East Liverpool, Ohio, ca. 1910.

Fig. 2.14 Clay shop employees at a Knowles pottery early in the century included many young children.

the definitions of skill and production. Rate cutting fostered price warfare, poor profits, and unsure investments. Stable bulk production was the most important goal for meeting the demands of the mass merchandisers. In spring 1900 the first uniform wage scale for the pottery industry was adopted by the USPA and NBOP.

Today's flea markets and secondhand stores are filled with the dishes left over from the early twentieth century, when inexpensive earthenware, cheerfully decorated with floral decals, could be had "for free" as premiums or for remarkably low prices through five-and-dime stores or mail-order catalogues. These vessels were created in a time when potteries depended on the tariffs to keep truly cheap foreign goods at bay and on their workers to turn out more ware for the same pay. These were efficiencies of cash. Standard manufacturing practices had not changed significantly since the eighteenth century. Indeed, not until World War I did the potteries finally tackle the harder issues of developing reliable domestic sources of raw materials and effecting manufacturing efficiencies to compete with each other. In part this was due to the reluctance of potters and owners to discuss their materials and methods. The American Ceramics Society, organized in 1899 by the technical experts in potteries to share practices, had trouble attracting members at the beginning because owners feared they would lose trade secrets.[82]

Homer Laughlin China Company

Fiesta, both as originally issued in 1936 and in today's revival, is Homer Laughlin China Company's most famous line, and *Fiesta*'s designer, Frederick Hurten Rhead, is among the most celebrated dinnerware designers in America.[1] Had *Fiesta* never been marketed, however, millions of American homes would still have had kitchen or tableware articles made by this pottery because it has been the largest and most productive American ceramics maker in the twentieth century. Both price and design aided the company in establishing widespread distribution through F. W. Woolworth & Co., J. C. Penney Company, W. T. Grant Company, and other five-and-dime stores as well as premium vendors, mail-order catalogues, and department stores. Families across the country have set their tables or furnished their kitchen cupboards with this pottery's products for more than a century.

Brothers Homer and Shakespeare Laughlin, along with their father, Matthew, sold imported and domestic ceramics through a china warehouse in New York. In 1873 they chose East Liverpool, Ohio, as the site of a whiteware factory. The Laughlins probably reasoned that by supplying goods for their New York warehouse outlet they could greatly enhance their profits; all middlemen would be eliminated and they would have a product that no competitors could sell. In addition the city of East Liverpool offered many inducements to attract a whiteware factory at this time.[2] The pottery opened late in 1874, and recognition of its superior product was immediate. At the 1876 Centennial Exposition in Philadelphia the Laughlins won top honors for their white, heavy-bodied ceramics. Following this early success, however, Shakespeare decided to work elsewhere and Homer began to sign his ware with his own name, using the mark that depicts the American eagle triumphantly defeating the English lion.[3]

For nearly twenty years Homer Laughlin operated the pottery as a sole proprietorship, but in 1896 he took as his partner W. Edwin Wells, who had been his bookkeeper since 1889. Laughlin gradually withdrew from the business, selling his interest over time to the Aaron family of Pittsburgh by 1897. Modernization of the factory and its products began slowly but gained momentum as the new owners' aggressive approach to the business was set in motion. Because the company had been founded by merchants, market satisfaction was the key goal of production, and Wells's superior cost analyses were critical to the firm's success. Wells, vice president Charles Aaron, and chief salesman George W. Clarke formed the company's design committee. Art director Arthur Mountford and the head of the decorating department, Edward L. Carson, were sometimes asked for advice, but they were primarily expected to follow the committee's orders. While many factors influenced

Homer Laughlin's design at the turn of the century, the demands of their principal customers, five-and-dime-store buyers such as Woolworth's Clinton P. Case, were at the fore (cat. 144).[4]

By 1902 Homer Laughlin China Company had three factories in East Liverpool. Between 1905 and 1910, the firm built a village and factory complex across the Ohio River in Newell, West Virginia, eventually constructing four factories in Newell operated by fourteen hundred workers. By 1912 the company's 110 kilns in East Liverpool and Newell supplied 10 percent of the U.S. ceramics market. Between 1923 and 1929 three new potteries were built in Newell, and the East Liverpool facilities were closed in 1929. Seven years earlier, an elaborate new showroom had been opened at the company's Newell headquarters (fig. 2.15).

Homer Laughlin China Company made semivitreous dinnerware, kitchenware, and novelties during most of its first seventy-five years of business. In 1925–26 it added an ivory earthenware body called Yellowstone, perhaps following on the fashion for ivory-colored dinnerware recently established by Lenox China and Salem Pottery Company. In 1959 Homer Laughlin introduced fully vitrified institutional china, which it has continued to improve throughout the past forty years. Today the manufacturer uses a 100 percent alpha alumina clay body and a completely lead-free glaze.

Much of Homer Laughlin's business in domestic dinnerware depended on volume production because the company sold its wares primarily through premium vendors and five-and-dime stores. Many lines were exclusive shapes or patterns for manufacturers such as Quaker Oats Company that used dishes as premiums. *Harvest, Tudor Rose, Wild Rose, Pastoral, Carnival,* and *Tea Rose* are among the most popular of Homer Laughlin's premium patterns. Lines were also made for sale through single retailers. *Fiesta,* for example, began as an exclusive for Gimbel Brothers, and Homer Laughlin's less expensive solid color line, *Harlequin,* was made exclusively for Woolworth's. J. J. Newberry's bought the *White Flower* pattern on the *Rhythm* shape. Homer Laughlin's dinnerware sets were also available through retail catalogues such as those of Sears, Roebuck & Co. and Montgomery Ward & Co.

In this high-volume sales environment manufacturing efficiencies were always important, and Homer Laughlin was among the earliest American potteries to modernize operations. Albert V. Bleininger, who had worked for the National Bureau of Standards in Pittsburgh, was hired in the early 1920s to establish quality control in production, and he played a vital role in the design and installation of the three factories built during that decade.[5] Especially significant was the introduction, with Bleininger's advice, of continuous tunnel kilns in the late 1920s. Shut down only for

Fig. 2.15 Homer Laughlin China Company's elaborate showroom, Newell, West Virginia, 1922.

sign was *Fiesta* (1936–72, revived 1985), his other important market introductions included *Wells Art* (1930) and *Century* shapes (1931), particularly the *Riviera* color range introduced in 1937 (cat. 26). Rhead was also responsible for developing the *Kitchen Kraft OvenServe* line (1937), the success of which proved vital to the company's financial health.

While Emerson was reworking the flow of ware through Homer Laughlin's factories, Rhead was analyzing the consumer market. His designs were keyed to the results of market analysis based on statistics about the popularity of patterns and manufacturers. This awareness represented a subtle shift in focus at Homer Laughlin away from retail merchants and toward the consumer. Instead of relying on design wishes of the retail industry, Rhead studied the consumer directly by collecting samples of the most popular wares in the market and analyzing the desires of the consumer. Rhead died in 1942.

Donald Schreckengost, design director for Homer Laughlin from 1945 to 1960, contributed *Jubilee* in 1947 (cat. 179) and its variations *Suntone* and *Skytone* in 1952. His *Epicure*, 1954, and *Rhythm*, 1955, were based on a coupe, or rimless, shape, and were offered in solid colors and with decals such as *American Provincial* (drawn from Pennsylvania German motifs designed by Schreckengost), *Golden Wheat*, *Rhythm Rose*, and *White Flower*. Other Homer Laughlin dinnerware lines of particular interest include *Historical America*, made from 1939 to 1958 and transfer printed with American scenes based on the art of Joseph Boggs Beale (cat. 174); and *Eggshell*, an earthenware body named for its light weight, which was introduced in 1937 and made in several shapes (*Swing, Theme, Georgian, and Nautilus*) over the next few years (cat. 54).

Many of these lines were extremely popular. In spite of its success in domestic dinnerware, however, Homer Laughlin decided in the late 1950s to curtail consumer products and concentrate on institutional ware. The company's managers could see that the influx of inexpensive porcelain from Japan would undercut Laughlin's markets. Rather than simply succumb to the competition, as most American makers of earthenware did, Laughlin decided to shift its production focus to the heavier institutional ware that was not then being imported from abroad in any quantity. In 1958 the

annual inspections and cleanings, these new kilns required continuous feeding of ware. Further improvements in the forming, glazing, and transportation of the ware throughout the factory were made over the following years in order to accommodate the new kiln technology. For these new operations the firm worked closely with Walter H. Emerson, a chemical engineer who had effected many improvements at the Mount Clemens Pottery in Michigan, a longtime Laughlin rival. During the 1930s Emerson introduced conveyors, trolleys, and robots to eliminate many unskilled jobs and move ware through the factory more efficiently.

As retailers like Woolworth's turned more frequently to foreign china manufacturers to fill their shelves, the five-and-dime-store trade declined in the early 1930s, calling for greater and greater efficiencies in Homer Laughlin's factories and a more aggressive design consciousness. Although many designers and craftsmen had worked for Homer Laughlin over the years, their contributions were continually blunted by the interplay between manufacturing and merchants and decal makers. During the late 1920s, however, the company became more aggressive about introducing new designs and leading the market rather than following it.

Frederick Rhead began to work for Homer Laughlin in 1927 as the art director.[6] He had emigrated from England to the United States in 1902 at the age of twenty-two and worked with several art potteries from Ohio to California during the early years of the twentieth century. His tenure at the American Encaustic Tiling Company in Zanesville, Ohio, beginning in 1917 drew the attention of Homer Laughlin's managers. Although Rhead's most enduring de-

Cat. 54 The *Nautilus* shape dish with *Della Robbia* pattern by Homer Laughlin China Company (1936) was the essence of conservative good taste in inexpensive dinnerware.

firm stopped making dishes for the home tabletop. The decision to specialize in the commercial market proved wise. Investing in a new tunnel kiln assured even greater efficiency during the 1970s and 1980s. Overall costs were reduced by 15 percent and inventories by 75 percent.

According to Homer Laughlin president Marcus Aaron II and chief executive officer Joseph Wells III, by 1987 the company was able to reduce its prices to the point of competing with foreign-made products. But in many ways it was the reintroduction in 1985 of the nearly fifty-year-old *Fiesta* that ensured the firm's survival. The partially restyled line sporting updated colors was responsible for 20 percent of the company's revenues. In 1993 Laughlin sold four million pieces of *Fiesta* worth about $10 million. Today the company is still privately owned by descendants of the Wells and Aaron families, and the pottery operation is one of the largest in the world, employing nine hundred people and supplying a major portion of America's institutional market for tableware in addition to the retail market for *Fiesta*.[7]

Notes

1. For more on Homer Laughlin China Company and Frederick Rhead, see Blaszczyk 1995; Cunningham 1998; Dale 1986; and Gates 1984.

2. Gates 1984, 77.

3. For a good compendium of Homer Laughlin's marks, see Gates and Ormerod 1982, 128–69.

4. On these issues, see Blaszczyk 1995, especially chap. 3.

5. On the introduction of new technologies at Homer Laughlin, see Blaszczyk 1995, especially chap. 4.

6. For an analysis of Rhead's work for Homer Laughlin, see Blaszczyk 1995, especially chap. 5.

7. Oliver 1994, 94.

AMERICAN POTTERS FIND A NICHE

The years surrounding World War I offered American potters tremendous new opportunities to improve their profits. With virtually no competition from European potteries and Japan's industry still in its formative stage, they were free to investigate and develop a broad range of possibilities. Disruptions in shipments of raw materials from abroad, for example, forced them to experiment more seriously with domestic materials. The absence of competition led to experimental launches of new designs and investigations of innovative ways to develop new products. American potters began to understand that competition based on quality and beauty would build a stronger domestic market than speed and cheapness. And, finally, growing national isolationism offered a prime opportunity to join the "Made in America" movement that swept the country between the wars.

New technologies added significant savings for the high-volume potteries and made investigation and invention a way of life in the other potteries. Innovative methods for performing old tasks were developed and new materials gave designers greater possibilities for shape and ornament. The introduction of tunnel kilns was of particular importance. First used in Europe, these new kilns fired continuously, rather than periodically, and promised to "revolutionize the industry . . . solve the labor problem of the kiln sheds, as well as reduce sagger and fuel costs."[83] Unlike traditional bottle kilns into which dishes protected in ceramic containers called saggers were stacked, fired, cooled, and unloaded (fig. 2.16), these new kilns moved ware loaded onto trolleys continuously through a brick tunnel. Cold ware was loaded at one end; red-hot ware was fired in the middle; and cooled ware was removed at the other end. In 1917 positive reports were already coming from Sebring, Ohio, where a new tunnel kiln was in operation. Three years later the USPA's president called for mechanizing all sorts of specialized operations in the factory, including sagger making, batting-out, casting, handle making, and dipping.[84] To feed these giant, continuous kilns, ware had to move efficiently through the pottery from start to finish. Therefore mechanical conveyors suspended from the ceiling on tracks were installed in some potteries. A concept borrowed from the automobile assembly line, these rolling conveyors enabled heavy pottery and saggers to be moved easily through the forming, glazing, and firing stages of ceramic production.

Simultaneously, the desire for color changed radically during the 1920s (see chapter 5), and consumers suddenly demanded tableware in a wide variety of vivid hues. To meet this demand, forward-thinking potteries invested in the development of new glazes and adapted spray-painting equipment from the automobile industry to their needs. Printing technol-

Fig. 2.16 Bottle kilns were used by some potteries until World War II.

ogy was also brought to the potter's aid. Stamping presses were now used to apply gold embossed ornament. Similarly, the silk screening process, already used to decorate glassware, was appropriated by potteries. Gold stamping and silk screening made it possible to feature brightly colored patterns without resorting to expensive decorative techniques like hand painting or gilding.[85]

The ceramics industry had for some time speculated that adapting products to new technologies would allow it to sprint past European rivals. But it was the advent of solid-color dinnerwares around 1930 that provided this leap forward, for vivid, solid hues depended as much on new color chemistry as they did on such seemingly mundane factory devices as automatic glaze-dipping machines and glaze-spraying operations. The fashion for color in interior decorating might have been the basis of the colored wares' popularity, but potters were pleased by the cost efficiency of a product that did not require a perfectly white body or legions of decorators to apply decals or paint flowers.

Retail advertising was another innovation of the interwar

Fig. 2.17 Onondaga Pottery Company appealed directly to consumers through advertisements in popular magazines as early as World War I.

years. Prior to this time most advertising had appeared in trade magazines because potters never sold directly to consumers (see chapter 4). The potters' customers were the buyers from department and five-and-dime stores, mail-order catalogues, and purveyors of premiums. But the first forays into "publicity," as the USPA called it, proved to be very fruitful (fig. 2.17). "It is gratifying to see an increasing number of American potters advertising to the American housewife through the magazines," declared the USPA president in 1927. "'Hall's Teapots' are becoming as familiar as 'Tetley's Tea,' and we gaze entranced at 'Cowan's Nymphs' disporting themselves 'mid flowery bowers on our dining tables. . . . Seriously, since our American periodicals are open to the advertisements of English, French, German, Japanese and every other sort of pottery, the ware made in the United States should receive much publicity."[86]

The addition of professional designers to the workforce of individual potteries on a more regular basis was especially noted during the 1920s and 1930s. The USPA saw the work of designers as a great benefit to business (see chapter 5). "It is not possible for many of the plants to employ an expert in this capacity," noted the USPA's Art and Design Committee in 1927, "but we feel sure that time and attention paid to this part of the business will lead to more satisfactory business on fewer decorations."[87] Complaints had circulated in the industry for years that potters were producing too many shapes and decorations and that this diversity was depleting resources rather than enhancing profits. The addition of designers to product development promised to streamline efforts. Furthermore, a more beautiful product would encourage the American housewife to buy American pottery: "Assuming that the average family consists of four people, the average housewife pays at retail approximately three dollars and fifty cents per year for all the dishes used in her home. More than half of these dishes were made abroad. If we can by beautifying our product, create in her a sufficient desire to make her purchase an additional fifty cents worth of American made dishes, we will have increased the demand for our product almost thirty percent."[88]

CALIFORNIA: A NEW RIVAL

In the early 1930s, when the Ohio potteries were moaning about loss of market from the depression, newly established California potteries transformed the aesthetics of American tableware. The public perception of color had changed radically during the late 1920s as the latest technologies provided the basis for new visual sensibilities. Bits of lively colored enamels were already being used to enhance Frank Holmes's exotic designs at Lenox China during the mid-1920s (cat. 147). But it was the California potteries that broke the color barrier in popular dinnerware in about 1930.

Although potterymaking had been going on since the nineteenth century in California, the earliest potteries produced utilitarian goods such as drainpipe, brick, and terracotta architectural elements. Gladding, McBean & Co., for example, was founded in 1875 by Chicagoans who saw great manufacturing potential in the refractory clay deposits of Placer County, California. Although this firm would eventually become known in the dinnerware market for its high-quality Franciscan Ware, its first product was drainpipe. Alongside such commercial operations, small art potteries were established beginning in the late nineteenth century by artists from the East Coast and Midwest who were attracted to the state's mild climate and easy lifestyle.

Of all the California potteries, the J. A. Bauer Pottery Company was especially important early on. The Bauer family, who had been making utilitarian pottery for several decades in Paducah, Kentucky, set up their operation in Los Angeles in 1909.[89] In California they continued to make the same

Cat. 55 In the 1930s French art deco dinner-ware was the inspiration for Metlox Potteries' rectangular *Pintoria*.

goods—jugs, jars, kitchen crockery, and flowerpots—while modernizing their design approach over the years. In 1916 Bauer hired the Danish immigrant Louis Ipsen who applied a matte green glaze to the firm's garden ware. In 1929, perhaps in response to developments at Catalina Clay Products, Bauer hired Victor F. Houser, a University of Illinois–trained ceramic engineer, to develop a range of colorful glazes for the firm's kitchenware. Shortly thereafter the company introduced a line of mix-and-match dinnerware (cat. 45). The combination of Bauer's matter-of-fact approach to ceramic forms, including coupe-shaped plates, and Houser's glaze chemistry set the ceramic industry spinning. By the mid-1930s, potteries across the country had responded with their own range of colors and shapes. Vernon Kilns and Gladding, McBean & Co. in California, Homer Laughlin in West Virginia, and Stangl Pottery in Trenton all had dinnerware lines with brilliant solid-color glazes (cat. 26).

Several California potteries began making dinnerware in the late 1920s and early 1930s. Like Bauer, most of these firms started in the building-supply business and used the special clay bodies developed for other purposes to produce dinnerware. Founded in 1925 on Santa Catalina Island off the coast of southern California, Catalina Clay Products initially made clay building products. Soon, however, it began manufacturing souvenirs and artware in a variety of colors for the tourist trade and initiated the craze for dinnerware in solid, bright colors in 1930. Catalina's *Plain* line probably contained the first coupe-shaped plate made commercially in America. Metlox Potteries based its early ware on a talc ceramic body patented in 1920 by Willis O. Prouty. In 1927 Prouty built a factory in Manhattan Beach to make outdoor ceramic signs but reorganized the factory's production in 1931 to make dinnerware (cat. 55). Pacific Clay Products of Los Angeles, which specialized in sanitary and technical ceramics (such as electrical fittings), introduced multicolored, solid-glaze tableware in the early 1930s.

Simultaneously, the drainpipe maker Gladding, McBean & Co. developed its Franciscan Ware line using a talc clay body called *Malinite* that had been invented by Andrew Malinovsky in 1928 (cat. 56). In 1937 Gladding, McBean & Co. acquired

Catalina Clay Products and made ware under that name until 1947. Vernon Kilns, based outside Los Angeles, was the other major California pottery. Unlike most of its West Coast rivals, this firm was established initially as a tableware pottery. Employing both fine artists and ceramic designers to create its products, Vernon Kilns made some of the most stylish of all American pottery during the 1930s, 1940s, and 1950s (cats. 57, 151, 171).

To better promote their wares nationally, the five biggest dinnerware makers in California united in 1937 to form the California Pottery Guild. Through this advertising association Bauer, Metlox Potteries, Pacific Clay Products, Vernon Kilns, and Gladding, McBean & Co. promoted their vivid dishes to millions of Americans. One of the guild's initial advertisements to the trade read:

> These California potteries perfected and popular-
> ized colored pottery. . . . Now they are collectively

and individually redoubling their creative and merchandising efforts to help you sell more of your most popular item—California Colored Pottery. Added to the universal acceptance of the pottery itself is all the romance of its California background—the most potent sales-promoter this country has ever known! Your customers are already sold on California Colored Pottery—give 'em what they want![90]

And sold they were. Americans consumed large quantities of California tableware during the 1930s and early post–World War II years. By the late 1950s, however, casual California-style wares of modern design had become standard among earthenware producers throughout the country. As a result many California potteries began to decline, ultimately dropping dinnerware production or going out of business altogether.

EARLY FINE CHINA

With few notable exceptions, little fine china manufacturing occurred in the United States before World War II. Onondaga Pottery Company, which made Syracuse China, continued to be successful and expanded its market and, consequently, its facilities. Even the 1930s was a time of creativity and growth that depended on the interplay of body, glaze, and process worked out so assiduously by James Pass during the first decades of the century and carried forward by the design genius of R. Guy Cowan during the depression.[91] But Syracuse China was mostly intended for institutional, rather than domestic, use. Not until the late 1930s was the company's thin American China aggressively marketed to householders.

Lenox China in Trenton, New Jersey, was the only company that was making fine china between 1906, when the product was introduced, and 1935, when other companies began to enter the market (see pp. 140–43).[92] Lenox's predecessor, Ceramic Art Company, was created as a large china art studio making the ivory body identified today as American Belleek and decorating it with lavish hand painting, gilding, and enameling (cat. 58). Gradually, beginning in 1902, it started making bone china tableware, first in the form of service plates ornamented as lavishly as the artware had been, and later under Walter Scott Lenox's leadership expanding the line to include whole table services in stock patterns (cat. 130).

Although by 1930 Lenox had developed a highly influential ivory-body dinnerware (ca. 1910), received a White House commission (1917–18), and produced many stylish patterns, the firm struggled to stay open during the depression. The executives took large pay cuts, and the workforce took smaller ones. Production was still dependent on periodic bottle kilns, which were fired only rarely. But the company kept experimenting with new alliances with other industries and new products: lamp bases for the lighting industry, tableware decorated with low-relief modeling rather than costly colored decals or gilding, china inserts for metal dish holders, perfume bottles and atomizers for DeVilbiss, and X-ray spools and transformer shields for Westinghouse (cat. 59).[93]

The "Buy American" campaign that swept the nation in the 1930s, combined with growing political instability in Europe, which fostered a new vitality in American earthenware potteries, encouraged more companies to bring fine china lines onto the market. Pickard Studios (later Pickard China Company), a Chicago decorating company that had relied on unornamented European blanks, introduced its fine china dinnerware to the market in 1937 after seven years of experiments to perfect a body and glaze. In the same year the company set up a manufacturing plant in nearby Antioch, Illinois.[94] Although this move could be seen as exhibiting a certain nervousness on Pickard's part about the continuing availability of European blanks (the firm had tried to buy a French pottery in the late 1920s), it also demonstrated confidence in the desire of American householders to purchase fine china. As Lenox had learned, painted giftware was passing out of favor. Both companies continued to offer sets of after-dinner cups and saucers and special editions of handpainted china plates into the early 1950s—Pickard's by Edward Challinor and Lenox's by Hans Nosek—but these products served the old-fashioned market and not the new boom in American fine china dinnerware nourished by a war and its aftermath.

Cat. 58 Ceramic Art Company (left) and Willets Manufacturing Company of Trenton produced porcelain of exceptional quality in the late 19th century.

Lenox China

Lenox China has been America's premier maker of fine china dinnerware since 1918, when President Woodrow Wilson ordered the first American-made White House service from the company.[1] Founded in Trenton, New Jersey, in 1889 as the Ceramic Art Company by Walter Scott Lenox, an American designer, and Jonathan Coxon, a practical potter, the firm made handpainted china artware and fancy tea, coffee, and chocolate sets during the 1890s (cat. 58).

At the turn of the century Charles Fergus Binns, son of Worcester Royal Porcelain Company's director Richard W. Binns, developed a bone china formula for dinnerware at Lenox. This body was initially used for service plates that were decorated by the same artists who embellished the large vases and dainty tewares; tableware was also made to order. This new product was called Lenox China to distinguish it from the artware. By 1906 the dinnerware was so successful that the company changed its name to Lenox China and its direction toward tableware (cat. 130). About 1910 the firm began to offer customers the choice of standard white bone china or the ivory-colored type that had been used exclusively for artware. After the Wilsons chose the ivory body for official White House china, the company's white bone china received so little attention that it was discontinued by 1920.

When Walter Lenox started Ceramic Art Company he intended to make only artware, a finely crafted ivory china (quite similar to the cream-colored body from the Belleek factory in County Fermanagh, Ireland) that was exquisitely painted by the leading decorators in America. Many of them, like William Morley and his nephew George Morley, Hans Nosek, Sigmund Wirkner, Bruno Geyer, and Lucien Boullemier, emigrated from England, Bohemia, Germany, and France. Each specialized in a particular type of subject: the Morleys were flower painters, Nosek painted putti and young women, Wirkner and Boullemier were figure painters, and Austrian artist Bruno Geyer specialized in bust portraits of beautiful women. These artists painted sets of service, fish, and game plates as well as vases.

The company also sold china blanks to be decorated outside the factory. While some of the blanks were embellished by leading independent decorators working in New York and Philadelphia, many others were decorated by amateurs and hobbyists. Tea sets and even whole dinner sets were painted outside the factory by independent decorators, especially in the 1910s and 1920s. In the same era Lenox china blanks were used by silver manufacturers for silver overlay, a process in which sterling silver is electrodeposited on the china in patterns previously applied by means of a substance that attracts the silver. Both artware and tableware shapes were decorated with silver overlay, especially vases and tea sets (cat. 69).

When the Lenox dinnerware line was introduced just after the turn of this century, each service was individually designed and decorated. Highly trained enamelers and gilders were responsible for the exquisite borders and monograms that adorned services made to order. As sales for this line increased, stock patterns were added to the repertoire beginning about 1910. These were often decorated with transfer-printed and filled patterns (The Virginian, 1910, cat. 25) or decals with added enameling (Coronado, 1922). Many of Lenox's current patterns still feature raised enameling added to the pattern by hand.

Prior to the Wilson commission, White House china had been made in other countries because no American firm could supply a high-quality service large enough for elaborate state functions. Following the commission, Lenox china services were requested by heads of state around the world. The Wilson service continued to be used in the White House until President and Mrs. Franklin D. Roosevelt ordered a completely new service in 1934. After World War II new services were designed for President and Mrs. Harry Truman in 1948 and President and Mrs. Ronald Reagan in 1981. The Reagan service, with brilliant red and gold borders, is still in use.

During this century the design of Lenox China has consistently been at the forefront of the industry. From 1905 until his death in 1954 Frank Graham Holmes was Lenox's chief designer (see chapter 5). Holmes had great facility with ornament and designed a wide range of patterns from historical styles to fashionable art nouveau and art deco designs. Some of his most popular patterns, like Ming (1917; cat. 133) and Autumn (1919), appealed to generation after generation of brides and homemakers as the epitome of traditional good taste. Ming was in production until 1966, and Autumn is still being made.

Winslow Anderson directed design after Holmes's death in 1954, and the department expanded greatly as the company's markets and fortunes grew. Among the most successful patterns issued under Anderson's leadership was Kingsley (cat. 60). Shortly after its release in 1954, the California-style pattern proved a huge triumph, especially in the bridal market, and it rivals Ming and Autumn as the company's all time best-seller. Charles Solt succeeded Anderson in the early 1980s, and Marcel Juillerat and Timothy Carder guided the department in recent years. As the staff grew larger, individual responsibility for specific designs was no longer recognized after Holmes's death.

Throughout the 1920s, 1930s, and 1940s, Lenox china was made for America's wealthiest families. Following World War II, however, the company changed its marketing and production substantially to appeal to a broad cross section of consumers who could not have purchased the ware pre-

Cat. 59 During the depression Lenox China controlled costs by producing designs with no hand decoration.

viously. Bridal registries allowed wedding guests to divide the purchase of a china set, and clever advertising made the product irresistible as a wedding present.

When John Tassie took over direction of manufacturing after the war, his first major effort was to revamp production by streamlining the company's line. Before the war, replacements for Lenox's patterns, no matter when they were introduced, could always be ordered. There were more than four hundred patterns in production. But in 1947 the company eliminated dealer exclusives and patterns with little contemporary appeal—only forty-seven patterns survived this cut.

Regional and national department store chains benefited greatly from this change, but shops specializing in luxury goods had difficulty competing for the Lenox consumer because they no longer could offer singular patterns unavailable in larger stores. Before the change a homemaker who had gotten her Lenox through Tiffany & Co. in New York or Marshall Field & Co. in Chicago would have to buy replacements from these retailers because their exclusive versions of Lenox patterns were slightly different from each other's and from all others on the market. After 1947 all

retailers who carried Lenox could order the same patterns. This move alone greatly expanded the company's access to consumers. In 1938, for example, 250 retailers handled Lenox wares; by 1950 that number had more than tripled to 767.

New china products have helped to broaden Lenox China's reach over the years. In 1963 the company introduced *Oxford,* a white bone china intended to expand sales beyond the signature ivory body by capturing some of the market for imported English china. After strong initial sales the line declined and was discontinued in the late 1970s. *Temperware,* Lenox's answer to casual stoneware, was introduced in 1972. Its durability was demonstrated in advertisements that showed a cup hammering a nail. Phased out in the 1980s, *Temperware* was replaced by *Chinastone* (1985), which is still made. *Chinastone* has a more refined overall appearance but features casual patterns.

Until 1954 all Lenox china was made in Trenton, but as production expanded rapidly after World War II, a new factory was built in Pomona, New Jersey, near Atlantic City, where natural gas and water were abundant. Manufacturing also continued in Trenton until 1964. Two more factories,

Cat. 60 Reserved and elegant designs like *Kingsley* (plate) from the mid-1950s made Lenox the best known china in America.

Fig. 2.18 Sister Clothilde shares a high school senior's joy at winning a prize in the Lenox table-setting contest, 1952.

built during the late 1980s, operate in North Carolina. Unlike the earthenware and vitreous china manufacturers that have fiercely competed with each other and with foreign makers on very close profit margins, Lenox has long had the luxury of continuing to use many old methods. Manufacturing at Lenox is still largely an artisanal operation in comparison with companies like Hall China, which rely heavily on elaborate robotic machines.

Advertising, marketing, and merchandising have contributed more to Lenox's success in the second half of the century than has extensive cost saving through mechanization. Drawing on the product's prewar reputation as a maker of luxury goods, managers of contemporary Lenox china have used modern advertising and clever promotional techniques to broaden brand recognition. Among brides and homemakers surveyed about fine china, more than 90 percent recognize the Lenox brand, an enviable position the company has enjoyed since extensive market testing began in the dinnerware business in the mid-1960s.

In the prewar years Lenox depended on its retailers to advertise and promote its wares. As with most other U.S. china manufacturers, Lenox's customers were retail buyers, and they in turn built the company's market. In 1940 Lenox hired its first advertising consultant; by 1950 the company's advertising budget was 400 percent larger than that of its closest competitor. The postwar advertising campaign stressed Lenox's modern design, quality of materials, and worldwide fame, but gradually the ads presumed these attributes and no longer mentioned them overtly. Perhaps most famous was Lenox's nine-year campaign in *Seventeen* magazine beginning in 1955, "You get the license . . . I'll get the Lenox" (fig. 4.27). But the company also advertised in *Bride's* as well as popular home furnishings magazines. Ads from the 1960s, 1970s, and 1980s typically showed a fashionably dressed hostess in a tasteful domestic setting, just at the moment when her guests will see her table set with Lenox. Such slogans as "Live the legend" and "Because art is never an extravagance" stressed Lenox's luxury status.

Although Lenox China continues to publicize its products heavily through bridal events and other wedding-related promotions, the company's most imaginative and successful ploy for building brand recognition was the National Table Setting Contest, which was launched in 1955 and continued until 1983. The contest was open to home-economics students in ninth grade and higher, including students in colleges and universities, and was administered by their teachers who directly benefited from awards to students. The contestant drew a table setting on the entry form, attached a swatch of cloth for the table linens, and noted choices for crystal, silver and Lenox china (after 1966 the crystal was also Lenox). Teachers selected the best entries for submission to Lenox, and the company in turn chose three to four hundred to present to panels of well-known lifestyle personalities, such as Polly Bergen or Bill Blass. The winner's table setting was styled for an exclusive feature in *Bride's* magazine. In the 1960s contests typically included three hundred thousand students from ten thousand schools (fig. 2.18).

While other U.S. manufacturers succumbed to foreign and domestic competition, Lenox has forged a strong position by building its brand on a significant past and knowing its market through careful analysis and testing. By 1960 Lenox China could claim 60 percent of the fine china market in the United States. Enjoying significant profits, Lenox China acquired the name and assets of Bryce Brothers in 1965. Lenox immediately changed the name of the glassmaker's domestic line to Lenox Crystal and began marketing the new name and product in association with its enormously successful china through bridal registries.

Although Lenox's venture in glassware was successful, its share of the U.S. fine china market declined considerably during the 1970s. Japanese products sold by the Noritake Company were especially competitive with Lenox during this period. Designed to resemble the American ware with a body and glaze of increasingly high quality, and priced more cheaply than Lenox china due to the yen's weak position against the dollar, Noritake succeeded at Lenox's expense. By 1981 industry reports revealed that of the total dollar market share for the fourth quarter of that year Noritake had 33.2 percent and Lenox 20.7 percent. However, by 1991 Lenox had boosted its sales and the two china makers were practically even in the United States. By the end of 1998 Lenox's dollar market share of department store sales was 42 percent, more than twice that of Noritake and four times that of Josiah Wedgwood & Sons.[2] Through high-quality products, constant consumer testing, and aggressive marketing, Lenox China has managed to survive and prosper in the hotly contested arena of the American tabletop.

Notes
1. For more on the history of Lenox, see Denker 1989.

2. Information from the Macomber Association Audit Reports provided by Lenox Archives.

REVIVAL AND REJECTION

The protracted conflicts of World War II gave American potters opportunities to capture a large share of the dinnerware market. With twenty years of research and modern technologies in hand, with advertising demonstrated as a viable way to build a customer base, and with the inspiring results of using factory and consulting designers to make their ware more attractive, America's potters were poised to prosper. War was the ultimate form of market protection, and while potteries had to participate in the war effort to maintain access to fuel and materials, they were also busy preparing for the great surge of business that would greet them at the other end of the hostilities. (See chapter 5 on their success in design during the immediate postwar years.) Mechanical improvements in firing, glazing, and moving ware through the factory had been worked into production in the potteries that survived the depression. Even Lenox had a continuous kiln up and running by the mid-1930s. First the depression and then war work encouraged even greater economies of manufacture and widespread automation of craft operations. The potteries had to turn out ever more ware with fewer workers because of the need to reduce payrolls during the depression and because so few workers were left on the home front to operate the factories during the war.

While the earthenware potteries shifted design focus in color and shape during the 1940s, new challengers to foreign dominance of the fine china market appeared. As noted above, Pickard Studios entered the market in 1937. Shenango Pottery Company took over production of certain shapes previously imported from France by Theodore Haviland & Co. in 1936 and three years later introduced the Castleton brand, which was distributed by the newly founded firm Castleton China (cats. 61, 188). The Franciscan Division of Gladding, McBean & Co. introduced its Masterpiece brand of fine china in 1941 using the vitreous body it had developed in 1939 for hotel ware (cat. 62). And the Flintridge China Company was founded in 1945 (cat. 63).

In addition Lenox China completely revamped its manufacturing and marketing between 1945 and 1948 to create a new product sold on its old reputation. As discussed above, production was streamlined by adopting manufacturing operations that required fewer skilled workers and by simplifying the product line. The most significant marketing changes that Lenox made had already started in other areas of the pottery business before the war. The bridal registry, developed in the mid-1930s and promoted extensively after the war, made even expensive tableware affordable by dividing the purchase of a set among many wedding guests (see chapter 4). At the same time the number of pieces considered necessary to form a place setting was radically reduced. For a former luxury producer like Lenox, a simple place setting had seven pieces, and a typical table service was not purchased by the place setting; rather, a service was bought as a whole set or in groups of six or twelve identical pieces. Add to that basic setting the additional forms necessary for breakfast and luncheon tables and there were literally scores of pieces in a service for twelve. The ultimate American table service, of course, was still that used in the White House, where nineteenth-century dining rituals never really went out of style. Lenox's service for Woodrow Wilson included twenty-one shapes. Sixty-three years later the Reagan service had nineteen. Following the lead of the earthenware potteries, John Tassie, who directed manufacturing at Lenox after the war, made the five-piece place setting standard for fine china in the early 1950s.

Simplification of the table service had been discussed in the earthenware potteries since the late 1930s, first as an effort to redefine work rules in manufacturing and later as a way to reduce the total cost of a table service. Potters made efforts to reduce the total number available to the consumer, who was beginning to question whether she actually needed separate sizes of plates for salad and dessert. Noting that "competition after the war" would rebound and that foreign factories "will be rebuilt on modern and economical ideas, which will bring us face to face with even greater competition," Vincent Broomhall, chair of the Art and Design Committee of the United States Potters' Association, asked at the 1942 annual meeting, "Since we have made great strides in production, isn't it possible that we could simplify merchandising? . . . If the number of items that go to make up the dinner service could be simplified, the change might be more practical, both for the manufacturer and the consumer."[95]

Advertising was another concept that fine china makers borrowed from the earthenware potteries and their competition. Before 1940 Lenox advertised its products to dealers but had not promoted itself directly to consumers. By 1950 Lenox was spending large amounts on advertising and was seen in almost all major home furnishing and teenage magazines in the 1950s and 1960s. Market testing, first used in the early 1930s to determine customer preferences, was promoted by the USPA in the early 1940s. In 1943 its Art and Design Committee suggested developing a "traveling nation-wide department store exhibit" that would be "accompanied by a capable person and questionnaires to determine the reactions of the public to the various styles in the exhibit."[96] At Lenox, John Tassie sent members of the company's rapidly growing design department to sit in key department stores and interview women, young and old alike, who were shopping in the china departments. The interviewer showed sample patterns and asked about the women's preferences. Also during the early 1940s the potteries became more sophisticated about tracking the market. The designer Frederick Rhead in 1940 described Homer Laughlin's practice of systematically collecting and studying the most popular patterns in the market.[97] The elaborate charts Rhead presented at USPA meetings shortly before his death in 1942 are an early example of the methods that would become standard after the war.[98] Since 1961 the industry has routinely tracked the top fifty patterns and manufacturer's market share through the Macomber Associates Audit Reports and uses sophisticated focus group interviews to define and predict the market.

Cat. 61 Starting in 1936 Shenango Pottery made
ware for the French firm Theodore Haviland &
Co. to sell in the United States.

Cat. 62 An example of Franciscan's Masterpiece china, the pattern *Westwood* (1942) emulated the thin, fashionable European ware unavailable during World War II.

Cat. 63 Among the Flintridge China Company's
products were innovative shapes and patterns
such as *Pagoda Lantern* (1959).

By introducing manufacturing economies and new advertising, marketing, and merchandising concepts to distribute and promote its product, Lenox easily led lagging foreign manufacturers in market share following the war and effectively squashed any competition from domestic manufacturers as well. In addition Lenox's advertising efforts had helped to make fine china the tableware of choice for formal and much casual dining in the majority of American homes. In large part the bridal registry had made this possible. When the Japanese manufacturers came back to the market in the early 1950s, offering porcelain (not earthenware) at low prices, the earthenware potteries could not compete realistically.

American-made fine china at the expensive end of the market and new, very cheap products at the low end, such as paper, plastic, and glass dishes, increased the pressure on the earthenware potteries, spelling their doom (see pp. 150–55). USPA president J. M. Wells Jr. remarked at the 1958 annual meeting, "When we lose 30% of our business in a single year something definitely is wrong."[99] A close watch over the tariff situation, made completely intolerable by the government's participation in the General Agreement on Tariffs and Trade (GATT) in 1947, improved methods of materials handling, and reorganization of product flow on the factory floor counted for little against the sea changes that the earthenware makers were facing.

Year after year the USPA noted declining membership, mostly because of business failures, but also because those companies that survived had already switched over to new products, while those making vitreous hotel and restaurant ware saw little advantage in staying with an organization that represented earthenware interests. The Homer Laughlin China Company is a good example. With its expert design department headed first by Frederick Rhead and later by Donald Schreckengost, Homer Laughlin had led the way from the mid-1930s, through the 1940s, and into the 1950s with successful design bolstered by efficient manufacturing. Then suddenly in 1959 the company changed direction, dropping consumer dinnerware, with the exception of *Fiesta*, in favor of institutional china as its principal product (cat. 64). In short, only the makers of vitreous tableware—fine china for domestic use and hotel ware for the institutions—ultimately survived the postwar changes in the American tabletop market.

Although this group was select, it was by no means poor. These potteries had learned to survive through many shifts and turns in a volatile industry plagued by high wages, low tariffs, and severe foreign competition. The companies that became ever more prosperous in the new marketplace for vitreous goods—Lenox, Syracuse, Homer Laughlin, Hall China, Mayer China, Flintridge, Shenango, Buffalo, and Gladding, McBean & Co.'s Franciscan Division—represented the cream of a very small industry. During the 1950s and 1960s, this close

group of survivors in the dinnerware market was joined by a new player. The Pfaltzgraff Pottery, the oldest family-owned pottery operating continuously in America,[100] entered the dinnerware business slowly, but methodically. Long a maker of utilitarian stoneware and redware flowerpots, this York, Pennsylvania, pottery introduced a line called *Country-Time*, designed by Ben Seibel in 1952. *Country-Time* was described as a "line of accessories," but it actually included dinnerware place settings along with serving dishes. The success of additional early dinnerware lines, *Country Casual* and *Heritage* (the latter designed by Georges Briard), convinced the company to create an in-house design department, which developed *Yorktowne* in 1967, a pattern still in production. Each time the company expanded its dinnerware lines, it also revamped production, introducing new machinery and rethinking the organization of the factory floor.

As the pottery industry began consolidating yet again with the entrance of low-wage Asian manufacturers into the market, Pfaltzgraff could afford to acquire factories, like Syracuse China in 1989. Syracuse had bought Shenango in 1988, which itself had acquired Mayer China in 1964. Shenango's remarkable "Fast Fire" kiln had revolutionized the vitrified china business in the 1960s by reducing firing times from an industry average of 36 hours to 1½ hours, but thirty years later this kind of technological breakthrough did not matter when Pfaltzgraff could no longer make Shenango profitable and closed the subsidiary in 1992.

OPPOSITE:
Cat. 64 Homer Laughlin China introduced *Epicure* in 1955 before it curtailed production of dishes for the home.

Plastic Dishes: A New Rival

During the twentieth century innovative materials and manufacturing processes gave rise to new types of tableware. From the introduction of inexpensive pressed glass in the late nineteenth century to the unveiling of Corning Glass Works' *Centura* dinnerware made from the hybrid material Pyroceram in 1962, glass and ceramics had long rubbed rims on the American tabletop. The new contenders, however, were the creations of unrelated industries. Paper plates and cups, spun and stamped aluminum, and turned and pressed wood all grew in popularity from the 1930s on. While serving food on and in paper eventually rose to dominance at fast food restaurants like Dairy Queen (est. 1940), Burger King (est. 1954), and McDonald's (est. 1954), plastic was the most important newcomer to the tablescape in the home.

Lightweight plastic dishes first existed in the form of picnic sets and a few services made for airlines in the 1930s. Research and development efforts, as well as the substitution of plastic for traditional ceramic and glass vessels by the U.S. Navy during World War II, greatly advanced the production and use of this new material in the United States.[1] Even before the war ended Ephraim Friedman of Macy's in New York exclaimed: "The 'Blitz' of the plastics is on. The panzer divisions of the synthetic resins have invaded the territories formerly occupied by ceramics, glass, metals, wood, and a host of other materials and they are there to stay."[2]

After the war the development of plastic dinnerware, and eventually stemware, moved very quickly. As rich and powerful chemical companies like E. I. du Pont de Nemours & Co., Union Carbide and Carbon Corporation, Monsanto Chemical Company, Allied Chemical and Dye Corporation, and American Cyanamid Company sought ways to sell the innovative raw materials they had developed, and entrepreneurs founded molding companies across the country, the plastics revolution was off to a bold start. Tupperware did more than any other product "to domesticate plastic" in the American consciousness. Working with Du Pont engineers, Earl S. Tupper experimented with molding items from polyethylene, a soft, waxy, flexible plastic. Soon he introduced the *Millionaire Line,* which included multicolored pitchers, coffee servers, cups and saucers, storage containers, and trays (cat. 65).

By 1949 the trade journal *Modern Plastics* was claiming that Tupperware had "taken the country by storm."[3] This new line embodied all that was exciting about plastic to midcentury Americans. True, it substituted for traditional materials, but more important, it possessed new qualities. Before Tupperware:

> People made do with storage dishes and water jugs of ceramic and glass. Heavy and breakable, they sweated condensation and became slippery;

the lids fell off and broke. Lightweight, unbreakable, and waxy-textured for a good grip, Tupperware solved all those problems while also introducing the crucial innovation of the air-tight seal. That it looked different, frankly new, and unprecedented simply reinforced its superiority to anything that preceded it.[4]

As women across the country began attending "Tupperware Parties" to view and buy Tupper's products, they were also being enticed by another type of plastic tableware—melamine.

Melamine, a carbon, nitrogen, and hydrogen compound, is produced from urea, which contains these three elements as well as oxygen. These components react with formaldehyde to create a versatile thermosetting resin. To produce plastic dishes, paper is impregnated with melamine-formaldehyde resin. The paper containing the resin is dried, crushed, and ground in a mill. Color pigments are added at this stage, and the mixture is formed into "pills." Once heated, these small pellets melt and the resulting plastic is pressed into the shape of tableware in metal molds.[5]

In the beginning there were several problems to be overcome. Initially, coffee and tea cups made from melamine stained more easily than their ceramic counterparts. Early plastic dishes scratched readily, although they stood up well during repeated washings. Most problematic of all were the limitations on applying surface decoration. The basic difficulties with durability were solved or at least lessened through technical research and the formation of industry standards. In 1951 molding companies across the country sent samples to a laboratory for evaluation. When the numerous trials were completed, *Consumer Reports* ranked the ware.[6] Such efforts both encouraged the correction of deficiencies and helped to standardize industry and consumer expectations of plastic tableware by the mid-1950s.

At the same time improvements in the plastics and lithography industries worked to solve the ornament issue. In the beginning melamine came only in solid colors. Reflective material could be mixed into the plastic to add sparkle, patterned decoration could be cut into the mold to produce an embossed effect, and the opaque surface could be shined, but decals would not hold up on the surface. As a result, the designs for plastic tableware in the late 1940s and early 1950s relied almost totally on shape and color. Given that the famous designer Russel Wright created the melamine prototypes for American Cyanamid in 1945, it is little wonder that early ware by many manufacturers drew inspiration from Wright's work in ceramics. Like most of his pottery designs, plastic dishes of the era tended to be

MODERN ⊕ PLASTICS

VOLUME 29   NOVEMBER 1951   NUMBER 3

THE
TABLEWARE
WAR

Absurdity of propaganda by Vitrified
China Association is shown by an
examination of simple facts

Institutions and schools recognized for their contributions to public health
through good nutrition are constantly proving the case for plastic tableware

Fig. 2.19 Potteries considered plastics an unwelcome addition to the American tabletop.

American Cyanamid "hoped to make a total of nearly 30,000,000 impressions . . . all selling Melmac dinnerware."[10] Through advertising, the brand name Melmac came to be synonymous with plastic dinnerware.

By 1950 there were at least twenty makers of plastic dinnerware in the United States.[11] The ones the industry rated as making the finest products at the time were Boonton Molding Company in Boonton, New Jersey; Plastics Manufacturing Company in Dallas; International Molded Plastics in Cleveland; and Watertown Manufacturing Company in Watertown, Connecticut.[12] From such firms and later ones came products that were sophisticated in both quality and design. By the late 1950s some products were so refined that manufacturers touted them as being on a par with china. Perhaps the finest of all was Russel Wright's *Ming Lace* pattern from the *Flair* line (1959; cat. 66). Belle Kogan's work for Boonton was also exceptional. Especially noteworthy were the *Belle* (1953) line made in Boonton's translucent *Candescent* body (1955) and the *Patrician* line (1957). Boonton stated in the press release for its *Candescent* body:

> This is the first time that such a quality has ever been achieved in Melmac. Besides its translucency, which has the appearance of fine bone china, *Candescent* sparkles with color. . . . The glowing quality of *Candescent* makes the new dinnerware suitable for casual table settings and for the most formal dinner. The pieces have a luxurious weight and luster, and the four rich colors that are available were chosen to give unlimited choice in the use of tablecloths, flowers, and other appointments.[13]

Manufacturers of ceramics were highly disturbed by such developments.

When plastic dishes first became a force to reckon with around 1950, the pottery industry went on the defensive (fig. 2.19). In 1951 Robert F. Martin, executive secretary of the Vitrified China Association, issued the inflammatory report "Plastic Tableware and Public Health." Furious over large contracts given to melamine tableware producers by the U.S. military at the start of the Korean War, potters claimed that scratches in plastic harbored bacteria, that the surface hindered washing because it could not be wetted properly, and that the ware released embalming fluid (formaldehyde).

organic in shape and colorful. Among these lines, those done by Belle Kogan for the Boonton Molding Company and by Wright for Northern Industrial Chemical were perhaps the most successful aesthetically (cat. 66).

Before long, decals were developed that could be applied to plastic. In 1954 International Molded Plastics introduced what was said to be "the first dinnerware to offer the consumer a really china-like multi-color decoration."[7] Initially rival makers held back to see whether this new product would be commercially successful before investing in equipment to ornament their plastic dishes. Within a few years colorful patterns were available from numerous firms. By the early 1960s plastic dinnerware was a riot of color and pattern.[8]

Just as it benefited from rapid technical and aesthetic development, plastic dinnerware reaped the rewards of strong marketing. Especially noteworthy in this respect were the efforts of the American Cyanamid Company. As one of the two primary producers of melamine pellets, the chemical giant had a vested interest in making sure the molding companies to which it supplied raw materials were successful.[9] To that end American Cyanamid trademarked its version of melamine, calling it Melmac, and began promoting its purported superior qualities to the trade. In 1949 the corporation launched a nationwide advertising campaign in trade journals as well as popular magazines like *House and Garden, Saturday Evening Post, New York Times Sunday Magazine,* and *Farm Journal.* Over the course of three months

Cat. 65 From Tupperware to Boontonware,
America embraced plastics in the 1950s.

Although each point was refuted in a dignified manner in the Society of the Plastics Industry's booklet *Public Health and Melamine Tableware,* the editors of *Modern Plastics* lashed out at their rivals when they summarized the potters' attack: "The Vitrified China Association is on a rampage . . . [and saying that] soon no doubt the citizens of this country will have an epidemic of plasticitis and the undertaker won't even be necessary because they will already be embalmed."[14]

The public apparently was not afraid of being permanently preserved by eating off of plastic dishes. Sold in chain, department, and discount stores, as well as distributed door-to-door and as premiums, melamine dishes were enjoying significant sales by the mid-1950s (fig. 2.20). Simultaneously, sales of plastic stemware and tumblers were advancing. Two of the most important lines of plastic drinking vessels were *Dallas Crystal Stemware* (1949) made by Plastics Manufacturing Company and *Laureline,* a Kogan design introduced by Boonton in 1956.[15] In total the plastic tableware market was estimated at $40 million in 1955 and a year later was claimed to be growing at the rate of $8 million annually. As a result of such strong sales, 90 percent of department stores carried the product by the mid-1950s. One anonymous buyer who participated in a survey at the time said that 23 percent of the gross volume in his china and glass department derived from plastic dinnerware sales alone.[16]

Because midcentury American women found plastic acceptable as a second or third set of dishes, some potters and glassmakers attempted to minimize their potential loss of revenues by going into the plastic business. Most notable of these efforts were those by Lenox China, Fostoria Glass Company, and Stetson China Company. In 1956, seeking profits in new fields, Fostoria decided to enter the competition in melamine. Plastic, it was believed, would not compete with Fostoria's traditional product line of glass tableware. The firm's directors in fact thought that specially designed plastic patterns displayed alongside Fostoria glass in department stores would both strengthen glass sales and tap the growing market for melamine dinnerware. The company hired the Chicago firm of Latham, Tyler, and Jensen as designer and Chicago Molded Products as manufacturer, and Fostoria Melamine Dinnerware was introduced in 1957.[17]

OPPOSITE:
Cat. 66 Molding companies such as Northern Industrial Chemical Company exploited plastic to produce novel shapes during the 1950s.

Fig. 2.20 Plastic dishes were touted as indestructible in midcentury advertising.

Lenox's interest in plastics was similar to Fostoria's. By the late 1950s Lenox's management felt the company had been so successful in the fine china business that it would be difficult to increase sales much further. Thus to expand and generate ever higher profits, Lenox decided to acquire companies making related products. In 1958 it secured a controlling interest in the Hellmich Manufacturing Company of Saint Louis, which produced plastic dishes under the brand name of Branchell (cat. 65). Shortly after the organization of Lenox Plastics, the Branchell lines of *Color-Flyte, Royale,* and *Prestige* were discontinued and an new initiative begun. Lenoxware was designed in New Jersey but made in Missouri and Puerto Rico.[18]

Stetson China of Chicago became far more identified with plastics than was Fostoria or Lenox. From its founding in 1919 by the Russian immigrant L. B. Stetson until World War II, the company produced and decorated inexpensive earthenware. Joseph W. Stetson, who purchased the pottery in 1945, changed the firm's direction. In the late 1940s and 1950s Stetson China became known for its painted dinnerware featuring both traditional and abstract patterns (cat. 175). Then around 1957 the company brought out a melamine line that it had made by molders in Chicago and Manitowoc, Wisconsin, and Benton Harbor, Michigan. By 1959 Stetson had mix-and-match lines that combined plastic Stetson Ware with its Linconite earthenware.[19] In 1965, however, Stetson's plastics division (Stetson Chemical) was sold to its raw material supplier Allied Chemical, which continued using the Stetson name on its fashion-oriented plastic dinnerware. Although Stetson China had just completed a record sales year, the pottery was closed within months of selling its plastic division. According to Philip R. Stetson, president and chief executive officer at the time, the decision was made because the future of U.S.-made inexpensive pottery looked bleak in light of competition from American plastic and Japanese pottery.[20]

Fostoria and Lenox's adventures with plastic ended unexpectedly as well. Because the raw material producers American Cyanamid and Allied Chemical licensed sizable numbers of manufacturers to produce melamine dinnerware in the 1950s and early 1960s, the price of plastic dishes fell dramatically due to increased competition during this period. Apparently, as prices declined, those customers who purchased the highest quality ware became disillusioned, causing sales of the most expensive lines to slacken.

Makers like Fostoria, Lenox, and Boonton—whose operating costs were driven up by investments in better equipment, raw materials, marketing, and design efforts—were the first to feel the crunch. Only two years after introducing its plastic line, Fostoria was forced to withdraw it in 1959, citing decreased demand for finer plastic wares.[21] After making profits at first, Lenox too found the plastics business a difficult one. In 1973 the Saint Louis plant was sold. A few years later the branch plant in Puerto Rico was also closed and its equipment moved to Mexico City and later Monterrey. Combined with a line of stainless, Lenoxware continued to be made in Mexico for the Central American market until the hyperinflation of the peso made the venture unprofitable in the late 1970s.[22]

The upscale plastic dinnerware that had so frightened potters in the early 1950s had largely run its course as a product for the dining room by the late 1960s as price cutting and declining demand forced American makers from the field. In May 1965 *Gift and Tableware Reporter* stated that "several melamine dinnerware producers [were] rumored 'on the rocks' financially—and may not hang on long enough to show at the summer markets."[23] Soon foreign manufacturers moved in to capture what was left of the market. By the 1970s plastic dishes made in Europe and especially Asia populated the patios of America.

Notes

1. "The Plastic Tableware Potential—Outgrowth of 'War Applications,'" *CGJ* 135:2 (Aug. 1944): 15.

2. "The Plastic Blitz Is On," *CGJ* 135:5 (Nov. 1944): 5.

3. "Plastics Supply and Demand," *MP* 26 (Jan. 1949): 142.

4. Meikle 1995, 158, 180–81.

5. Scribner 1950, 73. Information on making dishes from paper and resin provided by Billy Arcement, Melamine Chemicals.

6. "Ratings of Plastic Dishes," *Consumer Reports* 16 (Jan. 1951): 10.

7. "Plastics on the Table," *Industrial Design* 1 (Feb. 1954): 66.

8. For examples, see "Plastic Tablewares Reach Consumers through Many Retail Channels," *CGJ* 159:5 (Nov. 1956): 28–29; and "Melmac Measure of Quality," *GTR* (Nov. 1963): 14–15.

9. The other leading producer of melamine crystals was Allied Chemicals.

10. *CGJ* 145:1 (July 1949): 20–21.

11. For a list of most of them, see "Plastic Dinnerware," *CGJ* 146:3a (15 Mar. 1950): 110.

12. "Ratings of Plastic Dishes," *Consumer Reports* 16 (Jan. 1951): 10.

13. "Boonton Introduces New Candescent Line of Melmac Dinnerware," Boonton Molding Company press release, 1958, Belle Kogan papers.

14. "Dishes under Fire," *MP* 29 (Sept. 1951): 74 ff; and "The Tableware War," 29 (Nov. 1951): 73–76, 182.

15. For advertisements for these products, see *CGJ* 145:1 (July 1949): 24; and Kogan papers.

16. "The Market for Plastic Dinnerware," *CGJ* 157:1 (July 1955): 86; and "Plastic Tablewares Reach Consumers through Many Retail Channels," 159:5 (Nov. 1956): 28.

17. "Management Recommendation: Melamine Program" (23 Nov. 1956), Fostoria Archives. See also "Fostoria Announces Melamine Dinnerware," *CGJ* 161:2 (Aug. 1957): 44.

18. Information supplied verbally to Charles Venable by Ellen Denker, Lenox Archives, 21 Aug. 1999.

19. For information on Stetson, see "Stetson China Company Makes Marked Progress," *CGJ* 104:1 (6 Jan. 1927): 13; "L. B. Stetson Obituary," 109:2 (Feb. 1931): 58; and "New Patterns, Lines Keep Interest Focused," 165:1 (July 1959): 70.

20. "Plastics Firms Realign; Stetson-Allied in Deal," *GTR* (3 May 1965): 1; and Philip R. Stetson, letter to Charles Venable, 9 Oct. 1999.

21. "Factory Correspondence No. 19" (26 June 1959). Fostoria Archives.

22. Information supplied verbally to Charles Venable by Ellen Denker, Lenox Archives.

23. "Plastics Firms Realign; Stetson-Allied in Deal," *GTR* (3 May 1965): 4.

Hand versus Machine: Glass after 1880

For several years beginning in 1873 the country experienced a severe depression, which stunted production by domestic manufacturers. This economic downturn was especially hard on the market for luxury goods. In the glass industry the makers of pressed glass fared better than those who produced fine blown- and cut-glass tableware. Only a few companies were even making luxury glass at the time, including the stalwart Massachusetts glasshouses—New England Glass Company, Boston and Sandwich Glass Company, and Mount Washington Glass Company—along with Dorflinger Glass Works in Pennsylvania and Corning Glass Works in New York, which produced blanks for cutting by J. Hoare & Co. Some small cutting houses still operated in New York for the local market. Clearly the national glass market needed an event to capture the popular imagination and spur interest in these deluxe cut and engraved goods.

Forty-seven American glassmakers participated in the Philadelphia Centennial Exposition in 1876, or more than one-third of the total number of glass firms exhibiting. The Dorflinger Glass Works of White Mills, Pennsylvania, received the highest award for its decanter and thirty-eight wineglasses engraved with the seal of the thirty-eight states then in the Union.[101] The exhibition pieces of the New England Glass Company included chandeliers and a service of diamond-cut glass. Mount Washington showed chandeliers, an elaborate cut-glass table and a multitiered fountain. But it was the glasshouse erected by Gillinder & Sons behind Machinery Hall that was the most popular exhibit. In Gillinder's working factory visitors could see glass being blown, pressed, engraved, and cut. And afterward they could buy souvenirs, which the exhibit factory turned out by the thousands. "The whole process of manufacturing glass was shown here, and it was a very interesting and highly instructive exhibit," wrote one observer. "Many of the articles manufactured were especially designed as mementos of the great exhibition, and found a ready market. These included paper weights, upon which were stamped representations of different Centennial buildings, or public buildings of the city; busts of Washington, Lincoln and others, vases, colored ornaments and trinkets."[102]

Just as the potters were ignored at the fair by the art establishment, critics had little to say about the American glass exhibitors. After all, it was the era of gazing blindly at foreign wares and dismissing the American-made decorative arts. The popular press, however, made favorable comments, and the official Belgian report on the fair described the American

Cat. 67 Deeply cut and delicately engraved glass made by American workers was among the finest in the world early in the 20th century.

Fig. 2.21 Skilled workers cut a massive punch bowl at Libbey Glass Company, Toledo, ca. 1910.

glass as being second in quality only to the Bohemian displays, which may be taken as a great compliment, considering the importance of the Belgian and Bohemian glass industries.[103]

The displays of lavishly cut glass by the New England Glass Company, Boston and Sandwich Glass Company, and Dorflinger stimulated the American consumer's interest in cut glass. By the turn of the century, the high-end market was ravenous for the most elaborate, rich cut glass to be found. Despite the decades spent in development of mass production of the cheaper soda-lime glass, the lead-glass makers were able to create a new market niche for luxury tablewares and decorative objects in the late nineteenth century. As the population of the United States climbed from some 50 million in 1880 to about 170 million in 1920, the middle and upper middle classes swelled dramatically in numbers and proportion and clamored for fancy cut, engraved, and blown wares designed, produced, and marketed to satisfy their taste for opulence (cat. 67).[104]

Pressed-glass manufacturers from the western states hoped that the Centennial Exposition would have a positive effect on their business as well, and viewed the event as a chance to attract eastern customers for their cheaper wares (cat. 68). In spite of the mechanization of decoration that pressing technology had introduced into glassmaking during the mid-nineteenth century, most wares still required the attention of many workers (figs. 2.21, 2.22). By the turn of the century, however, the use of semiautomatic and fully automatic machines, such as tank furnaces and linear annealing

lehrs (long conveyor ovens that reduced the temperature of the glass slowly in order to stabilize it), had become widespread, and the design and marketing of vessels, tablewares, and accessories were dramatically different than in 1880.

Tank furnaces, being much larger than pot furnaces, provided molten glass continuously, eliminating the downtime necessary for melting new batches. With the tank furnace fueled by gas, new raw materials were added at one end while the glassmaker formed his ware from the molten glass at the other. Linear annealing lehrs also greatly lowered cost by decreasing the amount of time and attention given to the annealing process. Through the combination of the soda-lime formula, natural gas, continuous tank furnaces, and linear annealing lehrs, the potential of glass pressing was fully achieved.

RICH CUT GLASS

The fashion for rich cut glass (today called brilliant cut glass) during the last two decades of the nineteenth century might have been inspired by cut glass made earlier, but the new ware was much more elaborate. The *Russian* pattern, designed by Philip McDonald, a cutter for T. G. Hawkes & Co., and patented in 1882, was used for many years in the White House (1891–1918). *Russian* led the way as the most elaborate of the rich cut patterns. The combination of stars and raised rosettes in this pattern gave cut glass a brilliance not seen before, and its market potential was not lost on manufacturers or retailers. Despite Hawkes's patent, the pattern was widely made. During the 1880s and 1890s, it was pictured in

Fig. 2.22 Making stemware by hand, 1902.

Cat. 68 This *Goddess of Liberty* pressed glass compote is unusual for its green color.

catalogues of the New England Glass Company, Dorflinger Glass Works, and J. Hoare & Co. (the affiliate of Corning), and by 1900 the pattern was produced by all significant glass-cutting companies.[105]

One index of the high consumption of such elaborate patterns can be seen in the number of glass cutters working in Corning, New York. Five cutters worked in this glass center in 1870; by 1880 the number had grown to 39. In 1905, the height of the brilliant cut glass period, there were 490 cutters working in Corning.[106] Dorflinger Glass Works had 500 workers at its peak. The frenzy was fed in part by the success of Libbey Glass Company's pavilion at the World's Columbian Exposition in Chicago in 1893. Inspired perhaps by Gillinder's exhibit at the Philadelphia fair, Libbey went into debt to build, equip, and staff a building in Chicago. Although there were more than seventy glass exhibits, most were located in the Manufactures and Liberal Arts Building. The Tiffany & Co. pavilion won the most praise from critics, but visitors may have enjoyed Libbey's glass factory even more. To help defray the enormous cost of creating a separate pavilion, the firm decided to charge visitors, but deducted the price of the ticket from any purchases made in the shop. The exhibit was wildly successful for both cut glass and Libbey (cat. 70).[107]

The glass industry appealed directly to the consumer much earlier than the pottery industry. Gillinder's and Libbey's factories at the world's fairs are one example. The early practice of direct advertising to consumers by luxury glass-makers is another. For a long time the potters considered their customers to be the buyers for retailers rather than the actual end consumers. Glassmakers, on the other hand, went directly to the ultimate source of their profits. Thomas Hawkes was among the first cut-glass entrepreneurs to take advantage of trademarking and advertising, putting extensive resources into name recognition after his successful exhibit at the 1889 Paris world's fair.[108]

Hawkes, an Irishman, learned the glass-cutting business under John Hoare in New York. When Hoare moved his operation from Brooklyn to Corning, Hawkes went with him, serving for a time as supervisor of the glassworks. Hoare's operation was basically a cutting shop, as his blanks came from the Corning Glass Works.[109] In 1880 Hawkes set out on his own in Corning, having made an arrangement with Corning Glass Works for blanks. His business grew rapidly, expanding from an original retinue of seven or eight employees to between thirty and forty workers by 1882 and double again by 1890. By 1902 Hawkes's operation was the largest shop in Corning, employing about four hundred workers.[110]

Hawkes's trademark, which was only the second adopted for cut glass when it was introduced in 1891, was acid etched on the glass rather than merely printed on a paper label that could easily go astray.[111] In that same year Hawkes began to show photographs along with the trademark in his advertising, and he placed advertisements in both trade periodicals and popular women's magazines like Harper's Weekly, Century, Scribner's, and Ladies' Home Journal. The advertisements show a piece of glass with a line or two of text and the trademark. The slogan, "No piece without this trademark is genuine," fixed Hawkes's name in the popular mind.[112]

Consumers paid a high price for the opulence of cut glass. Blown and patterned art glasses such as Rose Amber and Burmese offered in the Pairpoint Manufacturing Company catalogue of about 1885–90 cost 50 to 100 percent less than cut glass in the same forms.[113] A big part of the price differential was the cost of producing these wares. In 1888 a master glassblower working in an American factory was paid a weekly wage of about $27. But cut glass also required the skill of a "rougher," who was the most skilled of the glass cutters and made $20 a week. In Germany, a glass cutter was paid $3 a week, while in England the same craftsman received $9 a week. Although the practice of paying high wages in American factories ensured an ample supply of highly skilled immigrant craftsmen to the American industry, some American companies reduced their costs simply by importing blanks from Europe. Small cutting shops with fewer than fifty employees proliferated between 1900 and 1910 using strategies such as this. Shortcuts and manufacturing efficiencies also helped American glasshouses compete. In the 1890s, for example, makers began using a combination of hydrofluoric and sulfuric acids as a polishing agent. Final polishing with acid took seconds instead of minutes, as it had with mechanical polishing, and most consumers could not tell the difference.

The most brilliant cut glass was made with free-blown blanks, although some shapes were attainable only by mold blowing, which imparted a certain overall dullness in the glass. To reduce costs even further, beginning in the early 1890s some cutting was done on pressed blanks, which greatly reduced the overall brilliance and clarity even with cutting and polishing. The greatest labor-saving method of making blanks, however, was introduced in the late 1890s or early 1900s. Pressing or mold blowing blanks with patterns gave the cutter a head start on cutting. With this simple expedient, production costs were reduced 40 percent because time was no longer needed to mark out the design before the beginning of cutting.[114]

The fashion for rich cut glass declined after 1905 when a deeply engraved style of glass that was often combined with deep cutting became stylish. This new taste was called rock crystal (cat. 67, goblet far left). At the same time the general technique of cutting declined further. Gang wheels, which made several parallel cuts at the same time, were introduced about 1910. These were often used to cut flowers on forms pressed with rich cut patterns. Furthermore, inexpensive glass after 1900 was pressed entirely with patterns that closely imitated rich cut glass and trademarked with the name given the line by each company (cat. 140). McKee & Brothers patented Prescut in 1904, for example. A. H. Heisey & Co. patented Plunger-cut in 1905, while Imperial Glass Company patented Nu-cut in 1914. Although some of the intricate pressed patterns sold under such brand names were technically remarkable, the glass was far inferior and much cheaper than the rich cut glass it imitated.[115]

With these innovations the job of the skilled glass cutter was finally in jeopardy. J. W. Ludlow, national representative of the American Flint Glass Workers Union, described the problem in 1926:

The pressed figured blank took the work away from the roughers and the quality of the work was not as good as that of the off-hand [blown] blank, as the latter was noted for its fine luster, and consequently this was eliminated. Firms sprang up everywhere which cut only half of the pattern on the articles and put them on the market as cut glass. Then came the semi-cut and near-cut glass. While the change this brought about made work for the press and mould making departments, it only lasted for a few years, when the "bootleggers" of the glass trade filled the department stores and pawn shops also with the cheapened ware until people were ashamed to say that they had any cut glass in their homes, and refused to buy it.[116]

As cut glass became less fashionable the whole industry declined after 1910, and many small and large shops closed.

In addition to cutting, high-fashion glassmakers also offered wares with copper- and stone-wheel engraving beginning in the 1870s. After 1885, when vessels were blown with thicker bodies and drawn lips, elaborate effects such as polished rock-crystal and unpolished matte-finish engraving were popular. As time went on, however, engraved decoration was simplified, the patterns becoming shallower and more open (cat. 67). For example, about 1920, Libbey introduced a new product called Light Ware, which featured open patterns executed with shallow engraving.[117]

GLASS FOR THE MASSES

The makers of midrange goods also had to resolve difficult issues during the early twentieth century. Not unlike the makers of expensive cut glass, they were often faced with the problem of having their most popular patterns copied or appropriated in some way. Despite patenting and copyrighting, imitation was rampant because there was so little enforcement of the law. There were even frequent disagreements over who copied what. In 1912 H. A. Marshall, a salesman for Fostoria Glass Company, reported in a letter to the president of Fostoria, W. A. B. Dalzell, that a Central Glass Works representative had boasted to him during a luncheon at Chicago's famous Palmer House Hotel about how many of Fostoria's patterns Central had copied. In the letter Marshall mentioned a Minton china pattern that Fostoria had been considering copying, but noted that Central was already making it exclusively for the Chicago department store Marshall Field & Co. He suggested to Dalzell that Fostoria make the same pattern but sell it to Marshall Field's competitors, Carson Pirie Scott & Co. and Mandel Brothers. The Central salesman had also told Marshall that his firm had copied Fostoria's pattern 1638, a hot fudge sundae dish, and sold it as an exclusive to Wanamaker's department store in Philadelphia. Finally, Marshall noted that

Central was making a handled stem brandy that was the same as Fostoria's pattern 810.[118]

Similar complaints were aired in a 1936 exchange of letters between officials of the Cambridge Glass Company and Fostoria. Carl Roe of Fostoria accused Cambridge Glass of copying Fostoria's 3500/64 pattern relish dish, noting that Fostoria's dish had actually been on the market for some time, and pointing out that "New Martinsville had copied it a year or so ago and that they have practically driven ours out of the market." Roe flippantly offered to Cambridge that Fostoria could "submit to you sketches of relishes that we have not made as we always have a few held back." Cambridge's secretary W. C. McCartney replied that Roe likely had not seen the relish in question since the handle and feet were quite different. "As a matter of fact," McCartney continued, "ours resembles more an oblong Relish Dish that Heisey made in his old 500 pattern, which was on the market prior to your own 3500."[119] Sometimes blatant imitation could occur even years after the initial introduction of a design. Cambridge's inexpensive pressed and blown pattern *Cambridge Square* is an instance of this practice. Introduced in 1952, *Cambridge Square* was a near direct copy of *Knickerbocker*, which Libbey had first marketed in 1933 (cat. 73). But where the public rejected the beautifully blown and cut surfaces of Libbey's product for being too expensive and modern, Cambridge's cheaper version was highly successful twenty years later when the average consumer was more interested in contemporary design.

Although piracy was indeed a problem, the greatest changes in glass tableware after 1900 can be traced to the dramatic developments in utilitarian glass. The Corning Glass Works laboratory, the first scientific glass laboratory in the United States, was established in 1908. Within only a few years it was developing a heat-resistant borosilicate glass, which was patented in 1915 as Pyrex, a pressed ovenware (cat. 22). Similarly, the H. C. Fry Glass Company of Rochester, Pennsylvania, produced a heat-resistant glass with a translucent mother-of-pearl color. By early 1922 they had developed a new line of inexpensive novelty glass using the same formula combined with applied glass of a contrasting color or iridescent crackled effects for home use as dinnerware and decoration. McKee & Brothers had its own line as well, called Glasbake.[120]

Benefiting from its own research and development effort, the Libbey Glass Company increasingly concentrated on production of machine-made bottles and tablewares. Michael J. Owens, who helped the company achieve solvency in 1890 by organizing the production of lightbulbs for General Electric, also developed the first of his many inventions to mechanize the blowing of glass. This first machine eliminated the need for boys to handle the molds for the bulb blowers. Further refinements resulted in the semiautomatic lightbulb blowing machine in 1894. And this was followed by development of a machine that made glass tumblers. When the new tumbler

OPPOSITE:
Cat. 69 The Rockwell Silver Company achieved artistic results by electrically depositing sterling on porcelain and glass made between the wars.

Fig. 2.23 Harnessing star power to sell dishes in 1952: Betty Hutton's movie *The Greatest Show on Earth* inspired Libbey Glass Company's *Circus* pattern.

machine and process were ready, they were sold to Fry Glass, and Owens went to work on lamp chimneys.[121]

Although Michael Owens is perhaps most famous for automating the lightbulb, bottle-glass, and sheet-glass (window) industries, it was his early machines for automated tumbler production that ultimately had the most profound effect on the making of table glass at Libbey Glass Company. While Owens was making money for the company through mundane mass-market products, Edward D. Libbey continued to work toward the goal of his father, William L., to reach the top of the luxury glass business (see pp. 163–66). As the glass industry mechanized, production moved gradually westward to western Pennsylvania, Ohio, West Virginia, and Indiana. In what proved to be a prescient decision, Edward Libbey relocated the New England Glass Company (the former name of the Libbey Glass Company) from East Cambridge, Massachusetts, to Toledo, Ohio, in 1888 to take advantage of newly discovered cheap gas reserves.

During World War I many independent cutting and engraving shops closed because their sources for blanks had been cut off. But there were deeper problems as well. Many established East Coast and mid-Atlantic glasshouses closed too, in part because of mechanization issues, but also because the elaborately finished object was passing from fashion. Dorflinger closed in 1921, Union Glass Works closed in 1924, H. P. Sinclaire & Co. closed in 1927, and Tiffany Studios closed in 1932. Steuben Glass Works, Pairpoint Manufacturing Company, and Libbey were among the few American firms that continued to make luxury wares with skilled labor (cat. 69). Ultimately the desire for luxury goods was eclipsed by the widespread availability of mass-market glass, and even the makers of midrange wares in the Midwest had instituted some economies of manufacture to compete with operations that were largely automated.

Mass production of glass in large mechanized factories required much more space than the hand production of luxury glass in small glasshouses. For the storage of raw materials alone, the mass producers needed a great deal more space. Rochester Tumbler in Rochester, Pennsylvania, for example, was turning out a half million tumblers a week by the late 1800s. Raw materials coming into the factory had to be mixed and melted, and once vessels were made, they had to be packed and held for shipment. Small wonder that a mass maker such as McKee & Brothers decided to build a factory and a town at the same time. In 1888 H. Sellers McKee moved his operation from Pittsburgh's south side to a new town he called Jeannette, after his wife, on farmland he had purchased in Westmoreland County near the Pennsylvania Railroad.[122]

Libbey Glass Company

The Libbey Glass Company traces its roots to the New England Glass Company (founded 1818) of East Cambridge, Massachusetts, for which William L. Libbey was agent or general manager beginning in 1872.[1] The company had long been known as a prosperous glasshouse that made extravagant blown and cut glass for the luxury trade. For most of its history the New England Glass Company, and later the Libbey Glass Company, employed some of the best cutters and engravers working in America. Louis Vaupel started with the company in 1856. Cutting and engraving glass in a colored casing, he created elaborate scenes of nature rendered in the Bohemian taste. A goblet showing a deer hunt engraved through red, now in the Toledo Museum of Art, is considered his masterpiece.[2] By the late 1820s New England Glass was pressing glassware as well. Indeed, some glass scholars credit the firm as being the first to explicitly describe and patent glass-pressing technology.[3] Ultimately, the pressing of glass in combination with the introduction in 1864 of a cheaper soda-lime formula developed by a West Virginia glasshouse served to undermine the company's prosperity.

By the time Libbey joined the company in the early 1870s, it was struggling to make money on its fancy goods. At the height of the company's success in 1865 five hundred men and boys worked in the factory; ten years later, in the midst of the depression caused by the Panic of 1873, only half that number were employed. The firm captured top honors at the Philadelphia Centennial Exposition in 1876, but that event failed to increase profits during the depression. The directors initially chose to close the factory in 1877, but then in 1878 leased the works to Libbey, who believed that he could make the company profitable even with fine lead glass as the primary product.

Edward D. Libbey, William's son, learned the business from childhood and became a partner with his father in 1880. After the elder Libbey's death in 1883 Edward Libbey brought out several lines of colored art glass that rescued the firm from complete failure. Although much of this work was intended for ornamental rather than utilitarian purposes, tablewares were available in all of these effects. Joseph Locke, who specialized in cutting cameos on colored grounds, was the glass craftsman and chemist who developed the special effects for the company. He worked for the Libbeys from 1883 to 1891. *Amberina,* which shaded from amber to ruby red, was the first of the colors, introduced in 1883. The shaded effect was achieved by reheating one end of the piece to draw out the red from the gold added to the glass mix. *Pomona,* an etched and stained glass introduced in 1885, featured nature motifs such as butterflies, pansies, and wild roses.

Wild Rose, patented in 1886, was New England Glass Company's version of *Peachblow,* introduced by Hobbs, Brockunier & Co. The name is a twist on the term "peach bloom," used to describe the two-tone glaze effect on Chinese porcelain popular among American collectors. (An extraordinarily high price was paid at auction in 1886 by collector William T. Walters of Baltimore for an antique Chinese vase from the collection of Mrs. Mary Morgan.) *Wild Rose* was a cased glass, white inside, that shaded from amber to rose, as did *Amberina.* Patented in 1887, *Agate* was achieved by splattering a *Wild Rose* glass piece with mineral stains that produced an amber, blue, or green marbled effect. *Maize,* patented in 1889, looked like corn on the cob, with green leaves at the bottom of each form.

The prosperity the glasshouse gained by selling this colored glass to high-end retailers like Tiffany & Co. was shallow, and Libbey saw that he could not support the high cost of making fine glass much longer. A bitter labor strike in East Cambridge forced him to close the factory, and he never reopened it. The discovery of natural gas in the Midwest attracted him to Ohio, and he moved the company to Toledo in 1888. He took with him those craftsmen who would follow and recruited additional workers from other Ohio valley glass factories.

The most important person Libbey hired turned out to be Michael J. Owens, who had started in the glass business in West Virginia as an apprentice at the age of ten. By fifteen he was a skilled journeyman glassblower. In 1888 he became shop foreman of Libbey's New England Glass Company factory in Toledo. When Owens tried to resign in the fall because the factory seemed to be failing, Libbey asked him to be superintendent. By the end of 1889 the pressure was easing and production schedules were being met, but the company was still running a deficit of $3,000. In an effort to turn a profit, Libbey agreed to make lightbulbs for General Electric when Corning Glass Works could not supply all they needed. New England Glass Company took over an existing glass factory in Findlay, Ohio, and made Owens manager. By the end of 1890 the company's profits were $75,000.

Besides contributing to this new profitability, Owens invented a machine to replace the mold-handling boys when they went on strike. The boys' job was to raise the bulb molds out of the water, hold them in position while the bulbs were blown by the glassblower, and open the molds when the blowers had finished shaping the bulbs. Owens created a machine to operate the entire process with a foot pedal. The blowers' hands were free for their work, and the handling of the molds was greatly simplified.

Despite the obvious profits in a utilitarian product like lightbulbs, Edward Libbey did not give up his dream of making beautiful glass. In 1892 he changed the name of the firm to the Libbey Glass Company and decided to build a glass factory for the World's Columbian Exposition in Chicago in 1893 to promote the new name. Although the effort

Cat. 70 Large pieces of cut glass like this
Libbey punch bowl were extremely time consuming to make and thus very expensive.

was costly, the firm sold enough glass to cover its expenses, and its large punch bowl and cups with a polished engraved hunt scene won the company a gold medal.[4]

For the Louisiana Purchase Exposition in Saint Louis in 1904, part of the Fine Arts Department was devoted to an applied arts section. About two dozen American and European glass displays were shown in this area, while about fifty-five more glass exhibits were included in the Varied Industries Building.[5] The Libbey Glass Company and the Quaker City Cut Glass Company had extensive cut-glass exhibits in the building, and both firms received grand prizes. The Libbey cut-glass display was part of the Golden Pavilion created by the Saint Louis jewelry company Mermod & Jaccard, Libbey's agent in that city. The display included a cut-glass table 24 inches in diameter (the cutting required fourteen weeks) and a gigantic bowl, also 24 inches in diameter, that had been cut by John Rufus Denman (cat. 70). In addition Libbey exhibited a large table service decorated with polished engraving, a plaque engraved with the theme Apotheosis of Transportation (copied from the doors of Louis Sullivan's Transportation Building for the 1893 Chicago fair), and a copy of a large punch bowl that the company had presented to President William McKinley in 1898.[6]

During this period Michael Owens invented a succession of automatic and semiautomatic machines to make lightbulbs (1894), tumblers (1895), lamp chimneys (1898), bottles (1903), and finally, sheet glass (1917). The Libbey company always shared in the profits of these inventions in some way, usually by creating a company through which to funnel money for research and development. Sometimes the new company would later sell or license the process and machinery to another company, and the pattern of profitable invention was used with each of the products listed above. Three great glass corporations of the twentieth century claim descent from Libbey Glass and Owens's inventions: Owens-Illinois Glass Company, Libbey-Owens-Ford Company, and Owens-Corning Fiberglass Corporation.

Still, Edward D. Libbey could not give up making art glass. When the fashion for brilliant cut glass was passing after World War I, Libbey's cutters kept the art alive by adding engraving—both polished and matte—to cutting in their elaborate creations. Even after Edward Libbey's death in 1925, the company's artisans continued to combine extravagant decorative techniques in vessels such as wineglasses that made these pieces available to only the wealthiest customers. Borrowing virtuoso effects from the famous Italian glasshouses in Murano that were popular in the 1920s, Libbey's artisans threaded stems with contrasting colors or made elaborate concoctions of knops and reels, and they added complex patterns of polished engraving to the bowls in clear glass or cut through stained surfaces.

In 1931 the company hired A. Douglas Nash, formerly of Tiffany Studios, to create a line of table and ornamental glass that would reestablish its leadership in this field. The Libbey-Nash series used all of the special effects known to glass craftsmen at the time, including cutting, engraving, application of contrasting colors, heat-sensitive color changes, and art glass in the style of the Durand Art Glass Company, Quezal Art Glass and Decorating Company, Tiffany Studios, and Steuben Glass Works. But the deepening depression doomed this effort, and in 1936 Libbey became a subsidiary of Owens-Illinois. Owens-Illinois, which had its headquarters in Toledo, continued to run the Libbey Division, although Libbey's artistic independence was eventually compromised for profitability.

In 1936 Owens-Illinois hired Edwin W. Fuerst to design a line of fine glass called Modern American, for which catalogues were issued in 1940 and 1942.[7] In a strong movement away from the colorful and ornate style of the 1920s and early 1930s, Modern American took its cue from the fashion for Scandinavian glass that was already informing the newest clear glass being made by Corning's Steuben Division—sleek monumental forms that emphasized the quality of the lead crystal. Elegant engraved decorations added to some pieces mimicked the style of the Scandinavian imports. The most famous design of the group was Embassy, used in the state dining room in the Federal Building at the 1939 New York world's fair (cat. 73). Modern American was discontinued during the war and not revived afterward.

In 1944 Libbey made an abrupt change in its market focus. The art lines were clearly unprofitable. Indeed, luxury glass had not been especially lucrative since the turn of the century, but the company's traditional commitment to the highest art of the glassmaker always held sway in any discussions of change. Now that Libbey Glass had been taken into the bigger Owens-Illinois, the bottom line became more important. The company would use its expertise in automatic processes for handling and forming glass to make table glass as well as bottles, and it could take advantage of the Safedge heat treatment developed to increase the resistance of institutional glass to mechanical and thermal shock. In other words, table glass would be considered a utilitarian product and no longer treated as an art form for fine dining. Ultimately, Libbey abandoned the traditional approach to table glass and undertook the automation and design development necessary to make glass for all types of consumers.[8]

To institute this change a design development department was assembled. Reassigned from Libbey and Owens-Illinois to this new enterprise were Lamson Rheinfrench, who had been head of premium and promotional sales; Willard Meyers, formerly with the Glass Container Division of Owens-Illinois; and Carl Fauster, former merchandising manager. Rheinfrench was made head of the new

department, Meyers became head of the art section, and Fauster was manager of advertising and merchandising. Working with the in-house staff were two consulting stylists: Virginia Hamill, a product stylist and home decorating consultant; and Freda Diamond, a designer who helped department stores coordinate their home furnishings so that shoppers would find harmonizing rather than competing patterns and colors in all departments.[9]

The work of the designer Freda Diamond for Libbey over a forty-year period took advantage of the latest inventions in shaping and decorating, yet coordinated with modern ideas of design (cat. 173). Silk screening with colors and gold and acid etching became hallmarks of Libbey's glass (fig. 2.23). Although it was no longer considered a prestige product, Libbey glass- and bar-ware featuring stylish decoration was ubiquitous in American restaurants and homes by the 1960s. Libbey closed the last of its hand-cutting shops in 1962 and escalated its manufacturing and marketing of mass-produced glass.[10] Selling much of its product in boxed "Hostess Sets," Libbey was extremely successful in the 1960s and 1970s. One of its patterns, *Golden Foliage* (1956) reached the thirty-million-piece mark before it was withdrawn from production in 1977. Similar success was seen in the 1980s (cat. 74).

By the early 1990s Libbey had acquired Syracuse China and had four thousand employees and five factories. In 1993 the firm became a publicly held company listed on the New York Stock Exchange, and reported sales in more than one hundred countries worldwide. The transformation from luxury-glass producer to a maker of machine-made utilitarian wares has been a successful strategy indeed for Libbey.[11]

Notes

1. For more information on the New England Glass Company and Libbey Glass, see Wilson 1972, Fairfield 1960, and Fauster 1979.

2. See Spillman and Frantz 1990, 40, for a color illustration.

3. Wilson and Nelson 1996, 753.

4. For an illustration of this bowl and cups, now in the Toledo Museum of Art, see Keefe 1968, 42; for more information on glass at the Chicago fair, see Spillman 1986, 42 ff.

5. For glass at the Louisiana Purchase Exposition, see Spillman 1986, 51 ff.

6. For illustrations of the table, punch bowls, and engraved plate, now in the Toledo Museum of Art, see Keefe 1968, 45–49.

7. For reprints of the Nash and Fuerst catalogues, see Fauster 1979, 314–400.

8. Diamond interview 1997. The Division of Ceramics and Glass, National Museum of American History, Smithsonian Institution, holds Diamond's personal collection of glass designed for Libbey and her business papers.

9. "Libbey Studies Post War Designs," *CGJ* 135:5 (Nov. 1944): 48.

10. "Industry News," *CGJ* 169:2 (Aug. 1961): 44.

11. Matranga 1997, 126–27.

A River of Glass

The importance of the skilled presser of glass tableware did not decline in the overall production scheme even as the mechanization of the typical table-glass factory increased. Unlike mechanization of the bottle factories, where the craftsman's job suddenly disappeared, the machines that eliminated the skilled presser were introduced over time. The transition was so gradual that only the increase in worker productivity gave any hint of changes in the production line. Most affected were the number of molds and the kind of power used. The rotary glass press consisted of a rotating table with four to six molds and a plunger above. In the early years the machine was operated by compressed air; later electric power was used. While the new source of power made the presser's work easier, it did not change the essential composition of the shop or the presser's role in the process. The shop's output, however, increased significantly. Some smaller jobs, such as warming-in, reheating, and glazing, which had been done by boys, were taken over by machines. Finishing conveyors, introduced in 1886, were fitted with hooded gas jets, which blew on the glass objects as they passed. By this process the edges of the piece were smoothed and polished at the same time: the jobs of two skilled boys were taken up by two semiskilled boys.

The truly revolutionary change in the making of pressed glass came with the successful introduction of the semiautomatic feeder in 1917. With the addition of this new machine the automatic press now consisted of a table that rotated intermittently, its motion synchronized with the feeder, which gave it gobs of glass, and the plunger, which pressed the glass into the molds. The job of the gatherer was completely eliminated, and the work of the presser was reduced to tending the machine, thus allowing manufacturers to replace the skilled presser with a semiskilled machine operator. The last step in mechanization came when an automatic removal was perfected and the job of the take-out boy, who removed the ware from the molds, was eliminated. The finishing processes that followed had already been largely mechanized and staffed by semiskilled workers. Shapes made by the automatic pressing machines included those that were flat or opened wide at the top, such as tumblers, bowls, trays, and small stemware, like sherbet and sundae dishes.[123]

Increasing automation of the glass tableware business continued through the early twentieth century, led largely by Macbeth-Evans Glass Company, which had bought Michael Owens's automatic machinery for making lamp chimneys in 1899. Following this purchase, Macbeth-Evans set its own mechanics to work on developing automated processes for making tableware. By 1930 the company's chief mechanical engineer, Charles Schuck, had developed an automated process in which machinery largely handled the material and molds for pressing patterned glass. Their advertisements heralded the development, proclaiming that their goods were "styled for quality . . . priced for volume."[124] Dogwood and Petalware, both introduced between 1925 and 1930, were among the first lines of tablewares to be made by automated

machines (cat. 32). Of course, Macbeth-Evans was not the only company to recognize the value of automation. Jeannette Glass Company turned out 50 tons of glass a day using continuous-melt tanks, mold and block cooling equipment, advanced polishing methods, and automatic lehrs.[125]

Color became a major fashion concern in table glass as it had in ceramics, starting slowly in the early 1920s as an accent and becoming prevalent by 1930 (see chapter 5). The desire for color that was so prominent in the 1880s, especially in art glass, was eclipsed by the dominance of rich cut glass by the turn of the century. In the 1920s, however, consumers began to choose colored glass again. Although this can be seen most clearly in the class of ware known today as depression glass, the makers of luxury goods also added color to their wares—as stems or bowls, inclusions, overlays, and the like (cats. 29, 71).

The technological changes described above in the chemical and mass-market pressed-glass industries were essential to the development and widespread use of colored pressed glass in the late 1920s and 1930s. With automated systems this glass was pressed by the ton in patterned molds beginning in the late 1920s. In some ware the color and overall pattern help to distract the viewer from the obvious impurities in the cheap soda-lime formula. In other patterns, which are modern, clean, and streamlined, extra care in the moldmaking gave greater clarity to the pattern. Plain shapes with solid colors, like Ovide by Hazel Atlas Glass Company or Royal Ruby by Anchor Hocking Glass Company, satisfied the same desire for large color accents in the home as the solid-color pottery of J. A. Bauer Company, Homer Laughlin China Company, and Stangl Pottery.[126] Like mass-market ceramics, this mass-produced glass was also distributed as premiums, and glassmakers like Anchor Hocking, Jeannette Glass Company, and Hazel Atlas became major competitors for the makers of discount goods in earthenware.

Color in glass virtually disappeared in the 1940s, probably from a combination of events and circumstances. Scandinavian glass, largely colorless, became fashionable in the high-end market (see chapter 3). In addition mineral coloring agents grew scarce during World War II, and shortages more or less obligated glassmakers to sell colorless glass to their customers. Thus they made it popular out of necessity. In February 1942 Fostoria warned its sales staff that the Ruby, Burgundy, and Regal Blue colors would not be made "owing to some recent rulings in regard to raw materials."[127] Cobalt for the blue and zinc oxide for the ruby hues were no longer available. Furthermore, restrictions on lead meant that the burgundy color could not be produced, since it required a lead-based glass rather than the soda-lime formula.

The interest in color returned during the 1950s, again due to a combination of circumstances. Among other considerations, the scarcity that had ruled wartime markets changed greatly: mineral coloring agents were available again, and rising family incomes of the 1950s enabled householders to update their home furnishings, including glass, and leave the drab, colorless war years behind. In 1952 Libbey advertised its new *Emerald Flair* glass sets as combining "the same shape selected for 'Good Design' by the Museum of Modern Art" and "the most popular glassware color—glowing emerald green." Anchor Hocking's *Forest Green*, a bold geometric design, was in production from 1950 to 1967.[128] Fostoria too introduced a series of new colors along with new shapes; these included the *Precedence* shape in *Black Onyx* and *Biscayne* in *Gold* (cat. 72).

STRATEGIES FOR SURVIVAL

After World War II American glassmakers enjoyed a period of prosperity because most European factories did not come back into production immediately and the Asian industry was still small. Gradually, however, the European factories resumed exports to the United States and were increasingly redesigned for automation. The Asian industry, especially in Japan and Taiwan, was strengthened to compete internationally, leaving the American luxury glass industry to die a slow,

Cat. 71 Morgantown Glass Works specialized in an almost infinite variety of barware.

painful death. Automation for the American companies at this late stage was expensive and offered little promise of return. And the market was so small to begin with that there was little ground to contest. In 1965, for example, France's 20 percent share of the market for imported crystal in America was worth hardly more than $500,000.[129] As a result American producers began to go out of business. One of the first major casualties was the venerable A. H. Heisey & Co. of Newark, Ohio, which closed in 1958.

One example typical of the traditional approach to table-glass making during this period is Fostoria Glass Company, which passed through the war years and emerged in much the same form as it had been in the 1930s—privately owned, independently operated, and making relatively high-end table glass with little automation (see pp. 174–78). During the 1970s, when the impact of foreign automation was beginning to be felt in the American industry, Fostoria chose to automate rather than die. In 1972 it upgraded its continuous tank to melt high-quality "crystal" glass and was among the first hand-method glass factories to do this. After installing the continuous-melt tank, the company began to automate many operations, hoping to prosper from using a combination of hand and machine methods.

While the increased production capacity might have been dramatic, the initial investment was large—so costly in fact that shops making glass by hand simply continued until there were no more orders, rather than try to compete with cheaper glassware made in automated foreign factories by lower-paid labor.[130] Despite efforts by quality glassmakers to teach retail sales staff and consumers that handmade glass had qualities unmatched by the machine-made alternative, the only difference apparent to consumers was the price. Fostoria closed its doors in 1986, preceded to its grave by other American quality glassmakers including Seneca Glass Company (closed 1983) and Tiffin Glass (closed 1984).

Although there was some modernizing during this period,

Cat. 72 During the middle years of the 20th century, Fostoria Glass Company provided a wide range of stemware, from clear to colored.

some firms survived by adapting in other ways to the difficult market conditions caused by less expensive imported glass. Bryce Brothers of Mount Pleasant, Pennsylvania, is a good case in point. The Bryce family's progenitor in glassmaking was James Bryce, who apprenticed to Bakewell, Page and Bakewell in 1827 and established his own glass factory in 1850 in Pittsburgh as Bryce, McKee and Company, which made the typical mix of flint-glass tableware, oil lamps, apothecary glass, and bottles. By the end of the nineteenth century the Bryce family was doing business as Bryce Brothers Company and had built a new factory in Mount Pleasant, southeast of Pittsburgh, housing more than four hundred workers who made a variety of ware (cat. 46). Like Fostoria and any number of other Ohio, West Virginia, and western Pennsylvania glasshouses during the early twentieth century, Bryce concentrated on barware in the early years, shifting production to domestic tableware with the coming of Prohibition in 1921. During the 1920s and 1930s Bryce's business was good, including even colored and cut table glass in the 1920s. Their pattern *Georgian* was used in the White House from 1933 into the 1940s, and a relationship developed with the U.S. State Department for Bryce to supply glass for the embassies.

During the 1950s Bryce made all the right moves for the survival of a traditional hand shop. Eva Zeisel designed *Silhouette* for them in 1952. Bryce stemware was included in the traveling exhibition *American Contemporary Glass* in 1954. And a brandy inhaler designed by Garth Huxtable for the famous Four Seasons restaurant in New York was selected by the Museum of Modern Art for its permanent twentieth-century design collection. Instead of automating its shop, the company instituted an apprenticeship program in the mid-1950s to ensure that traditional glassmaking skills would be perpetuated. All this time the company continued to be owned by the Bryce family and operated by family members. In the early 1960s Lenox China, with ready cash from its meteoric postwar rise to prominence in the American dinnerware market, was anxious to acquire a glass company in the hope of gaining control of even more of the U.S tabletop. Although the Dalzell family, who had controlled Fostoria since the turn of the century, decided to keep the firm independent, the Bryce family was ready to reap what financial rewards were to be had after more than a century in the glass business.

In 1965 Lenox China acquired the name and assets of Bryce Brothers. Lenox immediately changed the name of the domestic line to Lenox Crystal and went to work marketing the new name and tying the product to their enormously successful bridal registry efforts. At the same time, Lenox simplified the glass requirements for the proper tabletop in the same way that it had streamlined the modern upscale china table setting in the early 1950s. Retailers preferred to carry shorter lines with fewer stock units. Fostoria sales manager T. G. Lightner demonstrated similar market insight in 1966 when he proposed Fostoria could reduce the number of pieces in a place setting rather than charge more for dinner sets.[131] Furthermore, the consumer had some impact on changing the makeup of the stemware set for the table as well. For ex-

ample, *Gift and Tableware Reporter* published results of its study tracking a five-year trend in the early 1960s that showed wineglasses gaining on water goblets for the primary spot on the table among stemware shapes. Wine, goblet, and champagne stems were the basic shapes for the modern table according to bridal registries. The report from Atlanta was that "so many people have been abroad and learned that it's safe and smart to drink wine with meals" that a local retailer had doubled its sales of wineglasses over the past five years.[132] As discussed in the preceding chapter, the new interest in what to drink and how was spurred by the increase in home entertaining that was driving barware sales up as well during this period.

The younger shopper was a different buyer than her mother and grandmother. A 1961 survey of more than thirty-three thousand consumers by Jeannette Glass Company, a mass table-glass maker, showed that, "today's preference is for gay, colorful patterns. The trend is away from the dignified, quality look. Imitation cut glass, while still popular with the more mature shopper, has lost out to floral, bird and animal patterns with the younger set." The study also reported "a definite preference for less expensive glassware." For the older consumer the average household had one good set and one everyday set, but young buyers challenged these long-held notions and bought "different sets of glasses for various purposes—formal, informal, family, picnic, etc." The average American household contained three or four sets of glasses, comprising fifty to one hundred individual items in the cupboard. "Although there were taste differences between age groups," according to the report, "none was found to exist among the various income and ethnic groupings."[133]

By the early 1970s it was already apparent that young consumers were rejecting many of the homemaking standards of previous generations. Fine china, cut lead crystal, and sterling silver did not fit into the casual way of life that valued the function of objects more than their cost and care. Stoneware, machine-made glass, and stainless served the same purposes as china, crystal, and silver. The time needed to care for these finer materials could be better spent in more interesting ways.[134] In ceramics, companies like Lenox introduced casual high-fired products like *Temperware* (1972) and later *Chinastone* (1985) to answer some of these needs. In glass, foreign makers supplied Americans with stylish yet inexpensive wares.

Another approach to the postwar market was to dramatically change a company's product focus, remaining in the table-glass business but working the broad base of the market rather than the tiny tip at the top. Libbey, long a maker of elite tableware, ultimately gave up on its traditional market following the war. In 1936 Libbey Glass became a subsidiary of Owens-Illinois Glass Company, a container company spun off of Libbey years earlier during the era of Michael Owens's glass-processing inventions. Despite several attempts to establish design excellence in Libbey's products during the 1930s and early 1940s, the company decided finally that there was not enough breadth to the elite market to continue following the commitment of the Libbey family to traditional glass methods (cat. 73).

Cat. 73 Libbey Glass Company and its rival, Seneca Glass Company, enticed depression-weary shoppers with crystal of innovative design and fine workmanship.

OPPOSITE:

Cat. 74 Mechanically blown and decorated by silk screening, Libbey Glass Company's *Golden Foliage* was a smash hit when introduced in 1956.

In 1944, while the company was producing materials for the war effort, a small committee of in-house designers and managers and consulting stylists was revamping the company's focus. During the war Libbey made tubes for electrical devices and tableware for restaurants, hospitals, and other essential institutions. The company had developed a product enhancement by the trade name Safedge in which heat treating made vessels extra resistant to breakage by mechanical or thermal shock. In 1944 the company announced that it hoped to apply the development to retail lines after the war and instituted a new design development department to examine new products for the postwar period (cat. 74). The mass-produced glassware made by Libbey in the mid-twentieth century was extremely successful and allowed the company not only to survive but also to grow.

Fostoria Glass Company

Glass men from Wheeling, West Virginia, established the Fostoria Glass Company in December 1887 to take advantage of the free natural gas offered by the town fathers of Fostoria, Ohio, as an inducement to industrial users with the money to set up a factory. Operations started in 1888 in Fostoria, and the enterprise was immediately successful. Observers of the glass industry noted in January 1890 how Fostoria had chosen to imitate cut-glass products in order to make them more affordable to a broader audience of consumers:

> The Fostoria Glass Company . . . makes another encroachment of pressed ware upon the lines in which cut ware had been superior. Seen from a distance the magnificent Banquet Candelabra with its pendants, looks as rich and imposing as cut glass. This handsome ornament is now placed in reach of many who could not afford the enormous expense of the real cut glass article. It is matched by smaller ware intended for the same purpose and the whole line of ware ought to find eager purchasers.[1]

And indeed they did sell. However, the glass company's success doomed the village of Fostoria, which could not provide sufficient resources for production.

The gas boom in Ohio seems to have affected all the small towns that were anywhere near a gas field. Banners in Findlay, for example, boasted of the town's good fortune: "Findlay, Where Women Don't Have To Chop Wood."[2] Fostoria itself had no gas nearby, but it did have railroad access with five lines that converged in the town, and the village piped gas from faraway fields. Unfortunately for Fostoria, and nearby competitors, the fields that were tapped were rather shallow and not sufficient to supply the factory, which closed on December 31, 1891. The Dalzell family, who then had controlling interest, moved the factory to nearby Moundsville, West Virginia. The move to Moundsville did not adversely affect its profitability—quite the contrary.

Key craftsmen in the early period of the company included Henry and Jacob Crimmel, from Belmont Glass Company in Bellaire, Ohio, who had worked previously at Hobbs, Brockunier & Co. in Wheeling. Charles E. Beam, a moldmaker who later went to Indiana, where he worked for other glasshouses, may well have been responsible for the company's early work. As the mold shop foreman, Beam was also the designer of shapes, both molded and blown. When production was shifted from utility glassware to fine tableware and decorative pieces in 1925, a separate design department was established.[3]

Fostoria's significant early work includes the patterns *Victoria,* the most famous of the early period, and *Frosted Artichoke.* The cut-glass look-alike patterns, such as *Foster*

Block, which resembles heavy cane, were standouts for the company. In tableware the primary items were accessory pieces—cream and sugar sets, tumblers, spoon holders, and celery vases at the beginning. From the turn of the century until 1915 the company concentrated on oil lamps, "selling these colorful lighting devices by the thousands."[4] After lamps, Fostoria moved into commercial blown stemware and barware for institutions. But when Prohibition undercut the market for commercial barware, Fostoria switched to making domestic table glass, using its seasoned artisans to produce for the higher end of the market. During these early years of fine tableware production, with W. A. B. Dalzell and C. B. Roe at the helm, Fostoria became known for twisted work, deep-cut tableware, and etched glassware.[5] The company enlarged steadily and by 1926 had ten thousand different items in its catalogue, including some of the first glass dinnerware. The number of employees at this time—around 650—represented the peak in the company's workforce and the overall profitability of the firm before the depression and World War II dramatically changed the market.

Company president David B. Dalzell stated in 1950 that Fostoria's competition came "from three sources: other companies in the domestic trade, imports, and automatic machinery." At the time Fostoria was "even with the other top companies" in terms of price comparisons, but Dalzell noted that "machines are encroaching deeper and deeper into our field, a striking example of this being in the tumbler orders."[6] Although Fostoria was attempting to answer the automated competition with a continuous-melt tank for lead crystal, the firm would not add significantly to the automation of its shaping techniques for another twenty years.

Fostoria did initiate an aggressive design program during the 1930s and 1940s in an effort to stay ahead of its competition. In 1929 George Sakier was hired as a design consultant and charged with modernizing the firm's lines. A former art director at several important fashion magazines, Sakier was well aware of both European art deco and American streamline styling that were just becoming popular in the United States in the late 1920s. Soon after his arrival, Fostoria was producing Sakier's designs for modernist vases, giftware, barware, and stemware. Among the highlights of Sakier's early work for Fostoria were his *Mayfair* dinnerware (1930; cat. 75), the no. 4020 decanter (ca. 1930), and *Westchester* stemware (1934; cats. 72, 76). Bold in shape and often striking in color, such products attracted considerable publicity for Fostoria during the depression and helped establish its name as a maker of quality glassware.[7]

OPPOSITE:
Cat. 75 One of the earliest glass dinner services, *Mayfair* (1930) was declared "simply perfect for the most particular hostess."

Cat. 77 The acid-etched patterns on these 1930–31 pieces by Morgantown Glass Works and Tiffin Glass include art deco–style bathing beauties under palm trees.

Although Sakier remained for fifty years and Fostoria made some efforts to automate production, the company did not prosper in the 1950s (cat. 72). Imports increased steadily, and the products faced competition from metal, plastic, and wood tableware, although management's fears of alternative materials were probably exaggerated. The company's directors did notice that consumers were purchasing glass for gifts and expanded this category. These adjustments in technology and product likely made some impact on the bottom line; earnings during the 1960s showed much less volatility than during the previous two decades or the one that was to follow.[8]

In 1965 Fostoria bought the West Virginia Company Morgantown Glassware Guild (formerly Morgantown Glass Works). Morgantown, which had a long tradition of making

OPPOSITE:
Cat. 76 Classically elegant, this decanter and glass set was available in a range of colors from Fostoria Glass Company in the early 1930s.

fine stemware, had recently become famous as the maker of official White House table glass (cats. 6, 71, 77, 135). First Lady Jacqueline Kennedy had chosen Morgantown glass for its simple elegance and craftsmanship, and Fostoria sought to capitalize on the perception of Morgantown products as being youthful in design and spirit in contrast to Fostoria's reputation for old-fashioned quality. Morgantown was also very prominent in the commercial sphere of glass sales, supplying barware to a wide range of institutional customers. The White House connection would allow Fostoria to promote Morgantown to the lower end of the consumer market for handmade glass—the entry area populated by brides and young married women who wanted to entertain stylishly but could not afford luxury glass (cat. 36).[9]

Unfortunately, Fostoria had not anticipated the sea change in commercial accounts nor the reorganization of glass departments in retail outlets. For two years Morgantown was profitable, but then restaurants began switching to machine-made glass which was more economical to replace when broken. In addition department stores decided to eliminate secondary sources and concentrate their efforts on the major suppliers with high name recognition for consumers. Morgantown, already on the fringes of the domestic tabletop market, was dropped from glass departments across the country. After three years of struggling to stabilize Morgantown's sales, Fostoria gave up and closed the factory in 1971.[10]

In the same year Fostoria developed a retailing relationship with Pickard China Company to distribute a new coordinated line of china and crystal. For retail firms that agreed to stock and display a certain selection of patterns in main and branch stores, the companies would give discounts together. For example, the central store was expected to carry the whole new *Vision* line plus six patterns in the regular line.[11] Perhaps this was a way to achieve a tabletop coordination as Lenox China and Bryce Brothers (Lenox Crystal) had done during the late 1960s, but in the case of Fostoria and Pickard, one company did not have to buy the other.

Fostoria learned a great deal by looking critically at its unfortunate decisions in acquiring and marketing Morgantown Glassware Guild. When management surveyed the company's operations, they saw how far they were from the innovative production methods developed by their foreign competitors. The years after the war had been prosperous enough to encourage the company in its traditional approach to the tabletop, but by the 1970s the importation of automatically pressed lead-crystal tableware had increased sharply. Unfortunately, Fostoria had not fully anticipated these market changes by developing production facilities to

meet the competition. During this period the company concentrated on making the transition from the old Fostoria, which relied on hand methods, to a new Fostoria using combined hand and machine methods.

The transition was expensive. For example, a hand press cost about $15,000, and the equipment for a hand-blowing shop, about $13,000. In both of these hand operations, six to ten workers could produce four to six hundred good pieces of glassware per day. On the other hand, an automatic press cost $300,000, and using a continuous-melt tank with automatic equipment, three to fifteen workers could produce more than ten thousand good pieces of glassware in twenty-four hours. In addition, a set of molds for one stemware line made by either pressing or blowing cost $13,000 to $15,000, while the molds for an automatic press cost approximately $130,000.[12] Fostoria gambled that its investments in technology would pay off over time, but as it happened, the company was not in business long enough to reap the benefits.

Strikes during the early 1970s, in response to the automation of certain processes, put the company further behind by undermining its ability to deliver goods on time.[13] By 1980 Fostoria's commercial division was losing money rapidly, and the company's attempt to supplement its giftware program with imports was a disaster. Fostoria was sold out of family hands to Lancaster Colony Glass and closed altogether in 1986.[14] With the passing of Fostoria Glass, another giant in the American tableware field had fallen, leaving the market more susceptible to foreign dominance.

Notes

1. *Fostoria Review* (9 Jan. 1890), quoting from *National Glass Budget*, cited in Murray 1972, 12.

2. For background history on the village of Fostoria and other glass companies established in the town, see Murray 1972.

3. See "Fostoria Company History," unpublished typescript, ca. 1960, Fostoria Archives.

4. *American Glass Review* (15 Jan. 1963): 8.

5. Ibid.

6. Fostoria minutes, 26 Jan. 1950, Fostoria Archives.

7. For a lengthy discussion of Sakier's work for Fostoria, see Piña 1996.

8. David B. Dalzell, president of Fostoria, letter to stockholders, 1978, Fostoria Archives.

9. "Promotional Plans for Morgantown Glassware Guild, Inc.," unpublished typescript, 1966, Fostoria Archives.

10. "Fostoria Glass Company Closes Morgantown Glassware Guild, Inc.," press release, 1971, Fostoria Archives.

11. H. A. Pickard Jr., to D. Dalzell Sr., 25 Aug. 1971, Fostoria memorandum, Fostoria Archives.

12. David B. Dalzell, president of Fostoria, letter to stockholders, 1979, Fostoria Archives.

13. David B. Dalzell, president of Fostoria, letter to stockholders, 1975, Fostoria Archives.

14. David B. Dalzell, president of Fostoria, letter to stockholders, 1980, Fostoria Archives.

OUTPRODUCED AND UNDERPRICED: FOREIGN COMPETITION

As the English, French, and Germans rebuilt their glass industries after the war, several manufacturers saw the possibilities of automated tableware production. Chance Brothers and United Glass Bottle Manufacturers took the lead in Britain, producing tons of ware for the home market with machinery imported from the United States. United Glass, for example, purchased new technology from the Libbey Division of Owens-Illinois in 1948 to make automated stemware.[135] In the 1960s automated screen-printing equipment was exported to England from the United States. These are not isolated incidents of U.S. companies exporting technology to foreign markets. Corning sold the British Empire patent rights for borosilicate glass (Pyrex) to James A. Jobling of Sunderland in 1921.[136]

The association that ultimately exacted real damage to the homegrown American industry was the collaboration between Wheaton Industries of Millville, New Jersey, and J. G. Durand & Cie of Arques, France. As discussed in chapter 3, Durand is today the world's largest manufacturer of lead-crystal and glass tableware, bakeware, and cookware, with 12,000 employees producing nearly five million pieces of ware a day. The company exports 75 percent of its production, and the United States takes 25 percent of that exported ware. Given such massive production and marketing power, few American companies could compete. The one major exception was Corning Glass Works.

Having stressed research and development since the turn of the century, Corning built on the foundation it had established with Pyrex in the postwar years. In 1947 the company launched a line of kitchenware made of opaque glass decorated with color that was sprayed on before the final tempering process. This line was based on dishes that Corning had developed during the war for use in military mess halls and hospitals. Utilizing shock-resistant Pyrex glass, the line was soon broadened to include numerous forms suitable for use on the domestic table (cat. 78). These products were extremely popular and encouraged Corning to move further into the tableware market. In 1958 it introduced Corning-ware, which was made from glass first used in rocket nose cones. Four years later came *Pyroceram*, in the form of *Centura* dinnerware, followed in 1970 by the *Corelle* line, created from *Comcor* glass. This new substance was produced by laminating

Cat. 78 Although initially developed for military use, Corning Glass Work's shock-resistant Pyrex glass was eagerly embraced on the homefront in the postwar era.

together three layers of glass. To the chagrin of pottery-makers, all these products were extremely successful. In the 1960s and early 1970s *Centura* made serious inroads into the fine china market because it was designed to look like porcelain but was far more durable. By the mid-1990s 76 percent of American households owned Corningware.[137]

The United States has lobbied for the eventual opening of a worldwide marketplace for virtually all consumer goods since World War II through the GATT treaties; these agreements are negotiated regularly and have greatly reduced the tariffs that used to protect small industries like china- and glass-making. Although there is an identifiable American market, and manufacturers here and abroad use many market research techniques to understand it, America is now part of a much wider market of china and glass manufacturing. Japanese (Noritake) and French (Durand) manufacturers have learned this lesson, but with few exceptions American makers, for want of capital investment or vision, have yet to venture very far into the international arena except as exporters of glass technology and importers of goods manufactured for them abroad for sale in the United States under their brand names. Few American companies have made significant inroads into foreign markets, nor have they manufactured abroad to sell to those foreign markets.

Although the U.S. market for china and glass tableware is enormous compared to other places around the globe, the American producer has been relatively small compared to manufacturers of automobiles, structural steel, and other industrial goods. But the products of the tableware makers are among the most appealing of home furnishings, and the changes that have unfolded industry-wide over the past century are dramatic. Tariffs, invention and automation, design and marketing, and the persistence of craftsmanship offer fascinating stories, and the entrepreneurial nature of these industries is exhilarating. While few fortunes have been made by manufacturing china or glass, many have been lost. Numerous individual potteries and glasshouses have prevailed over long periods of time, but the general story of the industry is one of struggle and decline during the twentieth century. Using widely disparate market strategies, glass companies like Lenox Crystal, Libbey, and Corning and potteries like Lenox China and Homer Laughlin China have survived depressions, wars, and foreign and domestic competition. All of these firms have been blessed with inspired thinking at critical junctures. Ultimately, however, no history of a single company can account for the complex story of china and glass production in America.

Notes

1. For a general guide to ceramics in colonial homes, see Hume 1970.

2. Quoted in Schwind 1984, 33, from Rhinelander's records at the New-York Historical Society. On how foreign ceramics were traded in North America, see Blaszczyk 1984, 7–20; and Miller 1984b, 37–50.

3. For the history of Chinese export porcelain for the American market, see Mudge 1981.

4. French ceramics in the early United States are discussed in Detweiler 1982, 87–110; for nineteenth-century White House china, see Klapthor 1999.

5. For information on Limoges, France, as a center of china making, see d'Albis and Romanet 1980 and Meslin-Perrier 1996; illustrations of Limoges china popular in America can be found in Gaston 1996.

6. Haviland's Limoges operation is discussed in d'Albis 1988, Villa Terrace 1992, and Valiere 1992; for illustrations of Haviland's Limoges china, see Travis 1998.

7. For a review of American pottery before 1850, see Myers 1977, 1–13; for an analysis of the early potter in the American economy, see Myers 1984, 190–233.

8. Hume describes how he identified pottery excavated from the site of seventeenth-century Wolstenholme Town, Virginia, as having been made in colonial Virginia; see Hume 1987.

9. For Berkeley's Green Spring Plantation, see Caywood 1955; for the Coxe-DeWilde pottery, see Springsted 1985, 9–46.

10. Watkins 1968, 24–33.

11. For more on these vital trade networks for pottery, see Denker 1986, 21–36.

12. On Boston, see Watkins 1968, 40; for Bartlam, see South 1993; for Ellis, see Zug 1986, 71–72, and Bivins 1972, 24–26.

13. Stradling and Denker 1997. In addition to stoneware beverage vessels, the pottery also made pearlware plates in the 1830s decorated with blue transfer prints copied from the *Canova* pattern of William Ridgway's pottery in Staffordshire, England.

14. New Jersey 1972.

15. Bennett immigrated first to Jersey City to work for the Hendersons and later founded the pottery industry in East Liverpool, Ohio. See Stradling and Denker 1997 and Gates 1984, 30–33; for the Troy venture, see Stefano 1974, 553–55.

16. For background information on early porcelain making in America, see Frelinghuysen 1989, 6–8.

17. On Bonnin and Morris, see Hood 1972.

18. On Tucker, see Curtis 1972, 339–74; and Frelinghuysen 1989, 14–21, 83–105.

19. See Frelinghuysen 1989, for illustration of the Mead vase (p. 79), the DeCasse and Chanou tea set (p. 81), the Jersey City bowl (p. 82), and for text on all these pieces (pp. 11–14).

20. Stradling 1997, 88.

21. Frelinghuysen 1989, 24; for the Brooklyn porcelain makers, see 21–27 and 108–19.

22. For background on the development of Trenton's pottery industry, see Denker and Denker 1984, 56–67; and Denker 1989, 8–16.

23. On East Liverpool's pottery industry, see Gates 1984, 1–74.

24. Ibid., 33, 37.

25. Gates and Ormerod 1982, 3–5.

26. Cited in Goldberg 1983, 27.

27. *CGJ* 1:5 (23 Jan. 1875): 4–5.

28. For an illustration of this mark, see Gates and Ormerod 1982, 131.

29. Young 1878, 444–45.

30. Gates 1984, 77.

31. For general information on glass in early American homes, see Hume 1970.

32. For an overview of American glass history, see Spillman and Frantz 1990.

33. On Wistar, see Palmer 1976, 75–101.

34. On Stiegel, see Palmer 1989, 202–39.

35. On Amelung, see Lanmon et al. 1990.

36. Madarasz 1998, 36,144.

37. Madarasz discusses Bryce's history; see Madarasz 1998, 144. Through subsequent family partnerships and a move to Mount Pleasant, Pennsylvania, the current Lenox Crystal company is descended from Bryce's first enterprise.

38. Wilson 1972, 198–229.

39. Watkins 1945.

40. For more information on Mount Washington Glass Works, see Wilson 1972, 297–300.

41. *Commercial Gazette* (Boston), 13 Apr. 1818, cited in Wilson 1972, 230.

42. U.S. Census of 1820, cited in Wilson 1972, 230.

43. For the New England Glass Company, see Wilson 1972, 232–33.

44. For an illustration of the goblet, ca. 1870–75, that Vaupel considered his best work, see Spillman and Frantz 1990, 40.

45. Wilson and Nelson 1996, 753.

46. On the Boston and Sandwich Glass Company, see Wilson 1972, 261–84.

47. *Daily Evening Transcript* (Boston), 8 Sept. 1832, cited in Wilson 1972, 264.

48. For the Bloomingdale Flint Glass Works and Brooklyn Glass Works, see Revi 1965, 103; for the Jersey Glass Company, see Spillman and Frelinghuysen 1990, 707–17.

49. See ad illustrated in Spillman and Frelinghuysen 1990, 711.

50. For the Union Flint Glass Company, see Spillman and Frantz 1990, 24; for the Franklin Flint Glass Works and Gillinder Brothers, see Revi 1965, 255–56; for Dorflinger, see Feller 1988.

51. Blaszczyk 1995, 93.

52. Anderson 1938, 14.

53. USPA 1883, 8.

54. *CGJ* 1:5 (23 Jan.1875): 5.

55. *CGJ* 47:9 (3 Mar. 1898): 28.

56. Young 1878, 458.

57. Barber 1909, 180. Before his death, Carr contributed a serialized autobiography to *Crockery and Glass Journal* published in six installments in volume 53 (21 Mar.–25 Apr. 1901); Barber also notes that Carr had recently (ca. 1890) built retail stores on the land where his pottery had stood, "the rentals from which, he claims, yield him better returns than potting" (Barber 1909, 180).

58. Young 1878, 480.

59. *CGJ* 1:5 (23 Jan. 1875): 1.

60. Goldberg 1983, 50–53. Hagley Library has a Glasgow Pottery trade catalogue dated 1878.

61. For more information on Bloor, see Frelinghuysen 1989, 28; and Gates 1984.

62. USPA 1901.

63. *Daily State Gazette* (Trenton), 14 May 1879, 3. When Lenox formed his partnership with the engraver Ulrich, the latter had been convicted of counterfeiting U.S. currency. Lenox told the court he was willing to give Ulrich a second chance in return for access to his remarkable engraving skills.

64. Blaszczyk 1994, 145; and Blaszczyk 1995, 112.

65. "The National Potters' Association," *CGJ* 1 (23 Jan. 1875): 4.

66. *CGJ* 3 (20 Apr. 1876): 14. For examples of Edge's work, see Frelinghuysen 1989, 38, 39, 159. For pictures of these exhibition pieces by Müller and Broome, see Frelinghuysen 1989, 166–92.

67. *CGJ* 3 (1 June 1876): 15, cited in Stradling 1976, 148.

68. USPA 1883, 10.

69. USPA 1937, 15.

70. USPA 1894, 12.

71. Ibid., 18–21.

72. Young 1878, 462–63.

73. Reed and Skoczen 1997.

74. The Sebring brothers, of East Liverpool and later Sebring, Ohio, did not enter the pottery business until 1887 and were not making a vitreous china body until after 1900; see Pass and Binns 1930, 90.

75. *CGJ* 10:16 (16 Oct. 1879): 21.

76. The identity of the critical Greenwood wares for comparison with Onondaga's, especially in terms of the firing sequence and use of under- or over-glaze colors, has yet to be undertaken.

77. *CGJ* 7:4 (6 June 1878), 19.

78. Blaszczyk 1995, 252, 261.

79. For more on the subject of the skilled pottery trades in Trenton, see Stern 1994.

80. U.S. Industrial Commission, *Report*, 1901, 647, cited in Stern 1994, 113.

81. For detailed discussions of the history of the trade union movement, see Shotliff 1977 and Stern 1994.

82. For pertinent quotation by Herbert Wheeler, retiring president of the American Ceramic Society, 1900, see Stern 1994, 112.

83. USPA 1917, 13.

84. USPA 1920, 22.

85. For a discussion of these new technologies at Homer Laughlin, see Blaszczyk 1995, chaps. 4, 5; and McKee 1966, 12.

86. USPA 1927, 16.

87. Ibid., 36.

88. USPA 1929, 19.

89. For more information on Bauer, see Tuchman 1995.

90. *CGJ* 120:4 (Apr. 1937): 3; see also p. 50, "Five Firms Organize California Pottery Guild in Group Campaign."

91. See especially Reed and Skoczen 1997, chaps. 6, 7.

92. For more on the history of Lenox China, see Denker 1989.

93. Ibid., 48–52.

94. Reed 1995, 44–47.

95. USPA 1942, 54.

96. USPA 1943, 37.

97. USPA 1940, 49.

98. As an example, see USPA 1940, 52.

99. USPA 1958, 12.

100. The Pfaltzgraff Pottery was incorporated with this name in 1896; however, the family traces their company to the first Pfaltzgraff potter who set up shop in 1811. The company is still in business; see Pfaltzgraff 1989.

101. See Spillman 1986, 29, for a description of the fair and exhibit; for an illustration of the Dorflinger decanter and glasses, see Wilson 1994, 637.

102. J. S. Ingram, *The Centennial Exposition Described and Illustrated*, cited in Spillman 1986, 29–30.

103. For more on glass at the Philadelphia Centennial Exposition, see Spillman 1986, 29 ff.

104. Wilson 1994, 635.

105. For more information on the *Russian* pattern, see Spillman 1989, 97–105.

106. Wilson 1994, 638.

107. For more information on glass at this fair, see Spillman 1986, 42–44.

108. Spillman 1996, 141.

109. For more on Hoare, see Spillman 1996, 17 ff.

110. For more on Hawkes, see Spillman 1996, 44 ff.

111. Dorflinger's was the first trademark. It was used on their stationery for the first time late in 1888; see Spillman 1996, 141 ff, for an extensive review of Hawkes's advertising.

112. Spillman notes that the designs shown in these early advertisements are usually the patented ones, *Brazilian*, *Chrysanthemum*, *Grecian*, and *Venetian*, although *Imperial* and the cheaper *Strawberry Diamond and Fan* appear too; see Spillman 1996, 146. Many Hawkes advertisements are illustrated by Spillman, 141–61.

113. See Wilson 1994, 640, for a comparison of cut- and art-glass prices from a Pairpoint catalogue of about 1885–90 for two cruets and salt and pepper shakers: *Rose Amber* glass, $8.50; *Burmese*, $11.00; cut glass, $16.75.

114. See Wilson 1994, 640–41. Spillman uses extensive surviving Hawkes records to present detailed information about the technology and organization of making and using blanks in the cut-glass industry; see Spillman 1996, 95 ff.

115. Wilson 1994, 642.

116. "What Is Wrong with the Cut Glass Business?," *CGJ* 102:25 (24 June 1926): 16.

117. Wilson 1994, 645.

118. H. A. Marshall, Chicago, letter to W. A. B. Dalzell, Moundsville, Ohio, 12 Feb. 1912, Fostoria Archives.

119. W. C. McCartney, Secretary, Cambridge Glass Company, letter to Carl Roe, Fostoria Glass, 10 Jan. 1936, Fostoria Archives.

120. Wilson 1994, 648.

121. For more on Owens and Libbey, see Fairfield 1960.

122. Madarasz 1998, 51–52.

123. For more information about these machines and their introduction, see Pearce 1949, 227–29.

124. Advertisement, *CGL* (Aug. 1930): 7, cited in Madarasz 1998, 64.

125. Madarasz 1998, 65.

126. For illustrations of these and many other patterns, see Brenner 1998.

127. Memo No. 114, "To All Salesmen," from Merlin DuBois, dated 18 Feb. 1942, Fostoria Archives.

128. For an illustration, see Brenner 1998, 68; for the advertisement, see Libbey advertisement, *CGJ* 151:2 (Aug. 1952): 1.

129. "French Glass: Escalates 15% Yearly in U.S.," *GTR* (19 June 1967): 1, 26.

130. David B. Dalzell, Fostoria President, letter 1977, Fostoria Archives.

131. T. G. Lightner, Fostoria Sales Manager, letter to R. B. Stevenson, Ford Motor Company Car Sales Promotion, Dearborn, Mich., 7 July 1966. Ford was using Fostoria sets as premiums for Thunderbird owners; Fostoria Archives.

132. "Rise in Wine Glass Volume Tops Stemware Trends; Goblets Slip," *GTR* (1 June 1964): 1.

133. "Jeannette Polls Housewife," *CGJ* 169:3 (Sept. 1961): 29.

134. "New Life Styles—So; Now What?" *GTR* (Dec. 1970): 1.

135. Owens-Illinois owns United Glass today; see Jackson 1997, 74.

136. Jackson 1997, 78.

137. Ibid., 132–33.

Foreigners at Our Table: Imported China and Glass

Chapter 3

American made crockery is well known to be inferior to the English and French manufacture.

—Sears, Roebuck & Co. 1897 catalogue

Between 1880 and 1980 the United States emerged as a nation of voracious consumers of manufactured goods, and ceramic and glass tableware was no exception. Although statistics on overall foreign and American production are almost impossible to compare effectively, the United States was most likely the largest purchaser of tableware in the world during this period, until the recent economic unification of Europe brought together a larger number of affluent consumers.

Americans and their elaborate tables garnered the attention of manufacturers all over the world—especially makers of refined ceramic and glass tablewares. In 1901 about 30 percent by value of all ceramic tableware consumed in the United States was foreign made. Eleven years later imports had dropped to around 21 percent due to expanded domestic production. The total consumption of refined earthenware and porcelain had actually increased, however. By 1934, 32 percent by volume of the ceramic tableware consumed in this country was foreign made.

During World War II American producers made great inroads into their own domestic market, and thus foreign sales declined. In 1959 only 24 percent of combined earthenware and china consumption was accounted for by foreign dishes. In a little over a decade the trend had reversed again, and that figure had more than doubled, to 57.5 percent by volume.[1] Given that much of the pottery produced in the United States by midcentury was institutional ware for hotels and restaurants, the use of foreign dishes in American homes was likely even higher than indicated by these totals.

Judging from official government figures, foreign producers of glass had a more difficult time than ceramics makers gaining a place at the American table because the domestic glass industry was so strong. Although it is difficult to determine exactly how much foreign table glass was imported by Americans because the statistics do not separate table glass from other types of glass such as glass tubing, lighting devices, and electric lightbulbs, a general picture can be drawn. Glass imports peaked around 1890 and then declined through World War I, after which imports rebounded to about half their late-nineteenth-century high. They sank again during World War II and in the immediate decades thereafter. According to industry observers, at least half of all thin-walled blown tableware used in the United States before World War I was produced abroad. The high tariffs placed on imported blown-glass tableware in the late nineteenth and twentieth centuries were

OPPOSITE:
Japanese-inspired decoration (detail, cat. 83).

185

specifically aimed at protecting American production of this type from extinction by foreign competition (see p. 199).[2]

This situation changed as mechanical blowing and cutting transformed the domestic table glass industry. Adapting technology developed for the bottle industry, producers of generic blown glassware such as tumblers, barware, and inexpensive stemware were able to dramatically lower their production costs and thus successfully compete with foreign manufacturers of the same type of ware. Throughout the 1950s and 1960s, for example, imported glass made up less than 3 percent of all table glass used here. As foreign industry recovered somewhat in the early 1970s, this total rose to 5 percent in 1972.[3] Although these percentages were small, the American market was so huge by the mid-twentieth century that a share of it was still vitally important to many overseas producers.

The French

The outbreak of war in 1914 was a watershed event in the history of china and glass in America. During the four years of conflict, European manufacturers who had supplied the United States with substantial quantities of china and glassware retreated from this market, some ceasing exports altogether. In the case of glass and glassware, imports were at a twenty-two-year high in 1914 but had plummeted to a mere 22 percent of this total by 1916.[4] When shipments of china and glass resumed after the war, market conditions in this country had changed.

More than any other major tableware supplier to the U.S. market, France lost the most as a result of World War I. Thanks in large part to the efforts of David Haviland and his New York import house, Haviland Brothers & Co. (see pp. 193–98), French porcelain produced in Limoges had dominated the American market for expensive china since the mid-nineteenth century. Although before the war far more porcelain and earthenware came to the United States from England and Germany, American consumers found French ceramics the most fashionable and prestigious.[5] French imports set the standard against which rival domestic and foreign china was judged, and as a result sales of French porcelain to America's middle and upper classes were strong before World War I. Between 1892 and 1913 (excepting 1907) France's total ceramics exports to the United States ranked third by value in comparison to other nations' exports.[6]

The strength of the French position is further evidenced by the fact that in 1907 the American Potters Association successfully lobbied for an embargo on French porcelain because Limoges was shipping so much of its high-grade ware to the United States. French imports temporarily declined. Although the embargo lasted only from February to June, it dropped France from third place in overall U.S. imports of china and severely hurt Gallic manufacturers, who were dependent on the American market. This dependency is reflected in the sales of Theodore Haviland & Co. In 1914, for example, 70 percent of the firm's earnings were accounted for by U.S. sales.[7]

During the war and for a period afterward, French potteries were unable to ship ware to the United States due to labor, fuel, and transportation shortages.[8] This cessation acted as a catalyst for change in two ways. First, the traditional Limoges look of delicately molded shapes in white porcelain, often decorated with floral designs in light, pastel colors, went out of fashion (cats. 2, 79). Consumers in the post–World War I years preferred bolder, more geometric shapes and brighter colors. Second, the void left by the stoppage of high-quality French imports and the demise of a long-popular dinnerware aesthetic created opportunities for other foreign manufacturers, especially German, Czech, English, and above all Japanese potteries, to improve their positions in the U.S. market. American manufacturers also took advantage of the decline in French imports to bolster their own position in the marketplace.

American consumers ceased to view French porcelains as the most fashionable or prestigious product by the early 1920s, leading to the decline of the famous firm of Haviland & Co. (at that time a separate firm from Theodore Haviland & Co.) and its most important rivals, Charles Ahrenfeldt & Son and Vogt & Dose. While the Haviland story is well known, the history of the other firms is not. Charles Ahrenfeldt was a New York tableware importer who, like Haviland, realized the great potential in selling high-quality French porcelain to Americans.[9] Ahrenfeldt founded his firm in 1831 and made his initial trip to Limoges to secure better ware fit for the U.S. market in 1848. Working with potteries in Limoges for the next four decades, Ahrenfeldt commissioned lines of expensive tableware specifically designed for American consumers. Following his father's death, Charles Jules Ahrenfeldt took over and expanded the business. In 1896 he built a pottery in Limoges primarily to supply the firm's New York showroom. Although the firm won a grand prize at the 1904 Saint Louis world's fair, Ahrenfeldt & Son gave up distributing its own ware in the United States in 1910, and the importing house of Herman C. Kupper, Inc., became the French factory's sole American distributor.[10]

The history of Vogt & Dose is similar to that of Haviland & Co. and Ahrenfeldt & Son. John Vogt, a German immigrant, established a china import house in New York in 1840. Later he opened a porcelain decorating studio in Limoges and eventually another in New York. By 1865 the firm was trading as Vogt & Dose after John Vogt's son Charles and his nephew Frederic Dose entered the business. John Vogt's second son, Gustav, was managing the Limoges buying office and decorating shop by 1870. In 1891 Gustav Vogt and a partner, Emilien Tressemanes, purchased two small factories in Limoges and began producing porcelain for the U.S. market. Back in New York the import house was taken over by Dose in 1886 and then by Gustav Vogt, who installed his son Charly as manager while he remained in Limoges to oversee tableware production.[11] President and Mrs. Benjamin Harrison honored the firm with a commission for a White House service in 1892 (cat. 80).

Cat. 79 Before World War I, delicate French porcelain like this example from Haviland & Co. was the height of elegance in America.

IN THE WAKE OF WAR

By World War I, Haviland & Co., Ahrenfeldt & Son, and Vogt & Dose, along with Theodore Haviland & Co., L. Bernardaud & Cie., and Nathan Straus & Sons, dominated the market for French porcelain in the United States. Absence from the marketplace during the late 1910s and difficulty reacting to shifts in American taste injured all these firms, however. To reduce the cost of production, French companies simplified their lines. Herman Henjes, a salesman for Theodore Haviland & Co., recalled in 1931 that before World War I:

> There was much greater diversity in the lines of the china houses. . . . One hundred different decorations would come in from abroad at one time, with thirty different shapes represented. The same spray design would be reproduced ten times in ten different colors, for instance. Merchandise tended to be high priced or low priced, with little of the medium range. Sprays and conventional borders and acid gold treatments with slight variations were put out year after year. Now lines are simplified in the number of patterns carried.[12]

Despite such measures, the onslaught of the Great Depression forced some importers of French ceramics into bankruptcy.

This dire situation is reflected in government import figures. Although France maintained its lead in overall unit value, the country's export volume fell dramatically. In 1930 France shipped nearly 3.2 million pieces of tableware and kitchenware to the United States. The total had plummeted to about 350,000—a drop of almost 89 percent—by 1934.[13] Struggling to maintain market share through the 1920s and 1930s, French producers and importers fought the decline of their ware by engaging in "price cutting competition at the expense of their respective products' quality."[14] As a result of the simultaneous decline in price and overall quality, Limoges porcelains became even less fashionable among middle- and upper-class buyers. Once the effect of this situation was realized, some firms, including Theodore Haviland & Co., countered by introducing a limited number of new designs during the 1920s and early 1930s.

In 1927 Nathan Straus & Sons, which imported a mixture of tableware lines from Germany, England, and France, introduced *Madelon* from Limoges, a modernist twelve-sided

shape featuring a highly stylized floral center.[15] Similarly, L. Bernardaud, which had founded its own import house in New York in 1911, brought out in 1929 an art deco line that incorporated stylized floral ornament on a round body featuring rectangular flange handles and finials trimmed in gold (cat. 81). The modest efforts of Straus & Sons and Bernardaud were followed in 1930 by a major effort on the part of the Haviland China Company, the American arm of the French firm, when it introduced its ill-fated Paris Art Centre line.

Ahrenfeldt & Son took a similar tack. In 1928 the firm introduced an ivory-colored body that it marketed as *Ivoire de France*. Although it produced some modernist tableware, including examples by the well-known Parisian designers Jean Luce, Maurice Dufrêne, and Marcel Goupy, the firm's largest publicity effort in the 1930s was for a conservative line.[16] In 1931 Ahrenfeldt & Son's U.S. importer, Herman C. Kupper, Inc., unveiled the newly styled line in New York. In an advertisement titled "What Is the Matter with French or 'Limoges' China?" the firm noted that "the manufacturers at Limoges have not in the past years, with very few exceptions, produced anything distinctly new and desirable in line with the present day demand of the American public."[17] Ahrenfeldt & Son's new designs consisted of fourteen patterns on the *Riviera* shape. One pattern, *Chateaux de France*, featured images of chateaux along the Loire River.[18]

Cat. 81 The French art deco taste of the late 1920s is reflected in this covered vegetable dish by L. Bernardaud & Cie.

OPPOSITE:

Cat. 80 Designed in 1892 by First Lady Caroline Scott Harrison and her china-painting instructor, Paul Putzki, this plate was made in France for the White House.

In addition to introducing new designs, importers of French china tried to stem the decline of their ware in the United States in other ways as well. The Haviland China Company, for example, opened a new showroom in New York in 1927, and in 1930 the firm simplified its trademarks (fig. 3.1). But receding market share and growing economic pressure doomed most purveyors of Limoges products to the United States. L. Bernardaud & Cie. survived as a major producer of porcelain dinnerware in Limoges but closed its New York distributorship sometime after 1922. In 1929 Bernardaud tableware was listed along with German, Czech, and English wares in an advertisement for the well-known New York importer George F. Bassett & Co.[19] By 1947 the Bernardaud line was being distributed by the Crownford China Company of New York; by 1970 William Adams, Inc., handled it.[20] Similarly, Ahrenfeldt survived as a minor china line into mid-century, although its distributor, Herman C. Kupper, Inc., was forced to diversify into non-French merchandise.[21] The Ahrenfeldt factory was sold to investors in 1958 and closed in 1969.[22] Other firms did not survive at all: the venerable import firm of Vogt & Dose, famous before World War I for its T & V brand of French china, made an assignment to creditors and was liquidated at public auction in May 1931.[23] The Haviland China Company closed its doors three months later.

Another firm that succumbed to the depression was Guérin-Pouyat-Elite. Known for handling Baccarat crystal and middle-level French porcelain of its own make, the firm was founded by William Guérin, who started a factory in Limoges for making porcelain tableware for the U.S. market in 1877. During the late nineteenth century the French firm established its own import house in New York, William Guérin & Co. In 1921 the trading firm of Bawo & Dotter, based in New York and Montreal, purchased both the New York branch and the factory in Limoges and created Guérin-Pouyat-Elite. Crippled by flagging sales, this firm ceased operations in New York in 1932, and its factory in Limoges was demolished the following year.[24]

Although Theodore Haviland & Co. managed to survive, French porcelain as a whole never recaptured the imagination or the table of the American consumer it had held before World War I. From its preeminent status in the late nineteenth century, France assumed a minor role in the U.S. market compared to other exporting nations in terms of volume and overall value. Although the price of French products stayed relatively high, the country's share of the American tableware market dwindled in the post–World War II decades. By the mid-1960s and 1970s annual imports of French porcelain and earthenware contributed less than 1 percent in each category.[25] By value, however, French ceramics did slightly better. During the 1960s and 1970s porcelain made up 2 to 3 percent of total imports by value, and earthenware hovered at around 1 percent.[26] In 1969 one observer summed up the situation by remarking that French tableware sold "in dribbles" in the United States. Although they would have liked to change the situation, he postulated that, from the manufacturers' point of view, "America with its bizarre tastes, unreasonable demands, and price competition meant too much trouble for most of them."[27]

FRENCH GLASS

As French dinnerware settled into a minor role in the U.S. marketplace, the presence of French glass became more significant. A large part of France's success in the area of table glass during the second quarter of the twentieth century was due to its construction of several new and highly mechanized glass factories after the war. The machine-blown and molded tableware and barware that streamed from these efficient facilities could be sold in large quantities in the United States at a relatively low price point.

An example of this new investment in the French glass industry is J. G. Durand & Cie. of Arques, France. From its founding in 1815 through 1932 this firm made all of its glass by hand. After World War II, however, Durand emerged as a

Fig. 3.1 Haviland China Company's fashionable New York showroom overlooked Madison Square.

Cat. 82 French, Belgian, and Dutch crystal was imported for wealthy hostesses. Princess Grace of Monaco ordered the design in the center.

world leader in glass tableware research and mechanization. In 1958 it introduced tempered glass, and in 1960, mechanical production of annealed stemware. Durand's greatest achievement came in 1968, when it became the first manufacturer to begin fully automated production of 24 percent lead crystal (crystal with a lead content of 24 percent). Called Cristal D'Arques, the stemware line had sizes, shapes, and packaging customized for the American market and retailed for about $2.50 a stem.[28] This type of product, made with innovative machinery and processes, allowed Durand to gain greater market share in the United States, especially during the 1970s and 1980s. To ensure such growth in the U.S. market, Durand established Durand International as its American sales and marketing affiliate in the late 1960s and opened a permanent headquarters for the subsidiary in Millville, New Jersey, in 1970. By the mid-1990s, Durand was making 5 million pieces of glass a day in its French factories, of which about 25 percent was sold in the United States.[29]

While some Gallic firms sought to penetrate the middle-class market, others drew on their august traditions for producing exceptionally fine blown and cut glass to entice consumers. Before World War II, French table glass was highly prized by wealthy Americans, but because of its high cost it was imported only in very small quantities. Consider the world-famous Cristalleries de Baccarat, for example (cat. 82).

Originally founded in 1764 as the Sainte-Anne Glassworks in the town of Baccarat in northeastern France, Baccarat was exporting to many countries by the late nineteenth century. However, the great expense of its superb products placed them out of reach for all but the wealthiest Americans. In 1907 the firm's New York agent was fired because of "the few orders he had attracted," and in 1914 it was said that "the New York market remained of little importance."[30]

Although the importers A. Gredelue and Guérin-Pouyat-Elite distributed Baccarat in the United States and Canada in the 1920s, the line did not sell well.[31] In an attempt to finally establish itself in the United States, Baccarat opened its own New York showroom at Rockefeller Center in 1935 and appointed the young and innovative retailer Carole Stupell as director.[32] Thanks to the new showroom, the growing fame of Stupell's own china and glass shop, and Baccarat's participation in the 1939 New York world's fair with a display in the French Pavilion, its glass became much better known in the U.S. among wealthy consumers. This momentum was thwarted by World War II, however.[33] Baccarat appears to have been forced to close its New York showroom and end its relationship with Stupell because it was impossible to ship glass during the war. Soon after the fighting ended, A. N. Khouri & Brothers became Baccarat's representative in New York. Later the French manufacturer decided it once again needed a greater presence in the city, and in 1948 René de Chambrun, son of Baccarat's vice president, and his wife, Josée, opened a wholesale and retail showroom for the firm in New York.[34]

While Baccarat and other French producers of luxury glass, such as Lalique, used showrooms and agents during the early postwar years to build business with high-end retailers, it took a group effort on the part of French stemware producers to truly broaden the market for French crystal in the United States.[35] In 1967 "an ambitious program to hike French handmade lead crystal imports here by 15 percent per year, for the next five years" was undertaken by thirteen manufacturers. At the time France's crystal sales in America totaled $558,000, or 20 percent of all U.S. crystal imports. This sum represented 15 percent of all French crystal exports.[36] To improve on this base, the French makers of expensive stemware adopted the strategy of competing only at the topmost level and not challenging domestic products or firms like Durand. Also they hoped to take advantage of a large drop in U.S. import duties on glass following the Kennedy Round Agreements tariff reductions that took effect in January 1968 as part of U.S. participation in the General Agreement on Tariffs and Trade (GATT).[37] United in this effort were the glassmakers Baccarat, Bayle, Daum, Lalique, Romesnil, Schneider, Seiler, Sèvres, Saint-Louis, Vallerysthal et Portieux, Vannes-le-Chatel, Vianne, and Waltersperger. Over the ensuing years most of these glasshouses secured representatives in New York or opened showrooms. Together they published a book, *Cristal de France*, for U.S. distribution and introduced "French crystal styled for U.S. tastes."[38]

Of the producers involved, Baccarat was perhaps the best positioned to take advantage of the publicity and French government support surrounding this effort. Because it had maintained a presence, albeit a weak one, in the U.S. market for decades, the firm enjoyed greater name recognition and knowledge of American tastes. Baccarat had earlier introduced lines, including larger glasses than those used in Europe, "to accommodate the ice cubes that Americans mixed with their drinks."[39] Certain patterns such as *Colorado, Ohio,* and *Texas* were designed in the 1950s for distribution in the United States.[40] The result of such efforts was that sales in North America improved along with Baccarat's overall world exports. By the mid-1980s Baccarat's foreign exports, including those to the United States, amounted to 72 percent of its total production. In 1967, to help accommodate this growth, Baccarat was the first European factory to install a modern continuous-tank furnace. A second furnace was added in 1976, and a third in 1986.[41]

Because of continuing efforts on the part of a few luxury glass producers like Baccarat and because of the availability of inexpensive glass produced in highly automated plants like Durand's, French glass exports to the United States remained relatively steady during the course of the twentieth century, unlike those of ceramics. In 1911 France accounted for over 14 percent of all the ornamented table glass imported into America. After World War II, France's share continued to be significant hovering around 10 percent by value and as much as 15 percent by quantity in 1972.[42] By the mid-1970s France's glass exports to the United States ranked second behind Taiwan by quantity, and fourth by value behind West Germany, Ireland, and Italy.[43] Whereas their pottery counterparts failed to sustain the dominance in porcelain they had held in the American market before World War I, French glassmakers succeeded in building significant market share in the United States after World War II. Today millions of Americans use French glass—from Durand's line of *Arcoroc* food storage containers to Baccarat's most elegant cut crystal.

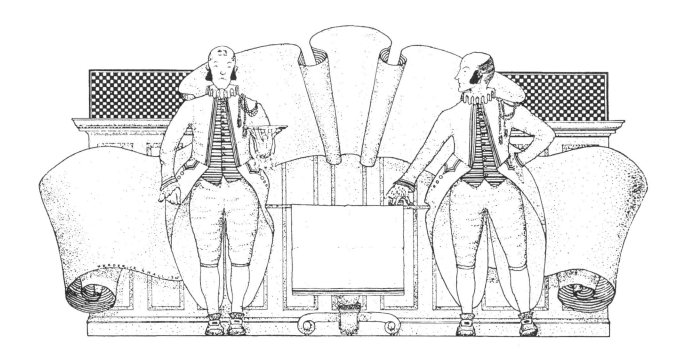

The House of Haviland

As the United States developed as an industrialized nation and world power during the nineteenth century, the rising standard of living led to an increased demand for refined ceramics. Among those who recognized a market for medium- and high-priced French porcelain designed for American tastes was David Haviland.[1]

Haviland first became involved with tableware in 1829, when at age fifteen he went to work for his older brother Edmond, whose New York shop included English earthenware among its stock. In 1838 David and another older brother, Daniel, founded their own firm at 47 John Street in lower Manhattan. Originally called D. G. & D. Haviland, the firm changed its name to Haviland Brothers & Co. in 1852 when brother Robert joined the company. Like Edmond, these Havilands also retailed English earthenware.

During the recession of the 1830s David and Daniel Haviland decided to try to sell French porcelains because of the slow turnover of their English goods. They soon discovered, however, that the tableware sent to them by merchants in France was not appropriate for the American market, and so David Haviland traveled to France in 1840 to establish business contacts. The next year he moved to France with his wife, Mary, and son, Charles. Settling in the potting center of Limoges in southwest France, David Haviland arranged for shapes and patterns adapted to American tastes to be shipped to his brother Daniel in New York. In 1847 he opened his own decorating shop and shortly thereafter started a second one. By 1855 Haviland had twenty muffle kilns in operation for firing on surface decoration. Haviland's timing was fortuitous. The late 1840s and 1850s were prosperous years in the United States, and more citizens could afford expensive French tableware. Imports of French china (much of it undoubtedly belonging to Haviland) rose from 753 loads in 1842 to 8,594 loads in 1853.[2]

Because so many of his best customers lived in the South, the American Civil War interrupted Haviland's plans to build his own china factory. By 1865 the situation had worsened, and Haviland Brothers in New York closed, leaving the decorating operation in Limoges to function on its own under the name of Haviland & Co. As soon as the American economy improved, the proposed factory was built, and David Haviland took his two sons, Charles and Theodore, into the business. Theodore Haviland was sent to the United States to rebuild a distribution network, while Charles assumed a managerial role at the factory. Both men were successful in their endeavors. Orders from America poured in during the 1860s and early 1870s thanks to Theodore's effort. Charles proved a brilliant businessman and assumed control of the Limoges factory in 1866. With the foresight of a visionary, he soon expanded production facilities and introduced new shapes and decorations. By the early 1870s, "400 barrels of china were shipped monthly to the U.S. . . . twice the 1866 volume, and 87 percent of the total output."[3]

During this period tableware by Haviland & Co. became highly fashionable among America's rich and powerful. Presidential services were created for the Lincoln (1861), Grant (1870), and Hayes (1879) administrations. At the same time great designers joined Haviland's staff, among them Joseph-Auguste (Félix) Bracquemond and Albert-Louis Dammouse (cat. 83). To help market its wares, Haviland & Co. exhibited at several world's fairs, including those held in Philadelphia in 1876 and Paris in 1878. With a growing export market, talented designers, and successful marketing to support the firm, Charles Haviland increased production capacity and in 1879 was able to stop subcontracting the production of ware. This consolidation allowed him to mark every piece he sold from then on with his own backstamp: *H & Co / L.* That same year Theodore Haviland returned from America to oversee production in Limoges.

In the 1880s English and German porcelain imported into the American market began to threaten Haviland & Co. Charles Haviland wrote to his brother Theodore in December 1882, "When plain whiteware was in demand, French porcelain had an advantage over British china; today it is decorated tableware that is wanted and the British can produce very cheap underglaze designs. We cannot rely on our own underglazes to see us through, they are the most costly."[4] The Limoges firm countered by introducing lines of complicated neorococo tableware designed by artists such as Edouard Lindeneher (cat. 79).

Although the exciting new shapes were successful in the marketplace, friction between Charles and Theodore Haviland led to the dissolution of Haviland & Co. in about 1891. Two new firms were founded. Charles's new company continued to use the Haviland & Co. name. Following the completion of a new factory in 1893, Theodore Haviland & Co. began marketing tableware in the United States through the New York importer William Briggs, who had been the original Haviland & Co. agent. After Briggs's death the business traded in New York under the name of Theodore Haviland & Co.[5]

Until World War I, Charles Haviland continued to be successful in America. To keep abreast of the company's primary market, family members regularly traveled to New York. Charles's son Georges was in the city "for a lengthy visit" in 1898, and Charles himself made his last of many journeys to New York in 1913.[6]

Following his father's death in 1921, Georges Haviland took over the firm and formed a new company in Limoges in 1925, the Haviland China Company. One of the assets of this new legal entity was the old Haviland & Co. showroom at 11 East Thirty-sixth Street in New York. In an effort to regain some of the prestige lost by French porcelain during World

Cat. 83 By the late 1870s Haviland & Co. enlisted great artists to create dishes for the finest tables. The oyster plate is from the 1879 Hayes White House service.

War I, Georges Haviland opened a new American showroom in 1927 under the name of his new company (fig. 3.1). Described as "modernly appointed and easily-reached," the location at 1107 Broadway at Twenty-fourth Street overlooking Madison Square was indeed central and highly visible.[7] A few years later Haviland China Company attempted to simplify its trademarks by ending the use of two backstamps on decorated wares.[8]

Simultaneously, Haviland China Company introduced new designs that it hoped would attract new customers. In early 1930 an article in the trade press announced the arrival of "A Twentieth Century Epoch—Haviland China in Art Moderne."[9] Designed by a group of Parisian artists, including Robert Bonfils, G. L. Jaulmes, André Marty, René Gabriel, Georges Barbier, and Drésa, this art deco ware was named Paris Art Centre so as to appear chic and progressive. To enhance their aura of sophistication, each piece was said to be "signed by the artist." Nevertheless, knowing that American consumers were rather conservative and did not like radical modernism, Haviland stressed "that the ultra-modern style [of the ware] should not be confused with true *art moderne*." In fact, none of the shapes or motifs were modern in spirit, although some of the patterns had art deco touches.

Under the weight of the Great Depression, new patterns, an updated showroom, and simplified trademarks could not save the Haviland China Company. "In order to immediately turn a large part of [its] New York stock into money," Haviland advertised to the trade in December 1930 that it was closing out twenty-five patterns and selling the stock at "large discounts."[10] Evidently the cash infusion was not sufficient because only four months later Haviland was reported to have disposed of all the stock in its New York showroom. The final sale to a "western department store" was described as "one of the largest in French china ever consummated in this country."[11] On August 1, 1931, the Haviland China Company discharged its remaining staff and closed its doors. The French factory was taken over by Porcelaine G.D.A. in Limoges, and retailers desiring stock to match patterns were instructed to contact the new owner directly.[12]

Theodore Haviland & Co. was more successful. From its founding in the early 1890s, the firm's products found favor in the United States. By 1906 the pottery employed eight hundred workers and was one of the largest in Limoges. Eight years later 70 percent of the firm's earnings were accounted for by U.S. sales.[13] Although World War I hurt Theodore Haviland & Co., as it did all Limoges potteries, this particular pottery managed to survive and prosper in comparison to its French rivals.

Like other French manufacturers, Theodore Haviland & Co. introduced new shapes after World War I in an attempt to regain lost market share. Appearing in 1923, for example,

was the up-to-date, octagonal *Pilgrim* shape, featuring bold surface decoration. In 1934 the company introduced a shape designed by Suzanne Lalique, the art deco *1937,* available with surface patterns such as *Nicole* (cats. 61, 136). The *1937* shape received substantial publicity in America because it was used to outfit the grand luxe suites on the famous luxury liner SS *Normandie.*[14] Just before the start of World War II, Theodore Haviland imported several streamlined shapes, including *Priscilla* and *Saint Raphael,* featuring conservative, pastel-colored surface decoration and gilt accents (cat. 84).[15] To ensure that the products it made for the U.S. market were likely to sell here, the firm employed an American, James H. Liberty, to design some of its ware.[16] Along with these new shapes and patterns Theodore Haviland & Co. attempted to find favor with American consumers, who during the late 1920s increasingly preferred ivory-colored ceramic bodies to white ones. Although it lagged several years behind American, German, and Japanese manufacturers, as well as Charles Ahrenfeldt & Son, Theodore Haviland & Co. brought out an ivory-colored body in late 1929.[17]

During the depression the firm implemented two strategies that allowed it to survive. First, Theodore Haviland broadened the line it carried in New York beyond French ceramics. In 1931 the company announced that it was the distributor for the well-known English pottery John Maddock & Sons of Burslem, Staffordshire.[18] Second, the firm began manufacturing much of its ware for the U.S. market in this country.[19] In 1936 Theodore Haviland contracted with the Shenango Pottery Company of New Castle, Pennsylvania, to produce china. Importing the ceramic formula, blocks, molds, and lithographic decorations from its factory in Limoges, the New York firm initially had its *Pilgrim* and *Ile de France* shapes produced in Pennsylvania. Over time, however, other Haviland wares were made at Shenango. The *Primavera* shape, for one, was made there in the 1950s (cat. 84).

By manufacturing ware in America, Theodore Haviland serendipitously could supply retailers during World War II, but apparently the company's reason for the move was to avoid import duties. The Fordney-McCumber Tariff of 1922 had set a duty on foreign decorated porcelain at 70 percent plus 10 cents per dozen pieces. As the depression worsened, French producers and their importers found this added expense difficult to bear. By producing locally much of the tableware it distributed in North America, Theodore Haviland competed on equal terms with U.S. manufacturers when setting prices and delivery fees. To enhance its position still

OVERLEAF:
Cat. 84 Theodore Haviland & Co. had wares made in both France and America for the U.S. market.

further, in 1941 the firm acquired the rights to all the marks and molds formerly used by the defunct Haviland & Co. back from Porcelaine G.D.A.; in 1948 it opened an office in Los Angeles for the convenience of West Coast customers; and in 1950 it began trading in the United States under the old name of Haviland & Co.[20]

In 1955 six new patterns designed in France and market-tested on American retail buyers were introduced. The firm expanded its factory in Limoges in the late 1950s when natural gas became available there for firing modern tunnel kilns. With larger, more efficient facilities planned, Haviland predicted that it could increase production for distribution in the United States by approximately 100 percent.[21] Haviland ceased subcontracting production of ware to Shenango

China, Inc., in 1958 and resumed importing from Limoges, a practice that continues today. In 1977 the Haviland family sold the company to Cerabati-Holding, a French producer of china and industrial ceramics. The transaction was said to be one of the largest in the history of Limoges.[22] The financial and industrial company FIDEI acquired Haviland in 1987, only to be bought out a year later by Dominique de Coster, a shareholder of FIDEI.

Although Haviland china is no longer as plentiful in the United States as it once was, the success of the Havilands has nonetheless been remarkable. In the course of a century and a half, this American-French family built an extraordinary porcelain empire that is still associated with quality at the dawn of a new millennium.

All Set for Breakfast!

Trays of Charming Wares That Will Gladden A Sleepy Beauty's Eyes

Notes

1. Unless otherwise noted, all general information in this section is derived from d'Albis 1988.

2. D'Albis 1988, 14.

3. Ibid., 24.

4. Ibid., 47.

5. "Chicago, West, All the Big Cities," *CGJ* 103:3 (Mar. 1931): 85.

6. *CGJ* 47:1 (6 Jan. 1898): 19; and 93:12 (24 Mar. 1921): 16.

7. *CGJ* 104:1 (6 Jan. 1927): 44.

8. *CGJ* 108:9 (Sept. 1930): 68. After 1930 ornamented wares carried the mark *MANUFACTURED / AND / DECORATED BY / Haviland / France,* and whiteware was stamped simply *Haviland / France.*

9. "A Twentieth Century Epoch—Haviland China in Art Moderne," *PGBS* 41:3 (20 Feb. 1930): 38–40; 25 (advertisement).

10. *CGJ* 108:2 (Dec. 1930): 163.

11. "Haviland Sells Stock," *CGJ* 109:4 (Apr. 1931): 33.

12. "Haviland China Office Closes," *CGJ* 109:8 (Aug. 1931): 38. The name of Haviland & Co. was briefly reintroduced into the American market in late 1939 by the New York importer Fisher, Bruce & Co. See *CGJ* 125:2 (Aug. 1939): 5. The initials G.D.A. stand for Gérard-Dufraisseix-Abbot.

13. Cameron 1986, 159; and d'Albis 1988, 69–70.

14. "S.S. Normandie Carries China and Glass Services for All Travel Classes," *CGJ* 116:6 (June 1935): 32, 38.

15. For an image of the *Priscilla* shape, see *CGJ* 127:3 (Mar. 1938): 35.

16. "They Got the Job: Maddock Dinnerware Goes to Theo. Haviland, Inc.," *CGJ* 109:5 (May 1931): 38. This article also noted that in France the firm used French designers to create "modernistic and conventional French patterns" for the home market. For a photograph of Liberty, see his article "Outline of Correct Table Arrangement," 110:12 (Dec. 1932): 48–49, 96.

17. *CGJ* 107:9 (Sept. 1929): 14.

18. *CGJ* 109:5 (May 1931): 5; and "They Got the Job," 109:5 (May 1931): 38.

19. *CGJ* 119:3 (Sept. 1936): 9; and "Famous as a 'Frenchman'—Really a Pioneer American," 119:3 (Sept. 1936): 16.

20. *CGJ* 142:1 (Jan. 1948): 14; and "Haviland Has New Name," 147:2 (Aug. 1950): 66–67. The latter article notes that "Haviland China will continue to be back-stamped 'Haviland—France' when made in France, and 'Theodore Haviland—New York—Made in America' when made in America."

21. "Haviland Develops New China," *CGJ* 157:5 (Nov. 1955): 45; and "Haviland Announces Expansion," 159:1 (July 1956): 82. Also see d'Albis 1988, 84.

22. "Family Drops Reins; Haviland a Sellout," *GTR* (May 1977): 1.

Tariffs and Tableware

Between 1880 and 1980 the U.S. government enacted numerous tariff laws that affected the importation of ceramic and glass tableware. The most notable of these tariffs and laws were: Mills Act (1883), McKinley Tariff (1890), Wilson Act (1894), Dingley Act (1897), Payne-Aldrich Tariff (1909), Underwood-Sherman Tariff (1913), Fordney-McCumber Tariff (1922), Hawley-Smoot Tariff (1930), General Agreement on Tariffs and Trade (GATT, 1947), Trade Expansion Act (GATT, 1962), and Kennedy Round Agreements (GATT, 1968–72).

Earlier, in 1864, the U.S. government placed a 40 percent ad valorem duty on imported earthenware, meaning that importers paid duty of 40 percent of the certified value of the goods. Porcelain was taxed at 45 percent for undecorated ware and 50 percent for decorated ware. In 1872 these rates were cut unilaterally by 10 percent. With the Mills Act of 1883, however, ad valorem rates for undecorated and decorated glassware were set at 40 and 45 percent, respectively. The duty on undecorated ceramic tableware was raised to 55 percent and on ornamented ware, to 60 percent.

The McKinley Tariff of 1890 retained the 1883 rates but required all imported ware to be marked with the country of origin. With the Wilson Act in 1894 the duty on glassware was reduced to 40 percent and dropped on ceramic dishes of all kinds to 30 percent for undecorated ware and 35 percent for decorated ware. But the Wilson Act was short lived, and in 1897 the rates were restored to their 1890 levels. The protectionist Payne-Aldrich Tariff of 1909 kept the 1890 rates, although it abolished most exceptions to the law. The liberal Underwood-Sherman Tariff of 1913 was the first to differentiate between refined earthenware and porcelain. In that year earthenware and stoneware were dutiable at 35 and 40 percent for undecorated and decorated ware, respectively. Porcelain was taxed at 50 and 55 percent, while the duty on glass was lowered to 45 percent ad valorem.

These lower rates had limited impact due to the onset of World War I. Most exporting nations, with the notable exception of Japan, were unable to supply the United States with goods because of the conflict. The isolationist Fordney-McCumber Tariff of 1922 raised import duties and was more detailed with respect to glass. Pressed glass was now taxed at 50 percent and blown glass at 55 percent. Duties on ceramics also rose. Earthenware rates were 45 and 50 percent for undecorated and decorated wares, while porcelain rates were 60 and 70 percent. For the first and only time, bone china was singled out with its own rates, 50 and 55 percent. In 1930 the tax on glass was increased by 5 percent for both pressed and blown categories, and ceramic tableware imports in both groups received a specific duty of 10 cents per dozen pieces.[1]

The signing of the General Agreement on Tariffs and Trade in 1947 ushered in a new era with respect to import duties. For the first time signatory nations acted in concert to promote free trade. In the case of U.S. duties on china and glass the long-term effect of GATT was decreased rates. Through a complicated series of tariff laws, including the Trade Expansion Act of 1962 and the Kennedy Round Agreements in 1968, ad valorem and specific duties on most types of ceramic and glass tablewares had been cut in half by 1972.[2]

Although on the surface it would seem that all nations exporting goods to the United States would suffer or benefit from American tariff policy equally, this was not the case. Because ad valorem taxes are sometimes assessed on the value of goods before they leave their country of origin, a manufacturer located in a country whose currency is devalued in relation to the U.S. dollar pays less duty. In addition the nature of the product affected the amount of duty paid. In 1922, when a separate and lower rate was included for bone china, the English benefited tremendously because they produced almost all the bone china shipped to America at the time. On the other hand the Japanese were hardest hit by the specific 10-cents-per-dozen tax levied in 1930. During the early 1930s Japan was exporting huge quantities of inexpensive porcelain to the United States. The recently increased duty of 70 percent on decorated porcelain tableware had limited impact on Japanese goods because the unit value was so minimal, but because the volume of imports was enormous, the specific tax on quantity hit hard.

Given these variables, the actual import rates paid by different countries varied significantly over time. In 1933 it was calculated that because they were subject to different circumstances, the earthenware, stoneware, bone china, and porcelain tableware of the five leading U.S.-supplying nations had average ad valorem rates as follows: Japan—100 percent; Germany—73 percent; United Kingdom—61 percent; France—68 percent; and Czechoslovakia—76 percent.[3] Given such realities and the sizable amount of money involved, it is little wonder that foreign producers and importers of tableware, as well as their American counterparts, regularly visited the hallowed halls of Congress, lobbying for legislation that would serve their purposes and increase their profits.

Notes

1. For general overviews of tableware's early tariff history, see USDC 1915, 80–84; USBFDC 1917, 334–36; Davis 1949, 245–46; and USTC 1936, 19–22.

2. "Tariffs Drop—It's Data Time," *GTR* (3 July 1967): 1, 35; "New Tariffs Spell B-I-N-D," (17 July 1967): 1, 33; "Tariff's 50% Cut in Five Equal Parts," (2 Oct. 1967): 1, 4.

3. USTC 1936, 20–22.

The English and Irish

For as long as the United States has been a nation, and even before, Great Britain has been a major source for the ceramics Americans use. For the most part, utilitarian wares of varying quality have made up this trade, which culminated in the vast quantities of whiteware known as ironstone or graniteware that comprised the bulk of English exports to the United States in the second half of the nineteenth century.[44]

Artistic wares and tiles were also a part of the export trade to the Americas, but to a much lesser extent. Decorative earthenware like majolica helped certain large firms in Staffordshire, England, such as Minton, Ltd., Josiah Wedgwood & Sons, and George Jones & Sons cater to the fashionable set in the 1860s and 1870s. When these potteries exhibited their wares at the Philadelphia Centennial Exposition in 1876, they prompted American manufacturers to attempt their own version of the popular colorful majolica glazes. Griffen, Smith, and Hill of Phoenixville, Pennsylvania; the Bennett and Chesapeake potteries in Baltimore; and Morley & Co. in Wellsville and East Liverpool, Ohio, were just some of the small-scale American potteries that had modest success with their majolica production (cat. 3). Most of their production came in the form of dinnerware and dessertware designs. Even so, these American firms could not compete with the quality and vast market share of the major English and continental factories.[45]

The interest in majolica in America, which reached its peak at the Philadelphia Centennial Exposition, began to fall off considerably in the 1880s.[46] Although majolica dinnerware was produced primarily for the American market during this period, nothing could stem the exodus from the previously popular ware. Wedgwood experimented with a more conservatively styled majolica type known as Argenta ware during the late 1870s and 1880s, in which the natural white body of the clay was allowed to show through and decorative glazes were applied only to relief ornament. Despite this attempt to respond to the new trends in majolica production, Charles Bachhoffner, Wedgwood's London agent, declared in 1878 that "majolica has had its day."[47]

A more lucrative response was Wedgwood's reintroduction of bone china production that year.[48] This ceramic body, developed and perfected in England during the last years of the eighteenth century, had been produced throughout the nineteenth century by leading manufacturers such as Minton, Worcester Royal Porcelain Company, Doulton & Co., and W. T. Copeland & Sons. However, Wedgwood found such success with its earthenwares that the bone china works were given over to earthenware production in 1815. By resuming production of bone china in 1878, the company positioned itself once again at the forefront of fine tableware manufacturing in Staffordshire.

The value of English exports to the United States remained high during the 1880s and 1890s, leading other countries by almost 3 to 1 until the Boer War of 1898 cut export production in half due to the loss of workers to military service.[49] From that point until World War I curtailed German exports to America, English production trailed that of Germany, although the British continued to outpace the French. Competition from American producers also began to affect the balance of trade in the tableware market during this period. The combination of growing competition from Germany and America gave rise to protectionist strategies in both England and America.

Tariff legislation was introduced on both sides of the Atlantic, resulting in a tightening of trade regulations that would drive the price of imported English tablewares to record levels in the first quarter of the twentieth century. Ironically, these higher prices ensured the success of the British pottery industry in America by propelling English wares into the high end of the market, making English goods synonymous with the highest quality in the eyes of many consumers. Since there was no demand for American tableware in England, the tariff changes were felt more by British manufacturers than by American ones.[50]

Another factor that contributed to rising costs in the British pottery industry was the birth of the trade union movement at the turn of the century. Studies have shown that a steady growth in output paralleled the successful development of unions. During periods of bargaining and agreement, production expanded. Conversely, acrimonious disputes prompted shutdowns and constricted manufacturing for export.[51]

Although the United States remained the most important foreign consumer of British tablewares in the first decades of the new century, its share of total British pottery exports actually declined.[52] Motivated by the instability of war and labor relations as well as the increased competition from other countries, some British manufacturers had begun to look closer to home for expanded sales, especially in France. Wedgwood and Minton in particular hired French designers to develop patterns for that market.[53]

The void in competition for American sales left by the stoppage of imports from continental Europe during World War I reawakened British pottery manufacturers' interest in their largest export market. Through steady efforts to produce designs that would appeal to the American taste for conservative, largely colonial revival and neoclassical motifs, English pottery manufacturers began to dominate the fine china and earthenware market in America. Limited output, or the sheer inability to make enough dishes to fill orders, began to plague potteries as demand for dinnerware increased around the turn of the century. A change in direction from utilitarian, lower-end wares to fine, expensive wares was not only essential but opportune. The shift provided British potteries a small but important niche that enabled them to compete with Japanese manufacturers, who steadily developed their own market share for porcelain dinnerware during the twentieth century aided by more modern factories and ever-increasing production levels.[54]

The British mantra was status, tradition, and quality.

Although British manufacturers repeatedly professed to filling orders in a timely manner, delays caused by labor disputes, dock strikes, military conflict, and outdated technology contributed to a constant frustration for U.S. importers and retailers. Yet, rather than causing the American consumer to look elsewhere, it seems that delivery delays did not significantly diminish demand for British tableware.

BRITISH REPRESENTATIVES IN AMERICA

Retailers, agents, and wholesale importers also contributed to changes in consumers' perceptions of English tablewares in the early years of the twentieth century. Their role in the success of British potteries in the American market cannot be overstated. For most companies trading in America these relationships between the home office in Staffordshire and importers in the United States were established in the mid-nineteenth century. One study has shown that "the outcome of Staffordshire ceramic distribution and the extent of adapted design for America might appear to be the same for both the minor firms and the extensive firms with their own American outlets, but it was achieved by different methods."[55] These methods, or the degree to which manufacturers relied on their own market research and that of their American importers, depended on the amount of working capital in the business. Small firms could not afford to undertake their own studies of taste and consumer demand. Instead they depended exclusively on their importers for design suggestions, or as in the case of teaware producers whose wares were highly specialized, they simply required a marketing partner.[56]

Larger potteries could and did establish their own agents in America, who provided enough reliable reconnaissance that managers and designers could assume a greater role in the firm's final designs. Marketing strategies were the domain of the American importer, however. Several manufacturers employed agents of this type early in the century but later established American branches that bore their own name as competition for brand recognition and market share increased.

One example of an American agent was Robert L. Johnson, sent to America around 1885 to represent his family's pottery, Johnson Brothers. He returned to England to resume work at the factory with his brothers in 1896. Responsibility for Johnson Brothers' American sales was then placed with nonfamily agents George Bartlett Jones and Edward Butler in New York. Jones became the sole agent after Butler's death and remained the company's representative until his own death.[57] At that time Johnson Brothers opened its own import house in New York. The firm's patterns remained a staple of the middle-priced earthenware market throughout the 1960s, even after the company was taken over by Wedgwood in 1968 (cat. 4).

Similarly, Doulton & Co. opened a U.S. sales branch in 1946, after having been represented for years by William S. Pitcairn in New York.[58] Worcester also chose this course in the 1940s, forming the Worcester Royal Porcelain Company and taking over American representation from Maddock & Miller, its long-time New York importer.[59]

The story of Maddock & Miller shows how some large producers in England set up a family agent in America who eventually gave control to an importer. In 1858 one of the sons of John Maddock established his family's business in the United States and served as its agent in New York until 1889. In that year John J. Miller was brought to the American office, and the importing firm of Maddock & Miller was formed. Miller's influence on the design of Maddock's products is evident from contemporary accounts, which attribute to him "development along the newer trends."[60]

Maddock & Miller became so successful that the firm took on the representation of other unrelated English potteries, including at various times those making the brands Royal Worcester, Shelley, Carlton Ware, Crown Ducal Ware, and Price Brothers teapots. This expansion proved detrimental to the success of John Maddock & Sons, the founding company of Maddock & Miller; in 1931 *Crockery and Glass Journal* announced that "owing to a conflict in selling their various dinnerware lines," Maddock & Miller was relinquishing its representation of John Maddock & Sons to Theodore Haviland & Co. in the United States.[61] Maddock's share of the American market was then reduced to little more than hotel and transportation wares.

Meakin & Ridgway in New York is another example of a large importing firm that began with one or two companies—in this case, J. & G. Meakin and Ridgway Pottery—and ended up representing several others. Both Meakin and Ridgway Pottery lost ground when the importing firm came to rely on Minton and William Adams & Sons for its lucrative bone china and earthenware trade. Regardless of the type of relationship between manufacturer and importer, no British manufacturer could succeed without the input of someone based in America. The degree to which a company understood and reacted to the changes in American taste determined its growth and survival in the vast American market.

THE IMPORTANCE OF DESIGN

Although the reasons for the success of English designs in twentieth-century America can be debated, the underlying fact is that by World War II, English bone china and earthenwares had become the most desirable choices for fine dinnerware by aspiring brides and housewives in the United States. Much of this success with consumers depended on "giving the lady what she wanted," as retail magnate Marshall Field liked to say.[62] And the department store Marshall Field & Co. did just that in 1913, opening what was hailed in the day as "the greatest display of Wedgwood ever shown in America."[63]

Most manufacturers saw the benefit of concentrating on traditional shapes and patterns for sale in America. Josiah Wedgwood & Sons and W. T. Copeland & Sons (which began trading in America under the name Spode in 1923) were particularly adept at producing earthenware shapes with long-lasting appeal; the shapes they introduced in the 1920s

remained popular with Americans through the 1950s (see pp. 211–17). Featuring heavily embossed or fluted rims, designs on shapes such as Wedgwood's *Edme* (1908), *Patrician* (1926), and *Wellesley* (1932) as well as Spode's *Chelsea Wicker* (1890), *Jewel* (U.S. patent 1926), and *Centurion* (1931) were hardly marketed in Britain, if at all (cats. 85, 86, 160). Spode went so far as to patent some of its most popular shapes for the American market to protect the growing popularity of its wares.

English potteries used the introduction of new shapes and patterns as opportunities to cater to the American desire for history and tradition in tableware design. One way they pursued this strategy was in the development of patterns that evoked eighteenth-century themes. Spode's *Fitzhugh* and *Gloucester* on a blue-gray stoneware body imitated Chinese export porcelain that came to America in the late eighteenth and early nineteenth centuries (cat. 92). Wedgwood's creamware patterns, especially its highly successful range of *Embossed Queens Ware*, also connected consumers with an eighteenth-century past. Also capturing this quality were Doulton's *The Granville* (cat. 159) and Mason's enormously successful *Vista* pattern. Even when sold next to far more sophisticated designs, *Pink Vista* remained the biggest seller at Neiman Marcus in Dallas throughout the 1950s, according to the former buyer, Barbara Boyd Wedgwood (cat. 174).[64]

Whereas traditional patterns were essential in the American market, tableware design in Britain before World War II favored more handpainted looks and streamlined shapes. Talented artists such as Clarice Cliff and Susie Cooper found success in the British home market with their strongly modernist shapes and colorful handpainted abstract designs (cat. 89). Doulton, Minton, Shelley, and W. H. Grindley & Co., and to a lesser extent Wedgwood and Spode, all developed modern shapes and patterns that were hailed in Great Britain and in the commonwealth countries such as Canada and Australia, where the lack of tariff restrictions allowed for a lower price in the stores. But in America, where customs duties continued to rise in the 1930s and domestic producers were able to make similar shapes for a fraction of the cost of the British imports, these modern designs were never as commercially successful as traditional ones (cats. 87, 88). For British manufacturers, traditional English-looking patterns with cottages, flowers, and brambles drove their American sales, and few producers—and perhaps more important, few agents and importers—wanted to upset that fragile equation.

OPPOSITE:
Cat. 85 The English firms Worcester Royal Porcelain Company and W. T. Copeland & Sons wooed Americans with attractive yet conservative patterns in the 1910s and 1920s.

BELOW:
Cat. 86 Spode earthenware dishes like the *Kerry* pattern of 1933 were so attractive that Americans considered the ware to be fine china.

Cat. 88 One of Doulton & Co.'s more radical
shapes was *Casino* of 1932.

OPPOSITE:
Cat. 87 Although known in the United States for
its floral patterns, Shelley Potteries occasionally
took on a modernist look, as with the *Vogue*
shape (1930).

Cat. 89 Clarice Cliff's bold modernist designs from the 1930s appealed to the hostess with a mind of her own.

WARTIME PRODUCTION

What did threaten to destabilize the industry was the growing cloud of another war looming over Europe. Indeed, World War II helped significantly to consolidate the British pottery industry into a coalition aimed at capturing and retaining the American market. The crisis, which developed in Britain as German bombs rained on the country, could have closed down the potteries, which would have ended the industry's export trade altogether.

The first domestic quotas were put into place in 1939 and 1940, reducing home market production to two-thirds the value of normal sales. This spelled doom for small producers with little export trade. The government thought that by reducing the sales to the home market and dominions, the potteries could turn their attention to export sales. However, many small potteries had long since given up competing with their larger counterparts for American sales and simply had no means of reentering the export market under such conditions.[65]

Faced with a continuing need to free up industrial labor for the war effort, the British Board of Trade moved to con-

solidate various industries in 1941. Only those potteries able to prove that they could function at 100 percent capacity and sell 70 percent of their total output overseas would be allowed to stay in production. Smaller firms that could not achieve this quota would be amalgamated with the larger firms, forming large collaborative potteries. The result was the consolidation of 131 potteries and the closing of 75 more in order to achieve the maximum export levels and free up 30 percent of the workforce.[66]

Minton was one of the potteries forced to close during the war. The Minton factory managed to reopen in 1946, but for many other firms, the loss of workers, and more important the loss of orders from America, resulted in permanent closure or takeover.[67] Although the government-imposed restrictions meant the end of many old, established potteries, the restructuring brought crucial dollars into the British economy and propelled the remaining manufacturers into the void left by the cessation of trade between America and the Axis powers, especially Germany and Japan.[68]

The larger firms quickly settled into wartime export production. When further restrictions limited the sale of decorated ceramics to dollar-based markets (the United States and Canada), the only concern for manufacturers was manning the kilns to fill orders fast enough. Contemporary notices in the trade journals during the war years by American agents of British manufacturers often caution their distributors and retailers to be patient. One article in 1943 reported that "supply ships on return trips regularly carry back English china" and that "china is coming through, and steadily."[69]

POSTWAR PRODUCTION

Their ability to continue exporting to the United States during the war gave the British producers a strong position in the market after the conflict had ended. Japan had outpaced Great Britain 4 to 1 in total value of American imports before the war, but that figure was reversed in 1947. The expected postwar consumer boom brought a brief moment of prosperity for British manufacturers. But with recovery in Germany and Japan underway, competition for the American import market soon resumed. Germany, Japan, and Great Britain once again claimed roughly equal market shares in 1948, each holding about 8 to 11 percent of total value of American ceramic imports.[70]

American importers and factory agents recognized the new cultural landscape that emerged after World War II and the importance of change in the pottery industry—shifts that few British companies were able to make or willing to accept. The decades of the 1950s and 1960s saw a gradual but steady decline in the U.S. market share for British manufacturers. Direct competition from Japan, labor strife in the potteries and on the docks, the failure to modernize, and the slow deliveries of orders all contributed to the closure and takeover of many British companies.[71]

U.S. retailers, who had earned substantial profits selling British pottery, tried valiantly to help British manufacturers keep pace with the changing times. A study conducted by Time-Life International in 1948 titled "The Market for United Kingdom China, Pottery and Glass in the United States" outlined opinions on the nature of the demand for British tablewares among leading department store executives and buyers. In the foreword to the survey, C. D. Jackson, vice president of Time, wrote, "It is hoped that this study will help British manufacturers plan their operations in the American market with greater confidence, and with a more specific idea of the methods to be used in achieving their full U.S. sales potential."[72] Such was the extent of retailers' concern over the success and failure of British goods in the American market after the war.

From this study, several facts emerge that help to explain the position of British tableware relative to other imported china and glass. The consumer demand for British ceramics remained high after the war due to the excellent quality of the product. Although British glassware at the time was relatively overlooked, one respondent noted that "English dinnerware with traditional designs is demanded by a certain class of purchasers because of prestige and a certain amount of glamour that goes with owning it." Another remarked, "A great percentage of Americans have the idea that such things as Wedg-

wood and Spode are better, something you buy knowing it will be in good taste" (see pp. 211–17).[73] The prewar marketing strategy of making British dinnerware synonymous with quality and prestige had obviously worked, as the notion was firmly planted in the minds of the consumer by this point. Home economy and etiquette manuals reinforced the image of quality and prestige.[74] The survey also revealed that consumers did not look to Britain for glass, and if they were to buy English glass, consumers would want cut patterns rather than pressed—a foreshadowing of the spectacular rise of Waterford Glass from Ireland over the next two decades (see pp. 218–21).[75]

The several criticisms revealed by the Time-Life study included slow delivery and high prices—both problems could be considered systemic in the British pottery industry during the twentieth century. Delivery delays had been a source of frustration since the late nineteenth century. By 1948 only one of the fifty-eight stores consulted rated British delivery times as "good or very good." The largest share, thirty-five stores, rated deliveries as "poor or very poor."[76] Many factors contributed to this problem, but the real source of production and delivery delays after the war was the general tendency to produce far more patterns and shapes than could be efficiently stocked. Before World War II British potteries, and in particular their American representatives, took pride in the fact that a pattern could be replaced for decades after it had been out of general production. One importer, Jones, McDuffee & Stratton Corporation of Boston, advertised in 1921 that "we carry our patterns for many years after they have ceased to be ready sellers" and supply "the wants of our customers who wish to replace broken pieces in the sets they bought years ago."[77]

Such a policy may well have contributed to the marketing image of longevity, tradition, and high quality before the war, when many consumers bought large sets of dinnerware that were supposed to last a lifetime. After the war, however, manufacturers felt the need to develop smaller sets that might be bought one year and replaced with another in the not-too-distant future. A policy of open stock and replacements was enormously inefficient from a production perspective and caused delays in delivery that frustrated consumers. Those companies, namely Wedgwood, that drastically streamlined production and did away with replacement policies and outdated patterns in the 1960s survived the treacherous postwar period. For most of the others, it was too late.[78]

Open stock policies contributed to higher prices at the retail level. Filling thousands of tiny orders for a few pieces of an outdated pattern took valuable time, and the financial cost of delays incurred by the manufacturer and the importer was passed along to the consumer. Rising labor costs after the war also escalated prices, as did high tariffs. Many of the department store respondents in this survey favored a general reduction in import tariffs so that they could lower prices on British products and increase their sales.[79] Some easing of tariffs would come in the 1960s but not enough to make a substantial difference in the price of English bone china and earthenware.

The difficult postwar years caused most of the large producers to send their own designers and executives to America to assess the situation and make recommendations for changes. Wedgwood dispatched Victor Skellern, chief of design, to the United States in 1949; Roy Midwinter toured Canada and California in 1952; John Harthill, chairman of Minton, visited the states in 1954; and Ronald and Robert Copeland made the journey for Spode in 1955. Their reports to the home office relayed the differences in taste and style across America, along with preferences for color, shapes, and patterns.[80]

Fascinating insights can be found in surviving diaries and reports compiled by Victor Skellern for Wedgwood and John Harthill for Minton.[81] These accounts focus on American technology, style, and taste as well as the competition from California potteries in the lower-cost earthenware market. Both Skellern and Harthill discuss the color palette in vogue in America, the enormous bridal market, and the frustration

OPPOSITE:
Cat. 90 Doulton & Co. hired an American designer to create its *Avon* shape in 1955.

BELOW:
Cat. 91 The British firm W. R. Midwinter joined the daisy craze of the 1970s with its *Flowersong* pattern.

with delays in filling orders. Skellern wrote, "A lot of business is being lost to Castleton, Lenox, Franciscan, etc. merely because the dealer is out of stock and waiting patiently for Wedgwood patterns." Harthill's account is even more extensive in its analysis of consumer likes and dislikes, motivations for purchasing fine china, and prospects for the future. Each man came away from his experience awed by the sheer size of the country and the vast array of differences among consumers in America, and with a healthy respect for the quality of American goods.

Skellern and Harthill also noted the pressure for modern designs, but most consumers still demanded traditional patterns from English manufacturers. The lack of any substantive market research and the constant criticism in the design press for more modernism led to costly experiments by many British companies in contemporary shapes and patterns, a crucial misjudgment of their U.S. consumers' preferences.

Some firms tried to answer the critics' call for modern design by employing American designers on a freelance basis. Doulton hired J. Russell Price, formerly a flatware designer with the Gorham Manufacturing Company, to develop a new shape based on the outcome of a market survey of five thousand college women in 1954. The result was the *Avon* line, which featured coupe-shaped plates and strong, simple patterns for both bone china and earthenware.[82] Only one of the

patterns, *Desert Star*, seems to have held any appeal for the American customer, however, and the line was withdrawn in 1964 (cat. 90). Wedgwood asked Clare Leighton to design a promotional series for Christmas featuring scenes of American industry that was even more of a failure in the face of traditional, lighthearted Christmas patterns. Later Wedgwood attempted once more to harness contemporary American taste by employing California designer Edith Kiertener Heath to develop a line of stoneware. Although initial requests from retailers looked promising and prototypes were produced, the venture never went past the design stage (cat. 177).[83]

One firm in Staffordshire, W. R. Midwinter, an old pottery founded in the nineteenth century, specialized in contemporary shapes after the war under the leadership of Roy and Eve Midwinter. They hired young British designers such as Jessie Tait, Terence Conran, and David Queensberry to challenge the accepted notions of style in dinnerware. Because Midwinter's product involved little hand painting and its small American sales network meant lower overhead, the pottery could produce wares at a lower cost than most British producers, and Midwinter's casually styled wares began to enjoy modest sales in America in the 1960s. The introduction of the *Stonehenge* shape in 1972, which capitalized on the look of handcrafted stoneware but was produced in earthenware, brought the company's greatest success with the American consumer (cat. 91).[84] Likewise, Joseph Bourne & Son, known commercially as Denby Pottery, made inroads into the American casual market with its stoneware patterns and enjoyed moderate appeal among consumers (cat. 203). The biggest success of this period was Portmeirion Potteries, formed in 1962 by designer Susan Williams-Ellis and her husband Euan Cooper-Willis. Portmeirion merged a conservatively modern shape with botanical prints in its pattern *Botanic Garden* (1972), a combination that would propel the firm to financial success among the top echelon of imported casual tableware manufacturers in the late 1970s and early 1980s.[85]

But such was not the case for the larger Staffordshire potteries that attempted to apply modern styling to bone china and fine earthenware. Companies such as Wedgwood, Minton, Doulton, and Spode had spent the better part of a century marketing their image in America as traditional, so their experiments in modernism were doomed from the start.

Spode's one attempt at contemporary bone china was the *Royal College* shape (1958) designed by students at the prestigious Royal College of Art in London (cat. 93). A clean, elegant design, it won a Design Council award and the Duke of Edinburgh's prize in 1960 but was nearly a complete commercial failure, especially in the United States. Similarly, a contemporary-style version of black basalt ware designed by Robert Minkin for Wedgwood in 1963 evoked no response in the American market. In retrospect, executives and designers alike, many still living and working in the industry, call attention to the failure of the British pottery industry to understand and listen to its customers rather than the art critics in the decades after World War II.[86] As a result companies faced with mounting labor costs brought about by inflation, the need to expend vast sums on modernization of factories, and the inability to connect with market demands in America were forced to merge or succumb to takeovers by conglomerates from other, unrelated industries. One by one they fell.

In 1964 the Lawley Group, itself a conglomerate of postwar failed potteries, was taken over by S. Pearson and Son, a group with interests in publishing and entertainment, to become Allied English Potteries. Allied English Potteries in turn acquired the Royal Crown Derby Company in 1965 and Shelley in 1966, only to be bought out again in 1972, this time by Doulton, which had already acquired Minton in 1968.[87]

Spode, badly in need of a cash infusion in 1966, sold out to an American industrial ceramics company, Carborundum Corporation, which provided the necessary capital to run the Staffordshire works until 1974, when Worcester acquired Spode. Although still run separately, the two firms are today under one large umbrella company, named Royal Worcester Spode.[88]

Led by an ambitious chairman, Arthur Bryan, Wedgwood became one of the largest conglomerates among the potteries during the 1960s. In rapid succession, it acquired Susie Cooper Pottery and William Adams & Sons in 1966, Coalport and Cauldon Potteries in 1967, Johnson Brothers in 1968, and Meakin and W. R. Midwinter in 1970. The firm's prodigious market share and strong capitalization made Wedgwood itself an attractive target for a larger company in the early 1980s. Wedgwood conceded to a hostile takeover bid in 1986 by Waterford Glass Group of Ireland, which had been acquiring many of its competitors since 1970.[89]

By 1990 the British pottery industry, which only a century earlier had consisted of several hundred family-owned firms concentrated in a five-town area in the heart of England, was reduced to a few conglomerates owned by businesspeople and stockholders around the world. The new capital enabled the industry to modernize and diversify; new executives forced changes in marketing strategies and design concepts. The consolidation of the potteries, the move away from costly traditional processes of manufacture, and the broadening of its international markets around the world have ensured the survival of the industry in Britain.

Two Approaches to the American Market:
Spode and Wedgwood

As the new century dawned pottery companies in Staffordshire, England, looked to the American market with renewed enthusiasm. Some firms sought American representation in the form of agents, who would market the factory's wares to distributors and retailers. These manufacturers, typified by the firm W. T. Copeland & Sons (the maker of Spode), did not want to invest large amounts of capital to set up a U.S. branch, with its attendant sales force traversing the country. Instead they relied on separate American import partners, who took on the sales and marketing responsibilities, thereby limiting the investment of the manufacturer.

Other companies, generally larger firms in Staffordshire such as Josiah Wedgwood & Sons, set up their own branch houses in America, usually headed up by a member of the owning family. In this way they established a closer connection to their market and exercised a greater degree of control over sales strategies. Firms like Wedgwood maintained a direct link to their retailers, enabling them to evaluate and respond more quickly to changes in consumer demand. Most agents, on the other hand, kept retailers and manufacturers apart in an effort to ensure their own position. Some agents went so far as to code the order sheets so that the manufacturer would not know the identity of the retailer placing the order.[1]

Although both Wedgwood and Copeland & Sons relied on American agents during the 1910s, Wedgwood's decision to establish a company branch in America would ultimately prove the more successful approach in the U.S. marketplace. The wisdom of this move would not become apparent until after World War II, when flexibility in response to market trends became essential. In the 1920s and 1930s, when English companies were expanding U.S. market share in fine tablewares, the Copeland approach succeeded as well.

In 1908 Copeland & Sons appointed its first agent in America, the Chicago firm of Burley & Tyrell. Prior to that Copeland & Sons had sold directly to retailers, whose china buyers sent orders by mail or chose patterns in person at the factory in Stoke-upon-Trent, in the Stoke-on-Trent region of Staffordshire. Burley & Tyrell's first advertisement in the *Chicago Tribune* announcing its exclusive arrangement to sell Spode, as the product was called in America, was published on September 21, 1908. The very next day one retailer wrote to the factory demanding confirmation of this appointment. As a result the best customers were still allowed to send their buyers to Stoke-upon-Trent to place orders, but they were charged a higher rate than the factory charged Burley & Tyrell. When these retailers paid their accounts, a credit for the rate difference would be placed on account with Burley & Tyrell, thereby providing retailers with an incentive to go through the agent the next time they ordered Spode dishes.[2]

Establishing a relationship between buyers and the agent proved difficult because retailers were unwilling to purchase from an agent when they had previously ordered directly from the factory. Copeland & Sons also experienced the trials of securing an agent who would strongly promote the firm's wares around the country, and especially in New York, where the wholesale trade was concentrated. In its five-year contract extension with Burley & Tyrell, Copeland & Sons allowed itself the option of assigning other agents in America and soon appointed Bawo & Dotter to be its representative in New York. At the same time the factory continued to sell directly to its best retail customers around the country, thereby undercutting the market control of its agents in Chicago and New York.

Finally in 1922, fed up with the frustrations of selling to both agents and retailers, the managing director, Ronald Copeland, made a change. He convinced Sidney E. Thompson, a buyer for one of Copeland & Sons' largest retailers in Canada, Cassidy's of Canada, to become the sole agent for the company in the United States. The import firm was renamed Copeland & Thompson. In Canada Copeland established Copeland & Duncan, which eventually came under the leadership of Sidney Thompson's brother, Harry.[3] In 1923 Sidney moved to New York and opened offices on Fifth Avenue, in the heart of the growing tableware importing district.

Thompson's influence over the Copeland firm in Staffordshire grew steadily as he took matters in hand to increase the profile and U.S. market share of the company's product—starting with the company name. Thompson believed that one of the factors limiting sales was confusion over the name. He convinced the company's board that the name Copeland was not as well-known in America as Spode. From the start Thompson marketed the company's wares as Spode, although both names remained on the backstamp until the late 1950s because the Copeland family was reluctant to remove its name from the product.[4]

Thompson also turned his attention to design. Even as he marketed Spode as synonymous with English tradition, prestige, and elegance, Thompson manipulated designs to reflect the qualities he was promoting. Every year Sidney Thompson and his son, George E. Thompson, who would succeed his father in the business, traveled to Staffordshire, spending much of their two-month stay poring over the old pattern books at the factory. Thompson instigated new embossed shapes, such as *Jewel, Mansard, Centurion,* and *Lowestoft,* as well as many patterns on existing shapes to suit American tastes (cat. 86, 92). Based on earlier nineteenth-century Spode china and earthenware designs, the patterns, which included *Buttercup* and

Billingsley Rose, became mainstays for Copeland & Sons. He also prompted the introduction in 1938 of Spode's all-time best-selling pattern, *Christmas Tree,* as a seasonal dinnerware to be used from Thanksgiving to Christmas (cat. 18).

The two decades before World War II were fruitful years for Spode in large part because of Thompson's influence. The company depended on Thompson's knowledge of the U.S. market and his experience in sales. Copeland & Thompson emphasized the quality of handpainted decoration and the vast array of patterns and shapes. As a result, Spode became one of the most recognized names in fine English bone china and earthenware in America.

This partnership worked well before the war, when both company and importer agreed on the approach to their biggest market. Troubles arose after 1950, however, when new leadership took over in each concern.[5] For example, higher labor costs led the company to push for using printed decals rather than handpainted decoration, but the importer could foresee only a decline in sales if the bedrock of tradition in manufacturing—handpainted decoration—was to fall to modernization.[6] Copeland & Thompson also complained

about costly experiments with contemporary design, such as the *Royal College* shape, that were aimed more at the European and British home markets than the United States (cat. 93).[7] The Copeland management felt that they had to do something to revive sales, which had fallen off sharply beginning in 1954 due to a perceived change in consumer demand away from "grandmother's china."[8] However, nothing could stop the downward spiral in sales that resulted.

Ironically the strong trading relationship between the company and its agent that supported the business earlier in the century contributed to the decline and eventual takeover of both companies in 1966 by the Carborundum Company of

Niagara Falls, New York. Although Spode continued in production, the Copeland family ceased to control the company's destiny.

Like most Staffordshire potteries at the turn of the century, Josiah Wedgwood & Sons attempted to establish a substantive trading link with the American market through an agent who was also handling ware from other firms. Edward Boote in New York first represented the firm until 1898, when the company tried another agent, J. A. Service. In 1906 Wedgwood undertook a reevaluation of its export market, and in that year the management sent a young family member, Kennard Wedgwood, to New York to establish a North American branch.

Kennard Wedgwood had already distinguished himself by initiating a change in direction from the production of the ornamental wares that had been the focus of the company's nineteenth-century production to an emphasis on tableware.[9] The new office in New York provided the company with a crucial family outpost in the middle of its fastest growing market. From this vantage point Wedgwood could be assured that its name and wares would receive the highest attention from its representative in New York.

Wedgwood's approach in seeking U.S. market share was more aggressive than that of any other Staffordshire company. Although other manufacturers eventually established New York branches, Wedgwood was one of the few British pottery companies to send a family member to head up their U.S. operations, and this personal connection gave the firm an advantage. The presence of an actual Wedgwood family member who could visit department stores and specialty shops across the country, giving lectures and signing plates, was an immeasurable asset in marketing the image of prestige and historical tradition. Kennard Wedgwood's appearances were treated as noted events in the local papers and on occasion were even reported in trade journals.[10] More important, he was able to oversee sales distribution and marketing from a company perspective.

From 1910 through the early 1920s, Kennard Wedgwood served as an importer, facilitating shipments to distributors around the country. Like those of Copeland & Sons, many of these trading relationships had been established in the nineteenth century, and thus the companies were resistant to the tighter marketing controls that Wedgwood wanted to implement. In short U.S. retailers did not want to go through a central source in New York, even if that agent was a member of the company family.

Brand recognition was a major goal for Wedgwood. The name Wedgwood was not confusing to the consumer as it was in the case of Spode, in which the name of the product was different from the name of the manufacturer, W. T. Copeland & Sons. The fact that the name of Wedgwood's agent was the same as the product was no doubt beneficial and

was marketed boldly during the 1920s.[11] A talented design team in Staffordshire headed by John Goodwin helped Kennard Wedgwood develop patterns and shapes especially for the American market. Inspired by the company's earliest wares, these new designs linked the modern firm with its eighteenth-century and nineteenth-century past. A testament to the success of this approach came when Wedgwood secured the license to reproduce *Queens Ware* for the much-acclaimed restoration of Colonial Williamsburg, Virginia, in 1937.[12] The commission brought them the imprimatur of colonial American tradition.

The early 1930s had been difficult years, precipitated by the stock market crash of 1929. The company's response was to lower costs by asking all employees to take wage cuts and to concentrate on new designs, particularly those that would help buoy the sagging American market. The first attempt to modernize design came in 1933, when the *Annular* shape was introduced with new matte glazes such as *Moonstone, Matte Straw,* and *Matte Green* and occasional painted decoration. The new shape was a collaborative effort between Clement Tom Wedgwood, John Goodwin, and Keith Murray. Murray was a talented architect and industrial designer who continued to develop mostly ornamental shapes and some tableware for Wedgwood throughout the 1930s. Although highly successful in Britain, Murray's designs held limited appeal in the American market because the shapes were so different from those American consumers usually associated with the name Wedgwood (cat. 94).[13]

As profits began to rise once again and the word came from America that the ability to fill orders promptly was foremost on retailers' minds, the directors of Wedgwood made the crucial decisions to relocate, expand, and modernize the factory to meet growing needs.[14] Other manufacturers, including Spode, Minton, and Doulton, remodeled or replaced various structures during this period, but none undertook such a daring move as Wedgwood.

The building of the new factory in the Staffordshire countryside at Barlaston began even as war engulfed the nation. Although most new construction in Britain was halted by the war, the Wedgwood factory was permitted to go ahead as scheduled because of its large export trade to the United States and Canada.[15] When wartime production restrictions were imposed, Wedgwood was ideally situated to lead the effort to target the American market. In 1940, to reassure North and South American retailers of its stability, the company took the extraordinary step of publishing in English and Spanish a hardbound book illustrating shapes and glazes that were guaranteed to stay in production

OPPOSITE:
Cat. 94 Classically simple, these designs from the 1930s were among Josiah Wedgwood & Sons' best-known modernist wares.

Fig. 3.2 Josiah Wedgwood & Sons' new showroom, warehouse, and office space, occupied five floors on 54th Street in New York.

through 1950.[16] With its new factory, production levels increased so much that, by 1948, output per man-hour was up by 40 percent over prewar levels.[17]

The strength of Wedgwood in America was evident when Kennard Wedgwood retired in 1947, handing over responsibility for sales in North America to Hensleigh Wedgwood. The next ten years were important ones for the company, as they were for every British manufacturer. All were struggling with the need to appeal to new audiences, attract younger consumers, and counter renewed competition from Japan. Companies that were unable to assess their U.S. market and adapt quickly to changes were doomed to takeover or total failure.

Wedgwood moved rapidly to study the postwar consumer landscape in America. In 1949 the design director, Victor Skellern, conducted an extensive study tour of the United States. His notes were essential in conveying the need for restraint in pushing modern shapes and patterns, the importance of the bridal market, and the rising popularity of domestic casual designs, particularly in California.

An independent study of retail opinion about British pottery and glass sales in the United States conducted at the same time reiterated that quality and tradition were the predominant factors governing sales of British products. For his part Hensleigh Wedgwood continued Kennard Wedgwood's practice of touring the country, giving lectures and demon-

strations in department stores. He worked to emphasize the longevity and tradition of the company by cooperating with museums, including the Brooklyn Museum of Art in New York, to organize exhibitions of Wedgwood ceramics. Hensleigh Wedgwood also oversaw the opening of a new showroom in 1949 at 24 East Fifty-fourth Street, New York (fig. 3.2).

Despite all efforts a recession in the U.S. economy spurred a downturn in sales to the American market beginning in 1957. Wedgwood took aggressive action by sending Arthur Bryan, then general sales manager, to report on the state of the market in the United States and Canada. This type of fact-finding mission was especially effective because Wedgwood acted as its own agent in North America. Changes could be made swiftly and decisively based on direct assessments of the market situation in a way that was impossible for Copeland & Sons and all the other companies that used independent agents in America.

Bryan's report convinced the company to opt for a change in leadership in America. Hensleigh Wedgwood retired in 1960 and Arthur Bryan succeeded him, taking a more aggressive approach to sales in America than ever before. Bryan focused more on a stronger sales force and less on the lectures and museum activities that had been the hallmark of both Kennard and Hensleigh Wedgwood. He concentrated the company's efforts on capturing three sectors of the market: brides, older matrons (women married twenty years or more who wanted a second dinnerware service), and gift-ware.[18] More Wedgwood displays were developed in major department stores, and in some cases a separate Wedgwood room was built within the larger china department. All these changes occurred in a short span of three years while Bryan directed the North American subsidiary.

In 1963 Arthur Bryan returned to Barlaston to become the first managing director of the company who was not a member of the Wedgwood family. Bryan continued the re-forms he had instituted in America, realizing that U.S. and Canadian imports had reached 65 percent of total sales.[19] He also began taking advantage of opportunities to reduce Wedgwood's competition by actively pursuing and acquir-ing struggling pottery companies. His first target was Copeland & Sons in 1964, but the high cost of buying out that firm's distribution contract with Copeland & Thompson in New York soured the deal.[20] By 1970 Wedgwood had ab-sorbed over a half-dozen potteries. Bryan also studied the possibility of acquiring several American companies. In 1979 he finally settled on the Franciscan Division of Glad-ding, McBean & Co. in California in order to acquire the rights to that firm's products, including *Apple* and the highly popular *Desert Rose,* which remains the best-selling Ameri-can dinnerware pattern of all time (cat. 39). Ultimately, Wedgwood's success in the U.S. market helped make it the strongest, most financially secure company in the British pottery industry before its own takeover by the Waterford Glass Group in 1986.

The achievement of Wedgwood in the twentieth century can be attributed to a combination of many factors, but none was so important as the decision early on to establish its own distribution arm in North America. When the market

Fig. 3.3 When designing this oversized glass in 1951, Waterford Glass had American ice cubes in mind.

began to change dramatically after World War II, companies such as Copeland & Sons that had relied too heavily on the advice of a separate American agent were not positioned to recognize those changes, much less respond to them before it was too late. The two approaches to the same vast market-place yielded radically different results.

Notes

1. Copeland 1989, 7.

2. Ibid., 1–3.

3. Ibid., 8.

4. Thompson interview 1997.

5. Beginning in the early 1950s, George E. Thompson ran the company for his father, Sidney, until the elder Thompson's death in 1958. In the same year Spencer Copeland succeeded his father Ronald Copeland and served on the board with his cousins, John Copeland and Robert Copeland.

6. Copeland interview 1997.

7. Thompson interview 1997.

8. Copeland interview 1997.

9. Batkin 1982, 119.

10. "Kennard Wedgwood Talks to Customers at Marshall Field's," *CGJ* 116:2 (Feb. 1935): 46; "Kennard L. Wedgwood Addresses 200 Women at Marshall Field," 126:5 (May 1940): 47.

11. *CGJ* 91:8 (19 Feb. 1920): 13; 93:5 (3 Feb. 1921): 17.

12. "Wedgwood to Produce Ware for Williamsburg Revival," *CGJ* 120:2 (Feb. 1937): 40.

13. Batkin 1982, 167–69.

14. For a thorough discussion of Wedgwood's move to Barlaston and the building of the new factory, see Gater and Vincent 1988.

15. In the last half-year before the war, from January to June 1939, sales to the United States and Canada were 53.8 percent of the company's total sales. See Gater and Vincent 1988, 59–60.

16. Wedgwood 1940.

17. Gater and Vincent 1988, 70.

18. Bryan interview 1997.

19. Ibid.

20. Copeland interview 1997.

Waterford Glass

The rebirth of the glass industry in Waterford, Ireland, after World War II and the meteoric rise of Waterford Glass in the three decades that followed could be attributed to a combination of vision, receptive market, and a healthy dose of luck. Although Ireland had been a leader in glass production throughout the eighteenth and early nineteenth centuries, no glass had been made there since 1851. In that year the last factory, the Waterford Flint Glass Works, owned by George Gatchell & Co., closed after sending entries to the Great Exhibition in London.[1] It would be another one hundred years before fine blown glass was produced commercially in Ireland again.

As the twentieth century progressed, Ireland saw its population endure nearly fifty years of political strife, beginning with a bloody struggle for independence from Great Britain in 1925 and continuing with an even more lethal civil war shortly thereafter. During this period the mass emigration to the United States that had begun with the potato famines in the nineteenth century continued apace. Much of the nation's remaining labor force was engaged in subsistence farming or political struggle—very little industry of any kind existed.

At the same time a mystique surrounding anything Irish and handmade developed both in Ireland and among Irish immigrants elsewhere. The colonial revival movement in the United States renewed stylistic interest in eighteenth- and early-nineteenth-century architecture and decorative arts of all kinds, including glass. The tendency was to classify all cut glass from this period as Irish, and more specifically Waterford, even though much of it had been made in England or Continental Europe.

In Ireland itself glass had become a symbol of a prosperous past, the Georgian period—ironically a time when Ireland was under total domination by Great Britain. Still, for many, owning a piece of old Irish glass was akin to possessing a precious relic. One jewelry store owner and silversmith in Dublin, Bernard J. Fitzpatrick, recognized the reverence for Irish glass, or glass that looked Irish, and began working in the late 1930s with a Czechoslovakian glass company near Prague owned by Charles Bacik to supply glass for sale in his store. When Europe was engulfed by war in 1939, Fitzpatrick helped his friend immigrate to Ireland, which had become officially neutral.

Although the country was spared the destruction and upheaval experienced by its neighbors, the Irish people emerged from the war eager to participate in the renewal of European industry that began in 1946. Fitzpatrick and Bacik decided that the time had come to resume glassmaking in Ireland as a way to promote nationalism and to capitalize on the interest in Irish glass they knew already existed. With little more than an idea, Bacik contacted his former chief designer in Prague, Miroslav Havel, and asked him to come to Ireland to help form a new company to produce glass.

Fitzpatrick and Bacik chose Waterford as the location for their new factory—not because they expected a ready source of experienced labor (there was none), but because they knew the town's name was inexplicably linked to the mystique of the old glass industry in Ireland.[2] So in 1947 Havel journeyed to Waterford, greeting Bacik for the first time since the war on the site where the small factory would be located.[3]

Havel and Bacik set about finding labor, designing machinery, and building furnaces, while Fitzpatrick worked in Dublin to secure funds for the venture. Over the course of the next year they struggled to locate materials made scarce by the war. Havel and Bacik finally convinced a Czech company to cast the first cutting wheels, and they purchased a quantity of Belgian glass to use in training future glasscutters. Havel approached the local priest to find six Irish boys in their midteens to begin training with Bacik and two Polish blowers, who had immigrated to England during the war. Meanwhile Havel traveled periodically to Dublin, where Fitzpatrick arranged for him to study genuine antique Irish glass in the collection of the National Museum of Ireland. Havel copied every detail of the glass in his drawings and brought the designs back to Waterford for the boys to learn to cut.[4]

By 1948 the factory was erected, the furnaces had been built to European specifications, and the workers were ready to begin. But on the very first day the furnaces were fired, and in the presence of dignitaries and townspeople who had come to see the first glass taken from the melting pot, the furnace collapsed in a fiery heap. Built by a French company with help from a Belfast foundry, it was not adequate for the amount of heat produced. Another year elapsed before experiments were completed and the first glass emerged.[5]

In the beginning only simple tumblers were produced because the inexperienced young cutters could manage nothing more complicated. Back in Dublin Bernard Fitzpatrick's resources had nearly run out when he found two investors, Joseph McGrath and Joseph Griffin, owners of the Irish Glass Bottle Company. McGrath and Griffin provided the Waterford venture with the necessary capital to continue its limited production until the workers were sufficiently skilled to make commercially viable glass. The newly formed Waterford Glass recruited thirty additional cutters and blowers from central Europe and moved the pilot factory to its present location on the outskirts of the town of Waterford.

In 1951 the first commercial tableware to be made included the patterns for which Waterford would become famous: *Sheila, Colleen,* and the best-selling *Lismore* (cat. 95).

These patterns were cut on shapes designed especially for the American market, such as large water goblets, saucer-shaped champagne glasses, and short cocktail glasses (fig. 3.3). One modern-style pattern, *Tralee,* was included but withdrawn after only a few short years of production. Contemporary cutting patterns did not fit the concept of traditional Irish patterns devised by Fitzpatrick and Bacik and would not be attempted again until the mid-1980s.

Early consumers were found mainly in the Irish home market after an initially lukewarm response in the United States. American department store buyers expected the new glass to have the bluish tint associated with old Irish glass. But the glassmakers considered the tint to be a flaw, an indication that the mix of materials was not quite right.

Although the company persevered in resisting blue tinting, it made a crucial discovery about the superficial nature of taste in the tableware market—flaws could be good, indeed desirable, if marketed properly. For the fledgling company in Waterford this concept was a boon because its glass was full of flaws, mostly in the form of bubbles. It was the bold idea of Waterford's sales director, Cornelius "Con" Dooley, to call these bubbles "the breath of the craftsman," and quality was never an issue again.[6] If the batch was particularly good on a given day, the foreman would order the cutters to produce the *Sheila* pattern, which featured broad, flat-cut panels. If the mix was very poor, the allover diamond pattern *Alana* was cut instead to mask imperfections. These two patterns took care of the extremes in quality, while most patterns, like *Lismore* and *Colleen,* could accommodate a few bubbles, which might be distracting in other patterns.[7]

Another factor initially troubled the master glassmakers Havel and Bacik: the blowers they trained could not produce thinly walled stemware like other glassware on the market. Havel and Bacik were evidently unaware of the survey produced for the British pottery and glass industry in 1948 that spoke of U.S. consumers wanting heavy glasses with deep cuts.[8] They soon discovered through experience, however, that thick, substantially weighted stemware, considered crude by glassblowers at the time, was what many Americans desired.

In 1952 the first orders were received from B. Altman & Co. in New York.[9] This single client kept the factory busy and growing for several years while sales director Dooley and others traveled to the United States, introducing buyers to the new stemware. Waterford was first represented by the Geo. Borgfeldt Corporation in New York, but by 1960 the Irish glassmaker had appointed the Horace C. Gray Company to act as its agent there.[10] Gradually department stores in Chicago and San Francisco carried Waterford stock, although Altman's remained the company's biggest customer until 1961. In that year Waterford followed the example set by Josiah Wedgwood & Sons earlier in the century and opened its own exclusive North American import house in New York under the name Waterford Glass. Overseeing its own sales and marketing in the United States, Waterford was better positioned to aggressively compete in the American market. The results were astounding: in 1967 Waterford announced that its sales had surpassed the previous year by over 45 percent, and as a result it had quadrupled its showroom space in New York.

In the early 1960s Waterford's marketing strategies followed the instinct of the company's founders—namely, to promote the connection between old Waterford glass and new. Magazine advertisements in 1963 quoted ads for Waterford glass from 1790 but featured an illustration of a new goblet.[11] At about this time Waterford changed the name of the product from "glass" to "crystal," and used provocative photography to feature sparkling prismatic effects—a strategy that instantly placed a mark of prestige on the product.[12]

Dooley stressed the Irishness of the product, appealing to the popularity of all things Irish inspired by the election of John Fitzgerald Kennedy, the first American president of Irish ancestry. By linking the new product with the rarity of the old, Dooley even managed to make delivery delays and shortages a profitable circumstance. According to one company executive, "If a lady wanted six goblets and she couldn't have them because the store had them on back order for weeks, she would often buy six wine glasses or even sherry glasses instead out of frustration just to own some Waterford—and Americans didn't even drink sherry!"[13]

The result of these efforts was the dramatic growth of Waterford's sales in the United States during the 1960s. Just fifteen years after the company began, it undertook a major expansion and built a new factory to accommodate the mounting orders.[14] The constant imbalance of greater demand than supply in fact masked a potentially fatal flaw in the structure of Waterford's production. At its formation the glasshouse adopted an old European system whereby a suite of twenty-four graduated pieces were made in each pattern every day. This production method was based on the premise that the best glass was at the top of the furnace pot at the beginning of each day, so the biggest pieces had to be made first. As the day wore on the blowers would be able to gather less and less good quality glass, meaning that forms had to be made in ever decreasing sizes, ending with the tiny liqueur glasses.

The problem with this method was that production drove marketing: the company had to make sherry and liqueur glasses regardless of whether the public wanted them. Otherwise the workforce would have to be idle after the first few hours until the furnaces were charged, a process that took hours and so was done overnight. The only solution was to market sherry and liqueur glasses as novelties and hope that demand for anything by Waterford would always outpace supply, a situation that in fact held true until the mid-1980s.

The company's steady rise in the American tableware market continued in the 1970s, expanding sales into every corner of the United States and Canada. Waterford soon became the acknowledged crystal of choice for wealthy brides, its popularity boosted by sales to famous women such as Patricia Nixon on the occasion of her White House marriage to Edward Cox in 1972. The first significant merger for the glassmaker came in 1970, when Waterford took over the English bone china producer John Aynsley & Sons to provide a tableware partner for marketing its stemware. Advertisements soon appeared showing Waterford goblets with Aynsley plates, reinforcing the notion that Waterford crystal went with English china, a further enhancement of the connection to tradition and prestige.[15]

In 1981 the West Virginia–based Fostoria Glass Company conducted a nationwide study of the American table glass market. In addition to determining that crystal was "strongly a high income market" and very limited—only 15 percent of adults had ever purchased such glassware—Fostoria discovered that Waterford dominated the field. When asked "What brand name comes to mind first when you think of crystal, stemware, or barware?," 37 percent of respondents said Waterford. Trailing the Irish maker were Fostoria (17 percent) and Lenox Crystal (13 percent). A full 25 percent said they already owned Waterford glass. But most telling of all was the researchers' conclusion that "Waterford is the closest to the qualities that people look for in crystal. A high percentage of respondents describe it as beautiful in design, high quality, and expensive."[16]

Despite its strong name recognition Waterford's growth slowed in the early 1980s, when labor strife afflicted the factory and sales began to lag in the United States. By this time the typical Waterford consumer was more sophisticated. She no longer bought whatever was on the shelf in her pattern just to have a piece of Waterford; instead, she purchased only what she specifically needed.[17] This shift left huge stockpiles back in Ireland of unsold sherry, cocktail, and liqueur glasses and other forms that were rarely used anymore by the American consumer. As a result the company undertook a massive renovation of its plants to accommodate new computer-driven furnaces that would produce glass of consistent quality, thereby eliminating the need to create unpopular forms.

In 1986, after a complete revision of its product lines, Waterford acquired another pottery manufacturer, Josiah Wedgwood & Sons. This bold move created one of the largest tableware producers in the world and finally united the most successful pottery and glass firms in Great Britain and the Republic of Ireland.

Cat. 95 Heavily cut lead crystal from Waterford Glass swept America in the 1960s.

Notes

1. Grehan 1981, 36–37.

2. Murphy interview 1998.

3. Havel interview 1998.

4. O'Leary interview 1998.

5. Ibid.

6. Murphy interview 1998.

7. Havel interview 1998.

8. Time-Life 1948, 13.

9. "B. Altman Has Waterford Crystal," *CGJ* 151:6 (Dec. 1952): 10; O'Leary interview 1998; and Giarracco interview 1997.

10. *CGJ* 160:5 (May 1957): 2; *GTR* (31 Mar. 1960): 65.

11. *GTR* (Jan. 1963): 96.

12. Much of the photography for print advertisements and other public relations was conceived and shot by Harry Pesin and in more recent years, Terry Murphy.

13. O'Leary interview 1998.

14. *GTR* (21 June 1965): 8.

15. *GTR* (June 1971): 4.

16. Internoscia 1982.

17. Ibid. According to this source 79 percent of respondents used "crystal" for entertaining, 61 percent used it for everyday meals, and 48 percent as barware. In these categories Waterford was used as follows: entertaining—22 percent; everyday—1 percent; and barware—7 percent.

The Germans and Czechs

Central Europe has been an important producer of earthenware, porcelain, and glass for centuries due to its abundant raw materials, efficient river transportation, and skilled labor force. By the early twentieth century, the German and Czech tableware industries were highly developed. Bohemian glass, one of Czechoslovakia's foremost exports, was world renowned. In the United States Bohemian glass was so well thought of in certain periods that not only was it imported in large quantities, but American glasshouses also sometimes purchased Czech blanks on which to do decorative cutting and even produced near-exact reproductions of Bohemian designs.[90]

Centered in northern Bohemia, the Czech glass industry employed thousands of workers making all types of glass articles, from goblets to window panes. In 1920 it was estimated that Bohemia had two thousand glasshouses with sixty thousand workers.[91] The German glassware industry was centered in eastern Germany in the regions of Saxony, Silesia, and Thuringia, across the border from Bohemia. Although Germans had produced high-quality glass since the Middle Ages, their glass industry grew dramatically during the twentieth century, as new technologies and export markets came into play. By 1970 fifty German glasshouses were producing tableware. Together they employed twenty-five thousand workers and annually produced about $105 million in glassware, of which about one-quarter went to the United States.[92]

The situation was reversed in the case of the German and Czech ceramics industries. Of the two, Germany's ceramics industry was larger and more highly developed, while that of Czechoslovakia greatly expanded after World War I. In 1925 it was reported that Germany had 1,588 factories producing table- and kitchen-ware. These potteries employed 92,035 workers. The Czech ceramics industry was significantly smaller, with seventy factories and seventeen thousand laborers in 1920.[93]

Like their glassworks, the Czech and German porcelain tableware factories were in fairly close proximity to one another. German porcelain manufacturing was concentrated in northeastern Bavaria and Thuringia, and to a lesser degree in Saxony and Silesia. Earthenware factories were more evenly distributed throughout both countries.[94] In addition to being geographically united, the German and Czech glass and ceramics industries were in many ways dependent on each other. German porcelain manufacturers relied heavily on Czech raw materials, especially high-grade white kaolin clay. Great quantities of quartz, feldspar, and coal were also imported into Germany from Bohemia. Skilled Czech workers crossed the border to labor in the plants of pottery centers such as Selb, Bavaria. The Czech glass industry in turn de-

Cat. 96 In the late 1920s and 1930s, the German potteries J. Uffrecht & Co. (rear plates) and Elsterwerda Earthenware Factory (tea set), supplied avant-garde dishes to American consumers.

pended on Germany for the critical ingredient potash.[95] Germany was a major investor in the Czech glass and ceramic industries, as well as a leading supplier of production technology. Before World War II many Czech factories were wholly owned or controlled by larger German firms such as Rosenthal & Co. and C. M. Hutschenreuther.

The amount of tableware made in Germany and Czechoslovakia typically surpassed what local inhabitants could consume. In 1927, for example, it was estimated that the domestic Czech market absorbed only 20 percent of the country's glass production. In the case of German ceramic tableware, exports averaged around 25 percent of the total output by value in 1935.[96] For some producers, especially producers of high-quality porcelain dinnerware, the percentage exported could be much higher—for example, in 1926 the leading firm of Lorenz Hutschenreuther exported 60 percent of its ceramics.[97]

Both Germany and Czechoslovakia sold ceramics and glass worldwide; the United States was one of their most important export markets between 1880 and 1980 and their biggest foreign buyer for much of this period. In 1897 Germany was responsible for the second largest amount of pottery imported into the United States, 30 percent of the total. By 1912 the Germans exported twice as many dishes to America as their main rival, the British. The total accounted for nearly one-quarter by value of all earthenware made in Germany and more than three-quarters of all porcelain.[98] A similar situation existed with respect to glass. In 1911 Bohemia, with one-third of the total imports, was the single largest supplier of foreign table glass to the United States. Germany followed close behind.[99]

After World War I the German and Czech shares of overall imports to America declined. In 1928 Germany's ceramics contribution was about 23 percent, but it fell to less than 10 percent after 1932 due to the depression and intense Japanese competition (cat. 96).[100] Although they never regained as great a share of the overall American market as they had held before 1930, the Germans reentered the American market after World War II and once again developed sizable sales.[101]

Because of the political changes wrought by World War II, the Czechs were most influential in the American market before 1945. Still part of the Austro-Hungarian Empire, Bohemia was consistently the fourth largest supplier of U.S. ceramic tableware imports between 1892 and 1905, after which time it was overtaken by Japan.[102] In 1913, on the eve of World War I, Bohemia was the second most important supplier of foreign decorated table glass to the United States. At the same time America was Bohemia's third largest foreign consumer of Czech pottery. Following behind Germany and Great Britain, Americans purchased nearly $500,000 in ware, virtually all of it porcelain (cat. 145).[103]

Following Czechoslovakia's independence in 1921, shipments to the United States increased. By 1929 Czech china exports had nearly doubled in value. At that time Czechoslovakia was America's fourth largest supplier of ceramic tableware, shipping nearly twice the quantity of ceramics to this country as was imported from France.[104] Having suffered declining sales during the depression, the Czechs tried to return to the American market in the postwar era, but exports of porcelain tableware to America were totally negligible during the next thirty-five years. Czech glass fared better after the war but declined over time.[105]

PROMOTION AND DISTRIBUTION

To ensure that as many potential domestic and foreign wholesale buyers as possible saw their wares, central European manufacturers employed the time-honored techniques of distributing multilingual trade catalogues, advertising in trade and popular magazines, and occasionally participating in world's fairs. Unlike most of their rivals, both the Germans and the Czechs developed highly sophisticated international trade fairs that took place semiannually. In Germany the most important of these fairs for the glass and ceramic industry was the Leipzig fair, which was established in 1895. In 1922 *Crockery and Glass Journal* noted 13,000 exhibitors, 700 coming from outside Germany. Further emphasizing the importance of this international event is the fact that 310,000 people visited Leipzig to view the merchandise. By 1925 the Leipzig fair was considered important enough to American trade that a U.S. sales center was opened by the American Leipzig Fair Association, headquartered in the F. W. Woolworth & Co. Building in New York.[106]

The Czechs' first international sample fair took place in 1920 at the Industrial Palace of Prague and featured the products of 2,100 manufacturers. Because of Prague's proximity to the heart of the Czech glass and ceramics industries, these commodities were always well represented.[107] Hence American china and glass buyers often timed their trips to Europe during the first half of the twentieth century to coincide with one or both of these trade fairs.

Because of the great number of German and Czech manufacturers exporting large quantities of ceramics and glass to the United States, a multifaceted distribution network developed. Some central European factories founded their own import houses in New York in hopes of gaining more direct access to the large U.S. market. Although importers of German and Czech tableware had existed before, the 1920s and 1930s were a particularly active period for them. Among the most notable in the interwar years were the Imperial Bohemia China Corporation, the Schumann China Corporation, the Overseas Mercantile Company, and the Wiener Werkstätte of America (cats. 97, 98).[108]

An example of such an import house about which some historical information is available is the firm of Heinrich & Winterling. The company evolved from the earlier import house of William C. Mueller, which represented a group of

OVERLEAF:
Cat. 97 German and Czech porcelain like these pieces featuring small modernist patterns appealed more to Europeans than Americans in the 1930s.

associated ceramics factories in Germany and Czechoslovakia, including the well-known firm of Heinrich & Co. In 1926 Mueller severed his connection with the company, and the name was changed to Heinrich & Winterling. Karl Lickhard, who immigrated to the United States in 1903 and was the treasurer for Mueller, became president and general manager of the new company.[109] During the next two decades Heinrich & Winterling carried a wide range of porcelain dinnerware and breakfast and luncheon sets, as well as earthenware and glass (cat. 148). Although Heinrich & Winterling introduced a line of American-made china in 1940, its inability to import wares from its German and Czech factories during World War II ruined the firm.[110] By 1948 it was likely out of business since its most significant lines were being handled by the Aristocrat China Company and Gustave Lap (cat. 99).[111]

The enormous porcelain and glass manufacturer Philipp Rosenthal & Co. had at different times both an exclusive distributor and its own import house in the United States (see pp. 234–44). Its foremost rival, Lorenz Hutschenreuther, did not establish its own American office and showroom until the early 1970s. Hutschenreuther was one of many firms that relied on the expertise of an independent importer in America—in this case, the well-known firm of Paul A. Straub & Co. Straub functioned as exclusive agent until the manufacturer established Hutschenreuther USA.[112]

Paul Straub personified the typical distributor of central European china and glass. Born in the United States of German parents, Straub spoke fluent German. In his late teens he joined the firm of J. Clingenberg, which specialized in Bohemian tableware imports, and about 1881 he left to join the staff of one of New York's biggest import houses, Bawo &

Dotter. In part due to his language skills, Straub became a resident buyer for the firm, operating out of Dresden for twenty years. When Bawo & Dotter was bought out by Cassidy's of Canada in 1915, he founded his own firm with his brother, Walter J. Straub, who had worked for the French porcelain importing firm of Vogt & Dose.[113]

Paul Straub acquired his first significant line of German porcelain, that of Tirschenreuth & Co, in 1915 when he took over its representation from Bawo & Dotter. Although initially handled in the 1920s by B. Tomby of New York, Straub became Hutschenreuther's exclusive distributor in 1932. As did many importers, Straub worked hard to ensure that the products he distributed would suit the American market. In the case of the Tirschenreuth brand, he was known to be in regular contact with the German pottery. In 1930 an observer noted:

> [Straub] essentially sends suggestions for adaptations for the American market. New patterns, shapes and decorations are constantly being tried out, and the recent growth in public preference for full dinner sets, with separate service plates, [after dinner] coffees, tea, salad, dessert and other additional occasional services, is answered fully in the prompt shipment of appropriate patterns and colorings of desired type.[114]

Through such diligent efforts, Straub and his German associates greatly expanded Tirschenreuth and gave it "distinctly English" styling. In 1915 the line included approximately

Cat. 98 Central European porcelain makers developed ivory-colored bodies for the U.S. market in the late 1920s and 1930s.

Cat. 99 Germans appreciated stark white dishes like Lorenz Hutschenreuther's *Apart* of 1957, but Heinrich & Co. added conservative decoration to *Anmut* (about 1950) for the American market.

twelve stock dinnerware patterns; by 1930 the line had grown to seventy-five patterns. Also the number of service plates had climbed in fifteen years to "200 designs ranging in price from $15 to $300 a dozen." Even when it came to naming patterns and creating a brand-name logo, an American point of view was taken. Tirschenreuth's patterns were given names like *Wilton, Oxford, Hanover, Derby,* and *Clermont,* and the design for the backstamp was derived from George Washington's coat-of-arms.[115]

With two leading lines of German tableware and less well-known lines from Italy, Austria, and England, Straub's business (known as PASCO by the mid-1950s) grew to the point that it needed a spacious showroom.[116] The firm moved into new quarters at 19 East Twenty-sixth Street in 1941 and opened a West Coast branch in the Brack Shops in Los Angeles in 1955. Straub could now distribute from each coast both conservative and modern-style tableware and giftware to retailers throughout the country.

Indicative of the wide range of German goods Straub carried were two Lorenz Hutschenreuther patterns featured in an advertisement in *Crockery and Glass Journal* in 1957. The *Richelieu*

pattern was based on rococo-revival French porcelain from the late nineteenth century; *Apart* was an avant-garde, triangular shape recently designed by Hans Achtziger (cat. 99). Such a product mix must have succeeded for Paul A. Straub & Co. because the firm survived as a leading importer in New York even after the Straub brothers' deaths in the 1950s.

Alongside firms such as Heinrich & Winterling, Rosenthal, and Straub that featured one or two major German or Czech china and glass lines, other firms in New York and a few in Philadelphia imported tableware from numerous countries, including central Europe. Some of the most prominent of these firms were George F. Bassett & Co.; Fisher, Bruce & Co.; Geo. Borgfeldt Corporation (fig. 3.4); B. Tomby; Justin Tharaud & Son; Fred C. Reimer Company; Koscherak Brothers; Otto Goetz, Inc.; Marks & Rosenfeld; Fraser's; and Ceramar (cat. 100).[117]

A few American companies designed their products in the United States, had them manufactured in central Europe, and then imported them back into the United States. The most prominent of these firms included Ebeling & Reuss (see pp. 289–90; cats. 5, 129), Graham & Zenger (cat. 101), Czecho

Fig. 3.4 Geo. Borgfeldt & Co. and other firms promoted a variety of Continental tablewares to the wholesale trade through ads such as this.

Peasant Art Company (cat. 13), and Block China Company (cats. 127, 207).[118]

THE POLITICS OF DISHES

Importers and the central European factories that supplied them overcame significant challenges to succeed in the American market. As with their French counterparts, U.S. tariff duties coupled with changes in the world economy made the cost of German and Czech tableware rise in America between 1880 and 1980 with few exceptions. By 1930 the duty on decorated china, for example, was 70 percent of value plus an extra 10 cents per dozen pieces. The major import house of Geo. Borgfeldt & Co. reacted to the new tariff that had raised duties to this new high when it advertised that the firm was downsizing "because of the tariff and other trade changes" and so was offering "at remarkable price reductions, for immediate delivery, large stocks" of china and glassware.[119]

In 1936 the situation deteriorated still further for the Germans when the U.S. Treasury Department suddenly increased the duty on German-made decorated porcelain by 22.5 percent. The resulting 92.5 percent total duty was enacted in retaliation for what the U.S. government believed to be unfair trade practices with respect to the importation of American

products. In the end the price of the finest German china went up 15 percent. One contemporary observer noted that as a result of this action the outlook for importers of German wares was "a glum one."[120]

During the 1920s and 1930s the Czechs fared somewhat better with respect to tariff duties but suffered from German competition. The hyperinflation that occurred in Germany during the 1920s devalued the German currency, and many foreign importers, including U.S. ones, switched their sources of supply for china and glass from Czechoslovakia to Germany. In 1922 it was reported that in Germany "large numbers of orders [for glassware] have been received from abroad, owing to the exceptionally favorable rates of exchange. It has only been possible to execute a portion of these orders, as all the glass works are working up to the full limit of their production."[121] The same situation existed in the German ceramic industry, resulting in great hardship for the Czechs.[122]

More helpful to Czech exports was the reciprocal trade agreement between the United States and Czechoslovakia, granting the young republic most favored nation status in March 1938. Although no change was made with respect to ceramics, this new accord reduced import duties on Czech handblown glass by 10 percent and on unpolished pressed glass by 50 percent. Because the new rates on glass in the U.S.-Czech agreement were by law applicable to all countries with most favored nation status, including Japan, American glassmakers were "greatly disappointed."[123]

WARTIME INTERRUPTION

Czechoslovakia's advantage in the American market was short-lived. In October 1938 the German army occupied the Sudetenland, where the major china and glass producers were located. Within weeks all ware being shipped from the occupied area had to be marked "Made in Germany," making it dutiable in the United States at the full tariff rate. In March 1939 the United States withdrew Czechoslovakia's most favored nation status altogether.[124]

Many American consumers and importers protested against German aggression by refusing to buy German and Czech products. One reporter noted:

> Several of the importing firms in New York have made surveys themselves or have had access to surveys of anti-German feeling from coast to coast in the United States. It has been discovered, they say, that the opinion that anti-German feeling is strong only in New York or in the larger Eastern cities is erroneous. In San Francisco, Los Angeles, Chicago, Cleveland, Cincinnati, and down in Texas they have had reports that the expectant sale of German goods in those cities has been reduced

OPPOSITE:
Cat. 100 Otto Goetz imported some of Schramberger Majolikafabrik's most radical ware into the United States in about 1930.

10 percent of what it was. Furthermore, in cases where the store heads themselves have not forbidden buyers the purchase of German goods, the consumer reaction has been too strong to warrant its handling.[125]

As the public outcry mounted, prices rose because of heavier taxation by the expanding Third Reich and escalating costs of raw material and labor. German and Czech products all but disappeared from store shelves in the United States by 1940.[126] American importers sought substitute products from other parts of Europe and increasingly from manufacturers within the United States for the duration of World War II.

Although they spurned postwar Japanese products, American consumers scarcely hesitated to buy German china and glass in the years following World War II. German tableware reappeared in this country relatively quickly after the war thanks in large part to the action of the U.S. government. Because the American army occupied Bavaria, it controlled the primary production centers for household and decorative porcelain. To partially finance the occupation and to rebuild the German economy, the U.S. Office of Military Government for Germany (OMGUS) established a policy by which DM 8 million worth of porcelain per month would be produced. Of that total 50 percent was for export, 25 percent for the American occupation forces, and 25 percent for the German home market.[127]

Apparently the United States consumed virtually all the German china exported in the late 1940s. To accomplish this feat, the Department of Commerce created the U.S. Commercial Company (USCC). Through its export-import division, the USCC facilitated exports from economically prostrate Germany, as well as from Japan. Sales of these products generated dollar credits that in turn were used "to import raw materials for additional production and for food items."[128] In the case of the German ceramics industry, the credits were initially used to purchase scarce kaolin clay and coal from Czechoslovakia, as well as gold from the United States for gilding.[129]

The USCC conducted surveys of American importers in 1946 to determine "what kind of china they would buy if they could get delivery" and used the results to guide German— and by extension Czech—production. The USCC also held exhibitions of German and Japanese wares in New York and invited potential buyers to visit displays of German tableware in Munich. Representatives from George F. Bassett & Co., Koscherak Brothers, and J. & I. Block (later the Block China Company) are known to be among those to have visited Bavaria.[130]

Beyond the 50 percent of German porcelain production that the U.S. Office of Military Government ordered to be exported, it directly oversaw the distribution of another 25 per-

cent through the Post Exchange (PX) network. The Army Exchange Service (AES) ran 190 PXs in Germany, Austria, France, Belgium, and England by 1949. As with other merchandise, the AES purchased German tableware at approximately wholesale rates. Because it did not pay taxes and did not have the overhead of typical commercial stores, the AES offered German, as well as Japanese and English, dinnerware to military personal at a substantial savings.[131]

The volume handled by these military stores was large. In 1947 the PX in Mannheim, Germany, which was one of the largest, had five thousand visitors a week with monthly sales of approximately $170,000. Among the merchandise offered was "exquisite china and glass, and fine table linen."[132] To buy and sell these wares effectively the AES published in its monthly magazine *Post Exchange* special articles such as "Buying and Selling Glassware for Every Occasion" and "Merchandise Facts to Help You Sell China and Earthenware."[133]

Being able to purchase expensive, high-quality china and glassware at reduced prices must have been an enticing opportunity for military personnel and their families. Certainly American retailers thought the opportunity would be irresistible. Even before the war was over merchants asked the government to restrict access to PXs because of the quantity of goods making its way to civilians through them. Given the large amount of merchandise, including tableware, that must have been purchased for loved ones in the United States, the merchants probably had reason to complain. In 1961 the government itself was worried about lost revenue and directed that all foreign-made products sold at PXs be acquired by its purchasing agents from an American importer. By enacting this rule the government ensured that duty was paid on merchandise.[134]

In spite of the fact that the U.S. government was capable of distributing large quantities of glass and ceramics shortly after World War II ended, obtaining reliable deliveries of stock was problematic. Although German potteries and glassworks were kept busy during the war supplying the Third Reich and their facilities suffered relatively little destruction from Allied bombing, production virtually stopped after the war due to shortages of raw materials and lack of manpower. Because Germany and Czechoslovakia were heavily dependent on one another in these vital areas, the creation of the Iron Curtain between the two nations meant that their china and glass industries had to adapt to new economic and political realities.

In the case of the German ceramics industry, the import-export division of the USCC initially arranged for deliveries of raw materials. Over time, however, German potteries had to develop new techniques for firing kilns using inferior domestic coal. Similarly, the majority of decal factories had been destroyed in air raids or were now in the Russian zone in the east, so West German potteries had to either develop new designs that did not require decal decoration or find new sources of supply.[135]

The Czech glass and ceramics industries suffered similarly after the war. As many as 75 to 80 percent of workers in Bohemian glasshouses were expelled from the country as ethnic Germans, creating crippling labor shortages. Also the nationalization of both industries ushered in mandatory price fixing and layers of inefficient bureaucracy.[136] The result of these changes was that china and glass prices were double or triple those before the war.[137]

The initial samples of German and Czech wares arrived in New York via different avenues. The china samples displayed by the USCC in New York in 1946 were from only a few leading manufacturers such as Rosenthal and the Krautheim Porcelain Factory.[138] At the time it was expected that samples of glass and earthenware would soon follow.[139] Because it was occupied by the Russians, Czechoslovakia did not receive aid from the USCC. Nevertheless the Czechs were enthusiastic about returning to the American market as soon as possible, especially with respect to the commodities that were their premier exports to the United States before the war, textiles and glass.[140]

In late 1945 the Czechs announced that they would revive the renowned Prague trade fair. In January 1948 Czechoslovakia became the first European country to hold a trade show in the United States after the war. Following that first event held in New York, another trade show was sanctioned by the U.S. State Department and was held in Boston in September 1949. At that fair 30 percent of Czech industry was represented, including glass and ceramics.[141] Shortly after the close of the fair the Czech government began advertising to the U.S. trade

a new state entity, the Czechoslovak Glass Export Company, known as Glassexport. A similar office, Czechoslovak Ceramics, was established to handle china sales in the United States. Through these efforts the Czechs did return to the American market. Glass stemware was being commercially distributed in the United States as early as 1947, but significant deliveries were achieved only in the 1950s. Ceramic tableware lagged behind and was not really reintroduced to American consumers until about 1960. Even then it sold only in miniscule amounts.[142]

As reflected in postwar export figures, Germany's return to the U.S. market was more significant in terms of both ceramics and glass. This success was partially due to the fact that many German producers were located in the western part of the country and thus could trade freely with the United States, unlike their Czechoslovakian counterparts. Unhampered by travel restrictions, the West Germans worked diligently to place their wares before potential buyers. By the early 1950s German manufacturers were represented at trade fairs and permanent showrooms worldwide, and all across the United States.

German producers and their American importers tried to analyze the preferences of American consumers and cater

Cat. 102 German, Czech, and Austrian makers continued to supply high-quality table glass to the United States after World War II.

to them. In 1951 the German trade periodical *Die Schaulade* reported on an exhibition in Stuttgart of modernist American household goods from the Museum of Modern Art's collection. Featuring tableware by designers such as Eva Zeisel, Freda Diamond, Walter Dorwin Teague, Russel Wright, Glidden M. Parker Jr., George E. Thompson, and Edith Heath, this show was believed to represent the best in American design and German producers were told to pay it close attention (cats. 177, 188). The reporter stated, "It is important for German industry and German trade to know what has developed in the world during the last twenty years and what has been discovered. He who will export must know the foreign world and its wishes."[143]

A RETURN TO THE MARKET

During the 1950s and 1960s German makers of china and glass tried very hard to "know" the American world and its wishes. Representatives from German firms regularly visited the United States, and market testing of new designs was often conducted. Initially the American consumer, hungry for products following the lean war years, drove imports of German glass and ceramics upward in the 1950s. Imports for German tableware in 1960, for example, had increased more than 20 percent over 1958 imports. But the fact that German glassware manufacturers were behind on U.S. orders because of high European demand forebode difficulties.[144]

From 1960 to 1963 German sales of high-quality china in the United States dropped by one-third, while sales within the European Common Market (ECM) rose over 500 percent. Since its founding in 1958 the ECM posed a dilemma for German glass and ceramics makers with respect to the American market.[145] When selling to member countries in Europe, import duties were lower, transportation costs less, and design development less complicated. Americans required patterns that could not be sold in Europe, and individual American consumers did not purchase porcelain dinnerware in large quantities in comparison to Europeans. One German sales manager summed up this contrast when he said in 1964, "Frankly speaking, the U.S. housewife is not a satisfactory china customer. She tends to reserve her 'good' dinnerware for important occasions. The Italian, German, and Lowland customers are better china users. I wish your people would break china like they do in Europe."[146] In 1973 another industry representative noted additional difficulties thwarting German success in America. According to him Germany was "not getting its just share of the American market" because of "the difficulty in getting distributors, of stocking the U.S., of tariff duties, and the high cost of advertising."[147]

At the same time the Germans faced other problems at home. As central European industry expanded, workers left the ceramics and glass manufactories for higher paying jobs. The result was escalating labor costs. But even with higher wages and an influx of workers from Greece, Italy, and Spain, many German potteries and glassworks could not meet demand.[148] With a shortage of product, deliveries to the United States began to lag and American retailers and consumers became increasingly disenchanted with German wares. In the end, "caught in a squeeze of growing sales potential in the Common Market countries, particularly France, and a limited labor supply at home," German china and glass manufacturers initially attempted to solve their problems in the American market in two ways. First, they simplified their operations by eliminating "less popular shapes and patterns to concentrate [their] production time on proven sellers." And second, for the most part they abandoned the lower- and middle-range markets to the Japanese and targeted "the big ticket, lower volume trade in the U.S." In 1964 one German china manufacturer said of this decision, "Labor cost represents 60 percent

Cat. 103 Villeroy & Boch lured Americans with playful progressive designs like this covered punch bowl in the 1930s.

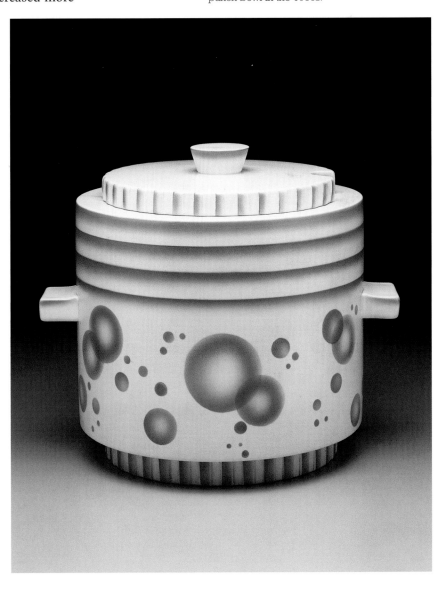

of our price. We can save ourselves a lot of worry by pushing prestige patterns" (cat. 108).[149]

The situation had worsened by the early 1970s. Labor costs continued to skyrocket, as expenses for raw materials increased. In an attempt to cut overhead the German ceramics and glass factories rationalized processes wherever possible with new forming equipment and mechanical glassblowing technology. In 1973 Dr. Traugott Malzan, marketing manager for the recently combined firms of Lorenz and C. M. Hutschenreuther, announced that 57 percent of his firm's annual sales were being "absorbed by wages and social security costs for its 5,000 workers." As a result, he concluded, "like potters all around the world, [we are] having to mechanize more stringently. That is where the future in dinnerware lies."[150] Meanwhile the industries themselves were made more efficient through mergers that brought greater economies of scale. In 1972, for example, Hutschenreuther and Kahla united and absorbed the Porzellanfabrik Arzberg and Tirschenreuth. Four years later Villeroy & Boch bought Heinrich & Co.[151]

During the early 1970s the German mark rose sharply against the U.S. dollar, making German china and glass more expensive in America. At the same time other countries were emerging as exporting nations. In 1974 a spokesperson said, "The [German] china industry has had to withstand serious competition from the East Block countries, Mainland China, and Japan. These currently offer their products on the ECC and U.S. markets at nearly 40 percent less than German industry can."[152] In the end German producers persevered.

A few firms made Herculean efforts to be successful in the United States. Villeroy & Boch is a good example. Headquartered in Mettlach, Germany, this giant firm had nineteen production facilities on three continents and eighteen thousand employees in 1973. Although Villeroy & Boch had exported small quantities of stylish earthenware to the United States before the war, it mainly supplied Americans with beer steins (cat. 103). Around 1970 efforts were launched to garner increased sales in the United States. This attempt was led by the young and dynamic Wendelin von Boch, who was then general sales manager, in association with other family members.

In 1973 Boch explained succinctly why his company was so eager to increase sales in the United States: "We are aware that the U.S. market is the most important in the world."[153]

During the 1970s Villeroy & Boch spent millions of dollars trying to succeed in the American market. First it secured Ceramar in New York as its U.S. distributor in 1969 and subsequently purchased the import house. Eventually Villeroy & Boch opened a showroom in New York under its own name. Designs were developed especially for American tastes in both traditional and contemporary patterns. In 1976 the American artist Matthew Delfino was hired to develop surface decoration. Villeroy & Boch undertook substantial advertising campaigns in hopes of enticing more Americans to buy its products. Initially there were successes. The pattern *Acapulco* (1969), for example, sold well in the United States and worldwide (cat. 204, right). But in the end the firm found America a difficult place in which to prosper given all the pressures facing German producers during that period.[154]

Luckily for Villeroy & Boch its domestic market absorbed 80 percent of its huge output. For many other German china and glass producers, American sales were vitally important. By 1957, for example, Lorenz Hutschenreuther was selling about 20 percent of its output in the United States.[155] In 1970 Americans purchased 38 percent of all the china made in Germany. But even when that figure plummeted to 13 percent of German ceramic tableware exports following a stiff rise in the value of the German mark, America was still important because its market was so large.[156] In the end it was German glassmakers who were most successful in the 1970s. As ceramic exports slowed, Germany's glassware sales in the United States rose dramatically. In 1965 that country's exports were 14 percent by value of total U.S. glassware imports. By 1972 Germany's share had grown to 21.5 percent, and German glassware sales in the United States surpassed those of china for the first time (cat. 102).[157]

Central Europe's relationship to the American tabletop has been long and complicated. Through war and economic turmoil, Germany and Czechoslovakia persevered to ensure that their products had a place on American tables. From frilly porcelains in the late nineteenth century to high-style art deco pottery and modernist crystal in the twentieth, Germany and Czechoslovakia shipped an extraordinary range of tableware across the Atlantic. Although neither the Czech Republic's nor Germany's sales are as large as they were in the past, the American consumer is still a key component in their global strategy today.

Fig. 3.5 The Porzellanfabrik Victoria in Bohemia, pictured in 1938, produced elegant porcelains for the American market.

Rosenthal & Co.

Of the many German firms that exported china and glass to the United States, Philipp Rosenthal & Co. has been the most aggressive. This huge porcelain manufacturing concern was founded in 1879 by Philipp Rosenthal. Before Rosenthal ever established his first factory, he was attuned to the tastes of the American consumer. Following his brother's example, in 1872 at age seventeen Rosenthal immigrated to the United States. After working in New York and Texas as a delivery boy, elevator operator, and cowboy, Rosenthal settled in Detroit, where he became a buyer for the porcelain import firm Jacob Meyer Brothers. Rosenthal's father had owned a china and glassware store, and Rosenthal was evidently a talented buyer.

In 1879 he returned to Germany to purchase stock for the Detroit importer. Once home, however, he decided to remain, and founded a small porcelain decorating shop in the town of Erkersreuth near the ceramics manufacturing center of Selb, Bavaria. By the time of his death in 1937 Rosenthal's firm had become a huge, publicly held company producing a wide range of ceramics products and owning plants and raw material resources throughout Germany as well as Czechoslovakia.[1]

Rosenthal's output was so great that it relied heavily on the export trade, and Philipp Rosenthal paid close attention to his foreign connections, especially his American ones. The Rosenthal family regularly entertained Americans in their home in Selb, and the firm participated in numerous world's fairs, including those in Saint Louis in 1904 and San Francisco in 1915.[2] Rosenthal was especially active at the annual Leipzig sample fair because it attracted china buyers from around the world, including the United States. Eventually Rosenthal also participated in the annual Pittsburgh china and glass show, as well as later shows in Atlantic City, Chicago, Los Angeles, Dallas, Atlanta, and Minneapolis.[3]

During the 1880s and early 1890s Rosenthal porcelain sold relatively well in the United States. Styled for the most part in imitation of florid French china or as adaptations of eighteenth-century German designs, Rosenthal was evidently an acceptable alternative to Limoges tableware (cat. 104).[4] However, the recession in the United States that lasted from 1893 to 1897 curtailed Rosenthal's U.S. exports, and the company's performance weakened until 1902. Except for setbacks in 1907–8 due to economic crises in America, the years 1903 to 1913 were extremely profitable.[5] During this period the firm continued to sell patterns based on French porcelain in addition to its own original designs. Some of these new designs, such as *Donatello,* found great favor with the American public (cat. 105). The declaration of war in 1914 changed the German pottery's fortunes. After its largest export market was cut off and the effects of a wartime economy were felt, the firm posted its first-ever financial loss in 1915.[6]

Following the war Rosenthal reentered the U.S. market relatively quickly. In 1920–21 Philipp Rosenthal was one of the first important German businessmen to travel to the United States during the postwar period. A contemporary observer reported that Rosenthal was in New York "in the interest of extending his business in America and in this connection will be at the headquarters of Graham & Zenger, his representatives in this country, where he will be glad to consult with the trade regarding the line."[7] Also in 1921 he began advertising his firm in American trade periodicals as "the largest factory of Quality-China of the world . . . offer[ing] the products of its seven different works direct to American importers—not through an agent."[8]

Apparently Rosenthal's relationship with the New York importer Graham & Zenger proved problematic, and exclusive distribution rights seem to have been revoked in the early 1920s.[9] By 1927 Rosenthal had established dual import firms, named the Rosenthal China Corporation and the Continental Ceramics Corporation, both located at 149 Fifth Avenue in New York. Louis E. Hellmann, a German immigrant who had come to this country in 1909, was president of both. Judging from entries in period trade directories, Rosenthal China imported ware produced under the Rosenthal name, whereas Continental Ceramics handled brands that were sold under its own name but that were in reality made at the Rosenthal factory or by subsidiaries. These allied brands included Thomas from the Porzellanfabrik F. Thomas in Marktredwitz, Bavaria (acquired by Rosenthal in 1908), and CCC Royal Bohemian from the Bohemia Keramische Werke in Neu-Rohlau bei Karlsbad, Czechoslovakia (affiliated with Rosenthal in 1922).[10]

Even before these corporate entities existed Rosenthal was attempting to adapt its products to American taste, just as it had prior to World War I. In 1925 the firm was one of the first foreign manufacturers to develop an ivory-colored porcelain body in response to an emerging demand for such a product in the United States (cat. 148).[11] Produced at several of its main factories and marketed as *Royal Ivory, Thomas Ivory,* and *Rosenthal Ivory,* the cream-colored body developed by the firm was widely advertised to the American wholesale trade, especially during the mid-1930s.[12]

Rosenthal was innovative in the U.S. market in other ways as well. In 1931 its New York importing house sponsored a public competition to find suitable designs for the American

PAGE 236:
Cat. 104 Philipp Rosenthal & Co.'s *Sanssouci* shape from the 1890s sold well in the United States throughout most of the 20th century.

PAGE 237:
Cat. 105 The *Donatello* shape of 1905 from Rosenthal reflected a movement toward bold, simple forms in German design at the turn of the century.

market. To ensure that the patterns and shapes it developed were protected, Rosenthal China patented many of them in the United States.[13] The New York import house also quickly adopted the practice of selling individual pieces from open stock. A 1935 advertisement for Rosenthal China, for example, invited buyers to "review [its] line of open stock patterns in all price ranges for immediate delivery" as well as "a wide range of special dinner sets popularly priced for promotional purposes."[14]

Rosenthal was one of the first manufacturers to obtain a dedicated boutique for display of its wares within a major department store. In 1937 the highly important china and glass division of Marshall Field & Co. in Chicago announced the opening of its new Rosenthal Room. According to contemporary descriptions the display included "samples of china used in the homes of various personages, including Pope Pius XI, Dowager Queen Marie of Romania, Tsar Boris III of Bulgaria, the Maharajah of Indore, and President Masaryk of Czechoslovakia." Furthermore, the turquoise-colored room was assigned to a special saleswoman, who assisted customers and supervised the daily resetting of a formal dining table that occupied the center of the space.[15]

Cat. 106 Castleton China's first line (left) was based on one of Rosenthal's most successful shapes (right) in America.

Rosenthal's efforts in the United States during the 1920s and 1930s were so successful that the firm was able to sell a wide variety of both German and Czech china, including some modernist designs (cat. 97, left coffeepot).[16] However, conservative shapes and patterns sold best. With its ivory body and simple, neoclassical ornament, the pattern *Empire* was perhaps the most successful before World War II. But despite successfully reentering the U.S. market after World War I, the 1920s and 1930s were not without difficulty for the German firm. The mid-1920s saw record profits for Rosenthal overall, but declining sales due to the onset of the depression in the early 1930s hurt the company as it did the firm's European competitors. All German and Czech china exports to the United States dropped dramatically between 1930 and 1932, and in 1931–33 Rosenthal posted its first corporate losses since 1915.[17]

Between 1932 and 1937 exports to America recovered somewhat, thereby allowing Rosenthal to return to profitability. As mobilization for war in central Europe restricted exports once again for the last two years of the decade, Louis E. Hellmann, president of Rosenthal China in New York, worked to ensure that Rosenthal-like patterns would be available in the United States during the coming war. Whether Hellmann's actions were sanctioned by his German employer is unknown, but in 1939 he founded Castleton China in New York and arranged for the Shenango Pottery Company in Pennsylvania to produce tableware based on Rosenthal's best-selling line (cat. 106). The Castleton product was introduced to the public in May 1940 using the nationalist slogan "Made in America / Made of America."[18] While these Pennsylvania-produced adaptations of Rosenthal were available during World War II and beyond, the U.S. government's freezing of German assets in America followed by its declaration of war on Germany in 1941 once again cut Rosenthal off from its premier export market.

As it had after World War I, Rosenthal was quick to return to the American market after World War II, with the aid of Joseph Block. Since the late 1920s Block had been in the housewares business in New York, and in 1945 he was among a group of businessmen asked by the U.S. government to aid Germany's economic recovery by buying German products. In addition to purchasing large quantities of Meissen and Rosenthal porcelain, Block negotiated an exclusive distributorship for Rosenthal in America that took effect the following year.[19] Having established the firm of J. & I. Block in New York to handle distribution in 1947, Block announced to the trade that the showroom at 26 West Twenty-third Street displayed Rosenthal dinnerware in "12 shapes [and] 125 patterns ranging from simple florals," as well as "Dinner Sets, Place settings and Starter Sets with Rosenthal's guarantee of pattern control and open stock availability."[20] Evidently

sales were strong enough to warrant opening a larger showroom at 1225 Broadway the following year.[21]

Joseph Block believed that a market existed for modern, although not overly avant-garde, German porcelain in the United States. Initially he carried innovative forms like Rosenthal's *Oval* coffee service (1950), but he quickly decided to initiate designs that were more likely to sell well in the United States.[22] The famous American industrial designer Raymond Loewy was engaged to create new patterns and shapes for production by Rosenthal. Next Joseph Block created the Rosenthal-Block China Corporation in 1952. Block was the majority owner, Rosenthal & Co. had a minority interest, and Raymond Loewy Associates had a 10 percent ownership. Loewy's company was one of the world's most prestigious design firms and commanded large fees that Block could not afford at the time. Raymond Loewy Associates received part ownership in Rosenthal-Block in return for its designs.

Initially Raymond Loewy Associates produced surface decoration, but the firm soon developed a series of new shapes that went into production during the early 1950s.[23] Of all the pieces it created for Rosenthal-Block China, the *Exquisit* (1951–52) and *Model 2000* (1952–53) shapes were the most popular in the United States and abroad (cat. 107). By 1962 Rosenthal had produced twenty million pieces of *Model 2000,* and by the time the line was discontinued in 1978, it had been executed with over two hundred different surface patterns.[24]

During the late 1950s Rosenthal-Block distributed these china lines widely, especially through department stores. In 1961 Joseph Block and Philip Rosenthal Jr. found themselves at odds. The son of the firm's founder, Philip Rosenthal Jr. had not played a major role in the business until 1950, after which he emerged as a power within the company and set the firm on a course of aggressively avant-garde tableware. In 1959 Rosenthal Jr. introduced the Studio concept. The goal of this initiative was to convince retailers to display Rosenthal products in specially designed display areas within their stores. This concept was followed in 1961 by the Studio-Line. Starting with products like those designed by Raymond Loewy Associates, this line grew to encompass a host of modernist, art-oriented ceramics, glass, and metalwares created by both in-house designers and a group of internationally known artists and designers (cats. 44, 108).[25]

While some distributors were enthusiastic about these innovations, others were not.[26] Many retailers resented having to allot a large amount of floor space exclusively to

OVERLEAF:
Cat. 107 The contemporary *Exquisit* (right) and *Model 2000* shapes were among the best-selling modern wares in America at midcentury.

Rosenthal, as well as having to take the entire Studio-Line. Joseph Block was one of these dissenters. Believing that many items being produced by Rosenthal would not sell well in the relatively conservative U.S. market, he refused to accept the entire line. As a part owner of Rosenthal-Block, Philip Rosenthal Jr. sued Block in 1961 in an effort to break Block's exclusive distribution contract with Rosenthal & Co. The court sided with Block, and Rosenthal was forced to purchase Block's and Raymond Loewy Associates' majority interest in Rosenthal-Block. Block, along with his two sons Jay and Robert, used the proceeds to found the Block China Company in 1963, which eventually developed its own ceramic and glass tableware lines (cat. 127).[27]

Once he was in control, Philip Rosenthal Jr. reorganized Rosenthal-Block with himself as president and renamed the firm the Rosenthal China Corporation after its 1930s predecessor. Plans to acquire new warehouses in New York and Los Angeles and to introduce the Studio concept were immediately made.[28] An aggressive advertising campaign followed, in which Rosenthal China stressed that it distributed *all* Rosenthal products and that "For the First Time in this

Cat. 108 After the war Rosenthal began making fine glassware designed by famous artists and sold it worldwide.

Country . . . the Rosenthal Studio concept of design will be projected from a single source, developed through one program, coordinated under a sole supervision." It went on to claim that new dinnerware shapes would be available "in a series of patterns designed for the American market."[29]

The first Rosenthal Studio shop in the United States opened in B. Altman & Co.'s department store in New York in December 1962.[30] Supported by an aggressive wholesale and retail advertising campaign, Rosenthal succeeded in placing Studio shops in a significant number of retail stores around the country and in building a modernist image for the line during the 1960s. A quote from Philip Rosenthal Jr. that frequently ran in advertisements sums up how the firm wanted to position its products in the marketplace:

> The true contemporary is neither ugly, crude, nor boring. It is varied, warm and elegant, but in contrast to the often hollow imitations of the great styles of the past, always a genuine expression of the artistic forces and of the spirit of our time.[31]

In the end the Studio concept and Studio-Line garnered much attention within the U.S. tableware industry but had trouble financially despite concessions to the American market. After learning that 80 percent of brides purchased white or cream-colored plates with gold or platinum trim, Rosenthal introduced competitive patterns into the bridal market in 1965.[32] The very next year, however, it announced a total overhaul of its strategy for the American market. The number of Studio shops would be reduced to ensure better service, and "U.S. salesmen would be replaced by a crew of European trained personnel to handle sales and Studio-Line education at retail accounts."[33]

Through the early 1970s Rosenthal followed this new strategy, concentrating its energy on outlets in extremely affluent shopping areas, where it hoped to attract sophisticated consumers who felt comfortable with avant-garde design. By 1971 Rosenthal was not quite halfway to reaching its goal of having 150 Studios in American department stores coast to coast. Even though Rosenthal tried in the early 1970s to make its wares more appealing to the U.S. market by hiring the Chicago-based designer Richard Latham, who had formerly done work for the firm when he was with Raymond Loewy Associates, to create new products such as its *Spectra* stoneware line (1971), Rosenthal's sales lagged in this country.[34]

As a result of this poor performance Klaus Vogt, president of the American import house that had recently been renamed Rosenthal USA, announced in 1975 that the Studio concept was being scuttled in the United States in favor of a traditional, broad-based marketing strategy. At the time it was noted that since the introduction of the Studio concept, Rosenthal accounts in America had decreased from over two thousand to a few hundred. Vogt said, "While the program worked well in Europe, where the people had a tradition for appreciation of contemporary, it did not succeed universally in the United States, with the exception of some few specialty stores (Neiman Marcus) and in cosmopolitan areas (B. Altman's and Bloomingdale's both in New York)." He added that a prime reason for the failure was "reluctance of many buyers in department stores to cooperate with their fellow gift-china and glass-silver buyers in merchandising the Studio Line as an ensemble." Vogt concluded, "In small, narrow jewelry stores it was not physically feasible for merchants who might want to install a Studio department to do so!"[35]

Shortly after this announcement Rosenthal sold its own tableware boutique, called the Studio-Haus, on Fifth Avenue in New York for $1 million to Julio Tanjeloff, an Argentine-born businessman.[36] The same year the German company reversed its decade-old policy of distributing only contemporary ceramics in the United States and reintroduced "typical Bavarian china patterns" under the name Porcelain Masterpiece Series. Klaus Vogt described the traditional patterns as appealing "to the volume market on a wide taste level." The youthful Vogt, who had been with Rosenthal in Germany, Canada, and the United States since 1959, simultaneously promised "an explosion of Rosenthal all over the country . . . in many shapes, forms and price ranges and for different taste levels."[37] Although the changes Vogt made in the distribution of Rosenthal china and glass in American were substantial and helped boost sales, the company nevertheless suffered from the basic problems of rising manufacturing costs and lagging U.S. sales that plagued all German tableware manufacturers during the 1970s and 1980s.

Notes

1. For histories of Rosenthal, see "Making a Milestone," *CGJ* 107:10 (Oct. 1929): 40–41, 77; Hilschenz 1982; and Schreiber 1980.

2. Schreiber 1980, 20.

3. For an advertisement announcing participation in the Pittsburgh show, see *CGJ* 119:6 (Dec. 1936): 4. For an advertisement noting participation in the other shows, see *GTR* (7 Dec. 1964): 33.

4. Before World War I Rosenthal produced very close copies of Limoges porcelain. For examples, see Hilschenz 1982, 7.

5. Schreiber 1980, 141–42, 144.

6. Ibid., 144.

7. "From Cowboy to China Manufacturer," *CGJ* 93:9 (3 Mar. 1921): 18.

8. *CGJ* 93:52 (29 Dec. 1921): 13.

9. For a Graham & Zenger advertisement featuring Rosenthal, see *CGJ* 92:13 (23 Sept. 1920): 9.

10. *CGJ* 104:2 (13 Jan. 1927): 32; and Hilschenz 1982, 206.

11. Hilschenz 1982, 206.

12. For advertisements for ivory porcelain, see *CGJ* 114:4 (Apr. 1934): 9; 117:6 (Dec. 1935): 13; and 119:6 (Dec. 1936): 4.

13. Hilschenz 1982, 206. For examples of patented designs, see "Patent Department," *PGBS* 41:16 (22 May 1930): 33. The designer noted in this source is George Wesp, but Wesp could have been either the actual designer or a company manager whose name was used for the patent application.

14. *CGJ* 117:6 (Dec. 1935): 13.

15. "Marshall Field's Directs Consumer Attention toward High-Quality Merchandise," *CGL* (Dec. 1937): 46.

16. For a 1936 advertisement noting ware available from three of Rosenthal's Czech factories being marketed as CCC Royal Bohemian, Princess China, and TK Thun, see *CGJ* 119:6 (Dec. 1936): 4.

17. "American Potters Can Build Foreign Markets, Says McCoy," *CGJ* 126:3 (Mar. 1940): 20; Schreiber 1980, 158.

18. Lehner 1988, 136–37; and *CGJ* 126:6 (June 1940): 4, 26.

19. Block interview 1998.

20. *CGJ* 141:6 (Dec. 1947): 101.

21. *CGJ* 142:5 (May 1948): 13.

22. Block advertised the *Oval* service in 1950; see *CGJ* 147:4 (Oct. 1950): 48.

23. Block interview 1998; "Loewy Designs Modern Dinnerware Patterns for Rosenthal China," *CGJ* 151:1 (July 1952): 71; and 152:5 (May 1953): 42.

24. *Rosenthal Verkaufdienst* 11 (Spring 1962): n.p.; Hilschenz 1982, 90.

25. Hilschenz 1982, 208.

26. For information about how many German retailers and rival manufacturers aggressively opposed the Studio concept, see *GTR* (16 Mar. 1964): 1, 9; and (4 Jan. 1965): 4.

27. Block interview 1998.

28. "Rosenthal Firms Merge," *CGJ* 169:5 (Nov. 1961): 44.

29. *CGJ* 169:6 (Dec. 1961): 6–7.

30. "Altman Opens Studio Shop," *GTR* (Nov. 1962): 76.

31. For advertisements including this quote, see *GTR* (Dec. 1963): 1; and (7 Dec. 1964): 33.

32. "Rosenthal Slants Patterns to Brides," *GTR* (4 Jan. 1965): 47.

33. "Revamp Sales Plan for Rosenthal Line," *GTR* (3 Jan. 1966): 1, 8.

34. "Rosenthal Coming Out with Stoneware," *GTR* (July 1971): 37.

35. "Broader Base Better: Vogt," *GTR* (June 1975): 1, 29. In reality, according to Stanley Marcus, Neiman Marcus did not sell Rosenthal profitably during this period; Marcus interview 1996.

36. "$1 Million Buys NY Studio Haus," *GTR* (Aug. 1975): 4.

37. "Broader Base Better: Vogt," *GTR* (June 1975): 29.

The Japanese

The success in the American marketplace of Japanese pottery and glass has been nothing short of extraordinary. Beginning as a maker of cheap novelties and imitative ceramics for export, by the third quarter of the twentieth century, Japan was America's foremost foreign supplier of porcelain and earthenware dishes, as well as a leading exporter of table glass. Japanese ceramics and glass had carried the stigma of being poorly made before World War II, but later many American consumers came to appreciate the best of Japanese ware as being of high quality.

Japan's ceramic tradition is a centuries-old and sophisticated one. However, because the country's geography and political history have with few exceptions isolated it from the West, the artistic influence of Japan was felt throughout the world only after the mid-nineteenth century. Following Commodore Matthew Perry's use of gunboat diplomacy to open the island nation to American trade in 1854, Japanese products became available for the first time in the United States and Europe in significant quantities. The ceramics that were included among the shipments of textiles, lacquerware, woodblock prints, and cloisonné between 1880 and World War I were in general decorative items like vases or teawares of a traditional nature.

During this early period the Japanese pottery industry was centered in three places. The ancient artistic capital of Kyoto specialized in high-quality artware for the domestic market, while the city of Seto produced utilitarian ceramics for both home and foreign markets. But it was Nagoya that came to dominate Japan's ceramics trade with the West. In 1921 the city produced about $7 million worth of ceramics for export, of which one-half went to the United States. By 1950 about twenty-five major potteries labored in Nagoya to satisfy the West's, and particularly America's, seemingly unquenchable thirst for Japanese tableware. At the end of the decade the U.S. government estimated that Americans consumed over 61 percent of all Japanese porcelain and earthenware exports. In 1963 the number of important Japanese factories producing ceramic dishes for American consumption reached sixty-seven.[158]

Establishing a Foothold in America

The development of the Japanese ceramics industry in relation to the U.S. market is a fascinating and amazing tale. Before 1900 potterymaking in Japan was for the most part a cottage industry. Between 1892 and 1902 Japanese ceramic tableware exports to the United States were consistently under $500,000, or less than one-half of 1 percent of total American imports.[159] However, the ceramics sector of the economy benefited greatly from the rapid growth Japan experienced following its victory in the Russo-Japanese War of 1904–5. During the ensuing four decades, the economy boomed. The population grew by 40 percent, and military expenditures soared as the nation assumed its role as a world power. As one scholar has pointed out, "Raw material output increased 300 percent and manufacturers' output more than 1200 percent. By the

1930s, exports had increased 2000 percent. More than 60 percent of all exports were finished goods."[160] Japan as a military ally of the United States and an enormously important purchaser of U.S. goods was granted special tariff reductions periodically in keeping with its most favored nation status.[161]

Within the context of this massive economic expansion, Japan transformed its ceramics industry and established a glass industry. Through the vision and entrepreneurial spirit of individuals like the Morimura brothers (see pp. 257–64), the availability of investment capital, and the introduction of European-style dinnerware as an export item, the city of Nagoya emerged as one of the foremost pottery centers in the world. In the first decade of the twentieth century, modern factories were constructed for the production of earthenware, stoneware, and porcelain gift- and table-ware, as well as sanitary and electrical ceramics. In 1912 Japan's export of ceramic tableware to the United States was 12 percent of total imports, while Japanese table glass shipped to the United States totaled a mere $1,721.[162] In 1914 the output of the entire Japanese pottery industry was valued at just under $8 million.

As an ally of the United States, Japan benefited from the stoppage of most European ceramic and glass exports to North America during World War I. By 1918 the value of Japanese pottery production had risen to over $22 million. Relatively unaffected by the recession of the early 1920s because of strong sales to the United States during the decade, the volume of Japanese ceramics continued to climb. In 1928 there were over seven thousand large and small potteries in Japan employing approximately 32,300 male and 12,500 female workers. The wares made in these factories were worth $35 million. A contemporary observer stated that "this figure is in excess of the total production of Germany, approximately 25 percent less than the United States production, and amounts to 40 percent of the production of Great Britain. Over two-thirds of all pottery manufactured in Japan is said to be produced in the Nagoya Potteries."[163]

Much of this increasing production was exported. Between 1908 and 1914 the Japanese shipped on average approximately $2 million worth of pottery overseas annually. Taking advantage of opportunities created for them by World War I, Japanese potteries increased their output, and by 1918 exports totaled $10 million and a decade later had climbed to $16 million. Of this total the ware produced in the Nagoya area accounted for over $10 million. In the late 1920s virtually all of this exported ware was destined for Pacific Rim countries.[164]

Devaluation of the Japanese yen vis-à-vis the U.S. dollar during the late 1920s and 1930s greatly influenced the Japanese ceramics and fledgling glass industries. Foreign borrowing to rebuild after the 1923 Tokyo earthquake and going off the gold standard in 1924 touched off a wave of inflation. By 1929, as its economy was recovering, the country went back on the gold standard only to abandon it again in 1931. Each time the government left the gold standard the yen fell in value, making Japan's exports cheaper abroad.[165] The export of tableware to the United States boomed. In 1928 the United

States consumed over 36 percent of all Japanese-made porcelain and earthenware.[166] A year later Japan accounted for almost 52 percent by quantity (86 million pieces) of all the earthenware, stoneware, and porcelain "household table and kitchen articles" imported into the United States.

TRADING WITH JAPAN BEFORE WORLD WAR II

Although total foreign imports dropped in 1931 and 1932 at the depth of the depression, rebounding in the years thereafter, the Japanese proportion of the total steadily rose. By 1934 Japan was making over 85 percent of the tableware and kitchenware shipped to America. The relative value of Japanese wares compared to those of its foreign rivals also climbed. In 1929 Japanese ceramics imports made up over 32 percent of the total value of imported dishes, and in 1934 the figure was nearly 60 percent.[167] Even in 1938–39, years that saw overall U.S. imports of domestic ceramics nearly cut in half as the world prepared for war, Japan was credited with over 84 percent of the porcelain (44 percent by value) and over 65 percent of the earthenware (nearly 26 percent by value) coming to America.[168] During the same decade Japan also expanded its exports of glassware to this country. In 1931 the country's nascent industry accounted for less than 2 percent by value of foreign table glass shipped here. Within three years the sum had grown nearly sixfold.[169]

While it was sending huge quantities of ceramics, and increasingly glass, to the United States, Japan purchased even more of America's products. A trade surplus with the United States in 1927 of ¥167 million in Japan's favor had reversed itself by 1936. In that year Japan imported ¥244 million more in products from America than it sold there.[170] Given its positive trade balance with Japan, the U.S. government was reluctant to curb Japanese exports of china and glass to this country, especially since the American industries producing such goods were relatively small and thus did not support a major sector of the economy. However, domestic producers of tableware were very vocal about what they considered unfair Asian competition.

This situation was aggravated by the implementation of the Roosevelt administration's National Industrial Recovery Act in 1933. Before the act was ruled unconstitutional in 1935 the National Recovery Administration (NRA) forced American potteries and glassworks to raise wages while cutting hours. In 1933 the minimum wage for unskilled labor was 45 cents per hour for a 40-hour week. The average pay for American potters was reported as "being $30 to $45 a week, while decorators in the United States receive as high as $14 a day." A contemporary U.S. government study of labor costs in Nagoya potteries stated: "The ordinary wages for a potter were ¥2.10 (63 cents) for eight and a half hours a day. . . . That is equal to $3.78 for the 51-hour week, or six days. The decorators are paid less for they receive ¥2.12 for a nine-and-a-half hour day. This is equivalent to $3.83 for a 57-hour week."[171]

Although the Japanese had relatively high raw material and transportation costs, their wages remained lower than American wages throughout this period. And since during the 1930s labor accounted for more than half of the total production costs of pottery and 65 to 70 percent that of handblown or decorated glass made in the United States, Japanese manufacturers had a substantial price advantage.[172] Less-expensive Japanese labor, coupled with a devalued yen in these years, meant that the only means of reducing these imports would have been for the Japanese to act voluntarily or for the United States to substantially increase tariffs.

For their part the Japanese did make efforts to alleviate the situation. They worked through their newly formed Manufacturers' Export Association to improve the climate surrounding tableware. During the early 1930s this organization "restricted the volume of china and earthenware shipments to [the United States] and raised price levels markedly." It also noted "a studied effort on the part of the Japanese to copy no American dinnerware designs."[173] American importers of Japanese china and glass were always represented at trade hearings in Washington, D.C., and so could tell their side of the story. Usually led by a representative from Morimura Brothers in New York, the Japanese version of these tense trade discussions appears to have impressed the U.S. government but only antagonized American producers. Although the Hawley-Smoot Tariff of 1930 did increase import duties on foreign glass and ceramics, it was not enough to significantly stem the flow of Japanese products, and no further official action was taken by the United States until 1939, when it renounced the U.S.-Japanese trade agreement of 1911 following Japanese aggression in Asia.

Given the economic stress that American manufacturers were under during the depression, it is little wonder that they tried diligently to convince the U.S. government to impose higher tariffs, especially on Japanese goods. In 1933 an article in *Crockery and Glass Journal* accused the Japanese of "dumping into this market, by virtue of its low-priced and pauper labor, depreciated yen and other considerations, more than seven times as much chinaware as all the world combined, and about three times as much earthenware."[174] By the end of that year the United States Potters' Association was asking President Roosevelt to use provisions in the NRA to protect American producers of tableware from Japanese competition. Joseph M. Wells of the Homer Laughlin China Company in Ohio, chairman of the association's code committee, pleaded, "We simply cannot continue unless protection is adequate. . . . Therefore, we beg of you to make such representation to the government as will secure relief for this industry."[175]

Over the course of those several years, potterymakers and glassmakers repeatedly called on the government for higher tariffs, documenting escalating imports and Japanese copying of American designs (fig. 3.6).[176] Although the Roosevelt administration responded with studies of the industries and foreign competition, no increase in the duty was forthcoming. As a result glass and ceramics manufacturers rekindled their support of the "Buy American" campaign that had been started by the American Legion. In 1936 Japanese importers were barred from exhibiting at the Pittsburgh tableware show.[177] Two years later, following the sinking of the U.S.

EXHIBIT PORTRAYING TYPICAL DESTRUCTIVE
JAPANESE COMPETITION IN GLASSWARE

MADE IN JAPAN

These items exactly duplicate in Style and Pattern
the American line shown below. This Japanese Ware
is Sold to Department Stores at 1.50 per dozen delivered,
duty (60%) paid. Wage rates for Japanese skilled glassworkers average $0.054 per hour.

MADE IN AMERICA

These items were exactly copied by Japanese. Direct Labor cost alone equals $1.47 per dozen.
Costs of material, fuel, packing, overhead expense (including taxes) and indirect labor must be added
Wage rates for American skilled glassworkers average $0.87 per hour.

Fig. 3.6 Using comparative diagrams such as this, the American Glass Association fought Japanese competition before the U.S. Senate, 1935.

Navy gunboat *Panay* by the Japanese, an anti-Japanese rally was held in the important pottery center of East Liverpool, Ohio. There in January 1938 three thousand pottery workers and sympathizers gathered to demonstrate against Japanese imports and to kick off a boycott. At the close of the event $20,000 worth of Japanese goods were burned in a bonfire (fig. 3.7).[178] Although this anti-Japanese sentiment was well covered by the American press and buyers at the 1938 Pittsburgh show were said to "refuse to even consider buying Japanese tablewares," its effects were short lived.[179] In the end it was Japan's attack on Pearl Harbor and the beginning of World War II that blocked the country's china and glass from the American market.

Because the United States occupied Japan after the war, America aided the recovery of Japan's china and glass industries. As it did with German products, in 1946 the Department of Commerce's subsidiary, the U.S. Commercial Company (USCC), organized exhibitions of Japanese products, including ceramics and glass. Initially potential American buyers had to bid through the USCC on these early postwar goods, but by mid-1947 the government was approving applications for travel to Japan so that importers could communicate directly with manufacturers.[180] Japanese dinnerware was also included among those commodities made available to U.S. military personnel through the Post Exchange (PX) system (cat. 109). But on the whole, unlike German china that re-

appeared on the U.S. market relatively soon after the war, Japanese tableware was slower to arrive because of severe shortages in Japan of raw materials, especially coal. The result was that potteries shifted away from inexpensive wares to more costly ones for export to the United States.

POSTWAR EXPANSION AND HIGHER QUALITY WARES

Higher priced Japanese tableware met resistance in America after the war. In fact, it took nearly twenty years for Japanese china to be totally successful at the highest end of the U.S. market. The trend towards more expensive ware was encouraged by several factors. Rising production costs during the late 1940s and early 1950s facilitated this change. The Korean War in 1950–53 drained fuel, raw materials, and labor away from industries like ceramics and glass, causing costs to rise. In 1950 it was reported that Japanese dinnerware prices were going to rise the next year from 5 to 15 percent because of increases in manufacturing costs. The cost of labor alone had increased 15 percent. Furthermore, production in these early postwar years lagged behind demand in the United States, also contributing to higher prices in the marketplace.[181]

As American consumers became more accepting of higher grades of Japanese tableware such as Noritake, the overall value of Japanese exports in this field rose. At the same time Japanese potteries became more efficient and production expanded. During the war the Japanese shut down many of their more inefficient factories.[182] In the 1960s and

Fig. 3.7 American potters torched goods in a demonstration against Japanese imports, East Liverpool, Ohio, 1938.

Cat. 109 Japanese porcelain was distributed through military PXs in large quantities following World War II.

1970s they repeatedly upgraded the remaining large-scale, mass-production potteries with innovative technology, building new, efficient plants when needed. And even though the cost of labor began to rise in the late 1950s, Japanese workers were still paid less than their American counterparts.[183] The effect of the acceptance of higher prices, increased production capabilities, and relatively low labor costs is reflected in postwar tableware import figures. In 1953, just six years after Japan surrendered to the United States, Japan accounted for 64 percent by volume of all chinaware imported into America.[184]

During the 1960s and 1970s the volume and value of Japan's exports of tableware to the United States rose and stabilized for the most part at very high levels. In the case of porcelain Japan's contribution represented on average 86 percent by quantity and 68 percent by value of all china sent to the United States during the late 1960s. Levels close to these highs were maintained over the next decade and later. Over the same period the quantities of Japanese earthenware fell somewhat in comparison to total imports. In 1967 Japan's contribution was 75 percent by volume, but it had declined to 67 percent by 1972. At the same time the overall value of total Japanese earthenware imports climbed from 52 percent to 59 percent.

This trend of escalating value for Japanese tableware is seen most clearly by examining the nation's exports to the United States on a per-unit basis. Between 1967 and 1972 the average worth of a piece of Japanese porcelain increased from $2.00 to $3.80, whereas earthenware rose from $1.48 to $4.21.[185] These substantial gains clearly reflect the growing acceptance of more costly Japanese tableware by American consumers during the second quarter of the twentieth century.

THE PROBLEM OF IMAGE

The success of higher quality Japanese china and glass achieved during the postwar decades required great resolve on the part of both manufacturers and importers. Much effort and planning was devoted to overcoming the stigma of producing poorly made, imitative ware. The creation in 1956 of the Japan Pottery Design Center in Nagoya was an important step toward improving quality and controlling exports in general. Directed early on by J. T. Mizuno, who had for ten years before the war been sales director for Morimura Brothers in New York, the Design Center served as a clearinghouse for tableware lines and for quality control. To prevent potteries from pirating the creations of fellow manufacturers or foreign firms, Japanese manufacturers had to submit their patterns to the Design Center for approval. If the designs were too close to a previously registered pattern, the copy was not allowed to be manufactured. If imitative ware was discovered to be already in production, it was banned from export. By the late 1960s approximately four thousand patterns were approved for registration annually.

Another organization to police the Japanese ceramics industry was founded around 1960. Called the Japan Ceramics and Industrial Federation, its purpose was to "impose production controls and price agreements" on its members, who joined voluntarily.[186] Other organizations that helped to monitor the Japanese ceramics industry and thus raise the quality of its products were the Japan Pottery Manufacturers' Federation, the Japan Pottery Export Association, and the Japan Pottery Inspection Association.[187]

In addition to the greater self-imposed quality control, the enhanced perception of Japanese tableware within the U.S. market reflected the emergence of a new attitude on the part of American importers after World War II. Historically the importers of Japanese tableware had been of two basic types. One group consisted of businesspeople of European ancestry who simply carried Japanese-made products among a large mix of European and American china lines, including such firms in New York as Geo. Borgfeldt Corporation; Fisher, Bruce & Co.; and Otto Goetz, Inc.

The other group generally consisted of individuals of Asian heritage who relied on personal connections with Japan to secure a wide variety of stock, among which might be ceramic vases and tea sets. The earliest of these importers were curio and fancy goods dealers who specialized in exotic Japanese and Chinese merchandise such as ivories, lacquerware, cloisonné, and carved furniture. Among this group of late-nineteenth- and early-twentieth-century dealers who often sold both wholesale and retail were H. Naito Company in Portland, Oregon; Japanese Art Store in Houston, Texas (fig. 3.8); and Morimura Brothers in New York.[188]

Following Morimura Brothers' highly successful introduction of porcelain dinnerware following World War I, other importing firms also added tableware to their inventory, while new firms led by Japanese Americans were founded to tap the growing market for Japanese porcelain and earthenware dishes. New York was the center of this activity by the 1920s and 1930s with enterprises like Takito, Ogawa & Co.; Tajimi Company; Mogi, Momonoi & Co.; Haruta & Co.; Imoto Brothers; Tuska Son & Co; Nagoya Seitosho; and Taiyo Trading Company.[189]

A few of these dealers, including Morimura Brothers, handled some Japanese ceramics of high quality, but the vast majority of the goods they sold were inexpensive and distributed though chain stores and for promotional purposes. The effect of this activity was to give Japanese ceramics the reputation of being of poor quality. This reputation proved difficult to overcome when higher quality wares began coming to America in increasingly large quantities after World War II. In late 1947 one observer commented on the first samples of these more expensive goods as follows:

> The sales of Japanese goods so far have been flops. At the start, the Japanese had high reserves of skilled labor, but little to work on. They did the obvious thing, applying a great deal of labor to a small amount of material, producing high quality wares. Unfortunately, the Japanese have built up a bargain-basement and not a quality patronage. Merchants interested in reviving the "Made-in-Japan" label do not have customers in the upper brackets. But the line of merchandise was changed before account was, or for that matter could have been, taken of distribution. It is as though Woolworth's suddenly took on some Saks-Fifth Avenue lines at Saks-Fifth Avenue's most reasonable prices.[190]

Clearly retailers were faced with the challenge of raising the image of Japanese tableware in the minds of the consumer.

Through the early 1950s the lingering perception of Japanese tableware as being cheap and of low quality persisted. In 1950 Gladys Miller wrote an article for *Crockery and Glass Journal* titled "Is There a Place for Japanese-Made Ceramics and Glass in Our Country?" In it she stated that the Japanese were "confused," that they were slavish copyists, and that the ware they made was often of poor quality.[191] In the next issue the manager of Tuska Merchandise Company in New York, M. B. Tuska, challenged Miller's assumptions and conclusions. Explaining that Nagoya had at the time about twenty-five factories making wares in a wide variety of forms and quality, and that the American importer and ultimately the consumer determined what the Japanese manufacturer made, Tuska argued:

> [The importers] are principally the chain stores and promotionally-minded buyers. These stores, naturally desire low [priced] and conventionally styled merchandise, since one does not introduce modern shapes as a promotional item. Looking at this from the point of view of the American customer who sees nothing but inexpensive chinaware with the "Made in Japan" label, he thinks that the converse is also true, namely, that all Japanese ware is inexpensive. . . . Only when the finer stores carry Japanese ware on a non-promotional basis and in the higher price brackets and be successful in this type of merchandising can we importers feel secure in importing a modern and conventional style china.[192]

Tuska's words were prophetic.

During the late 1950s and 1960s a small but growing number of American importers and Japanese manufacturers saw the potential for finely made Japanese tableware in the United States. As early as 1960, one commentator remarked:

Fig. 3.8 Rows of imported porcelain on display at the Japanese Art Store, Main Street, Houston, Texas, ca. 1911.

The news that has captured interest of U.S. retailers is the tremendous up-grading surge going on in Japan. There have always been imports from Japan of high grade, and moderately expensive tablewares. And there will always be a good supply of any promotional goods coming from the country. In some unexpected places, however, we find evidence of better business for the top quality product, than for the frankly lower priced. Thus we have old-line importers of Japanese ware (in the promotional brackets) saying that price is "not the important fact in Japanese imports that everyone is led to believe." One U.S. importer told C&GJ he is now so convinced that price is a secondary factor that his firm "has embarked on a whole program of making merchandise highly styled, of the finest quality and is not considering price as a major selling point."[193]

The observer concluded by noting that much of the new esteem for high-quality Japanese goods was due to the confluence of manufacturers' efforts to deliver the best work possible and to American designers and importers who aided producers in making ware for the upper levels of the U.S. market.

An early example during the postwar period of a well-known American designer working with a U.S. importer and a Japanese manufacturer is the United China & Glass Company. Founded in New Orleans in 1850, this firm built up a trade supplying merchants in the Mississippi River valley. By the 1930s the firm's territory encompassed twelve southern states. In 1932 a vice president of the company, Sol A. Stolaroff, traveled to Japan for the first time and contracted for United China & Glass's first line of imported dinnerware.

Although the firm returned to selling domestic products during the war, it aggressively reentered the Japanese trade in the early postwar years. In 1947 one report stated that "Mr. Stolaroff returned to Japan and had the distinction of signing the first purchase contract with the Supreme Command Allied Powers and the Japanese Board of Trade." It further revealed that by that point the company had become "one of the largest importers of Japanese chinaware, [bringing] into the United States the largest variety of china dinnerware, tea sets, coffee sets, fancy chinaware, novelties, and gifts."[194] Distributing such wares proved so profitable that foreign-made china and glass accounted for 75 percent of the firm's total sales volume in the late 1940s.

To expand its business United China & Glass opened showrooms for its imported lines in New York, Chicago, and Dallas, and displays were presented at the annual Pittsburgh china and glass shows. The firm also established an office in Nagoya with a staff of fifteen. By having permanent representatives in Japan the company could work closely with potteries and their staffs to produce wares that it hoped would sell well at a higher price in the United States.

The first completely new line that resulted from this close collaboration between producer and distributor was *Norleans China* (cat. 110). Created to celebrate the centenary of United China & Glass, the shapes were commissioned from the well-known contract designer Eva Zeisel. With subtly undulating walls the forms were especially modern in feel. The surface patterns, which may have been designed by artists at Meito China, were more conventional. Given its early date and the difficulties under which Japanese potteries labored for several years after the war, the *Norleans China* line was well made, with especially fine gilding.

JAPANESE AND AMERICAN INNOVATIONS

In the early postwar period United China & Glass's anniversary line and some of the lines of its huge rival Noritake Company were progressive in design and of relatively high quality, but it took new firms led by young, creative entrepreneurs to fully comprehend the possibilities with respect to Japanese tableware. Two such innovative firms were Mikasa and Fitz and Floyd China. In 1948 Japanese American George Aratani and several partners, including Alfred Funabashi, established an importing business named American Commercial in Los Angeles. This parent company had two subsidiaries, Kenwood Electronics and Mikasa Dinnerware. The latter purportedly was named in honor of Prince Takahito Mikasa, the youngest brother of Emperor Hirohito. Dinnerware soon became an important part of the business, and American Commercial opened an office in New York, where it represented several important Japanese dinnerware manufacturers, including Nagoya Shokai, Narumi, and Yamato. With access to some of the finest potteries in Nagoya, the Mikasa Dinnerware division developed products that were modern in concept and fashion-oriented. One of its most decisive moves was into the area of bone china in 1965. The Mikasa line was made by the high-quality manufacturer Narumi and featured eleven surface patterns. It was introduced to the market in fifty-three-piece sets (services for eight) that retailed from $100 to $150.[195]

By 1969 Mikasa Dinnerware claimed to hold a 10 percent share in the U.S. market for bone china and was projecting gross sales for 1971 of $20 million from all its dinnerware categories. In addition to bone china, Mikasa distributed porcelain, stoneware, and ironstone made in Japan, as well as some ware produced in England and France. To design its Japanese patterns and shapes Mikasa worked closely with the staffs of potteries such as Narumi, which created many of Mikasa's early lines. In 1969 one of Narumi's leading designers, Tomiyasu Sugihara, was sent to Mikasa's New York office to learn how to design "American style" and then take that knowledge back to Japan.[196] Such efforts worked. By 1970 the firm had 350 active patterns in its lines, ranging in price from $35 to $600 for services from eight to twelve.

To show off its extensive collection Mikasa opened a new showroom in November 1969. Housed at the Los Angeles headquarters of American Commercial, Mikasa's new space was described as avant-garde, even "mod." Interior designer Robert Winquest outfitted it with "open-end Plexiglas cubes as individual modules" that "provided settings for hanging displays on three sides, plus a set-up [space for a place setting] in the open interior space." Winquest noted at the time that he wanted "to discard all showroom clichés" and that the Plexiglas cubes provided "unlimited spatial possibilities in the shapes and heights" they created and achieved "a background of texture and color to enhance the china."[197] During the 1970s and 1980s Mikasa worked with suppliers in Japan and eventually around the world to develop dinnerware that was highly fashion conscious (cats. 111, 209).

Following leading trends in color and pattern, Mikasa's primary customers were for the most part relatively wealthy and sophisticated in their taste. They typically purchased Mikasa dinnerware as a fashion statement, knowing that they would tire of it in a few years. The firm catered to this cyclical consumption pattern by introducing numerous patterns, few of which stayed active very long. Customers with several sets of china and sophisticated tastes liked this marketing tactic, but many others, especially brides, did not. Most brides needed time after their marriage to complete their pattern, and so designs that went out of production quickly were not popular.

According to Joseph Giarrocco, longtime china buyer for the B. Altman & Co. department store in New York, Mikasa's

Cat. 110 The *Norleans China* shape of 1949 was a highly successful porcelain made in Japan for the American market immediately after World War II.

patterns were so popular during the late 1960s and 1970s that eventually nonbridal buyers accepted the fact that stock in the patterns they chose would not be available for long. Shoppers were encouraged to and did purchase entire sets of dishes all at once. Eventually this trend made the open stock concept almost extinct for all but the most expensive patterns.[198]

Mikasa was also an important force in the spread of the "factory outlet" concept. Dansk Designs had opened an outlet store in 1968, and Mikasa, under the leadership of Alfred J. Blake, who became its president in 1976, unveiled its first outlet store in Secaucus, New Jersey, in April 1977. Because they did not have the overhead of a department store, Mikasa's stores successfully moved large volumes of imported goods and set a trend among importers and domestic manufacturers that continues today.[199]

Although its wares had a different look from Mikasa's, Fitz and Floyd China filled a similar niche in the market. The firm was founded in Dallas in 1960 by Patrick Fitz-Patrick and Robert Floyd. The two men had met in college and were sales representatives at the Dallas Trade Mart. With an initial investment of $2,000 each, they founded Fitz and Floyd's Sales Agency in 1960. The company represented Otagiri, a San Francisco–based importer of high-quality Japanese ceramics, and other compatible lines. In 1964 Otagiri asked Robert Floyd to come to Japan and assist in creating designs for that firm. Floyd accepted once both parties agreed that Otagiri would allow Fitz and Floyd to design and import a separate line of its own. Although Otagiri never had a financial interest in Fitz and Floyd, the two importers built a close working relationship that lasted over fifteen years.[200]

Initially Fitz and Floyd designed and marketed a line of ceramic and papier-mâché novelties. However, an early successful venture with the internationally known Dallas retailer Neiman Marcus encouraged Fitz and Floyd to add the coffee mug, a relatively new and increasingly popular ceramic form, to its portfolio of products. In 1960 Roger Horchow, then the gift buyer at Neiman Marcus, returned from England with a coffee mug designed by Susie Cooper. Because the mug would have too high a price if it were imported from England, Horchow challenged Patrick Fitz-Patrick to make a related version in Japan. Working through Otagiri, a mug of similar shape was produced, and Neiman Marcus sold thousands of them. By the late 1960s Fitz and Floyd was well known in the trade for its stylish coffee mugs, which were typically sold in boxed sets of four as giftware.[201]

Patrick Fitz-Patrick died prematurely in 1970, leaving Robert Floyd in control of the firm. Although trained as an actor, Floyd had developed a strong sense of visual style during the early years of the firm. During his first trip to Japan in 1964 in search of products to import he was extremely taken with Japanese culture and design. Embracing this Asian influence, Floyd worked with several staff designers, especially Dale Hodges and Ken Kondo, to develop bold surface decorations that were applied to shapes produced primarily by the Chunichi factory in Nagoya. Early successful experiments included

sets of salad plates meant to be used by the customer with china already owned.

In 1975 Fitz and Floyd introduced its first important line of dinnerware. Featuring service plates with banded surface decoration called *Rondelet* and dinner plates named *Imperial Crest*, the patterns were produced in a range of harmonious colors and were meant to be "mixed and matched." The concept of interchangeable tableware had been popular before, as in the 1930s and 1940s when mixing variously colored dishes was in vogue. Robert Floyd's reinvention of mix-and-match evolved out of his enthusiasm for traditional Japanese table settings, in which a variety of different shapes and patterns of dishes are combined to give an elegant and cohesive effect. During the late 1970s mix-and-match dinnerware became very popular and Fitz and Floyd flourished, and as a result in 1976 Robert Floyd was named Importer of the Year by the Dallas Trade Mart. At that time the firm employed more than ninety people with sales of more than $10 million annually.[202]

By the time Robert Floyd sold the firm in 1985, Fitz and Floyd had produced numerous successful dinnerware lines based on the mix-and-match principle (cat. 112). Interestingly, almost none of these products utilized custom-designed shapes. Rather, Fitz and Floyd, like many other importers of Japanese tableware, produced exclusive surface patterns and color schemes that were then applied to preexisting shapes available at a specific Japanese factory. According to Dale Hodges, who has been head of design at Fitz and Floyd since 1967, he and Ken Kondo, and sometimes other members of the design staff, would travel to Japan two to three times a year for about six weeks at a time. Robert Floyd was there so frequently that he maintained an apartment in Nagoya. Together, Floyd and his staff would meet with representatives from the Chunichi pottery to select appropriate shapes and go over artwork for the surface patterns to be applied to them.

Fitz and Floyd had a reputation among the Japanese for being difficult to work with because the firm was very particular about such things as patterns fitting the shapes perfectly and the color being exactly the right hue. As a result this collaborative process could be a long and tiring one. Once standards were successfully met and samples were available, Floyd would usually place a minimum order for a particular item and then return to the United States to see whether significant demand existed among retail buyers to warrant increasing his quantities.[203] Because Neiman Marcus was Fitz and Floyd's premier account, buyer Roger Horchow often met Floyd in Hawaii to view his new samples so that he could make Neiman's selection before rival buyers ever saw the collection at the Dallas showroom or at tableware shows.[204]

Fitz and Floyd's efforts succeeded to a great degree. Bloomingdale's in New York was eventually added as a major

OPPOSITE:
Cat. 111 Mikasa's *Country Gingham* line of the mid-1970s would have been purchased as a fashion statement and replaced in a few years.

Cat. 112 Fitz and Floyd China became famous
for its high quality mix-and-match porcelain in
the 1970s and 1980s.

account and by the early 1980s was selling enough of Fitz and
Floyd's tableware and giftware to warrant opening a boutique
dedicated to the Dallas firm. Like Neiman's, Bloomingdale's
also periodically commissioned exclusive designs, such as the
Tutankhamun pattern in 1978. Augmenting the firm's notoriety
was the White House commission it received in 1981 from the
Reagan administration for dinnerware for use in the private
quarters and on the presidential plane, *Air Force One* (cat. 113).
With national publicity and prestigious stores in Dallas and
New York as well as a host of other stores across the country
promoting its dinnerware, Fitz and Floyd was able to sell expensive, well-made Japanese porcelain to relatively wealthy
customers in major cities throughout the United States. Given
that thirty years before American consumers had considered
the great bulk of Japanese ceramics imported to the United
States to be of little value, the achievements of firms like
Mikasa and Fitz and Floyd were extremely noteworthy.

THE JAPANESE LEGACY

In the end the extraordinary success of Japanese tableware in
the United States after World War II drove most domestic producers out of the middle and high-end dinnerware business.
Thanks to a fine-quality product and extensive advertising,

Lenox China was able to survive and even flourish during this
period, but Lenox was an exception. By the mid-1950s most
American producers of earthenware, and to some extent porcelain, realized that the Japanese were going to dominate the
U.S. market within a brief period of time.

As a result a gentleman's agreement was struck between
the high-volume producers of earthenware in East Liverpool,
Ohio, and their Japanese counterparts. The Japanese agreed
not to export to the United States institutional ware for use in
hotels, hospitals, and restaurants, and in return firms like
Homer Laughlin China Company and Hall China Company
curtailed production of tableware for the home. This voluntary agreement was honored until the 1980s, when the American firms of Mikasa and Lenox introduced institutional china
lines manufactured for them in Japan.[205] With this act the
domination of Japanese ceramics in the U.S. market was virtually complete. No longer constrained by the thirty-year-old
agreement, Japanese producers moved into the one remaining
stronghold of American potteries.

OPPOSITE:
Cat. 113 For the 1981 Reagan White House
commission, Fitz and Floyd drew inspiration
from an antique blue and white plate.

Fig. 3.9 A huge Noritake factory belches smoke in a Morimura Brothers ad of 1920.

Morimura Brothers and the Noritake Company

In 1876 Ichizaemon Morimura founded the export house Morimura Gumi (Morimura Group) in Tokyo. In the same year his younger brother, Toyo, established himself in New York. Two years later Toyo Morimura opened a retail store on Sixth Avenue. The name of this store, the Hinode Company, was soon changed to Morimura Brothers.

Initially the American branch handled a variety of merchandise, including lacquerware, vases, antiques, and fancy goods. Around 1882 Toyo Morimura realized that porcelain goods might be a profitable line, and his brother in Japan arranged for vases, tea sets, and other giftware to be shipped to New York from several potteries in the Seto district in Aichi Prefecture. The most important supplier during this early period was the Harumitsu Katoh Pottery, which produced ware with a grayish-colored body.[1]

In 1889 Ichizaemon Morimura attended the Paris world's fair and was greatly impressed by the high quality of European ceramics exhibited there, as well as the sophistication of the factories that produced them. Because the New York store's sales of gray-bodied porcelains were declining, and on the advice of a New York department store owner, the brothers decided to switch to a pure white ceramic body. At the same time the German-born salesman Charles Kaiser, who had joined the firm in 1901, encouraged the brothers to add dinnerware as a product line.[2] A test kiln was constructed at one of the firm's decorating factories, and research was conducted in the development of white porcelain.

When perfecting the technique proved difficult, the company brought in outside expertise. In 1902 members of the Rosenfeld family were consulted. The Rosenfelds were well positioned to help Morimura Brothers solve its production problems, as they were operators of the well-known Porzellanfabrik Victoria in Altrohlau, Bohemia (fig. 3.5), and partners in the Czech export firm of Lazarus & Rosenfeld, which had offices in London and New York. Initially Benedikt Rosenfeld, president of the London company, visited Morimura Brothers in New York to discuss how the Japanese firm might successfully produce white-bodied dinnerware. Soon thereafter his sons Abraham and Louis Rosenfeld traveled to Nagoya, Japan, to inspect the facilities, while representatives from the Morimura Group visited the Rosenfeld's Czech factory and the Seger Institute for Ceramic Research in Germany. With this central European foundation, the pure white, hard-paste porcelain body called *Nitto 3 • 3* was developed.[3]

Following the reorganization and consolidation of the family's facilities in Nagoya, in 1904 the Morimura Group established the Nippon Toki Kaisha (Nippon Porcelain Company) in a district of the city of Ohaza Noritake (now Noritake-cho). Construction began immediately on a factory for the sole production of white-bodied tableware for the U.S. market (fig. 3.9). Although much of the ware made at the new plant proved satisfactory and sales of gray-bodied wares were stopped, the facility was hampered by the fact that it could not successfully produce the standard-size dinner plates integral to all sets of china sold in the United States.

The Morimura engineers were dispatched once again to the Seger Institute in Germany, and advice was sought from the Rosenfeld family. Louis Rosenfeld agreed to construct a modern factory that would make use of German technology in exchange for a portion of the factory's output.[4] Completed around 1912, this factory used high-grade kaolin clay imported from central Europe. With the addition of modern technology, more refined white clay, and improved shapes, the Noritake factory was able to complete its first ninety-three-piece dinner service in 1914, after two decades of research and development. The pattern was called *Sedan*.

Like other Japanese potteries, the Morimura Group benefited from the cessation of most European ceramic exports to America during World War I as well as from the favorable trading conditions that Japan garnered from the United States in the first decades of the twentieth century. During the interwar years the Morimura Brothers American operation became very sophisticated. To ensure that its products were appropriate for the U.S. market, a design staff was assembled in New York. Until the 1920s efforts concentrated on adapting the contemporary art nouveau style to American taste and producing it more cheaply than European potteries (cat. 114).

In the 1920s the head designer, English-born Cyril Leigh, and Charles Kaiser, then merchandise manager, took the firm in new directions. With a keen eye on the competition, the New York team, in association with its counterpart in Japan, developed two distinct product lines during four month-long visits to Nagoya.[5] The giftware and specialty tableware line was the more visually exciting of the two (cat. 161). Drawing inspiration from popular magazines such as *Harper's Bazaar, Ladies' Home Journal, Vogue,* and *Vanity Fair,* as well as from contemporary applied and fine art from England, France, Germany, and Czechoslovakia, the designers created brightly colored and boldly designed giftware in the art deco style.[6]

Conversely, in the 1920s and 1930s the dinnerware lines were more conventional. Based on conservative English prototypes, these wares typically featured white centers framed with floral borders. To keep current with fashion trends in the United States and to improve its position in the marketplace, Morimura Brothers introduced service plates and an ivory-colored body in 1927 and a bone china body in 1933. The latter was marketed as *Royal Bone China* line (cat. 115).[7] To protect its investment the firm regularly patented its designs in the United States.[8]

Cat. 114 The Noritake No. 175 pattern sold steadily from about 1918 until the late 1980s.

The advertising and sales programs that Morimura Brothers built following World War I were prodigious. To give added brand recognition to its dinnerware line, Morimura Brothers began marketing its china under the name Noritake in the early 1920s.[9] Led by men such as Charles Kaiser and Yasukata Murai, who joined Morimura Brothers in 1879 and was president of the firm by the 1910s, a vast distribution network was established. By 1924 the company had two hundred sales representatives, including some of the largest secondary wholesalers in America.[10]

One innovation that Morimura Brothers did not adopt until much later was selling china by the piece, or as open stock. When buying Noritake, the customer had to purchase a complete set of dishes. The firm was able to avoid selling open stock because Noritake maintained a very low price point in comparison to rival European or American brands of porcelain or earthenware. Most middle-class consumers who purchased Noritake china could afford an entire set.

Only in times of great economic hardship did this policy come under attack. During the Great Depression, retailers did not want to keep large amounts of china in stock for fear of not being able to sell it. Morimura Brothers counteracted this trend by increasing the amount of merchandise carried in its various U.S. warehouses. This stockpiling meant that china buyers did not have to commit to large orders but instead could simply rely on prompt deliveries from Morimura Brothers to satisfy their customers.[11]

Morimura Brothers weathered the economic decline of the 1930s relatively well thanks in large part to its ability to remain extremely price-competitive in the United States while improving the quality of its products. After inspecting sixty-three American potteries and several in Europe, Morimura management decided in 1929 to reduce its overhead and raise the quality of its dinnerware by replacing the twenty-eight old fashioned bottle kilns at its Noritake factory with modern tunnel kilns. Between 1932 and 1938 four tunnel kilns were constructed and new conveying machinery was installed.[12] The reduced manufacturing costs coupled with a weak yen allowed Morimura Brothers to sell complete sets of dinnerware at a time when other manufactures and distributors could not move dinnerware even by the piece.

Japan's invasion of China in 1938 marked the beginning of difficulties for all Japanese exporters to the United States. Although in April 1941 Morimura Brothers extended the lease on its showroom at 53–57 West Twenty-third Street in New York for another three years, the U.S. government froze the firm's assets in September. That same month Japanese businesses were forced to operate under the supervision of a short-term license system that greatly curtailed business activities. In response to this situation Morimura Brothers advertised to the trade: "Due to present conditions we may be unable to complete delivery of the balance of Fall import orders on time. We urge our customers to consider the substitution of our stock merchandise to make up the unfilled balance of their import orders."[13] After the United States declared war on Japan following the Japanese attack on Pearl Harbor, Morimura Brothers ceased operations in the United States.

During World War II the Noritake factory almost exclusively produced ceramic grinding wheels and abrasives for the Japanese war effort. These government contracts must have been profitable, because in 1946 the investment capital in the Morimura Group's subsidiary, the Nippon Toki Kaisha, which owned the Noritake factory, was three times greater than the level in 1938. Furthermore, the main plant survived Allied bombing virtually undamaged. At the close of the war the pottery was one of the largest in the world, covering 135,000 square meters and employing 2,700 workers. With intact facilities and increased capital the Nippon Toki Kaisha was anxious to return to the U.S. market as quickly as possible. Exactly one year following Japan's surrender to the United States, the production goal for Noritake china was set at 1.2 million pieces per month.[14]

The Morimura Group planned its return to the American market very carefully. Because the initial output from the Noritake factory did not meet prewar quality standards, the company protected its brand name by selling the first substandard wares under the name Rose China in 1946. Soon after the Noritake pottery was producing high-quality tableware, and the Noritake brand name was reintroduced into the United States through both the military Post Exchange (PX) system and regular commercial channels (cat. 109, bamboo design). Within two years, three import houses—Metasco, Adline Trading Company, and Noritake Company (the new name of Morimura Brothers)—were distributing the Noritake brand in New York. The first of these entities to advertise in trade literature was probably Metasco, whose initial advertisement in *Crockery and Glass Journal* announced:

> Beginning in January 1948 the Nippon Toki Kaisha, Ltd., will resume production of the genuine "Noritake" quality dinnerware. The "Noritake" trademark will again appear on the bottom of each piece of this fine china. Chinaware buyers are urged to see the new samples of the pattern for 1948 at the Metasco, Inc., showroom, 1440 Broadway, Fourth Floor. Act now as quantities available are limited. CHARLES KAISER will be glad to welcome you.[15]

Apparently the presence of longtime employee Charles Kaiser, who must have been over seventy years old by then, was used as a means to help overcome anti-Japanese sentiment in the United States after the war.[16] Although it handled

the Noritake line for only a few years, Metasco continued into the early 1950s, importing what it called "Grade A inspected, first quality dinnerware from Japan."[17]

Another firm that handled Noritake china immediately after the war was the Adline Trading Company, located at 39–41 West Twenty-ninth Street. Adline's distribution of the ware appears to have been short-lived, however. In March 1949 it was announced to the trade that the Noritake Company was now the exclusive distributor of Noritake china.[18] The president of the new firm from 1948 to 1963 was Riutaro "Reo" Matsushita. Born in California and educated in Boston and New York, Matsushita worked for Morimura Brothers before the war but left the firm to join the U.S. Army. Aided by his brother-in-law, Kyuichi Sugihara, who also worked for the firm, Matsushita is credited with having "returned the Noritake Co. to national prominence following World War II."[19]

The three decades between 1950 and 1980 were heady ones for the Noritake Company and its supplier, the Nippon Toki Kaisha. Charles Gifford, who joined the Noritake Company in 1964 as sales representative for the Pacific Northwest and western Canada and who served as president from 1990 to 1996, remarked that "Noritake grew after the war with tremendous products, pattern, delivery, and price."[20] Working with the Noritake Company in America, the Japanese manufacturer invested heavily in research and development, in terms of both new products and new manufacturing facilities in the postwar years. In 1953 *Fine China,* a refinement of the Noritake white porcelain body, appeared (cat. 109, covered dish). Six years later an improved ivory body was unveiled.

Both of these new ceramic bodies were of such high quality that the California firm of Gladding, McBean & Co. contracted with Nippon Toki Kaisha to supply it with fully decorated ware based on its own designs. Between 1958 and 1960 white porcelain was imported from Japan and marketed as Franciscan Cosmopolitan China. For three years starting in 1961 ivory-colored tableware was delivered to California and sold as Franciscan Porcelain.[21] Unfortunately for Gladding, McBean & Co. these two lines did not sell well, and so they were discontinued. The Nippon Toki Kaisha continued producing the new bodies and fully integrated them into their product lines, however. According to Charles Gifford, "This decision changed the destiny of the company." Sales of the Noritake versions soared over the next thirty years.[22]

Other ceramic innovations followed. In 1964 heat-resistant reinforced porcelain was developed, and in 1966 it was introduced to the U.S. consumer as Noritake Progression China. Shortly thereafter several types of refined stoneware were added, including *Nitto* (1970), *Folkstone* (1971), *Primastone* (1971), and *Stoneware* (1975). Although it had subcontracted with other potteries to produce earthenware for many years, starting in 1972 Nippon Toki Kaisha undertook the manufacture of the material itself, bringing out ware named *Craftone* (1972), *Keltcraft* (1980), *New Decade* (1984), and *Primachina* (1988). Bone china, which had been perfected at the Noritake factory in the early 1930s, was reintroduced to the United States in 1967 and became the focus of a major marketing effort to enter the bridal market in 1979.

Although American designers were occasionally used as consultants during the postwar period, the vast majority of these new products were designed by a chief designer and five junior designers in the United States in association with their colleagues in Japan.[23] By the end of the period under consideration in this study, the Noritake Company employed around thirty-five designers, five of whom lived in the United States. According to Osamu Tsutsui, who was recruited as a designer by Noritake and sent to the United States in 1957, Japanese designers typically knew little about American culture and thus had difficulty designing for the U.S. market unless they were able to travel and mix with Americans. Tsutsui himself spent two years in the New York office, two years in Los Angeles, and one year in Chicago.

By moving from the national headquarters to regional offices, designers were able to learn about regional preferences in dinnerware. For example, East Coast buyers generally liked traditional English-looking patterns, whereas California customers preferred brighter, more contemporary patterns (cat. 116). Although Noritake attempted contemporary patterns, its designers and management found the concept of a casual lifestyle difficult and, on the whole, focused on conservative, traditional design concepts. In summing up the situation, Charles Gifford remarked that although "Noritake's designers were fine artists, they did not know when to make the square plate with a hole in it! . . . They [produced] the same surface design that concentrated on 'little details' for forty years."[24]

As long as Noritake dinnerware could be delivered quickly at a low price, it was successful in the United States. To maintain these conditions, the company organized an extensive system of seven regional warehouses and offices. The corporate headquarters were in Manhattan. In 1955 the showroom at 212 Fifth Avenue was expanded to include space on two floors, giving Noritake "one of the largest display areas for dinnerware and artware in the country."[25] The Seattle office was of particular importance because it

served as point of entry for all Noritake tableware shipped from Asia. Once in the Pacific Northwest, the dishes were transported by rail or truck to regional warehouses and showrooms in Cincinnati, Atlanta, Dallas, Chicago, and Los Angeles. Because Noritake maintained stock and salespeople throughout the country, it could provide its customers quick deliveries and good service.

Noritake prided itself on delivering quality products at a low price. To achieve this goal the Noritake Company and its allied potteries pursued a supply-driven business policy that relentlessly sought to increase efficiency and output while containing costs. In 1961 the monthly output of Noritake china was 2.6 million pieces.[26] By the 1980s the company had ten factories making tableware, as well as its own decal plants producing surface decoration. Most of these facilities were in Japan, but as labor and raw materials costs rose at home, potteries were built or acquired abroad. In the early 1970s Noritake built new factories in Sri Lanka and the Philippines. In 1975 the company purchased a large interest in the Arklow Pottery in Ireland for the production of ironstone, and in 1977 it opened a new facility there. The Japanese giant's overseas operations also included joint ventures in Iran and Colombia.[27]

The largest of the Noritake potteries produced more than 1 million pieces of tableware per month, while others operated at a rate of 600,000 to 700,000 pieces per month. To manage this ever-expanding enterprise the company became the first Japanese corporation to import an IBM computer.[28] Eventually Noritake china *had* to be sold in huge quantities in order to absorb the continuous stream of porcelain flowing from the company's kilns around the world. If sales declined, workers would have to be laid off and factories closed—realities that Japanese corporate leaders avoided at all costs.[29]

To utilize this enormous production capacity, Noritake china was made in hundreds of patterns. At the company's height in the 1970s and 1980s, approximately sixty new dinnerware patterns on a variety of body types were introduced annually. Thanks in large part to an inexpensive Japanese yen in comparison to the U.S. dollar before 1985, Noritake china could be sold more cheaply than almost all European or American porcelain or earthenware of similar or even inferior quality.[30] Consequently, the Noritake Company was able to capture the lion's share of America's middle-class market. As Charles Gifford remarked, "Noritake was as big in Walla Walla per capita as in San Francisco . . . Lenox could sell $100 place settings in San Francisco, but it couldn't in Butte, Montana, or Walla Walla, Washington. We

Cat. 116 In the 1950s and 1960s sparse modernist decoration was a hallmark of Noritake china designed for Americans who liked the contemporary look.

were for everybody. We kept our designs and our price for everyone, but we had the advantage of the low yen. That made a hell of a difference."[31] And indeed it did. By 1977 Noritake's annual worldwide sales for its domestic and foreign affiliates totaled $192 million.[32] High-quality products, a huge variety of patterns, dependable delivery, and low prices culminated in Noritake china becoming one of the top-selling brands of china in most china and glass departments in America from the late 1960s on. In 1981 Noritake led in the U.S. market with a total dollar market share of 33 percent. Although the rise in the value of the yen against the dollar made its products more expensive and thus reduced the company's sales in the late 1980s and 1990s, Noritake is still a major force in the American tableware market today.[33]

Notes

1. The main sources for information in this section are Noritake 1997, 2–9; and Hida and Unno 1996, 6.

2. "When West Meets East: A Sidelight on the Career of Charles Kaiser," *CGJ* 107:9 (Sept. 1929): 29. For a photograph of Kaiser, see 110:6 (June 1932): 23.

3. It is not clear which member of the Rosenfeld family first met with the Morimuras. One source states that "B. Rosenfeld, the President of Rosenfeld Company, London, visited New York in 1902" (Noritake 1997, 3). However, research done by the Noritake scholar Judith Schwartz and communicated verbally to Charles Venable suggests that Louis was the family member who was involved with the Morimuras. For information on Lazarus & Rosenfeld see Hartmann 1997, 685–86. Around 1935 the New York branch became Marks & Rosenfeld.

4. Schwartz and Schwartz 1991, 42.

5. "'Fisherman of Ideas' Back from Orient," *CGJ* 110:6 (June 1932): 23.

6. For an overview of the art deco giftware, see Washington 1982, 21; and Schwartz and Schwartz 1991.

7. *CGJ* 104:20 (19 May 1927): 5; and Noritake 1997, 4.

8. For examples of patented designs, see *PGBS* (11 Dec. 1924): 35; and (13 Feb. 1930): 33. The last source identifies the designer of the dinnerware as Urasaburo Tomita of Astoria, New York. It is not known whether Tomita was the designer or a member of Morimura Brothers management staff.

9. For an early advertisement using the name Noritake, see *PGBS* (14 Aug. 1924): 22–23.

10. "Y. Murai," *CGJ* 118:4 (Apr. 1936): 32; 107:9 (Sept. 1929): 77; and Schwartz and Schwartz 1991, 42.

11. "Morimura Brothers' Stock Policy," *CGJ* 112:3 (Mar. 1933): 27.

12. "'Fisherman of Ideas' Back from Orient," *CGJ* 110:6 (June 1932): 23.

13. "Leases Renewed by Morimura," *CGJ* 128:4 (Apr. 1941): 43; "Japanese Licenses," 129:3 (Sept. 1941): 14; and 129:3 (Sept. 1941): 46.

14. "'Noritake' Ware Being Made in Japan Again," *CGJ* 139:3 (Sept. 1946): 50.

15. *CGJ* 142:1 (Jan. 1948): 32.

16. For another advertisement that mentions Kaiser's presence, see *CGJ* 143:1 (July 1948): 98.

17. *CGJ* 151:6 (Dec. 1952): 2. This advertisement announced that Metasco would be exhibiting at the Pittsburgh and Los Angeles tableware shows in January 1953.

18. *CGJ* 144:1 (Jan. 1949): 28; and 144:3 (Mar. 1949): 70. The first Noritake Company showroom was at 125 East Twenty-third Street in New York.

19. "Reo Matsushita," *GTR* (Sept. 1969): 9.

20. Gifford interview 1997.

21. Noritake 1997, 5.

22. Gifford interview 1997.

23. For an example designed by the Californian Richard Rummonds, see "Noritake Breaks with Tradition; U.S. Designer Name on Backstamp," *GTR* (19 Oct. 1964): 4.

24. Gifford interview 1997.

25. "Noritake Expands Line, Showroom," *CGJ* 157:3 (Sept. 1955): 44.

26. "Noritake: What We Are in Brief" (Nippon Toki Kaisha, Ltd., promotional brochure, 1961): 3.

27. "China's a Joy; Forget the Limits," *GTR* (July 1977): 55.

28. Gifford interview 1997.

29. Tsutsui interview 1997.

30. Following the Plaza Accord between the United States and Japan the value of the yen escalated dramatically, making Japanese exports much more expensive in the United States.

31. Gifford interview 1997.

32. "China's a Joy; Forget the Limits," *GTR* (July 1977): 55.

33. Sales figures derived from the Macomber Association Audit Reports and furnished by Lenox Archives.

Occasional Guests

France, England, Ireland, Germany, Czechoslovakia, and Japan provided over 90 percent of all foreign-made tableware used in America between 1880 and 1980, but literally hundreds of factories from around the world exported china and glass tableware to the United States during this period (cat. 117). The vast majority of these smaller exporters never truly succeeded in this market. Small potteries and glassworks generally could not afford to enter the U.S. marketplace to any serious degree. Doing so required increased investment for creating additional shapes and patterns designed specifically for American tastes, higher packing and shipping expenses, and advertising. Only firms with relatively large production capacity could hope to service such a vast market. Importers and retail establishments, like department stores, demanded good service and prompt deliveries. If a supplier had trouble meeting commitments, buyers typically spent their money elsewhere the next year.

The most important exception to this general rule was that some foreign makers of expensive luxury goods found America a highly receptive and important market. Because of the amount of hand labor required to produce lead crystal or gilded porcelain, the output of these firms was often small by definition—and so was the number of people who could afford their products. With its large population and growing economy, America was home to a sizable portion of the world's most elite consumers. As a result, if a foreign or domestic luxury china and glass producer could attract the wealthiest American clientele, its product often became a trendsetter, influencing less expensive wares made by larger factories.

THE SCANDINAVIANS

The northern European countries of Norway, Sweden, Finland, and Denmark have long maintained respected ceramics and glass traditions, but for the most part the factories that emerged during the nineteenth century were relatively small. Even those that expanded production through mergers and increased technology during this century typically found it difficult to compete against their rivals to the south, much less against Japan, in the American market. The most important exception to this reality was Swedish glass during the 1950s and 1960s.

Cat. 117 Before the Russian Revolution in 1917, the Brothers Kornilov Factory in St. Petersburg sold porcelain through America's most fashionable tableware retailers.

Swedish stemware was certainly offered for sale in American shops before World War II. In the 1920s and 1930s New York importers such as J. H. Venon, George F. Bassett & Co., and G. Torlotting offered crystal stemware created by the Swedish glasshouses Alsterfors Glasbruk, Boda Bruks, Johannsfors Broakula, Kosta Glasbruk, Pukeberg Glasbruk, and Vebo.[206] Judging from advertisements, the glass imported from these factories was stylish cut and handblown stemware that would have sold in tiny quantities due to its price.[207] After the war, sales of Swedish glass in the United States increased. Because Sweden had been neutral during World War II, Swedish industry was not physically damaged by the conflict. Nevertheless, the blockade that cut Scandinavia off from transatlantic shipping in 1940 effectively halted its export trade. During the early 1940s Swedish producers survived by making "preserving jars, bottles, techno-chemical glassware and . . . ordinary household articles" that were sold for the most part domestically.[208]

By the war's end the Swedish market was saturated, and glassmakers turned immediately to the United States for sales. Although hampered in some cases by lack of raw materials, most glass factories in Sweden were working at full capacity by late 1946. Representatives from New York distribu-

Cat. 118 Swedish glass with clean lines was particularly popular in America in the postwar years. Elvis Presley owned yellow stemware like the piece seen here.

tors such as the Vaco Company, D. Stanley Corcoran, Frederik Lunning, Enright Le-Carboulec, and Finland Ceramics & Glass Corporation traveled to Scandinavia shortly after the war to negotiate distribution contracts. Alsterfors, Boda, Hovmantrops Glasbruk, and Kosta were some of the first glass lines these distributors carried after the war. At the same time Fisher, Bruce & Co. of Philadelphia and New York began importation of Orrefors Glasbruk glass.[209] Robert F. Brodegaard was a particularly interesting importer of Swedish crystal. In the 1950s Brodegaard hired the American designer Belle Kogan to design glassware that Brodegaard then had manufactured in Sweden (cat. 118, second and third from left).

The Swedish producers' ability to satisfy the pent-up demand for imported tableware that existed in America in the late 1940s gave them an initial postwar advantage. This capability, coupled with a general rise in U.S. appreciation of Scandinavian design, caused Swedish glassware sales to the United States to climb between 1945 and 1965. In 1956 Sweden produced 12 percent by value of all the foreign glassware imported to America. Sweden's share of world glass exports to the United States declined to 7 percent in 1965 and fell to 5.2 percent in 1972.[210] Despite this decrease the United States remained Sweden's number one buyer of glass stemware. In 1973 Sweden had about twenty-five glasshouses that primarily produced handmade stemware. American consumers purchased a full third of their total output.[211]

The Scandinavian style was an easy one to copy, however. In 1963 a reporter for the trade periodical *Gift and Tableware Reporter* noted, "Though it is flattering that everyone—American, European, and Japanese alike—now sees fit to emulate the once unique Scandinavian look, this turn of events has created a new problem: 'Scandinavian' is flooding the market—often at lower prices."[212] Challenged by cheaper, imitative products, particularly from eastern Europe, Swedish and other Scandinavian glass producers had to become more competitive.

Some firms merged to gain economies of scale, installed mechanical blowing equipment, and opened showrooms in New York. Royal Krona, a firm that was created to market glass from five small to medium-size factories, is an example of this strategy. It opened a New York showroom in 1972, one year before Orrefors acquired a controlling interest in Fisher, Bruce & Co, its U.S. distributor.[213] A merger in 1970 created Sweden's largest glassmaker, Kosta-Boda-Afors, which by 1973 was working to mechanize some of its production. Taking an opposite tack, some smaller producers such as Reijmyre recommitted themselves to "a rigid policy of strictly handmade glass," believing that they "must feature designs that cannot be made by machine in order to remain competitive."[214] Glassmakers in Denmark (Holmegaards Glass), Finland (Notsjoe and Karhula-Iittala Glassworks), and Norway (Magnor Crystal) faced the same challenges as did their Swedish rivals, although each country accounted for less than 1 percent of total U.S. glass imports during the entire post–World War II period.[215]

Unlike Swedish glass, ceramic tableware from Scandinavia never accounted for a large portion of U.S. imports. At the height of its popularity during the 1950s and 1960s, earthenware from Finland made up around 1.5 percent of imports by value, while imports of ware from Denmark and Sweden were under 1 percent. Porcelain imports from all these countries were consistently under 1 percent throughout the twentieth century.[216] But despite their small volume and overall value, Scandinavian ceramics were influential in America. In the 1920s and 1930s, the importers of Scandinavian glass also distributed pottery, as did Royal Copenhagen Porcelain & Danish Arts. Scandinavian factories selling earthenware and porcelain in the United States included Gefle, Gustavsberg, Linköping, and Rörstrand Porslins Fabriker (Swedish); Bing & Grøndahl Porcelaenfabrik, Kähler Ceramics, and Royal Copenhagen Porcelain Factory (Danish); and Kupittaan Savi and Arabia (Finnish).[217] During the 1930s and the years immediately following the war, Scandinavian dinnerware designs featuring banded decoration with central floral or leaf motifs were most popular and were imitated by American manufacturers. Patterns like *Quaking Grass* (1933) by Royal Copenhagen, with its green border and botanical center, for example, must have inspired the Franciscan Division of Gladding, McBean & Co. in California to introduce *Westwood* (1942, compare cats. 62, 119).

As with glass Scandinavian ceramics reached their peak of popularity in the United States during the twenty years following World War II. During the late 1940s and early 1950s "peasant" motifs, with colorful borders and broadly painted floral designs, were produced by firms such as Arabia of Helsinki. These patterns influenced earthenware designs produced at American factories such as Southern Potteries and Stangl Pottery (cat. 184).[218] At the same time modern-style ware came to the United States from Finland, Sweden, Norway, and Denmark.

Although they were not copied to any great extent in the United States, patterns that received significant attention in the U.S. marketplace included *Kilta* (1948) by Arabia and *Blue Fire* (1949) by Rörstrand (cat. 120). But it was Scandinavia's earthy, stoneware look that truly swept America in the third quarter of the twentieth century. Heavy, thick-walled, and intentionally unrefined, these ceramics exuded a handmade quality that belied their factory origins. By 1960 products like Dansk Designs' *Flamestone* (1957) had become popular with upscale American customers (cat. 121). Domestic and foreign manufacturers imitated such designs, especially in terms of shape and weight (cats. 205, 208). Although their glaze patterns may not have been directly inspired by Scandinavian prototypes, ceramics made by firms such as Fabrik in Seattle, Washington, and Decor Pottery in Rimouski, Quebec, owe much to Scandinavian design (cat. 122).

Of the firms that distributed Scandinavian ceramics in the United States after World War II, Frederik Lunning, Inc., and Dansk were particularly interesting. Frederik Lunning was born in Denmark and worked as the head of sales for Georg Jensen Silversmithy in Copenhagen. After immigrating to the United States around 1922, Lunning opened an American subsidiary for Georg Jensen on Fifth Avenue to sell silver and

Cat. 120 The potteries Arabia AB in Finland
and Rörstrand in Sweden offered these wares
to Americans in the late 1940s and 1950s.

OPPOSITE:
Cat. 119 Scandinavian tableware like these Royal
Copenhagen examples were too expensive to sell
well in the United States when made in porcelain
but were mimicked by American makers.

Cat. 121 Dansk Designs' *Flamestone* (1957), with a matte finish and elegant form, was a highly acclaimed stoneware line.

Cat. 122 Scandinavian stoneware influenced design worldwide, including these examples from Quebec (mugs) and Washington State.

Royal Copenhagen porcelain.[219] During World War II Lunning was unable to import products from occupied Denmark, so he stocked American-made merchandise and added lines of girls' dresses and perfume. This action "precipitated a long dispute with his Copenhagen suppliers." As a result Lunning left Georg Jensen and established Frederik Lunning, Inc., where he came to be known as "the best salesman on Fifth Avenue."[220] During the late 1940s and early 1950s, Frederik Lunning sold Royal Copenhagen porcelain and patterns such as *Lunning Lily* that were produced in the Scandinavian style by English potteries especially for the New York store.[221]

In 1957 the firm, now led by Frederik's son, Just Lunning, acquired its rival distributor Waertsila Corporation. This purchase made Frederik Lunning, Inc., the largest distributor of Scandinavian merchandise in the United States, selling ceramic lines from Arabia, Gustavsberg, and Royal Copenhagen, as well as glass from Karhula-Iittala, Notsjoe, and the German maker Süssmuth. The firm also carried Danish, Swedish, and German stainless steel flatware.[222] By the mid-1960s Frederik Lunning had been acquired by Georg Jensen, but it operated under the Lunning name as a subsidiary for some time thereafter.

Dansk Designs was founded in 1954 by Americans Martha and Ted Nierenberg.[223] During a trip to Denmark in 1950 the couple met award-winning designer Jens Quistgaard, whose work inspired the Nierenbergs to try to sell elegantly designed Scandinavian products in the United States. Operating out of Mount Kisco, New York, Dansk worked with several important Scandinavian designers, as well as a few designers of other nationalities, to develop lines of coordinated stainless steel flatware, enamel cookware, wooden objects, silver plate, glassware, and pottery. Not a manufacturer itself, Dansk had these products made in Scandinavia (and later elsewhere) for distribution in the United States and abroad.

The Nierenbergs' first major success came in 1954, with a stainless steel flatware pattern named *Fjord*. Popular ceramics and glassware lines soon followed. Especially notable were the *Flamestone* line (1957) by Quistgaard and Niels Refgaard's stoneware patterns *Generation* (1967) and *Bistro Christianshaven* (1978), both of which are still in production today (cat. 121). Selling ceramics that lessened "the distinction between fine and casual china," along with other successful products, Dansk's sales grew substantially. Between 1954 and 1970 gross volume grew from $1 million to $10 million. In 1968 Dansk initiated the outlet store concept when it opened a store in Kittery, Maine. Having built a profitable importing company, the Nierenbergs sold Dansk in 1984. Dansk purchased Gorham Silversmiths in 1989, and both of these firms were in turn acquired by Brown-Forman in 1990 for its portfolio of tabletop brands, which also included Lenox.[224]

THE BELGIANS AND DUTCH

Like their Scandinavian counterparts, Dutch and Belgian potteries never exported tableware to the United States in large quantities between 1880 and 1980, although some of their products were certainly sold in America. Earthenware from the Dutch factories of Gouda, Leiderdrop, De Sphinx, and the Société Céramique was imported by the New York distributors Schoemaker & Co. and the Geo. Borgfeldt Corporation before World War II. A few lines, including those from the Mosa and Fris factories in Holland, were imported by the Foreign Advisory Corporation in the postwar era.[225]

Belgian and Dutch glassmakers were more successful than their Scandinavian competitors in the U.S. market. In 1911 Belgium accounted for 10 percent and the Netherlands 3 percent by value of ornamented glassware imported into the United States.[226] In a greatly expanded market Belgium consistently produced about 2.5 percent of all the table glass shipped to the United States in the third quarter of the twentieth century. The Netherlands, however, declined from 3 percent in 1956 to less than 0.5 percent by 1972.[227] Of the glass imported from these countries three brands were by far the most important in terms of quality and visibility in the marketplace—Val St. Lambert, Royal Leerdam, and Royal Netherland. All these brands were expensive and typically featured extensive hand cutting (cat. 82). St. Lambert and Royal Leerdam are known to have been distributed in New York before World War II. St. Lambert was carried during this period by the wholesaler Alfred B. Gunthel, and Royal Leerdam was handled by Graham & Zenger and Schoemaker & Co. After the war the main importers of the Dutch lines were Justin Tharaud & Son in New York and New Jersey (Royal Netherland) and A. J. Van Dugteren & Sons in Maryland (Royal Leerdam).

In 1950, in an attempt to greatly expand its sales in America, St. Lambert opened its own showroom in New York, as well as branches in Dallas, Chicago, and Los Angeles.[228] This direct investment in the U.S. market evidently was not profitable, and by the mid-1960s the showroom had closed and St. Lambert was being handled once again by two American distributors, Jackson Internationale in New York and J. M. Gilbert Company in San Francisco.[229] By the time the national distribution house of William Adams, Inc., took over the brand around 1970, it was to promote St. Lambert's newly introduced machine-blown stemware. Having invested $2.5 million in up-to-date technology, the Belgian producer could make lead-glass blanks using mechanical blowing or pressing techniques and then decorate and polish the pieces by hand. The end result was a goblet that retailed in the United States for $3.50 to $5.00, whereas handmade competitors cost from $8.00 to $11.00.[230]

THE ITALIANS

The United States was an important market for Italy as well. In 1911 Italian glasshouses contributed 2 percent by value of all the ornamented glassware imported by Americans. During the postwar period the use of Italian tableware and decorative glass grew dramatically in the United States. From a starting point of 10 percent in 1956, Italian glass imports swelled to 27 percent in 1965 and then receded to 11 percent in 1972. Italian ceramics were never sent to America in such large quantities. Imports of Italian porcelains always remained under 1 percent,

Cat. 123 Glass made in Murano, Italy, was favored by wealthy Americans. Princess Grace of Monaco received pink glassware as seen here as a wedding gift.

while earthenware declined from a high of 16 percent in 1956 to 4 percent in 1972.[231]

Early in the century several New York importers featured Italian glass and pottery. In 1935 *Crockery and Glass Journal* listed six firms distributing glass from Italy. Those same importers plus another five firms handled Italian earthenware. Out of the eleven companies, four marketed Italian porcelain tableware. Apart from Venetian glass from Brower & Co. and earthenware from A. Zen & Figlio, Italian tableware lines are not noted in this directory, suggesting that Italian tableware was seen as a specialty item and had little brand recognition among American china buyers and consumers.[232] This conclusion is supported by the fact that prewar advertisements and discussions of Italian tableware seldom mention the manufacturer.[233] With the notable exceptions of the Richard-Ginori and Ernestine lines, this situation of non-branded marketing continued throughout the second half of the twentieth century.

As for glassware Americans have long had a tradition of thinking of all high-end Italian stemware generically as Venetian glass from Murano, the island near Venice, even though the Italian glass industry was very diverse by the twentieth century (cat. 123). In 1968 Italy was said to have five hundred glasshouses employing approximately thirty-six thousand people. The chief centers of tableware production were Turin, Milan, and Rome. In 1963, 28 percent of all the table glass made in Italy was exported to the United States.[234] A fraction of this total was crystal, but most of the glassware that came to America from Italy was inexpensive ware used in homes and in bars and restaurants across the United States. Simple in design and anonymous as to brand, such glass was in many ways interchangeable with much middle-level contemporary Czech, French, German, Swedish, and American glass. In fact, in 1967 one outraged manufacturer said of American importers shopping for products in Italy, "Only three out of ten Americans here are genuine buyers. . . . The

rest want samples, which they take home to have copied in Japan."[235]

In the end the number of Italian glass and ceramics producers that were able to build brand-name recognition in the American market were few. During the early 1970s Cooperative Emploese Vetrai and Vetreria Artistica Valdesana, two large glassmakers in Empoli, Italy, tried to establish themselves in the United States as makers of higher quality stemware. Hoping to effectively compete with the Germans and French, the Italians claimed that their new product was of "a quality not previously seen in the U.S." The new crystal lines were said to be made from 30 percent lead glass that had been press-molded and then cut with a pattern in the traditional manner.[236] Although it was purported to be cheaper than its European rivals and was often of very high quality, upscale Italian stemware never became widely popular in America (cat. 126).

The Italian pottery Richard-Ginori Società Ceramica Italiana was more successful. Richard-Ginori was founded in Milan in 1896 when the earthenware manufacturer Giulio

OPPOSITE:
Cat. 124 In the 1950s Richard-Ginori drew inspiration from 18th-century porcelains for its patterns *Italian Fruit* and *Perugia* (plate).

BELOW:
Cat. 125 Colorful pottery by American designer Ernestine Cannon was produced in Italy and sold in the United States from the 1940s to the 1980s.

Cat. 126 Italian glasshouses provided both clear and colored stemware of innovative shape to the high end of the American market from the 1950s to the 1970s.

Richard acquired the famous Doccia porcelain factory (est. ca. 1735) near Florence from the Ginori family. Although tableware and artware by Richard-Ginori may have been exported to America earlier, the firm's products seem to have first appeared here when Fisher, Bruce & Co. of Philadelphia and New York began handling the line. In the 1930s the importer advertised Richard-Ginori's modernist wares designed by Giovanni "Gio" Ponti. In 1946 Fisher, Bruce & Co. became the Italian pottery's exclusive American distributor for "Ginori China Dinnerware."[237] Richard-Ginori's sales through this distributor were apparently not strong enough. In 1960 Pasmantier & Co. in New York replaced Fisher, Bruce & Co. as Ginori's exclusive American distributor. To shorten delivery time, tableware was now stocked in New York, Chicago, and San Francisco, and a national advertising campaign was launched.

Two years later Richard-Ginori opened its own retail store at 711 Fifth Avenue in New York, leaving wholesale distribution with Pasmantier & Co. At the time Ginori also operated thirty-one stores in Italy and one in Paris.[238] To further "consolidate manufacturing facilities, to improve distribution, to eliminate duplication and to prepare the way for new product development," Ginori merged with its important rival Società Ceramica Laveno in 1965.[239]

As a result of these efforts in production, marketing, and distribution, the Richard-Ginori brand of porcelain did become known among elite consumers during the postwar era. Of all the many shapes and patterns it sold in the United States, the company's first real success came in the mid-1950s, when two rococo-revival shapes were introduced—*Antico Doccia* and *Vecchio Ginori*. These shapes were decorated with a wide range of eighteenth-century-style patterns, including *Italian Fruit* and *Perugia* (1950s, cat. 124). In the 1960s and 1970s Richard-Ginori was also successful with a French-empire-style shape called *Impero* decorated with various classical patterns, including *Pompeii* and *Pincio*.

Along with Richard-Ginori, a second Italian tableware manufacturer achieved name recognition in the United States—Ceramica D'Arte Ernestine Cannon-D'Agostino. Very little information is available about the founder of this pottery, Ernestine Cannon. According to one source Cannon was an American who lived in Salerno, Italy, throughout World War II. Appalled by the poverty she saw there after the war, she started a pottery to create jobs for local citizens. Executed to Cannon's own designs, the eye-catching earthenware featuring botanical motifs was discovered by American buyers in Italy and then introduced to the trade at the 1949 Pittsburgh tableware show by Fisher, Bruce & Co., the exclusive U.S. representative.

Cat. 127 Block China Company's *España* shape
(left) of 1964 was made in Spain, and its *Transition*
shape (right) of 1968 was produced in Switzerland.

Progressive department stores such as Neiman Marcus in Dallas and specialty shops like Carole Stupell, Ltd., in New York added the Ernestine line (cat. 125).[240]

Edward Marcus of the department store Neiman Marcus was struck by the bold surface decoration and purchased large quantities of Ernestine directly from the factory around 1950. According to Barbara Boyd Wedgwood, china buyer for the store from 1952 to 1959, the line's thick glaze often crackled (or crazed) terribly, and it was in reality not popular with their customers. Although Neiman Marcus heavily promoted the pottery, in the end the store had to drastically discount its stock of Ernestine in order to sell it.[241] But despite its cold reception in Texas in the early 1950s, many affluent New Yorkers evidently admired the ceramics, which sold well at Carole Stupell's shop. By the mid-1960s Ernestine was being distributed in America by Laveno Italian Ceramics in New York and had gained in popularity as mainstream taste shifted to brighter colors and bolder patterns. In 1972 a columnist for the trade periodical *Gift and Tableware Reporter* called the Ernestine line "an American favorite." Although her statement may have been an exaggeration, given Neiman Marcus's early experience, Ernestine's trendy designs nevertheless caught the attention of enough American buyers and consumers to allow it to survive as a line until at least 1980.[242]

Fig. 3.10 For those who liked fish, New York importers could fulfill their wish!

THE PARTY CONTINUES

Virtually any country that produced ceramic and glass tableware attempted to export it to the United States at some point. Although the nature and quantities of their exports changed over time, France, England, Ireland, Germany, Czechoslovakia, and Japan were by far the most frequent guests at the American table. While the economic unification of much of Europe in 1993 created a market for goods of all kinds that was larger than the United States's approximately 275 million consumers, America nevertheless remains of exceptional importance to foreign tableware manufacturers.

The world of tableware has changed. In the late 1960s production began to shift from country to country in the quest of cheaper labor and raw materials. As a result new nations came to sit at the American table. In the 1960s Mexico emerged as a source for inexpensive glassware, while Portugal and Spain supplied higher quality porcelains and glassware (cat. 127). As Eastern Europe opened to the West at the end of the 1960s and early 1970s, many glass and ceramics importers left the Iberian Peninsula in search of cheaper production facilities, and Poland, Hungary, Yugoslavia, and Romania began exporting to the United States.

Following President Richard Nixon's watershed trip to China in 1974, the geopolitics of tableware shifted again—this time to Asia. Since the late eighteenth century, American merchants had imported porcelain tableware from China. As late as the 1920s, the New York import house of Soy Kee & Co. claimed to have "the most extensive showing of Chinese wares in America," including large quantities of the ever-popular *Blue Canton* and *Gold Medallion* patterns.[243] When communist China opened to the West in the late 1970s, many American importers and manufacturers invested in Chinese factories staffed by low-paid workers. As production standards rose, these businesses transferred their supply line from Europe to China. By the 1980s other Pacific Rim countries had joined in the business of producing ceramics. Today Indonesia and Malaysia have sophisticated tableware industries manufacturing dishes for export to America and beyond.[244]

Notes

1. USDC 1915, 74; USTC 1936, 44; and GTR (Aug. 1973): 25.

2. In 1889 the proportion of foreign glass of all types consumed in the United States reached a pinnacle of 16 percent. By 1914 this total had shrunk to 6 percent, and it declined further during World War I. Foreign glass imports rebounded in the postwar era (7 percent by 1929), only to decline again following World War II. If non-table glass were eliminated from these figures and domestic tableware production compared solely to similar imports, the percentage of foreign ware would be much higher. Davis 1949, 243, 248.

3. USBFDC 1917, 335; Davis 1949, 244; and GTR (Aug. 1974): 29.

4. USBFDC 1917, 334. The total for 1914 imports of ornamented tableware was $1,151,875, whereas that for 1916 was $282,783. Exports of French pottery were also dramatically reduced. According to a 1922 article in Crockery and Glass Journal, France's total pottery and glassware exports in 1913 were 262 million units. In 1919 they were 85 million units, and by 1921 they were still only 129 million units. "The French Ceramic Trade," CGJ 94:16 (20 Apr. 1922): 17.

5. Gates notes that in 1896 England and Germany were the leading exporters of tableware to the United States. Out of total pottery imports to America, England accounted for 48 percent and Germany for 40 percent. Gates 1984, 267.

6. USDC 1915, 85.

7. D'Albis 1988, 69–70.

8. Ibid., 70.

9. The information given here on Ahrenfeldt is taken from "Ahrenfeldt China: The Story of a Dream That Came True," CGJ 107:1 (Jan. 1929): 36–39, 82; and Cameron 1986, 11.

10. The New York branch of Ahrenfeldt & Son was still in business in 1908. "The New York Crockery and Glass District," CGJ 67:2 (9 Jan. 1908): 29.

11. Cameron 1986, 340–41.

12. "Chicago, West, All the Big Cities," CGJ 109:3 (Mar. 1931): 25.

13. White 1994, 210. Between 1930 and 1934 the value of French ceramics per "unit" ranged from $2.28 to $2.79. Values for England, France's closest competitor, ranged between $1.07 and $2.10.

14. "The Rejuvenation of French China," CGJ 109:2 (Feb. 1931): 25.

15. CGJ 104:9 (3 Mar. 1927): 9.

16. "Ahrenfeldt China: The Story of a Dream That Came True," CGJ 107:1 (Jan. 1929): 36–39, 82. For examples of Ahrenfeldt ceramics designed by Luce, see "S.S. Normandie Carries China and Glass Services for All Travel Classes," CGJ 116:6 (June 1935): 32, 38; and McCready 1995, 76–78.

17. CGJ 109:2 (Feb. 1931): 6–7.

18. "The Rejuvenation of French China," CGJ 109:2 (Feb. 1931): 25.

19. CGJ 107:2 (Feb. 1929): 19.

20. Cameron 1986, 45; CGJ 140:2 (Feb. 1947): 74; GTR (Dec. 1970): 1; and (Jan. 1972): 43.

21. "Imported Lines," CGJ 142:4 (15 Apr. 1948): 170. Ahrenfeldt is listed as a china line represented by Kupper in 1966; see GTR 7:16 (15 Aug. 1966): 199. For a Kupper advertisement depicting Hampton Ivory English earthenware, see CGJ 109:8 (Aug. 1931): 37.

22. Cameron 1986, 11.

23. "Vogt & Dose End Long Career," CGJ 109:5 (May 1931): 36.

24. Cameron 1986, 149.

25. In 1939 French imports of china tableware and kitchenware accounted for 2 percent by quantity; overall value was 3.5 percent. Even though quantities and overall value fluctuated periodically, French exports to the United States maintained a steady, but low, rate from the late 1940s onward. In 1955 French imports accounted for only 2 percent by quantity of all foreign porcelain shipped to the United States, whereas the total for earthenware was 4 percent.

26. These figures were derived from data published in CGJ 143:6 (Dec. 1948): 66–67; 162:5 (May 1958): 27; GTR (15 Aug. 1966): 32–34; and (Aug. 1973): 23–26.

27. "More from France than Appears—U.S.," GTR (6 Jan. 1969): 16.

28. "Glass 'First' Hits Market," GTR (1 July 1968): 1.

29. General information on Durand is taken from Matranga 1997, 114–15.

30. Sautot 1993, 69, 72.

31. CGJ 93:1 (6 Jan. 1921): 8; 94:8 (23 Feb. 1922): 14.

32. Stupell 1932.

33. Sautot 1993, 81.

34. CGJ 142:4 (Apr. 1948): 61; and Sautot 1993, 85.

35. Starting in January 1963, Lalique was exclusively represented in the United States by Jacques Jugeat. For an advertisement announcing this arrangement, see GTR (Jan. 1963): 23.

36. "French Glass: Escalate 15% Yearly in U.S.," GTR (19 June 1967): 1, 26.

37. Ibid.; and "Tariffs Drop—It's Data-Time," GTR (3 July 1967): 1, 35.

38. "French Glass: Escalate 15% Yearly in U.S.," GTR (19 June 1967): 26.

39. Sautot 1993, 81.

40. Baccarat 1995.

41. Sautot 1993, 87.

42. In 1955, 8 percent by value of all imported table and art glass was French in origin. By 1972 that figure had risen to 11 percent.

43. Figures derived from USBFDC 1917, 339; CGJ 162:5 (May 1958): 27; and GTR (Aug. 1973): 23–26.

44. For a comprehensive and insightful look at ceramics imports from Staffordshire to America in the nineteenth century, see Ewins 1997, 1–154. See also Miller 1984a and Collard 1967.

45. Dawes 1990, 154–73.

46. Jones 1993, 150.

47. Wedgwood Archives (WA)-28000A-38, cited in Dawes 1990, 108.

48. Batkin 1982, 90.

49. USDC 1915, 86.

50. A thorough explication of American and British tariff responses up to the 1930s can be found in Jones 1934, 211–46.

51. Whipp 1990, 30–38.

52. Export figures for 1900 show that the United States received 28.95 percent of total British pottery exports; in 1925 the figure had fallen to 14.97 percent. See Whipp 1990, 31.

53. One of these talented designers was M. A. Leger, who worked for Wedgwood from 1898 to 1904 and created patterns intended for the French market that were given French names. Collaborative efforts were also achieved through French retailers with other French artists, including Paul Follot and Marcel Goupy, who created designs before World War I, but the designs were not produced until after cessation of hostilities. Léon Solon joined Minton in 1895, designing in the fashionable art nouveau style until his departure in 1905.

54. Barely 3 percent of all ceramics sales was fine china and earthenware by the end of the twentieth century.

55. Ewins 1997, 129.

56. The major importers representing this type of Staffordshire producer in New York during the 1920s included Edward Boote, representing Cauldon China, Wood & Sons,

and Gibson & Sons Teapots; John Davison; Hugh C. Edmiston, sole agent for Mason's Patent Ironstone China; Edward B. Dickinson, an importer of generic teawares, Booth's dinnerwares, and Rockingham teapots; A. J. Fondeville & Co.; Robert Slimmon & Co., representing A. J. Wilkinson's, Bourne & Leigh, R. Sudlow & Sons, Shorter & Sons, Royal Aller Vale, and Watcombe Pottery; and Justin Tharaud, Inc., sole agent for Myott, Son & Co. but also selling German and French wares.

57. *CGJ* 104:12 (24 Mar. 1927): 26.

58. *CGJ* 138:3 (Mar. 1946): 19.

59. *CGJ* 142:4 (Apr. 1948): 61.

60. "The House of Miller," *CGJ* 107:12 (Dec. 1929): 179.

61. *CGJ* 109:15 (May 1931): 3.

62. "'Give the Lady What She Wants,'" *CGJ* 151:2 (Aug. 1952): 36.

63. Ibid., 40.

64. Wedgwood interview 1996.

65. Hannah 1986, 71–72.

66. Ibid., 72–73.

67. Jones 1993, 297.

68. Lend-lease supply arrangements with the United States required Britain to pay in dollars, so any industry that had a promising export trade to the United States, such as the pottery industry, was a prime target for Board of Trade restrictions.

69. "British Export Operation Under Wartime Conditions," *CGJ* 132:6 (June 1943): 15.

70. "Made in U.S.A. Wins Stamp of Approval," *CGJ* 143:6 (Dec. 1948): 66.

71. Hannah 1986, 85.

72. Time-Life 1948, 2.

73. Ibid., 6.

74. See Sprackling 1941.

75. Time-Life 1948, 12.

76. Ibid., 8.

77. *CGJ* 93:52 (29 Dec. 1921): 10.

78. Copeland interview, 1997; Bryan interview 1997.

79. Time-Life 1948, 17.

80. Wedgwood Archives, Barlaston, "Report on Visit to America by Victor Skellern"; Jenkins 1997, 12–13.

81. Minton Archives, Stoke-upon-Trent, no. 3111, "Diary and Confidential Report of Mr. Harthill's Journey in the United States with Mr. Bruce Ridgway, October to November 1954."

82. "Doulton Launches New Coupe Shape," *CGJ* 155:7 (Jan. 1955): 59.

83. Sir Arthur Bryan, letter to Stephen G. Harrison, 8 Oct. 1998.

84. Midwinter interview 1997.

85. Niblett 1990, 57.

86. Queensberry, Midwinter, Copeland, Bryan, and Wood interviews 1997.

87. Niblett 1990, 60–72.

88. Ibid., 75.

89. Ibid., 79–87.

90. For examples of American makers doing this, see "Glass Novelties from Bohemia," *CGJ* 93:7 (17 Feb. 1921): 41; and "Reproductions of Bohemian Glassware," 93:20 (19 May 1921): 16.

91. "Bohemian Glass Plants to Resume," *CGJ* 91:17 (22 Apr. 1920): 20.

92. "Germany's China Exports to U.S. Continues Strong," *GTR* (Jan. 1970): 2. The exact figure was 26 percent.

93. Holdridge 1950, 9, 15; "Bohemian Glass Plants to Resume," *CGJ* 91:17 (22 Apr. 1920): 20.

94. For maps showing the geographic distribution of the German and Czech pottery industries and raw material sources, see Holdridge 1950, 49–52.

95. Holdridge 1950, 8; "Bohemian Glass Plants to Resume," *CGJ* 91:17 (22 Apr. 1920): 20.

96. "Czechoslovak Glass Products Enjoy Worldwide Reputation," *CGJ* 104:10 (10 Mar. 1927): 10; Holdridge 1950, 12.

97. Siemen 1989, 62; and "Wachsende japanische konkurrenz erschwert den porzellan-export," *Schaulade* 33:9 (Sept. 1958): 615. Jungeblut notes that worldwide exports of German earthenware gained steady ground after 1920 and had begun to equal prewar totals by 1926. Exported porcelain sales were stronger, surpassing prewar totals by 1925 and continuing upward into the late 1920s (Jungeblut 1928: 368–69).

98. USDC 1915, 85–86, 479–80. In 1912 the United Kingdom contributed 22 percent of all foreign dishes imported to the U.S., whereas the Germans tallied 41 percent. The actual totals for U.S. consumption of German tableware were 23 percent (pottery) and 77 percent (porcelain).

99. USBFDC 1917, 339. Bohemia's total was 32 percent and Germany's 29 percent.

100. USTC 1936, 29. Due to changes in the way the government counted ware and the categories of ceramics included at a given time, these figures are not strictly comparable, but the general trend in losing market share by volume to the Japanese is accurate.

101. In 1956 West Germany accounted for 15 percent ($3.2 million) of china imports. A decade later that sum had declined to 11 percent, and by 1972 it had decreased further, to 10.5 percent. Figures derived from statistics reported in *CGJ* 162:5 (May 1958): 27; *GTR* (15 Aug. 1966): 32; and (Aug. 1973): 24.

102. USDC 1915, 86.

103. Ibid., 557; and USBFDC 1917, 339.

104. USTC 1936, 29. In 1929 Czech imports to the United States were slightly higher than France's by value as well as being 6.4 percent of total imports vs. France's 6.1 percent. By quantity the totals were 5.4 percent versus 3 percent.

105. In 1956 imports reached 7 percent by value of all glassware shipped to the United States. By 1972 Czechoslovakia's share of U.S. glassware imports had fallen to 3 percent. Figures derived from statistics reported in *CGJ* 162:5 (May 1958): 27; *GTR* (15 Aug. 1966): 32; and (Aug. 1973): 24.

106. "Good Demand for China at Leipzig Fair," *CGJ* 94:14 (6 Apr. 1922): 21; and "Leipzig Fair to Open American Sales Center," 100:24 (11 June 1925): 22.

107. "The Prague Sample Fair," *CGJ* 92:20 (11 Nov. 1920): 14; "Bohemian Fair to be Held," 93:1 (6 Jan. 1921): 18; and "The Prague Fair," 100:20 (14 May 1925): 21.

108. The Imperial Bohemia China Corporation was active in New York in the early 1930s and represented the china manufacturers Haas & Czjzek of Schlaggenwald, Czechoslovakia (*CGJ* 113:1 [July 1933]: 4). The Schumann China Corporation was active in the early 1930s, marketing tableware from the Schumann factory in Bavaria. The line was sold under the two brand names Dresdner Art China and Schumann Bavaria (*PGBS* 41:3 [20 Feb. 1930]: 37; and *CGJ* 113:2 [Aug, 1933]: 4). The earliest advertisement depicts a pattern named *Cotswold* that is described as an "exclusive English Pattern on IVORY CHINA."

The Overseas Mercantile Company, active in New York in the late 1930s, was run by Lewis R. Werner and represented several important Czech makers of glassware and dinnerware, including the Pirkenhammer factory and EPIAG (*CGJ* 121:1 [July 1937]: 55; and 122:6 [June 1938]: 3, 27). The Wiener Werkstätte branch shop was located at 581 Fifth Avenue and was run by Josef Urban. It opened in 1922 and closed in 1924 (Fahr-Becker 1995, 212, 215, 239).

109. "All in the Day's Work: A Personal Interview with Karl Lickhard," *CGJ* 108:5 (May 1930): 16–17, 73.

110. For advertisements noting the lines carried, see *CGJ* 123:6 (Dec. 1938): 19; 116:6 (June 1940): 25; and 128:1 (Jan. 1941): 61.

111. *CGJ* 145:3 (Sept. 1949): 25, 33; and 146:1 (Jan. 1950): 83.

112. Siemen 1989, 80–81.

113. For histories and obituaries of the Straubs, see *CGJ* 144:4 (Apr. 1949): 56; 155:9 (4 Mar. 1955): 35; 152:1 (Jan. 1953): 69; and 164:1 (Jan. 1959): 50.

114. "The Story of Tirschenreuth a Business Romance," *PGBS* 41:13 (1 May 1930): 13, 33.

115. Ibid.

116. For an advertisement noting other countries from which Straub imported, see *CGJ* 165:1 (July 1959): 47.

117. George F. Bassett & Co. was active in New York from 1869 until about the 1930s. It handled lines from Holland, England, and France and eight lines from Germany and Czechoslovakia. For a list of what was carried, see *CGJ* 107:2 (Feb. 1929): 19. According to *CGJ* 93:17 (28 Apr. 1921): 16, the firm was incorporated in 1921 following the death of the last surviving partner, Frederick H. Doremus.

Fisher, Bruce & Co. was active in Philadelphia from 1872 until after 1976. The firm incorporated in 1923 and eventually opened showrooms in New York, Los Angeles, San Francisco, and Seattle. During its existence Fisher, Bruce & Co. carried lines from England, America, Italy, and Sweden as well as the Bohemia brand of Czech china and the German Baronet dinnerware line. In 1976 a controlling interest in the firm was purchased by the Swedish glassmaker Orrefors Glasbruk. Fisher, Bruce & Co. had represented Orrefors glass in this country since 1946.

Geo. Borgfeldt & Co. was active in New York from 1881 apparently into the 1970s. It imported an enormous range of German and Czech china and glass, including ceramic lines by EPIAG, Beyer & Bock, Rudolstadt, and Reinhold Schlegelmilch, along with ware from France, England, Italy, Holland, Japan, and the United States. One article stated that Borgfeldt provided "doubtless the trade's largest and most varied display of china and glassware" ("New Borgfeldt Home Occupied Last Month Brings Approval of Visitors," *CGJ* 109:2 [Feb. 1931]: 40). Another article states that in 1949 Borgfeldt had branch offices in San Francisco, Toronto, and San Juan, Puerto Rico ("75 Years of Progress," *CGJ* 145:3 [Sept. 1949]: 89).

B. Tomby was active in New York from the 1910s to the 1920s and imported mainly central European ceramics, including Meissen, Hutschenreuther, and Paul Mueller dinnerware and hotelware. Tomby was allied with the Royal Dresden Porcelain Corporation, located at the same address, 9 East Forty-seventh Street, for the distribution of Meissen in the early 1920s.

Justin Tharaud was active in New York from 1915 until around 1980. It carried at various times well-known lines from France, England, Holland, Czechoslovakia, and Germany, including Royal Bayreuth dinnerware and hotelware from Porzellanfabrik Schönwald.

Fred C. Reimer was active in New York in the 1920s. It distributed Italian glass and ceramics, French pottery, and several lines of German and Czech dinnerware and glassware, including Royal Nymphenberg and Theresienthal crystal. One source notes that Theresienthal Glassworks and Reimer copyrighted its products in the United States and sold colored glass dinner services as well as stemware ("Generation of Craftsmen Have Made Theresienthal Glass," *PGBS* 41:3 [20 Feb. 1930]: 56–58).

Koscherak Brothers was active in New York from the 1920s to the 1950s. It carried some Italian and German dinnerware, but specialized in Venetian and Bohemian glassware and fancy goods.

Otto Goetz was active in New York from the 1920s to the 1930s. It sold lines such as Royal Bayreuth porcelain and Schramberger earthenware.

Marks & Rosenfeld was active in New York from the late 1930s to the 1950s. It was the exclusive agent for Victoria China, produced by Altrohlauer Porzellanfabriken in Altrohlau, Czechoslovakia (*CGJ* 122:1 [Jan. 1938]: 11).

Fraser's was active in New York and Berkeley, California, from the 1950s until apparently the 1970s. It carried several important German lines, including *Urbino* from the Königliche Porzellan-Manufaktur (KPM) in Berlin and tableware from the Schönwald Porcelain Factory.

Ceramar was active in New York in the 1960s and 1970s. It was the U.S. distributor of Villeroy & Boch. Founded by Carlo Piccoli, the firm also imported the Italian lines of Cantagalli, Este, Mancioli, and Ernestine. In 1976 Villeroy & Boch purchased Ceramar as part of its plan to increase sales of its ceramics and crystal in the United States. When Villeroy & Boch acquired rival Heinrich & Co. in the same year, that line was also picked up by Ceramar.

118. Graham & Zenger was active in New York from 1906 to ca. 1936. William P. Graham founded the firm in 1906. Zenger joined the company in 1910, and the name was changed to Graham & Zenger. Although Zenger left the firm in 1912, the name remained the same until 1936, when it was changed to Black Knight China. In 1925 the firm was incorporated, with several employees having interests. In 1936 Graham again took over control of the company. Graham & Zenger evidently did well until the early 1930s, when it had to liquidate much of its stock, and it appears to have gone out of business sometime soon after 1936. The showroom was located at 104 Fifth Avenue in New York. Over the years this importer carried Italian and Dutch crystal, as well as numerous German and Czech products, including Rosenthal china in the 1920s, Theresienthal and Schaffgotsch stemware, and a line of German dinnerware called *Black Knight* that it designed in the United States. The high-quality Black Knight line was introduced about 1925, and the logo was trademarked in 1927.

For information on the Czecho Peasant Art Company, see cat. 13.

For early information on the Block China Company and its precursor, see pp. 235–44. Following the dispute with Rosenthal, the Block family used several American designers to create china and glass lines that were then manufactured in Europe for the most part, including porcelain at the Fabrique de Porcelain Langenthal in Switzerland and Arzberg in Germany. Block China is still active today, although it is no longer owned by the Block family.

119. *CGJ* 108:10 (Oct. 1930): 2.

120. "New Duties on German Goods Will Raise Price 15 Per Cent," *CGJ* 119:1 (July 1936): 64.

121. "The German Glass Industry," *CGJ* 94:2 (23 Mar. 1933): 27.

122. "Czechoslovak Glass Products Enjoy Worldwide Reputation," *CGJ* 104:10 (10 Mar. 1927): 10; and "Das Neue 'Bohemia' Service," *Schaulade* 5:2 (Feb. 1929): 77.

123. "What About the Czecho Treaty?," *CGJ* 122:4 (Apr. 1938): 34; "China and Glass Trades to Have Hearing on Proposed Czech Treaty," 121:4 (Oct. 1937): 34; and "Swapping with the Czechs," 122:4 (Apr. 1938): 15.

124. "Made in Czecho-Slovakia," *PGBS* (Mar. 1939): 2.

125. "Resourcefulness Marks Czechoslovak Importers' Course in Sudeten Problem," *CGJ* 123:6 (Dec. 1938): 34; "Importers Await Final

Word on Czechoslovakia," 123:4 (Oct. 1938): 17; and "Made in Czecho-Slovakia," *PGBS* (Mar. 1939): 7.

126. "American Buyers Will Avoid Central Europe, Says Proctor," *CGJ* 124:4 (Apr. 1939): 19.

127. Holdridge 1950, 49.

128. "News from the AES in Europe," *Post Exchange* 7:1 (Apr. 1947): 34.

129. "Der Produktions- und Exportplan für die Porzellan Industrie," *Schaulade* 21:2 (July 1926): 29–30.

130. "Poll Results Guide Foreign Production" and "Americans Invited to View German Wares," *CGJ* (Dec. 1946): 72; and Block interview 1998.

131. "The EUCOM Exchange System," *Post Exchange* 8:12 (Mar. 1949): 43–51.

132. "News from the AES in Europe," *Post Exchange* 6:10/11 (Dec. 1947): 37.

133. *Post Exchange* 6:13 (Mar. 1947): 16–26; and 8:7 (Oct. 1948): 36–37.

134. "Limit Post Exchanges," *CGJ* 132:2 (Feb. 1943): 44; and "PX to Sell Foreign Ware," 168:3 (1 Mar. 1961): 46.

135. "Bavarian China Producers Recovering Despite Shortages, New York, Chicago Importers Report," *CGJ* 143:1 (July 1948): 81.

136. "European Industry Slowly Returning to Production," *CGJ* 139:3 (Sept. 1946): 76.

137. "Bavarian Pottery Prices Double or Triple Prewar," *CGJ* 140:4 (Apr. 1947): 50.

138. The Krautheim Porcelain Factory exported tableware to this country under the trade name of "Franconia China." See *CGJ* 167:1 (July 1960): 20; and "Rosenthal to Debut $7 Million Factory," *GTR* (2 Oct. 1967): 1.

139. "U.S.C.C. Furthers Plan to Import Japanese and German Tableware," *CGJ* 139:6 (Dec. 1946): 67.

140. "Czech Trade with U.S. Seen Gaining in '47," *Stars and Stripes* (10 Mar. 1947): 2.

141. "Czechs Plan Trade Fair," *CGJ* 137:6 (Dec. 1945): 62; and "Czech Fair Held in Boston," 145:4 (Oct. 1949): 68.

142. *CGJ* 145:6 (Dec. 1949): 128–29; and "Czechoslovakia," 166:5 (May 1960): 36.

143. "Neues Hausgerät in USA," *Schaulade* 26:6 (June 1951): 192–93.

144. "Germany," *CGJ* 166:5 (May 1960): 26–27.

145. "'Die Schaulade' and the Common Market," *Schaulade* 33:5 (May 1958): 333.

146. "Labor, Sales Baffle Europe's Pottery Men," *GTR* (7 Sept. 1964): 6.

147. "Germany's Wares Missing Full U.S. Sales Potential," *GTR* (Feb. 1973): 2.

148. "Bavaria Is Home for German Potteries," *GTR* (Oct. 1962): 92.

149. "Labor, Sales Baffle Europe's Pottery Men," *GTR* (7 Sept. 1964): 6.

150. "Germany's Wares Missing Full U.S. Sales Potential," *GTR* (Feb. 1973): 2.

151. "German Firms Enter Merger," *GTR* (Oct. 1972): 5; and "Acquires Pottery" (May 1976): 1.

152. "German Trade Put in Focus," *GTR* (Feb. 1976): 7.

153. "Villeroy & Boch—Why the Time Is Now," *GTR* (July 1973): 36.

154. "Von Boch: Why Not Contemporary & Traditional?," *GTR* (Feb. 1971): 35; and "Villeroy & Boch—Why the Time Is Now," (July 1973): 33–36.

155. "Centennial Celebrated by Hutschenreuther," *CGJ* 161:2 (Aug. 1957): 46.

156. "Germany's China Exports to U.S. Continues Strong," *GTR* (Jan. 1970): 4; and "Crystal Sales Pass China," (Feb. 1972): 1.

157. *GTR* (15 Aug. 1966): 32; (Aug. 1973): 24; and "Crystal Sales Pass China," (Feb. 1972): 1.

158. "Japan Makes and Ships That Which the U.S. Orders," *CGJ* 146:6 (June 1950): 9; USDC 1961, 1, 6; and "Credit U.S. Habits with Increasing Japan Ware Mfrs.," *GTR* (15 Feb. 1965): 18.

159. USDC 1915, 86.

160. Washington 1982, 16.

161. Livingston et al. 1973, 372. According to this source, by 1936 "Japan was absorbing half of all United States exports to Asia—or as much as the whole continent of South America."

162. USDC 1915, 86; and USBFDC 1917, 339.

163. "The Making of Japanese Pottery in Modern Factories," *PGBS* (15 Aug. 1929): 11.

164. Ibid.

165. Washington 1982, 17.

166. "The Making of Japanese Pottery in Modern Factories," *PGBS* (15 Aug. 1929): 11.

167. USTC 1936, 29.

168. "Made in U.S.A. Wins Stamp of Approval," *CGJ* 143:6 (Dec. 1948): 66.

169. "Act to Stem Foreign Competition," *CGJ* 116:5 (May 1935): 13.

170. Livingston et al. 1973, 372.

171. "Imports Hearing at Tariff Commission Reveals Interesting Figures and Percentage," *CGJ* 115:1 (July 1934): 58.

172. USTC 1936, 21, table 16; and "Act to Stem Foreign Competition," *CGJ* 116:5 (May 1935): 14.

173. "U.S. Potters Appeal for Direct Relief from Japanese and English Competition," *CGJ* 113:3 (Sept. 1933): 15.

174. "Potters Complain of Japanese and English Competition," *CGJ* 113:2 (Aug. 1933): 15.

175. "U.S. Potters Appeal for Direct Relief from Japanese and English Competition," *CGJ* 113:3 (Sept. 1933): 15.

176. See "Domestic Potters and Foreign Competition—A New Appeal?," *CGJ* 117:1 (July 1935): 36, 56, 58.

177. "Wm. Penn Hotel to House Entire Exhibit, Japanese Importers Excluded," *CGJ* 118:1 (Jan. 1936): 39.

178. "Potters and Labor Unions Inaugurate Boycott of Japanese Merchandise," *CGJ* 122:1 (Jan. 1938): 64; and Gates 1984, 320–24.

179. Gates 1984, 323.

180. "Commerce Department Will Import Japanese China," *CGJ* 139:5 (Nov. 1946): 60; and "Lift Ban on Business Travel to Japan; Visits Begin Aug. 15," 141:1 (July 1947): 72.

181. "Japanese Dinnerware Prices to Rise," *CGJ* 147:5 (Nov. 1950): 43.

182. "Japs to Push Costlier China," *CGJ* 139:5 (Nov. 1946): 60.

183. In 1954 testimony was given before the Tariff Commission in Washington, D.C., that the average Japanese pottery worker earned 20 cents per hour compared to $1.70 in the United States. "The Japanese labor myth" states that real wages for Japanese workers went up 21 percent between 1955 and 1959. In 1959 wages rose 7 percent, and in 1960, another 5 percent. *CGJ* 169:5 (Nov. 1961): 5.

184. Hinckley and Ridgway 1954, 1.

185. These statistics compiled from government data are reported in *GTR* (19 Aug. 1968): 26 ff.; (Aug. 1971): 22 ff.; and (Aug. 1974): 27 ff. Figures for Japanese glass imports are less readily available, but in 1967 Japan contributed 22 percent by volume and 10 percent by value to U.S. glass imports.

186. "Archivist Sink 'Ships' of Pirates," *GTR* (Aug. 1969): 16–18; and "Japan," (May 1960): 23.

187. USDC 1961, 1–2.

188. For information about these firms and others, see White 1994, 10–11; and especially Brandimarte 1991.

189. For representative advertisements from some of these firms, see *CGJ* 93:7 (17 Feb.

1921): 10; and 93:30 (28 July 1921): 15. Judging from the names of firms noted in Brandimarte 1991, many of the retailers of Japanese goods were of Chinese heritage.

190. "Sale of Japanese Goods Lagging," *CGJ* 141:4 (Oct. 1947): 58.

191. *CGJ* 146:4 (Apr. 1950): 37–38.

192. "Japan Makes and Ships That Which U.S. Orders," *CGJ* 146:6 (June 1950): 9.

193. "Japan," *GTR* (May 1960): 22.

194. "1850–1950: A Century of Progress in Both Domestic and Import Fields Is Being Marked by United China & Glass Co.," *CGJ* 145:6 (Dec. 1949): 122.

195. "What ACI's Bone China Looks Like," *GTR* (18 Jan. 1965): 4.

196. "Japanese Designer Likes U.S.'s Color, OK of Ideas," *GTR* (14 Nov. 1969): 6.

197. "Mikasa Opens New Facility; Goes 'Mod,'" *GTR* (Dec. 1969): 4.

198. Giarrocco interview 1997.

199. The original outlet store was in Mikasa's warehouse. In 1982 the firm moved into a new headquarters building in Secaucus, New Jersey. The financial and accounting departments that had remained in Los Angeles moved to New Jersey in 1998, according to company sources.

200. Otagiri founded his firm in the late 1940s. For many years Ray Hirokawa was president and Bob Wang national sales representative. By the early 1970s Otagiri had showrooms at 1400 Folsom Street in San Francisco and 11 East Twenty-sixth Street in New York, as well as a warehouse in New Jersey. The firm went out of business in 1994.

201. For an early advertisement of Fitz and Floyd mugs, see *GTR* (Apr. 1970): 20.

202. "Honors to Floyd, Importer of Year," *GTR* (June 1976): 27. This source states that Floyd made his first trip to Japan in 1965, but Floyd himself says it was 1964 (Floyd to Venable correspondence, 1 June 1999).

203. Hodges interview 1999.

204. Horchow interview 1998.

205. Gifford interview 1997; and Noritake 1997, 9.

206. These glasshouses are listed among the lines carried by New York importers in *CGJ* (Dec. 1935): 108–10.

207. *CGJ* 91:8 (19 Feb. 1920): 19; 125:1 (July 1939): 28; and *PGBS* (19 Sept. 1929): 6.

208. "Swedish Glass Products," *CGJ* 134:4 (Apr. 1944): 36.

209. *CGJ* 138:2 (Feb. 1946): 13; "Swedish Glass Factories Working at Full Capacity," 139:4 (Oct. 1946): 62; and "Corcoran Reports on Glass Production in Sweden," 144:3 (Mar. 1949): 68.

210. Figures derived from statistics reported in *CGJ* 162:5 (May 1958): 27; *GTR* (15 Aug. 1966): 32; and (Aug. 1973): 24.

211. "Swedish Glass—The 1973 Change in Pace," *GTR* (July 1973): 22.

212. "What's Next for Scandinavia?," *GTR* (Oct. 1963): 23.

213. "Orrefors Buys Fisher, Bruce & Co.," *GTR* (Apr. 1973): 1.

214. "Swedish Glass—The 1973 Change in Pace," *GTR* (July 1973): 22.

215. According to *Crockery and Glass Journal*, the following Danish, Finnish, and Norwegian glasshouses were selling ware in New York before the war: Holmegaards, Iittala, Karhula, and Osakeyhtio Riihimaki. *CGJ* 117:6 (Dec. 1935): 108–10.

216. Figures derived from statistics reported in *CGJ* 162:5 (May 1958): 27; *GTR* (15 Aug. 1966): 32; and (Aug. 1973): 24.

217. For period advertisements, see *CGJ* 123:3 (Sept. 1938): 14; 124:3 (Mar. 1939): 23; 124:6 (June 1939): 35; 124:5 (May 1939): back cover. For a listing of lines imported in 1935, see *CGJ* (Dec. 1935): 108–10.

218. For Scandinavian-inspired designs by Southern Potteries see Newbound and Newbound 1989. For images of the Scandinavian imports, see *CGJ* 141:6 (Dec. 1947): 36; and 142:1 (Jan. 1948): 23.

219. Sources conflict on the date and situation surrounding Lunning's first shop. His obituary says the shop opened in 1922; other sources give 1924. Jensen 1980, 17.

220. *CGJ* 151:4 (Oct. 1952): 60.

221. *CGJ* 143:3 (Sept. 1948): 63.

222. "Frederik Lunning Buys Waertsila," *CGJ* 160:1 (Jan. 1957): 52; 8 (advertisement).

223. For a brief history of Dansk, see Eidelberg 1991, 370.

224. *Dansk* 1994, n.p., notes the opening of the outlet store as 1972. Gura 1999, 107, states that the outlet store opened on the Fourth of July 1968. According to Ted Nierenberg, the 1968 date is correct (phone conversation with Charles Venable, 3 Sept. 1999).

225. For listing of lines imported in 1935, see *CGJ* (Dec. 1935): 108–10. For Mosa tableware, see "Europe: Modern Designs Appeal to Americans," *CGJ* 160:5 (May 1957): 40. The

Fris factory is listed in the 1966 directory of imported lines. See *GTR* (15 Aug. 1966): 194.

226. *USBFDC* 1917, 339.

227. Figures derived from statistics reported in *CGJ* 162:5 (May 1958): 27; *GTR* (15 Aug. 1966): 32; and (Aug. 1973): 24.

228. *CGJ* 147:1 (July 1950): 117.

229. *GTR* (15 Aug. 1966): 199.

230. "Machine-pressed Crystal Tethering Costs?," *GTR* (Dec. 1970): 1.

231. Figures derived from statistics reported in *CGJ* 162:5 (May 1958): 27; *GTR* (15 Aug. 1966): 32; and (Aug. 1973): 24.

232. *CGJ* (Dec. 1935): 108–13.

233. For a typical example, see *CGJ* 108:2 (Feb. 1930): 7.

234. "Murano, Si! Plus More Italy Glass," *GTR* (22 Jan. 1968): 14.

235. "Italy—A Worn-out Welcome?," *GTR* (1 May 1967): 1.

236. "Italy's Export to America Holding Steady," *GTR* (May 1972): 2.

237. For an advertisement, see *CGJ* 125:3 (Sept. 1939): 25. For an announcement of the appointment, see *CGJ* 139:3 (Sept. 1946): 5.

238. *CGJ* 167:1 (July 1960): 4; 167:3 (Sept. 1960): 15; "Richard-Ginori Names U.S. Firm," (July 1960): 90; and "Ginori Opens NYC Store," *GTR* (June 1962): 84.

239. "Italy's Name Brands Join in Merger Talk," *GTR* (15 Mar. 1965): 1.

240. *CGJ* 143:6 (Dec. 1948): 108; and 144:3 (Mar. 1949): 8. Basic biographical information on Ernestine Cannon provided by Keith Stupell, son of Carole Stupell, in a phone conversation with Charles Venable, 8 Aug. 1999.

241. Wedgwood interview 1995.

242. *GTR* (15 Aug. 1966): 194.

243. *CGJ* 91:3 (15 Jan. 1929): cover; and 93:7 (17 Feb. 1921): 55.

244. Block interview 1998.

"The Trade's Printed Salesman"

POTTERY
GLASS & BRASS
SALESMAN

ISSUED WEEKLY BY
THE O'GORMAN PUBLISHING CO.
NEW YORK

VOL. XLI, No. 6

Entered as second-class matter Feb. 3, 1910, at P. O., New York, N. Y., under Act of Mar. 3, 1879.
Subscription in the United States, $2.00 a year and upward.

MAR. 13, 1930

From Warehouse to Your House: Tableware Marketing

Chapter 4

Hundreds of women are eager to venture forth with bright, interesting tables, but they've been afraid. . . . It's to the buyer's advantage to teach [them] to dare!

—KATHERINE L. VEDDER, buyer, Neiman Marcus, 1932

Refined china and glass have long been produced at a great distance from the final consumer. For centuries western Europeans used tableware made in potteries far from their homes. This was especially true for colonists in the New World, who lived thousands of miles from European and Asian sources of ceramics and glass. Even domestic wares came from far away. Because American tableware production was concentrated in a few places during the nineteenth and early twentieth centuries, U.S. producers created a distribution system to move china and glass from factories to homes throughout the country.

The Wholesale Trade

SALESMEN

Dispersing fragile eating utensils across such a great expanse was complicated, involving multiple steps and many people. At its most basic, however, the process was divided into wholesale and retail levels. During most of the nineteenth century selling glass and ceramics was a rudimentary affair.[1] Factories as well as domestic distributors and import houses typically sent out traveling salesmen with a few samples and perhaps a printed price list or trade catalogue in hand. Visiting countless cities and towns to call on merchants who might place orders for their goods, these salesmen suffered the travails of nineteenth-century travel. With a few urban exceptions, journeying through America was difficult and sometimes dangerous, as travelers moved along the nation's rivers and roads and took accommodations in boarding houses and primitive hotels. Although some men might have enjoyed the freedom inherent in such a roaming existence, the work was often tiring and difficult.

Between 1880 and 1980 the selling of ceramics and glass was transformed. Early in this period, factories, domestic distributors, and importers divided the country into "territories" to which they assigned specific salesmen. Several times a year sales representatives traveled through their respective territories to call on retailers. In this manner salesmen built up close relationships with clients that ideally translated into orders.

The life of the wholesale salesman improved in many ways. Special trunks were designed to carry samples (fig. 4.2). A greatly improved and efficient railway (and later highway) network emerged to carry salesmen and their samples across the

OPPOSITE:
Fig. 4.1 Cover, *Pottery, Glass and Brass Salesman*, 1930.

285

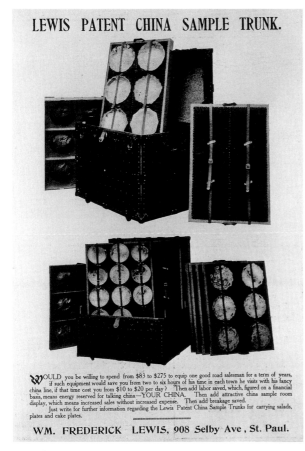

LEWIS PATENT CHINA SAMPLE TRUNK.

WOULD you be willing to spend from $83 to $275 to equip one good road salesman for a term of years, if such equipment would save you from two to six hours of his time in each town he visits with his fancy china line, if that time cost you from $10 to $20 per day? Then add labor saved, which, figured on a financial basis, means energy reserved for talking china—YOUR CHINA. Then add attractive china sample room display, which means increased sales without increased expense. Then add breakage saved.
Just write for further information regarding the Lewis Patent China Sample Trunks for carrying salads, plates and cake plates.

WM. FREDERICK LEWIS, 908 Selby Ave., St. Paul.

Fig. 4.2 Salesmen traveling by rail in the early 20th century kept their goods safe in custom-fitted trunks.

Fig. 4.3 The twenty-ninth annual banquet of the Pottery, Glass, and Brass Salesmen's Association, Hotel Astor, New York, 1921.

nation, while standardized time zones implemented by the railroads in 1883 helped keep them on schedule. Simultaneously, a host of relatively comfortable hotels and restaurants sprang up to accommodate their needs. The newly instituted national telephone system and dependable postal service benefited traveling salesmen as well, allowing them to keep in touch more easily with both home offices and clients. Finally, a support system emerged from within the ranks of salesmen. In 1880 a group of glass salesmen founded what became the Pittsburgh glass and pottery trade show. Twelve years later the Pottery, Glass, and Brass Salesmen's Association was established (fig. 4.3). Led by well-known sales representatives such as Alex G. Menzies of the Cambridge Glass Company, this organization held annual banquets at which the "Knights of the Road," as they called themselves, discussed business conditions and other pertinent issues.[2]

SHOWROOMS AND WAREHOUSES

Although most producers continued to employ traveling salesmen well into the twentieth century, the need for them lessened over time with the emergence of permanent showrooms, intermediate wholesalers, and trade shows. During the first half of the twentieth century, when ceramic and glass tableware production was at its height in the United States, many manufacturers maintained their own showrooms. Almost without exception the factory site included a sample room. Early on it was common for buyers to travel extensively through New Jersey, Pennsylvania, Ohio, and West Virginia, visiting factories and placing orders. In the case of large and profitable firms like the Homer Laughlin China Company, these local showrooms could be grand indeed (fig. 2.15). A few producers in this class showed their wares in such local display spaces exclusively. Lenox China is the most noteworthy example of the practice; until 1997, when the firm opened a space in New York, buyers had to view Lenox products at the company's New Jersey headquarters or in temporary displays at trade shows.[3] This practice was the exception, however.

Producers and importers typically were represented in New York, the center of the U.S. tableware market (see pp. 289–90). Other regional distribution centers developed over time, but New York always remained supreme. From the mid-nineteenth century until today the heart of the china and glass market has been in lower Manhattan where Fifth Avenue crosses Broadway. Along the thoroughfares bounded by Twenty-second and Twenty-sixth Streets, millions of dishes have been bought and sold in the scores of showrooms that dot the district. Anchoring the area were several high-rise buildings that vied for the title of most fashionable. Before World War II three structures competed for important clients (figs. 4.4). The Fifth Avenue Building at 200 Fifth Avenue was billed as the "Uptown Headquarters for the Pottery, Glass, China, Metal Goods and Housewares Trades," while the Flatiron Building at 1107 Broadway was heralded as "The New China and Glassware Citadel!" in 1929. These leading addresses were followed in significance by the seventeen-story

Fig. 4.4 The Fifth Avenue Building was home to scores of tableware showrooms before World War II.

Fig. 4.5 The showroom of Fostoria Glass Company boasted the latest modern decor when it opened in 1952.

structure at 1140 Broadway.[4] After World War II all of these showroom locations were eclipsed by the building at 225 Fifth Avenue and eventually by 41 Madison. This last facility was erected in 1972 and became the home of the New York Merchandise Mart. Today it is the most prestigious location for china and glass showrooms in the country.

As with the displays at factories, some of the exhibits presented in these New York buildings and elsewhere could be elaborate. The Fostoria Glass Company, for example, went all out in 1952 when it opened a new, modernist space at 225 Fifth Avenue. Created by the Chicago designer Harper Richards, the showroom was meant "to show how to show glass" in retail stores (fig. 4.5).[5]

Domestic producers that could not maintain exclusive display spaces in New York usually relied on the services of wholesaler distributors, or "jobbers." These firms, like those that handled imported wares, typically displayed several lines of pottery and glass in a single showroom and maintained a traveling sales force to sell the combined lines of goods nationally (see chapter 3). By the early 1920s there were numerous firms in New York performing this role. Among the most notable were Horace C. Gray Company, which at one time represented Southern Potteries, Paden City Pottery Company, Fenton Art Glass Company, and Indiana Glass Company and many others (cat. 14). Cox & Co. was another importer and

domestic distributor. Occupying the entire fifth floor of 120 Fifth Avenue in the 1920s and 1930s, this wholesaler was the agent for several important manufacturers, including the Homer Laughlin China Company and Imperial Glass Company. Through the decades these distributors became increasingly sophisticated. In the 1950s, for example, Richards-Morgenthau retained showrooms in both Chicago and New York, laid out by the well-known designer Edward J. Wormley, and commissioned tableware lines such as *Raymor Modern* (cat. 128).[6]

To distribute china and glass efficiently, producers, domestic wholesalers, and importers maintained warehouses from which they filled orders. Many firms had single warehouses in the vicinity of their main showrooms, but some larger distributors had more. The American branch of the Japanese firm the Noritake Company, for example, maintained seven warehouses across the country to ensure prompt deliveries nationwide (see pp. 257–64). More typical were East Coast firms that in the early post–World War II years opened warehouses and sometimes showrooms in California to better serve the western part of the country.

OVERLEAF:
Cat. 128 The distributor Richards-Mogenthau & Co. commissioned *Raymor Modern* in 1952 and had it made at the Roseville Pottery in Ohio.

Ebeling & Reuss

Ebeling & Reuss is one of the longest surviving china and glass import houses in the United States. Frederick W. Ebeling, born in Hanover, Germany, immigrated to America in 1872 and eventually became a traveling salesman for the Philadelphia china and glass firm of Zeh & Schenck. Following Schenck's departure in 1886, Ebeling became a partner in the firm along with another top salesman, Theodore Reuss, and the name was changed to Zeh, Ebeling & Reuss. After Zeh's retirement in 1900 the firm became Ebeling & Reuss, located at 440 Market Street.[1] In the early twentieth century Ebeling & Reuss moved into expanded quarters with an adjacent warehouse at 707 Chestnut Street. Following Frederick Ebeling's death, his son Henry became president, and Theodore Reuss Jr., vice president. Henry Ebeling is said to have "quickly become the company's buyer and premier salesman, bringing new lines of dinnerware."[2] In 1933 the Ebeling family bought out Reuss but retained the firm's joint name.

Ebeling & Reuss opened its first New York showroom in the newly completed Empire State Building in 1932. Robert W. Ebeling, who like his brother Henry had entered the business in 1926 as a traveling salesman, was appointed manager. Five years later the showroom was moved with the offices to 225 Fifth Avenue, in the heart of New York's housewares district. During the ensuing decades offices and display spaces were opened in the Chicago Merchandise Mart (1938) and at 527 West Seventh Street, Los Angeles (ca. 1948). A warehouse in Pasadena, California, was added in 1955 to improve deliveries to the firm's western customers.

From the firm's earliest days, a large part of Ebeling & Reuss's business was in giftware. In the late nineteenth century stock included specialty items like ceramic mustache cups and smoking sets. In the mid-twentieth century the firm was best known as the U.S. distributor of Hummel figurines from Germany. Along with giftware, Ebeling & Reuss marketed a wide variety of glass and ceramic tableware. Some merchandise was conceived by contract designers hired by the American importer and then produced in Europe. Belle Kogan's work for Ebeling & Reuss was especially interesting. Created primarily in the mid-1930s, Kogan's dinnerware patterns, including *Berkeley, Regatta,* and *Metropolis,* were manufactured in Germany (cat. 129).

In 1935 Kogan designed a new logo for the firm incorporating the word "ERPHILA," which stood for Ebeling & Reuss, Philadelphia. The logo was used on the company's wares for years.[3]

Most of the wares the company sold, however, were selected from available stock. Building on the European connections of its founders, this import house carried sizable lines of tableware and giftware from Germany, Czechoslovakia, England, France, Belgium, Denmark, Italy, Finland, and Sweden by the late 1930s (cat. 5).[4] Given the firm's dependence on European suppliers, World War II was hard on the business. To survive, Ebeling & Reuss imported ceramics from South America, Mexico, and China. The import house also developed an exclusive line of domestic dinnerware, St. Regis American Porcelain.[5] Soon after the war the importer reintroduced many of the types of wares it had handled before the hostilities. German porcelains from the Schumann, Jaeger, and Heinrich factories, for example, were sold in the late 1940s and 1950s (cat. 99). During the same period Ebeling & Reuss distributed English chintzware by Royal Winton and James Kent, Ltd., as well as Tuscan China.[6]

Through the 1960s the importer appears to have prospered, and by 1966 showrooms had been added at the Dallas Trade Mart and the Atlanta Merchandise Mart. However, rising production costs in Europe began to reduce profit margins during the next decade. In 1976 president Henry Ebeling stated that "the economic problems facing European countries have caused the company to re-evaluate its present lines and to keep introducing new lines. In some instances lines have had to be dropped from our distributorship because they no longer could be priced within a competitive market."[7]

The Ebeling family apparently gave up control of the company in the early 1980s. At the time of Ebeling & Reuss's centennial in 1986, the importer was operating from offices in Devon, Pennsylvania, but was reported to be in financial difficulty. In 1992 Ronald D. Rapelje, who had been named president two years earlier, purchased the firm, moved it to Allentown, Pennsylvania, and refocused the company's product line away from giftware and back to dinnerware. Today Ebeling & Reuss distributes Royal Doulton as well as other English tablewares.[8]

Cat. 129 Ebeling & Reuss had the geometric pattern *Metropolis* manufactured in Germany, Czechoslovakia, and the United States in the 1930s.

Notes

1. "Obituary: Frederick W. Ebeling," *CGJ* 104:14 (7 Apr. 1927): 38, cited in "After 90 Years Life's Easier," *GTR* (Feb. 1976): 9. The 1976 article records different dates; it says Schenck left the firm in 1905 and that Ebeling and Reuss became partners at that time.

2. "After 90 Years Life's Easier," *GTR* (Feb. 1976): 9.

3. "Do You Know These Trade Marks?," *CGJ* 115:1 (July 1934): 67.

4. *CGJ* 123:3 (Sept. 1938) 14; and 125:1 (July 1939): 13.

5. *CGJ* 129:2 (Aug. 1941): 31.

6. For representative advertisements, see *CGJ* 142:1 (Jan. 1948): 1; 145:3 (Sept. 1949): 29; 146:4 (Apr. 1950): 2; and 156:6 (June 1955): 13.

7. "After 90 Years Life's Easier," *GTR* (Feb. 1976): 9.

8. Ronald D. Rapelje, letter to Charles Venable, 10 Aug. 1999.

TRADE SHOWS

Along with the creation of sales forces, showrooms, and warehouses, the advent of organized trade shows made the distribution of tableware at the wholesale level much more efficient. The earliest, and for many years the most important, of all such events was the Pittsburgh glass and pottery show held each January from 1880 to 1958 (see pp. 293–95). This show was strategic in both location and timing: Pittsburgh was in the heart of the region where glass and ceramic tableware were produced, and because January was a slow time for retail sales, buyers were free to travel.

Although the Pittsburgh trade show was paramount for decades, it was not unrivaled. Of the other shows, those in Chicago, New York, and Atlantic City were the most important. Because it was scheduled annually for early February, Chicago's Winter Gift Show (founded 1921) was Pittsburgh's greatest rival (fig. 4.6). Located in a major metropolitan center with attractions for buyers and sales representatives alike, this show drew many buyers who were unable or unwilling to travel to Pennsylvania so soon after the New Year holiday. Although not a direct threat to the Pittsburgh show, the Chicago Gift Show (founded 1900) took place in late July and early August.[7]

New York was also host to important sample fairs. One of the first was the New York Houseware Exhibit, initially held in July 1920 at the Hotel Imperial. Although this fair included tableware, that was not its main focus. In 1933 the New York China and Glass Show was inaugurated to take advantage of the fact that many buyers for home furnishings departments who visited Manhattan for the houseware exhibit also bought tableware for their stores. The new show was held in late July and early August in order to coincide exactly with the home furnishings show. At some point in the 1930s these complementary events apparently merged; in 1940 the New York Housewares Manufacturers' Association announced that for the first time it would hold its home furnishings show that July in Atlantic City, New Jersey. Promoted as taking place in "the city of show, sun, and ocean breezes" serviced "through sleeping cars from all points West," Atlantic City's show grew in importance after World War II. Attesting to the advantage of being near New York when most buyers traveled there to order fall and holiday merchandise was the fact that three thousand buyers attended the very first Atlantic City summer show.[8]

As a result of the summer exhibit's success, a winter China and Glass Show was held every January in Atlantic City following the demise of the Pittsburgh show in the late 1950s. Both the winter and summer trade events in Atlantic City continued until the end of the 1970s. By then the New York Gift Show was being held in August to counter the one in Atlantic City, and in 1979 a January exhibit staged in New York directly competed with the neighboring show to the south. Weakened by these rival events, as well as rising hotel rates following the influx of casinos, Atlantic City relinquished its role as successor to Pittsburgh around 1980.[9]

Beyond the premier shows in Pittsburgh, Chicago, New York, and Atlantic City, dozens of others occurred annually. By midcentury trade periodicals listed scores of china and glass exhibits held in cities as diverse as Boston; San Francisco; Omaha, Nebraska; and Amarillo, Texas. At first these events were staged in hotels, but gradually permanent trade marts hosted more of them. The model for these regional market halls was the Chicago Merchandise Mart. Specializing in home furnishings, this huge facility opened the doors to its 4 million square feet of display space in 1930. Unlike a periodic trade show, "The Mart" and its numerous showrooms were open year-round so that buyers could examine tableware lines whenever they were in Chicago. The concept of the merchandise mart spread relatively rapidly across the country. By 1950 important regional sales centers had developed around permanent facilities, including those in San Francisco, Dallas, and Atlanta.

Attending "market" was and still is a vital event in the lives of those in the trade. Showing off and catching glimpses of new merchandise were two of the main reasons for going. Receiving a large order or finding a new item that would attract potential customers to a buyer's shop was an exciting moment. Seeing colleagues, however, was equally important. As in most industries, the buying and selling of china and glass were as much about personal relationships as anything else. Friendships between manufacturers' representatives and buyers could well determine what store distributed a particular product, enjoyed prompt deliveries, or received an extra discount. Whether you were a seller, buyer, or member of the trade press, building and maintaining a personal network within the field were critical pursuits. Consequently, gift giving—or bribe taking, depending on one's point of view—was common. Furthermore, the big parties thrown at trade shows by leading manufacturers and department stores were more than entertainment. Amid the rich food and liquor, trade intelligence was communicated through serious conversation and gossip. Friends were embraced and enemies shunned. Powerful buyers made their entrances with entourages of assistants, while eager purveyors of dishes hovered around like moths circling a flame.

Fig. 4.6 Rival trade shows tempted buyers with striking graphic design, as seen in this 1930 ad..

The Pittsburgh Show

For three-quarters of a century, the annual china and glass exhibit held in Pittsburgh was the most important of all trade shows for the U.S. tableware market.[1] Since the early nineteenth century Pittsburgh had been a center for glassmaking, and by 1880 it was home to numerous important glassworks. Consequently, wholesale and retail buyers regularly traveled to the city to view glassware displayed in local factory showrooms. Two salesmen are credited with founding the Pittsburgh trade show—William B. Ranney of the Co-Operative Flint Glass Company of Beaver County, Pennsylvania, and S. C. Dunlevy of the LaBelle Glass Company of Ohio.

Dissatisfied with the sales of his firm, which was located 35 miles northwest of Pittsburgh, Ranney surmised that buyers coming to inspect the showrooms of large glasshouses in the city would view a display of wares from outlying firms if it was staged in Pittsburgh. For six weeks in January 1880 a voluntary exhibition of glass was organized by salesmen and manufacturers at the elegant Monongahela House Hotel. Although a few potteries joined in the very next year, the annual affair remained primarily a glassware trade show until the early twentieth century. By 1889 the event included displays by seventeen out-of-town factories. Nine years later the show was better organized, included twenty-four manufacturers, and was attended by a respectable number of buyers primarily from the northeast, Midwest, and mid-Atlantic regions.

The size of the show had nearly doubled by 1909, with fifty-one exhibitors, and had doubled again by 1918. In that year the show was well established, with 101 producers represented. Of those participating, fifty-seven were domestic glassmakers, while the remainder consisted of potteries (20), importers (17), and a few makers of other types of goods (7). A decade later 131 purveyors of tableware attended, including a sizable contingent selling English, Continental, and Japanese wares. In 1942 more than one thousand buyers traveled to Pittsburgh for the show, and after the war that number rose as the event expanded. Twelve hundred buyers from all over the United States and Canada attended the 1950 show; the displays at the William Penn Hotel that year occupied six floors and filled additional spaces in the lobby.[2]

Through the decades the trade show evolved in several ways. The exposition changed locations as it required addi-

Fig. 4.7 Fostoria's Crystal Room of 1922 illustrates how manufacturers transformed hotel rooms at trade fairs.

tional space and more up-to-date facilities. In 1909 manufacturers transformed rooms in four hotels into temporary showrooms (fig. 4.7). Although the Monongahela House was still the lead facility that year, the Fort Pitt Hotel across town (strategically located near the Pennsylvania Railroad station and local glass showrooms) soon emerged as the favored site (fig. 4.8). Along with spaces in other hotels—including the Neville, Schlosser, Anderson, Seventh Avenue, and Henry —the Fort Pitt Hotel held sway from 1910 until 1936, when the entire show moved to the William Penn Hotel.[3]

Besides location, the duration of the Pittsburgh exhibit also changed over time. In its earliest years the show lasted from a month to six weeks. As traveling became easier in the late nineteenth and early twentieth centuries, the show evolved into a two-week event usually held during the second and third weeks of January. In 1936 the sample fair was shortened to one week at the request of buyers, but the month never changed.[4] Before the advent of the Pittsburgh show, January was an extremely slow period for glassmakers and potteries. Most purchases had traditionally been made in the fall before the holidays and in the spring in anticipation of the wedding season. By bringing large numbers of wholesale buyers into contact with American and foreign manufacturers or their representatives, the Pittsburgh pottery and glass show was central in transforming the languid winter months into one of the busiest times of the year. In January 1920, for example, an observer at the show noted, "The volume of business booked this year . . . set new high records. Some orders . . . call for 1921 delivery. Manufacturers will be taxed to the utmost for the first six months of this year. On account of inability to take care of

Fig. 4.8 For many years the Fort Pitt Hotel played host to the Pittsburgh china and glass show.

more business a number of firms removed their samples last week."[5]

The organization of the event shifted over time as well. Originally, the exhibit was loosely structured with relatively minor glass and ceramics firms voluntarily participating. But after World War I, as nationally known firms began to exhibit, a more professional structure was needed if the event was to reach its full potential. At the 1921 show a group of American producers formed the Associated Glass and Pottery Manufacturers. Beginning the next year the association assumed responsibility for the show's organization. One innovation was to further separate the exhibitors into groups: by 1916 domestic manufacturers were showing their wares at the Fort Pitt Hotel, while importers took showrooms in the William Penn. Starting in 1923 the Fort Pitt was officially reserved for American products only. When in 1936 the entire show was held in the William Penn Hotel for the first time, the two types of exhibitors were reunited.

Although there were occasional conflicts between the domestic and import camps—as in 1936 when Japanese ware was banned from exhibit in support of the "Buy Ameri-

can" movement—importers played an increasingly important role in the show, especially after World War II.[6] The show held in 1948 (following a five-year hiatus at government request) was bigger than ever. The exposition was renamed the Keystone Show in 1949. The number of importers grew until by 1951 the majority of exhibitors displayed foreign wares.[7]

Although on the surface the Pittsburgh show seemed extremely vibrant in the early postwar era, it was actually in a slow state of decline. The domestic industries it supported, especially ceramics, were entering a period of great disruption. Most American potteries were no longer producing tableware for the home by the early 1960s. Furthermore, several important trade shows began to rival Pittsburgh for the attention of buyers and manufacturers. The earliest and perhaps most critical of these was the Winter Gift Show, which started in 1921 and was held in Chicago during the first week of February.[8] The Chicago fair was an important competitor—it was in a bigger city that by 1930 also contained a major home furnishings market with scores of permanent showrooms. In response to this competition the

Associated Glass and Pottery Manufacturers increased its advertising efforts, developing slogans such as "See it first in Pittsburgh."[9]

During the interwar years the association's tactics worked, but new rival shows in Atlantic City and New York, as well as gift and housewares exhibitions and permanent trade marts throughout the country, eventually crippled the Pittsburgh show. The city of Pittsburgh itself ceased to be an asset over time. A leading center of coal, steel, and glass production, the city was bleak in January. Barbara Boyd Wedgwood remembers as a young china buyer for Neiman Marcus how dirty she found Pittsburgh: "Exhibitors had to change the white sheets with which they covered their display tables one or more times a day because of the soot that came through the windows into the hotel rooms."[10]

Despite the soot, traveling to Pittsburgh to sell or buy was a major event in the lives of hundreds who worked to market china and glass in America for more than eighty years. In 1950 one longtime attendee wrote:

> The Pittsburgh show is more than a trade show. It is an annual reunion of the affiliated trades.... Many a buyer made the first real purchase of his career in Pittsburgh. Many of the present day producers first displayed their products there. There is an aura about the show that cannot be described; but it is there. There are thousands in this country who feel, somehow . . . that they belong to the glassware and pottery industry once they have been to Pittsburgh.[11]

While perhaps nostalgic, this description has much validity. One came to Pittsburgh in cold January not just to exhibit or view merchandise, but to make new contacts, network with old ones, and scoop one's rivals. The salesmen's and manufacturers' organizations typically held gala meetings, while buyers were feted at great parties given by important producers. Even Barbara Boyd Wedgwood, who vividly recalls the grayness of Pittsburgh in winter, also remembers the lavish parties at which she watched the powerful and the meek vie for attention. The grandest of these events was sponsored in the mid-1950s by United States Glass Company and was held at a local men's club. The then-Miss Boyd, along with other female buyers, had to enter the building from a side door, but once inside was treated to extravagant food and entertainment. As Wedgwood laughingly recalled, "I had my first oysters at that party and then 'went wild.'"[12]

Ironically the gala events Wedgwood recalls were some of the last ever staged in Pittsburgh by the tableware industry. Within a few years, competition from other shows and turmoil among American manufacturers killed the Pittsburgh show. The last china and glass exposition was held there in 1958.[13]

Notes

1. For histories of the Pittsburgh show, see "The Good Old Days," *CGJ* 141:6 (Dec. 1947): 66–69; "Pittsburgh Shows, 1880–1950: The 'Good Old Days' Get Better," 147:6 (Dec. 1950): 88–89; "Looking Back at Fifty Years of Importing," 147:6 (Dec. 1950): 94; "Pittsburgh Glass Exhibit 43 Years Old Next January," *CGL* (6 Nov. 1922): 11–12; and Madarasz 1998, 78–84.

2. Madarasz 1998, 79; "The Pittsburgh Exhibit," *CGJ* 47:1 (6 Jan. 1898): 15; 47:2 (13 Jan. 1898): 21; "The Pittsburgh Exposition," 87:1 (3 Jan. 1918): 17–18; "Many Changes in Pittsburgh's March of Progress," 94:10 (9 Mar. 1922): 17; "List of Exhibitors at Pittsburgh Show," 106:1 (5 Jan. 1928): 36; "Looking Back at Fifty Years of Importing," 147:6 (Dec. 1950): 94.

3. "The Good Old Days," *CGJ* 141:6 (Dec. 1947): 68.

4. "Wm. Penn Hotel to House Entire Exhibit, Japanese Importers Excluded," *CGJ* 118:1 (Jan. 1936): 39.

5. "The Pittsburgh Exposition," *CGJ* 91:5 (Jan. 1929): 15.

6. "Wm. Penn Hotel to House Entire Exhibit, Japanese Importers Excluded," *CGJ* 118:1 (Jan. 1936): 39.

7. "Looking Back at Fifty Years of Importing," *CGJ* 147:6 (Dec. 1950): 94.

8. One source (*CGL* [23 Oct. 1922]:19) states the second of these shows was held in 1922, but another source ("China, Glass and Gift Show," *CGJ* 107:1 [Jan. 1929]: 61) says the fourth show was to be held in 1929. The discrepancy in dates is probably due to a change in management or name of the event in 1925. The first source states the name of the show as the Glass, Pottery, Lamps, and Housefurnishings Exhibit.

9. The slogan "See the New Wares First in Pittsburgh" was also used; "Golden Jubilee for Pittsburgh Exhibit with January, 1930, Show," *CGL* (Dec. 1929): 42.

10. Wedgwood interview 1995.

11. "Pittsburgh Shows, 1880–1950: The 'Good Old Days' Get Better," *CGJ* 147:6 (Dec. 1950): 89.

12. Wedgwood interview 1995.

13. There is TV footage of the 1958 trade show, and it is known that the dates were set for the 1959 show; however, no reports of the event for 1959 have been found. Thus it is likely that the 1959 show never actually took place.

Retail Selling

BUYERS

The link between the wholesale and retail markets was the buyer. As retailing became more sophisticated and increasingly complicated in the late nineteenth and early twentieth centuries, individuals who selected merchandise for stores assumed greater authority and responsibility. By the mid-twentieth century the industry's most important buyers could influence fashion by following their taste or cripple a factory by canceling a large order. Because of their power, buyers were simultaneously admired and hated.[10]

The life of a good buyer was an active one. China and glass sales tended to be cyclical, with the majority of profits coming during wedding season before June and at Christmas time. To increase sales during the rest of the year, special promotions were offered to entice shoppers to buy tableware at slow periods. Valentine's Day, Passover, Mother's Day (first observed in 1914), Columbus Day, Halloween, Election Day, and Thanksgiving as well as general summer entertaining were occasions for boosting china and glass sales. What the consumer did not realize was that the buyer and his or her colleagues planned well in advance for such promotions. Merchandise had to be viewed, selected, and ordered. Barrels and later cartons of china and glass needed to be received, unpacked, inspected, and placed in inventory. Breakage, which could be as high as 3 percent in a busy store, was monitored and reduced if possible.[11] Advertising departments had to be consulted and newspaper copy written. Store displays were created and showrooms maintained, and retail saleswomen and men hired and fired.

This activity gave a certain rhythm to the life of a buyer. In the slow retail month of January staff took inventory and buyers traveled. They visited the Pittsburgh and, later, Atlantic City trade shows, and then spent a week or more in New York to inspect imported lines not shown at the pottery and glass shows. Much travel also followed the late spring bridal season. Trips were made to New York and the houseware shows in Atlantic City and Manhattan. Overseas travel often took place at this time as well; the most important buyers in the mid-twentieth century traveled in style aboard ships like HMS *Queen Mary*. If required, buyers made additional trips abroad in a given year.[12]

The power of a great buyer, however, did not stem from these outward activities alone. As longtime tableware buyer Joseph Giarrocco explained, the best buyers used numerous tactics to help make their departments profitable.[13] Giarrocco was one of the most famous of all twentieth-century buyers. Beginning as a stock boy at B. Altman & Co. in New York in 1937, he became head of the china and glass department ten years later. When he assumed control, the department's annual gross sales were $600,000. By the time Giarrocco retired in 1984, Altman's gross sales of tableware had climbed to $7.5 million. As a result of such growth, the store ranked third nationally in tableware sales and had the most comprehensive tableware department in New York. At its height the store stocked approximately seven hundred dinnerware patterns

alone. Having such a wide selection set the store apart from its Manhattan rivals. As Giarrocco explained, "Even if they ended up not buying their tableware at Altman's, they had to come to our department to look first because we had more on display than anyone else in the city. That brought in traffic, which was good for the store overall."[14]

To achieve such success Giarrocco gained every advantage he could for his store with the manufacturer. From the retailer's perspective it was especially important to coerce the producer not only to give the greatest possible discounts in return for large orders, but also to extend to the retailer sizable allowances for advertising. During the 1960s and 1970s Giarrocco was even able to convince makers to pay for sales representatives who worked in his department's "shops within a shop," thereby reducing his staff's workload in taking inventory, placing orders, and making sales to customers.

Ensuring that your store received first right of refusal on particular patterns and shapes was also of the utmost importance. During the first half of the twentieth century, when exclusive rights to specific designs were being granted, buyers used all their leverage to obtain control of the merchandise they thought would sell well. Obviously, retailers who ordered in large quantities or had prestigious names received the best treatment. Thus buyers like Joseph Giarrocco at Altman's, Barbara Boyd (later Wedgwood) at Neiman Marcus, and Roger Horchow at Foley's and later Neiman's, usually had the upper hand with respect to their colleagues at lesser stores. This advantage helped when it came to returns as well. Periodically a manufacturer would approach a buyer about displaying a new pattern to see how it would sell. Giarrocco recalls that when this happened he retorted, "If you want me to try the new pattern then you have to take back the one of yours we have in stock that won't sell!"[15] In this fashion slow-moving stock was replaced with potentially profitable goods.

From the manufacturer's point of view, of course, such tactics were anathema. As early as 1930 producers were complaining about what they considered unreasonable requests from buyers.[16] Charles Gifford, who served as chief executive officer of the Noritake Company, has recalled how debilitating the cumulative effect of deals made with key buyers could be. By the 1980s, according to Gifford, no department store wanted to keep large amounts of stock on hand, and they all wanted the producer to take back whatever did not sell:

> Eventually buyers wanted everything boxed for display. Noritake resisted that move initially, but was forced into it by retailers. We got away with resisting such developments when our lines were hot, but once [Noritake] started to cool, retailers stopped buying until we came along and made concessions. When a Walmart does $80 billion a year [in sales] you'd better join up or get out of the way. The giants of today have amazing operations, but you have to meet their needs of pushing merchandise through their systems in specific ways.[17]

With few exceptions, American producers "got out of the way" of mass retailers. As early as 1964 an editorial in the *Gift and Tableware Reporter* quoted one manufacturer as saying, "The department stores want too much from you. They demand free freight, ad allowances and guaranteed sales."[18] Within a decade of this statement, few potteries in this country produced anything at all for the home, while the domestic glass industry had greatly curtailed its production of all but the cheapest tableware.

SPECIALTY AND JEWELRY STORES

China and glass buyers represented a variety of retailers. At one end of the spectrum were stores that specialized almost exclusively in china and glassware. Before World War II such stores were relatively common in American cities. Although their numbers decreased in the decades following the war, firms like Gump's in San Francisco, Tatman's in Chicago, and C. Reizenstein Sons in Pittsburgh catered to the needs of the affluent in their regions. C. Reizenstein Sons, for example, became well known regionally under the leadership of glassware connoisseur and sometime designer Louis Reizenstein. The Pittsburgh firm used the slogan "If you want tables set in good taste, come to Reizenstein's." On a national level in the late 1940s, Reizenstein's marketed the exclusive Reizart brand of glassware designed to match famous china patterns.[19]

Yet as prosperous as some regional stores were, the firms in New York set the standards. Among the most prestigious were William H. Plummer & Co., Ovington Brothers, and Gilman Collamore & Co. At its height before World War I, Collamore's was possibly the most prestigious china and glass shop in the country.[20] The firm was known for its exceptional inventory of the finest glass and china available (cat. 130, plate). Indicative of its prestige, Collamore's purportedly never held a sale of marked-down merchandise until its liquidation during the Great Depression. The store relied on the patronage of the wealthiest customers, who desired china and glass tableware of the utmost quality and were willing to pay high prices for it. In the end it took the worst financial crisis in the nation's history to close Collamore's. In late 1931 the new owner, Armin Riley, held several auctions to rid the firm of outdated merchandise. A year later he sold all that remained to the Boston department store Jordan Marsh and closed the famous New York establishment.

Other firms soon took the place of the venerable house of Collamore at the high end of the market. In 1929 young Carole Stupell founded the Cocktail Shop, a specialty store located in New York's Hotel Barclay. Having gained notoriety selling barware during prohibition, Stupell expanded her stock to include a wide assortment of tableware and began trading solely under her own name in 1934. Coupling business sense with her flair for decorating tables, Stupell opened branch stores in Washington, D.C., and Boston and achieved relative fame as a retailer and a wholesaler during the depression. From the beginning she worked with foreign and domestic manufacturers, especially the glassmakers Baccarat and Dorothy C. Thorpe, to create exclusive patterns specifically for sale at Carole Stupell, Ltd. But what the shop became most famous for was the drama Stupell brought to the table: by the 1950s her exuberant styling was christened the "Carolated" look.[21]

A few specialty firms that emerged in the 1950s and 1960s rose to national prominence in the ensuing decades by catering to youth and the casual lifestyle. One such store in Chicago, Crate & Barrel, was founded by Carole and Gordon Segal in 1962. As its name implied, everything in its first store was displayed on a crate or in a barrel, reinforcing the concept of casual entertaining (fig. 4.9). The same attitude was inherent in the name of its rival, Pottery Barn in New York. An offshoot of the Barn, an import housewares store established on Tenth Street on Manhattan's West Side in 1950, Pottery Barn was born in 1968 on the posh Upper East Side at 227 Sixtieth Street. Part-owner Tony Brush explained at its opening that the store was intended to be informal yet sophisticated: "Aside from greeting each shopper, and giving him any information or help he needs, we leave him alone. We have a very casual approach. The Barn downtown, and even here to an extent, is kind of a browsing store."[22] By embracing a generation of consumers who rejected the formal lifestyles of their parents and grandparents, Crate & Barrel and Pottery Barn— along with other stores that carried large amounts of tableware, like Pier 1 Imports (founded in 1962, in Fort Worth, Texas)—were hugely successful. Today Crate & Barrel, still based in Chicago, has eighty stores around the country. Pottery Barn currently has ninety-eight retail outlets.[23]

The type of retailer that came closest to a traditional china and glass specialty shop without being one was the jewelry store. Such stores made their greatest profits from selling jewelry, but because jewelers supplied wedding rings, they could attract collateral bridal business. This was especially true in small towns, although famous jewelry stores that sold tableware certainly existed in major urban centers.

Perhaps the most notable example is Tiffany & Co. in New York, which over the years has maintained a thriving china and glass department (cats. 25, 92; fig. 4.10). Black, Starr & Frost and its successors was another Manhattan jewelry store that carried large inventories of tableware. Over time, however, these firms became increasingly elite exceptions. As early as 1935 a commentator in the *Crockery and Glass Journal* noted, "In large metropolitan cities, it has not been usual to see china and glass in the average jewelry store for some years. Such merchandising continues to be prevalent and profitable, however, in almost every town and city of moderate population in the country—and logically so. In the larger cities—the department store—and, mildly, the china and glass specialty shop, hold sway."[24]

Traditional, locally owned jewelry stores did indeed survive longer outside of urban centers. Be it Westmoreland Jewelry Store in Huntsville, Texas, or Boswell Jewelers in Tulsa, Oklahoma, the local jewelry store profited as long as competition from department stores and, later, jewelry discount firms was minimal. While there was still a niche in the marketplace, the best jewelry stores tried hard to capture as much of the local fine china and crystal business as possible. To that

Cat. 130 Porcelain by Pickard China Company (pitcher) and Lenox China were sold by America's finest retailers. The plate was sold by Gilman Collamore & Co., New York.

Fig. 4.9 Crate & Barrel really used crates and barrels in its retail display when the store opened in 1962.

Fig. 4.10 Dishes covered every surface of Tiffany & Co.'s china-selling floor in the late 19th century.

end storeowners had to attract women, and thus much effort was put into developing the bridal business, and especially bridal registries, between 1930 and 1970. This practice was particularly common in the South, where conservative families appreciated organized bridal services.[25] When successful, such sales could be sizable. In 1932 C. Kendall, head of the china and glassware department at Arthur A. Everts Company in Dallas, claimed the jewelry store "often supplies 75% of the gifts sent to one wedding."[26] To help achieve such strong sales, jewelry stores generally tried to have the best selection of patterns possible. In the mid-1930s L. W. Moon, owner of the Moon Jewelry Company in Tallahassee, Florida, said: "To my mind there is nothing that attracts women more than a beautiful display of china and glass. We ourselves, in developing these two items, always include an attractive sterling pattern in the general make-up. With a little thought in the selection of attractive, well-known lines of china and glass, enough business can readily be worked up to pay for the entire overhead of the average store."[27]

DEPARTMENT STORES

The concept of one large store containing a wide variety of goods was revolutionary in the nineteenth century. Following the Civil War, local entrepreneurs in the nation's foremost cities founded department stores. While their primary focus was and would always remain ready-to-wear clothing, household goods soon were added to the merchandise mix. China and glass departments were standard features in some department stores early on. In 1874 Rowland H. Macy subcontracted with the firm of L. Straus & Sons to open a large china and glass shop in his New York department store, R. H. Macy & Co.[28] By 1900 virtually all American department stores were selling tableware. It was in the interwar years, though, that their china and glass departments became significant enough to rival jewelry stores and specialty shops.

Great strides were made during the depression, when sales of expensive tableware plummeted. Because department stores typically sold larger volumes of merchandise and thus garnered price concessions from manufacturers, they could often offer goods at lower prices than smaller stores. Consequently, in the 1930s a generation of customers searching for bargains learned to shop for ceramics and glass at department stores.

Beyond having cheaper prices, these stores beckoned shoppers with elaborate displays, lectures, and large sales forces. As seen in the history of Marshall Field & Co., department stores offered highly efficient bridal registries and knowledgeable consultants by the late 1930s. Some upperclass stores even developed specialized areas within the tableware division that grouped goods thematically or featured the products of a single manufacturer. In 1962, for example, Altman's in New York installed a "Craft House." Described as "the only retail store duplicate of the Williamsburg (Va.) Craft House" the display included among other items Blenko glass, Wedgwood dinnerware, and Royal Doulton figurines (cat. 131).[29]

Upscale department stores generally set the standard for in-store promotions of china and glass. Over the years representatives from virtually all major manufacturers worked the department store circuit, lecturing to women about the superiority of their products while etiquette experts taught the finer points of dining. Certain stores, such as Neiman Marcus, were particularly good at such events. Founded in Dallas in 1907 Neiman Marcus became the Southwest's most fashionable retail store by capitalizing on the influx of money into the regional economy resulting from the Texas oil boom of the 1930s.[30] Thanks largely to the leadership of Stanley Marcus, who joined the firm in 1926, the store became nationally and ultimately internationally recognized as a trendsetter in merchandising.

Among Marcus's most significant achievements as president of the store from 1950 to 1975 was the series of international "Fortnights" begun in 1957, each of which saluted a particular country or region. By staging these gala events in mid-October, Neiman's increased sales during what was traditionally a slow retail period before the holiday season. Furthermore, every department including china and glass was involved, so stronger sales occurred throughout the store. Besides the storewide Fortnights the Dallas retailer also periodically held promotions focusing on tableware—for example, from March to June 1956, Neiman's hosted six sequential exhibits of fine china. Included were Lenox, Wedgwood, Spode, Rosenthal, Pickard, and Royal Crown Derby. Featuring representatives like Hensleigh Wedgwood, president of Josiah Wedgwood & Sons' North American division, and W. P. C. Adams, president of Royal Crown Derby, the promotions were heavily advertised in the press. According to trade sources hundreds of shoppers attended from within a 60-mile radius. The in-house goals of the program were "1) to create a wider, more intense awareness of imported and domestic fine china; 2) to determine the public's preferences by showing every current pattern in each line at one time and having the public vote; 3) to increase the store's china sales over a long range period."[31] Barbara Boyd Wedgwood, the buyer in charge of these activities, remembers the promotions as being very successful.

Not all department stores could afford to invest in such lavish promotions for their china and glass departments. Furthermore, stores supplying the middle and lower strata of the market had less need for such publicity because their sales were driven more by low prices than by brand recognition and perceptions of quality. Indeed the range of department stores during much of the twentieth century was rather striking. In terms of sales of high-end tableware, the country's leading stores were, in order of volume, Marshall Field & Co. (Chicago), J. L. Hudson & Co. (Detroit), and B. Altman & Co. (New York). Below these top three was a host of stores with regionally significant china and glass departments (see list p. 302).

OPPOSITE:
Cat. 131 Blenko Glass Company revised history in its "reproductions" for Colonial Williamsburg in the late 1930s and 1940s.

Selection of Regional Department Stores Selling Tableware

Northeast
Abraham & Straus, Brooklyn
Bloomingdale's, New York
Gimbel Brothers, New York
Jordan Marsh, Boston
R. H. Macy & Co., New York
Saks Fifth Avenue, New York
Shepard Company, Providence
Stern Brothers, New York

Mid-Atlantic
Hecht & Co., Washington, D.C.
Hutzler Brothers, Baltimore
John Wanamaker's, Philadelphia
Strawbridge & Clothier, Philadelphia

South
Cain-Sloan, Nashville
D. H. Holmes, New Orleans
Goldsmith's, Memphis
Hearn's, Shreveport
Ivey's, Charlotte
Miller & Rhoads, Richmond
Pfiefer's, Little Rock
Rich's, Atlanta

Midwest
Carson Pirie Scott & Co., Chicago
F. & R. Lazarus, Columbus
Hall's Department Store, Kansas City
Kaufmann Brothers, Pittsburgh
L. S. Ayres, Indianapolis
May Department Store, Saint Louis

Southwest
Brown-Dunkin Company, Tulsa
Denver Dry Goods, Denver
Foley Brothers, Houston
John A. Brown, Oklahoma City
Joske's, San Antonio
Neiman Marcus, Dallas
Sanger-Harris, Dallas
Zion's Co-operative Mercantile Institute,
    Salt Lake City

West Coast
Bon Marché, Seattle
Breuner's, Oakland
Broadway Department Store, Los Angeles
Bullock's, Los Angeles
Emporium, San Francisco
Frederick & Nelson, Seattle

During the middle decades of the twentieth century a few middle-class and low-end retailers maintained branches across the country. Among these were J. C. Penney Company, Sears, Roebuck & Co., and Montgomery Ward & Co. To service the rural customer as well, these firms also issued mail-order catalogues containing china and glass selections that could be shipped to a farm or ranch (cats. 132, 174; figs. 1.15, 1.16; see pp. 35–37).

Marshall Field & Co.

For nearly one hundred years Marshall Field & Co. in Chicago was the largest retailer of china and glass tableware in the United States.[1] Founded as P. Palmer & Co. in 1852 by Potter Palmer, the general merchandise store grew quickly in the bustling frontier town on Lake Michigan. Marshall Field moved to Chicago from Massachusetts in 1856 and began work as a clerk in the dry goods store Cooley, Wadsworth & Co. Because of his great skill for the business, Field became a partner in 1862, and the name of the reorganized wholesale firm was changed to Farwell, Field & Co. two years later. In 1865 Palmer took Field in as a partner along with Levi Z. Leiter, who had worked with Field as a bookkeeper. However, Palmer was consumed with his real estate investments, and the partnership was dissolved in 1867. Newly named Field, Leiter & Co., the firm erected an imposing store in 1868 on State Street. Known in Chicago as the "Marble Palace," the store was an anchor edifice among others developed in this newly fashionable shopping district.

Along with much of Chicago the "Marble Palace" burned in 1871, resulting in a $3.5 million loss for the partners. Although Field and Leiter immediately reopened the store using salvaged stock and later erected an even grander store in 1873, it too was destroyed by fire in 1877. Undaunted, the partners built yet another structure on the corner of State and Washington Streets.

In 1881 Levi Leiter retired, and the firm's name was changed to Marshall Field & Co. The store flourished under the leadership of Field. In 1887 it opened the architecturally significant wholesale warehouse designed by H. H. Richardson, and in 1892 the structure that forms the core of the current downtown building was erected. Following Field's death in 1906 the store continued to expand. In 1929 a suburban branch was opened in Evanston, Illinois, followed two years later by another in Lake Forest. Most important for the housewares industry, however, was the erection by Marshall Field & Co. in 1930 of the mammoth Merchandise Mart in Chicago. This structure eventually became the center of the wholesale tableware trade in the Midwest.[2]

With exceptional customer service and innovative policies that allowed for goods to be sold "on approval" and returned if need be, Marshall Field's had a long history of selling home furnishings. Establishing a china and glass department, however, evidently proved to be a challenge for Field and his staff initially. In the 1890s manufacturers of high-quality products did not want to sell tableware to department stores, preferring to distribute through specialty china and glass shops. To increase the amount of merchandise available under one roof, Field's buyers searched Europe for manufacturers that would sell sets of fine porcelain and expensive service plates directly to the Chicago store. As sales boomed, the china and glass department grew, and manufacturers and importers gradually changed their minds about supplying Marshall Field's as well as other department stores.

In the twentieth century the china and glass department of Marshall Field's retained its national edge by being innovative: during World War I when imports were curtailed, the store encouraged the public to purchase smaller quantities of ware in services for six to eight and by the piece. The Chicago retailer's willingness to sell open stock encouraged the practice throughout America. This pattern of setting precedents continued during the depression. To boost lagging sales, Marshall Field's arranged with Lenox China to sell its patterns by the place setting rather than by the dozen. By the late 1940s acquiring china and glass in place settings was standard practice throughout the industry.

Introducing inventive products and displays was another hallmark of this Midwest firm. Marshall Field's was one of the first, if not the first, stores to introduce Lenox's ivory-colored china to the public after World War I. Within a

Fig. 4.11 China buyer and his dishes, Marshall Field & Co., Chicago, 1919.

Fig. 4.12 By 1952 dishes covered nearly an entire floor at Marshall Field's.

decade ivory-bodied dinnerware was being made in porcelain and earthenware both here and abroad for the American market. The same was true for brightly colored mix-and-match wares during the depression. The Harlequin look, which Marshall Field's sold as early as 1933, was popular throughout the country by the end of the decade.

Another trend encouraged by the store was that of specialty areas within the china and glass department. In 1913 "the greatest display of Wedgwood ever shown in America" was unveiled, followed in 1930 by an exhibition of antique Wedgwood objects loaned by the pottery itself. The emphasis on Wedgwood continued through lectures and appearances by representatives of Josiah Wedgwood & Sons American branch.[3] The strong sales that resulted from such exhibitions and publicity led to specialty areas in the department during the interwar years. In 1929 what was likely the first "Lenox Room" in America opened (cat. 133).[4] Others followed at Marshall Field's, including rooms for Steuben (ca. 1934), Rosenthal (1937), and Wedgwood (ca. 1940). Major department stores from coast to coast copied the boutique concept.

Of all Marshall Field's innovations perhaps the most far-reaching was the creation of a formal bridal registry. The "Bride's House," erected in 1935, contained not only a display of stock from which brides and gift-givers could make selections but also a registry of brides' chosen patterns. The bridal registry concept had swept the country by World War II.

Marshall Field's china and glass department wielded formidable power in the postwar years. Boasting the highest volume of tableware sales in the country, its buyers, unlike those from most other stores, could demand concessions from manufacturers for merchandise selection, delivery, and advertising allowances. Reflecting this power are the advertisements run in trade journals by domestic and foreign manufacturers in honor of Marshall Field's one hundredth anniversary. The celebratory ads in 1952 were placed by Theodore Haviland & Co., United China & Glass Company, Paul A. Straub & Co., Geo. Borgfeldt Corporation, and Southern Potteries.[5] Their respect was warranted. The store carried $3 million of inventory in the china and glass department in 1930. This high investment meant that Marshall Field's was the foremost account for many producers and importers. The Fostoria Glass Company, for example, surveyed its top one hundred accounts in 1971 and found that Marshall Field's was number one, having bought $72,726 worth of glassware the year before. With the single exception of J. L. Hudson & Co. of Detroit, which ordered more than $65,000 in glass, Marshall Field's surpassed its closest rivals by roughly 50 percent or more.[6]

To generate such large sales, Marshall Field's expanded beyond its downtown and two suburban locations. As early as 1929 Frederick & Nelson, one of Seattle's biggest department stores, had been purchased. By the time the Chicago retailer celebrated its centennial in 1952, it was planning its first branch in a shopping center. The Park Forest store opened in 1955, and another was built in the Old Orchard Shopping Center in Skokie, Illinois, the following year. Through the 1960s and 1970s Marshall Field's expanded aggressively in the Midwest, Pacific Northwest, and Texas. In 1990 Dayton Hudson Corporation of Minneapolis bought Marshall Field's, and today it has twenty-four stores nationwide.

Fig. 4.13 Marshall Field's ninth floor tempted shoppers with "the machinery of good living" in 1929.

Notes
1. Unless otherwise noted the information used here is derived from "Give the Lady What She Wants!," *CGJ* 151:2 (Aug. 1952): 36–40.

2. The dates for these events are taken from "Brief Historical Outline of Marshall Field & Company" provided by the firm. The Merchandise Mart was sold in 1945.

3. "Wedgwood Collection Displayed by Marshall Field & Co.," *CGJ* 108:6 (June 1930): 60; "Kennard Wedgwood Talks to Customers at Marshall Field's," 116:2 (Feb. 1935): 46; and "Kennard L. Wedgwood Addresses 200 Women at Marshall Field," 126:5 (May 1940): 47.

4. "The *Lenox Room* at Field's," *CGJ* 107:5 (May 1929): 61, 66–67.

5. *CGJ* 151:2 (Aug. 1952): 11, 13, 15, 28, 55.

6. "Top 100 Accounts, 1 Mar. 1971." Fostoria Archives.

OPPOSITE:
Cat. 133 Selling large quantities of patterns like *Ming* and *Mandarin* (1917), Marshall Field's was one of Lenox China's foremost customers.

STORE DISPLAYS AND SELLING TECHNIQUES

A few top stores could afford to stage elaborate promotions in their china and glass departments. While these events were often copied on a smaller scale by average retailers, many display and selling techniques were used by virtually all retailers of china and glass across the country. On the most basic level tableware departments benefited from general improvements made throughout American retailing during the early twentieth century. The introduction of electricity into stores was a great boon. Because ceramics and glass reflect and refract light so well, illuminating shelves of cut glass or rows of china made such merchandise more appealing (fig. 4.14). Incandescent lighting, coupled with the emergence of professional display artists in the 1920s and 1930s, made exterior store windows more useful. By the second quarter of the century window-shopping could be an extraordinary experience in America when elaborate display techniques were employed (fig. 4.15).

Inside stores developments more specific to tableware were afoot. In the late nineteenth century china and glassware were usually kept separate in stores, and giftware was displayed in a third area. In addition shops that specialized in china and glass often set aside areas for thematic presentations and special product lines. Ovington Brothers, for example, claimed in 1931 that its yachting tableware section had equipped "more than 1,000 vessels."[32] In department stores and some large jewelry stores related merchandise like silver-

ware and linens were displayed in separate spaces as well. If a retailer was big enough, different buyers managed these divisions, resulting in little coordination between merchandise categories. Over time this situation changed. As retailing became more competitive and ways were sought to decrease overhead costs, all but the biggest stores reduced the number of buyers on the payroll. Thus one buyer might handle tableware as well as silver and gifts. At the same time the physical spaces allotted to tableware became less distinct. China and glassware were combined early on in most stores. Silver, and especially flatware, was folded in after World War II. A special boutique for giftware was sometimes kept, but often this category was merged as well.

Amid these shifting boundaries, one feature remained fundamental to nearly every tableware department—the "Great Wall of China." To allow early-twentieth-century shoppers to view and compare each ceramic and glass pattern, managers began erecting rows of shelving where they placed

Fig. 4.14 Pittsburgh's Kaufmann Brothers department store used new-fangled lightbulbs to make their cut glass glisten in 1908.

Fig. 4.15 Window dressing was an art form in the 1930s, as demonstrated by John Wanamaker's New York store, 1931.

Fig. 4.16 "The Great Wall of China" was a fixture in every store by the 1950s.

In addition to the "Great Wall of China," all but the lowest level retailers employed the bridal registry as a potent marketing tool (see pp. 311–13). The bridal registry was developed as a means to increase sales across several product lines at once. Created in the 1930s and perfected after World War II, the registry concept enabled all levels of retailers to increase sales of china, glass, silver, and linens. By enticing brides-to-be to register at their stores, managers garnered much of the gift business generated by weddings.

a dinner plate, cup, and saucer in each pattern alongside complementary glassware. On the reverse of each dinner plate was adhered a list of all the forms available in that pattern and the price by piece, place setting, and set. By midcentury the shelves were typically of glass, and fluorescent lighting illuminated the displays. Often drawers were constructed below waist level for storage of extra pieces like gravy boats, vegetable dishes, and teapots. Because almost all stores used this system, managers sought ways to make their firms' displays appear different. Some divided their stock by manufacturer; others, by style.

In the early 1960s May-D & F, a Denver department store, divided its wall display by price. One wall featured expensive fine china and crystal elegantly spaced on glass shelves before a dark blue-green grass-cloth background. Conversely, the less-expensive, but brightly colored, casual patterns were mounted flush against closely spaced beige panels (fig. 4.16). According to a 1962 description by George Linton, Mays' dinnerware buyer:

> By separating the patterns into two basic price ranges, the store . . . simplifies customer decisions. If the shopper's needs are simple ones, she is not confused or delayed by the presence of more elegant patterns. However, if she is in the market for fine china, the choices available are set off for her easy selection. . . . Furthermore, by creating two distinct groupings, coordinated glassware and accessory pieces may be displayed conveniently near appropriate patterns, thus increasing tie-in-sale potential. With each fine china design are placed two or three suitable stemware shapes. On the counter beneath the informal dinnerware, decorated barware suggest possibilities for mixing or matching.[33]

This segregating of stock by price—and thus customers by class—apparently worked. Mays' tableware sales reportedly rose at both the high and low ends.

While the bridal registry was developing as a fundamental marketing technique, so too was the table-setting display. Specialty shops likely used the technique first, but it was the department store that popularized the concept across the nation's retail landscape. In 1930 a market observer commented that over the last year or so there had been a "decided tendency among large department stores to successfully merge, at least for display purposes, such departments as china and glassware, silverware, table linens, and furniture." He went on to write, "Today the public is being told through demonstration, by display and by articles in magazines of decoration, that the china, glassware, table linens, furnishing and hangings of the dining room must all be in accord. If any one of the various factors be selected in poor judgement, then the entire ensemble is lost."[34] Both shopper and merchant loved the table-setting concept. Seeing fully set and coordinated tables taught a woman how to decorate a table and gave her the confidence to entertain formally in the home. By helping potential customers visualize the finished appearance of their own tables, retailers sped up decision making in stores and encouraged women to purchase goods they otherwise might not. Likewise, by forcing buyers and display managers from various departments to cooperate, the table-setting technique boosted all sales of china, glassware, silver, linens, and furniture.

Initially elaborate table-setting displays were done as special promotions in conjunction with coordinated window dressing and lectures. In one of the first large exhibitions of table setting in the country, Gimbel's in New York decorated its nine exterior store windows along Broadway as well as the entire linen department with dining tables in the fall of 1930 (fig. 4.17). The interior display featured theme tables in styles described as Georgian, Modern, Italian, and "Pent House." Audrey Denness Cooper of the Irish and Scottish Linen Guild addressed each style in her twice-daily talks on "New Fall Fashions in Table Settings."[35] The success of such events resulted in the rapid spread of this marketing technique. By the end of the decade table exhibits were important annual events at many retailers. The Fall Table Show at exclusive Gump's in

Fig. 4.17 The New York department store Gimbel Brothers led the way in 1930 by featuring table displays.

San Francisco was one of the best. In just six days in late 1940 the remarkable count of eighteen thousand people viewed the thirty display tables arranged by the store.[36]

To generate such crowds, enormous amounts of energy and investment went into the table decorations. At first the floor staff arranged the tables, but by the end of the 1920s professional stylists emerged.[37] Some stylists, such as Carole Stupell, owned their own businesses and acted as consultants. Others, like Rhoda Sande with Iroquois China Company, worked for manufacturers and arranged their products on retailers' tables.[38] As a result of the success of this marketing strategy, many retailers, especially department stores, permanently allocated space for table-setting displays. One of the earliest was Neiman Marcus's L'Hexagone Room. The renowned Katherine (Kay) L. Vedder, who managed the so-called Decorative Galleries at Neiman's from 1932 to 1952, once stated in the early 1930s the goal of the table displays in this area:

> Teach the ladies to use their imaginations! Hundreds of women are eager to venture forth with bright, interesting tables, but they've been afraid. It's up to the china and glassware buyers to overcome that fear. We're not urging housewives to be bizarre in table decorating any more than we're urging them to be conspicuous by walking down Main Street backward, but we are insisting on their using imagination in setting their tables. . . . Why, every hostess has little bits of Dresden and little knick-knacks around that she would like to use to make her table decorations different, and it's to the buyer's advantage to teach her to dare![39]

By World War II employing table-setting displays to sell tableware and related merchandise was standard practice throughout the country in all but the most inexpensive stores. Simultaneously, table setting became a major topic of conversation and concern for women of all social levels. At female gatherings of every kind etiquette and dining-room decor were discussed. Some manufacturers encouraged this activity by providing programs for women's clubs. For example, in the early 1940s the Fostoria Glass Company produced a series of table-setting slides featuring its products. Using as a tag line the old joke "What are the three fastest means of communication? Answer: Telegraph, telephone, and 'tellawoman,'" Fostoria told its retailers in 1942 that more than 1,400 clubs and "more than 70,000 'tellawomen'" had seen its colored slide lectures and thus learned about its glass. Promoted and distributed through the national magazine *Better Homes and Gardens*, the popular slide program reportedly had to be booked nearly a year in advance.[40] Table setting remained important, as evidenced by the ten thousand teenage girls who participated in *Seventeen* magazine's national "Taste-Setter Tablesetting Contest" in 1957, in which contestants "studied tablewares, designs, and the etiquette of formal and informal table setting."[41] Because of such marketing efforts as well as genuine interest, American women were setting the most elaborate tables in the Western world by midcentury.

Fig. 4.18 Slides of table settings taken by a Texas family at holiday and wedding festivities in the 1950s.

The Bridal Registry

The ritual giving of wedding gifts has long been of seminal importance to the china and glass industries. For hundreds of years in Western culture the presentation of precious objects like fragile, expensive ceramic and glass vessels has been associated with the marriage ceremony. During the twentieth century the American retailing establishment exploited this tradition to the extent that it ultimately became heavily dependent on the bridal business. By the late 1960s the bridal market accounted for approximately one-third of all dinnerware and glassware sales in the United States. In the category of fine china the figure was nearly double— 64 percent, or $111 million in sales.[1]

During the late nineteenth and early twentieth centuries, it was not uncommon for the bride's or groom's parents or another close relative to give the young couple a complete set of china at the time of their marriage. However, as purchasing entire services of tableware became less popular after World War I, this practice changed.[2] The situation that emerged vexed retailers all across the country. In the 1920s and early 1930s relatives and friends of the bride and groom were prone to visit the jewelry store, specialty shop, or department store of their choice and select wedding gifts at random. As a result fewer sets of china or glass were sold, and inventory had to be increased so that potential purchasers could have immediate delivery of the merchandise they selected. Furthermore, couples returned many of the uncoordinated gifts and exchanged them for items they truly wanted.

To increase the usefulness of wedding presents and to avoid what retailers called the "'pest' of exchanging wedding gifts," clever brides and purveyors of china and glass manipulated the gift-giving ritual.[3] In 1931 the trade press noted:

> Some brides, an increasing number, make the rounds of the china, glass and other departments of their local stores and tell the buyers that if friends inquire what to buy for her to show them certain merchandise.
>
> In this manner modern brides are saved from receiving a mayonnaise set of French china, a tea pot of English earthenware, six Japanese tea cups, sugar and creamer from Bavaria, bone china cream soups of English make and a Delft ware jug while the humiliation of having to set a table with four Waterford reproduction tumblers, a hobnail butter dish, cut rock crystal stemware in goblets and etched glass finger bowls is obviated at a stroke. Today she receives an ensemble instead of a hodge-podge.[4]

Aggressive retailers capitalized on this behavior. They increased their share of bridal profits by systematically "cap-

turing" brides and the gift business that they brought with them.

By attracting most of the business for a particular wedding a retailer was in a position to coordinate the purchases, thereby limiting the amount of stock that had to be carried and the number of returns. Furthermore, if the main store at which a bride registered happened to be a department store, profits could be large indeed because the couple and their attendants and relatives were often likely to purchase their wedding clothing at that store. Stanley Marcus, former president of the elite department store Neiman Marcus in Dallas, recalled that by midcentury an expensive wedding might be worth $30,000 to a high-end department store like Neiman's if it could capture all of the associated business, from ring to dress and china to silver.[5]

During the 1920s and early 1930s retailers in small towns and urban areas escalated their efforts to attract bridal business by capturing brides themselves. Merchants regularly scanned newspapers for engagement announcements and queried customers about future weddings in their families. Lists were compiled of brides-to-be who soon received letters or telephone calls encouraging them to visit a particular store for advice about etiquette, formal entertaining, and home furnishings for their new abodes. Most important, stores asked these young women what they would like to receive as gifts. If a bride accepted the offer and came to the store, sales representatives discussed her preferences. During this process a good sales clerk steered the young woman away from patterns the store might not have in sufficient quantity or that might not fit the family's economic position. The appropriate selections were recorded, and the bride was asked to supply her list of wedding guests. Those individuals in turn were invited to the store and told of the bride's choices.

Working in concert in this fashion, the bride and retailer

Barbara's
wedding date
is June

Her china pattern is Wedgwood "Grapevine"; her silver, "Trousseau"; her crystal, "Rhythm"; the color scheme of her kitchen, yellow and white . . and all these decisions are registered with our Wedding Secretary. For Barbara, being a bright young woman, has come to Field's Bride's House and looked over the fascinating things for her new home. Her friends and relatives have but to ask the Secretary to learn exactly what Barbara wants.

This convenient service Field's is giving brides and their relatives and friends this season. A chance to see the lovely things that make a new home, assembled in one spot. A chance for every bride to leave with us a record of the things she wants. A chance for relatives and friends to refer to it. But aside from its extreme usefulness, you'll love the smart merchandise and bright ideas so romantically collected in the

Bride's House Eighth floor.

MARSHALL FIELD & COMPANY
Headquarters for Brides

Fig. 4.19 Marshall Field's Bride's House of 1935 was perhaps the world's first bridal registry.

controlled the gift-giving ritual to their mutual advantage. Stores avoided returns and often sold more expensive stock because items were now being purchased by the piece or place setting. Brides received coordinated gifts that were not only suited to their tastes but often more costly than if entire sets of china or glassware had been purchased by individuals.

The logical extension of this act of control was the creation of the bridal registry. Although numerous stores actively sought bridal business, the first true bridal registry appears to have been developed by Marshall Field & Co. In spring 1935 the gigantic Chicago retailer installed the "Bride's House" on its eighth floor among other model rooms. The trade press reported:

> It is a complete house, completely furnished to give the bride suggestions as to her new home from kitchen to bedrooms. And as if the wedding was just about to occur there is one room devoted to the wedding gifts. Here, attractively arranged on tables and shelves, are the gifts which the bride has supposedly received. Instead of the card of the donor each one carries the price card.[6]

No selling was done in this room, but engaged women and potential customers were directed to the appropriate departments to discuss possible selections with a departmental "adviser to the bride." However, in this space occurred the formal registration of a bride's wedding gift preferences. Previously records were kept and gift givers counseled; now there was an official "registration bureau."[7]

Marshall Field's Bride's House was extremely popular among shoppers and rival retailers. While most stores could not erect a model house to promote their bridal business, they could institute a formal bridal registry christened with myriad names and staffed by so-called bridal consultants, advisors, secretaries, or coordinators. Registries had sprung up in stores of all sizes from coast to coast by 1940. During the postwar years the concept was refined and integrated into elaborate bridal promotions usually held in the spring months leading to June. By the 1950s recording your selections at a bridal registry had become a marriage ritual in itself.

The concept of registering gift preferences expanded to the point that teenage girls, aided by bridal consultants, began selecting patterns and acquiring tableware long before they were engaged. In 1969 it was reported that "one in five has begun to hoard flatware, one in six owns china, and one in ten are collecting crystal. Sterling silver is the first acquisition at a median age of 14 years 6 months. China and crystal follow at 16, and such practicalities as linens, towels and stainless flatware at the sensible old age of 17."[8]

Fig. 4.20 Imperial Glass Company seduced brides with its glass "trousseau treasures," in the 1950s.

Although the registry's popularity began to decline as more and more newlyweds adopted casual lifestyles in the late 1960s and early 1970s, the traditional bridal registry promoting the classic gift categories of china, glass, silver, and linens was not seriously challenged until the 1980s. In response to competition, sellers of china and glass have become more efficient in serving the bridal market. Choices are now computerized so that relatives near and far can consult a bride's registry information at any branch store. Computerization has allowed retailers to reduce their investment in stock to a bare minimum. When stock runs low, the computer reorders. Today most china and glass purchased through a bridal registry is "drop-shipped," meaning that it is shipped directly from a central warehouse to the bride, accompanied by a packing list and notification of the purchaser's identity. Unfortunately for sellers of tableware, the gifts that arrive in the mail today are often not china or glass. With annual wedding gift sales now estimated at over $15 billion, retailers of all kinds, including sellers of sporting goods, tools, CDs, and liquor, have established registries in hopes of increasing profits. Tradition is giving way to the realities of modern life.[9]

Table Trousseau Treasure

FOREVER BEAUTIFUL! Imperial Candlewick Crystal service . . . for her wedding table, for the important anniversary dinners, for every festive dining occasion in her own home. Table trousseau treasure collecting means a dream realized. Leading stores all over the nation are helping, year 'round, to fill hope chests from their complete, open-stocks of this original, one-and-only beaded pattern that radiates loveliness because of its untiring simplicity.

Hand-crafted by the Imperial Glass Corporation, Bellaire, Ohio

Notes

1. The figure of 31 percent for total dinnerware and glassware sales was reported in 1969 by *GTR* (Sept. 1969): 36. The figure for fine china comes from *GTR* (Sept. 1970): 33.

2. "Store Image? Texas Retailers Show How to Build Up a Reputation," *CGJ* 166:1 (Jan. 1960): 43. According to Joseph Giarrocco, china and glass buyer for B. Altman & Co. in New York from 1947 to 1984, many Jewish and Italian families, as well as other ethnic minorities, continued to purchase entire sets of dishes for their children well into the twentieth century. See Giarrocco interview 1997.

3. "More about Gifts for the Bride," *CGJ* 118:5 (June 1936): 14.

4. "250,000 June Brides Will Receive Wedding Gifts: How Many Will Be Bought in Your Shop?," *CGJ* 109:5 (May 1931): 44.

5. Marcus interview 1996.

6. "Field's Erects Bride's House for Wedding Gift Promotion," *CGJ* 116:6 (June 1935): 41.

7. Ibid.; and "More about Gifts for the Bride," *CGJ* 118:5 (June 1936): 14.

8. "Not So Flighty Teenagers Stocking Hope Chests," *GTR* (June 1969): 29.

9. "New Life Styles—So Now What?," *GTR* (Dec. 1970): 1; and "Wedding Gifts Finally Come of Age," *Forbes* 158:7 (23 Sept. 1996): 39–40.

Fig. 4.21 Retail packaging and presentation became increasingly important in the 1950s.

OPEN STOCK, PLACE SETTINGS, AND PACKAGING

Once enticed by marketing methods like walls of china, table-setting displays, and bridal registries, customers had to decide how many dishes to buy. This act was fundamentally altered by the introduction of selling "open stock." Sometime soon after 1900 a few wholesale and retail merchants began keeping large quantities of popular patterns in stock that a customer could purchase at any time by the dozen and eventually by the piece. It is unclear who devised open stock selling and when the practice was first adopted. In 1921 the Boston importer of English and Japanese dinnerware Jones, McDuffee & Stratton Corporation claimed to have originated the idea. But in 1952 a historian of Marshall Field's suggested that the Chicago department store's early-twentieth-century practice of dismantling sets of china to sell replacements for broken pieces gave rise to the open stock concept.[42] Regardless of its origin the practice was widespread by the early 1920s, and by 1930 it was called "the backbone of the china business." While customers liked being able to buy replacements for several years after their initial purchase, retailers often disliked open stock because it required them to carry much larger inventories. As late as 1949 some store buyers were still ranting about the burden of having to keep patterns that could be purchased by the piece. In the late 1930s, however, the idea of selling tableware by the place setting came about and solved some of the problems of open stock selling.

The basic place setting consisted of five pieces: dinner plate, salad plate, soup bowl, bread-and-butter plate, and cup and saucer. By convincing consumers to build complete sets out of individually purchased place settings, retailers were able to manage their stock better and increase sales. Middle-class consumers evidently liked being able to purchase china and glass in affordable yet sizable units, and many more began to buy fine china and crystal in the post–World War II years. Even Americans with small incomes could acquire more expensive sets of matched dishes, thanks to low-end manufacturers applying the place-setting idea to inexpensive earthenware. In 1940 Homer Laughlin introduced the "Add-A-Place" campaign for its Eggshell ware (cat. 54). A place setting sold for $1.[43]

After the war selling tableware in standardized units dominated retailing. In 1948 an article on how to plan one's mix of merchandise in a china and glass department advised, "High priced china is better sold by place setting, since not many of today's customers will buy a service for 12, or even for eight."[44] To accommodate this shift in purchasing habits, some manufacturers such as Castleton China introduced club marketing plans in which participants took home a new place setting of china each time they made a specified cash payment toward the entire set. These plans were often targeted at consumers who had little money but a desire to own fine china. As Castleton told retailers in 1956, its plan attracted "prospects you couldn't sell before . . . teen-age girls, engaged couples, young marrieds. . . . [They] now become cash customers."[45] To make place-setting sales even more convenient,

Fig. 4.22 Most tableware was packed and shipped in wooden barrels until the 1950s.

special gift boxes were designed to contain the five basic pieces (fig. 4.21).

Fine china makers produced packaging for place-setting sales partly from their desire, and that of retailers, to make the shipping, handling, and selling of china and glass more efficient. Until the mid-twentieth century most tableware was transported from factory to store in wooden barrels packed with straw (fig. 4.22). Although a few low-end producers used cartons in the interwar period, it was during the late 1930s that some manufacturers of higher quality merchandise experimented with shipping tableware in cardboard boxes.[46] In 1939, for example, Fostoria informed retailers that it had started shipping glass in newly designed octagonal cartons that equaled one-half a barrel in volume. Although the new shipping method doubled Fostoria's packing time, retailers saw significant savings in freight charges; the paper containers were much lighter than the wooden ones and were more easily disposed of after unpacking. Within a decade Fostoria was shipping even its finest cut stemware in specially designed cardboard boxes.[47]

Paper packaging of sets of dishes went still further. During the 1920s and 1930s food-store chains began packaging commodities of all types for easier consumption in the home. By 1931 one writer observed that "packaging goods for retail selling has become a science and the decoration of the con-

tainers an art" and went on to predict correctly that similar packaging of sets of china and glass "was on the horizon with the prospect of prepackaging open stock goods just over the hill."[48] By the 1950s virtually all middle and low-end ceramics were sent to stores preassembled in units of four or six place settings known as "starter sets," while glassware came in small sets as well. Engineered and produced for manufacturers by specialized packaging firms like Flintkote Company of Los Angeles, boxes emblazoned with advertising and featuring innovations including "fold-back tops" and luggage-type handles also began to appear in stores nationwide (fig. 4.23).[49] Almost everyone loved them. Only purveyors of the most expensive goods resisted this movement, but by the 1970s and 1980s even they had followed suit. Regardless of price, today much dinnerware and glassware is prepackaged as giftware and sold by the piece.

Brand Awareness and the Rise of Advertising

Packaging china and glass in containers bearing the name of both manufacturer and product as well as advertising slogans and striking graphic designs was part of an overall trend toward brand awareness. Producers and retailers began their efforts to make the buying public associate a specific name or symbol with a particular product in the late nineteenth century. Early attempts at "branding" merchandise included affixing backstamps or paper labels to mark products with one's name, location, and logo. Sales aids like

Fig. 4.23 Single dishes and boxed sets line the shelves of McCrory's, Baton Rouge, Louisiana, 1958.

JOSIAH WEDGWOOD & SONS. L.T.D. ETRURIA.

Cat. 134 In the early 20th century Josiah Wedgwood & Sons and other firms gave retailers plaques from which customers selected monograms for their china.

ceramic name plates and monogram plaques were displayed alongside products to increase name recognition (cat. 134). Important commissions like those for the White House and well-known ocean liners were sought for the publicity they generated (cats. 80, 83, 135, 136). Supplying the weddings of famous brides and the households of celebrated personalities such as Queen Elizabeth of England, Princess Grace of Monaco, Lynda Bird Johnson, and Patricia Nixon could also heighten brand awareness for the lucky manufacturer and retailer (cats. 82, 118, 123, 137).

The emergence of professional advertising agencies after World War I brought these traditional efforts together with a host of new strategies. Manufacturers traditionally advertised at the wholesale level in the trade publications *Crockery and Glass Journal* (1874–1961), *Pottery, Glass, and Brass Salesman* (1910–42, fig. 4.1), *Gift and Tableware Reporter* (1962–78), *American Pottery and Glass Reporter* (1879–93), *National Glass Budget* (est. 1896), and *China, Glass and Lamps* (1890–1941). National advertising firms propelled manufacturers who could afford the cost directly into millions of American homes through newspapers, radio, television, and above all popular magazines. Starting around World War I advertisements associating fine living with china and glass began to appear. By the 1920s and 1930s many tableware makers used advertising to entice consumers to purchase their products at local stores. From Pyrex to Steuben and from Homer Laughlin to Lenox, American readers were bombarded by declarations of how new dishes would improve their lives (fig. 5.1). Keeping abreast of the rising tide of magazine publishing, manufacturers were spending millions annually on national advertising by midcentury.

During the height of World War II Fostoria ran advertisements in the April, May, and June issues of *American Home, Better Homes and Gardens, House Beautiful, Mademoiselle, Ladies' Home Journal,* and *Guide for the Bride.* Together these periodicals had a circulation of more than twenty-three million readers. Ten years later Gladding, McBean & Co. ran a similar campaign that added the magazines *Life, Sunset,* and *Gourmet* to the mix with the result that thirty-nine million women likely saw its advertisements for Franciscan Ware.[50] Some campaigns were so successful that women still remember them decades later. Lenox's advertisements in *Seventeen* during the late 1950s and early 1960s are such an example. Created by Phyllis Condon of D'Arcy, the agency that took over the Lenox account in 1955, the slogan "You get the license . . . I'll get the Lenox" appealed so strongly to teenage girls that many still remember it fondly after forty years (fig. 4.27).[51]

National advertising was on the whole very beneficial to leading producers because it increased their power in the retail marketplace. In 1945 G. E. Minard, the buyer for Stern Brothers department store in New York, remarked, "We find more people looking for branded goods such as Wedgwood, Spode, Haviland, Syracuse, Fostoria, Cambridge and Heisey. The merchandise is easier to sell with an advertised brand name. In the post war period I feel we will be able to get a better turnover, with less chance of markdowns. We are planning

Cat. 135 Morgantown Glassware Guild changed the name of one stemware line to *The President's House* after the White House ordered it in 1961.

Cat. 136 Theodore Haviland & Co.'s art deco style *Shape of 1937* was used aboard the luxury steamship SS *Normandie*.

Cat. 137 Designed in the 1930s, the Wedgwood pattern *Persephone* (platter) became well known after being used at the coronation of Queen Elizabeth II in 1953.

to give more display space to advertised brand lines."[52] Minard was not alone in this observation; his colleagues across the country also promoted "branded" china and glass lines more than ever before following World War II.

There were tradeoffs, however. The most important of these was that producers stopped granting exclusive distribution rights for particular patterns to specific stores. Exclusive distribution was prevalent for expensive merchandise before the war. Having singular patterns in a store helped a buyer distinguish his or her department from others. Unique patterns also required customers to return to the same store for extra or replacement pieces. Increased demand generated by national advertising made certain brands so strong that their manufacturers could end the practice of granting "exclusives." From the maker's point of view exclusive patterns were costly to produce and complicated to distribute; eliminating them would decrease overhead. In the late 1940s Lenox was the first major fine china maker to end exclusives. The rest of the industry quickly followed suit.

As nationally advertised brands became stronger manufacturers often forced retailers to display their products in specific ways. Stanley Marcus of Neiman Marcus recalls how the exclusive boutiques that began to appear in upscale department stores in the late 1920s often resulted from a

Fig. 4.24 Morimura Brothers chose a holiday theme to sell dishes in 1921.

Fig. 4.25 Drama and dishes meet in a 1925 Edwin M. Knowles China Company ad.

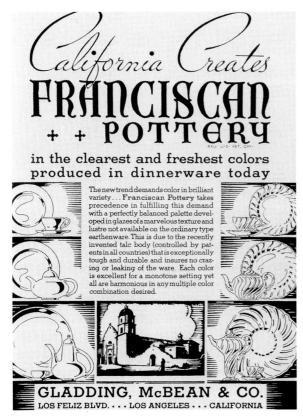

Fig. 4.26 Franciscan evoked the romance of old California in 1935.

Fig. 4.27 Young women were swept off their feet by Lenox China's most famous tag line introduced in 1955: "You get the license . . . I'll get the Lenox."

manufacturer's coercion. Well-known brands like Steuben starting in 1934 and Rosenthal beginning in 1962 demanded that stores display their products separately from those of other manufacturers. This stipulation meant that the manufacturers received more floor space and had their name and prestige reinforced in the eyes of the consumer. Makers did help defray the costs of such specialized shops within a shop by partly paying for construction, staff, and advertising, and giving markdown allowances, but increasingly manufacturers became forces to be reckoned with.[53]

Although retailers lost exclusive patterns and had to make display concessions in order to ensure a supply of popular branded merchandise, national advertising did increase retail sales overall. Between 1950 and 1970, for example, the volume of imported fine china sold in the United States rose 318 percent. By value the rise was even more dramatic—503 percent. Although sales of American-made fine china fell 48 percent in volume over the same twenty years, this category rose 30 percent by value. Successful national advertising was largely responsible for allowing makers to maintain and even increase prices while production fell. Lenox was so accomplished at maintaining its image and price points through advertising and distributor controls during this period that the Federal Trade Commission alleged in 1966 that the china maker was, in effect, fixing prices.[54]

The rise of national advertising in the tableware industry was not a panacea. While the increased name recognition for certain products did help sell them, other factors worked against many china and glass retailers during the twentieth century. At its most basic, selling tableware was not particularly profitable. Looking back over decades of retailing, Stanley Marcus recently observed:

> The china and glass business, I think, is unprofitable. The china business in particular is unprofitable for everybody, including most of the manufacturers. They have to constantly bring out new patterns. You have to buy the patterns, [while] you still have the old ones because people who bought them three years ago want replacements five years later. . . . As a result your stock is constantly outgrowing your sales.[55]

Couple that problem with high breakage rates and low profit margins and, according to Marcus, most department stores would never have carried china and glass. But women expected such stores to sell tableware, and so they did, with the hope that a woman who came to look at dishes would also purchase items, like clothing, that yielded solid profits.

Times of financial stress greatly accentuated the problem of small profit margins. By the late 1920s many china and glass retailers were losing money. In August 1929 Louis Hoening wrote an article titled "What Is Wrong with China and Glassware Departments?" in which he attributed the losses to "unintelligent buying and poor stock-keeping." Yet the fact remained that many department stores and other types of stores were not turning a profit selling tableware.[56] Following the stock market crash later that year, the situation became bleak indeed. For eleven long years most china and glass retailers lost money due to low stock turnover rates (less than two annually), tremendous display space requirements, and high overhead. These problems were finally overcome after the economy improved in 1941. That year china and glass departments averaged profits of 2.0 to 4.7 percent.[57] Wartime government spending in the 1940s fueled strong tableware sales, especially of American-made merchandise.

The middle decades of the twentieth century brought complications for manufacturers and retailers. A huge issue confronting them was the decentralization of U.S. cities. The slow movement of retail establishments from city centers that began in the late 1920s sped up dramatically after World War II. In November 1946 *Crockery and Glass Journal* posed the question "Is Main Street Moving?" in a lead article of the same title. The author further commented on the problems of store location:

> Our manufacturers now have the capacity to produce twice as [many] consumer goods as ever before but the retailer and his employees already jam Main Street with their own cars and keep the customer cruising around, burning up gas and patience, while trying to find a place to park. Streamlined store fronts alone will not solve this distribution problem. More cars on the street will aggravate the problem.[58]

According to this writer the solution to crowded inner city shopping districts was the shopping mall.

Following a spate of mall construction throughout the country, the same publication found itself seven years later fending off gloomy predictions of downtown retailing when it published "The Downtown Department Store Is Not Doomed."[59] In 1953 the department store might not have been doomed, but it certainly was wounded, and rival downtown sellers of china and glass were in fact doomed. Locally owned urban jewelry and specialty stores often found the move to the suburbs difficult, especially in light of ever increasing competition from better financed jewelry store chains and department stores. Even department stores that made the move to the malls (and most did) had to invest millions of dollars in new stores and expanded staff and stock. Now with multiple china and glass departments to manage, head buyers and managers faced a more difficult task. Increased overhead also meant that store owners looked harder at the bottom lines of tableware departments.

In the midst of these changes discount distributors eroded the core market for china and glass in the post–World War II years. There had always been nonretail sales outlets and low-end chain stores that distributed inexpensive tableware. During the late nineteenth and early twentieth centuries soap makers, movie houses, and sellers of tea gave away dishes to customers. By the 1950s, however, nonretail distri-

Cat. 138 Porcelain dishes featuring Native Americans were given as purchase premiums in the 1950s at Knox gas stations in Oklahoma.

bution was a $2 billion market, of which china, crockery, and glass comprised 15 percent. Furthermore, much of the distribution through club plans, door-to-door sales, coupon redemption, trading-stamp schemes, gift promotions, party plans, and supermarket and gas station give-aways competed directly with goods sold in average retail stores (cat. 138).[60]

Chain and discount stores also rivaled traditional retailers. A 1932 article in the trade press declared "Woolworth Invades Dinnerware Field." The giant chain store, which had long been a major distributor of cheap tableware, had begun to sell more expensive pottery as part of a move to add 20-cent items to its traditional "five and dime" mix. Thus one hundred-piece sets of pottery were offered at less than $15.[61] Some ware was even specially designed for F. W. Woolworth & Co. to compete with the brightly colored *Fiesta* line that was popular in the 1930s and 1940s (cat. 26). The S. S. Kresge Company, which sold dishes made in its own pottery, similarly challenged middle-class retailers in 1962 when the giant chain store began discounting tableware in its fast-growing string of discount stores called Kmart. Unlike Kresge's main

stores, Kmarts offered only dinnerware sets and no open stock patterns. But because prices were low, the middle-class customer that the discount chain targeted was content to make prepackaged bulk purchases.[62]

In addition certain manufacturers and import houses, such as Dansk Designs and Mikasa, opened outlet stores that directly competed with the middle- and upper-level retailers who distributed those firms' tableware. Finally, mail-order operations—conceived in the late nineteenth and early twentieth centuries by the likes of Sears, Roebuck & Co. and Montgomery Ward & Co.—went upscale to rival mainstream retailers. Roger Horchow, for example, founded the now well-known Horchow Collection catalogue in 1973 after purchasing the fledgling Kenton Mail Order of New York.[63] Soon mail-order catalogues featuring tableware from Horchow and a host of other firms were arriving in thousands of mailboxes from coast to coast.

By the 1980s retailing china and glass was a far cry from what it had been before World War II. America's small specialty tableware shops had largely disappeared, replaced by a few successful chains like Crate & Barrel and Pottery Barn. Most locally owned jewelry stores had also been absorbed by national chains or gone out of business. The same was true for department stores: in the postwar decades many family-run stores were purchased by a few large firms like the May Department Stores Company, Federated Department Stores, and Dayton Hudson Corporation. The nature of tableware retailing in these stores changed simultaneously. To ensure profitability, management reduced china and glass stocks, staff size, and display space in tableware departments. At the lower end of the retail scale Kmart and its challenger Target survived, but Kresge's and Woolworth's did not. These dramatic shifts were reflected in data on store failures among retailers of china, glassware, and housewares. While relatively low in the early 1950s, failure rates had doubled by 1954 and tripled by the end of the decade. Failures occurred at this high rate through the mid-1960s after which they fell back to an uneasy plateau of seven to nine bankruptcies a year in the early 1970s.[64] By 1980 selling china and glass in America had definitely become a challenging, if not precarious, task.

Notes

1. For early- and mid-nineteenth-century examples of selling glass tableware, see Madarasz 1998, 68–77.

2. Menzies was a founder of the organization and served as its secretary in 1895. For an overview of Menzies's life, see "Alex G. Menzies Dead: For Years One of Glassware Trade's Most Popular Salesmen," *CGJ* 100:11 (12 Mar. 1925): 21. For a description of the association's first banquet, see "Our Salesmen Royally Dine," *CGJ* 35:2 (14 Jan. 1892): 1.

3. "Homer Laughlin China Co. Opens New Sample Room," *CGJ* 93:52 (29 Dec. 1921): 16, 25; and 94:6 (9 Feb. 1922): 25. For an image of the elegant showroom opened by Lenox in 1920, see Denker 1989, 47.

4. For images of and information on these buildings, see *CGJ* 91:8 (19 Feb. 1920): 48, 58–59; 107:1 (Jan. 1929): 81; and 112:1 (Jan. 1933): 4–5.

5. "Fostoria Brings Innovations in Glass Display with New 225 Showroom," *CGJ* 151:4 (Oct. 1952): 40–41.

6. For a list of the glass and pottery lines carried by Gray Company and Cox & Co., see *CGJ* 93:30 (28 July 1921): 17; and 91:8 (19 Feb. 1920): 59. For a description of Richards-Morgenthau's new showrooms, see *CGJ* 151:2 (Aug. 1952): 58.

7. For advertisements of these Chicago shows, see *CGL* (23 Oct. 1922): 19; *CGJ* 107:1 (Jan. 1929): 61; and *CGJ* 146:6 (June 1950): 10.

8. For the New York and Atlantic City shows, see *CGJ* 91:23 (3 June 1920): 16–17; "New York Welcomes Its First China and Glass Show," 112:5 (May 1933): 34; "The Show of the Year! New York Housewares Show," 126:4 (Apr. 1940): inside cover; "Expect 5,000 Attendance at Atlantic City Show," 127:1 (July 1940): 42; and "Three Thousand Register at China and Glass Show in Atlantic City Auditorium," 127:2 (Aug. 1940): 17.

9. "Apple Promotion: New York Aims at Its Southern Neighbor," *GTR* (Aug. 1978): 110–11, 145.

10. Although the author primarily deals with apparel buyers, Marcus 1993b, 129–43, provides interesting insights into the lives of buyers.

11. Giarrocco interview 1997. B. Altman & Co. had a 3 percent breakage rate.

12. For a calendar of activities in an ideal china and glass department, see "A Year Round Merchandising Calendar," *CGJ* 117:6 (Dec. 1935): 54–55.

13. Giarrocco interview 1997.

14. Ibid.

15. Ibid.

16. "Substituting Live Patterns for Dead," *CGJ* 108:9 (Sept. 1930): 21, 62.

17. Gifford interview 1997.

18. "Blame It on the Patterns: Says Who?," *GTR* (16 Nov. 1964): 23.

19. See "Louis Reizenstein," *CGJ* 141:2 (Aug. 1947): 47; and "Newspaper Advertising Pays Off," 143:3 (Oct. 1948): 29–30.

20. Led successively by Gilman Collamore, John Gibbons, and Armin W. Riley, the store occupied fashionable quarters through the years at 677 Broadway, 731 Broadway, 19 Union Square, Fifth Avenue at Thirtieth Street, and 15 East Fifty-sixth Street.

21. "Carole Stupell Heads Hospitality Drive," *CGJ* 155:2 (Aug. 1954): 54. General information taken from Stupell 1932.

22. "Crate and Barrel—A Most Unusual Store," *GTR* (June 1963): 9–10; and "A Browsin' Barn Gets New Look for Manhattan's Swingin' 60s," (4 Mar. 1968): 8.

23. Pottery Barn was sold to the clothing retailer the Gap in the 1970s and again in 1986 to the San Francisco–based kitchen store Williams Sonoma.

24. "China, Glass—And a Diamond Ring," *CGJ* 116:1 (Jan. 1935): 83.

25. "Dixie: Love That Bridal Registrar," *GTR* (20 June 1966): 6.

26. "We Often Supply 75% of the Gifts Sent to One Wedding," *CGJ* 110:4 (Apr. 1932): 28.

27. "China, Glass—And a Diamond Ring," *CGJ* 116:1 (Jan. 1935): 84.

28. "The 100th Year for Macy's," *CGJ* 162:3 (3 Mar. 1958): 32–33.

29. "Altman's Opens Craft House," *GTR* (Dec. 1962): 55.

30. For a history of Neiman Marcus, see Marcus 1993a.

31. "Neiman-Marcus Stages Fine China Promotion Program," *CGJ* 158:5 (May 1956): 42–43; "N-M Promotes 75 Wedgwood Patterns," 158:6 (June 1956): 40–41; and "Six Famous Names in Fine China Were Emphasized in Dramatic Wide-scale Presentations," 159:2 (Aug. 1956): 33–36.

32. "This Company Has Equipped 1000 Yachts with China and Glassware," *CGJ* 109:5 (May 1931): 24.

33. "Class Conscious about China?," *GTR* (Oct. 1962): 28.

34. "Dinnerware and Company," *CGJ* 108:12 (Dec. 1930): 54.

35. Ibid.

36. "18,000 View Gump's Fall Table Show," *CGJ* 127:6 (Dec. 1940): 19, 40.

37. For an early description of a stylist's duties, see "Buyer vs. Stylist: Part I," *CGJ* 107:5 (May 1929): 21–22, 74; and "Part II," 107:6 (June 1929): 25, 33.

38. "Rhoda Sande Joins Iroquois China Co.," *CGJ* 151:2 (Aug. 1952): 74.

39. "Teach the Ladies to Use Their Imaginations!," *CGJ* 110:12 (Dec. 1932): 45.

40. "Factory Correspondence No. 124" (2 July 1942); and "No. 132" (6 Jan. 1943). Fostoria Archives.

41. "Teenagers Study Tablesetting," *CGJ* 160:6 (June 1957): 45.

42. *CGJ* 93:52 (29 Dec. 1921): 10; and "Give the Lady What She Wants!," 151:2 (Aug. 1952): 40.

43. "Place Set Idea Dramatically Applied to American China," *CGJ* 126:6 (June 940): 11.

44. "Creating a Balanced Stock," *CGJ* 142:4 (15 Apr. 1948): 70.

45. "Selling Open Stock Dinnerware," *CGJ* 107:2 (Dec. 1929): 80, 186; "Service and Distribution," 108:5 (May 1930): 15 and 72; "Open Stock Selling," 144:2 (Feb. 1949): 34–35; "Place Set Idea Dramatically Applied to American China," 126:6 (June 1940): 11; "It's a 3-Way Profit Package," 146:3 (4 Mar. 1950): 13; and "New! Castleton China Club Plan," 158:4 (Apr. 1958): 15.

46. McKee 1966, 15.

47. "Memo for More Sales" (Mar. 1939); and "Factory Correspondence No. 8" (17 May 1950). Fostoria Archives.

48. "Is Factory Prepackaging a Way out of the Red," *CGJ* 109:10 (Oct. 1931): 13.

49. "Packaging Can Speed Sales of China, Earthenware, and Glass and Reduce Operating Costs," *CGJ* 160:2 (Feb. 1957): 50–53; and "Packaging Progress in Tableware," 161:5 (Nov. 1957): 19–21.

50. "Factory Correspondence No. 132" (6 Jan. 1943). Fostoria Archives; and *CGJ* 151:6 (Dec. 1952): 18.

51. Denker 1988, "Name Recognition Fostered in Teens," n.p.

52. "Buyer Survey Indicates Brand Name Preference," *CGJ* 136:5 (May 1945): 45.

53. Marcus interview 1996.

54. "U.S.'s Import Craving to Affect Tariff Verdict," *GTR* (Jan. 1972): 20; and "Lenox Denies FTC Pricing Charges" (5 Dec. 1966): 27.

55. Marcus interview 1996.

56. "What Is Wrong with *China and Glassware* Departments?," *CGJ* 107:8 (Aug. 1929): 76, 104.

57. "Fall Business Increases Fail to Bring China and Glass into Profit Columns," *CGJ* 125:1 (July 1939): 39; and "China and Glass Department Breaks Profit Records in 1941," 131:2 (Aug. 1942): 15.

58. "Is Main Street Moving?," *CGJ* 139:5 (Nov. 1946): 45.

59. "The Downtown Department Store Is *Not* Doomed," *CGJ* 152:5 (May 1953): 64.

60. "The Non-Retail Picture," *CGJ* 162:1 (Jan. 1958): 31–36.

61. "Woolworth Invades Dinnerware Field," *CGJ* 110:3 (Mar. 1932): 17, 38.

62. "K-Mart Is Discounting Tablewares Now . . . Giftwares Next?," *GTR* (Nov. 1962): 24–25, 88–89.

63. "Horchow Obtains Catalogue Operation," *GTR* (July 1973): 3; and "Horchow: Let Mailman Do It," (Jan. 1975): 39.

64. "Failures among Retailers of China, Glassware and Housewares, 1950–1973," *GTR* (Aug. 1974): 38.

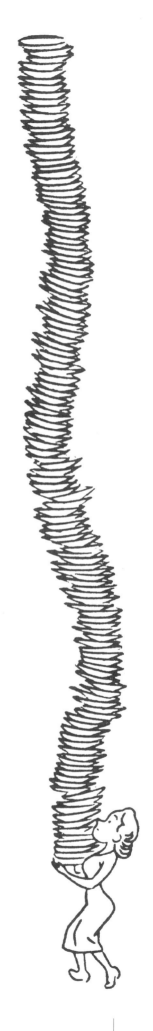

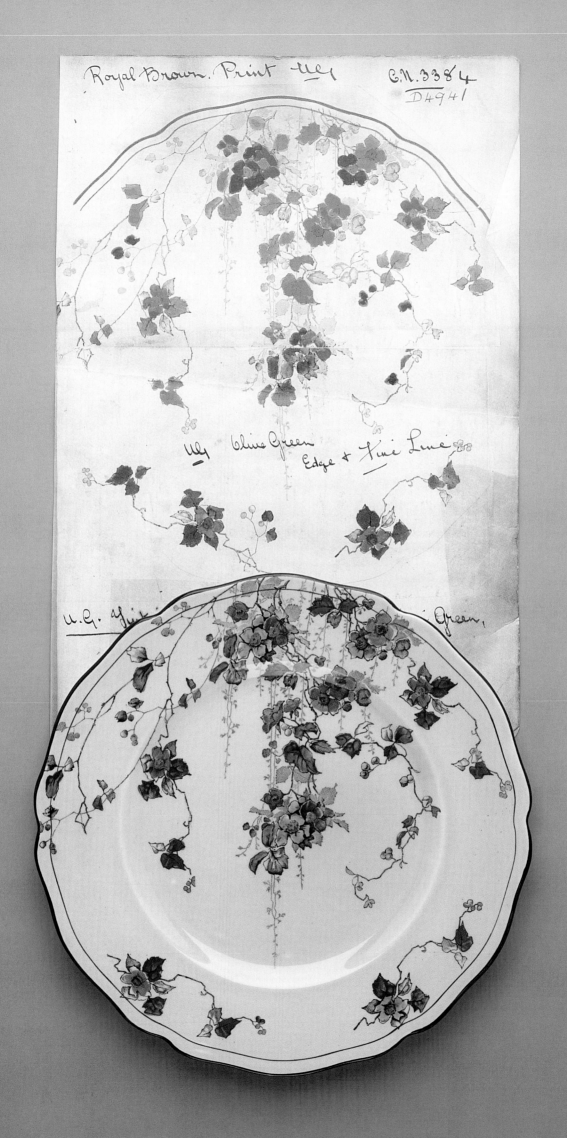

Design, Industry, and the Consumer

> *I believe that good design should keep the consumer happy and the manu-*
> *facturer in the black. . . . The designer must be a businessman as well as*
> *an artist, and must accept the responsibility of his position as a liaison*
> *between management, engineering, and the consumer.*
>
> —BELLE KOGAN, designer

Industrial designers are not artists in the traditional sense. In many respects the task of creating objects for mass production is more difficult than that of the artist. While a painter, sculptor, or studio craftsmen might receive direction from a patron or be limited by materials, the work of an artist is at its best one of unbridled imagination. In contrast the creative drive of an industrial designer is constrained by numerous outside forces. Practical concerns about size, weight, durability, and function form the parameters within which an industrial designer must work. Less obvious are a designer's limited ability to manipulate the more malleable qualities of objects—shape, color, and texture. While great designers can certainly produce tableware of startling originality, they do so within the realities of factory production and the retail marketplace. Designs that cannot be produced successfully are failures, as are designs that the public will not buy.

During the course of the century between 1880 and 1980 certain restrictions affecting tableware design remained constant. Although it was refined in many ways, the basic technology of making glass and ceramic tableware remained much the same. A designer in the industry always had to create objects that could be produced in a cost-effective way using the available manufacturing processes. More radical was the impact of factors such as consumer testing; market testing limits variety. Over time and especially after World War II, industrial designers in many ways found their range of artistic expression increasingly restricted by a more thorough knowledge of consumer preferences.

The Gilded Age

During the late nineteenth and early twentieth centuries, tableware in potteries and glasshouses around the world was generally designed not by professionals but by factory owners and highly skilled craftsmen who worked together to create new wares. Some establishments were fortunate enough to have owners or managers who were also talented designers. One of the most notable in America before World War I was Walter Scott Lenox. For the majority of manufactories, however, it was the moldmaker who was most central to the design process. Workers who had the skill to turn blocks of hardened steel into molds for pressing glass, or to make

OPPOSITE:
Cat. 139 Designers produced detailed drawings of patterns before they were made. This piece by Doulton & Co. is called *Kew.*

325

the "blocks" or models used to produce master plaster molds for casting ceramics, were always in short supply in virtually every production center. As late as 1920, for example, it was estimated that in all of England there were no more than fifty fully trained modelmakers and that in the county of Staffordshire "only some half dozen were apprenticed to serve 300 factories."[1]

In the United States modelers for the pottery industries were often English immigrants who had independent shops and worked for different potteries simultaneously. Isaac Broome, active in New Jersey in the second half of the nineteenth century, is an important example of a modelmaker who was sought out by leading firms such as Ott & Brewer to create many of their most exceptional products.[2] Because making prototypes and molds required great skill, these men were highly paid, especially in the glass industry. Men like native-born Thomas T. McCoy working in Pittsburgh and German immigrant John Oesterling of Wheeling, West Virginia, cut patterns in metal molds for shaping molten glass; this ability gave skilled craftsmen great power over product design well into the twentieth century.[3]

Along with the scarcity of skilled modelmakers, the limited production of some materials also constrained design. This was especially true with respect to lithographic decorations. The technique of transferring monochromatic ornament from a printed sheet of paper to the surface of a vessel had been perfected in England in the eighteenth century. In the 1890s, English and French printers transformed the decorative technique of transfer printing, as it was called, by perfecting the use of lithographically printed multicolored ornament that also could be transferred from printed sheet to object. By about 1905 the use of these "lithos," or decals, had virtually replaced transfer printing in America.[4] Building on their expertise in the fields of printing and chemical dyes, German firms were the leading producers of lithographic ornament before World War I. In both the United States and England, and probably in other countries as well, some large producers may have ordered sheets of decorative designs directly from Europe. Typically, however, an import house acted as middleman. In America the firm of Palm, Fechteler & Co. served such a role. The New York branch was established in 1856 by German immigrants, who imported materials and decorations for glass- and pottery-makers, as well as for amateur china painters.[5]

The other American firms that produced sheets of decal decorations in the early twentieth century were Palm Brothers Company of Cincinnati and Stoke-on-Trent, England, Meyercord Company of Chicago, and Rudolph Gaertner in Mount Vernon, New York.[6] Of all these firms, Gaertner's was probably the most important early in the century. Established in about 1901, the company initially imported German and English decals.

Although men like Rudolph Gaertner served as important mediators of design for ceramics and glass manufacturers and foreign decal makers, total customization of ornament was rare before the 1920s. Developing surface decoration in the late nineteenth and early twentieth centuries was a process in which "selection rather than development was the rule." American, and to a large extent English, manufacturers simply chose new patterns from among the selections decal makers presented, be they native or foreign. As a result it was common for numerous potteries and glasshouses simultaneously to produce objects featuring the same decoration.[7]

World War I was a catalyst for change. Because German supplies of lithographic decals were cut off during the war, entrepreneurs outside central Europe moved to fill the void. In America Palm Brothers began producing decals. By 1920 the firm was advertising "Classy and Snappy Patterns" for application to glass and pottery, "Made Specially for American Ware" in its Staffordshire and Ohio factories.[8] Similarly, Rudolph Gaertner founded a lithographic printing plant in Mount Vernon, New York, during World War I. By the time this company was incorporated in 1938 as Commercial Decal, it had an annual output of one million sheets of decoration and was the most important of all American lithographic transfer printers. Due to the stoppage of imports again during World War II, Commercial Decal continued to expand, until in 1950 its capacity had grown to eleven million sheets per year and had, it claimed, "made the American potter independent of European production."[9]

Before "independence" increased the ability of American manufacturers to be more original in their surface patterns, and while modelers and moldmakers were still a scarce commodity, the U.S. tableware market was deeply stratified. At the top were a very few domestic firms such as Ott & Brewer, Lenox China, Libbey Glass Company, and Dorflinger Glass Works that competed with numerous English and continental potteries and glasshouses for the luxury market. During the course of the late nineteenth century, however, American manufacturers came to dominate some important sectors of the middle-class and lower-class markets. U.S. glasshouses were unmatched in their production of pressed-glass tableware. Thanks to the ingenuity of moldmakers and the severe price competition that existed among glass producers, Americans had a huge variety of pressed glass from which to choose in the late nineteenth and early twentieth centuries (cat. 140).[10]

Similarly, domestic producers came to dominate the middle and lower range of ceramic tableware. By 1900 American potteries were making 71 percent of the ceramics consumed in the United States. Following the import restrictions in World War I, by 1918 domestic potteries had 91 percent of the market when measured by value.[11] But despite growing production prowess the appearance of tablewares used in America before World War I was highly dependent on European design.

During the last two decades of the nineteenth century many older styles were still in production in the middle and lower levels of the marketplace. English-type brown glaze (or Rockingham) wares, plain whitewares, and majolica, all of which had been fashionable in the 1860s, were still being imported into America. Similar ceramics were also being produced in the United States (cat. 3). English transfer-printed wares in single and sometimes multiple colors that had first come to the United States in the second quarter of the century continued to be imported as well. In this class of goods, underglaze decorations in blue were still the most popular. A variation of this decorative scheme known today as "flow-blue" was highly successful in America between 1880 and 1914 (cat. 141).

THE AESTHETIC MOVEMENT

While middle-class and lower-class consumers participated at the end of these earlier traditions, wealthy purchasers of luxury goods led design in new directions. Throughout the 1880s and a bit beyond, the Aesthetic movement that had dominated the prior decade was still a potent force. Drawing their inspiration from numerous sources, including Japanese influences, wares in this style typically featured naturalistic motifs. Images of flora and fauna delicately arranged on the surface or molded into the body of pottery and glass decorated the wares made both here and abroad for the American market. France—the first nation to assimilate Japanese art into its native artistic efforts—produced some of the most exceptional porcelain in the potting center of Limoges (cats. 83, 142).

Some English and American firms rivaled the French with elaborately printed, enameled, and gilded work on a variety of bodies, including bone china, Belleek, and earthenware. In the United States, producers in New Jersey marketed the most elaborate wares, featuring intricately modeled forms and finely decorated surfaces. Although they had difficulty competing in terms of price due to high labor costs, works by Ott & Brewer, Ceramic Art Company, Willets Manufacturing Company, and eventually Lenox China were often equal to their foreign rivals in quality (cats. 48, 49, 58). Although the Asian-influenced Aesthetic taste had fallen from the peak of fashion by about 1890, the style continued for a while in cheaper wares. English and American firms produced whiteware decorated with delicate flowers and gilding until the turn of the century (cats. 50, 141).

While the Aesthetic movement played itself out, firms in Limoges adapted the vocabulary of delicate flowers and birds to a ceramic style of their own. Featuring white porcelain bodies in frilly, undulating shapes and pastel flower decals, these French wares resembled fragile sugar confections on the table. Between 1890 and 1914 such wares made by Haviland & Co., Theodore Haviland & Co., and others became extremely popular in America. Furthermore, competition from rival French, German, and Austro-Hungarian potteries drove prices down. By the first decade of the new century, middle-class Americans from Maine to Mississippi and beyond could afford delicate, foliate porcelain dinner services for their homes (cats. 2, 79).

The vogue for delicate white porcelains was mirrored by the popularity of heavy, elaborately cut glass. Some specific types of glassware were imported from England and the Continent. So-called rock crystal, for example, which was tradi-

tionally produced by Bohemian and English craftsmen using copper engraving wheels, was often imported (cat. 67, goblet at left). In contrast, most of the heavily cut glass used in America was supplied by domestic makers. Whether at large factories like Libbey, which made their own blanks, or in cutting shops like T. G. Hawkes & Co., which bought undecorated glass from others, domestic artisans made some of the finest cut glass in the world between 1880 and 1920 (cats. 67, 70). By the late 1880s brilliant cut glass, as it is now called, was so popular that makers of pressed glass copied the patterns, making them available to middle-class consumers at a fraction of the cost of the real thing (cat. 140).[12]

STYLE AT THE TURN OF THE CENTURY

As the fashion for delicate French porcelain and bold cut glass entered its final phase, new influence from Europe was felt in the U.S. tableware market. Although it had begun earlier, the retrospective Arts and Crafts movement, which was dependent on German, English, and American idealism for its sustenance, finally came to influence mass-produced tableware, especially pottery. In the United States, Arts and Crafts designs were most important in the area of art pottery. But some small firms, like the Dedham Pottery in Massachusetts, made ware in this taste that emphasized a handmade look through imperfect finishing, elementary painting, and crackle glazes. More important were large English producers such as Doulton & Co. that exported numerous lines of Arts and Crafts–influenced tableware (cat. 143). Because the Arts and Crafts aesthetic lent itself to less refined earthenware, few manufacturers of fine porcelain adopted the style.

In addition to the Arts and Crafts movement, the "New Art" styles of French art nouveau and German Jugendstil, along with the Austrian Secession and the Mackintosh School in Glasgow, Scotland, were known to Americans. Through European travels, periodicals, and museum exhibitions such as *German Applied Arts*, which was organized by the Newark Museum in New Jersey and toured the United States in 1912–13, the most sophisticated Americans were made aware of these avant-garde movements.[13] However, when these styles appeared in the United States they typically did so in the form of decorative ceramics such as vases, clock cases, and tiles, not tableware.

Some influence was nevertheless felt through imports and domestic production. The graceful curving lines and naturalistic motifs of art nouveau design appeared on costly French ceramics and on inexpensive earthenware from Ohio and Japan alike (cats. 114, 144). At the same time the more rigid, geometric shapes and patterns of German, Austrian, and Scottish origin arrived at the American table from several U.S. potteries. (cats. 53, 130). These styles also came on imported wares, but in general only the least expensive of them found success in North America (cats. 105, 145).

OVERLEAF:
Cat. 140 Late 19th–early 20th century American pressed and mold-blown glass took some highly specialized forms.

Cat. 142 The asymmetrical decoration and images
from nature on these pieces from Limoges reflect
the French appreciation of Japanese art in the
second half of the 19th century.

OPPOSITE:
Cat. 141 For 300 years Americans have loved
blue and white dishes. This "flow blue" platter
by Wedgwood is an example of a type admired
in the late 19th century.

The Interwar Years

World War I was a defining event in the history of the American tableware market. Domestic firms, as well as their Japanese counterparts, exploited the stoppage of European imports during the war. Reflecting on wartime production increases, *Pottery, Glass and Brass Salesman* announced that 1919 had been the "best American pottery year."[14] By the early 1920s foreign china and glass were pouring back into the country. With the exception of introducing brightly colored glass and a few ceramics in the late 1920s, progressive tableware manufacturers sought to improve their profits by reducing the cost of production rather than by developing innovative designs. In the area of hotel ware producers examined their product lines to determine whether they were overly large in number. Working in concert with the Vitrified China Manufacturers Association, the U.S. Department of Commerce published a series of reports between 1924 and 1926 demonstrating how the services being made for use in hotels, restaurants, hospitals, and trains could be radically reduced. Of the seven hundred types and sizes of institutional china then in use, 540 were declared redundant.[15] Following a spate of new product introductions in the early 1930s to combat lagging sales, makers of domestic ceramics reduced the number of shapes and decorations produced in the 1930s and 1940s, both in the United States and England.[16]

Cat. 143 Bold shapes and stylized naturalistic patterns by Doulton & Co. were influenced by the Arts and Crafts movement of the late 19th and early 20th centuries.

INDUSTRIAL DESIGNERS

It was during the interwar years that designers not strictly trained within a craft tradition first came to work in the U.S. tableware industry. To some extent the appearance of design departments, staff designers, and consultant designers was the result of the immigration to America of well-trained individuals from abroad, especially from England. The technical schools in Staffordshire produced a series of graduates who greatly influenced American design. Increasingly, however, graduates of specialized schools and technical departments in the United States became important in the industry. In this country, several centers of learning were important in the area of tableware design before World War II, including Ohio State University; Rutgers University and Trenton School of Industrial Art in New Jersey; Philadelphia Museum and School of Industrial Art; Rhode Island School of Design; and Alfred University, Cooper Union, and Pratt Institute in New York State. In 1935 the Carnegie Institute of Technology founded the first college program in industrial design in the country. Led by German-born designer Peter Müller-Munk, the institution was located in Pittsburgh, the heart of pottery and glass country, and was well positioned to influence American tableware.[17]

Cat. 144 Homer Laughlin China's inexpensive tureen (ca. 1905) brought the curvilinear art nouveau style to thousands of American tables.

OVERLEAF:
Cat. 145 From expensive Czech glass and porcelain to cheaper English earthenware, a wide range of modernist European tableware was available in America around the turn of the century.

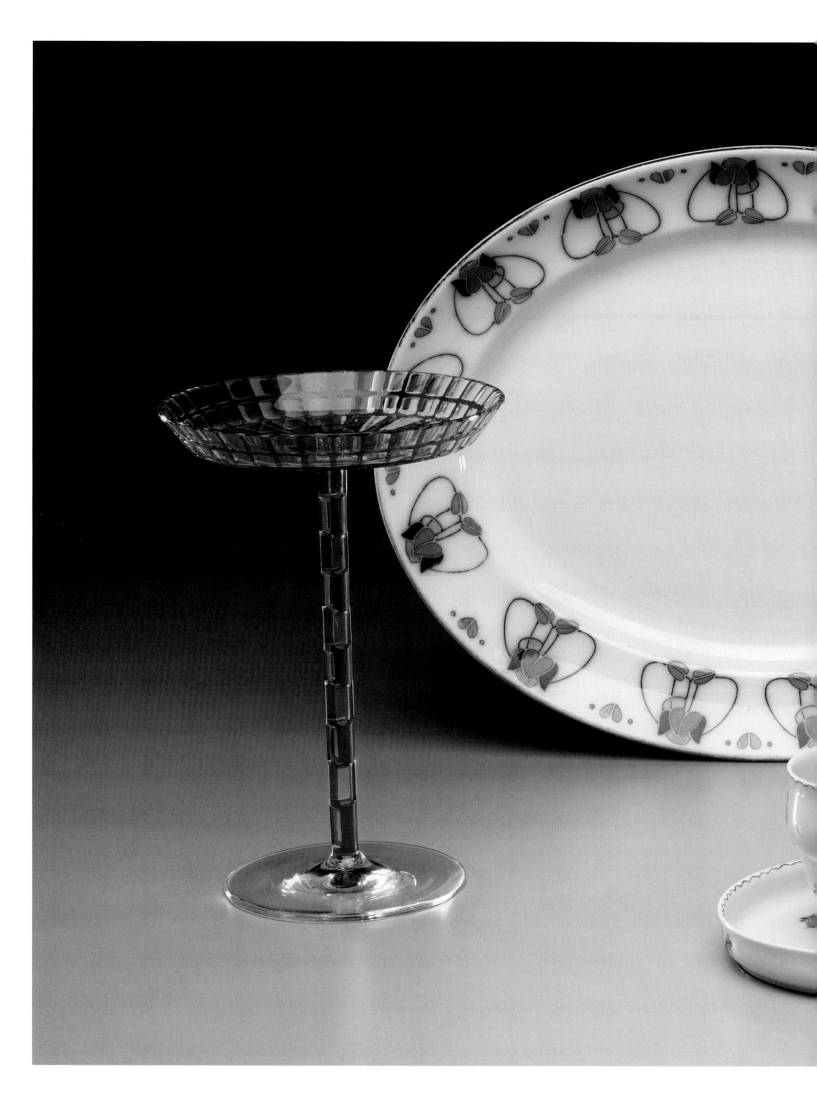

The entrance of professional designers into the tableware industries was uneven. Robert A. May, designer for Duncan & Miller Glass Company, stated as late as 1936 that "only a few glass companies are today using industrial designers on even a consulting basis and the number using them full-time is even smaller."[18] During the 1920s and especially during the economically depressed 1930s, more and more progressive firms began to place greater emphasis on product design as a means to increase sales. The designers who initially rose to fame and thus to power within the tableware field were trained in traditional art and technical schools before going to work for manufacturers. Americans Frank Graham Holmes (see pp. 338–41) and Gale Turnbull, along with Englishmen Leon Victor Solon, Frederick Hurten Rhead, and Joseph Palin Thorley, were leading figures among these early designers; of these Rhead was the most influential.[19]

Born into a family of Staffordshire potters, Frederick Rhead was educated at the Stoke-on-Trent Government Science and Art School and Brownfield's Pottery in Cobridge. From 1899 until his departure for America, he worked as art director for Wardle Art Pottery and taught design at the Longton Government Art School. In 1902 the young Englishman immigrated to the United States. After gaining experience in American production methods by working in potteries in California, Missouri, and Ohio, Rhead was appointed in 1921 to the Art and Design Division of the American Ceramics Society. Six years later Rhead became art director for the country's largest dinnerware manufacturer, Homer Laughlin China Company. Until his death in 1942 Rhead used his energy and prominent position to advance the cause of research and design within the industry. In numerous lectures and articles Rhead called for the need to emphasize design within potteries and glasshouses through the creation of art departments staffed with individuals who had both artistic and practical training. Through their employment Rhead believed the tableware industry would achieve "saleable and profitable quantity production."[20] He claimed that unfortunately while "technical and engineering departments can obtain university graduates who in reasonable time can be industrial material, a graduate from a ceramic art school—with too rare exceptions—must have years of factory experience before he is of any industrial value."[21] Rhead felt the same was true of contract designers, and thus he generally opposed their use by manufacturers.

The modern concept of the consultant industrial designer was developed from 1927 through the early 1930s.[22] Unlike their counterparts on staff at potteries and glassworks in the United States and abroad, this new breed of designer did not typically have extensive experience in production methods and materials gained through practical experience on the factory floor. Rather, pioneer industrial designers who eventually worked in the tableware industry, such as Walter Dorwin Teague, Raymond Loewy, and Russel Wright, often came from the fields of fine art, theater design, and advertising. Other early consultant designers who became important to the field of ceramics and glass were hybrids. Belle Kogan

(see pp. 342–43) had both fine art and practical training, as did George Sakier, who started as an engineer and machine designer and eventually became a prominent glass designer for Fostoria Glass Company.[23]

The economic collapse of the Great Depression advanced designers and the role of product design within the tableware industry. Manufacturers who had improved profits in the 1920s through greater efficiency watched their gains evaporate as consumers stopped buying. In a 1934 article titled "Product Design—The Answer to Price Advance," W. Frank M. Hawe, designer for the United States Glass Company, reflected on the difficulties of the early 1930s: "Here was a buyers' market without buyers. Prices knew no bottom in this battle for survival. The outlook for both the manufacturer and dealer was a persistent blue until the end of the fiscal year, when the deficit gave it an irritating reddish cast."[24] In hopes of reviving sales many firms increased the use of staff designers and contract designers to create new products that might catch the eye of reluctant shoppers. To do this successfully designers, no matter what their backgrounds, had to be attuned to the consumer's changing needs and desires.

The ability to predict what shape or pattern would be a hit in the marketplace was always more of an art than a science before highly sophisticated market research methods were developed much later in the century. During the interwar period, well-financed firms led the way by adding market research personnel to their payrolls. Corning Glass Work's development and promotion of its wondrous new oven-to-table glass, Pyrex, is an excellent example of such early efforts. Developed as part of Corning's extensive scientific research and development efforts before World War I, Pyrex was put on the market in 1915. Thanks to help from domestic science and cooking specialists such as Mildred Maddock, head of the Good Housekeeping Institute, and Sarah Tyson Rorer, founder of the Philadelphia Cooking School, Pyrex was initially successful with middle-class and upper-class consumers. Its novelty soon waned, and sales dropped. To devise ways to make Pyrex more appealing to American women, Corning created a home economics department in the late 1920s. Here men and women worked together with designers, advertising agents, and scientists to make Pyrex a household word in the 1940s and 1950s (cats. 22, 78; fig. 5.1).[25]

To a great extent manufacturers began using designers in the late 1920s and 1930s to divine what would be successful in the marketplace as much as to solve production problems. In 1928 one writer for *Ceramic Industry* proposed that "what a number of ceramic plants need today is an artist who can sense the trend of the times and who has the ability to create original ideas and who can meet the rapidly changing modes as fast as they appear."[26] Peter Müller-Munk was more direct in describing the period when he said, "Industry discovered that the designer was a practical tool through which to win the consumer's favor."[27] The ability to create objects that would sell well required designers to know their audience.

Increasingly during this period the element in society that garnered attention from manufacturers and thus designers of consumer products as the arbiters of American taste were white urban women. After World War I this group had more leisure time and more money than ever before:

> [These women] assumed an unquestioned role in shaping the production of goods, material, humanities, literary, and artistic. They were the chief spenders of money. . . . It was estimated that they bought personally at least seven-tenths of all the manufactured commodities sold each year in the country. Books, magazines, newspapers, and moving pictures were modeled to suit their purses and their fancies. Lines of automobiles and plans of houses were drawn to please their imaginations. Objects of domestic adornment—rugs, wall papers, lamps, chairs, tables, curtains, and pictures —had to conform more and more to their standards of taste.[28]

China and glass were no exception.

To understand these new arbiters of taste, designers explored the world of the urban woman. The best designers, as well as salesmen and marketing personnel, read popular magazines, observed women shopping in department stores, and attended fashion shows to determine what colors would be in vogue next year.[29] In the home furnishing field, they visited trade shows attended by furniture, carpet, wallpaper, textile, and paint manufacturers.

Museum and department store exhibitions also became important sources of information and inspiration for both consumers and designers. Building on its strong track record, the Newark Museum exhibited German, Austrian, and Czech decorative art in 1922. Meanwhile the Metropolitan Museum of Art in New York mounted exhibitions of modern French furnishings in 1919–20. Six years later the Metropolitan displayed material that had been shown at the 1925 Paris International Exposition of Modern Decorative and Industrial Arts, followed in 1927 by contemporary Swedish work. In the late 1920s the museum's design exhibitions were restricted to work by American residents and became popular annual events. The 1934 show was attended by 130,000 visitors.[30]

In addition to the Newark Museum and the Metropolitan Museum of Art, other institutions hosted design exhibitions that excited the public and industry. The Art Institute of Chicago displayed British Arts and Crafts design (1921) and contemporary Austrian decorative arts (1923). The Philadelphia Museum of Art set the standard for the 1930s with *Design for the Machine* (1932), and New York's Museum of Modern Art presented *Machine Art* in 1934, which was followed by a similar show at the Detroit Institute of Arts two years later. At the same time some of the country's most influential department stores held museumlike design exhibitions. The first of these was *Art in Trade*, held at Macy's in New York in 1927. The next year New York shoppers and designers were treated to *Exposition of Modern French Decorative Arts* at Lord & Taylor's, while at Marshall Field's in Chicago visitors could tour industrial designer Buckminster Fuller's revolutionary Dymaxion House.[31]

Fig. 5.1 Corning Glass Works associated Pyrex with fine dining in the 1920s.

Frank Graham Holmes, Staff Designer

Frank Graham Holmes was chief designer at Lenox China from 1905 until his death in 1954. During his lifetime he was awarded the Craftsmanship Medal of the American Institute of Architects (1927), the Binns Medal from Alfred University (1928), the Award for Excellence from the National Alliance for Art and Industries (1932), and the silver medal of the American Designers Institute (1943). Holmes designed three sets of china for the White House and, in 1925, was appointed by Secretary of Commerce Herbert Hoover to the commission that reported on the International Exposition of Modern Decorative and Industrial Arts in Paris. An enthusiastic practitioner of contemporary design, he collaborated with such avant-garde architects as Eliel Saarinen and Josef Urban during the 1920s on works for industrial arts exhibitions held at the Metropolitan Museum of Art in New York.

During his long tenure as chief designer for Lenox China, Holmes created at least four hundred patterns in a variety of historic and contemporary styles. In 1947 the company, in an extraordinary effort to remake itself, reduced the number of available patterns to forty-seven. Of the patterns that were retained, the majority had been designed by Holmes between 1932 and 1942. But Holmes's most innovative work of the 1910s and 1920s in the elegantly fashionable and colorful styles of those decades—the patterns for which he won contemporary fame and awards—was largely forgotten. Holmes's surface designs for the luxury trade set the image of the product as one of "good" taste and high quality; the company used this image after World War II to build a dominant brand name while expand-

ing its marketing from a wealthy clientele to middle-class households.[1]

Before Holmes's arrival in 1905 in Trenton, New Jersey, Walter Scott Lenox had been Trenton's premier designer of artware for Ott & Brewer, Willets Manufacturing Company, and his own Ceramic Art Company. During the 1890s Ceramic Art Company's fame grew dramatically, and although the firm had good years and bad, the general momentum was forward. Most of the forms it produced were decorative—vases, clock cases, dressing table accessories, and so forth. The range of tableware was limited to services for tea, coffee, and chocolate, and even these were probably used primarily for display (cat. 58). Standard dinner services were not made. Holmes was hired as chief designer in 1905, signaling two changes at Ceramic Art Company. First, the pottery had decided to follow Charles Fergus Binns's suggestion to expand the product line to tableware using the bone china body Binns had developed in his brief tenure with the company. Second, another designer was needed to develop the new product because Walter Lenox was going blind.

Born in Pawtucket, Rhode Island, in 1878, Holmes had been apprenticed to a silver designer as a youth and later attended the Rhode Island School of Design and the New York School of Art, where he was a student of Robert Henri and Frank Dumond. In his early professional work Holmes designed silver for the Howard Sterling Company in Providence, Rhode Island, beginning in 1898 and, when that firm went out of business in 1901, for Dominick and Haff of New

Fig. 5.2 Frank Graham Holmes in his studio, Trenton, ca. 1920.

York and Newark, New Jersey. Holmes later confessed that his initial plans were somewhat different from the events that eventually transpired: "Like everyone else at that time, I had the desire to study abroad. Just as I was about to leave America, or rather while I was hoping for a windfall in the way of funds so that I might go abroad, a friend suggested that I look into an opportunity with Lenox. The founder of Lenoxware was losing his eyesight, and was looking for some person to take over the work of designing."[2]

Holmes's arrival at the Ceramic Art Company marked a new beginning for Lenox's wares as he created designs that appealed to contemporary consumers. Even if Walter Lenox had not been losing his vision, the firm would have needed a new design concept that combined a knowledge of shapes and motifs from the ancient past with modern sensibilities of order, balance, and color, and at the same time fulfilled the desires of wealthy patrons for richly ornamented surfaces. Moreover, Holmes's youth and formal art training promised that his designs would continue to reflect current tastes and an awareness of contemporary art movements.

The company, renamed Lenox China in 1906, continued to offer exclusive designs and decorations for its wealthiest consumers, although now for the table more than the mantel. The first dinnerware catalogue, a small booklet published in 1908, illustrated a few of the shapes available and suggested the various types of decorations that could be ordered, including fish and fowl designs, monogramming, and gold etching. All dinnerware made at this time was individually designed by Frank Holmes (cats. 130, plate; 146).

Holmes's most celebrated commissions were, of course, those for the White House. He designed three of the four Lenox White House services: those for Woodrow Wilson (1918), Franklin D. Roosevelt (1934), and Harry S. Truman (1951). (The fourth Lenox service was for the Reagan administration.) The first, for President and Mrs. Woodrow Wilson, defined a new simplicity and elegance in official White House china and set the style for the rest of the century. The service plates for the Wilson, Truman, and Reagan (1981) services are remarkably similar, with their gold-etched rim border enclosing a wide colored band and splendid Great Seals in raised gold paste. Only the Roosevelt service differed in detail because of the Roosevelts' desire to include the rose and feather motifs from their family coat of arms and because the service needed to be decorated entirely with decals in order to reduce cost during the depression.[3]

In each phase of Lenox's development as a dinnerware maker in the twentieth century, Holmes created designs to fit the need for growth. When stock patterns were required, he designed printed-and-filled patterns such as *The Virginian* (1910, cat. 25, rear plate). When the company decided to move toward decal decoration, he designed *Ming* (1917), *Mandarin* (1917), *Autumn* (1918), and many other colorful

exotic offerings for the Lenox ivory body (cat. 133). When ware was needed in the 1930s and 1940s for a market that could not afford to pay for the extra steps of decorating, he designed *Washington-Wakefield* (1927), *Terrace* (1932), *Three Step* (1932), and *Beltane* (1936)—all patterns that depended on relief-molded rims to carry the design (cats. 25, front plate; 59). When Lenox expanded its market after World War II and eliminated many skilled operations in the plant, thereby causing inconsistencies in quality, Holmes designed *Westwind* (1953) to spread asymmetrically across the plate, heralding a new design era for Lenox and at the same time providing broad coverage of the plate's surface to hide any flaws in the ceramic body.

Holmes believed that design was foremost in the industry, followed by the cost to produce the design and its salability: "I have often been asked how we know a new decoration will sell. We do not know. In most cases, we take a sporting chance . . . and we seldom mention failures."[4] He was frequently asked by reporters for his source of inspiration, but rarely gave substantive answers. In 1937 a public relations specialist, Enid Day, from Davison-Paxon, a high-end department store in Atlanta, elicited information from Holmes in a radio interview:

> Inspirations for design come from all kinds of sources. The periods of ornament must be studied —dating back as far as possible. And that's pretty far . . . [including] the artisans of Egypt, Greece, and Rome, India and Persia, China and Japan, long before the wares of Europe and America challenged the masterpieces handed down from the past. The study of museum specimens, not only of chinaware but of fabrics, silverware, jewelry—in fact all of them, furnish inspiration for design. Or it might be a costume motif inspired by something one sees in a theater. Quite often an inspiration for design will come from nature itself—I carry always with me a pencil and a pad, so that I may jot them down whenever these ideas come.[5]

Examples of Holmes's use of historic ornament include *Maryland* (1922), based on faience from Rouen, France, that he saw at the Metropolitan Museum of Art, and *Ming* (1917), influenced by standard Chinese export patterns of the eighteenth century. Elsewhere he cites nature as the source for *Florida* (1922) and notes that *Coronado* (1922) "meets the modern desire for more vivid coloring" (cat. 147).[6]

The *Fountain* pattern was designed in 1926 after Holmes returned from the 1925 Paris exposition. Although Herbert Hoover had declined the invitation for the United States to exhibit, he sent to Paris four commissioners, Frank Holmes among them, who encouraged American trade groups and manufacturers to attend and build liaisons with foreign

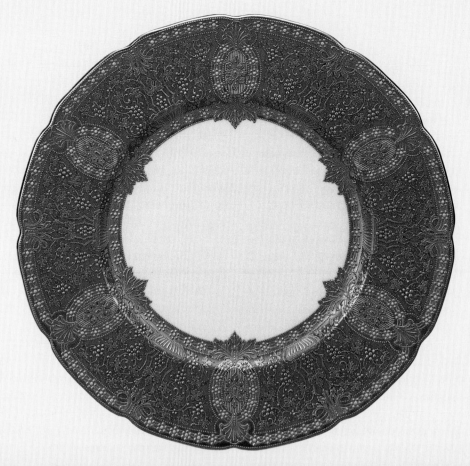

experts in their fields. This was a great honor for Holmes, and he must have been excited by the opportunity to see modern design first-hand. Holmes had begun working with new expressions and bright colors, as seen in his patterns *Florida* and *Coronado*. He claimed that *Fountain* was based on designer Edgar Brandt's gates for the Porte d'Honneur at the Paris exposition. However, an interior designed by Brandt and Henri Favier contained a screen by Brandt that seems a more likely design source, as the central motif of Holmes's dinnerware pattern is remarkably similar.[7] The fountain motif was seen frequently at the exposition and elsewhere at this time in the work of René Lalique and in the interior of the Parfumerie Française, designed for the exposition by Raguenet and Maillard.

Many of the patterns that Holmes created after 1925 incorporated overtly modern color schemes and design ideas, including *Pasadena* (1926, cat. 147) and the unnamed pattern nos. A 391 (1926) and E 347 (1930). In addition to contemporary fashion, he also had in mind the contemporary woman, no doubt embodied for him by his second wife, Louise Allen. A reporter for the *American Mercury* when Holmes met her in the early 1920s in New York, she later became the advertising manager for the women's section of the *Herald Tribune*.

Holmes's patterns of the 1930s, 1940s (*Lenox Rose,* 1934; *Rhodora,* 1939; *Rutledge,* 1939; *Harvest,* 1940), and early 1950s seem to lack the vibrancy and stylishness of his earlier work. There was, however, little impetus from the market for dinnerware design to be inventive. Austerity and conservatism were the keynotes for the 1930s due to the depression. Dinnerware production was mostly curtailed during the early 1940s in favor of war work, and postwar tastes favored clean lines and spare ornament (*Starlight,* 1950). Perhaps Holmes was fulfilling his own analysis of the market for decorative design in America. In 1927 Holmes observed:

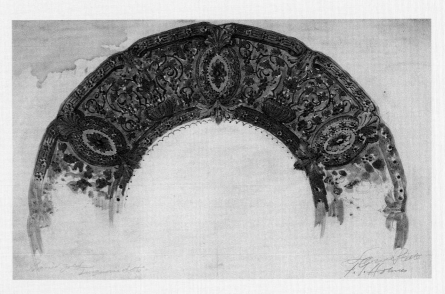

By creating along conservative lines, it seems to me that [a household product] is bound to reach a greater buying public. I do not mean that a concern should not take a flier in producing lines to meet fads. Vivid color combinations, unique and fanciful designs are a necessary part of a line; they are usually made to meet some popular demand of the moment, and the manufacturer has to get a run for his money as quickly as possible, before the fad passes out.[8]

Holmes's greatest ability as a designer was to adapt to all of these conditions in his work for Lenox and to do it creatively—from the highest style for the luxury trade to designs created for mass production. Through his sure grasp of style and ornament he defined design in American dinnerware for more than half a century both for Lenox and its imitators.

Notes

1. For more on Lenox China and Holmes, see Denker 1989. This profile does not include Holmes's contribution to three-dimensional design at Lenox because the company's shape records are not as explicit in citing the designer as are its surface design records.

2. Holmes interview 1937; *Who Was Who in America,* vol. 3, 1951–60, "Holmes, Frank Graham." Howard Sterling Company entered receivership in 1901 or 1902; see Rainwater 1975, 75.

3. For more on these White House services, see Klapthor 1999.

4. Holmes 1927.

5. Enid Lawson Johnston, "Trenton China Designer and His Work Attract Wide-spread Attention at Exhibition in the Metropolitan Museum of Art," *Trenton Sunday Times-Advertiser* (25 May 1924).

6. Ibid.

7. For illustrations of the Brandt and Favier interiors and the Raguenet and Maillard perfume shop, see Battersby 1998, 57, 39.

8. Holmes 1927.

OPPOSITE:

Cat. 146 Designed by Frank Holmes in 1923, this labor-intensive decoration was expensive to execute. Lenox charged $800 per plate.

Cat. 147 Holmes's patterns *Florida* (left), *Fountain* (right), and *Pasadena* (bowl at right) from the 1920s featured colored enamels and gilding.

Belle Kogan, Contract Designer

Belle Kogan was one of the very first professional female contract industrial designers in America (fig. 5.4).[1] Born in Russia in 1902, Bella, as she was then called, immigrated at age four with her family to the United States. While working in her father's jewelry store in Bethlehem, Pennsylvania, she took up drawing. The jewelry and silverware salesmen who called on the shop encouraged Kogan to pursue her efforts, as did her schoolteachers. Bella had been the only girl ever to study mechanical drawing at Bethlehem High School, and due to her exceptional talents soon after her graduation in 1920 she was asked to teach the introductory course in that subject. The next year Kogan entered Pratt Institute in New York only to withdraw several months later to enter the family business, which had recently been relocated to New York.

Although her father found the move to Manhattan traumatic, Kogan thrived. For the next eight years she worked in the store, gaining much business and design acumen, while studying painting at the Art Students League. In 1929 she received her first formal training in design during a summer course at New York University. According to Kogan, that experience made her aware "that design didn't just grow, it had to be developed. . . . It was wonderful, like a puzzle, all the parts fitted in; the business training, the painting, the color study and an intense interest in mechanics, machinery and production problems."[2]

That same year Kogan got her first job as an industrial designer, working with a plastics company as a color consultant. By the end of 1929 she was a full-time employee at the Quaker Silver Company in Massachusetts. After studying the firm's production processes for three months and

more formal training at the Rhode Island School of Design, Kogan began designing new wares. The company soon sent her to Europe for fifteen months to learn about Continental design and to study at the School for Applied Arts in Germany's silverware and jewelry production center, Pforzheim. Although she continued to design for Quaker Silver until 1959, her talents quickly outgrew the firm's needs, and Kogan began working for other clients.

Firmly committed to a career in the nascent, male-dominated field of industrial design, Kogan decided early on never to marry or have children.[3] In 1931 she began working as an independent contract designer and two years later opened an office at 185 Madison Avenue in New York, where she and an assistant specialized in home furnishing design. Business was scarce during the depths of the depression, but Kogan's firm, which eventually became Belle Kogan Associates, soon attracted several important clients, including the silver manufacturers Reed & Barton and Towle Manufacturing Company. Her association with Towle Manufacturing allowed her to travel for six weeks to nineteen cities throughout the United States, speaking with store buyers and young college women about the market for both traditional and modern silver patterns.[4]

Kogan's most important early clients for tableware were the Philadelphia import house Ebeling & Reuss and Red Wing Pottery in Minnesota. During the 1930s she designed several ceramic shapes and decorations as well as a new logo for Ebeling & Reuss (see pp. 289–90). As with most designs, inspiration came from a variety of sources, though the client's wishes were foremost. In 1935 Kogan was asked by Ebeling & Reuss to create two new dinnerware lines—one "conservative and ornamented, the other severely modern." *Berkeley* and *Metropolis* were the result (cat. 129).

These two concepts were meant to appeal to different tastes in the marketplace. For the conservative woman *Berkeley* featured lobed melon-shaped bodies, scale decoration, and leaf-like curls on the finials and handles. According to Kogan this traditional shape was based on an Austrian or Czech tea set she had seen in a book. Conversely, *Metropolis* was very modern in its bold geometry, like the avant-garde objects Kogan had seen while in Europe.[5] Only the most adventuresome of consumers would have been comfortable serving dinner on such an austere product.

Kogan's relationship with Red Wing Pottery was longer lived than her association with Ebeling & Reuss. From 1938 to 1963 she produced numerous designs for vases, giftware, and tableware. Among her most significant contributions at Red Wing were the dinnerware shapes *Fondoso* (1938) and

Fig. 5.4 Belle Kogan in her New York office, ca. 1948.

Fancy Free (1951), along with the surface patterns *Caprice, Country Garden, Desert, Iris, Lanterns, Plum Blossom,* and *Zinnia* (cat. 169). Concerned about possible tension arising between the contract and staff designers, the management at the pottery took great care to keep Kogan and staff designer Charles Murphy apart when she was there, though Kogan says there was no need for such caution. She remembers many cordial phone conversations with Murphy about work at the factory that took place without management's knowledge.[6]

In addition to Ebeling & Reuss and Red Wing, Kogan produced designs for many other tableware manufacturers, including Libbey Glass Company, United States Glass Company, and the importer R. F. Brodegaard & Co. (cat. 118, second and third from left). Some of her most successful designs were for Federal Glass Company and the Boonton Molding Company. Designed in 1946, Federal's *Star* shape featured a faceted motif in the base. The successful production of this highly popular glassware resulted from Kogan's intimate knowledge of advanced glass production techniques using sophisticated machine tooling and high-grade metal dies. Her designs for plastics also benefited from her technical knowledge. After working in the 1930s for the Bakelite Corporation, Kogan became an important force in the industry. By the time she worked with Boonton between 1949 and 1962 to develop lines of plastic dishes and stemware, Kogan was one of the most experienced designers in the plastics field. Of her creations for Boonton the *Belle* (1953) and *Patrician* (1957) shapes found the most success in the marketplace (cat. 65, bowls).

In many ways Belle Kogan seems to have been a near ideal member of her profession. Unlike some of her fellow contract designers she clearly understood the requirements of mass-produced merchandise and the limitations with which the designer had to work. In 1946 she wrote in *Crockery and Glass Journal:*

> In designing for this vast market, the designer must always be aware of two things: First, he or she must know who the ultimate consumer is likely to be and cater to the various tastes of the different sections of the country. Secondly, in designing for this [lower] priced market there must be a realization of the limit to what can be done with color and form, and the extent to which embellishment or applied decoration will influence sales. Designs must be practical not only for satisfactory manufacture, but practical from the standpoint of their utilitarian and esthetic appeal to the public.[7]

Later Kogan put her design philosophy even more simply: "I believe that good design should keep the consumer happy and the manufacturer in the black."[8]

For three decades at midcentury, Kogan espoused her beliefs through teaching, preaching, writing, and cajoling. As Helen Rice has written, "She educated the manufacturer, the merchant, and the consumer by explaining current events, design history, customs, and marketing trends. She introduced each to the other, explaining the role and needs that each had, while constantly stimulating her audience."[9] Through these efforts Kogan furthered the young profession of industrial designing. In 1940 she helped found the New York chapter of the Chicago-based American Designers Institute (ADI), initially serving as the organization's secretary. She became chair in 1946 and by 1949 was an ADI fellow. In 1994 Kogan received the Personal Recognition Award from the organization's successor, the Industrial Designers Society of America.

Beyond such official roles Belle Kogan was an important role model for other women in the design field and for women in general. As the first female American industrial designer to establish her own independent consulting firm, she realized how important it was for her to succeed in a man's world, both in and outside the office and factory. Once at the end of a long day at the Pittsburgh tableware show, after listening to too many sexist remarks from the fifteen Red Wing Pottery salesmen treating her to dinner, she jumped up and led the men out of the restaurant in a conga line, waving the check—a bold step at the time.[10]

In 1970 Belle Kogan closed her New York office and moved to Israel to work for the Koor Corporation. By the time she retired two years later, Kogan and her associates had designed tableware and a host of other products for more than fifty manufacturers—a truly significant career.[11]

Notes

1. For general information on Kogan, see Rice 1982, Rice 1994, CTE [1980?], and Reiss 1996, 105–7.

2. Rice 1982, 4.

3. Kogan interview 1997.

4. Ibid.

5. Ibid.

6. Ibid.

7. "Let Design Be Worthy of the Body," *CGJ* 138:1 (Jan. 1946): 56.

8. CTE [1980?], [1].

9. Rice 1982, 7.

10. Kogan Interview 1997.

11. For a list of clients see CTE [1980?], [9].

Inspired by magazines, architecture, interior design, film, and exhibitions, tableware, like many other commodities, became increasingly fashion-oriented in the 1920s and 1930s—and color was the most important fashion statement of the period. During the mid-1920s brightly colored consumer goods took America by storm. In 1926 fifty new paint shades for automobile bodies were unveiled at the Detroit Motor Show. As one observer remarked, "Household goods that had been traditionally commonplace for generations blossomed out as *objet d'art*. Dishpans suddenly appeared in mauves and yellows. . . . Bathrooms went Renaissance and Pompeian, with ornamental bases, mirrored tubs and inlaid tile to match the colors of the walls."[32]

Although color fads, such as the taste for ruby, amber, and yellow glass in the 1880s and 1890s (cat. 140), were nothing new, the impact of color on tableware was more pervasive between the wars.[33] Color manifested itself in tableware in many ways; one of the most important of these was the advent of a distinctively American preference for ivory-colored ceramics, as well as bright saturated hues, in both pottery and glass. The development of an ivory ceramic body occurred initially in high-quality decorative wares made in New Jersey from a so-called Belleek-type body that resembled its famous Irish namesake (cat. 58). Around 1910 Lenox began making ivory-colored dinnerware in addition to its white bone china. By the time it switched exclusively to an ivory body around

1920, Lenox was known as the finest of all American china manufacturers.[34]

Whether the Sebring Pottery Company in Ohio hoped to borrow some of Lenox's prestige by marketing inexpensive ivory-colored wares is unknown, but after several years of research, in 1923 the pottery introduced its own version of ivory-bodied dinnerware named *Barbara Jean*. This line proved popular, and other Ohio Valley potteries brought out ivory-colored lines within a few years. By 1927 *Crockery and Glass Journal* published an article titled "Manufacturers Certain Ivory Body Has Come to Stay for Long Time."[35] The claim proved true. By 1930 most foreign potteries exporting to America had developed ivory dinnerware lines designed exclusively for the U.S. market (cats. 84, 98, 115, 148). Although pottery was also marketed in rose, green, and yellow during the 1920s, ivory-bodied wares came to dominate the American market after World War II.

An interest in bright, saturated colors ran parallel to the demand for ivory-bodied wares. Thanks to advances in the chemical, glass, and pottery industries, a new palette became available to tableware producers in the early twentieth century. Formerly staid fine china designs, for example, often featured vibrant colors and elaborate gilding on ivory grounds by the

Cat. 148 The German firms Philipp Rosenthal & Co. (covered dish and plate) and Heinrich & Winterling (tea set) made ivory-colored bodies in the 1920s and 1930s for the American market.

Cat. 149 Handmade with elaborate coloring techniques, tableware from Tiffany Studios (large bowl) and Steuben Glass Works (goblets, bonbon dish) were extremely costly.

late 1920s. A Marshall Field & Co. catalogue entitled *Color Follows Color as Course Follows Course: The New Vogue in Dinnerware* highlighted the bold designs of Black Knight China in 1930 (cat. 101).[36] Glass producers, however, were the ones to take up the color challenge most aggressively at first. Early on luxury glassmakers such as Steuben Glass Works and Tiffany Studios experimented with exotically colored art and tableware (cat. 149), but these were expensive goods that only the rich could afford.

In 1924 Fostoria Glass Company made colored glassware available to millions of middle-class Americans when it introduced dinnerware in an array of appealing hues and shapes. While most firms were still hawking clear pressed or cut glass, Fostoria launched a nationwide advertising campaign enticing American women to purchase entire sets of pink, green, blue, and yellow glass dinnerware. Building on its initial success Fostoria hired the consultant designer George Sakier to bring modern styling to its wares, eventually appointing him art director (cats. 75, 76).[37]

Other firms soon followed Fostoria's lead. Within a few years many American glasshouses were producing brightly colored vessels of all kinds, while foreign competitors shipped loads of colored blown glass to the United States (cats. 29, 123, 150). Due in large part to its range of color, inexpensive glassware became so popular that a government study of the domestic pottery industry in the late 1920s and early 1930s noted that many ceramic items for kitchen and table use had been replaced by glassware.[38]

Potteries fought back with a color barrage of their own. Progress made by some of the country's leading chemical firms, including B. F. Drakenfeld & Co., the Roessler & Hasslacher Chemical Company, and E. I. du Pont de Nemours & Co., caused the color range and vividness of both decals and glazes to improve greatly during the interwar years.[39] Brightly colored tableware was first made in California. Soon after its founding in 1925 Catalina Clay Products began making souvenirs and artware in a variety of hues in keeping with the Spanish colonial revival then taking place in southern California. Encouraged by its sales of multicolored products, in 1929 the pottery added a line of simply shaped tableware in hot colors. Perhaps aware of the innovations taking place at Catalina the J. A. Bauer Pottery Company began production of its *Plain* line (late 1920s) and later *Ring* ware (introduced 1933) in green, blue, yellow, and orange (cat. 45). The *Plain* lines of

Catalina and Bauer included what were probably the first coupe-shaped plates made for general sale by an American commercial pottery.

With the West Coast emerging as the nation's leading edge of fashion, this rustic mix-and-match dinnerware proved popular for casual dining. Other California potteries soon entered the field, producing solid-colored tableware in both vivid and pastel hues. Metlox Potteries introduced its lines *California Pottery* (1932), *"200" Series* (1934), *Mission Bell* (1935), and *Pintoria* (1936, cat. 55). Vernon Kilns entered the market for solid-colored dishes with *Early California* (1936), *Modern California* (1935), and *Sierra Madre* (ca. 1937, cat. 151), and the Franciscan Division of Gladding, McBean & Co. jumped in with *Coronado* (1935) and *Metropolitan* (1939, cats. 56, 152). In 1937 Pacific Clay Products introduced *Coralitos* ware in "verdure green, dorado yellow, cielito blue, and mission ivory."[40]

California's colors were indeed a hit. In 1931 an editor for *Crockery and Glass Journal* remarked that while some white-bodied ware was being marketed, the demand for colored-glaze and colored-bodied ware dominated the retail trade.[41] Eager to boost profits during the depths of the depression, Ohio Valley potteries soon introduced solid-colored lines. Midwestern potteries had several advantages over their California rivals: shipping ware east from the West Coast increased freight costs, and no California pottery had large

OPPOSITE:
Cat. 150 This colorful jug by Tiffin Glass was designed to hold lemonade and iced tea cooled by ice cubes, a novelty in the 1920s.

Cat. 151 Vernon Kilns joined the color craze with its streamlined wares in the mid-1930s.

Cat. 152 Franciscan's rectilinear shapes were highly acclaimed by design critics. Two-toned *Metropolitan* of 1939 was the first to appear.

enough production capacity to supply the entire middle-class market. (The West Coast potteries did not advertise much nationally until five of the biggest firms unified as the California Pottery Guild in 1937.) In contrast, the Ohio River valley was more centrally located and was home to America's largest potteries. Homer Laughlin, for example, had a capacity of thirty thousand pieces of ware a day in 1931.[42] Ohio and West Virginia potteries with sizable capacities and easy rail access to everywhere but the West initiated production of colored mix-and-match ware in the 1930s.[43]

With Frederick Rhead, who had once run his own pottery in California, as art director, Homer Laughlin introduced in 1930 colored dinnerware featuring Wells Art Glazes in rose, brown, and green. The following year the firm unveiled its vaguely modernist *Century* shape, covered in a smooth, matte, ivory-colored glaze called *Century Vellum* (cat. 26). Although conservative compared to their California counterparts, and related to the fashion for ivory-colored earthenware, these wares were definite steps in Homer Laughlin's progression toward a bright-color palette.

The triumph of this effort was *Fiesta* (cat. 28). Having

invested significant effort and resources into developing a rainbow of bright, saturated colored glazes, in 1936 Homer Laughlin introduced the *Fiesta* line, which consisted of forty-two streamlined shapes in five colors—bright green, yellow, blue, ivory, and orange-red. The line proved so successful that within a year the firm was manufacturing thousands of pieces of *Fiesta* daily. Building on this great success, Rhead designed similar lines for the company, such as *Harlequin* (introduced 1938), and updated the *Century* shape with strong colors to produce *Riviera* (introduced 1938).[44]

While the giant Homer Laughlin had *Fiesta*, rival potteries in the area had their own versions of colorful tableware. Salem China Company's *Tricorn* (1934, cat. 153) came in radiant "Mandarin red." Harker Pottery Company's *Cameoware* (ca. 1935) was available in vivid blue and pink. Hall China Company, like some glass producers, adorned the interiors of refrigerators and the tops of tables with its vibrant leftover dishes and teapots (cat. 30). As Homer Laughlin did with *Century*, other potteries simply updated shapes already in production by applying colorful glazes. Paden City Pottery Company brought out the *Caliente* line (1936) using its *Elite* shape in

Cat. 153 Salem China Company's *Tricorne* and
Streamline were radical brightly colored wares
of the mid-1930s.

orange, yellow, blue, and green, and the Edwin M. Knowles China Company did the same with *Deanna*. Among the most successful transformations of this type was Taylor, Smith & Taylor's creation of *Lu-Ray Pastels* (1938) using pastel glazes on a combination of shapes from the older *Laurel* and *Empire* lines (cat. 154).

By the late 1930s a riot of color had exploded on the American tableware market as a result of this competition among ceramics manufacturers and glassmakers. In fact many in the home furnishings industry thought there was too much color. To bring order out of chaos, the National Bureau of Standards of the U.S. Department of Commerce met with manufacturers of housewares and bathroom fixtures in 1937 to standardize colors. The hues selected during the conference as having the most potential in the marketplace were to be reproduced on color chips and made available to the industry and retailers so that both manufacturers and consumers could coordinate their products and purchases.[45]

During the late 1930s Russel Wright combined the notion of mix-and-match solid colors with innovative, organic shapes that pointed toward the future post–World War II era.

Working with his wife, Mary, Wright designed *American Modern* in 1937 (cat. 24). Containing an early example of the coupe-shaped plate and hollowware pieces in undulating, biomorphic forms, Wright's creation was so radical that two years elapsed before a pottery agreed to produce it. In 1939 the then-bankrupt Steubenville Pottery Company began production of the line in four colors developed by students of Donald Schreckengost at Alfred University—*Chartreuse Curry*, *Granite Grey*, *Seafoam Green*, and *Bean Brown*. Like *Fiesta*, *American Modern* was a smash hit in the marketplace. Whereas Frederick Rhead's work looked backward to streamlined designs of the early 1930s, Wright's creation was futuristic in both shape and color and thus appealed to the young, well-educated, urban consumer who in the postwar period would come to dominate the debate over "good taste."

MODERN ART IN THE NOT-SO-MODERN HOME
Stating that the United States had no products designed in the "modern" taste, Secretary of Commerce Herbert Hoover declined the French government's invitation to the United States to participate in the 1925 International Exposition of Modern

Cat. 154 Taylor, Smith, & Taylor gave older shapes new life in 1938 when it covered them with *Lu-Ray Pastels.*

OPPOSITE:

Cat. 155 Josiah Wedgwood & Sons' *Prairie Flower* from 1928 featured a floral motif specifically designed to appeal to Americans.

Cat. 156 The patterns *Gobelin* (1929) from Spode and *Montrose* (1939) from Minton evoked the romance of 18th- and 19th-century England.

Decorative and Industrial Arts in Paris. Although there were a few exceptions in the field of tableware, including some of Frank Holmes's early designs for Lenox (cat. 147), Hoover was correct as far as dishes were concerned. Before the late 1920s very few designs in America were contemporary in spirit. During most of the interwar period domestic manufacturers produced and importers brought in designs that were based on conservative English shapes covered with a seemingly endless variety of scroll and floral motifs (cats. 139, 146, 155, 156). The ultimate in these flower designs was Chintzware, which featured vegetation from edge to edge (cat. 157). In stemware, glass cut and etched with floral sprays and architectural borders was also popular and remained so through the immediate postwar period (cat. 158).

Cat. 157 An example of "chintz" patterns, *Festival* (ca. 1927) by A. G. Richardson & Co. features exuberant plant life and Japanese lanterns.

Cat. 158 *Language of Flowers* (introduced 1942) combined pottery, glass, and linens decorated with floral motifs inspired by book illustrator Kate Greenaway.

Although an interest in tableware that hearkened back to the nation's colonial heritage had begun earlier (cat. 25), colonial revival designs became increasingly popular between the wars. Some, like Lenox's *Washington-Wakefield* (1927), were closely patterned on authentic eighteenth-century objects. Most designs, like Homer Laughlin's *Della Robbia* (1937, cat. 54) and Edward M. Knowles's *Williamsburg* (1941), were loose adaptations of colonial artifacts or were patterned after nineteenth-century prototypes (fig. 5.5). Foreign countries that could draw from long, rich histories of ceramic and glass production were especially adept at producing retrospective patterns for the American market (cats. 104, 159, 160). In 1937 Josiah Wedgwood & Sons, along with Blenko Glass Company of West Virginia, received its first commission from Colonial Williamsburg for Georgian-style tableware (cat. 131).

Fig. 5.5 Many glass companies, including Macbeth-Evans Glass Company, blended Victorian-style glassware with America's colonial past, 1933.

Cat. 159 Doulton & Co. based its brightly colored and traditionally styled *Granville* (1929) on 19th-century floral patterns.

Cat. 160 Inspired by 18th-century prototypes,
Wedgwood's *Edme* shape has been popular
in America since its introduction in 1908.

ART DECO AND THE STREAMLINED LOOK

The impact on general taste of modern architectural forms such as the skyscraper and radical art movements like cubism was significant, although perhaps not as important as art historians have stated.[46] Sizable numbers of American artists, designers, and consumers were exposed to avant-garde ideas at various special events held during the interwar period. The most important of these included the *International Exhibition of Modern Art* (the so-called Armory Show), which traveled in 1913 to New York, Chicago, and Boston and featured European and American contemporary art; the 1925 Paris International Exposition of Modern Decorative and Industrial Arts, where luxurious art deco buildings and furnishings were displayed; and the *International Exhibition of Modern Architecture* at the Museum of Modern Art in 1932, which toured more than thirty cities throughout the country. Some American visitors were inspired by and accepted these new concepts. Frank Holmes, a member of the official U.S. commission reporting on the Paris exposition, returned home to design ware in the high art deco taste (cat. 147).

But unlike Lenox's use of the elegant French style, other makers drew from more radical sources. Designs such as Reuben Haley's creation *Ruba Rombic* (1927) and some foreign imports owed much to the fractured surfaces of cubism and the geometry of the German Bauhaus (cats. 87, 103, 161–163). Although more sophisticated shoppers might have found the novelty of such fantastic creations appealing, the vogue soon withered and died. By 1932 Richard F. Bach, director of the Industrial Arts Department at the Metropolitan Museum of Art, was able to say in hindsight:

> For a time, we passed through a period unhappily called "Modernistic" in which manufacturers, seizing on the public demand for products designed in the new manner, wildly seized on new forms and produced monstrosities. Angles and geometric figures dominated all forms of industrial art. We were flooded with unsightly "modernistic for the sake of modernism." Happily that era passed, killed by the depression.[47]

In a trade advertisement two years later the W. S. George Pottery Company was more aggressive, declaring: "The early failure of modern art in America can be attributed to the Dadaistic, Surrealistic, and Cubist forms of art abhorrent to the average layman. . . . The European deformation of reality as a means of expression is not America's conception of modern art."[48]

While some Americans found this new spirit exciting in fine art, few embraced the concept in everyday consumer products. The "bizarre lines and madness of colors" of strident modernism were generally rejected in the home.[49] A buyer from Madel Brothers department store in Chicago summed up the situation in 1934: "Extreme Modern does not

Cat. 161 The angular shape and faceted motifs of this Noritake bowl from the 1920s were possibly influenced by avant-garde Czech cubist designs.

Cat. 162 The cubist style *Ruba Rombic* tableware (1927) from Consolidated Lamp & Glass Company was far too wild for most American women.

OVERLEAF:
Cat. 163 Bauhaus-trained Margarete Heymann-Marks applied avant-garde concepts to this tea set design from about 1930.

sell. People have to live intimately with their china and glassware and the designs they will use must be livable. . . . Consumers are interested in the more conservative Modern design because they think it is something new, but it takes them much longer to make up their minds to buy it than other styles in glassware and china."[50] The success of Clarice Cliff's plainer wares and the failure of her more eccentric designs in the U.S. marketplace reflect this reality (cat. 89).

Although extreme concepts were unsuccessful in the marketplace, conservative forms of modernism fared better. As a strategy to combat increased domestic and foreign competition in the 1920s and to revive flagging sales during the depression, many manufacturers increased the number of lines they had in production during the interwar years. Unlike producers of ware for restaurants and hotels, makers of dishes for the home believed that increased variety would result in increased sales. Many of these new wares were traditional ones with floral motifs or antique elements, but others had streamlined shapes and featured geometric or solid-color surfaces.

Of all the new patterns that appeared during these years, the wares produced at Leigh Potters in Alliance, Ohio, were among the most interesting. Leigh Potters was one of several potteries owned by the Sebring family. Frank A. Sebring had built the Sebring Pottery Company into a large and modern operation; by the 1920s his son Charles Leigh Sebring was

an important force of innovation within the firm. As noted above, the Sebring Pottery Company was one of the first American firms to introduce an ivory body in earthenware. Additional changes occurred following Charles Sebring's appointment as president of the Crescent China Company in 1929. This factory, which Charles renamed for himself using his middle name Leigh, became young Sebring's testing ground for new ideas. Under his leadership Leigh Potters engaged in a progressive product development and marketing program.[51]

To design his new ware Charles Sebring in 1928 hired Joseph Palin Thorley, who had formerly worked for Wedgwood. Although Thorley's tenure at the Leigh factory lasted only about a year, his contributions were significant. Working with the plant's technical staff, Thorley developed a beige-colored body called *Umbertone* that soon was available in a line known as *Leigh Ware* (cat. 164). In mid-1929 Thorley left to become head of the newly formed conglomerate the American Chinaware Corporation. Shortly thereafter Sebring engaged Gale Turnbull as head designer at Leigh Potters. Turnbull was an art-school-trained American painter who had already consulted with Thorley on designs for the line. Through the

Cat. 164 To catch the shopper's eye, Leigh Potters applied images of modern architecture and cubist paintings to plates around 1930.

Cat. 165 *The Aristocrat* (ca. 1932, left) and *Ultra*
(ca. 1929) by Leigh Potters were progressive
art deco designs produced in America.

efforts of these men, Leigh Potters introduced three of the
most innovative dinnerware shapes on the American market
between 1929 and 1932—*Leigh Ware*, *Ultra*, and *The Aristocrat.*

A massive advertising campaign was launched to promote the new Leigh line, along with related designs from
other Sebring potteries. In both the trade and popular presses
Sebring ran full-page advertisements touting the attributes of
its ware (fig. 5.6; cat. 165). The advertisements linked the designs to European modernism by mentioning Turnbull's extensive travels and studies in Europe, especially Paris, but
great pains were taken to distance the line from radical modernism. The ads stated: "Everything that smacks of the bizarre, the freakish has been discarded" and "only the best
expressions of modernism have been retained." One article
noted that "there are no freakishly shaped cups, no angular
plates, no fantastic curves in platters and deep dishes, running counter to all accepted ideas of what rounded outlines
should be . . . nothing to annoy the eye or distract the mind."
In short, "Leigh Ware is not grotesque."[52]

Leigh Ware was at first relatively successful in the marketplace thanks to its modern yet restrained design, the

Fig. 5.6 Leigh Potters promoted its products
with modernist graphic designs, 1929.

Fig. 5.7 Nostalgic images of America's past softened the modernist edge, 1939.

advertising campaign, and extensive pretesting of the line. In 1930 the firm attributed its success to the staff's "thorough and comprehensive study of the taste trends of the modern woman."[53] By 1934, however, Leigh Potters was closed. It seems competition in the early 1930s from new American pottery featuring streamlined forms and brightly colored surfaces, and from imported work by foreign high-style designers such as Clarice Cliff, Jean Luce, and Keith Murray, resulted in declining sales of Leigh Ware (cat. 94). Although production of the original Leigh Ware shape and that of Ultra were evidently abandoned, the Sebring Pottery Company did take up manufacture of the Aristocrat line for a few years, even offering it in solid-color glazes.[54]

In 1934 the Sebring Pottery Company itself noted the fierce competition among American manufacturers during the early 1930s when it stated in an advertisement that "about 1500 new patterns were announced in January by the potters of the United States."[55] Joining Leigh Ware were all the solid-color lines, colonial revival designs, and patterns that combined modernism with retrospective elements. Designs like Limoges China's Triumph (1936), Salem's Victory (1937), and Homer Laughlin's Swing (1937) perfectly illustrate how companies took simple, modern shapes and made them more appealing to conservative customers by applying ornament (cats. 27, 132). In their most basic forms the overall effects were rather chaste. To broaden the potential audience for the shapes, colored bands were added in all three lines, while floral or colonial revival decals were applied to create patterns such as Colony, Colonial Kitchen, and Godey Ladies (cat. 20; fig. 5.7). By remaining flexible, firms like Homer Laughlin, Salem China, and Limoges China Company maximized the appeal of their products with a minimum of expense.

Circumstances in the glass industry were similar to those in the potteries. The 1920s and 1930s were awash with patterns and colors of all descriptions. While Blenko Glass Company created colonial revival ware, Consolidated Lamp & Glass, Indiana Glass Company, and the Morgantown Glassware Guild produced some of the most avant-garde work (cats. 14, 71, 162). At the core of the industry large firms such as the glass companies Fostoria, A. H. Heisey, Duncan & Miller, Hazel Atlas, Anchor Hocking, and Macbeth-Evans led the way with popular and well-designed items in the middle and lower price ranges (cats. 166, 167).

The situation with luxury glass was not as positive. Steuben Glass Works, Tiffany Studios, Libbey Glass, and Seneca Glass Company, for example, saw sales dwindle during this period (cats. 73, 149). Producers of costly handblown and cut glass faced stiff competition from abroad, in addition to a declining customer base due to the depression. Numerous attempts were made to cope with this situation. Once a purveyor of colored glass, Steuben discontinued producing it and embarked on a massive overhaul of the firm's marketing strategy. Steuben became known for the world's purest clear crystal, designed by modernists Walter Dorwin Teague and Sidney Waugh (cat. 168). Rather than sell its wares through many outlets, Steuben crystal was available at only a handful of

Cat. 166 Hazel Atlas Glass Company's *Modern-tone* glassware (ca. 1934, front) and A. H. Heisey & Co.'s patterns *Ridgeleigh* (ca. 1934) and *Stanhope* (ca. 1935, cup and saucer) brought pizzazz to middle-class tables.

Cat. 167 *Manhattan* (ca. 1938) by Anchor Hocking Glass Company used concentric rings to disguise flaws in the glass while adding dynamism to the design.

Cat. 168 Perfect for the bar or office shelf, *Lust* and *Sloth* Steuben's goblets from the *Seven Deadly Sins* series (1947) were masculine presentation gifts.

America's finest retailers by the mid-1930s.[56] Libbey took the exact opposite tack. Famous for producing exquisite cut glass, the Toledo, Ohio, firm eventually dropped its high-end lines after World War II in favor of the cheap, mechanically produced lines designed by Freda Diamond and others (cat. 74). These products were distributed by retailers coast to coast.

EXOTICA: MEXICO AND HAWAII

Among the myriad styles that populated the American table during the interwar years a few were especially exotic. Of these, the two most significant were the Mexican and Hawaiian styles. During the late 1930s and into the 1940s many firms introduced handpainted or decal-decorated patterns featuring brightly colored images of Hispanic peasants, adobe dwellings, cactus, and Indian pottery. Such wares were appropriately christened *Mexicana*, *Old Mexico*, *Adobe*, and *Navajo*. Even in glass, screen-printing and enameling, along with names like *Sierra*, made vivid the warm regions of the southwestern United States and Central America (cats. 29, 169). The same was true for Hawaii and the Pacific. As more Americans visited the beautiful Hawaiian Islands on cruise ships, motifs of tropical fish and exotic plants came to decorate kitchens and dining rooms across the country (cat. 170). Some patterns had evocative names like Vernon Kilns' *Hawaiian Flowers* (1938).

By the late 1930s the enormous variety of tableware available on the American market had become a burden. Not only did customers find selecting a particular pattern a bewildering process, but also domestic and foreign manufacturers came to realize that by increasing their selection of shapes and decorations they were hurting profits rather than boosting them. As early as the mid-1930s insiders were calling for the industry to "regulate and control shape and pattern production." In 1936 delegates to the United States Potters' Association convention in Cleveland even discussed imposing a two-year moratorium on new shapes "with the idea . . . of devoting more attention to the production and merchandising for profitable sale of shapes and patterns already created."[57] Although no group action stemmed the proliferation of tableware patterns, as had been the case with hotel ware in the mid-1920s, simple economics forced individual manufacturers to take steps. Makers who simplified their product lines and increased the efficiency of production, marketing, and distribution shortly before or after World War II greatly

OVERLEAF:
Cat. 169 U.S. glassmakers and potteries decorated wares with stereotypical images of the American Southwest and Mexico in the 1930s and 1940s.

Cat. 170 Palm trees and tropical fish on wares by A. H. Heisey & Co., Purinton Pottery, and Vernon Kilns lend an air of the exotic.

increased their chances of survival in the competitive 1950s. With few exceptions the firms that continued to produce large lines in endless variation died during the depression or were killed off by midcentury by competition from better-managed domestic and foreign rivals.

World War II and Beyond

Between 1939 and 1946 foreign imports to America declined sharply while the world was engulfed in conflict. The advantage to domestic producers was greater than it had been during World War I because the Japanese, who had made dramatic gains in the United States during the 1920s and 1930s, were now cut off from the U.S. market. The British, who continued to ship wares across the Atlantic competed primarily with domestic fine china makers rather than with most U.S. potteries, which produced earthenware. With the weakening of competition and the help of government defense contracts, American china and glassmakers expanded both their production and prestige within the marketplace. In 1929 it was estimated that domestic potteries supplied 50 percent of the dishes used in the United States. By 1940 that total had risen to 80 percent and was increasing as imports declined.

The same year, 1940, *Life* magazine ran the four-page story "American Dishes: Home Product Fills Gap Made by War and Boycott." Illustrated with a wide variety of wares, including striking handpainted designs by Southern Potteries and the boldly drawn work of Rockwell Kent for Vernon Kilns, the article lauded American potteries for the advances they had made and predicted a bright future (cats. 57, 171, 172).[58] Further progress came slowly, however. Certainly a few new lines were introduced during World War II. Much more common were prewar shapes that were simply updated with new decals or colors. Even the old *Fiesta* shape was dressed up in red and white stripes during the 1940s.

This lack of initiative on the part of manufacturers worried some in the industry. In discussing the proper role of an industrial designer, Frederick Rhead said in early 1941:

> As far as the future is concerned the time to give deep and serious consideration to creative developments is under such conditions that we are experiencing right now, while our factories are still busy and loaded with orders, because with our present product, good as it is, we will not be able

Cat. 171 The illustrator Rockwell Kent provided iconic images of the country's regions for Vernon Kilns' *Our America* tableware (ca. 1939).

Cat. 172 This 17-inch chop plate featuring a map of the United States was the centerpiece of the *Our America* pattern.

Cat. 173 Industrial designers Eva Zeisel and Freda Diamond were employed by tableware makers from the 1940s to 1960s to design glass and ceramics for mass production.

to compete with what will arise from the ashes of the present conflict abroad.[59]

Although Rhead had a vested interest in firms introducing new wares, his words nevertheless proved prophetic. What rose from the ashes of Europe and Japan was formidable indeed.

Some firms were ready for combat. Libbey Glass had formed a design development department that, starting in 1942, worked with designers Virginia Hamill and Freda Diamond to prepare the company for the return to peacetime production of domestic tableware (cat. 173).[60] At the end of the war, however, most tableware manufacturers suffered greatly from foreign competition. Designers who had become much better organized as a profession during the early 1940s and whose livelihoods depended on the profitability of the china and glass industries were extremely vocal about solving the problems at hand and regularly commented on the need to improve manufacturing, marketing, and design.[61]

As early as 1943 H. Garver Miller, designer for Taylor, Smith & Taylor, passionately urged manufacturers and retailers to simplify, simplify, simplify. Observing that producers for home consumption were slow to adopt the reforms begun by makers of hotel ware in the mid-1920s, Miller suggested a "simplification and standardization combining manufacturing process, shape designing, and decorative design." By reducing the number of pieces in standard sets, he argued, the cost savings would be sizable to the maker, retailer, and consumer.[62]

Ten years later Freda Diamond touched on related issues. In an address before the China, Glass, and Pottery Association of New York, Diamond said:

> The most obvious trend in the dinnerware field is a shocking one. It's toward self-annihilation! . . . With all the perplexing domestic and foreign problems confronting both American china and glass manufacturers today, we seem determined to play the ostrich and continue on a course of self-destruction. As competition gets tougher—and it's getting tougher every day as the percentage of import business rises—we seem to bury our heads deeper in the sand and come up with some of the most unrealistic solutions that bear out the indicated trend.[63]

If the industry was going to survive, Diamond stressed, the multitude of available patterns on the market had to go. The solution was to move away from the system of open stock patterns to a situation in which tableware was a fashion commodity. Diamond believed that through training and advertising buyers would come to change their china and glass periodically as they would replace an older-model car, thus eliminating the need to maintain huge inventories of patterns in open stock. If this situation could be achieved, both manufacturing and retailing would be greatly simplified. Diamond also asserted that the glass and china industries were going to have to "get together" and market their wares jointly, rather than compete with each other for the consumer's attention.

On the subject of design Belle Kogan sounded the alarm in 1946:

> There is no good reason why, with our present methods of production, we cannot counteract and surpass foreign appeal and quality. We can do it only if the stop-light is taken from the drawing boards of the designers, and the pottery manufacturers spend the time and money necessary to pioneer new designs. . . . By insisting on an adherence to stereotyped conceptions, we are achieving a dangerous monotony of American design—a danger which cannot be over-estimated as to its future effect.[64]

The most progressive manufacturers heeded the warnings of Miller, Diamond, and Kogan. Lenox is a good example. Under the leadership of John M. Tassie, the company reduced its number of active patterns from four hundred to forty-seven during the 1940s. Next the New Jersey firm introduced highly popular modern shapes and patterns based on contemporary California wares made by Franciscan and Flintridge China Company and built a new plant in which to produce these wares (cat. 60).

Lenox expanded its advertising budget as well. By 1950 Lenox was spending far more on advertising than its nearest competitor. At the same time the pottery expanded its design department and by 1960 had twenty designers on staff. In 1958, in a move that must have pleased Freda Diamond, Lenox acquired a maker of plastic dishes, the Branchell Company of Saint Louis, and soon introduced its own synthetic brand, Lenoxware. The 1965 purchase of the well-known crystal maker Bryce Brothers of Mount Pleasant, Pennsylvania, gave birth to Lenox Crystal.[65]

Fig. 5.8 Castleton China sought women's opinions in market testing, 1952.

MARKET RESEARCH AND POPULAR TASTE

Few firms were as successful as Lenox in creating new products and brand-name recognition in the postwar years, but those that survived for any length of time had to find solutions to the complicated problems that designers and managers articulated in the 1940s and early 1950s. One strategy that most producers came to rely on was market research. Although some large firms like Fostoria were probing the potential acceptance of their new products by the public in the early 1930s, market testing came of age in the 1950s. In 1952 Castleton China announced to the trade that its newest patterns had been market tested first with "design, production, and retailing experts."[66] Next a research team took fifty potential patterns to eight major U.S. cities, where female consumers examined them. Only four patterns survived (fig. 5.8).

Initially some designers had mixed feelings about market research because of its potential to limit their artistic freedom, but because professional consumer testing took much of the risk out of introducing new lines of tableware, manufacturers quickly came to rely on it. In 1955 one observer compared the "Golden Age of Design," when industrial designers were novel and thus had more power, to the present, when designers "are taken for granted, and must fight for their rights among the other industrial groups that seek to control the product." He continued, "Worst of all, new witch doctors have arisen with their own arcane ritual for the charming of executives; not the least of these are the high priests of consumer research. Many a designer, knowing he can't lick them, has eagerly decided to join them."[67]

By joining with market researchers, designers and manufacturers came to know their potential customers better than ever before. What they found was a market of great complexity and increasing sophistication. Whereas the strata of high, middle, and low had been discussed for decades, now the discussion centered on how to appeal to specific niches in the market. California was recognized as having the most casual and colorful taste in the country, whereas the South was much more formal and traditional. West Coast customers favored brighter colors and bolder shapes for their outdoor parties, and southern girls clung to the bridal registry and English-style china for use in formal dining rooms.

Consumers at the two extremes of the price spectrum had the most conservative taste. Ironically, the richest and poorest Americans wanted similarly florid tableware in traditional shapes. High-end wares included expensive English bone china or earthenware sold at stores like Carole Stupell, Ltd., or Neiman Marcus. At the bottom end were inexpensive dishes from Ohio that might have been offered as premiums at the grocery store or sold by J. C. Penney Company or F. W. Woolworth & Co. (cat. 174).

In the middle were a vast number of consumers who would accept contemporary design under certain circumstances. There was the sophisticated crowd that one writer has described as "professional, with little money, but plenty of taste."[68] They were practically the only people in the country who would purchase all-white tableware in avant-garde

Cat. 176 Eva Zeisel's shapes *Tomorrow's Classic* (1949) and *Century* (ca. 1955) were among Hall China Company's most progressive.

OPPOSITE:
Cat. 174 Sold by J. C. Penney & Co., *Historical America* and *Early American Homes* (left) mimicked expensive earthenware patterns such as Mason's *Pink Vista* (right).

Cat. 175 Stetson China Company's *Holiday* shape (ca. 1954) was primarily sold as premiums by grocery stores and other merchants.

shapes. A larger but related sector of the market would buy white dishes when a bit of color and pattern was added (cat. 176). Middle-income buyers, like their wealthier counterparts, could also have multiple sets of dishes if they desired and were able to afford them. Americans could acquire tradition and history through fine china and crystal but simultaneously free themselves from those very bonds by using casual dishes in unusual shapes or with abstract patterns (cats. 33, 175). Plus new sectors of the market were emerging. One was teenage girls, who according to contemporary sources were most interested in building sets of fine china, crystal, and silver in anticipation of marriage. Another emerging element in the marketplace were African Americans, who seemed most responsive to well-known brand names.[69]

Designers and manufacturers coped with such diversity using two basic strategies. Some chose niche markets and catered to them. Edith Kiertener Heath and Dorothy C. Thorpe consistently appealed to sophisticated shoppers who were relatively wealthy and well educated and so did not change their styles much over time (cats. 177, 178). Numerous foreign firms and import houses, including Spode, Dansk Designs, and Rosenthal (beginning in the 1950s), also went after specific sectors of the market. Rosenthal and Dansk wanted the

Cat. 177 Edith Heath's *Coupe* shape of the mid-1940s was so well thought of that Wedgwood considered producing it in England in 1965.

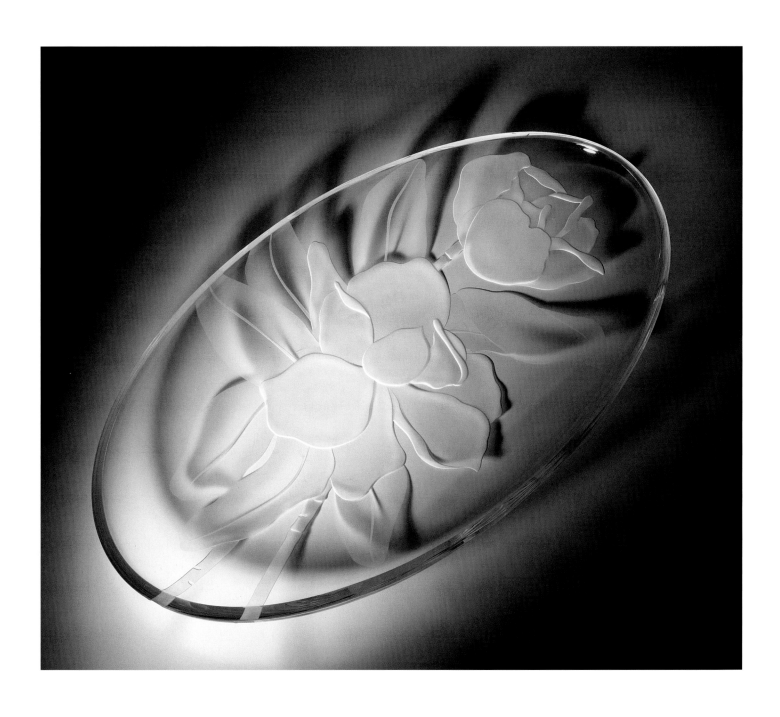

Cat. 178 Dorothy Thorpe's sophisticated sandblasting of glass was widely imitated after its
introduction in the 1930s.

wealthy sophisticate, and Copeland sought the wealthy traditionalist (cats. 92, 108, 121).

Some large U.S. firms like Libbey, Lenox, Heisey, Fostoria, and the Franciscan Division of Gladding, McBean & Co. used a different approach. Rather than attack a small area of the market, they tried to reach as large a portion as possible by developing and test-marketing patterns that would appeal to a wide array of tastes simultaneously. Franciscan's Masterpiece china brand, as well as much of its earthenware, for example, was "fine" enough to please the wealthy consumer and just modern enough to tap the sophisticated element in the middle market (cats. 62, 152, 193).

As diverse as American consumers were, certain commonalities helped forge them into a single overall market. During the postwar years, the United States became increasingly unified as a society thanks to better transportation systems, national retail stores and restaurant chains, and above all telecommunications. Traveling in trains on a well-developed railway grid, by plane in the emerging commercial aviation network, and in private cars motoring across the country on an expanding national highway system, as well as experiencing the world through television, Americans were able to explore their own country and foreign lands as never before.

As they became increasingly mobile, Americans were exposed to endless varieties of entertaining and tableware. Restaurants along the highway featured theme china for steaks and seafood, while trains and planes had their own services (cat. 52). Department stores and five-and-dime chains displayed shelf after shelf of china and glass. Museums and trade associations beckoned the public with displays of dishes. In 1948 the United States Potters' Association launched the First National Dinnerware Exhibit, which traveled to department stores across the country.[70] Meanwhile institutions like the Museum of Modern Art sought to "improve" the public's taste through annual juried shows such as its Good Design exhibitions, which began in 1950.

Perhaps most important of all was the influence of television. In 1950 fewer than 9 percent of American households owned a television. Ten years later 87 percent of families were tuning in to shows like Leave It to Beaver, I Love Lucy, and Father Knows Best on their black-and-white sets.[71] Vicariously participating in the lives of television stars and endlessly viewing the fictitious interiors of middle-class and upper-class white families served to unify tastes across the country, all the while making Americans more aware of style as a concept. In 1957 designer Donald Schreckengost noted, "Statistics support the fact that consumers are far more conscious of style today than ever before, and for this reason eye appeal . . . seems to have a greater influence on their choice of a product than does utility or function."[72]

Television commercials and magazine advertisements for brand-name consumer goods like dishes and dishwashers had the same effect. First introduced by Kitchenaid in 1949, within a decade dishwashers were a major force of change in the tableware industry.[73] During the early 1950s chemical companies and decal manufacturers worked with china and glass makers to produce wares that would not fade, craze, or chip while being washed by machine. Thanks to technical and design advances the "oven-to-table" phenomenon of the 1920s and 1930s now came full circle, with glass and ceramic containers that could honestly live up to the claims "oven to table to dishwasher" and "dishwasher-safe" (cat. 78).

PREWAR SURVIVORS AND AN ELUSIVE AMERICAN STYLE

In 1941 the patriarch of American tableware designers, Frederick Rhead, published an article titled "The Full Meaning of an 'American Design,'" which began with the statement, "Many of the so-called American traditional types are no more American than is Hitler or Mussolini." Rhead noted that America had made several important contributions in the field of tableware—in particular, the high-fired earthenware (which he called semivitreous), bright solid-color glazes, and silk-screened decoration. Although the list could have been expanded to include innovative glass-pressing and -blowing equipment, Rhead's point was that while Americans had made great progress in the areas of materials and technical processes, they had not developed their own aesthetic, or "typical American feeling or theme." He concluded: "When I try to think in terms of an American decorative type—in tableware—I mentally review what has been done and excepting the pottery wares of the American Indian, I fail to recognize a pottery type which can be honestly classified as distinctly American."[74] Although there were a handful of exceptions by the early 1940s, Rhead's assessment on the whole was correct. However, by the end of the decade an American aesthetic was emerging.

With the return of foreign competition and the enhanced position of American ceramics and glass during the 1940s, the U.S. tableware market was again flooded with choices in the 1950s. At the beginning of the decade Belle Kogan stated, "There has never been, in the history of these wares in this country, such a wide price range, so many styles, trends, and colors to choose from."[75] Some of the major trends were holdovers from the prewar period. Solid colors and texture remained as popular as they had been before World War II. But from the late 1940s until the 1960s, bright, saturated colors gave way to lighter pastels and mottled earthy hues. In some lines solid colors were simply an alternative to surface pattern (cats. 179, 180). In others the colored surface was as important as the shape (cats. 128, 181, 182).

Wares with textured surfaces were more complicated. In some respects ceramics and glass that mimicked radically different materials like textiles, wood, or stone were part of a more general movement toward a totally coordinated tablescape that had begun in the 1930s.[76] Thanks to savvy retailers like C. Reizenstein Sons in Pittsburgh, which had glassware made to match famous china patterns in a brand named Reizart (ca. 1945–55), and Duncan & Miller, which distributed booklets such as Everywoman's Guide to Harmonizing Patterns: Crystal, China, Silver (1952), the initial phase in this process was

Cat. 179 Donald Schreckengost designed *Jubilee*
in 1947 to celebrate Homer Laughlin China's
75th anniversary.

Cat. 180 Hall China's *Tri-Tone* of 1954 featured sprayed decoration that looked hand dipped.

OVERLEAF:

Cat. 181 Russel Wright's *White Clover* (1951) for Harker Pottery was acclaimed by critics for its good design but was a commercial failure.

Cat. 182 The designs provided to Sovereign Potteries (left) and Edwin M. Knowles Pottery (right) in the mid 1950s by Mary and Russel Wright were innovative but unpopular with the public.

Cat. 183 Introduced by Royal China in 1950, the *Colonial Homestead* line featured romanticized views of an 18th-century interior that proved highly popular with consumers.

Cat. 184 Stangl Pottery's peasant-style patterns of 1948, *Golden Harvest* (plate) and *Amber-Glo,* were meant to be mixed and matched.

aimed at coordinating eating utensils. Soon linens were brought into the mix, and thus ceramics and glass designers came to pay great attention to the color and patterning of contemporary textiles. An early example of such efforts was the line called *Language of Flowers* (1942). To realize this concept, Duncan & Miller, Limoges China, and Leacock, Inc., cooperated to produce coordinated glass, pottery, and linens based on floral designs adapted from the earlier work of the illustrator Kate Greenaway to create an aesthetically controlled tabletop (cat. 158).

Textiles became increasingly important to the tableware industry in the postwar period. In the mid-1940s designers began to create more textiles that were meant to match specific tableware lines. Russel Wright, for example, designed *American Modern* table linens in 1946. Soon this concept grew to include upholstery fabric as well.[77] As a result American women at midcentury could purchase many tableware patterns that were named after fabrics such as plaid and tweed. Some actually had textile weaves silk screened or molded onto

their surfaces, as in Red Wing Pottery's *Capistrano* (1953, cat. 19). Others simply hinted at fabric or bark through their abstract, handpainted surfaces (cat. 175).

Like the desire for color, the American love affair with eighteenth-century England and its colonies continued unabated through the 1940s and 1950s. At midcentury dishes depicting colonial kitchens were given away at grocery stores across the country (cat. 183). Although not directly associated with the birth of the nation, the related "peasant look" did evoke a quieter, less complicated past. Peasant-type wares had first appeared in the 1920s and continued to be produced after World War II, with initially primitive modeling and often handpainted decoration (cats. 13, 125, 184). Of all the patterns that were part of this rustic style, *Apple* (1939), *Desert Rose* (1940), and *Ivy* (1947) by Franciscan were especially successful. *Desert Rose* was in fact one of the most popular patterns of dinnerware ever distributed in the United States. By 1964 Franciscan had sold sixty million pieces of it (cat. 39).[78]

Not unlike colonial revival and peasant-style designs,

Cat. 185 Syracuse China conjured the exotic
tropics with its pattern *Flamingo Reeds* in 1951.

tableware in the Scandinavian taste was in many ways also a legacy of the prewar era. It was during the 1930s that glass and ceramics from Europe's far north first entered the country in large quantities. Generally undecorated, the clear glassware was often of bold form, while china was typically painted with a central floral motif and an outside border (cat. 119). Using these imports as models, and calling on designers who had seen Scandinavian tableware in Europe, American manufacturers created Nordic lines. By the early 1940s, as foreign imports were disappearing from the market, companies as diverse as Southern Potteries, Tiffin Glass, Steuben, and Franciscan were vying for the Scandinavian niche in the U.S. marketplace (cat. 62).[79]

After World War II, Scandinavian tableware, especially glass, returned to America. Some lines were wholly foreign in origin; others were actually designed by Americans for manufacture in northern Europe; and still others were domestic products that evoked Scandinavian aesthetics (cat. 118). A good example of the latter type was the Indiana Glass Company's *Norse* line of the mid-1950s.[80] By the end of the decade the "Swedish and Danish Modern" movements that were characterized at the time by refined, crystal-clear glass and restrained pottery gave way to an earthier craft look. In tableware this look would be manifest in the nationwide vogue for stoneware and textured glass that began in the 1950s but reached it zenith in the 1960s and early 1970s.

In addition to the sophisticated forms of Scandinavia, styles of other cultures still fascinated Americans just as they had before the war. In the 1940s and 1950s tropical motifs, such as Syracuse China's *Flamingo Reeds* (1951) and Purinton's pattern with palm trees (ca. 1950), continued to appear (cats. 170, 185). Similarly, the 1920s and 1930s affinity for southwestern designs was continued in patterns like Red Wing's *Desert* (1951, cat. 169) and Metlox's *Navajo* (1956). This theme broadened to embrace a full-blown western decorating craze. In tableware for the home, Vernon Kilns' *Winchester '73* (1949) pattern and its accompanying glassware by Heisey are fine examples of the western theme. But it was in commercial ware that images of the Old West appeared most frequently, thanks to the proliferation of steak houses across the country after the war (cat. 38).

In keeping with this fascination for things western, brightly colored California pottery remained popular and grew in stature in the marketplace until the mid-1950s. California-made tableware in the postwar era was a complicated mixture of styles united in their evocation of the casual life. The variety of West Coast pottery that was closest to prewar work embodied the look of studio crafts. Working in this genre were producers as diverse as Dorothy Thorpe and Edith Heath (cats. 177, 178). Of the two, Thorpe achieved greater national prominence. By the late 1930s and 1940s her elegant sandblasted glass was carried by high-end department stores and gift shops across the country and touched off a national vogue for glass with frosted decoration that lasted into the 1950s.

Other firms that evoked the craft aesthetic were Max Weil of California, Winfield Pottery, and American Ceramics Products Company. To suggest a handmade quality in their massproduced wares, these potteries produced thick-walled, somewhat primitive plates and tumblers ornamented with solid glazes and handpainted or incised motifs (cat. 186). This particular variety of the California craft look had an impact on some non–West Coast commercial makers. Although its wares certainly had a distinctive quality, the aesthetic developed by Glidden Pottery in Alfred, New York, for example, owed much to its California counterparts.

REVOLUTION AT THE TABLE

As the numerous stylistic currents that survived World War II to flourish in the diverse midcentury marketplace demonstrate, there was much truth in Frederick Rhead's statement in the early 1940s about the lack of originality in American design. But the seeds of change had been planted by the time Rhead made his remark. Russel Wright's *American Modern*, which appeared three years before, was arguably the first embodiment of a truly American aesthetic. In the 1940s and 1950s, American designers gained international fame through the creation of innovative shapes. Building on the success of *American Modern*, Russel and Mary Wright designed a series of fresh concepts in glass, ceramics, and plastic, all of organic or circular form and produced in colors ranging from white to earthy hues with names like *Nutmeg* and *Pepper*. Among his most outstanding designs were *Casual China* (1946), *Pinch* (1949), *Highlight* (1948), *White Clover* (1951), *Residential* (1953), *Esquire* (1955), and *Flair* (1959, cats. 66, 181, 182, 187).

These innovative wares, but especially *American Modern*, which remained in production for twenty years, transformed the American tabletop. More educated and wealthier than ever before, the American middle class often found the casual nature of such designs greatly appealing. The coupe-shaped plate that Wright featured in all of his pottery lines could be stacked to save space in the smaller houses and apartments of the era, and was perfect on buffet tables. Buffet-style dining had been introduced before World War II, but it became the norm in the 1940s and 1950s in many households, and as a result many designers incorporated rimless, stackable plates into their lines.[81]

In addition to Wright, one other designer greatly expanded the frontiers of American tableware—Eva Zeisel. Born in Hungary, Zeisel worked in Germany and Russia before coming to the United States in 1938, later obtaining a teaching post at Pratt Institute in New York (cat. 100). The strongly opinionated Zeisel gained stature in the design field through her teaching, lecturing, and writing. Following her creation of *Stratoware* (ca. 1941) for Sears, Roebuck & Co., Zeisel received her first major commission in tableware in this country in 1942–43, when Louis E. Hellmann of Castleton China asked her to design a dinner service (cats. 31, 188). The commission was sponsored by the Museum of Modern Art, and the vessels were to be overtly modern and the ultimate in educated good

| chapter five

Cat. 186 Pottery from Winfield in California and Glidden in New York State were designed for casual dining in the 1940s and 1950s.

Cat. 187 Russel Wright's *Casual China* for Iroquois
(1946), seen here with a *Highlight* bowl (1948), was
a sturdy and popular ware that was in production
until the 1960s.

taste. *Museum*, as the service was called, was marketed as the first truly modern example of American-made fine china. To create *Museum*, Zeisel drew from her extensive knowledge of prewar European modernist ceramics, especially German and Scandinavian designs, but the result was new and innovative. Made from warm, white-colored porcelain and less geometric than its European antecedents, Zeisel's design was a study in graceful curves. Once production began in 1945, *Museum* quickly became famous among critics around the world as the epitome of casual American modernism.

Like Wright, Zeisel took full advantage of her notoriety to gather other interesting commissions. Less formal than *Museum* were the multicolored *Town and Country* (ca. 1945, cat. 12) and *Tritone* (1954, cat. 180) lines, as well as the clear glass shape *Prestige* (1953, cat. 173, far left). Although they were more curvilinear than *Museum*, Zeisel's designs for *Tomorrow's Classic* (1949) and *Century* (ca. 1955) offered the customer the elegance of the earlier service at a lower cost. To Zeisel's dismay most American women found her work in its undecorated state too stark. Consequently, manufacturers applied a host of decal decorations and glazes to her shapes.

With Wright and Zeisel's work as the benchmark, some foreign competitors tried to develop wares that would compete in the American marketplace for the consumer who wanted contemporary design. England and Germany were by far the most successful in this effort. Although most English potteries continued to export traditional designs to the United States after the war, a few took great pains to develop modern lines complete with coupe-shaped plates specifically for the North American market. In 1952 Roy Midwinter of W. R. Midwinter in Staffordshire visited the United States to gain firsthand knowledge of consumer preferences. Impressed by the casual lifestyle emanating from the West Coast and by the informal creations of designers like Wright and Zeisel, Midwinter developed the *Fashion* shape for the Stylecraft brand (cat. 189). With its flaring rim and outswung handle the *Fashion* shape was heavily based on *Tomorrow's Classic* by Eva Zeisel. Furthermore, combining solid colors with striking decals was in keeping with the decorative practice Hall China used for Zeisel's lines.

While *Fashion* was consciously patterned on American prototypes, the contemporary designs produced by most English potteries were less stridently imitative. Although few designs were as imitative as *Fashion*, a significant number of English firms did invest in producing modern wares (cats. 90, 93). Like Roy Midwinter, Tom Arnold at Ridgway Pottery traveled to the United States and was inspired by the contemporary pottery he saw there. Upon his return to England he designed the somewhat conservative, but nonetheless modern, *Sapphire* shape for production in bone china. Following the suggestion of a buyer for B. Altman & Co. in New York, the shape was produced in earthenware with various surface

Cat. 188 Eva Zeisel's *Museum* was critically acclaimed in both America and Europe when introduced in 1946.

patterns, including *Homemaker* (ca. 1957), which interestingly was copied by Homer Laughlin in Ohio (cat. 190).[82]

Germany's most important contribution to the American tabletop at midcentury was actually achieved in collaboration with an American importer and an American design office. In 1952 the Rosenthal-Block China Corporation in New York commissioned the well-known firm of Raymond Loewy Associates to create a series of designs for distribution in the United States. The first of these was *Exquisit* (1951–52), quickly followed by the *Model 2000* shape (cat. 107). Produced by Rosenthal and available in a wide range of colors and patterns, these lines were immensely popular among young sophisticated consumers for nearly two decades. Although other German companies tried to emulate this success with contemporary designs in white porcelain, none achieved the widespread distribution in the United States of the Loewy lines (cat. 99).

Drawing inspiration from this shape revolution, numerous domestic and foreign manufacturers brought out lines that were oriented less toward timeless elegance and more toward current fashion. A number of California firms were

Cat. 190 Ridgway Pottery's *Homemaker* pattern (ca. 1957) and Homer Laughlin's copy (bowl) were both produced by sophisticated printing technology.

OPPOSITE:
Cat. 189 *Tomorrow's Classic* (1949, left) was the inspiration for W. R. Midwinter's *Fashion* shape (ca. 1954).

OVERLEAF:
Cat. 191 Prototypes like this tea set by Viktor Schreckengost for a California pottery (ca. 1950) were integral to the design process.

foremost in offering tony fashion pottery for ultramodern living. Some of these wares were even suitable for the coming space age. During the 1950s firms like Vernon Kilns, Metlox Potteries, and Franciscan produced shapes and decorations that celebrated the freedom of a casual lifestyle (cat. 192). The work of Frank Irwin, Bob Allen, and Mel Shaw at Metlox was particularly interesting. Featuring angular and cantilevered shapes for hollowware and coupe-shaped plates, these designs were given upbeat, carefree, and sometimes exotic names like *Freeform* and *Confetti*, with surface decoration such as *California Aztec* (1955).

Some of these designs pushed beyond the simply casual to evoke the worlds of contemporary art and outer space. Metlox's *California Mobile* and *California Freeform* patterns (1954–55) were reminiscent of artist Alexander Calder's famous kinetic sculpture, while Franciscan's *Starburst* (1954) and the more formal *Starry Night* (1952) looked to the heavens that would soon be alive with satellites and rocket ships (cats. 193, 194). On examples of china and glass from other areas of the country, shooting stars, atomic particles, and scientific imagery also appeared. Inland Glass Works' *Modern* carafe (1949) and Hall China's atomic-inspired *Fantasy* (ca. 1950) reflected this taste for the scientific and the heavenly (cats. 23, 176).

The combination of revolutionary shapes and the casual California look unleashed a nationwide trend for contemporary ceramics and glass. In 1952 Alfred Duhrssen, president of Commercial Decal, commented, "The ratio of present patterns is tipping more and more in favor of modern—and particularly to a new kind of modern, one which offers us the chance to tap a vast market."[83] Soon inexpensive, American-made dishes that were stylish in their decoration and modern in their shape streamed from numerous factories throughout the country. In 1955 an editor for *Crockery and Glass Journal* proclaimed that "Ohio Valley dinnerware . . . is a tremendously 'new' product. . . . In short, the Ohio Valley dinnerware industry . . . is a completely revitalized one."[84] The same could have been said for Red Wing Pottery in Red Wing, Minnesota; Southern Potteries in Erwin, Tennessee; Tamac Pottery in Perry, Oklahoma; and Stetson Potteries in Lincoln, Illinois (cats. 195, 196).

Virtually every pottery in America that serviced the middle-range and lower-priced markets produced lines during the late 1940s and 1950s that were contemporary in spirit. To capture this quality, most used pastel colors and surface patterns that were overtly artistic in their asymmetry and bold graphic quality. Plates were almost invariably coupe shaped, sometimes even square or asymmetrical, and hollowware was often nontraditional in form (cat. 197). Among the most interesting of these designs was Viktor Schreckengost's *Primitive* pattern on his *Freeform* shape (1955, cat. 198). The surface decoration of Stone Age hunters and animals was based on ancient cave paintings. Like *Primitive*, the *Freeform* shape was also very animated. Especially interesting was the use of tripod spiked feet to support teapots and cups.

CASUAL ELEGANCE FOR THE FORMAL TABLE

While sometimes radical imagery from the outer reaches of space, the visible world of earth, and the hidden worlds of science and the imagination was making its way onto less-expensive earthenware and glass in the late 1940s and 1950s, a more conservative transformation was occurring at the highest end of the market. Because the porcelaneous bodies of true porcelain and bone china were more expensive to produce than earthenware, they tended to be more traditionally styled. Designs like Eva Zeisel's *Museum* and Raymond Loewy Associates' *Exquisit* and *Model 2000* shapes were the exceptions, not the rule. Whereas consumers could afford to tire of an inexpensive set of earthenware dishes featuring fashion-oriented or novelty decoration (see pp. 54–56), those who spent large amounts on fine china knew they would have to live with their decision, often for a lifetime. As a result most consumers were far less inclined to gamble with unfamiliar modern trends. Nevertheless, makers of fine china were affected by contemporary design, and the same was true of crystal stemware.

Because of shortages of foreign goods caused by World War II, American production of fine china and crystal expanded. In the 1940s and 1950s Lenox, Franciscan, Syracuse China, Pickard China Company, Flintridge China Company, and Shenango Pottery Company all expanded or initiated production of fine china, while glassmakers like Tiffin, Fostoria, Heisey, Seneca, and Bryce Brothers tried to take over more of the market for high-end stemware. The most popular glass designs, which were typically more conservative than those of pottery, featured either acid-etched flowers or cut abstract patterns. Inspired by more freeform Scandinavian and Italian contemporary glass, some firms ventured beyond tradition. Fostoria, for example, produced fashion-oriented colored glass in modern shapes during the 1950s and 1960s (cat. 72).

Developments in fine china were more multifaceted. The tradition of the ivory body remained standard among American producers, and the coupe-shaped plate became a viable option in fine china. As in earthenware, lighter colors prevailed, sometimes celadon or gray. By the early 1950s wares produced in California with solid color bodies were highly influential (cat. 8). Similarly, platinum trim that would match their sterling flatware became all the rage among brides around 1951. America's fine china makers, who were heavily dependent on the bridal market, quickly introduced patterns trimmed with the silver-colored metal rather than the traditional gold (cats. 60, 193). The same was true of European china producers. Having seen their production peak and then decline in the mid-1950s, the English were especially interested in preserving their share of the U.S. fine china business. They too introduced American-style coupe-shaped plates and a limited number of modern shapes. In the end, however,

OPPOSITE:
Cat. 192 Taking a cue from modern art in the 1950s, Metlox Potteries offered some of the most animated tableware shapes ever made in America.

Cat. 194 The casual pattern *Starburst* was a resounding success for Franciscan during the 1950s.

OPPOSITE:
Cat. 193 Franciscan's *Starry Night* pattern (ca. 1952) makes dramatic use of heavenly imagery, yet apparently failed with the buying public.

Cat. 197 Taylor, Smith, & Taylor's *Conversation*
shape (1949) featured a distinctive squared
plate.

OPPOSITE:
Cat. 195 Franciscan's *True China* shape (ca.
1958) included lively hollowware designs and
surface patterns, such as *Lute Song* (1959).

Cat. 196 Tamac's tableware line of the same
name (ca. 1946) recalls natural formations and
was especially suitable for outdoor dining.

Cat. 198 Sporting tripod feet and ancient hunting scenes, Viktor Schreckengost's *Free Form* shape with *Primitive* pattern stood out from the crowd in 1955.

most Americans wanted tradition when they bought bone china by Spode, Minton, Wedgwood, Doulton, or Worcester (cat. 199).

Although it was not considered as desirable as American or European china, Japanese porcelain also made steady gains in the United States during the 1950s. Because leading brands such as Noritake were much less expensive than anything offered in fine china by competitors, Americans began to buy large quantities of it. In addition its hard body held up better than earthenware in dishwashers, and its design was invariably a mix of conservatism with a hint of the contemporary. Low cost, appealing design, and durability were features that Americans loved. By the early 1980s Noritake China led in the United States, accounting for a full third of total department store fine china sales (cat. 116).

The Reign of the Consumer
The trend begun in the 1950s emphasizing design in both pattern and shape in glass and ceramic tableware, continued apace in the 1960s but was tempered in the 1970s by an increased awareness of the consumer. The tableware industry found itself in a design flux as fashion dictated contemporary-

style shapes and art-conscious surface decoration while the market continued to reveal a steady propensity for conservative, traditional patterns.

The influence of industry-heralded designers, who enjoyed a degree of popular fame due to marketing schemes aimed at associating sophistication with "designer" goods, could be seen throughout the 1960s. Designers and buyers alike clamored for a complete rethinking of style and aesthetics. "What we need is a wider selection with more frequent changes, and a fashion look," commented one buyer for Gimbel Brothers in Philadelphia.[85] Textile designer Marion V. Dorn complained at the time that "dinnerware designing has fallen into a rut."[86] As the 1960s progressed, the call for change prompted many manufacturers to hire freelance designers, whose names could be used as a part of the design concept itself, to develop new shapes, bodies, and fashion-conscious surface decoration.

FOREIGN FASHIONS FOR THE UNITED STATES
During the late 1950s and 1960s, as the Japanese ceramics industry captured the inexpensive china market and squeezed most American potteries out of business or drove them to

Cat. 199 With *Josephine* (1943, plate) and *Wildflower* (1945) Wedgwood encouraged conservative Americans to buy English bone china during World War II.

Cat. 200 After initially producing its own porcelain, Jackson Internationale had its designs manufactured in Japan by 1960.

OPPOSITE:
Cat. 201 In 1952 Jean Luce's *Butterflies* pattern gave a hint of color to this classic Arzberg shape from 1931.

consolidate and concentrate on hotel and restaurant ware, European manufacturers, along with a few remaining American companies, competed for the sophisticated consumer. Following Rosenthal-Block's lead in hiring Raymond Loewy Associates to design dinnerware in the early 1950s, some firms employed well-known freelance designers to revamp their looks with new shapes and decoration. For example, in 1952 the Arzberg factory in Germany introduced a series by the famous Parisian designer Jean Luce; the company hoped the new airy surface patterns for its stark white porcelain would make it more appealing. Four years later Jackson International had Paul McCobb radically overhaul the look of its product, which was then being made in Japan rather than the United States (cats. 200, 201).

The British tried especially hard to gain market share in America during the 1960s and 1970s. One of the leaders of the avant-garde in British tableware design throughout this period was the firm of W. R. Midwinter, led by the husband and wife team of Roy and Eve Midwinter. Together with David Queensberry, a professor of ceramics at the Royal College of Art, they developed a new look that was at once casual and refined.[87] The most successful of their collaborations was the *Fine* shape of 1962 (cat. 204, coffeepot at left). The form recalled the earlier can-shaped designs of Susie Cooper (cat. 205) along with the designs of Hans Theodor Baumann and Tapio Wirkkala for Rosenthal. Queensberry's shape, with its straight sides and concave neck, was a much more controlled design than the fluid forms of the previous decade.[88] It related most closely to that of a butter churn. By evoking such a warm and comforting image, the shape appealed to both modern

and traditional sensibilities and became very popular, though primarily in Britain. In 1964 Midwinter launched the line in America with a publicity tour by David Queensberry, whose celebrity status was no doubt helped by his dashing good looks and the fact that, as the Marquess of Queensberry, he was a member of the British aristocracy.[89]

Although Midwinter never achieved a large market share in the United States, its influence had an impact on the general look of British ceramics in the American market. Critics championed the new styles and created the inaccurate impression that modern design was what the consumer wanted from Britain. Large manufacturers there felt pressure to respond not only to Midwinter's and Rosenthal's success among sophisticated consumers but also to the growing demand for Scandinavian designs in both the British home market and America. An experimental move toward severe, straight-sided or angular-sided shapes developed. In bone china this shift was an almost complete disaster. Spode's *Royal College* shape (1958, cat. 93) limped along, with little success either at home or abroad, despite its many design awards. In 1963 Wedgwood produced a modern-style version of its traditional black basalt body designed by Robert Minkin that failed to sell altogether. Far more commercial were cylindrical shapes by American companies like Red Wing (*Cylinder*, 1962) and Metlox (*Studio Potter*, 1969, cat. 208). Expensive versions like Lenox's *Innovation* shape (ca. 1969, cat. 202) failed, while earthenware potteries relied on their lower prices and tradition for contemporary design to succeed in the marketplace.

The failure of large British manufacturers to produce successful contemporary lines was in part due to the designs themselves, the timid marketing effort put forth by the producers, and the impenetrable will of the consumer to accept only traditional designs from old-line British manufacturers.[90] The only sector of the market that was receptive to modern British designs chose casual stoneware, a heavy clay body that enjoyed enormous popular appeal across the board in America. The use of casual stoneware grew dramatically in the 1960s, having been introduced from Scandinavia in the late 1950s. Until that time stoneware had been used in America mostly by studio potters, and so the recognizable hard clay body was identified in the mind of consumers with handmade artistic pottery. It was this association that made stoneware

ideally suited to the trend in casual dining that developed in postwar Europe and America. Factory-produced stoneware supplied the look of expensive hand-thrown studio pottery at a fraction of the cost. Followers of the fashion to go "back to nature" in everything from clothes to food to lifestyle in the 1960s and 1970s embraced stoneware designs with their rough-hewn textures and handcrafted looks. Simultaneously, the gourmet cooking movement that began in the 1960s and spread through American kitchens and retail stores in the next decade heightened the desire for stoneware.

Mugs were among the first forms in stoneware to appear in large quantities on the market. In the early 1960s the American importer Otagiri distributed handsome, substantial vessels that recalled the look of ancient Japanese ceramics. These vessels were so stylish that they were suitable for use in entertaining and helped further the trend for using stoneware on social occasions as well as for everyday family meals.

Pottery manufacturers in America, Britain, Europe, and Japan all contributed to the casual trend in tableware with stoneware lines that were smart enough for evening entertaining. The epitome of the so-called Danish Modern look was established first through Dansk's *Flamestone* line (1957), with a stark form and matte finish (cat. 121). In the United States,

Cat. 202 Lenox China went modern with its *Innovation* line in 1969, but women in search of traditional patterns rebuffed it.

Cat. 203 With names like *Arabesque* and *Samarkand* (1962–63) and *Potter's Wheel* (1973, plate), Denby brought to mind handmade ware from exotic lands.

Edith Heath Ceramics, Franciscan, and Iron Mountain Stoneware led the way with stoneware production (cat. 177). By the early 1970s even Lenox had entered the field with its *Temperware* line.

The most successful British producers of stoneware were smaller potteries such as Portmeirion Potteries and Joseph Bourne, which was marketed simply as Denby after the town in rural Derbyshire where the factory was located. Among Denby's first stoneware lines to be marketed in the United States were *Ode* (1961), which won a gold medal for excellence at the California State Fair the year it was introduced, and *Echo* (1962) in very subdued pastel gold and blue.[91] They were followed by the introduction in the U.S. market of the more radical designs *Samarkand/Arabesque* (1962–63, cat. 203) and *Chevron* (1963).[92] Midwinter joined the stoneware trade in 1972, with the development of its highly successful *Stonehenge* shape. Although it looked like stoneware, in reality it was made of an earthenware body covered with experimental iron oxide glazes that created the look of pitted stoneware.[93] Portmeirion was more successful in Britain but exported its stoneware to America, as did many other foreign makers in the mid-1960s and early 1970s. Noritake Company introduced its first stoneware body—*Nitto*—in 1970. Rosenthal entered the field the following year.

A WEALTH OF COLOR AND PATTERN

Along with the call for new directions in shape and body, the early 1960s brought a desire for new approaches to surface decoration. As the decade dawned, simplicity still reigned in formal china design for the bridal market—classic white or ivory bodies with simple gold or platinum bands. Less formal styling used leafy patterns dispersed randomly or in borders. Tall, thin stemware was sometimes made to match ceramic patterns, as in Bjørn Wiinblad's *Romance* (1962–64) designed for Rosenthal (cat. 108). The influence of Scandinavia could be seen as well, especially in casual glassware and barware, which favored simple unadorned forms in clear or sometimes smoky colors.

During the 1960s and early 1970s more exotic use of color and pattern prevailed in casual tableware. "Back to nature" and the "country look" were catchphrases for a resurgence in the use of browns and earth tones in tableware color. In 1965 Block China introduced Gerald Gulotta's *España* shape, which was available in a dark brown matte glaze called *Tierra*, or "earth" in Spanish. English producers also favored these colors, using them as stripes and all-over glazes. Midwinter's *Flowersong* (1972) on a rustic milk can shape is a particularly vivid example of this aesthetic (cat. 91). Along with earthy tones, bold colors were soon widespread in contemporary pottery and glass design. Hot, bright hues typical of a Mediterranean or Central American palette found their way onto tableware in designs with pattern names to match, such as Midwinter's *Sienna* (1962) and Villeroy & Boch's *Acapulco* (1969), evoking the romance of travel and exotic locales (cat. 204, right).

In glass the third quarter of the century saw bright colors reemerge, along with bolder, more angular shapes. Taking advantage of their long tradition for whimsical, colored glassware, Italian stemware manufacturers contributed a host of exciting vessels to the American table in the 1960s and 1970s (cat. 126).

The latest crazes in the fashion and art worlds spilled over into tableware design as well. The Op Art movement gave rise to a plethora of patterns that created optical illusions with superimposed geometric shapes in varying degrees of saturation, such as Gerald Gulotta's *Evolution* pattern on Jack Prince's shape *Transition* (1968) for Block China (cat. 127, right). The Op Art movement lasted about two years, culminating in the important exhibition of British artist Bridget Riley's work at the Museum of Modern Art entitled *The Responsive Eye* (1965), but the impact on surface pattern design lingered for several years. Susie Cooper's *Diablo* pattern (1969) for Wedgwood clearly owes its inspiration to an Op Art aesthetic (cat. 205, cup and saucer). Artists themselves got into the act, applying silkscreened transfers of their work to tableware, as in the series of plates for Wedgwood (1968–69) with prints by Scottish artist Eduardo Paolozzi. The Italian artist Piero Fornasetti also applied his designs to ceramics in this way (cats. 204, 206).

Clothing fashions were a logical source for designs during the 1960s and 1970s. The same bright "psychedelic" colors and wild patterns found on the backs of runway models in New York, Paris, and London emerged on the rims of plates, mostly in inexpensive earthenware production, but with a few notable exceptions in porcelain such as Lenox's patterns *Fantasies* and *Firesong* (1971, cat. 202).[94] Some designers even came from the world of fashion, textiles, and the graphic arts, such as Mary Quant and Barbara Brown in London, and Jack Prince and Peter Max in New York.[95] The popularity of hot colors was tempered in the early 1970s by a debate in the press over poisoning from lead and cadmium in ceramics. Some designs, including Gulotta's and Prince's highly innovative *Chromatics* (1970, cat. 207), had to be withdrawn from sale altogether when alternative ways to produce them could not be found. The overall result was a move toward softer, less-saturated colors that mitigated concerns over contamination by using colors that were free of toxic chemicals (cat. 42).

Like fashion, other aspects of popular culture infiltrated surface design in the 1960s and 1970s. "Flower power" sprouted daisies on everything from placemats to coffee mugs in 1965 and lasted through the early 1970s with patterns such as Midwinter's *Flowersong* (1972). Poppies became "groovy"

Cat. 204 Bright colors and wild patterns were all the rage in the 1960s, as reflected in wares by Midwinter (left), Wedgwood (center), and Villeroy & Boch (right).

when the Metlox pattern *Wild Poppy* (1972) showed up on
the breakfast table of America's favorite singing family, television's *The Partridge Family* (cat. 208). Emphasis on the great
outdoors and the environmental movement brought the
Mother Nature look and "mushroom mania" in patterns like
Ernestine Pottery's *Champignons* (ca. 1975, cat. 125), while the
"Age of Aquarius" ensured a demand for zodiac designs
throughout the early 1970s. The U.S. bicentennial in 1976
gave rise to red, white, and blue designs like Interpace's *Independence* shape (1973, cat. 41), and even the advent of the block-
buster museum exhibition prompted a tableware response
when *Treasures of Tutankhamen* traveled the country in 1976
and 1977.[96]

All of these trends lasted no longer than a few years at a
time and none was more significant than the others, but taken
together they indicate the type of frenzied pace and random
choice that characterized contemporary tableware design in
this period. Perhaps the ultimate expression of this direction
was the reinvention in the mid-1970s of the mix-and-match
concept by Robert Floyd of Fitz and Floyd. Service plates,
which had not been popular since before World War II, suddenly reappeared, now updated with solid bands of color. On
top would be set a smaller plate with an elaborate all-over design or patterned border that allowed yet another plate to be
laid on top of it (cat. 112). The result was a visual feast of
dishes in which the tableware design could change with every

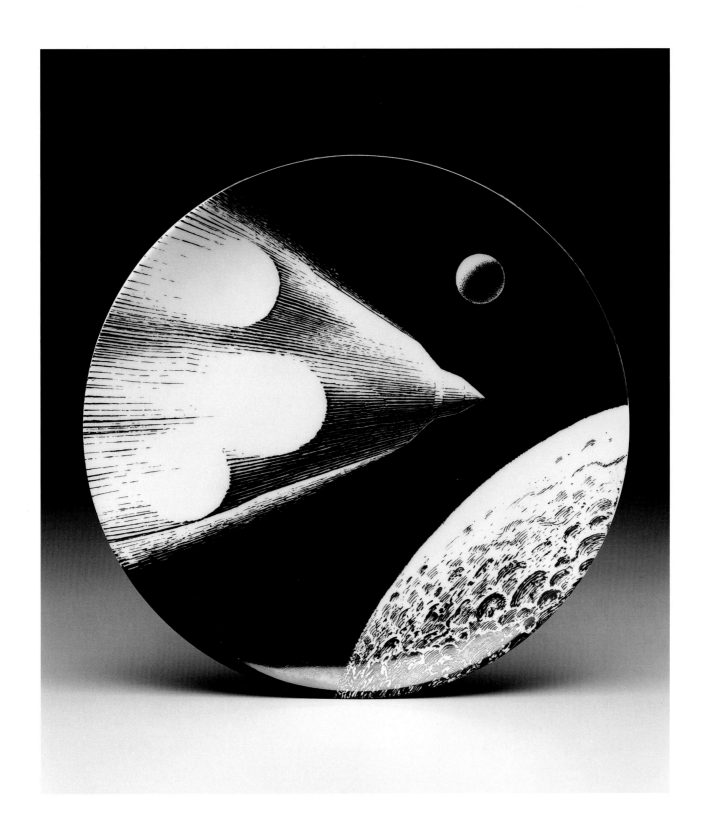

Cat. 206 Piero Fornasetti's *Man in Space* series
(1966) demonstrated his bold and often surreal
application of graphic design to tableware.

Cat. 207 *Chromatics* (1970) by Block China was acclaimed for its sophisticated color schemes and clever stacking design.

Cat. 208 Trendy Day-Glo colors appropriately adorned Metlox Potteries' *Wild Poppy* pattern of 1972.

course. Ironically, this new, fresh concept hearkened back to the elaborate multiple-course meals of the turn of the century, an idea spurred by the growing emphasis among some people on sophisticated gourmet dining and formal entertaining in the 1970s and 1980s.

Yet this mix-and-match concept could be applied to casual tableware with equal ease. Stackable lines were very popular, and most companies, particularly Mikasa and Block, were designing suites of coordinating dishes, placemats, and glasses that recalled the harlequin sets of the 1930s (cat. 207). This sense of flexibility was the one enduring contemporary stylistic legacy to survive into the 1980s. All other attempts by designers and manufacturers to modernize the American tableware consumer seemed destined to fail in the long term. The result was a consolidation of the entire industry from top to bottom. Patterns were dropped, and companies merged or closed. Ultimately by the 1980s, when corporate restructuring placed a priority on the bottom line, the consumer voice would prevail, and traditional styling would signal the end of fad-driven design.

TRADITION SPELLS SUCCESS

While industrial designers called for an "out with the old, in with the new" approach to tableware design in the 1960s, most consumers never strayed from conservative "good taste," especially where expensive tableware was concerned. There was no risk in choosing patterns that linked the present with the past, and in almost every survey reported by industry publications, consumers time and again made their preferences known. Yet designers and, more important, manufacturers persisted in attempting to move the consumer along a more contemporary path, targeting much marketing to the younger audience of brides. The problem for manufacturers was that many younger brides may well have wanted to entertain less formally than their mothers, but they also wanted to maintain their social status as a good housewives. One survey reported in 1969 that more than 78 percent of young women rated being a homemaker an important career and that six out of seven girls considered the ability to "entertain graciously" as "very important."[97] That meant that most young brides would probably continue taking very little risk when it came to purchasing sets of formal china and glassware, perhaps considering contemporary looks only for less expensive informal tableware.

In 1960 the bride had much to choose from, as jewelry and department stores were still stocking many prewar patterns. This situation changed as the decade wore on when British, European, and American companies succumbed to rising costs and increased competition from Japan. Manufacturers eventually consolidated and withdrew many pre- and post-war lines and patterns just as the industry itself underwent massive corporate restructuring. What remained were the traditional best-sellers—patterns in earthenware like Franciscan's *Desert Rose* and *Apple*, Mason's *Vista*, Wedgwood's *Embossed Queens Ware*, and Spode's *Jewel* and *Buttercup*, as well as patterns in fine china featuring fruit, flowers, and ivy borders

Fig. 5.9 Wedgwood beckoned female consumers with 18th-century elegance.

or simple gold and platinum bands (fig. 5.9). Another twenty years elapsed before most of these patterns were withdrawn. During the 1960s and 1970s they were the mainstays of formal tableware production. Among British manufacturers, the two greatest success stories from this era, Wedgwood and Waterford, recognized their niche and never strayed far from that path. Most of the other firms were swallowed up in the futile attempt to drive the consumer down another, more contemporary path.

From the outset in 1960 advocates of traditional design delineated three necessary tenets of tradition in tableware: "a feeling of warmth; formality and elegance; and classical themes."[98] The conservative consumer found instant reinforcement of these characteristics in the guise of the new first lady, Mrs. John F. Kennedy. With her handsome husband and growing young family, Jacqueline Bouvier Kennedy embodied the ideal housewife on a mission to create a beautiful life for her family. That beauty was epitomized in her decision to restore the new family home, the White House, with a sense of formality and elegance. The style to be used? Without a doubt, it had to be early American.

It is no wonder that practically every housewife (and by extension, every tableware consumer) in the United States tuned in on the evening of February 14, 1962, to view the televised tour of the White House restoration conducted by the first lady herself. It was the largest television audience in history, and for weeks afterward the pages of home furnishings publications were alive with articles on her choices for everything from fabrics to tableware.[99] When Kennedy filled the White House with traditional classical antiques, she provided the decorative model for the average consumer—even if one could not afford originals, reproductions gave the same look. Against such a traditional backdrop, she used Lenox china from the White House collection, antique flatware, and simple clear stemware from Morgantown Glassware Guild in West Virginia. The subsequent commercial success of Morgantown's *President's House* line after 1961 was assured (cat. 135).

Although Jacqueline Kennedy chose a domestically produced stemware, the occupancy of the White House by its first president of Irish ancestry is often credited with creating interest in Waterford crystal in America in the early 1960s. Before then Waterford had been a little-known specialty line in exclusive department stores in a few major cities. According to company executives working at the time, John Kennedy's much-heralded visit to Ireland in 1963 awakened massive pride across America in traditional Irish crafts, including handcut glassware (see pp. 218–21).[100] Whatever his influence, the fact remains that the heavy cut crystal of Waterford found a newly receptive audience in the American consumer, who had previously preferred thin, plain, or etched stemware. By 1969 a survey reported that nearly 75 percent of young brides preferred "hand cut glass or crystal."[101] By 1982 another survey placed Waterford as the "number one crystal brand" and termed it the "standard against which all other brands are compared."[102] Much of the crystal's appeal no doubt rested on its resemblance to old Irish glass, and indeed many of Waterford's shapes were reproductions of antique glass.

The same preference for antiques could be found in the popularity of museum reproductions and patriotic adaptations in tableware. The leading producer of reproduction china was the firm of Mottehedah. Antiques dealers for over forty years before going into the ceramics business, this husband and wife team fashioned their first products in 1962 after designs in books and antique pieces in their personal collection. Employing slogans like "reproductions for connoisseurs by connoisseurs," the Mottehedahs began with reproductions of French transfer-printed earthenware from Creil and continued with Chinese export porcelain and Old Paris porcelain from the early nineteenth century (fig. 5.11).[103] Their wares joined others on the market that recalled eighteenth- and early-nineteenth-century patterns or shapes and provided the look of the antique at an affordable price, including Spode's prewar *Lowestoft* line and Richard-Ginori's *Antico Doccia*, *Vecchio Ginori*, and *Impero* shapes of the 1950s and 1960s (cats. 92, 124).

While no other first lady had quite the influence on tableware trends that Jacqueline Kennedy did, the choices of subsequent first ladies were always reported and discussed—especially Rosalynn Carter's decision to used handmade stoneware and blown stemware for a White House luncheon in 1977.[104] Her attempts to make the White House less formal were later reversed when Ronald Reagan succeeded Jimmy Carter as president in 1980. The new first lady, Nancy Reagan, ordered the largest, most complete dinner service in the history of the White House from Lenox in a regal, traditional style. Even the ware from Fitz and Floyd used in the executive offices, private quarters, and *Air Force One* was classically elegant (cat. 113).

Despite marketing efforts throughout the 1960s that directed modern designs toward younger consumers, buyers in 1970 reported that "the traditional bride, and her traditional choices are still very much in evidence."[105] That sentiment remained unchanged in the early 1980s, when consumer testing revealed an overwhelming desire for simple, classic designs.[106] Much had stayed the same: although changes in fashion between 1880 and 1980 periodically dictated brighter colors, bolder patterns, or more modernist shapes in costly fine china and crystal, the nature of these products was con-

Orchid SETS THE STYLE FOR SMART TABLES

The fashion-wise woman completes her costume with a carefully selected accent — a smart dash of color — an exquisitely set jewel. Beautiful hand-wrought crystal brings that same added styling to an attractive table setting. Its graceful lines complimented by a dainty, etched design, Heisey ORCHID *pattern is the perfect jewel-like accent for your own table ensemble. For your gala party occasions or your simpler everyday needs, choose charming* ORCHID *crystal at your Heisey dealer. A. H. Heisey & Co., Newark, Ohio.*

THE FINEST IN GLASSWARE, MADE IN AMERICA BY HAND

Fig. 5.10 A. H. Heisey employed subliminal sexual imagery to draw attention to its *Orchid* glassware pattern from the 1950s.

Fig. 5.11 Mottehedah's ceramic reproductions of the early 1960s looked back to the 18th century.

sistently conservative. Whether hosting luncheons in the 1920s or holiday meals in the 1970s, women typically preferred plain dishes of traditional shape and color in formal situations.

The opposite was often true in the case of cheaper wares used for occasions that were not as important and ritualized. When less was at stake, the attitude could be more casual and the dishes more fashion- and fad-oriented. Thus bright colors swept across America every thirty to forty years beginning in the 1880s. Botanical motifs ranged from delicate blossoms at the turn of the century to geometric art deco flowers in the 1930s to free-form fungi in the 1970s. It was easy and fun to dress up your table as you might yourself with something that was understood to be transitory, meant to give a few years of pleasure before being replaced. In the end the parallel strands of formal conservatism and casual playfulness wove a complex cover for the American tabletop.

Notes

1. Hannah 1986, 31.

2. Blaszczyk 1987, 23–24.

3. Madarasz 1998, 95–97; and Blaszczyk 1995, 144.

4. Blaszczyk 1995, 112.

5. "Decal Firm Is 100 Years Old," CGJ 158:6 (June 1956): 53. Palm, Fechteler & Co.'s factory was in Weehawken, New Jersey.

6. McKee 1966, 13.

7. For information on Gaertner, see Blaszczyk 1995, 239–40, 255. On decorating in the late nineteenth century, see Blaszczyk 1987, 26.

8. CGJ 92:6 (June 1920): 6.

9. "The New Commercial Decal, Inc.: American Decals for Americans," CGJ 143:6 (Dec. 1948): 8–11. The archives of this firm are at the National Museum of American History, Washington, D.C.

10. For design and competition in the pressed glass industry, see Blaszczyk 1995, chap. 2.

11. Ibid., 257.

12. For information on brilliant cut glass, see Spillman and Farraf 1977.

13. For a discussion of the Newark show, see Shifman 1998.

14. "1919 Best American Pottery Year," PGBS 22 (19 Aug. 1920): 8–9.

15. For the first of several reports on the subject, see USDC 1924.

16. For a discussion of how Wedgwood reduced its lines, see Buckley 1990, 83 ff.

17. For a discussion of the work done at the Carnegie Institute, see "Carnegie Tech School Advances Ceramic Design," CGJ 118:6 (June 1936): 17, 36; and Streichler 1963, 177 ff.

18. "The Industrial Designer Takes His Place in the Sun," CGJ 119:1 (July 1936): 26.

19. For a discussion of Rhead's importance, see Blaszczyk 1987, 54 ff.

20. "The Organization of a Decorative Ceramics Research Department," PGBS 26 (14 Dec. 1922): 109.

21. USPA 1940, 49.

22. For a thorough discussion of the rise of early industrial design in the United States, see Streichler 1963.

23. For information on Sakier, see Piña 1996.

24. CGJ 114:3 (Mar. 1934): 28.

25. For a discussion of Pyrex's development, see Blaszczyk 1995, chaps. 7–9.

26. "The Industry Needs Ceramic Artist," CI 10 (May 1928): 147.

27. "The Future of Product Design," MP 20 (June 1943): 76.

28. Beard and Beard 1928, 722, cited in Streichler 1963, 36.

29. V. Schreckengost interview 1995.

30. Streichler 1963, 73.

31. For a discussion of museum and department store shows, see ibid., 70–90; and Shifman 1998, 28.

32. From C. Merz's And Then Came Ford, cited in Streichler 1963, 38.

33. For a discussion of color in tableware, see Blaszczyk 1987, 101–15.

34. Denker 1989, 37.

35. CGJ 104:2 (19 May 1927): 10.

36. Marshall Field [1930].

37. For discussions of Fostoria's colored line, see Blaszczyk 1987, 592–94; and Piña 1996.

38. USTC 1936, 87.

39. For information on Du Pont's acquisition of Roessler & Hasslacher in 1930, see "Roessler & Hasslacher Acquired by E. I. Du Pont de Nemours & Co.," CGJ 108:4 (Apr. 1930): 66–67. On Du Pont's advances in the 1930s, see "Du Pont Shows New Effects in Color," 120:5 (May 1937): 47; and "Du Pont Pre-Tests Ceramic Colors," 122:3 (Mar. 1938): 2.

40. "Right from the Kiln," *CGJ* 121:5 (Sept. 1937): 27. For an informative advertisement see 138:1 (Jan. 1946): 30.

41. "New Dinnerware Spurs Domestic China Production," *CGJ* 109:4 (Apr. 1931): 37.

42. Blaszczyk 1987, 156.

43. The members of the California Pottery Guild were Bauer, Gladding, McBean & Co., Metlox, Pacific Clay Products, and Vernon Kilns; see "Five Firms Organize California Pottery Guild in Group Campaign," *CGJ* 120:4 (Apr. 1937): 50.

44. For a detailed discussion of developments at Homer Laughlin in this period, see Blaszczyk 1987, 148–62.

45. "Conference Adopts Standard Colors," *CGJ* 120:5 (May 1937): 20.

46. For a discussion of this early phase of modernism, see Davies 1983.

47. "Is the Depression Raising Decorating Standards?" *CGJ* 110:2 (Jan 1932): 61.

48. "Some Definitions and a Bit of History of Modernism," *CGJ* 114:2 (Feb. 1934): 12.

49. "West Awakens to Modern Lamps," *CGJ* 107:2 (Feb. 1929): 48.

50. "Buyers Talk About Modern Dinnerware," *CGJ* 114:4 (Apr. 1934): 16–17.

51. For a discussion of these efforts, see Blaszczyk 1987, 131–43.

52. *CGJ* 107:10 (Oct. 1929): 7; "Leigh Ware," 107:4 (Apr. 1929): 29; and "Modernism," 107:9 (Sept. 1929): 13.

53. *CGJ* 108:1 (Jan. 1930): 29.

54. According to *CGJ* 116:5 (May 1935): 32, Leigh Potters reopened in 1935. It is no longer listed in trade directories after 1938. For an advertisement of the colored glazed ware, see *CGJ* 114:3 (Mar. 1934): 8.

55. *CGJ* 114:3 (Mar. 1934): 8.

56. For a discussion of the changes at Steuben see Blaszczyk 1995, chap. 8.

57. "Regulate and Control Shape and Pattern Production," *CGJ* 118:3 (Mar. 1936): 14.

58. "The Ceramic Designer in Wartime," *CGJ* 131:1 (July 1942): 46, written by J. P. Thorley; "American Dishes: Home Product Fills Gap Made by War and Boycott," *Life* 9:11 (9 Sept. 1940): 76–79.

59. "The Full Meaning of an 'American Design,'" *CGJ* 128:3 (Mar. 1941): 43.

60. For information on the design team, see "Libbey Studies Post War Designs," 135:5 *CGJ* (Nov. 1944): 48.

61. On how designers became more organized as a profession, see Streichler 1963, chap. 7; "Designers Listed," *CGJ* 132:2 (Feb. 1943): 46; and "Designers 'Bill of Rights' Drafted Against Chisellers," 135:1 (July 1944): 39, 68.

62. "Can Dinnerware Design Be Streamlined? Can It Be Standardized, Simplified?," *CGJ* 132:1 (Jan. 1943): 68.

63. "Accentuate the Positive," *CGJ* 152:5 (May 1953): 30.

64. "Let Design Be Worthy of the Body," *CGJ* 138:1 (Jan. 1946): 56.

65. For more on Lenox see Denker 1989.

66. "Factory Correspondence No. 213" (6 July 1933). Fostoria Archives. "Castleton's Patterns Research-Tested," *CGJ* 151:6 (Dec. 1952): 32–33, 90. For additional examples, see "Pre-Show Testing," 147:6 (Dec. 1950): 95; and "Industry News: New Pattern in the Market," 161:5 (Nov. 1957): 44.

67. Larrabee 1955, 62.

68. Buckley 1990, 120.

69. The African American market emerged as its own niche at the beginning of the 1960s; see "Selling the Negro Market," *GTR* (Jan. 1963): 84; "A Look at the Negro Market" (4 Apr. 1966): 2, 4; and "Sales Appeal Is to Blacks" (Oct. 1969): 20.

70. "First National Dinnerware Exhibit Opens," *China, Glass & Decorative Accessories* (May 1948): 32–33.

71. Matranga 1997, 46.

72. "American Dinnerware Designers Report Major 1957 Designs Trends," *CGJ* 160:1 (Jan. 1957): 37.

73. For a history of Kitchenaid, see Matranga 1997, 150–51.

74. "The Full Meaning of an 'American Design,'" *CGJ* 128:3 (Mar. 1941): 12.

75. "Here Are Fall's Design-Trends as Leading Designers See Them," *CGJ* 149:1 (July 1951): 98.

76. For an early effort in coordinating the tabletop, see the advertisement for Community China and Crystal in *CGJ* 112:2 (Feb. 1933): 12; "China, Glass, Linen Alliance Profitable," 128:1 (Jan. 1941): 40.

77. For an early example of dishes matching furnishing fabrics, see *CGJ* 145:6 (Dec. 1949): 140.

78. "Franciscan Feat," *GTR* (7 Dec. 1964): 4.

79. *CGJ* 128:5 (May 1941): 1; and 130:1 (Jan. 1942): 71.

80. *CGJ* 155:5 (Nov. 1954): 8.

81. For general information on Wright and his wares, see Hennessey 1985 and Kerr 1990.

82. For a history of the *Homemaker* pattern, see Moss 1997.

83. "Are Today's Design-Standards Slipping?," *CGJ* 151:6 (Dec. 1952): 96.

84. "Ohio Valley Dinnerware: American Styled for American Taste," *CGJ* 156:4 (Apr. 1955): 26.

85. "Good Design Makes a Difference," *GTR* (Jan. 1963): 34.

86. "The Designer Talks Facts of Life to the Tableware Industry," *GTR* (Nov. 1961): 9.

87. Jackson 1998, 59–69.

88. Ibid., 69–70.

89. "English Modern Gets a New Look," *GTR* (21 Sept. 1964): 30.

90. Bryan interview 1997; Queensberry interview 1997; Copeland interview 1997; and Midwinter interview 1997.

91. Hopwood and Hopwood 1997, 72.

92. *GTR* (Dec. 1962): 18; (17 Feb. 1964): 23; (3 Aug. 1964): 24; (1 Mar. 1965): 6, 28.

93. Hannah 1986, 95.

94. Midwinter interview 1997; Queensberry interview 1997.

95. Hannah 1986, 89; "Artist Peter Max Takes a Trip with Gifts," *GTR* (3 Apr. 1967): 7.

96. Fitz and Floyd designed a line of dinnerware for Bloomingdale's to coincide with this exhibition (Floyd interview 1997).

97. "Not So Flighty Teenagers Stocking Hope Chests," *GTR* (June 1969): 29.

98. "The Three Faces of Traditional," *GTR* (Jan. 1960): 34.

99. "White House Profile: Taste in Tableware," *GTR* (Apr. 1962): 36–37.

100. Murphy interview 1998; O'Leary interview 1998.

101. "Not So Flighty Teenagers Stocking Hope Chests," *GTR* (June 1969): 29.

102. Internoscia 1982, 1.

103. "Where Do New Ideas Come From?" *GTR* (Mar. 1962): 108–9; "Creil: Reproductions for Connoisseurs by Connoisseurs" (Mottehedah trade catalogue), 1964, cover.

104. "Handcrafts were Rosalynn's Choice for White House Party," *GTR* (July 1977): 9.

105. "New Life Styles—So; Now What?" *GTR* (Dec. 1970): 1.

106. Internoscia 1982.

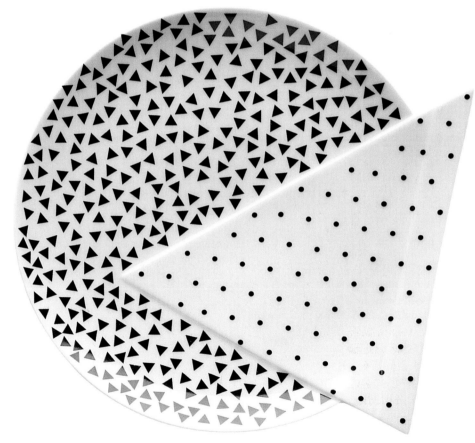

The years between 1880 and 1980 were momentous ones in the tableware industry, as the preceding chapters have shown. New manufacturing and marketing techniques transformed the production and distribution of consumer goods, while American consumers were themselves transformed. Dramatic changes in commerce and culture did not cease in 1980, however. Many processes set in motion earlier continued to evolve unabated. The introduction of mass-production technology into potteries and glasshouses in the late nineteenth and early twentieth centuries gave rise to computer-driven equipment of astounding sophistication.

The consumer testing of midcentury has become a multibillion-dollar industry. While costly mistakes can still occur due to the public's sometimes fickle nature, today's china and glass, along with virtually everything else one can buy, are now designed for a market that is endlessly probed and therefore well understood. No longer envisioned as a legion of homogeneous, white, middle-class consumers, the American market is recognized as richly diverse, having been recently influenced by immigrants from the Pacific Rim, Eastern Europe, the Middle East, and Africa. In response, the vision of mass-production has come to be one of great flexibility. On the one hand, the practice of the past continues—making standardized products and altering their surfaces to create the appearance of variety. On the other hand, manufacturers are developing techniques of mass customization. Employing new technology and accurate information about the desires of specific niche markets, producers are becoming more adept at satisfying individual wants. In many ways the cycle has come full circle—from small production runs and specialty shops, to mass production and mass marketing, to mass customization of both product and distribution.

Even more dramatic has been the evolution of Americans themselves. At the end of the twentieth century there are 265 million people in the United States. Of these, 45 million are members of the so-called Generation X. In their twenties and early thirties, these individuals are not as interested in material possessions compared to their parents and grandparents. Rather, they crave exciting experiences and entertainment. Along with their younger counterparts, graying Baby Boomers often feel pressed for time; more than ever before, women are especially busy outside the home. In the 1940s and 1950s, 66 percent of American families had a stay-at-home mother, whereas only 17 percent of families did in 1994. By the mid-1990s, women made up 46 percent of the workforce. Of twenty-five- to fifty-four-year-old women, 75 percent had paying jobs.[1] Repercussions in the country's kitchens and dining rooms have been profound.

With less time to spend at the stove and table, Americans consume more prepackaged food than home-cooked meals. To accommodate this change microwave ovens have entered the kitchen. Invented in the 1970s, microwaves appeared in one-third of American households by 1983. By 1995 that number had increased to 90 percent. In author Victoria Matranga's words, "This phenomenon reshaped eating habits, food preparation, cooking utensils, and a mother's traditional role as provider of after-school snacks and family feasts."[2] The early twentieth-century journey for dishes from "oven to table" had lengthened once again. Now dishes have to be freezer, oven, microwave, and dishwasher safe, and still look attractive on the table!

With smaller homes, less time to spend eating, and new priorities, Americans need fewer dishes. No longer are fine china and crystal at the top of the list for wedding gifts. Bridal registries have expanded to include a wide variety of goods, including sporting equipment and tools. Often one set of sturdy dishes will do for all occasions. While Americans might still enjoy romantic images of the past or of idyllic nature on their dinner plates, they generally do not want a wide variety of forms. The proverbial five-piece place setting has in many cases dwindled to three—a plate, a bowl, and a mug.

OPPOSITE:
Cat. 209 With eccentric shapes and bold geometric patterns, Mikasa's *Millennium* tableware of the early 1980s was meant to make a brief fashion statement before being replaced by a trendier design.

Adapting to such dynamic shifts has been difficult for manufacturers and distributors alike. As the demand for new dishes lessened, production and marketing costs simultaneously rose. This situation forced many American manufacturers out of business during the 1960s and 1970s. As some European currencies and the Japanese yen reached new postwar highs against the dollar, and labor costs soared in the 1980s and early 1990s, tableware producers in Europe and Japan had to reduce costs to remain competitive. Some constructed factories in countries that still had abundant cheap labor. Thus, dishes in America are now as likely to have been made in China, Indonesia, or Sri Lanka as in England, Germany, or France.

In recent decades the distribution of dishes has also changed radically. Whereas department stores were the prime sellers of tableware and housewares twenty years ago, now discount stores like Wal-Mart dominate. Founded in Arkansas in 1962 by Sam Walton, Wal-Mart generated sales of nearly $140 billion from its nearly three thousand U.S. stores in 1999.[3] Together the discount retailers Wal-Mart, Kmart, and Target account for more than one-third of all housewares sales. Department stores such as Sears, Montgomery Ward, and Macy's represent another 11 percent, while specialty retailers like Crate & Barrel, Pottery Barn, and the Container Store contribute 10 percent of sales.[4] To move enormous quantities of goods through their distribution systems, these mass retailers require manufacturers to meet exacting criteria. In the case of tableware, this often means prepackaging dishes in small units. Potteries and glassmakers now sell a large quantity of their product in units of one.

In many ways tableware has become giftware in the eyes of the consumer. Whereas a shopper might have bought a dozen cups and saucers fifty years ago, now a customer is likely to purchase a single coffee mug boxed by itself. Producers and retailers who need to sell more dishes to make money encourage the perception of tableware as giftware. Gifts are special whether one buys them for a friend or for oneself. Small quantities of attractive tableware encased in enticing packaging is the final stage of tableware's movement into the realm of fashion that began in the 1950s and came of age in the 1970s and 1980s. Since 1980, fashion industry giants like Ralph Lauren and the House of Dior, as well as proponents of radical design concepts like Memphis (cats. 44, 209), have taught consumers to think of tableware as fashion. The result is that style changes are more rapid than ever before in the ceramics and glass industries. To keep pace and try to ensure success, industrial designers use CAD (computer aided design) software that allows them to create "virtual" tableware. Before a single pot is thrown from wet clay or vessel blown from molten glass, consumer-focus groups pass judgment on multiple variations of patterns and shapes that do not yet exist.

In an ironic twist, as Americans have come to rely on tableware less and less in their daily lives and treat it more as a disposable, fashion-oriented product, many have become increasingly attached to the dishes of the past. Even if they actually use them very seldom, Americans are buying old dishes as never before. This desire to make the past tangible can be seen in the rise of the pattern matcher. In 1965 the editor of the trade periodical *China, Glass and Tablewares* told readers that his office was receiving an increasing number of letters asking how to obtain replacements for china and glass patterns that were out of production. He recommended that retailers try hard to obtain replacements from producers, and if that failed, they should sell their customers new patterns that harmonized with the old ones. Seeing an opportunity, J. Allen Murphey of Princeton, Illinois, founded one of the first pattern-matching services in 1960. Within two years his small shop, Patterns of the Past, was handling 1,190 discontinued patterns.[5]

In the following decades the number of women searching for discontinued patterns grew, along with the choice of firms catering to their need. In 1981 Bob Page of Greensboro, North Carolina, founded a company called Replacements, Ltd., which eventually brought order and sophistication to the selling of old tableware. Taking full advantage of computer technology for stock acquisition and inventory control, while adapting innovations in telemarketing, Replacements, Ltd., has grown from gross sales of $125,000 in 1981 to $64.3 million in 1998. Today five hundred employees labor in a warehouse of 225,000 square feet containing 5.5 million pieces of china, crystal, and silver. Currently, the firm has 2.5 million customers on file who are searching for more than 121,000 different patterns of tableware.[6]

With the recent economic unification of Europe, the United States is no longer the largest single market for tableware in the world. However, even if Americans buy fewer new dishes these days and use those they do have less and less, they still love dishes. Perhaps, though, they appreciate them more today as links with the past. Vessels connect the hurried participants in the present with the seemingly quieter past: life in small towns and on farms, Sunday supper at Grandmother's—worlds in which women demonstrated their talent and proved their worth by arranging flowers and elaborate table settings. How else can one explain the need felt by so many ordinary Americans to amass large quantities of "depression glass," *Fiesta* ware, or California pottery? How else can one justify stockpiling sets of china and glassware that are virtually never used? If the truth be known, America is awash with countless dishes. In cabinets and cupboards throughout the land rests the legacy of thousands of men and especially women who labored to make, market, acquire, and preserve china and glass of infinite variety. Silent and safe, these objects wait for us to give them meaning, to awaken them as conveyors of culture and history from those long dead to those yet unborn through the living present.

BREAKFAST

LUNCHEON

FAMILY DINNER

FORMAL DINNER

Notes

1. Matranga 1997, 84.

2. Ibid., 85.

3. Information from the Internet address www.wal-mart.com/newsroom/data.html.

4. Ibid., 87.

5. "Grandmother's China," *China, Glass & Tablewares* 83:12 (Oct. 1965): 9; and "Mr. Murphey Did Something about Pattern Hunters," *GTR* (Feb. 1962): 53, 56.

6. Information from the Internet address www.replacements.com/press.html.

Catalogue Documentation

Note to the Reader

The conventions outlined here are used in the following catalogue entries.

Titles: Shape and pattern names are italicized if they were used at the time of manufacture for sales purposes. Some line names (for example, Continental China and Hallcraft) are distinguished by roman typeface and refer to broader categories of goods that encompass more than one shape. The term "shape range" denotes the entire group of individual pieces that together constitute an overall shape carrying a specific name (*Museum, Tomorrow's Classic*). In the case of objects for which a single name describes both the shape and surface ornament (*Fiesta, American Modern*), the modifiers "shape" and "pattern" are not used. A number that identified a shape or pattern in the wholesale trade is not italicized unless the manufacturer treated it as the formal name of the ware. When the word "plate" is used in a title without a modifier such as "salad" or "dessert," the item is a dinner plate. When known, specific glaze names and body types are italicized and noted in the entry text.

Dates: Unless otherwise noted, the date that follows the title indicates when the shape was designed, not when the surface pattern was created or the ware was introduced to the market. In virtually all cases the shape was created first, sometimes many years before the pattern. When known, the date of the surface decoration is noted in the entry text.

Designers: When the information is available, designers of specific shapes and patterns are listed. However, design departments were often organized so that a particular design would be credited to a single designer even if several individuals contributed to its creation. When no specific designer can be identified, the reader should assume that the object was created in the design department of the glass house or pottery cited.

Makers: If no specific designer, importer, or distributor is listed, the maker of the object is named without the designation "maker" following it. Since firm names often changed over time, care has been taken to give the correct names of the makers, importers, and distributors at the time the object in question was produced. In the case of English firms producing wares in the five-village community of Stoke-on-Trent in the county of Staffordshire, the particular village in which the relevant pottery was located is indicated in the entry text. The five villages are Barlaston, Burslem, Hanley, Newcastle, and Stoke-upon-Trent.

Media: Because of the exceptionally complicated nature of glass and ceramic body compositions during the period under consideration, broad categories of body types are used here. Glass is called "lead glass" when it is known to contain that element; otherwise it is simply described as "glass." Five basic divisions of ceramic body types are employed: "Earthenware" denotes anything relatively low fired and porous. "Whiteware" designates a wide range of higher-fired wares that are fully vitrified and hard but not translucent. This group includes ware commonly known today as graniteware and hotel ware in addition to particularly hard, highly vitrified wares produced in the United States for home use. If a manufacturer identified its ware as "stoneware," that term is used. "Porcelain" denotes wares made of the most refined clays, thinly potted and very highly fired. The term "bone china" describes porcelains that were marketed as such by the manufacturer and that contain bone ash. Glaze compositions are not noted. Decorative techniques have been simplified for brevity; for example, ornament produced by transfer printing, decal application, or screen printing is simply referred to as "printed decoration." Similarly, "painted decoration" encompasses all techniques used to apply surface ornament by hand, including enameling and hand painting under the glaze.

Size: Measurements are given only for the tallest item in each photograph of catalogue objects unless otherwise indicated.

Marks: Words, numbers, and images on objects are transcribed as accurately as possible. Slashes signify line breaks. Marks of all types are italicized. Explanations of marks appear in parentheses and are not italic. The unitalicized word "and" indicates that the subsequent marks are not associated with the preceding marks.

Cat. 1

Carrara Modern cup and saucer, ca. 1954.
Iroquois China Company, Syracuse, N.Y.
Earthenware with painted decoration.
Both marked: *Carrara | Modern | CHINA |
BY IROQUOIS*. Dallas Museum of Art,
20th-Century Design Fund, 1996.123.

Carrara Modern was available in brown, white,
and charcoal glazes. While the ware is reflective of the emergence of the New York School
of abstract painting in the late 1940s and
1950s, especially the drip paintings of Jackson
Pollock, its relatively low cost was what the
manufacturer stressed in advertising. A complete service for four cost $14.95 when the
line was put on the market in 1955.[1]

Ballerina coffeepot, 1948. Universal Potteries,
Cambridge, Ohio. Earthenware; h. 9¾ in.
(24.8 cm), w. 9 in. (22.9 cm), d. 5½ in.
(14 cm). Unmarked. Dallas Museum of Art,
20th-Century Design Fund, 1997.145.

Ballerina was extremely popular during the
decade following its introduction in January
1949. It was produced in several colors and
adorned with a wide variety of decal decorations. The original glazes were *Periwinkle Blue,
Jade Green, Jonquil Yellow,* and *Dove Grey*. Consumers could mix and match the colors as
desired. In 1960 *Ballerina*'s production was
taken over by the Edwin M. Knowles China
Company when Universal Potteries stopped
making dinnerware.[2]

Skyline shape teapot with Marbella pattern,
1949. Southern Potteries, Erwin, Tenn. Earthenware with painted decoration. Unmarked.
Dallas Museum of Art, 20th-Century Design
Fund, 1998.2.

At the Pittsburgh trade show in 1950 the *Skyline* shape was introduced to the market with
fifteen surface patterns.[3] Southern Potteries
was known for its handpainted, peasant-style,
floral decorated Blue Ridge Dinnerware. The
stark two-tone nature of this design is highly
unusual. When new in 1955 the maker advertised *Marbella* (or sometimes *Marble*), available in several colors, as "MASTERPIECES
IN MARBLE . . . Blue Ridge reflects the lovely
lustre and classic beauty of fine sculpture in
these distinctive new marble patterns. Every

piece of flatware is individually Hand decorated for a true replica of nature's finest creation, on backgrounds of coral pink, turquoise blue, sandstone gray or snowy white.
Holloware of solid onyx black and charcoal
gray lend striking contrast for a table that is
always the topic of conversation."[4]

1. *CGJ* 155:82 (Feb. 1955): back cover.
2. *CGJ* 166:2 (Aug. 1960): 39.
3. *CGJ* 145:6 (Dec. 1949): 94.
4. *CGJ* 156:5 (May 1955): 41.

Cat. 2

Covered muffin dish and plate, ca. 1890.
Coiffe et Touron, Limoges, France, maker;
Straus, Lewis & Sons, New York, importer.
Porcelain with printed, painted, and gilded
decoration; plate: h. 1 in. (2.5 cm), diam.
9½ in. (24.1 cm). Both marked: •LS&S • |
LIMOGES [all between two concentric circles] |
FRANCE. Dr. and Mrs. L. M. Harrison, Jr.,
Collection.

Delicate, lacy patterns featuring soft patches
of color and gilded garlands were typical of
French porcelain patterns favored by American consumers at the end of the nineteenth
century. These pieces are from the wedding
china of Mary Anna Jelks and Anthony Fly of
Summit, Mississippi, and were probably purchased in New Orleans in 1891. Another plate
in this set bears the mark of Coiffe et Touron.

Cat. 3

Covered jug, ca. 1867. Attributed to Frederick
Bret Russel, designer; Josiah Wedgwood &
Sons, Etruria, England, vessel maker; Gorham
Manufacturing Company, Providence, lid
maker. Earthenware with painted decoration.
Jug marked: *WEDGWOOD | A* and *GJC* (date
mark for 1874) | 24 and 1360 |. Lid marked:
[lion] [anchor] G | GORHAM & CO. | STERLING | I
(date mark for 1876). Dallas Museum of Art,
anonymous gift, 1991.412.49.

Popularly known as the *Caterer* jug, this form
came in several sizes both with and without
lids. The motto around the side of the jug is a
quote from William Shakespeare's *Comedy of
Errors*: "What tho my gate be poor | Take it in
good part | Better cheer may you have | But
not with better heart" (III, 1). The presence
of a sterling lid made by an American silver
manufacturer suggests that a retail store
commissioned the lid from Gorham to place
on Wedgwood jugs so that the pieces could
be monogrammed, a common practice in
this example.

**No. 668 shape covered game pie dish with
liner,** 1873. Possibly Paul Comelera, designer;
Minton, Ltd., Stoke-upon-Trent, England,
maker. Earthenware with painted decoration.
Dish marked: *MINTON* and *j* and (date mark
for 1873) and 6 • and *668* (shape number).
Liner marked: 6. Cover marked: 34. Dallas
Museum of Art, anonymous gift in memory
of Sophia Taubman, 1993.62.

In 1873 Paris-born Paul Comelera came to
Minton, where he specialized in modeling
figures of animals, many life-size, for use
with majolica glazes. One of these, a large
standing figure of a peacock, exhibits some
of the same motifs, particularly the trailing
ivy, that can be seen in this game pie dish.
He left the factory in 1876 but continued to
work for the company on a freelance basis.[1]

Jug, 1883. Frederick Hackney, designer; D. F.
Haynes & Co., Baltimore, maker. Earthenware; h. 7¾ in. (19.7 cm), w. 5½ in. (14 cm),
d. 4¼ in. (10.8 cm). Unmarked. Dallas Museum of Art, gift of the 1990 Dallas Symposium, 1990.185.

After David Francis Haynes purchased the
Chesapeake Pottery in Baltimore, he hired
English potter Frederick Hackney to develop
artistic wares similar to those produced in
England at the time. Hackney produced Carlton ware (illustrated), which featured bands
of geometrical embossing and dark glazes of
blue or green. The decoration recalls Rhenish
stoneware of the late Middle Ages; Doulton &
Co. also produced similar wares.[2] Before
being bought by Edwin Bennett in 1890,
D. F. Haynes found success with two types
of majolica in addition to its artistic wares.
Like Carlton ware, its Clifton ware and Ava-
lon faience copied leading English majolica
production—specifically the distinctive white
ground Argenta ware of Josiah Wedgwood &
Sons. The Baltimore company won recognition at the 1904 Saint Louis world's fair but
struggled after Haynes's death in 1908. The
works were eventually sold to the American
Sugar Refining Company, which closed the
factory in 1914.[3]

**Shell and Seaweed jug and Cauliflower plate
and teapot,** ca. 1880. Griffen, Smith & Co.,
Phoenixville, Pa., maker. Earthenware
with painted decoration. Jug marked: [star]
ETRUSCAN [star] | GSH [conjoined in a circle] |
MAJOLICA [all within a circle] | E 26 and t. Plate

marked: [star] ETRUSCAN [star] / GSH [conjoined in a circle] / MAJOLICA and M [surrounded by a star] and 60. Teapot marked: GSH [conjoined] / E 13 and 18. Heidi B. Hollomon Collection.

Collectors still refer to this company as Griffen, Smith & Hill, although it had that name only between 1879 and 1880. William Hill had left the firm by 1880, and the name was changed to reflect his departure although the factory continued to use the mark GSH on its wares.[4]

Like other American pottery manufacturers of the late nineteenth century, Griffen, Smith & Co. closely modeled its wares after English prototypes in order to compete with the popular majolica and artistic wares being imported to America. The firm's *Shell and Seaweed* was a copy of one of Wedgwood's Argenta ware designs of 1879; *Cauliflower* recalled the earlier eighteenth-century tureens made in Strasbourg, France, and Chelsea, England, and more directly the early teawares of Thomas Whieldon and Josiah Wedgwood I. Griffen, Smith & Co. quickly rose to prominence with its adaptations of English majolica, culminating in an acclaimed display at the 1884 World's Industrial and Cotton Centennial Exhibition in New Orleans. Unfortunately the rapid change in taste away from majolica glazes around 1890 coupled with a disastrous fire at the factory in 1889 contributed to the firm's demise in 1892.[5]

1. For a description of Comelera's work for Minton and an illustration of his famous peacock, see Jones 1993, 138–41.
2. Frelinghuysen 1986, 208.
3. Karmason and Stacke 1989, 166–67.
4. Ibid., 145.
5. Ibid., 145–61.

Cat. 4

Symmetry shape platter with Fish pattern, ca. 1955. Johnson Brothers, Hanley, England, maker; Johnson Brothers, New York, importer. Earthenware with printed and painted decoration; h. 1¼ in. (3.2 cm), w. 16 in. (40.6 cm), d. 12¼ in. (31.1 cm). Marked: FISH / [image of a fish] / MADE IN ENGLAND BY / JOHNSON BROS / A GENUINE HAND ENGRAVING / ALL DECORATION UNDER THE / GLAZE DETERGENT & ACID / RESISTING COLOUR / PAT PEND. Dallas Museum of Art, gift of George Roland in memory of Annabelle and Charles Thomas Roland, 1997.62.

When first advertised in 1955, *Symmetry* was described as a shape "to fulfill today's needs and to anticipate the needs of tomorrow."[1] *Symmetry* was Johnson Brothers' response to the call for modernism, yet the first six patterns were all very conservative floral scenes— *Azure Rose, Floating Leaves, Sunny Fields, Lace, Titania,* and *Snow Crystals.* At about the same time, Johnson Brothers issued the *Fish* pattern on the shape to appeal to the American market for sets of dishes used at informal fish

suppers. The expansive surface of *Symmetry* perfectly accommodated the asymmetrical scene of several large fish swimming through weeds at the bottom of a lake.

1. CGJ 157:1 (July 1955): 33.

Cat. 5

Platter, plate, and three ramekins, ca. 1935. Unknown factory, Czechoslovakia, maker; Ebeling & Reuss, Philadelphia, importer. Earthenware (platter and plate) and porcelain (ramekins) with painted and sprayed decoration; platter: h. 1¾ in. (4.4 cm), w. 7¼ in. (18.4 cm), l. 16⅜ in. (41.6 cm). Platter marked: 7604 and MADE IN / CZECHOSLOVAKIA. Plate marked: same as platter except without 7604. Crab ramekin marked: Made in Czechoslovakia • / PV. Lobster ramekin marked: ERPHILA / CZECHOSLOVAKIA and M. Second lobster ramekin marked: same as plate. Dallas Museum of Art, 20th-Century Design Fund, 1997.164.1–4.

As suggested by the crab, lobster, and shrimp imagery, such sets were used for serving seafood. A 1938 photograph of a display at a San Francisco retailer shows a "lobster service" with identical plates, as well as a tureen and salad bowl featuring lobster-shaped handles.[1] Because the ramekins are made of porcelain, they could be used in the oven.

1. CGJ 123:1 (July 1938): 61.

Cat. 6

Champagne glass with Queen Anne shape stem and Manchester Pheasant pattern, ca. 1930. Morgantown Glass Works, Morgantown, W. Va. Glass with etched and printed decoration; h. 5¼ in. (13.3 cm), diam. 4 in. (10.2 cm). Unmarked. Dallas Museum of Art, 20th-Century Design Fund, 1996.22.

Duo-tone silk-screen printing was introduced as a decorative device on Morgantown glassware in 1928. Appearing two years later, the *Manchester Pheasant* pattern was one of only two silk-screened motifs ever used by the firm. The twisted *Queen Anne* stem first appeared in Morgantown catalogues in 1931.[1]

1. Gallagher 1995, 66, 135. Because the Morgantown Collectors Association has assigned names to patterns and shapes for which no original is known, it is difficult to know which published terms are period ones.

Cat. 7

Oyster plate, ca. 1880. Union Porcelain Works, Brooklyn, maker; Richard Briggs, Boston, retailer. Porcelain with painted decoration. Marked: U.P.W. / [eagle's head holding letter S] / Pat. Jan. 4, 1881 and Richard Briggs / Boston / Mass. Dallas Museum of Art, gift of the Friends of the Decorative Arts' 1993 Maryland trip in honor of Heidi and Alen Hollomon, 1993.64.

No. 3389 pattern covered pickle jar on stand with tongs, 1885. Jar: Unknown factory, United States or Bohemia. Stand: James W. Tufts, Boston. Silver-plated base metal and glass; h. 12 in. (30.5 cm), w. 5 in. (12.7 cm), d. 4¼ in. (10.8 cm). Glass unmarked. Stand marked: JAMES W. TUFTS / BOSTON / [T in a star] / WARRANTED QUADRUPLEPLATE / 3389 (pattern number). Dallas Museum of Art, gift of W. C. and Sally Estes in memory of Dr. and Mrs. T. G. Estes, 1995.89.

Stylish Victorian tabletops included a wide variety of specialized forms in china, glass, and metal that held luxury foods for elegant dining. Oysters were served as a separate course, and special plates for their service were typically purchased by the dozen. Fancy pickles were available as condiments with the main courses.[1] The tongs hanging from the stand allowed diners to extract the delicacies without dirtying their fingers. The metal manufacturers ordered glass inserts made to their specifications and retailed the assembled product. A trade catalogue for James Tufts wares, from about 1888, shows an identical metal stand. However, that source depicts a pickle container that was described as "imported decorated glass in colors." Selling for the relatively large sum of $5, the jar depicted had a metal lid that could be suspended from the top knob of the frame.[2] Inherently fragile, pickle jars were easily broken and often replaced, as in this case.

1. For an illustration of another pickle jar, see Frelinghuysen 1989, 53.
2. Tufts' Quadruple Silver Plated Ware (James W. Tufts trade catalogue, ca. 1888), 26, item no. 3389.

Cat. 8

Encanto shape coffee and tea set with Sandalwood pattern, 1949. Mary C. Grant, shape designer; Franciscan Division, Gladding, McBean & Co., Glendale, Calif., maker. Porcelain with platinum decoration; coffeepot: h. 7½ in. (19.1 cm), w. 9 in. (22.9 cm), d. 5½ in. (14 cm). Pots and sugar bowl marked: Franciscan fine China / MADE IN CALIFORNIA U.S.A. [in an oval surmounted by a Spanish mission] / GLADDING, McBEAN & CO. Creamer marked: FRANCISCAN Fine CHINA [in an oval surmounted by a Spanish mission] / MADE IN CALIFORNIA. Dallas Museum of Art, 20th-Century Design Fund, 1996.120.1–4.

At the time of *Encanto's* introduction, the simple lines of the shape were well received by critics. In 1952 *Encanto* was included in the *Studio Year Book.*[1] The shape was produced without printed decoration in several colors, including *Willow* (chartreuse), *Dawn* (aqua), *Twilight* (light blue), *Teak* (black), *Spruce* (dark green), *Magnolia* (pink), and white. *Sandalwood* remained in production at least through the 1950s.[2] These interesting color effects were achieved through the use of solid colored bodies, not colored surface glazes. In the late 1950s a few changes were made to the line, including the addition of a new, taller cup, and the name was changed to *Encanto Nuevo*.

1. Holme and Frost 1952, 103.
2. For images of all the colors, see Snyder 1996.

Cat. 9
Clockwise from left:
Accent shape snack plate and *Criterion* shape cup with *Ebonette* pattern, 1954. Edwin M. Knowles China Company, Newell, W. Va. Earthenware with painted decoration. Both unmarked. Dallas Museum of Art, 20th-Century Design Fund, 1995.129.1–2.

Typically the *Ebonette* pattern was used on the *Criterion* shape, which included square-shaped plates with rounded corners. The lobed *Accent* shape plate (illustrated) was likely used for the snack set because such sets were sold as specialty giftware and were not part of the regular dinnerware line.

Plate with *Mardi Gras* pattern, ca. 1962. Salem China Company, Salem, Ohio. Earthenware with printed decoration; h. ⅞ in. (2.2 cm), diam. 10 in. (25.4 cm). Marked: *Salem [in an oval featuring a cup] / OVENPROOF / Mardi Gras © / [two stars] 62 Z (date mark for 1962).* Dallas Museum of Art, gift of Michael E. Pratt, T42376.

The *Mardi Gras* pattern was used on four forms—dinner plate, salad plate, bowl, and cup and saucer. Each featured a slightly different version of the abstract design.

Ranchero shape teapot with *Cloudburst* pattern and plate and cup and saucer with *Tahiti* pattern, 1937. Simon H. Slobodkin, shape designer; Cavitt-Shaw Division of W. S. George Pottery Company, East Palestine, Ohio, maker. Earthenware with sprayed decoration. Teapot marked: *CLOUDBURST / BY / CAVITT-SHAW / DIVISION / W.S. GEORGE / 15 UA.* Plate and saucer marked: *W.S. George / HALF CENTURY OF FINE DINNERWARE / 1904– 1954.* Cup unmarked. Dallas Museum of Art, gift of Michael E. Pratt, T42334, T42620.

The *Ranchero* shape was very popular and was produced for at least twenty years. Originally it was decorated with southwestern motifs and advertised as "An interpretation of the primitive American cultural background, this ware combines the Puritanism of New England with the sweep and color of the Southwest; a sturdiness of form with grace of line; simplicity with a plastic decorative effect which is completely native in theme."[1] These examples were made after World War II. *Cloudburst* was available in several colors, including this *Sunlight Green*. *Tahiti* was one of a series of striped designs that included *Caravan*

(chartreuse), *Tango* (green), *Carnival* (brown), and *Holiday* (blue). *Caravan* was introduced in 1951. All were advertised until at least 1955.[2]

1. "Cavitt-Shaw Potters," PGBS (Dec. 1937): 39–41.
2. CGJ 148:2 (Feb. 1951): 25; 152:6 (June 1953): inside cover; 155:9 (4 Mar. 1955): inside cover.

Cat. 10
Terrace cup and saucer, plate, goblet, champagne glass, tumbler, and juice glass, ca. 1935. Duncan & Miller Glass Company, Washington, Pa. Glass with pressed decoration; goblet: h. 6⅝ in. (16.8 cm), diam. 3⅛ in. (7.9 cm). All unmarked. Dallas Museum of Art, 20th-Century Design Fund, T42468.1–6.

Although very little is known about *Terrace* glassware, it is nonetheless one of the best designed of all mass-produced table glass made during the 1930s. The designer of these simple, elegantly terraced shapes is unknown, but he may well have been Robert A. May. May graduated from Washington and Jefferson College and then studied in the School of Fine Arts of the Carnegie Institute of Technology in Pittsburgh before being put in charge of design at Duncan & Miller in the mid-1930s. During this period he was an outspoken proponent of the "new" profession of industrial design.[1]

1. Robert A. May, "The Industrial Designer Takes His Place in the Sun," CGJ 119:1 (July 1936): 26.

Cat. 11
Caribbean punch set, ca. 1935. Duncan & Miller Glass Company, Washington, Pa. Glass with pressed decoration; bowl: h. 5¾ in. (14.6 cm), diam. 11¾ in. (29.8 cm). Ladle labeled: GENUINE / Duncan. Dallas Museum of Art, 20th-Century Design Fund, 1996.185.1–14.

When introduced in 1936, *Caribbean* benefited from inclusion in a national advertising campaign launched by Duncan & Miller that year. Images of this punch set appeared in magazines such as the *New Yorker* and *American Home* along with the slogan "Picture this lovely Duncan Glass from you—among the Bride's gifts."[1] The *Caribbean* line was in production until 1955 and included a wide variety of forms available in clear or light blue glass. Punch cups and ladles were made with colorless, red, blue, or amber handles.[2]

1. CGJ 118:6 (June 1936): 3.
2. For a list of forms, see Florence 1995, 56–59.

Cat. 12
Town and Country teapot, creamer, cruet, salt and pepper shakers, and syrup jug, ca. 1945–46. Eva Zeisel, designer; Red Wing Pottery, Red Wing, Minn., maker. Earthenware; teapot: h. 5⅛ in. (13 cm), w. 11⅝ in. (29.5 cm), d. 7⅛ in. (18.1 cm). All unmarked. Dallas Museum of Art, 20th-Century Design Fund, 1995.119.1–6.

In the mid-1940s the president of Red Wing Pottery, Hubert Haddon Varney, asked Eva Zeisel if she could design in a "Greenwich Villagey" fashion. By that he meant create a design that was a bit eccentric and would appeal to young consumers who were embracing a casual lifestyle after World War II. The result was the *Town and Country* line that Red Wing introduced in 1947 and made through the early 1950s. Free-form in shape and meant to be mixed and matched on the table, Zeisel's design was akin in concept to Russel Wright's *American Modern* (see cat. 24). In its sales literature Red Wing promoted the line as "luncheon ware" and said that it was created by "Eva Zeisel, one of America's foremost designers." It went on to say, "Town and Country is made in six colors: Dusk Blue, Forest Green, Metallic Brown, Chartreuse, Grey, and Rust. Each color was selected for its individual smartness as well as its ability to blend with any one or all of the other colors. Unusual and distinctive table settings can be arranged from this selection of colors, the versatility of which lends itself equally to modern interior or outdoor serving." In short, *Town and Country* was promoted as "contemporary, functional, colorful, smart."[1]

1. See period brochure illustrated in Reiss 1997, 15. For a discussion of the aesthetics and history of this design, see Eidelberg 1991, 105–6; and Montreal 1984, 36–44.

Cat. 13
Cup and saucer, plate, covered bowl with underplate, coffeepot, and mug, ca. 1927–30. Joseph Mrazek, designer; J. Mrazek Peasant Art Industry, Letovice, Czechoslovakia, maker; Czecho Peasant Art Company, New York, importer. Earthenware with painted decoration; plate: h. ¾ in. (1.9 cm), diam. 9⅜ in. (23.8 cm). Cup unmarked. Saucer marked: *PEASANT ART INDUSTRY / J Mrazek / MADE IN CZECHOSLOVA-KIA [all in a circle]* and 229.A. Plate marked: *Made in / Czechoslovakia / Letovice [all in a stylized oval]* and 821.A. Covered bowl marked: same as plate except with 817. Underplate marked: *MADE IN CZECHOSLOVAKIA • P.A.1. / 282 [all in a circle]* and *PEASANT ART INDUSTRY / [bird] / MADE IN CZECHOSLOVAKIA [all in a circle].* Coffeepot marked: same as saucer except with 801.B. Mug marked: same as saucer except with 260.K. Dallas Museum of Art, 20th-Century Design Fund, 1997.163.1–5.

The Czech immigrant Joseph Mrazek began importing Czech goods to the United States in 1918. In 1922 he initiated pottery production at an existing factory in Czechoslovakia and in 1926 built his own facility. The following year the Czecho Peasant Art Company began importing the type of colorful ware illustrated. According to trade advertisements, Mrazek himself designed the line and oversaw its production by "the peasants in the colony of Letovice, Czechoslovakia." It was used in the "largest and most important tea rooms" in New York and was available for sale in tea room gift shops.[1] In addition, "For summer porch or sun-parlor [the designs] are decidedly useful and ornamental, giving a bright note of color to the outdoor room."[2] By 1929 this ware was distributed nationally through agents in New York, Chicago, Minneapolis, Cleveland, Pittsburgh, and Los Angeles.[3] The depression forced Mrazek to stop production and he closed the Czech factory in 1931 or 1932.[4]

1. "Czecho Pottery for Tea Rooms, CGJ 104:9 (3 Mar. 1927): 42.
2. "Colorful Czecho Ware for Summer Use," CGJ 104:14 (7 Apr. 1927): 30.
3. CGJ 107:1 (Jan. 1929): 80.
4. General biographical information provided by Bill Mrazek, son of Joseph Mrazek, conversation with Charles Venable, 14 Sept. 1999.

Cat. 14

All pieces: ca. 1925. Indiana Glass Company, Dunkirk, Ind., maker. Glass with pressed decoration. Unmarked.

Pyramid pitcher. H. 9½ in. (24.1 cm), w. 8¾ in. (22.2 cm), d. 6 in. (15.2 cm). Dallas Museum of Art, 20th-Century Design Fund, 1996.156.

Tea Room goblet and pitcher. Dallas Museum of Art, 20th-Century Design Fund, 1996.157.1–2.

Both of these designs were introduced in 1926 and discontinued around 1931–32. Pyramid was made in clear, pink, green, and yellow, and Tea Room was produced in green and pink glass.[1] Although used in homes, these lines were primarily intended for "Tea Room or Soda Fountain Use."[2] Unlike most pressed glass of the period, which featured traditional floral patterns, the angular lines of Pyramid and Tea Room were in keeping with avant-garde design of the late 1920s.

1. For variations, see Florence 1986, 136, 196.
2. CGJ 107:12 (Dec. 1929): 74.

Cat. 15

Snack set, ca. 1925–40. Nippon Toki Kaisha, Nagoya, Japan, maker; Morimura Brothers, New York, importer. Porcelain with printed and painted decoration; platter: w. 8½ in. (21.6 cm), d. 7⅛ in. (18.1 cm). Cup and saucer marked: NORITAKE | M [in wreath] | HAND-PAINTED | MADE IN JAPAN. Dallas Museum of Art, gift of Margaret E. (Peg) O'Neill, 1997.50.

This snack set, or "tea and toast set" as the Japanese sometimes called this form, was intended for use during mah-jongg games. A simplified version of this Chinese game became popular in America in the mid-1920s, especially among women. The surface decoration on this set depicts the ivory or Bakelite game pieces used in mah-jongg.[1]

1. Lovegren 1995, 87–88.

Cat. 16

Casino bridge set, ca. 1950. Limoges China Company, Sebring, Ohio. Earthenware with printed decoration; cake plate: h. 1⅜ in. (3.5 cm), w. 10 in. (25.4 cm), d. 12¼ in. (31.1 cm). Cups marked: AMERICAN LIMOGES | CHINA CO. | © ALC CO. Other pieces marked: CASINO | by AMERICAN LIMOGES | © ALC CO. Dallas Museum of Art, 20th-Century Design Fund, 1995.172.1–11.

Casino is noteworthy for the way in which the bridge theme is expressed in elements of the design. The shapes used in the set—hearts (saucers), clubs (cups), diamonds (creamer, sugar bowl, and cake plate), and spades (plates)—follow the suits in a deck of cards. The printed ornament further carries out the theme.

Cat. 17

New Era saucer champagne glass, rye bottle, and wineglass, 1934. Rodney C. Irwin, designer; A. H. Heisey & Co., Newark, Ohio. Glass, pressed and etched decoration (rye bottle); rye bottle: h. 8¾ in. (22.2 cm), w. 4 in. (10.2 cm), d. 2¼ in. (5.7 cm). All unmarked. Dallas Museum of Art, 20th-Century Design Fund, 1996.160; 1996.186; 1996.188.

Originally named Modern Line by Heisey, New Era was the perfect glassware complement to an art deco tabletop or bar. With its square bases, plates, and saucers, this pattern clearly followed the fashionable European trend for alternatives to traditional round forms. Earlier versions in earthenware by Jean Luce (see cat. 55) and Clarice Cliff (see cat. 89) no doubt influenced Irwin's design for Heisey. Available in a wide range of bar and tableware shapes, the pattern served as the blank for a number of cuttings and came in both colorless and cobalt versions, as in these examples.[1]

1. For more information on Heisey and the New Era line, see Bredehoft 1987 and Stout 1985.

Cat. 18

Regimental Oak shape plate with Christmas Tree pattern, ca. 1945. Harold Holdway, pattern designer; W. T. Copeland & Sons, Stoke-upon-Trent, England, maker; Copeland & Thompson, New York, importer. Earthenware with printed and painted decoration; h. 1 in. (2.54 cm), diam. 10½ in. (26.7 cm). Marked: COPELAND | SPODE | ENGLAND | S2133 (pattern number) | 52 (date mark for 1952). Dallas Museum of Art, gift of Stephen Harrison in honor of George Roland, 1997.181.

Designed in 1938, Christmas Tree became the best-selling Spode pattern of all time. Though Copeland & Sons originally produced Christmas Tree on the Kailess shape as a printed and handpainted design, the company switched to the Regimental Oak shape (with narrower rim)

after the war and then to a more efficient lithographed decal in the early 1960s.

Cat. 19

Both pieces: Attributed to Charles Murphy, designer; Red Wing Pottery, Red Wing, Minn., maker. Earthenware with painted decoration.

Anniversary shape casserole dish with Capistrano pattern, 1953. H. 6⅞ in. (17.5 cm), diam. 9¼ in. (23.5 cm). Marked: Red Wing | U S A. Dallas Museum of Art, 20th-Century Design Fund, 1996.38.

Futura shape casserole dish with Random Harvest pattern, 1955. H. 4¾ in. (12.1 cm), w. 11¼ in. (28.6 cm), d. 7⅜ in. (18.7 cm). Marked: Red Wing | U S A. Dallas Museum of Art, 20th-Century Design Fund, 1995.108.

These shapes reflect the playful quality of many of Red Wing's best products during the postwar period. Anniversary is particularly interesting because of its textilelike surface decoration. The exterior molded ornament was described as "basket-weave"; the texture on the top resembles burlap. An overall beige version was named Tweed-Tex.

Although the shapes are rather avant-garde, the surface pattern is not. The hand-painted birds and plants reflect the fact that most consumers would not accept overtly modern shapes without traditional surface decoration.[1]

1. For images of all the patterns available on these shapes, see Reiss 1997, 20–21; 24–25.

Cat. 20

Swing shape plate with Yellow Organdy and Colonial Kitchen patterns, 1937. Shape attributed to Frederick H. Rhead, designer; Homer Laughlin China Company, Newell, W. Va., maker. Earthenware with printed decoration; h. ¾ in. (1.9 cm), diam. 9⅞ in. (25.1 cm). Marked: Homer Laughlin | EGGSHELL [in a ribbon] | MADE IN U.S.A. | M 42 N (date mark for 1942). Dallas Museum of Art, 20th-Century Design Fund, 1996.121.

Surface patterns like Colonial Kitchen were added to the relatively restrained Swing shape to improve its sales (see cat. 27). Numerous other brightly colored and traditional decals were also used.

Cat. 21

Vogue shape plate with Stormy Weather pattern from the Melody series, ca. 1951. Alf Robson, designer; Universal Potteries, Cambridge, Ohio, maker. Earthenware with painted decoration; h. 1 in. (2.5 cm), w. 10¾ in. (27.3 cm), d. 10¾ in. (27.3 cm). Marked: E-39 | OVEN-PROOF | UNIVERSAL POTTERIES, INC. CAMBRIDGE, OHIO | Vogue | UNION MADE IN U.S.A. [all in a Vogue shape plate outline] | [musical notes] MELODY SERIES [musical notes] |

STORMY WEATHER. Signed *Robson* in decal. Dallas Museum of Art, gift of Charles L. Venable in honor of Susan Green, T41754.

When introduced to the market in 1952, the *Vogue* shape was advertised as "the dinnerware shape of tomorrow . . . today!" and was well thought of by art critics.[1] The shape appeared in the *Studio Year Book* for 1953–54.[2] Originally *Vogue* was available in solid colors called *Coffee Brown* and *Mist Green* that could be mixed and matched. Starter sets for four people sold for $6.95. The *Melody* series on the *Vogue* shape also appeared in 1952, but sixteen-piece sets cost a dollar more due to the added cost of the decoration. Each plate featured a different popular song. In addition to *Stormy Weather*, the other tunes depicted were *My Blue Heaven*, *Stairway to the Stars*, *Red Sails in the Sunset*, *Moonlight and Roses*, and *Betty Co-ed*.

1. Unidentified ad from 1952 and ad clipped from BH&G (May 1952).
2. Holme and Frost 1954, 75. The designer is incorrectly listed as "Alf Rosen" in the caption.

Cat. 22

No. 5901 casserole dish, ca. 1929–30. S. W. Farber, Inc., Brooklyn, designer/maker; Corning Glass Company, Corning, N.Y., maker. Glass with pressed and engraved decoration and chromed steel with stamped decoration; h. 6½ in. (16.5 cm), w. 10 in. (25.4 cm), d. 8 in. (20.3 cm). Glass marked: T.M. REG. | $ [reversed] | PYREX | $ [reversed] | U.S. PAT. OFF. [all in a circle] and 673-B and A–C (model number). Lid marked: PYREX 673 C A–C and DES. PAT. NO. 82736. Holder marked: FARBER WARE | BROOKLYN N.Y. Dallas Museum of Art, gift of the Friends of the Decorative Arts' 1996 Chicago Trip, 1996.146.

Before World War II, Corning Glass made custom inserts for three outside companies, including Farber and the Gorham Manufacturing Company. Farber had Corning Glass produce three Pyrex inserts for metal Farberware holders. One of these was rectangular rather than octagonal. The illustrated model was available in 1- and 1½-quart sizes and was probably designed at Farber since that firm held the design patent (no. 82,736). In a 1930 catalogue the dish is described as "modern." Both the bold angular shape and the floral panels are similar to high-style French art deco work.[1]

1. Jerry Wright, letter to Charles Venable, 10 July 1996. A 1930 Farberware catalogue showing this model and the original drawings for the glass insert survive at the Corning Museum of Glass, Corning, N.Y.

Cat. 23

Modern carafe on stand with four individual carafes, 1949. Ernest L. Lilja, designer; Inland Glass Works, Chicago, maker. Glass, plastic, and steel with platinum decoration; carafe on stand: h. 16 in. (40.6 cm), diam. 6½ in.

(16.5 cm). Large carafe marked: INLAND XXX | PATENT NO. | DES. 106,186 | 16 CUP | HAND BLOWN [all in a circle]. Others unmarked. Dallas Museum of Art, 20th-Century Design Fund, 1996.1; 1997.9.1–6.

While examples were produced before World War II, the use of laboratory glass for domestic purposes, especially for serving coffee, did not become popular until the late 1940s and 1950s. The original label on this set states that it was made of "hand blown TRIPLE XXX heatproof glass" onto which the platinum decoration was fired "to make it long wearing under constant use." Inland Glass Works was a division of Chamberlain when this design was introduced, but was later owned by Club Aluminum Products of Chicago. Inland Glass Works also made oil and vinegar bottles from scientific glass.[1]

1. CGJ 146:2 (Feb. 1950): 70; and 146:4 (Apr. 1950): 66.

Cat. 24

***American Modern* tableware,** ca. 1937. Russel Wright, designer; Steubenville Pottery, Steubenville, Ohio, maker; Wright Accessories, Inc., New York, and Richards-Morgenthau, Chicago and New York, distributors. Earthenware; pitcher: h. 10⅝ in. (27 cm), w. 8⅛ in. (20.6 cm), d. 8⅛ in. (20.6 cm). All marked: *Russel | Wright | MFG. BY | STEUBENVILLE.* Dallas Museum of Art: (pitcher) General Acquisitions Fund, 1988.50; (cup and saucer) gift of the Friends of the Decorative Arts' 1991 Twilight Zone Trip, 1991.90; (teapot, demitasse cup and saucer, bread plate, and luncheon plate) gift of Rozwell Sam Adams in memory of Herndon Kimball Adams and Loither Iler Adams, 1991.99.1–4; (gravy boat, covered casserole dish, sugar bowl, plate, and bowl) gift of Glenn Lane, 1994.15.1, .4, .5, .7, .8.

It took Russel Wright two years to find a pottery that would produce his radical shapes. Nevertheless, *American Modern* became one of the best-selling dinnerwares of all time. In production between 1939 and 1959, it is said to have grossed $150 million, and Steubenville Pottery expanded twice to keep up with orders for the ware. Over time it was offered in eleven colors, including those illustrated: *Chartreuse, Seafoam,* and *Coral.*[1]

1. For discussions of this line, see Kerr 1990, 74–84; and Eidelberg 1991, 36–37.

Cat. 25

***Washington Wakefield* luncheon plate,** 1927. Frank Holmes and Ernest Henk, designers; Lenox China, Trenton, maker. Porcelain. Marked: L [in wreath] | LENOX | WASHINGTON | WAKEFIELD. Dallas Museum of Art, 20th-Century Design Fund, 1996.130.

No. 1445 shape plate with *The Virginian* pattern, ca. 1905–09. Frank Holmes, pattern

designer; Lenox China, Trenton, maker. Porcelain with printed, painted, and gilded decoration; h. ¾ in. (1.9 cm), diam. 10½ in. (26.7 cm). Marked: L [in wreath] | LENOX | THE VIRGINIAN DECORATION | COPYRIGHT. Newark Museum, gift of Walter Scott Lenox, 1915, 15.780.

Although the no. 1445 plate shape featuring a scalloped rim was designed between 1905 and 1909, *The Virginian* surface ornament was created in 1910.

No. 670 shape demitasse cup and saucer and no. 742 shape teapot with *The Mt. Vernon* pattern, ca. 1900–05. Frank G. Holmes, pattern designer; Lenox China, Trenton, maker; Tiffany & Co., New York, retailer. Porcelain with painted and gilded decoration. All marked: L [in wreath] | LENOX | TIFFANY & CO. | THE | MT. VERNON. Cup and saucer also marked: 670 (shape number) | H.48 (pattern number). Pot also marked: 742 (shape number) | H48 (pattern number). Dallas Museum of Art, 20th-Century Design Fund, T42481.1–2.

Although *The Mt. Vernon* pattern was introduced in 1911, the shapes illustrated here were conceived several years earlier. Both the cup and saucer shape and that for the teapot date to the first few years of the century.

The colonial revival style was so popular by 1910 that a name alone could convey a sense of tradition. Lenox's *The Virginian* and *The Mt. Vernon* patterns have little, if anything, to do with colonial American life, but the names evoke the past and the patterns suited the idea of traditional elegance during this period. *Washington Wakefield*, which was designed more than ten years later for "lovers of Colonial art as well as history," shows a more historical approach to the past. For this pattern, Lenox's designers copied salt-glazed stoneware shards retrieved from archaeological digs on the grounds around Wakefield, the birthplace and boyhood home of George Washington, which burned to the ground on December 25, 1780. Although the service was designed "at the request of" the Wakefield National Memorial Association, which was organizing the reconstruction of the estate in the late 1920s, the *Washington Wakefield* pattern was widely sold as a standard Lenox product for those who wanted "to eat with ancestors, inspire appetite with imagination and flavor food with romance and tradition."[1]

1. "The Washington Wakefield" (Lenox sales brochure).

Cat. 26

All pieces: Frederick H. Rhead, designer; Homer Laughlin China Company, Newell, W. Va., maker. Earthenware.

Harlequin plate, cup and saucer, jug, salt and pepper shakers, ca. 1936. Jug: h. 4¾ in.

(12.1 cm), w. 6½ in. (16.5 cm), d. 3⅜ in. (8.6 cm). All unmarked. Dallas Museum of Art, gift of Drs. Sylvia M. and Charles L. Venable in honor of Alice Lane Venable, 1992.526.1–5.

Harlequin was developed as a less expensive version of *Fiesta* (cat. 28). Although the line had been designed earlier, it was not introduced until 1938. *Harlequin* was sold exclusively through F. W. Woolworth & Co. stores until it was discontinued in 1964. The line was reissued with some modifications in 1979, on the occasion of Woolworth's centennial, but it remained in production for only a few years.

Century shape soup bowl with no. C22 pattern, 1931. Earthenware with painted decoration. Marked: *HL [conjoined] | HOMER LAUGHLIN | MADE IN U.S.A. | [illegible]* and *Wells [peacock logo] | MADE IN U.S.A.* Dallas Museum of Art, 20th-Century Design Fund, 1995.160.

In 1930 Homer Laughlin developed its *Wells Art Glaze* line. Among the colors in this line was an ivory glaze called *Vellum*, which is seen on this bowl.

Riviera luncheon plate and covered casserole dish, 1931. Both unmarked. Dallas Museum of Art, 20th-Century Design Fund, 1995.156, 1995.98.

The *Riviera* line was introduced to the market in 1938. However, most of *Riviera*'s forms were taken from the *Century* shape range (1931), while the salt and pepper shakers came from *Tango* (1937). A few new shapes were designed to harmonize with the older ones, but what made *Riviera Riviera* was its glazes. Meant to be mixed and matched at the table, the colors were green, mauve, blue, red, and yellow.

Cat. 27
Swing shape cup and saucer with Pink Organdy pattern and coffeepot, creamer, and sugar bowl, 1937. Attributed to Frederick H. Rhead, designer; Homer Laughlin China Company, Newell, W. Va., maker. Earthenware; coffeepot: h. 6¾ in. (17.1 cm), w. 6⅜ in. (16.2 cm), d. 4 in. (10.2 cm). Saucer marked: *HLC | SWING | Eggshell | U.S.A. | B 41 N 5* (date mark for 1941). Coffee set marked: same except with *K 38 N 5* (date mark for 1938). Dallas Museum of Art, 20th-Century Design Fund, 1995.106, 1996.230.1–3.

Swing was the third shape produced in the *Eggshell* body. When introduced in 1938 it was available with green, blue, or pink handles, and with a variety of banded and decal decorations. Homer Laughlin's initial advertisements for the ware stated: "Music and dance are typical of American living these days. And here is music in tableware . . . a new, high-spirited shape called 'Swing' to suit the tempo

of the times. Swing is distinguished by its simple, modern, smooth-gliding lines and its dynamic, youthful, appeal. It is made in the famous Eggshell, . . . remarkable for its light weight, its delicacy and its craze-proof glaze. . . . We invite you to inspect this new Homer Laughlin development. Swing into bigger profits with Swing."[1] The shape was sold into the 1950s.

1. *CGJ* 122:1 (Jan. 1938): 36. For general information see Jasper 1993, 126–33.

Cat. 28
Fiesta tableware, 1935. Frederick H. Rhead, designer; Homer Laughlin China Company, Newell, W. Va., maker. Earthenware; plate: h. ⅞ in. (2.2 cm), diam. 9⅜ in. (23.8 cm). Pitcher, cup and saucer, plate, and bowl marked: *GENUINE | fiesta | HLCo USA.* Carafe marked: same except *GENUINE* omitted. Shakers unmarked. Dallas Museum of Art: (carafe) 20th-Century Design Fund, 1995.157; (others) gift of Drs. Sylvia M. and Charles L. Venable in honor of Alice Lane Venable, 1992.525.1–6.

Fiesta was one of the most popular tableware lines ever made. Capitalizing on this commercial success, Homer Laughlin produced a wide range of forms in the design, including vases and candleholders. The color range was also broad. The original hues were blue, green, ivory, red, and yellow. In 1937 turquoise was added, but in 1943 red had to be dropped because the pottery could not obtain the uranium oxide needed for the glaze during the war. By fall 1951 green, blue, and ivory had been replaced by chartreuse, forest green, gray, and rose. In 1959 red was reinstated and a new color, called medium green, was added. In an effort to make the line more contemporary, it was restyled in late 1969 and produced only in red as *Fiesta Ironstone* (discontinued in 1972). Fourteen years later Homer Laughlin reintroduced *Fiesta* with updated shapes and glaze colors. This version is still in production.[1]

1. For more information on *Fiesta*, see Cunningham 1998, 159–71.

Cat. 29
Sierra bowl, ca. 1930. Jeannette Glass Company, Jeannette, Pa. Glass with pressed decoration; h. 3½ in. (8.9 cm), diam. 8¼ in. (21 cm). Unmarked. Dallas Museum of Art, 20th-Century Design Fund, 1996.161.

Jeannette Glass began the automatic production of clear and colored pressed glass in 1927. *Sierra* was introduced in 1931 and discontinued in 1933. Also available in pink glass, the line consisted of at least sixteen different pieces.[1]

1. For illustrations of numerous forms, see Florence 1986, 187.

Cat. 30
All pieces: Hall China Company, East Liverpool, Ohio. Stoneware.

Sundial covered casserole dish, ca. 1937. Marked: *HALL [in a circle] | MADE IN U.S.A. | 2068 | [illegible].* Dallas Museum of Art, 20th-Century Design Fund, 1995.121.

Hercules covered pitcher, ca. 1939. Westinghouse Electric Company, Pittsburgh, distributor. H. 9¼ in. (23.5 cm), w. 7¼ in. (18.4 cm), d. 3½ in. (8.9 cm). Marked: *MADE EXCLUSIVELY FOR | WESTINGHOUSE | BY | The Hall China Co. | MADE IN U.S.A.* and *03.* Dallas Museum of Art, gift of David T. Owsley, 1997.42.

General covered leftover dish and covered butter dish (far right), ca. 1938. Westinghouse Electric Company, Pittsburgh, distributor. Both marked: *Made | Exclusively for | WESTINGHOUSE By | The Hall China Co. | Made in U.S.A.* Leftover dish also marked: *3.* Dallas Museum of Art: 20th-Century Design Fund (orange leftover dish), 1996.4; anonymous gift in honor of Douglas Hawes (green butter dish), 1995.88.

Nora pitcher, ca. 1954. McCormick & Co., Baltimore, distributor. Dallas Museum of Art, gift of Mr. and Mrs. Jeremy L. Halbreich, 1995.81.

This pitcher was sold as a premium for $.89 with the purchase of McCormick tea bags in the mid-1950s.[1]

Airflow teapot, 1937. Marked: *Hall [in circle] | MADE IN U.S.A.* Dallas Museum of Art, 20th-Century Design Fund, 1995.158.

Although some sources state that the *Airflow* design was introduced in 1940, *Crockery and Glass Journal* announced its appearance in January 1938.[2]

Plain covered casserole dish, ca. 1951. Westinghouse Electric Company, Pittsburgh, distributor. Marked: *HALL [in a circle] | MADE | EXCLUSIVELY | FOR | WESTINGHOUSE.* Dallas Museum of Art, gift of Mr. and Mrs. Robert F. Venable, 1995.48.

Hall China specialized in producing extremely durable ceramics through a process that required a single firing. The shock-resistant stonewarelike body that resulted was well suited for use in kitchens, and especially in refrigerators, where breakage due to constant handling was a major problem.[3]

1. For an image of a 1955 tea advertisement showing the pitcher, see Whitmyer and Whitmyer 1994, 187.
2. *CGJ* 122:1 (Jan. 1938): 47–49.
3. For more information on Hall's refrigerator ware, see Whitmyer and Whitmyer 1994, 187–93.

Cat. 31

Stratoware covered pitcher, salt and pepper shakers, creamer, and sugar bowl, ca. 1941. Eva Zeisel and Pratt Institute students, designers; Universal Potteries, Cambridge, Ohio, maker; Sears, Roebuck & Co., Chicago, retailer. Earthenware; pitcher: h. 8¼ in. (21 cm), w. 6 in. (15.2 cm), d. 3½ in. (8.9 cm). Pitcher, creamer, and sugar bowl marked: *Stratoware* / *MADE IN U.S.A.* [with image of an airplane in clouds]. Shakers unmarked. Dallas Museum of Art, 20th-Century Design Fund, 1995.166.1–3, 1996.31.1–2.

Created for sale through the Sears mail-order catalogue, this ware was designed for the middle-class market, which demanded "beauty, utility, and economy." Thus except for cups, the handles were integral with the body for ease of manufacture and reduction of breakage. The ring handles on the cups were designed so that the vessels stacked easily. The 1942 Sears catalogue said: "Stratoware is as in key with modern living as the newest TWA Stratoliners. Distinguished ware that is practical enough for everyday. Two beautifully blended colors on every piece. Four air-minded trim colors: Horizon Blue, Flare Yellow, Wing Brown, and Airport Green. Body is contrasting San Diego Sand color. . . . Design created exclusively for Sears by the Industrial Design Dept. of Pratt Institute."[1] A twenty-piece service for four sold for $3.29.

1. For a reproduction of the ad and for comments on *Stratoware,* see Montreal 1984, 31–32. Zeisel stated that the ware was made by Universal (Zeisel interview 1996).

Cat. 32

Petalware creamer, sugar bowl, plate, salad plate, cup and saucer, ca. 1930. Macbeth-Evans Glass Company, Charleroi, Pa., or Corning Glass Works, Corning, N.Y. Glass with pressed and painted decoration; sugar bowl: h. 3⅜ in. (8.6 cm), w. 5 in. (12.7 cm), d. 3⅜ in. (8.6 cm). All unmarked. Dallas Museum of Art, 20th-Century Design Fund, 1996.29.1–5.

Macbeth-Evans began producing machine-made tableware during the late 1920s. Two of its most popular lines were *American Sweetheart* and *Dogwood.* These dishes, along with *Petalware,* were rivals to inexpensive pottery being made in the Ohio Valley for the low end of the marketplace. *Petalware,* for example, is known to have been marketed by Corning Glass (which purchased Macbeth-Evans in 1936) to manufacturers for use as premiums.[1] Until its discontinuation around 1940, the line was available with a variety of surface motifs and colors. Ivory-colored glass, or what Corning called *Ivrene,* was the base for most of the enameled decoration. Unlike the illustrated examples, *Petalware* was more commonly ornamented with floral and fruit patterns. It was

also made in clear glass and several striking solid colors including dark blue and red.[2]

1. "Corning Ivrene Petalware: Catalogue 407" (Corning sales brochure, 1938).
2. For an image of various decorative schemes, see Florence 1986, 152–53.

Cat. 33

Constellation creamer, sugar bowl, plate, salad plate, and covered pitcher, ca. 1952. Viktor Schreckengost, designer; Salem China Company, Salem, Ohio, maker. Earthenware with printed decoration (salad plate); pitcher: h. 8¼ in. (21 cm), w. 6½ in. (16.5 cm), d. 5¾ in. (14.6 cm). Creamer, sugar bowl, plate, and covered pitcher unmarked. Salad plate marked: [stylized door logo] / HARMONY HOUSE [in a ribbon] / [two stars] 54W. Dallas Museum of Art, gift of Viktor Schreckengost, T42113.

The *Constellation* shape was available with numerous surface patterns, including the traditional *Shaker Brown Lime* and abstract *Jackstraw* (both ca. 1952–53). The unidentified pattern featuring a rooster as an accent on some pieces was made for Sears, Roebuck & Co. and marketed under the store's Harmony House brand name. When the shape was introduced, Salem called the two-tone glaze effect a "'day and night' art texture."[1]

1. CGJ 153:6 (Dec. 1953): 54.

Cat. 34

Corn set, ca. 1930–40. Unknown factory, Nagoya, Japan. Earthenware with painted decoration; large platter: h. 1 in. (2.5 cm), w. 11⅛ in. (28.3 cm), d. 8½ in. (21.6 cm). All marked: MADE IN / SS [within a diamond] / JAPAN. Anonymous collection.

Although made of low-quality earthenware, this set is nonetheless interesting for its realistic representation of corn through molded and enameled decoration. Corn sets became popular in the 1930s, and both foreign and domestic makers supplied these uniquely American specialty items. The main platter was designed to hold six ears of corn, which would be transferred to the individual plates at the table.

Cat. 35

Champagne pitcher, ca. 1870–88. Attributed to Boston and Sandwich Glass Company, Sandwich, Mass., or New England Glass Company, East Cambridge, Mass. Lead glass; h. 11½ in. (29.2 cm), w. 5½ in. (14 cm), d. 5½ in. (14 cm). Unmarked. Dallas Museum of Art, Dallas Glass Club Collection, gift of the Dallas Glass Club, 1996.106.

This pitcher has a bladder located at the base of the handle that could be filled with ice so that liquids would be cooled but not diluted.

The icelike surface was created during the blowing process by rolling the molten bubble of glass in crushed glass, which adhered to the surface. This type of glass is called "overshot."[1]

1. For a discussion of overshot glass and images of examples from Sandwich, see Barlow and Kaiser 1983, chap. 6.

Cat. 36

Normandie martini mixer with rod, ca. 1958. Morgantown Glassware Guild, Morgantown, W. Va. Lead glass; pitcher: h. 9¾ in. (24.8 cm), w. 5¾ in. (14.6 cm), d. 4 in. (10.2 cm). Labeled: Genuine / Old / Morgantown / Lead [goblet logo] Crystal. Dallas Museum of Art, 20th-Century Design Fund, 1995.176.

In an effort to regain its pre–World War II reputation for producing fine glassware, in 1958 Morgantown launched a new line called Décor, available in seven colors. Décor featured a wide range of barware, including eight martini pitchers or "mixers." *Normandie* was available in three colors—*Steel Blue* (illustrated), *Crystal,* and *Lime.* Morgantown sold the pitchers as part of eight-piece sets, which included six glasses. The glasses that came with the *Normandie* pitcher are conical with a small base. Although the designer of *Normandie* is unknown, Ben Seibel was designing contemporary-style glassware for Morgantown in the mid-1950s and might have executed this design.[1]

1. CGJ 155:1 (July 1954): 68; and 162:5 (May 1958): 51. For images of the other shapes of pitchers and colors, see Gallagher 1995, 19, 179, 183.

Cat. 37

Cocktail plate with Down the Hatch pattern, ca. 1933. Unknown factory, Nagoya, Japan, maker. Earthenware with printed and gilded decoration. Marked: M [within an] M / [two leafy branches] / HAND PAINTED / JAPAN. Anonymous collection.

This plate is based on a series of cocktail or hors d'oeuvres plates made in England for the importer Maddock & Miller. When they were introduced to the market in late 1932, *Crockery and Glass Journal* said of the English prototypes: "These are not limited to bar use—far from it—as they will make a gay addition to any party and they certainly have loads of appeal as gift sets."[1] Like the Maddock & Miller plates, the Japanese versions, which were of the same shape, featured raised, molded ornament on the rim and drinking scenes in the center. However, whereas the English plates illustrated nineteenth-century bar interiors, the Japanese series sported scenes in the style of the contemporary cartoonist John Held, Jr. Held's work for publications like *Life* was very well known, and the Japanese appropriated his style to ensure the popularity of these inexpensive sets of cocktail plates.

Cocktail plate with *Hot Toddy* pattern from the *Cocktail Hour* series, ca. 1937. Gale Turnbull and Jane Bennison, shape designers; Vernon Kilns, Los Angeles, maker. Earthenware with printed decoration; h. 1 in. (2.5 cm), diam. 8½ in. (21.6 cm). Marked: COCKTAIL HOUR / by / Vernon Kilns / U.S.A. Dallas Museum of Art, 20th-Century Design Fund, 1997.65.

This plate is one of several sold by Vernon Kilns around 1950 as part of the *Cocktail Hour* series. Each featured a border depicting the names and images of popular drinks and a different woman in a suggestive pose in the center. The name of this particular plate—*Hot Toddy*—is a clever play on words describing both a cocktail and the sexy woman. Examples are known on which colored enamels have been added over the printed decoration.

1. "Right Out of the Kiln," *CGJ* 110:11 (Nov. 1932): 18.

Cat. 38
Cup and saucer and luncheon plate with *El Rancho* pattern, ca. 1950. Wallace China Company, Los Angeles. Stoneware with printed decoration. Plate marked: *Wallace / CHINA / 14-X / LOS ANGELES, CALIF.* and *EL RANCHO PATTERN.* Cup and saucer marked: same except ® above *Wallace* and 7-S (cup) and 9-S (saucer). Dallas Museum of Art, 20th-Century Design Fund, 1997.224.1–2.

This ware was made for use in restaurants and thus is especially heavy for durability.

Snack plate and mug with *Country Modern* pattern, ca. 1950. B. J. Brock & Co., Lawndale, Calif. Earthenware with sprayed decoration. Plate marked: *Brock / OF CALIFORNIA.* Cup unmarked. Dallas Museum of Art, 20th-Century Design Fund, 1997.123.

Brock produced several patterns and shapes in a series called Farmhouse Provincial. The first of these appeared in about 1950 and was called *California Farmhouse.* Advertising material for this pattern stated that it was styled "for all types of home, because here at last is a truly American dinnerware; California designed for modern living, without losing the quaint charm of its 'Early American' heritage."[1] By 1952 three other related patterns had been added—*Country Lane, California Chanticleer,* and *Country Modern* (illustrated). In *House Beautiful* Brock described these new patterns as "Pretty and oh, so practical, these dishes and accessory pieces are modern in shape, provincial in design . . . right for contemporary and traditional homes."[2]

Wagon Wheel plate and dessert bowl and underplate, ca. 1941–42. Frankoma Pottery, Sapulpa, Okla. Earthenware. Plate marked: FRANKOMA. Dessert bowl marked: FRANKOMA and 94XO. Underplate marked: same as bowl except 94E. Elizabeth and Duncan Boeckman Collection.

Wagon Wheel was one of several Western-style lines produced by Frankoma. Others included motifs like arrowheads and barrels.[3]

Montecito shape plate and covered casserole dish with *Winchester '73* pattern, ca. 1935. Vernon Kilns, Los Angeles. Earthenware with printed and painted decoration; plate: h. ¾ in. (1.9 cm), diam. 10½ in. (26.7 cm). Both marked: *Winchester / 73 / [crossed rifles] / Hand Painted / Under Glaze / By / Vernon Kilns / U.S.A.* [all in a circle]. Dallas Museum of Art, 20th-Century Design Fund, 1997.26.1–2.

While the *Montecito* shape was introduced around fifteen years earlier, *Winchester '73* first appeared in 1950. Early advertisements proclaimed: "All the romance of the winning of the West is in this attractive new pattern . . . designed with a particular eye to masculine tastes . . . for casual dining any time, anywhere. WINCHESTER '73 has he-man appeal, with its bold Western scenes . . . cowboys . . . covered wagons . . . in dramatic colors on a soft green background. WINCHESTER '73 will be introduced simultaneously with the great new Universal-International picture, 'Winchester '73' starring James Stewart and Shelley Winters and will tie in with tremendous studio promotion of the new film!"[4] Three years later Winchester Repeating Arms Company sued Vernon Kilns for using its name. Consequently, the name of this pattern changed to *Frontier Days.*

1. "California Farmhouse" (Brock sales brochure, ca. 1950).
2. HB 94:11 (Nov. 1952): 22.
3. For more information, see Bess and Bess 1995, 63.
4. CGJ 146:6 (June 1950): 5.

Cat. 39
Desert Rose plate and coffeepot, 1940. Mary Jane Winans, designer; Franciscan Division, Gladding, McBean & Co., Glendale, Calif., maker. Earthenware with painted decoration; plate: h. 1 in. (2.5 cm), diam. 10⅝ in. (27 cm). Both marked: FRANCISCAN / MADE IN / CALIFORNIA / U.S.A. / HAND DECORATED / GLADDING, / McBEAN / & Co. / OVEN-SAFE. Dallas Museum of Art: gift of Gary D. Wooley in honor of the renewed friendship of Mary Thompson and Jerry Wooley (plate), T42641; 20th-Century Design Fund (coffeepot), T42626.

In 1940 Franciscan released *Apple,* the first in a series of casual peasant designs featuring relief molding and handpainted decoration.

This initial pattern was followed by *Desert Rose* (introduced 1941) and *Ivy* (introduced 1948). Of the three, *Desert Rose* was the most popular. In fact, it is among the most popular American dinnerware patterns ever made—by the end of 1964 the pottery had made over 60 million pieces in the pattern.[1]

1. "Franciscan Feat," GTR (12 Dec. 1964): 4. For early ads for *Apple* and *Desert Rose,* see respectively CGJ 126:4 (Apr. 1940): 5; and 128:5 (May 1941): 7.

Cat. 40
Fine China shape teapot with *Roman Coin* pattern, ca. 1955. Sascha Brastoff, designer; Sascha Brastoff Products, Inc., Los Angeles, maker. Whiteware with printed and gilded decoration. Marked: [rooster logo] / Sascha Brastoff / FINE CHINA / CALIFORNIA / USA / ©. Dallas Museum of Art, 20th-Century Design Fund, 1997.10.

Roman Coin was introduced to the market in mid-1956 as part of Brastoff Products' new *Fine China* line. Made of a highly vitrified and thinly potted body, these wares initially came in at least eight patterns. A contemporary catalogue stated that the line was "created for the connoisseur."[1] *Roman Coin* was one of the most sophisticated of the patterns offered, featuring a matte gray glaze and concentric black and gold circles. The shape of the teapot, as well as the coupe-shaped plates and teacups and saucers, is strikingly similar to those designed in 1931 by Trude Petri as part of her famous *Urbino* service. Made by the Staatliche Porzellan-Manufaktur in Berlin, the *Urbino* shapes were imported into the United States in the early 1950s by Fraser's in Berkeley, California, and thus were likely copied by Brastoff or another staff designer.[2]

Plate and cup and saucer with *Laguna* pattern and sugar bowl and creamer with *Monterrey* pattern, ca. 1965. Dorothy C. Thorpe, designer; Crown Lynn Potteries, New Zealand, maker; Dorothy C. Thorpe, Inc., Sun Valley, Calif., importer. Earthenware; plate: h. 1 in. (2.5 cm), diam. 10⅜ in. (26.4 cm). Plate and cup and saucer marked: *Laguna / Pat. No. 484 / DESIGNED BY / Dorothy C. Thorpe / of California / CROWN LYNN POTTERIES / NEW ZEALAND / DETERGENT PROOF COLOURS.* Others marked: same except pattern name *Monterrey* at beginning and patent number 473. Dallas Museum of Art, gift of Carole Stupell, Ltd., T42624.27–28.

These shapes are some of Thorpe's most playful. Animated by their ball handles and two-tone color schemes, the designs have an almost cartoonish quality. In addition to *Laguna* and *Monterrey,* the patterns *Pine, Santa Barbara, Brocade, Palm Springs,* and *Golden Rain* were applied to this shape. Except for *Laguna* and *Pine,* which was $5 less, the line cost

$34.50 for a twenty-piece starter set.[3] This ball-handled shape is known to have been produced for Thorpe in France and in New Zealand. A cup and saucer made from a coarse porcelain decorated in pink and blue and marked "Porcelain du Paris" is in the collection of the Brooklyn Museum. For customers who did not want cups with spherical handles, versions featuring loop handles were available in all patterns at no extra charge.

1. Conti, et al. 1995, 297, 304–5, 318.
2. *CGJ* 151:4 (Oct. 1952): 65.
3. "Sophisticated Tableware from New Zealand by Dorothy C. Thorpe" (Thorpe sales brochure, [1966]); *China, Glass and Tablewares* (Feb. 1967): 12.

Cat. 41

All ceramic pieces: ca. 1961. W. Craig McBurney, designer; Nippon Toki Kaisha, Nagoya, Japan, maker; Interpace Corporation, Parsippany, N.J., importer. Whiteware with printed decoration. All marked: [*eight stars*] | [*image of Independence Hall, Philadelphia*] | *1776* [*within banner*] | INDEPENDENCE | © IRONSTONE ® | INTERPACE | JAPAN [*all within octagon*].

Independence shape salad plate with *Pillow Talk* pattern. Dallas Museum of Art, 20th-Century Design Fund, 1997.210.

The *Pillow Talk* pattern was introduced in 1975.

Independence shape cup and saucer and plate with *Yankee Doodle* pattern. Dallas Museum of Art, 20th-Century Design Fund, 1997.209.1–2.

The *Yankee Doodle* pattern was introduced in 1973.

Independence shape water goblet and sherbet glass. Glass with pressed decoration. Labeled: INDEPENDENCE | GLASSWARE | COPYRIGHT | JAPAN. Dallas Museum of Art, 20th-Century Design Fund, 1997.191.1–2.

Independence shape coffeepot with *Blue Tulip* pattern. H. 12¾ in. (32.4 cm), w. 8½ in. (21.6 cm), d. 5¾ in. (14.6 cm). Dallas Museum of Art, 20th-Century Design Fund, 1997.211.

The *Independence* line was introduced in 1961 by Castleton China, which was owned and operated by Shenango China Company beginning in 1951. Modeled as an adaptation of early American pewter and ceramic forms, it became one of that pottery's most popular products and remained popular after Interpace purchased Shenango and merged with Gladding, McBean & Co. in 1968. The name, the shape, and the patterns all targeted the traditional consumer through the 1960s and 1970s. The date of its design coincides with the national interest in Jacqueline Kennedy's much-publicized restoration of the White

House. Later, the shape adorned with the *Yankee Doodle* pattern in the colors of the American flag was perfectly suited to the fervor surrounding the American Bicentennial. The irony of the line's being manufactured overseas in Japan was apparently lost on the public amid patriotic marketing.

Cat. 42

Plate and cup and saucer with *Shalimar* pattern, 1972. Otto Lund, pattern designer; Franciscan Division, Interpace Corporation, Glendale, Calif., maker. Stoneware with printed and platinum decoration; plate: h. ⅞ in. (2.2 cm), diam. 10¾ in. (27.3 cm). All marked: SHALIMAR and [*in an oval*] INTERPACE | © ® | *Franciscan* | MASTERPIECE | CHINA | MADE IN U.S.A. Dallas Museum of Art, 20th-Century Design Fund, 1996.119.1–2.

Shalimar was one of five flamboyant surface patterns introduced by Franciscan in 1973; the others were *Madrigal, Ondine, Mandalay,* and *Minaret.* All of these exotic designs derive from Near Eastern and Asian ornament. A sales brochure referenced these origins when it said of the patterns: "They speak of the world of Byzantium. As fanciful as a minaret. As sumptuous as an Oriental carpet. As exotic as a sari. They are our newest patterns, bringing a welcome opulence to china design."[1]

1. "Franciscan Sets Your Table with Masterpieces" (Franciscan sales brochure, 1972?), back cover.

Cat. 43

Taylorton shape bread tray with *Autumn Splendor* pattern, ca. 1958. John Gilkes, designer; Taylor, Smith & Taylor Company, East Liverpool, Ohio, maker. Stoneware. Marked: *Taylorton* | American Fine China [*within a tray-shaped logo*] | A John Gilkes Design | Oven Proof-Craze Proof-Detergent Proof | TAYLOR SMITH & TAYLOR CO. U.S.A. Dallas Museum of Art, 20th-Century Design Fund, 1996.3.

The introduction of *Taylorton* in 1959 was accompanied by a substantial advertising campaign. An ad in *House Beautiful* proclaimed: "Taylorton is for you, for everyday use, because it combines the feel and the look of fine china with a most practical body—it will not stain or scratch . . . it is unharmed by harsh detergents. And it is *oven-proof.*"[1] Such statements reflect the fact that increasingly in the late 1950s women were using dishwashers to clean their dishes and therefore needed tableware that was not fragile. Ads also noted that the shape was available in all-white as well as in "four distinctive modern or traditional patterns." These patterns were called *Rose Sachet, Masterpiece, Silver Wheat,* and *Autumn Splendor.* This last design featured tumbling fall foliage on all the forms except the bread and relish trays (illustrated). It appears that *Taylorton* was in production until the mid-1960s.

Informal shape coffeepot with *Harvest Time* pattern, ca. 1957. Ben Seibel, designer; Iroquois China Company, Syracuse, N.Y., maker. Stoneware with printed decoration; h. 12 in. (30.5 cm), w. 7½ in. (19.1 cm), d. 5½ in. (14 cm). Marked: *Informal* | TRUE CHINA BY | Iroquois [*all within a flame shape*] | A Ben Seibel DESIGN | FLAMEPROOF FOR COOKING | MADE IN USA. Dallas Museum of Art, 20th-Century Design Fund, 1996.232.

When introduced in 1958, *Informal* was promoted as usable on the stove and in the oven thanks to its highly vitrified stoneware body. One sales brochure asked, "What is Cookmanship in China? Imagine scrambled eggs served piping hot in the same decorative fry pan in which they were cooked. That's 'cookmanship' for you. Your Iroquois INFORMAL china not only fries, but bakes, broils, roasts and serves with gourmet distinction. Created by gifted designer Ben Seibel, INFORMAL fulfills your every requirement for informal dining and entertaining—and eliminates washing all those extra pots and pans."[2] Besides *Harvest Time, Informal* was also available in the patterns *Blue Vineyard, Old Orchard, Georgetown,* and *Rosemary.*

1. HB 101:6 (June 1959): 152.
2. "Start Cooking with China!" (Iroquois sales brochure, 1958).

Cat. 44

Flash shape covered bowl and platter with *Flash One* pattern, ca. 1984–87. Dorothy Hafner, designer; Rosenthal Glas und Porzellan, Selb, Germany, maker; Rosenthal USA, New York, importer. Porcelain with printed decoration; covered bowl: h. 6⅛ in. (15.6 cm), w. 9¼ in. (23.5 cm), d. 5⅜ in. (13.7 cm). Both marked: *Rosen* [X surmounted by a crown] *thal* | studio-line | GERMANY and Dorothy Hafner [*worked into decal design*]. Dallas Museum of Art, 20th-Century Design Fund, 1995.59.

The original *Flash* shape, designed by New York studio potter Dorothy Hafner, was introduced as a tea service in 1985. That year it received the Westerwald Prize for best new ceramic design. In 1987 Rosenthal expanded *Flash* to a full line, which received the "Design '88" award from the design center in Stuttgart the following year. In addition to the original *Flash One* surface pattern (illustrated), several others were applied to this shape, including *Flash Frisco, Flash Marking,* and *Biscayne.* Hafner's designs, part of Rosenthal's Studio-Line, were marketed to the most avant-garde consumers who were willing to invest sizable amounts of money in tableware. In 1994 this covered bowl and platter sold for $325 and $175, respectively.[1]

1. "Rosenthal Studio-Line 'Flash'" (sales brochure and price list, 1994).

Cat. 45

Back to front:

Plate, ca. 1929. Catalina Clay Products, Santa Catalina Island, Calif. Earthenware; h. ⅞ in. (2.2 cm), diam. 11¼ in. (28.6 cm). Marked: *CATALINA | ISLAND.* Dallas Museum of Art, 20th-Century Design Fund, T42619.

This type of plain coupe-shaped plate coated in brightly colored glazes was revolutionary when introduced. It not only encouraged rival California firms like J. A. Bauer Pottery Company to produce similar products, but also influenced major, high-volume potteries like Homer Laughlin China Company in Ohio to develop lines of mix-and-match colored dishes by the mid-1930s. Although Catalina was small compared to its midwestern competitors, the firm was successful in distributing its dinnerware nationally. A historian of Chicago's Marshall Field & Co. claimed it was the first department store to introduce solid-colored tableware to the public when in 1933 it began selling dishes "conceived by the chewing gum king, William Wrigley."[1] Wrigley was the owner of Catalina Island and of the pottery. Early glazes used at Catalina were *Descanso Green* (illustrated), *Mandarin Yellow, Catalina Blue, Toyon Red, Pearly White, Sea Foam,* and *Monterey Brown,* as well as turquoise.[2]

Salad and bread and butter plates, ca. 1933. Louis Ipsen, designer; J. A. Bauer Pottery Company, Los Angeles, maker. Earthenware. Both marked: *BAUER | MADE IN | U.S.A. | LOS ANGELES.* Dallas Museum of Art, 20th-Century Design Fund, T42598.1–2.

What collectors now call "Ringware" was the second line that Bauer made in a range of bright, solid colors. However, the line was originally marketed along with Bauer's plain dinnerware simply as Bauer California Pottery. The first colors in which the line appeared were *Jade Green, Delph Blue,* and *Chinese Yellow;* shortly thereafter it appeared in black, white, and orange.[3]

1. "Give the Lady What She Wants!" *CGJ* 151:2 (Aug. 1952): 40.
2. For more information on Catalina, see Chipman 1992, 24–25.
3. For more information on Bauer, see Tuchman 1995 and Chipman 1998.

Cat. 46

Pleat and Panel bread tray and Lorne covered butter dish, ca. 1885. Bryce Brothers, Pittsburgh, maker. Glass with pressed decoration; bread tray: h. ⅞ in. (2.2 cm), w. 13 in. (33 cm), d. 8½ in. (21.6 cm). Both unmarked. Dallas Museum of Art: Dallas Glass Club Collection, gift of Virginia Gilbert (bread tray), T42327; Dallas Glass Club Collection, gift of Betty Bell (covered butter dish), T42326.

Amethyst was among several "jewel-tone" colors, including sapphire blue, ruby red, and emerald green, that were popular in pressed glass production during the last decades of the nineteenth century. These pieces are pictured in the 1891 catalogue of the United States Glass Company, a conglomerate of glass companies formed in 1890 that included Bryce Brothers in Pittsburgh.[1] Bryce Brothers had been making these shapes for a number of years prior to that date.

1. Heacock and Bickenhouser 1978, 82.

Cat. 47

Wine cooler, ca. 1811. Josiah Wedgwood & Sons, Etruria, England. Whiteware with applied decoration; h. 9¾ in. (24.8 cm), w. 10 in. (25.4 cm), d. 7½ in. (19.1 cm). Marked: *WEDGWOOD | D* (date mark for 1875 or 1901). Dallas Museum of Art, anonymous gift, 1991.412.84.

Wine coolers of this shape were produced as early as 1811 according to recorded orders from the London sales office, although the date mark shows that this example could be from either 1875 or 1901.[1] The longevity of the essentially neoclassical shape, as well as the applied grapevine border, which appeared on *Queens Ware* dinnerware for the American market throughout the twentieth century, is a testament to the enduring fashion for traditional shapes and patterns.

Soup bowl and Elephant shape tureen with no. 2206 pattern, 1886. James Hadley, shape designer; attributed to Edward Raby, pattern designer; Worcester Royal Porcelain Company, Worcester, England, maker; Ovington Brothers, Brooklyn and New York, importer. Whiteware with printed, painted, and gilded decoration. Both marked: *OVINGTON BROTHERS [within a banner] | [crown] | [four intertwined Ws, C, and 51 at the center of the mark] | X | Rd No 36114 | W 2206* (pattern number). Dallas Museum of Art, gift of Rozwell Sam Adams in memory of Herndon Kimball Adams and Loither Iler Adams, 1998.126.1–2.

Much of the tableware imported to America from England in the late nineteenth century was not bone china but a durable form of whiteware often called ironstone or graniteware. The illustrated tureen, with its elephant handles, Japanese-inspired daisies, and muted pink color, is indicative of the taste for exotic decoration that was favored by many tableware manufacturers during this period.

1. Reilly 1989, 483.

Cat. 48

Two dessert plates and a compote, ca. 1882–93. Ott & Brewer, Trenton, maker; Tiffany & Co., New York, retailer. Porcelain with painted and gilded decoration; square plate: h. 1 in. (2.5 cm), w. 8¼ in. (21 cm), d. 8¼ in. (21 cm). All marked: *TIFFANY & CO. | BELLEEK | O & B [on crescent with] TRENTON | N.J.* Newark Museum, gift of Mrs. W. Clark Symington, 1965, 65.8.

Ott & Brewer was the first Trenton whiteware company to set up a separate studio for making and decorating the delicate ivory-colored porcelain. Developed commercially under the company's design director, Walter Scott Lenox, in 1882, the body was marketed as *Belleek.*[1] The paste and production methods were perfected under William Bromley Sr. and his son, who were brought in from the Belleek factory in Ireland. Experienced English and Continental decorators embellished the extravagant shapes. While the very earliest Ott & Brewer pieces are nearly indistinguishable from Irish *Belleek,* Lenox quickly developed a signature Trenton style that married the ivory-colored Irish body with Aesthetic-style decoration characteristic of the Worcester and Minton factories. The motifs on these pieces are in the Anglo-Japanese taste popular in the last quarter of the nineteenth century.

1. Denker 1989, 14–15; Frelinghuysen 1989, 43–49.

Cat. 49

Plate with Erie pattern, ca. 1880. Thomas Till & Sons, Burslem, England. Earthenware with printed and painted decoration. Marked: *TRADE [star] MARK | ERIE [within a globe] | TILL & SONS | 3362 | 6.* Anonymous collection.

Plate with Drapeau pattern, 1886. Possibly F. Winkle & Co., Stoke-upon-Trent, England. Earthenware with printed and painted decoration. Marked: *DRAPEAU | Rd No 46496 [within a rectangle] | F.W.C and 4 and 3999.* Anonymous collection.

Plate, ca. 1885. Ott & Brewer, Trenton. Whiteware with printed, painted, and gilded decoration; h. ⅞ in. (2.2 cm), diam. 10¼ in. (26 cm). Marked: *OPAQUE | O [globe logo with WARRANTED across it] B | CHINA.* Dallas Museum of Art, Discretionary Decorative Arts Endowment Fund, 1997.144.

Innumerable combinations of birds, flowers, bamboo, and geometric ornament in the Japanese taste were applied to dinnerware made in English and American potteries for the American market. By the 1880s most of the larger potteries had added decorating departments that could produce these complex decorative designs quickly.

Cat. 50

Covered tureen, stand, and ladle, ca. 1885. Mercer Pottery, Trenton. Whiteware with printed and painted decoration; stand: h. 1½ in. (3.8 cm), w. 13½ in. (34.3 cm), d. 10 in. (25.4 cm). Stand marked: [globe enclosing] MERCER / WARRANTED / CHINA. Others unmarked. Newark Museum, gift of the Overseas Ministries Study Center, 1969, 69.99.

One of the first Trenton factories to add a decorating department, John Moses's Mercer Pottery turned out enormous quantities of whiteware and cream-colored ware in the 1870s. By 1880, however, the firm was advertising "Hotel Ware" and "Thin Ware," which may have been closer to stoneware in its formulation, or at least had a glaze that did not craze, or crackle, as readily as softer earthenware glazes.[1] The newer ware was suitable for "HOTEL AND DOMESTIC PURPOSES." This tureen with its stand and ladle are decorated in the Japanese taste with asymmetrical branches of blooming prunus.

1. For these advertisements, see CGJ 2:36 (23 Sept. 1875): 30; 11:26 (24 June 1880): 20; and 12:26 (23 Dec. 1880): 19.

Cat. 51

Plate with Zembo Temple pattern, ca. 1930. Thomas Maddock's Sons Company, Trenton. Porcelain with printed and gilded decoration; h. 1 in. (2.5 cm), diam. 9¾ in. (24.6 cm). Marked: Tho's Maddock's Son's Co. / Trenton, N.J. and ZEMBO TEMPLE / [Shriner's symbol] / HARRISBURG [within a medallion flanked by quarter moons]. Dallas Museum of Art, 20th-Century Design Fund, T42458.

Thomas Maddock's Sons Company made a specialty of creating commemorative items for fraternal organizations such as the Shriners during the early twentieth century. Although plates were a popular form, tankard sets were also made. This example features the extravagant interior of Zembo Temple in Harrisburg, Pennsylvania, surrounded with a border of symbols and symbolic activities associated with the Shriners. According to marks on this plate, Zembo Temple was designed by architect W. F. Wise, whose name appears on the front of the piece. However, other sources list the architect as C. Howard Lloyd. Construction of the temple began in 1929, and the structure was dedicated a year later.[1]

1. For a brief history of Zembo Temple, see Zembo 1976, 5.

Cat. 52

Child's plate and mug, ca. 1940. Warwick China Company, Wheeling. Stoneware with printed and painted decoration. Both marked: SANTONE / WARWICK CHINA / MADE IN U.S.A. Dallas Museum of Art, 20th-Century Design Fund, 1997.182.1–2.

The amusing images of roller-skating animals and vegetable creatures on these pieces are found on ware from several potteries. In 1941, for example, Syracuse China used them on an order from the Great Northern Railroad.[1] Each pottery simply bought the same decal designs from the same printer and applied them to its own shapes.

Morwel shape plate with Deep Sea Fish pattern, ca. 1935. R. Guy Cowan, shape designer; Onondaga Pottery Company, Syracuse, N.Y., maker; S. W. Stinemetz, Washington, D.C., retailer. Whiteware with sprayed decoration. Marked: 3-EE (date code for March 1950) / SYRACUSE / China / U.S.A. William Swann and William Leazer Collection.

Deep Sea Fish (Shadowtone pattern no. 18) was designed for the Neptune Room restaurant in Washington, D.C., and was ordered by that establishment from 1938 to 1963. The Shadowtone ornamental technique was developed by the head of Onondaga's decorating department, Harry Aitken, and was introduced in 1938; the pottery produced nearly three hundred patterns in this line using a sophisticated decorative process that employed stencils and air-brushed glazes. The Econorim shape range was introduced in 1933. Morwel was the same as Econorim except that it lacked the molded decoration on the rim. Morwel was in production from 1935 until 1997.[2]

Plate, ca. 1930–40. Sterling China Company, East Liverpool and Wellsville, Ohio. Whiteware with printed decoration; h. 1¼ in. (3.2 cm), diam. 10⅜ in. (26.4 cm). Marked: MEDALLION / STERLING / CHINA © / L-8 (date code for April–June 1976). William Swann and William Leazer Collection.

The logo of a winged streamliner locomotive was probably designed for the Union Pacific Railroad before World War II. However, dishes with the design were produced for use in the line's business cars by numerous potteries, including Homer Laughlin China Company, Scammell China Company, and Onondaga Pottery Company. Sterling China Company made this particular example in 1976.[3]

Pilgrim shape plate with Aeroplane pattern, 1932. Bertram Watkin, shape designer; Onondaga Pottery Company, Syracuse, N.Y., maker; Nathan Straus-Duparquet, New York, retailer. Whiteware with sprayed decoration. Marked: O.P.C.O / SYRACUSE / CHINA / 4-U (date code for April 1940). Dallas Museum of Art, gift of William Swann and William Leazer, T42593.

The Pilgrim shape was made between 1932 and 1997. However, Aeroplane (Shadowtone pattern no. 35) was designed in 1940. The surface decoration was commissioned by the Air Lines Terminal restaurant in New York, which used the pattern until 1946.

1. Reed and Skoczen 1997, 19.
2. For information on Shadowtone and Syracuse hotel ware, see ibid., chap. 4.
3. For information on this and other railroad china, see McIntyre 1990.

Cat. 53

Plate with Bangor pattern, ca. 1905. Buffalo Pottery, Buffalo. Earthenware with printed and painted decoration; h. ⅞ in. (2.2 cm), diam. 10⅛ in. (25.7 cm). Marked: SEMI-VITREOUS / [image of a buffalo] / BUFFALO POTTERY and 1372 and 1906 (date). Dallas Museum of Art, 20th-Century Design Fund, T42391.

Plate with Vienna pattern, ca. 1915. Buffalo Pottery, Buffalo. Earthenware with printed decoration. Marked: SEMI-VITREOUS / [image of a buffalo] / BUFFALO POTTERY / VIENNA and TT. Dallas Museum of Art, 20th-Century Design Fund, T42388.

The creators of Bangor and Vienna were heavily influenced by turn-of-the-century central European design. Between 1900 and 1920 highly stylized floral motifs such as these were applied to everything from textiles to building facades in cities like Prague and Vienna. As with most of Buffalo Pottery's early patterns, Vienna was made as a premium for the Larkin Soap Company and appeared in that firm's 1915 catalogue. However, Bangor was never featured in a Larkin catalogue and evidently was sold through standard retail channels.[1]

1. Altman and Altman 1969, 158.

Cat. 54

Nautilus shape covered casserole dish with Della Robbia pattern, 1936. Homer Laughlin China Company, Newell, W. Va. Earthenware with printed decoration; h. 5¾ in. (14.6 cm), w. 11 in. (27.9 cm), d. 7½ in. (19.1 cm). Marked: HLC [conjoined] Eggshell / NAUTILUS / U.S.A. [all in a shell] / D 37 34 4 (date mark for 1937). Dallas Museum of Art, 20th-Century Design Fund, 1996.5.

Nautilus was the first shape produced in Homer Laughlin's new lightweight body called Eggshell. Before its introduction in 1937, much effort had gone into the new body's development. According to a period source, the Eggshell ware "has extraordinary advantages due to its light weight and the rigid control exercised throughout every stage of its manufacture. Each piece is far more uniform in quality than has heretofore been possible."[1]

Like the *Eggshell* body, *Della Robbia* appeared in 1937. Designed for middle-class consumers who shopped at stores like Montgomery Ward & Co. and Sears, Roebuck & Co., this pattern was highly traditional. In advertising it, Homer Laughlin stressed the name's connection to the famous fifteenth-century Florentine sculptors and potters of the della Robbia family, claiming that "DELLA ROBBIA is one of the most appealing numbers in the Eggshell Nautilus line. Breathing the joyous spirit of the Italian Renaissance, yet brilliantly modern in conception and execution, Della Robbia combines in one ware two strong sales appeals . . . traditional beauty and up-to-the-minute practical qualities at a reasonable price."[2]

1. Duke 1995, 412.
2. CGJ 121:2 (Aug. 1937): 10.

Cat. 55

Pintoria luncheon plate, 1936. Metlox Potteries, Manhattan Beach, Calif. Earthenware; h. ⅞ in. (2.2 cm), w. 10⅝ in. (27 cm), d. 8⅝ in. (21.9 cm). Unmarked. Dallas Museum of Art, 20th-Century Design Fund, 1997.185.

This line was available initially in a range of vivid colors—*Delphinium*, *Turquoise Blue*, *Rust*, *Canary Yellow*, and *Poppy Orange* (illustrated).

Plate and luncheon plate, ca. 1933. Jean Luce, designer; unknown factory, Limoges, France, maker. Earthenware with platinum decoration. Both marked: [conjoined J and L within a rectangle] / FRANCE and JEAN LUCE / [conjoined J and L within a rectangle] / FRANCE. Dallas Museum of Art, 20th-Century Design Fund, T42463.1–2.

Square plates became a fashionable alternative to the more conventional round shape early in the 1930s as designers sought to express a new vocabulary of geometrical forms inspired by the Machine Age. Difficult to produce without sagging corners or warped edges, these shapes were technologically and aesthetically challenging. Jean Luce was among the first tableware designers to be associated with the art deco movement; his creations could be found on the most sophisticated tables, including those on the chic French ocean liner the S.S. *Normandie*. The illustrated plates carry a monogram, illustrating the range of custom design that was possible when purchasing from an exclusive shop like Carole Stupell's in New York. Stupell is known to have carried this design as late as the early 1960s, indicating that a market continued to exist for high modernism well after the war.[1]

1. Undated advertisement, Stupell 1932.

Cat. 56

Coronado demitasse cup and saucer and coffeepot, 1935. Mary K. Grant, designer;

Franciscan Division, Gladding, McBean & Co., Glendale, Calif., maker. Earthenware. Coffeepot marked: MADE IN / U.S.A. Cup unmarked. Saucer marked: GMcB [in an oval] / MADE IN / U.S.A. Dallas Museum of Art: gift of Gary D. Wooley and R. Gene Lewis (cup and saucer), T42564; 20th-Century Design Fund (coffeepot), T42450.

Early advertising material for *Coronado* stated that it was "reminiscent of California's formal Spanish spirit" and available in ivory, turquoise, yellow, maroon, coral, turquoise green, and light yellow.[1] In 1940 the design appeared in the *Studio Year Book*.[2]

El Patio shape chop plate and teapot with *Padua* pattern, ca. 1933–34. Mary K. Grant, designer; Franciscan Division, Gladding, McBean & Co., Glendale, Calif., maker. Earthenware with painted decoration; chop plate: h. 1⅛ in. (2.9 cm), diam. 12 in. (30.5 cm). Plate marked: FRANCISCAN / • • • WARE / MADE IN U.S.A. Teapot marked: GMcB [in an oval] / MADE IN / U.S.A. Dallas Museum of Art, 20th-Century Design Fund, 1996.165.1–2.

The El Patio shape was originally introduced in 1934 in eight brightly colored solid glazes. Using this older shape, *Padua* was marketed in 1937 as the pottery's first handpainted pattern.[3]

Rancho shape cup and *Montecito* shape saucer and plate with *Geranium* pattern, ca. 1937. Franciscan Division, Gladding, McBean & Co., Glendale, Calif. Earthenware with painted and printed decoration. Cup marked: MADE IN U.S.A. Saucer and plate marked: FRANCISCAN / MADE IN / CALIFORNIA / U.S.A. / • WARE • [all in a circle]. Dallas Museum of Art, 20th-Century Design Fund, 1996.164.1, 3.

The *Rancho* shape range was developed by Catalina Clay Products, bought by Gladding, McBean & Co. in 1937. The *Montecito* shape range was created by Franciscan the same year. In 1939 the firm introduced the *Geranium* surface pattern on a group of shapes that were drawn from both the *Rancho* (cup) and *Montecito* (flatware) shape ranges. *Geranium* was one of the pottery's first patterns to use a printed decal rather than handpainted design.

1. "Coronado Ware" (Franciscan Division sales brochure, ca. 1936).
2. Holme 1940, 104.
3. For an early ad for *Padua*, see CGJ 120:1 (Jan. 1937): 13.

Cat. 57

Chop plate with *Salamina* pattern, ca. 1937. Gale Turnbull and Jane Bennison, shape designers; Rockwell Kent, pattern designer; Vernon Kilns, Vernon, Calif., maker. Earthenware with printed and painted decoration; h. 1 in. (2.5 cm), diam. 16¾ in. (42.6 cm). Marked: SALAMINA / Designed by / Rockwell Kent /

VERNON KILNS / Made in U.S.A. Dallas Museum of Art, 20th-Century Design Fund, 1996.108.

Salamina was the only handpainted, and consequently the most expensive, of three dinnerware patterns that Rockwell Kent designed for Vernon Kilns in the late 1930s—the other patterns were *Moby Dick* and *Our America* (see cat. 171).[1] With scenes adapted from illustrations in Kent's book *Salamina*, published in 1935, the pattern depicted images of Greenland and the native Inuit woman named Salamina whom he met there. Salamina became Kent's housekeeper and friend, and the two shared a close bond. Kent's description of Salamina as "the most faithful, noble, and most beautiful, most altogether captivating" of all the women in north Greenland was used in the advertisements for the pattern. His regard for Salamina can also be seen in the sensitive, dignified way she is depicted in his illustrations.[2] *Salamina* was introduced in 1939, and its production was cut short in 1941 by the war.

1. Nelson 1994, 178–204.
2. For a thorough analysis of the imagery in *Salamina* as well as its cultural context, see Weisman 1996.

Cat. 58

No. 47 shape chocolate pot, ca. 1889. Ceramic Art Company, Trenton. Porcelain with painted and gilded decoration; h. 10 in. (25.4 cm), w. 6 in. (15.2 cm), d. 5 in. (12.7 cm). Marked: [painter's palette logo] CAC [conjoined] / BELLEEK. Dallas Museum of Art, gift of the Dallas Antiques and Fine Arts Society, 1991.23.

This shape appears in a Ceramic Art Company trade catalogue from 1891.[1] It was probably designed in 1889 by Walter Scott Lenox or William Wood Gallimore, an English modeler who worked in both England and Ireland before coming to New Jersey. The decoration, executed between 1889 and 1896, may have been designed by Lenox. The word "Belleek" marked on the chocolate pot's bottom refers to the ivory-colored body, which was reminiscent of porcelain made at the famous Irish Belleek factory.

Chocolate pot, ca. 1887–93. Possibly Walter Scott Lenox, designer; Willets Manufacturing Company, Trenton, maker. Porcelain with painted and gilded decoration. Marked: BELLEEK / [snake in the form of a W] / WILLETS. Newark Museum, Members Fund, 1979, 79.19.

Chocolate cup and saucer, ca. 1887–93. Possibly Walter Scott Lenox, designer; Willets Manufacturing Company, Trenton, maker. Porcelain. Unmarked. Dallas Museum of Art, Discretionary Decorative Arts Endowment Fund, 1997.180.

Walter Scott Lenox, who worked as art director for Willets Manufacturing Company from

1886 to 1889, founded the Ceramic Art Company in 1889.[2] The aesthetic ideas embodied in this group reveal his concept of American fine art porcelain at this time. The ware combines ideas from Worcester and Minton in England and mixes them with motifs and forms in the Japanese taste that was popular at the time.

1. *Ceramic* 1891, 14.
2. Denker 1989, 15–16, 21–26.

Cat. 59

All pieces: Frank G. Holmes and Ernest Henk, designers; Lenox China, Trenton, maker. Porcelain. All marked: L [*in a wreath*] LENOX.

Terrace covered casserole dish, 1932. Dallas Museum of Art, 20th-Century Design Fund, 1996.127.

Three-Step plate and cup and saucer, 1932. Plate: h. ½ in. (1.3 cm), diam. 10½ in. (26.7 cm). Cup also marked: 2300 (shape number). Dallas Museum of Art, 20th-Century Design Fund, 1995.136; 1996.124.

The Lenox design department's ledger records the shape range of which these pieces are a part as the "Stepped Edge Service." Subsequently, however, the various stepped shapes that made up the line were referred to as *Terrace* generally, and as *Three-Step* and *Five-Step* according to the number of rings. Both banded versions were probably introduced so that the company could offer new ware without adding costly colored decal decoration. Adding a decal meant that the ware had to pass through another department and another firing, both of which increased production costs substantially. The salmon bands on the *Three-Step* pieces are actually clay instead of glaze. Colored slip was added as part of the slip-casting processes used to form the ware. With this technique, the banded decoration did not have to be fired separately. In late 1932 the National Alliance of Art and Industry gave these designs the award of merit for excellence in design.[1] In 1933 an undecorated casserole dish retailed for $10.70.[2]

1. *CGJ* 110:11 (Nov. 1932): 21, 25.
2. *CGJ* 112:4 (Apr. 1933): 46.

Cat. 60

All pieces: Winslow Anderson and Lenox Design Department, designers; Lenox China, Trenton, maker.

Plate with Kingsley pattern, ca. 1900–1910. Porcelain with printed and platinum decoration; h. ¾ in. (1.9 cm), diam. 10⅝ in. (27 cm). Marked: L [*in wreath*] | KINGSLEY | BY LENOX | X-445 (pattern number) | MADE IN USA. Dallas Museum of Art, 20th-Century Design Fund, T42506.

The *Kingsley* surface pattern was introduced in 1954. However, the "standard" shape of this dinner plate dates to the first decade of the century. The pattern was in production until 1980.

No. 1620 shape cup and saucer with Jewel pattern, ca. 1905–8. Porcelain with printed, painted, gilded, and platinum decoration. Both marked: L [*in wreath*] | JEWEL | © BY LENOX | A-557 (pattern number) | MADE IN USA. Dallas Museum of Art, 20th-Century Design Fund, T42487.

The *Jewel* pattern was designed in 1956; however, many of the shapes to which it was applied were much older. This cup and saucer, for example, was designed about fifty years earlier. When introduced in early 1957, a five-piece place setting of *Jewel* retailed for $24.95.[1] The pattern was produced until 1970.

Coupe shape coffeepot with Glendale pattern, ca. 1940–45. Porcelain with gilded decoration; h. 8⅛ in. (20.6 cm), w. 7⅞ in. (20 cm), d. 4⅜ in. (11.1 cm). Marked: L [*in wreath*] | GLENDALE | BY LENOX | X-559 (pattern number) | MADE IN USA. Dallas Museum of Art, 20th-Century Design Fund, T42488.

The *Coupe* shape range was designed in the early 1940s and incorporated coupe-shaped plates of earlier design. Following World War II numerous surface patterns were applied to this shape range. *Glendale* was designed in 1954 and available until 1969. When introduced in early 1955 it was said to "appeal to both contemporary and traditional tastes." The color used on the handle, spout, and finial of this pot and the shoulder of the plates was called *Smokey Green*.[2]

Lenox began making tinted body colors in the 1930s. By the 1950s, when these patterns were designed, the company's artisans were expert at producing shapes like the *Kingsley* dinner plate and the *Jewel* cup and saucer shown here, for which they would slip-cast the tinted body first and then slip-cast the ivory body in effect "behind" it. For the *Glendale* coffeepot, the handles and spout were cast in separate molds and applied to the cover and the main body of the pot. *Kingsley*, among the first American patterns to use a solid color border, was one of Lenox's most popular patterns.[3] Although Lenox is generally identified with traditional taste, its work in the 1950s had a stylish, contemporary look.

1. *CGJ* 160:2 (Feb. 1957): 35.
2. *CGJ* 155:8 (Feb. 1955): 37.
3. Anderson interview, 1997.

Cat. 61

Pilgrim shape coffeepot and demitasse cup and saucer with Bourbon pattern, 1923. Theodore Haviland & Co., Limoges, France,

designer; Shenango Pottery Company, New Castle, Pa., maker; Theodore Haviland & Co., New York, distributor. Porcelain with printed and gilded decoration; coffeepot: h. 7½ in. (19.1 cm), w. 8¾ in. (22.2 cm), d. 5 in. (12.7 cm). All marked: THEODORE HAVILAND | NEW YORK and Bourbon. Dallas Museum of Art, 20th-Century Design Fund, 1997.106.1–2.

The *Pilgrim* shape was designed in 1923 for export to the United States. The pattern used here was created at an earlier date, October 1922, and initially called *Rajah*. It was renamed *Bourbon*, as indicated by the marks on these examples. The character of the marks also indicates that these pieces were made in 1936 by Shenango Pottery Company using molds and decals imported from France.[1]

1. D'Albis 1988, 125; and Chantal Meslin-Perrier, letter to Charles Venable, 2 Oct. 1998.

Cat. 62

Ovide shape cup and saucer, teapot, creamer, and sugar bowl with Westwood pattern, 1942. Franciscan Division, Gladding, McBean & Co., Glendale, Calif. Porcelain with printed and painted decoration; teapot: h. 5 in. (12.7 cm), w. 10½ in. (26.7 cm), d. 4½ in. (11.4 cm). All marked: FRANCISCAN | CHINA [*words inside an oval surmounted by a Spanish mission*] | MADE IN CALIFORNIA | WESTWOOD. Dallas Museum of Art, gift of Mr. and Mrs. Robert F. Venable, 1995.16.1–4.

In 1941 Franciscan introduced a brand of translucent fine china called Masterpiece. The first shape to be produced was *Merced* (1940). *Ovide* (also called *Redondo*) appeared in 1942 and was available in several patterns including *Westwood*, *Elsinore*, and *Shasta*. The *Ovide* shape was made through at least 1949. The Hunt Glass Company (location unknown) decorated stemware with enamels to match the *Westwood* pattern.[1]

1. *CGJ* 145:5 (Nov. 1949): 24; 144:6 (June 1949): 84.

Cat. 63

Town & Country shape coffeepot and cup and saucer with Pagoda Lantern pattern, ca. 1955. Attributed to Nan Hogan, designer; Flintridge China Company, Pasadena, Calif., maker. Porcelain with printed decoration; coffeepot: h. 10½ in. (26.7 cm), w. 8⅝ in. (21.9 cm), d. 5 in. (12.7 cm). All marked: FLINTRIDGE CHINA | [*F on an arrowhead flanked by lion supporters*] | U.S.A. | MADE IN CALIFORNIA | Bon-Lite | PAGODA LANTERN | © 1959 FLINTRIDGE CHINA CO. Dallas Museum of Art, 20th-Century Design Fund, 1996.117.1–2.

Flintridge introduced the *Town & Country* shape in January 1956. Initially it appeared in various two-toned color schemes called "Matchmakers Colors."[1] By 1959, when the patterns *Pagoda Lantern* and *Open House* were introduced, the shape was part of what Flintridge called "Bon-Lite Budget translucent china." In that year *Open House*, which was all white except for colored finials on the hollowware, sold for $6.30 per five-piece place setting.[2] In addition to *Pagoda Lantern*, Flintridge produced several other abstract patterns on this shape featuring vertical bands of color, including *Chinese Garden, Imperial Chess, Jade, Rose Quartz, Sapphire,* and *Topaz*. Flintridge China Company was founded in 1946 by Thomas Hogan and Milton Mason, both of whom had worked for Gladding, McBean & Co. The firm's dinnerware was highly successful during the late 1940s and 1950s. According to an article in *Crockery and Glass Journal*, Nan Hogan, wife of Flintridge president Thomas Hogan, was "responsible for the patterns in this fine dinnerware."[3]

1. *CGJ* 158:1 (Jan. 1956): 15.
2. *CGJ* 164:4 (Apr. 1959): 20.
3. "Designs for Living in America," *CGJ* 162:2 (Feb. 1958): 43.

Cat. 64

Epicure coffeepot, 1954. Donald Schreckengost, designer; Homer Laughlin China Company, Newell, W. Va., maker. Earthenware; h. 10 in. (25.4 cm), w. 9½ in. (24.1 cm), d. 4¾ in. (12.1 cm). Unmarked. Dallas Museum of Art, 20th-Century Design Fund, 1995.169.

Epicure was available in four colors—*Dawn Pink, Snow White, Charcoal Grey,* and *Turquoise Blue*. When it was introduced in 1955, Homer Laughlin called *Epicure* its "newest and smartest dinnerware for casual dining! Its superb styling with textured glazes in charming colors . . . creates an incomparable table setting. Sturdy, . . . Multi-purpose, . . . Ovenproof. . . . Meeting America's demand for function and beauty at modest prices."[1] According to Donald Schreckengost, the design was selling well when Homer Laughlin withdrew it from the market as part of its agreement with the Japanese to discontinue production of domestic tableware and to concentrate on hotel ware production.[2]

1. *CGJ* 155:8 (Feb. 1955): 4.
2. D. Schreckengost interview 1995.

Cat. 65

Color-Flyte sugar bowl and creamer, ca. 1950. Hellmich Manufacturing Company, Saint Louis. Melamine. Both marked: DESIGNERS | DINNERWARE | [surrounded by stylized clouds] FASHIONED OF | Melmac | A | Color FLYTE [over three converging lines] | by | BRANCHELL | ST. LOUIS. MO. Anonymous collection.

Hellmich marketed its *Color-Flyte* line under the name of the Branchell Company. Available in several colors, the line was discontinued in January 1959, following Lenox China's acquisition of Hellmich.[1]

Millionaire Line set of six cups and saucers, ca. 1949. Earl Tupper, designer; Tupperware Corporation, Farnumsville, Mass., maker. Polyethylene. Cups marked: TUPPER [in an oval] | Millionaire Line | 1 [or 2] #121 | PATS. APPL'D FOR. Saucers marked: TUPPER [in an oval] | #151 | Millionaire Line | PATS. APLD. FOR. Dallas Museum of Art, anonymous gift in honor of Debra Wittrup, 1995.83.1–6.

The *Millionaire Line* was one of the first produced by Tupper. Also available was a covered beverage server and tray.

Deluxe serving bowl and divided vegetable bowl, 1949. Belle Kogan, designer; Boonton Molding Company, Boonton, N.J., maker. Melamine; serving bowl: h. 2⅛ in. (5.4 cm), diam. 10 in. (25.4 cm). Serving bowl marked: MADE IN | Boonton | N.J. | U.S.A. | 604-10. Divided vegetable bowl marked: same except 605-10. Dallas Museum of Art, gift of Michael E. Pratt, T42378.

While on contract as a designer to Boonton between 1949 and 1962, Belle Kogan designed three full sets of dinnerware, of which *Deluxe* was the first. The line was very successful and established Boonton as a leader in plastic tableware.[2] These bowls could be purchased with or without a cover.

Debonaire creamer, 1956. Kenro Corporation, Fredonia, Wisc. Melamine. Marked: *Debonaire | MELMAC ® | dinnerware | PAT. 2 761 176.* Dallas Museum of Art, anonymous gift, 1995.46.1.

This creamer and its matching covered sugar bowl were introduced to the market in January 1957 to augment Kenro's plastic dinnerware line, which was available in four textured colors: brown (*Cocoa*), pink, white, and yellow. A service for eight cost $29.95.[3]

1. *CGJ* 163:1 (July 1958): 22.
2. The addition of the divided vegetable bowl to the line is noted in *CGJ* 146:2 (Feb. 1950): 57.
3. *CGJ* 16:1 (Jan. 1957): 50.

Cat. 66

All pieces: Russel Wright, designer; Northern Industrial Chemical Company, Boston, maker.

Front to back:

Residential covered vegetable and soup bowls, 1953. Melamine. Both marked: *Russel | Wright | RESIDENTIAL | by | Northern | Boston 27.* Dallas Museum of Art, 20th-Century Design Fund, 1995.165.1–2.

Flair shape platter with *Ming Lace* pattern, ca. 1959. Melamine with embedded leaves; h. 1½ in. (3.8 cm), w. 15 in. (38.1 cm), d. 12 in. (30.5 cm). Marked: *Russel | Wright | FLAIR | by | Northern | Boston 27.* Dallas Museum of Art, 20th-Century Design Fund, 1996.53.

Residential was both a commercial and a critical success. Originally produced in gray and in colors called *Sea Mist, Lemon Ice, Black Velvet,* and *Copper Penny,* the line was later produced in the colors white, light blue, and salmon. By 1957 the line was the best-selling door-to-door tableware in America, with gross sales of $4 million. Simultaneously it was acclaimed as the most artistic of early plastic dinnerware designs. The Museum of Modern Art gave *Residential* a Good Design Award in both 1953 and 1954. Capitalizing on this success, Wright and Northern Industrial brought out *Flair* in 1959. In addition to the shapes being different, this line had pattern. The designs were called *Golden Bouquet, Spring Garden, Woodland Rose, Arabesque,* and *Ming Lace* (illustrated). This last pattern, the most unusual in the group, was created by embedding real leaves from the Chinese jade orchid tree in the plastic.[1]

1. For more information about these lines, see Kerr 1990, 131–32.

Cat. 67

Goblet from the Elbert H. Gary service with no. 8675 pattern, ca. 1900–16. Hieronimus William Fritchie, engraver; attributed to Stevens & Williams, Stourbridge, England, maker; T. G. Hawkes & Co., Corning, N.Y., distributor. Lead glass with cut and engraved decoration. Marked: *Fritchie* and G [monogram]. Dallas Museum of Art, Dallas Glass Club Collection, gift of the Dallas Glass Club, 1993.39.

A large service in this pattern was originally ordered for E. H. Gary, first president of U.S. Steel, from Tiffany & Co. sometime between 1900 and 1910. Most likely Tiffany's asked Hawkes to supply the service, and Hawkes in turn either ordered the blanks fully engraved from Stevens & Williams, who designed the shape and pattern, or else procured the blanks and decorated them in its Corning works. It is unknown who might have engraved the original service, although the names Hall, W. Kny, and Fritchie are variously found on surviving pieces. Confusion about the origin of the engraving has arisen because William Kny worked for the English firm of Webb Corbett.

This goblet may have been fully or partially (just the initial) engraved by Hieronimus William Fritchie, who worked at Hawkes as an engraver between 1900 and 1916. It seems unlikely that he would have signed his name if he had engraved only the initial; however, he might well have fully engraved the piece to match the set as a replacement. Fritchie's name should not be confused with that of William Fritsche, a fellow Bohemian who engraved for Thomas Webb & Co. in England. Regardless of the confusion over the origin of this set, the goblet remains a remarkable example of the Bohemian style of three-dimensional polished engraving known as "rock crystal," which represented the ultimate in glass decoration at the turn of the century.[1]

Champagne glass, ca. 1900–15. Unknown factory, United States, maker; attributed to T. G. Hawkes & Co., Corning, N.Y., decorator. Lead glass with cut decoration. Unmarked. Dallas Museum of Art, gift of the estate of Kathleen Bass Tewes, T42577.

The shape of this goblet is included among Hawkes's profile drawings used for ordering blanks from other companies, which would then be cut or engraved by the Hawkes cutters.[2]

Decanter, ca. 1890–1910. Unknown factory, United States. Lead glass with cut decoration; h. 12 in. (30.5 cm), diam. 5½ in. (14 cm). Unmarked. Dallas Museum of Art, gift of the estate of Kathleen Bass Tewes, T42579.

Ice cream tray, ca. 1880–1900. Attributed to Libbey Glass Company, Toledo. Lead glass with cut decoration. Unmarked. Dallas Museum of Art, gift of the estate of Kathleen Bass Tewes, T42576.

Although this tray is unmarked, its shape and dimensions match those of Libbey's shape no. 285 in its 1896 catalogue.[3] An ice cream set included a large oblong tray, such as the one pictured, and matching round dishes usually numbering a dozen.

Claret jug, ca. 1880–1900. Attributed to Libbey Glass Company, Toledo, maker; unknown factory, United States, decorator. Lead glass with cut decoration. Unmarked. Dallas Museum of Art, gift of the estate of Kathleen Bass Tewes, T42581.

The fact that this jug is not marked indicates that it was probably a Libbey blank (no. 300) that was sold to another company to be cut— a frequent practice. The term "claret jug" is used in the 1896 Libbey catalogue to denote tall jugs such as this one with narrow necks and a flared base. Similar narrow but straight-sided jugs are called champagne jugs in the same catalogue. Wide-necked jugs have no appellation except capacity and were probably intended for lemonade or other nonalcoholic drinks.

Water jug, ca. 1880–1910. Unknown factory, United States. Lead glass with cut decoration. Unmarked. Dallas Museum of Art, Dallas Glass Club Collection, gift of Eugenia Reedy in memory of her parents, Mr. and Mrs. Frank Reedy Sr., 1992.475.

Tumbler with *Chantilly* pattern, ca. 1903–18. Attributed to Frederick Carder, designer; Steuben Glass Works, Corning, N.Y., blank maker; T. G. Hawkes & Co., Corning, N.Y.,

decorator. Lead glass with cut and engraved decoration. Unmarked. Dallas Museum of Art, 20th-Century Design Fund, 1997.199.

Delicate, thinly cut tableware patterns such as *Chantilly* were popular during the first quarter of the twentieth century and were less expensive than the more dramatic rock crystal patterns.

Compote, ca. 1920–40. Unknown factory, United States. Lead glass with cut and engraved decoration. Unmarked. Dallas Museum of Art, Dallas Glass Club Collection, gift of Mrs. G. W. Hayes and Mrs. LaVere Tremblay, 1992.508.1.

Teapot, ca. 1915–30. H. P. Sinclaire & Co., Corning, N.Y. Lead glass with engraved decoration. Marked: S [*within a circle*]. Dallas Museum of Art, Dallas Glass Club Collection, gift of the Dallas Glass Club, 1993.38.

Due to their fragile nature, glass teapots are uncommon from any age, although a handful of examples date back to the eighteenth century. This teapot is decorated with rough engraving, which was popular in the 1920s.
    The examples of cut and engraved glass in this photograph illustrate the wide range of such tableware available in America during the late nineteenth and early twentieth centuries. From extraordinarily expensive rock crystal designs, to brilliant deep cutting, to less expensive wheel-engraved patterns, sparkle on one's table could be procured at many economic levels from American companies by the 1920s.

1. Spillman 1996, 253–54; and Farrar 1977, 728.
2. Spillman 1996, 97.
3. "The Libbey Glass Co. Cut Glass" (trade catalogue, 1 June 1896), 6.

Cat. 68
***Goddess of Liberty* compote,** ca. 1880–85. Challinor, Taylor & Co., Tarentum, Pa., maker. Glass with pressed decoration; h. 7⅝ in. (19.4 cm), diam. 8½ in. (21.4 cm). Unmarked. Dallas Museum of Art, Dallas Glass Club Collection, gift of the Dallas Glass Club, T42324.1.

This type of compote has come to be known among collectors as "Jenny Lind," but the figure on the stem bears little resemblance to the famous nineteenth-century chanteuse. Examples of this compote are quite rare, particularly in color, although it is known to have been produced in white, purple marble, caramel (amber) marble, transparent amber, and blue. This example in green is the only one known in a public institution and may have been an experimental color trial. Two versions of base designs are known on this shape, a ribbed base or a floral band (illustrated). Another example of a compote with

a similar base but a different bowl has been attributed to the Crystal Glass Company.[1]

1. Madarasz 1998, 102.

Cat. 69
Plate, ca. 1925–35. Pairpoint Manufacturing Company, New Bedford, Mass., and Rockwell Silver Company, Meriden, Conn. Glass with silver overlay decoration; h. ⅞ in. (2.2 cm), diam. 10¾ in. (27.3 in.). Unmarked. Dallas Museum of Art, 20th-Century Design Fund, T42457.

No. 1306 shape demitasse cup and saucer and no. 1960 shape coffeepot with *Moderne* pattern, ca. 1908–19. Lenox China, Trenton, and Rockwell Silver Company, Meriden, Conn. Porcelain with silver overlay decoration. Cup and saucer marked: [*painter's pallet*] / L. Cup also marked: 1306 (shape number) / LENOX and R. S. Co. Coffeepot marked: 12 / *Moderne* and L [*in wreath*] / LENOX. Dallas Museum of Art, 20th-Century Design Fund, 1997.8.1–2.

Although the decoration on these porcelain pieces dates to around 1930, the shapes were designed much earlier. The cup and saucer shape was introduced about 1908, and the design for the coffeepot was produced in 1919.
    The fashion for silver applied to ceramic and glass objects was strongest between 1910 and 1930. Although the look of the final product was controlled by the silver manufacturer who applied the decoration and sold the object, fine china and handblown glass were frequently used as blanks. Often the silver company purchased stock shapes from the glass- and china-makers, as was the case here. Occasionally, however, a shape was designed especially for a particular silver company. Silver overlay on tableware is confined primarily to forms used for dessert and beverage service, the type of tableware on which householders were willing to spend a little extra to make a statement about their wealth and taste.[1]

1. For more information on silver overlay, see Stokes 1990.

Cat. 70
Punch bowl and stand with *Grand Prize* pattern, ca. 1905. Libbey Glass Company, Toledo. Lead glass with cut decoration; h. 14½ in. (36.8 cm), diam. 14⅞ in. (37.8 cm). Bowl marked: *Libbey* / [*sword*] / 117. Stand marked: 117. Dallas Museum of Art, 20th-Century Design Fund by exchange, 1997.140.

Punch bowls were items of prestige in a glass-cutting firm's line at the turn of the century. They were often sold as wedding or anniversary presents and usually cost several hundred dollars, more than the price of some cars at the time. This example is a smaller version of Libbey's enormous punch bowl made for the 1904 Louisiana Purchase Exhibition in Saint

Louis, which took top honors at the show. From that point on the cutting pattern was marketed as *Grand Prize* in the firm's catalogue. The pattern required so much cutting that the price was prohibitively expensive and only a few are known to have been made. For middle-class consumers, the look of expensive hand-cut glass could be achieved at a fraction of the cost in pressed glass. As a result, traditional punch bowls continued to reign over the buffet table well past World War II. Duncan & Miller Glass Company, for example, kept pressed versions of cut-glass punch bowls in their catalogue through the 1950s.[1]

1. "Duncan & Miller Catalog no. 93" (trade catalogue, 1955?).

Cat. 71
All pieces: Glass with pressed decoration. Unmarked.

Champagne or sherbet glass, ca. 1933. Attributed to Morgantown Glass Works, Morgantown, W. Va. Dallas Museum of Art, 20th-Century Design Fund, 1996.18.

This glass has been attributed to Morgantown based on the fact that its blue color is seen in other Morgantown products and because its stem shape is closely related to one called *Palazzo*, which first appeared in the firm's catalogues in 1933.[1]

Wineglass with *Paragon* shape stem, ca. 1928. George Dougherty, designer; Morgantown Glass Works, Morgantown, W. Va., maker. Dallas Museum of Art, 20th-Century Design Fund, 1996.24.

George Dougherty of Morgantown, West Virginia, applied for a patent on this stem shape in 1928 and was granted design patent no. 77,943 the next year.[2]

Champagne glass with *Courtney* shape stem, ca. 1928. George Dougherty, designer; Morgantown Glass Works, Morgantown, W. Va., maker. Dallas Museum of Art, 20th-Century Design Fund, 1996.23.

George Dougherty also applied for a patent on this stem profile in 1928 and was granted design patent no. 77,942 the next year.[3] However, the use of a rectangular motif like this one was likely derived from a French crystal shape called *Hagueneau*. Designed in 1924 by René Lalique, that pattern's stem features a square superimposed over a rectangle.[4] Dorothy C. Thorpe is known to have sold the American version with a frosted stem, which was achieved through sandblasting.

Goblet with *Art Modern* shape stem, ca. 1928. George Dougherty, designer; Morgantown

Glass Works, Morgantown, W. Va., maker. H. 7¾ in. (19.7 cm), diam. 3½ in. (8.9 cm). Dallas Museum of Art, 20th-Century Design Fund, 1996.25.

Design patent no. 77,227 was granted to Dougherty for this stem shape in 1929. Reflective of the lukewarm reception that modern designs were having in the marketplace in the late 1920s, an advertisement for this glass stated, "Our new 7640 line of stemware may be 'Modern' in design but, beyond and in spite of that, it is beautiful as well."[5]

Champagne glass with *Yale* shape stem, ca. 1932. Morgantown Glass Works, Morgantown, W. Va. Dallas Museum of Art, 20th-Century Design Fund, 1996.20.

***Walpole* cocktail glass,** ca. 1932. Morgantown Glass Works, Morgantown, W. Va. Dallas Museum of Art, 20th-Century Design Fund, 1996.17.

Morgantown began calling its cased glass stems "filament stems" in 1931. A known example of this glass shape bears an original label "PAT 1933."[6]

The variety of bowl shape, stem profile, and color seen in the glasses reflects the high quality of the best of Morgantown stemware. Few other glasshouses in America competed at this level—Morgantown's main rivals were European.

1. Gallagher 1995, 142.
2. Ibid., 130.
3. Ibid., 131.
4. The Lalique design was reintroduced in the mid-1980s as *Tosca*.
5. *CGJ* 107:3 (Mar. 1929): 73. Also see 107:2 (Feb. 1929): 39.
6. Gallagher 1995, 35.

Cat. 72
All pieces: Fostoria Glass Company, Moundsville, W. Va., maker. Glass with pressed decoration.

***Westchester* shape cordial glass and wineglass with *Festoon* pattern,** ca. 1934. George Sakier, designer. Wineglass: h. 6⅞ in. (17.5 cm), diam. 3¼ in. (8.3 cm). Both unmarked. Dallas Museum of Art: 20th-Century Design Fund (cordial glass), 1996.136; gift of Eason Eige (wineglass), T42318.11.

When the *Westchester* shape was introduced in the fall of 1934, *Festoon* was one of the original cuttings available. The line also came in what Fostoria called its "new Oriental Ruby" color (see cordial glass).[1] In addition, the shape was made over time in burgundy and hues called *Empire Green* and *Regal Blue*. Although the colored versions were dropped in the 1940s, *Westchester* was produced until 1970 in colorless glass.

***Capri* plate, sherbet glass, and iced tea glass,** ca. 1952. George Sakier, designer. Plate labeled: *Fostoria | MADE [goblet logo] IN U.S.A.* Glasses unmarked. Dallas Museum of Art, 20th-Century Design Fund, 1996.134.1–2, 1996.135.

Capri was in production from 1952 until 1965; however, it was produced only with *Bitter Green* or *Cinnamon* colored bases for six years following its introduction.[2]

***Precedence* champagne glass and plate,** ca. 1967. Glass marked: *Fostoria.* Glass labeled: *Fostoria | PRECEDENCE.* Plate unmarked. Dallas Museum of Art, 20th-Century Design Fund, 1996.141.1–2.

Precedence, made from *Onyx* colored glass, was produced from 1967 to 1974. The line was also available in clear and *Gray Mist.*[3]

***Biscayne* sherbet glass,** ca. 1971. Marked: *Fostoria.* Dallas Museum of Art, 20th-Century Design Fund, 1996.140.2.

Biscayne was available from 1971 to 1973 and came in the colors gold (illustrated) and blue, as well as *Nutmeg, Onyx,* and *Snow.*[4]

1. *CGJ* 115:3 (Sept. 1934): 5. For more information, see Long and Seate 1995, 83–84.
2. Long and Seate 1995, 104.
3. Ibid., 133.
4. Ibid., 139.

Cat. 73
***Knickerbocker* tumbler and sherbet glass,** ca. 1932. A. Douglas Nash, designer; Libbey Glass Company, Toledo, maker. Lead glass. Both marked: *Libbey [in a circle].* Dallas Museum of Art, 20th-Century Design Fund, 1995.131.1, 3.

Both *Knickerbocker* and *Malmaison,* discussed below, were part of the new luxury line introduced by Libbey in 1933. *Knickerbocker* was commercially successful enough to be included in the firm's *Modern American* line of 1939, but later and cheaper copies of the design sold best. In 1952 Cambridge Glass Company introduced *Cambridge Square,* a nearly identical and less expensive copy of the Libbey design that seems to have sold well.[1] Another copy of the Libbey design was made in 1968 by the Japanese firm Sasaki Glass.[2]

***American Prestige* wine, cordial, and water glasses,** ca. 1938. Edwin W. Fuerst, designer; Libbey Glass Company, Toledo, maker. Glass with cut and pressed decoration. All marked: *Libbey [in a circle].* Dallas Museum of Art, 20th-Century Design Fund, 1996.143.1–3.

In its catalogue Libbey claimed that through this glass, "The designer tells a story of craftsmanship—a bubble of glass becomes the bowl, a block of crystal the stem, while two small terraced rings in the foot indicate the rolling motion of a footsetter's tool."[3]

No. 476 goblet with *Moderne* pattern, ca. 1930–40. Seneca Glass Company, Morgantown, W. Va. Glass with cut decoration. Unmarked. Dallas Museum of Art, 20th-Century Design Fund, 1996.196.

Indicative of the wide variety of patterns available to consumers in the 1920s and 1930s, Seneca produced at least fifty cut designs on the no. 476 shape alone. Some were traditional in style, but many, like *Moderne* and *Rhythm*, with their clear geometric motifs, were quite contemporary in nature.[4]

No. K13 shape goblet with *Malmaison* pattern, ca. 1932. A. Douglas Nash, designer; Libbey Glass Company, Toledo, maker. Glass with pressed and engraved decoration. Unmarked. Dallas Museum of Art, 20th-Century Design Fund, 1995.57.

Embassy water, cordial, and sherbet glasses, ca. 1938. Edwin W. Fuerst and Walter Dorwin Teague, designers; Libbey Glass Company, Toledo, maker. Glass with pressed decoration; water glass: h. 8¾ in. (22.2 cm), diam. 2⅞ in. (7.3 cm). All marked: *Libbey.* Dallas Museum of Art, gift of the Dallas Antiques and Fine Arts Society, 1989.18.1–3.

In addition to being part of Libbey's *Modern American* line, *Embassy* is noteworthy for having been used in the State Dining Room of the U.S. Government Building at the New York world's fair in 1939. The examples that were used there featured a crest incorporating the American eagle and thirteen stars. Along with the rest of the tableware that Teague selected for use at the fair, *Embassy* appeared in the 1940 *Studio Year Book.*[5] Although Teague was frequently cited as the designer, the extent of his contribution to the creation of this stemware is not known at present.

1. For information on *Cambridge Square*, see Florence 1996, 212–13. According to this source, the product was illustrated in a 1949 company catalogue, but it does not seem to have been marketed extensively until 1952.
2. GTR (23 Dec. 1968): 11.
3. Fauster 1979, 396.
4. Page and Frederiksen 1995, 34–37.
5. Holme 1940, 104.

Cat. 74
Pilsner, tumbler, and beverage glasses with *Golden Foliage* pattern, 1956. Freda Diamond, designer; Libbey Glass Company, Toledo, maker. Glass with pressed, printed, and gilded decoration; pilsner: h. 8½ in. (21.6 cm), diam. 2⅞ in. (7.3 cm). Pilsner unmarked. Tumbler and beverage glass marked: L. Dallas Museum of Art, 20th-Century Design Fund, 1997.197.1–3.

Golden Foliage, a pattern silk-screened onto *Safedge* glass, was the most popular of all Libbey's "Hostess Set" patterns. It was produced continuously between 1956 and 1977. In all, more than thirty million examples were made and sold in groups priced at eight glasses for $4 and $6.50 for a boxed set. A 1958 ad for the design stated: "Shimmering golden leaves on a band of pearly frosting—can't you picture the gaiety and sparkle Golden Foliage glassware by Libbey will bring to your family table? Rimmed and trimmed in 22K gold—these glasses are so handsome your family will want to use them *every* day. And they can!—each sparkling piece has the Libbey chip-defiant rim."[1]

1. Fauster 1979, 144.

Cat. 75
***Mayfair* compote,** 1930. George Sakier, designer; Fostoria Glass Company, Moundsville, W. Va., maker. Glass with pressed decoration; h. 5¼ in. (13.3 cm), diam. 5½ in. (14 cm). Unmarked. Dallas Museum of Art, 20th-Century Design Fund, 1996.197.

When this line was introduced, Fostoria touted it as "Simply Perfect for the Most Particular Hostess." A sales brochure promoted its modernity and tastefulness: "Mayfair is one of the newest designs in a complete dinner service. It has a modern smartness—expressing the tempo of our age. Beautiful in its simplicity. Always appropriate. Always in excellent taste. Effective in any scheme of decoration, but particularly so in modern surroundings. It may be had in a warm rose, a rich amber, clear green, brilliant topaz and sparkling crystal."[1]

1. "Mayfair" (Fostoria sales brochure, 1930?).

Cat. 76
No. 4020 shape decanter with four glasses, ca. 1929–30. George Sakier, designer; Fostoria Glass Company, Moundsville, W. Va., maker. Glass with pressed decoration; decanter: h. 11⅜ in. (28.9 cm), diam. 4 in. (10.2 cm). All unmarked. Dallas Museum of Art, 20th-Century Design Fund, 1997.16.1–5.

When in November 1929 George Sakier received design patent no. 81,301 for the shape of the illustrated glasses, the design was already in production. Although glasses of various sizes featuring square bases were made immediately, the matching decanter was not produced until 1930. In early 1931 the decanter was illustrated in the *Crockery and Glass Journal*, which said that it resembled the work of René Lalique.[1] The bases of both the decanter and glasses were pressed in several colors. The blown upper sections were also available in various hues and with a variety of etched ornaments.[2] The line was discontinued in 1940.

The no. 4020 shape was admired by contemporary design critics and widely exhibited in the early 1930s. In 1933 one writer went so far as to say that this shape was responsible for "the disintegration of the European glass monopoly in America" and that before Fostoria introduced the line "none in this country could compare with imported examples from the standpoint of design compatible with price."[3]

1. "Infinite Variety in Fostoria Smartness," *CGJ* 109:3 (Mar. 1931): 28; "Fostoria Introduces New Line," 107:8 (Aug. 1929): 67.
2. For examples see Long and Seate 1995, 57–59; 180.
3. Harry V. Anderson, "Contemporary American Designers," *Decorators Digest* (July 1933): 39; quoted in Piña 1996, 16.

Cat. 77
Goblet with *Lexington* shape stem and *Fairwin* pattern, ca. 1931. Morgantown Glass Works, Morgantown, W. Va. Glass with pressed and etched decoration. Unmarked. Dallas Museum of Art, 20th-Century Design Fund, 1996.19.

An advertisement in *Crockery and Glass Journal* said of this pattern in October 1931: "There's Magic in these Stems—Shoppers become 'Crystal gazers' when they see this delicately blown (cased) stemware on display. Even the salespeople never quite get over their wonder at the way the Ritz-blue filament so mysteriously illuminates these dainty fluted Crystal stems. If you want to speed up your sales tempo, display 'Fairwin' before the Holidays."[1]

No. 15,039 shape liqueur glass with *Vogue* pattern, ca. 1930. Tiffin Glass Division, United States Glass Company, Tiffin, Ohio. Glass with pressed and etched decoration. Unmarked. Dallas Museum of Art, 20th-Century Design Fund, 1996.189.

Water or iced tea glass with *Nasreen* pattern, ca. 1930. Morgantown Glass Works, Morgantown, W. Va. Glass with etched decoration. Unmarked. Dallas Museum of Art, 20th-Century Design Fund, 1996.15.

Goblet with *Legacy* shape stem and *Superba* pattern, ca. 1931. Morgantown Glass Works, Morgantown, W. Va. Glass with pressed and etched decoration; h. 8¼ in. (21 cm), diam. 3½ in. (8.9 cm). Unmarked. Dallas Museum of Art, 20th-Century Design Fund, 1996.21.

The etched decoration on all of these glasses is characteristic of glass created by American stemware producers in the very late 1920s and early 1930s. The decorative motifs range from stylized foliage (left) to geometric art deco designs (center) to tropical figural scenes (right).[2]

1. *CGJ* 109:10 (Oct. 1931): 2.
2. For a full rendering of *Superba*, see Gallagher 1995, 94.

Cat. 78

Hostess casserole dish, ca. 1949. Corning Glass Works, Corning, N.Y. Glass; h. 3½ in. (8.9 cm), w. 8⅝ in. (21.9 cm), d. 7⅞ in. (20 cm). Marked: 515B-015 1½ QT. | T M. REG | PYREX | A - 2 | MADE IN U.S.A. | OVENWARE. Dallas Museum of Art, 20th-Century Design Fund, 1995.112.

The introduction of heat- and shock-resistant opaque glass kitchenware for domestic use grew out of Corning's development of glassware for use in military mess halls during World War II. In 1947 the company introduced brightly colored Pyrex mixing bowls made of white glass onto which colored enamel was sprayed before the final tempering process. This casserole dish was put on the market in 1949 and came in four colors—yellow, blue, pink, and red. Originally it would have been part of a "hostess set" consisting of the casserole dish and four 7-ounce uncovered ramekins. The set sold for $2.95, and a larger covered casserole dish was available for $1.95. The *Hostess* design was taken out of production by 1955.[1]

1. Rograve and Steinhauer 1993, 106.

Chapter 3
Foreigners at Our Table: Imported China and Glass

Cat. 79

Marseille bowl, ca. 1880–85. Edouard Lindeneher, designer; Haviland & Co., Limoges, France, maker; Haviland China Company, New York, importer. Porcelain; h. 3⅞ in. (9.8 cm), w. 10⅜ in. (26.4 cm), d. 8½ in. (21.6 cm). Marked: H & Co | L | France and E and 2. Dallas Museum of Art, 20th-Century Design Fund, 1997.108.

Lindeneher probably designed the *Marseille* line in the early to mid-1880s. The mark on this example was in use between 1888 and 1896.[1]

1. D'Albis 1988, 44–45, 122.

Cat. 80

Plate from the Harrison White House service, 1892. Caroline Scott Harrison and Paul Putzki, designers; Tressemanes & Vogt, Limoges, France, maker; Dulin & Martin Company, Washington, D.C., retailer. Porcelain with printed and gilded decoration; h. ⅞ in. (2.2 cm), diam. 9½ in. (24 cm). Marked: DECORE | PAR | LIMOGES | TV [in a bell] | POUR | Dulin, Martin Co. | WASHINGTON | LIMOGES | FRANCE | HARRISON 1892. Dallas Museum of Art, gift of the Friends of the Decorative Arts, 1994 Connoisseurship Class, 1994.21.

An avid china painter, First Lady Caroline Scott Harrison designed the new White House service herself, with the help of Paul Putzki,

her teacher of china painting. When Harrison moved to Washington in 1889, she prevailed upon Putzki to accompany her to continue her lessons and set up a regular china painting class in the White House for selected ladies of Washington.[1] The shapes for the service and the eagle and shield in the center were based on designs used for the earlier Lincoln service, but the border of corn and goldenrod was intended to remind diners of the Harrisons' Indiana roots. The service continued to be used during the administrations of Presidents William McKinley and Theodore Roosevelt. This particular plate was made in 1908 as a replacement during the Theodore Roosevelt administration. The retailer of the first examples was the firm of M. W. Beveridge of Washington, D.C., of which William Martin was a partner.

1. Klapthor 1999, 127–31, 150–51.

Cat. 81

Covered vegetable dish, ca. 1929. L. Bernardaud & Cie., Limoges, France, maker; George F. Bassett & Co., New York, importer. Porcelain with printed and gilded decoration; h. 5½ in. (14 cm), w. 10¼ in. (26 cm), d. 8½ in. (21.6 cm). Marked: B & Cie and LIMOGES | FRANCE | 28 | L. BERNARDAUD & Cie | Limoges. Dallas Museum of Art, 20th-Century Design Fund, T42464.

This was one of two shapes introduced by George F. Bassett & Co. in the spring of 1929. Having witnessed a backlash against designs that were radically modern, the importer carefully noted in its advertisements that "These treatments are not extreme but rather are the type that will fit into most any scheme of interior decoration." This simple style of "Modern Art is a definite school of design itself" and "cannot, and must not, be confused with the so-called Futuristic or Cubistic Art. . . . The production of dinnerware by L. Bernardaud & Co. has not been just a hit or miss creation. The designer . . . is a graduate of the school of design in Paris, and is at the present time, spending three or four days each month in this school, keeping in touch with the latest trends in this contemporary art. The lines and decorations . . . have been pronounced by many art critics as perfect examples of this particular school of art."[1]

1. "Art Moderne as Applied to Dinnerware," CGJ 107:4 (Apr. 1929): 75.

Cat. 82

Sherry glass with Buckingham pattern, ca. 1939. Cristalleries de Baccarat, Baccarat, France. Lead glass with cut decoration. Unmarked. Dallas Museum of Art, 20th-Century Design Fund, T42474.

Champagne glass with Malmaison pattern, 1910. Cristalleries de Baccarat, Baccarat,

France. Lead glass with cut decoration. Marked: BACCARAT | [logo with glass, decanter, tumbler] | FRANCE. Dallas Museum of Art, 20th-Century Design Fund, T42475.

According to trade literature, *Malmaison* was one of Baccarat's most famous panel-cut designs and was consistently popular among wealthy consumers throughout the century. In 1979 the pattern cost the large sum of $80 per stem.[1]

Tumbler with Marennes pattern, ca. 1899. Cristalleries de Baccarat, Baccarat, France. Lead glass with cut and engraved decoration. Unmarked. Dallas Museum of Art, 20th-Century Design Fund, T42476.

Capri goblet, 1969. Cristalleries de Baccarat, Baccarat, France. Lead glass; h. 7⅛ in. (18.1 cm), diam. 3⅛ in. (7.9 cm). Marked: BACCARAT | [logo with glass, decanter, tumbler] | FRANCE. Dallas Museum of Art, 20th-Century Design Fund, T42473.

Capri was adapted from a design originally created in the late nineteenth century for the Maharani of Baroda in India. What influenced U.S. sales, however, was the fact that H.S.H. the Princess of Monaco, Grace Kelly Rainier, selected the pattern for use in the royal palace.[2]

Tumbler with Blarney pattern, ca. 1955. Cristalleries de Val St. Lambert, Val St. Lambert, Belgium, maker; Val St. Lambert, Inc., New York, importer. Lead glass with cut decoration. Unmarked. Dallas Museum of Art, 20th-Century Design Fund, T42470.

Goblet with Rondo pattern, ca. 1955. N. V. Kristalunie Maastricht, Maastricht, Netherlands, maker; Justin Tharaud & Son, New York, importer. Lead glass with cut decoration. Unmarked. Dallas Museum of Art, 20th-Century Design Fund, T42472.

Finger bowl with Netherlands pattern, ca. 1950. N. V. Kristalunie Maastricht, Maastricht, Netherlands, maker; Justin Tharaud & Son, importer, New York. Lead glass with cut decoration. Unmarked. Dallas Museum of Art, 20th-Century Design Fund, T42471.

This selection of cut crystal from France, Belgium, and the Netherlands is representative of the high quality of stemware that was often imported from Europe to the United States. The amount of cutting required to produce such elaborate stemware was costly, however. In 1952, for example, B. Altman & Co. in New York advertised Royal Netherland brand stemware. Regularly priced at $84 per dozen pieces, the *Netherlands* shape was reduced to $63 per dozen for this special sale.[3]

1. "Baccarat: 'The Crystal of Kings'" (trade catalogue and price list, 1979).
2. Ibid.
3. Clipping from *New York Times* (19 Oct. 1952), page unknown.

Cat. 83

Oyster plate from the Hayes White House service, 1879. Theodore R. Davis, designer; Haviland & Co., Limoges, France, maker; Haviland & Co., New York, importer. Porcelain with painted and gilded decoration; h. 1 in. (2.5 cm), diam. 8½ in. (21.6 cm). Marked: FABRIQUE PAR | HAVILAND & Co. | d'apres les dessins | DE | Theo: R. Davis and H & Co. [underlined twice]. Dallas Museum of Art, Charles R. Masling and John E. Furen Collection, gift of Mr. and Mrs. William Rubin, The Arthur A. Everts Company, and Arthur and Marie Berger by exchange, 1991.101.23.

Early in 1879 Mrs. Rutherford B. Hayes chose Haviland & Co. to make a new state dinner service for the White House. By coincidence, Theodore R. Davis, an artist and reporter for *Harper's Weekly*, was introduced to Lucy Webb Hayes as she was reviewing some proposed designs from Haviland. Davis remarked that it was a pity the new service was not being produced in America, but even if it had to be made elsewhere, surely it should incorporate American flora and fauna in the design. Hayes is said to have been so taken with the idea that she immediately asked Davis to supply the artwork and later sent word to Haviland that Davis was now in charge of the design. Not surprisingly, there were time extensions and cost overruns, so the entire service was not complete when it was delivered in June 1880.

Later that year the exquisite oyster plates were sent to the White House, and the set was eventually completed. Additional orders were placed by President Chester Arthur in 1884 and President Grover Cleveland in 1886. Haviland also produced sets for public sale, resulting in much public notice of the beautiful handpainted White House tableware. The oyster plate, with its realistic depiction of bluepoint oysters and seaweed, generated wide acclaim and coincided—indeed probably influenced—a fashion for such plates with individual oyster wells during this period.[1]

Dessert plate, 1879. Albert Dammouse, shape designer; Joseph-Auguste (Félix) Bracquemond, pattern designer; Haviland & Co., Limoges, France, maker. Porcelain with painted decoration. Marked: HAVILAND & Co. | LIMOGES [within a circle] and H & Co. | L. Dallas Museum of Art, gift of Mr. and Mrs. John Rogers in memory of Charles Haviland, George Haviland, and Marthe Haviland de Bruchard, 1994.185.5.

One of the many celebrated artist-designers working in the ceramics industry during the latter half of the nineteenth century, Félix Bracquemond is perhaps most noted for his exquisite designs in the Japanese taste. He was one of the first to embrace this new style, called *japonisme*, and caught the eye of the critics at the 1866 Paris exposition with a Japanesque faience service for the Creil factory. His work for Haviland & Co. continued in this mode during his tenure as design director from 1872 to 1882. The asymmetrical placement of a bird in flight balanced by foliage, as seen in this dessert plate, is characteristic of Bracquemond's fluid handling of the style, as is the sweeping ribbon found also in other designs for the factory. The combination of Bracquemond's gentle scenes and Dammouse's subtle forms produced plates that were strikingly close to authentic Asian designs, making them quite desirable among fashionable consumers. This particular example and four others of variant design in the museum's collection descended in the Haviland family and were brought to the United States by a family descendent.

1. A thorough analysis of this service can be found in Klapthor 1975, 97–109.

Cat. 84

***Primavera* shape cup and saucer with *Ebb Tide* pattern and plate with *Meadow Lace* pattern,** 1952. Theodore Haviland & Co., Limoges, France, designer; Shenango Pottery Company, New Castle, Pa., maker; Haviland & Co., New York, distributor. Porcelain with printed decoration; plate: h. 1 in. (2.5 cm), diam. 10½ in. (26.7 cm). Cup and saucer marked: THEODORE HAVILAND | NEW YORK [in oval cloud shape] | MADE IN AMERICA | Ebb Tide. Cup also marked: 27. Plate marked: same except pattern name *Meadow Lace* and 51 and 0. Dallas Museum of Art, 20th-Century Design Fund, 1997.12, 1997.109.

The *Primavera* shape was introduced in 1953 and described as "an entirely new conception of modern design, classic in its simplicity." It stood for "enduring good taste and fine quality for so long a characteristic of Haviland China."[1] A five-piece place setting in plain white sold for $9.50, while one with decoration cost $13.55.[2]

***Saint Raphael* shape teapot, demitasse cup and saucer and luncheon plate with *Primrose* pattern,** ca. 1935–50. Theodore Haviland & Co., Limoges, France, maker; Theodore Haviland & Co., New York, importer. Porcelain with gilded and printed decoration. All marked: Haviland's | Primrose and Haviland | France. Teacup, cup, and plate also marked: T*H [surmounted by a ribbon]. Dallas Museum of Art, 20th-Century Design Fund, 1997.107.1–3.

The *Saint Raphael* shape was probably designed in the 1930s. It is similar to the *Priscilla* shape that was available in America in 1938.[3] However, the marks on these examples indicate that they were made between 1946 and 1957. It is likely that Haviland exported this somewhat passé art deco design to the United States in the late 1940s before the firm had had time to develop new shapes for the postwar era.[4]

Covered bowl with *Astoria* pattern, ca. 1930–40. Theodore Haviland & Co., Limoges, France, maker; Theodore Haviland & Co., New York, importer. Porcelain with gilded decoration. Marked: T*H [surmounted by a ribbon] and PATE IVOIRE | THEODORE | HAVILAND | FRANCE [all in a shield] and Theodore Haviland | Limoges | FRANCE | Astoria. Dallas Museum of Art, 20th-Century Design Fund, 1997.110.

1. CGJ 152:3b (16 Mar. 1953): 107.
2. CGJ 152:2 (Feb. 1953): 27.
3. CGJ 127:3 (Mar. 1938): 35.
4. D'Albis 1988, 124–25; and CGJ 140:1 (Jan. 1947): 53.

Cat. 85

Clockwise from left:
***Stratford* shape chop plate with *Chinese Chippendale* pattern,** ca. 1910. Worcester Royal Porcelain Company, Worcester, England, maker; Maddock & Miller, New York, importer. Bone china with printed and painted decoration; h. 1 in. (2.5 cm), diam. 12½ in. (31.8 cm). Marked: [crown] | [four intertwined Ws within a circle; C and 51 at the center] | ROYAL WORCESTER ENGLAND | (date mark for 1912) | Rd No 612812 [within a rectangle] and xx | 9882/1 and 14 and 1 and 1M. Dallas Museum of Art, 20th-Century Design Fund, T42469.

A genuine interest in the American colonial past grew steadily in the early twentieth century with such notable events as the sesquicentennial in 1926 and the restoration of Colonial Williamsburg shortly thereafter. Articles about eighteenth-century Chinese porcelains appeared almost monthly in one magazine or another and inspired modern pottery manufacturers to create patterns that were either reproductions or adaptations of Chinese ceramics. In this case, Worcester's *Chinese Chippendale* (introduced ca. 1912–13) reminded the American consumer, both in name and decoration, of the English cabinet-maker who had championed the Anglo-Chinese style, Thomas Chippendale. Lavishly hand-enameled, this pattern was available in several color combinations.

***Prince* shape plate with *Chantilly* pattern,** ca. 1920. Worcester Royal Porcelain Company, Worcester, England, maker; Maddock & Miller, New York, importer. Bone china with printed and painted decoration. Marked: [crown] | [four intertwined Ws within a circle; C and 51 at the center] | ROYAL WORCESTER | [diamond] (date mark for 1929) | MADE IN ENGLAND | CHANTILLY. Dallas Museum of Art, gift of George Roland in memory of Annabelle and Charles Thomas Roland, 1997.202.

In an attempt to compete with the growing popularity of ivory-colored porcelain produced by Lenox China, English manufacturers experimented with patterns that incorporated an all-over ivory glaze over the traditional white bone china body. Introduced around 1929, *Chantilly* was Worcester's version of a Lenox-like pattern. It apparently sold reasonably well in the United States and was available in five different color schemes.

Jewel shape plate with *Heath & Rose* pattern, ca. 1924. W. T. Copeland & Sons, Stoke-upon-Trent, England, maker; Copeland & Thompson, New York, importer. Earthenware with printed and painted decoration. Marked: SPODE'S JEWEL | COPELAND | SPODE [*within boxed reserve*] | ENGLAND | REG No. 70392 | U. S. PATT JUNE-15th 1926. | "HEATH & ROSE" and *Copeland* | *Spode* | *Imperial* | 41 (date mark for 1941) and S117 (pattern number) | 4. Dallas Museum of Art, 20th-Century Design Fund, 1996.194.

The distinctive embossed design of the *Jewel* shape was modeled from a dessert plate in an extensive table service made for Queen Victoria in 1857. The original service included plates that incorporated actual paste jewels set into the tiny embossed recesses. The modern version is a typical adaptation prompted by Copeland's American agent, Sidney Thompson: take a distinctive element from an earlier Spode pattern—in this case, the heavily embossed border; add a new design feature—the painted floral center; and a new pattern is born that appeals to the American appetite for traditional wares.[1] With *Jewel* the Copeland factory (which produced Spode) found a winner—the shape was in production for over sixty years. *Heath & Rose* is almost identical to the most popular pattern on the shape, *Billingsley Rose*.[2]

1. Thompson interview 1997; Copeland interview 1997.
2. Copeland 1993, 166–67.

Cat. 86

Centurion shape covered vegetable dish with *Kerry* pattern, 1931. W. T. Copeland & Sons, Stoke-upon-Trent, England, maker; Copeland & Thompson, New York, importer. Earthenware with printed and painted decoration; h. 7⅛ in. (18.1 cm), w. 11¾ in. (30 cm), d. 10½ in. (26.7 cm). Marked: SPODE'S | CENTURION | UNITED STATES DESIGN | LETTERS PATENT No. 84384 | Rd. No. 762857 | COPELAND | SPODE | GREAT BRITAIN | "KERRY" | S211 (pattern number) | F | 34 (date mark for 1934) | *Copeland* | *Spode*. Dallas Museum of Art, gift of George Roland in memory of Annabelle and Charles Thomas Roland, 1997.207.

The *Centurion* shape was designed in 1931 as a revival of the earlier *Walpole* shape and became the vehicle for a number of patterns derived from eighteenth- and nineteenth-century de-

signs in the Spode pattern books. *Kerry*, which was introduced in 1933, with its gently dispersed sprays of colorful, handpainted flowers, was just the sort of pattern that spelled tradition and "good taste" to American consumers. In an era of nostalgia for the past, the name itself was a not-so-subtle attempt to link the pattern with an image of "ye olde Ireland," further establishing a connection for some Americans to their Irish or English ancestry.[1]

1. Copeland interview 1998.

Cat. 87

Vogue shape tea set with *Sunray* pattern, 1930. Eric Slater, designer; Shelley Potteries, Longton, England, maker. Bone china with painted decoration; teapot: h. 4½ in. (11.4 cm), w. 8½ in. (21.6 cm), d. 5 in. (12.7 cm). All marked: *Shelley* [*within a shield*] | ENGLAND | Rd. 756533 and 11743 (pattern number). Plate marked: same except without registry mark. Dallas Museum of Art, 20th-Century Design Fund, 1996.145.1–4, .6.

An early interpretation of modernism in commercially produced English tableware, the *Vogue* shape and its close relatives *Mode, Eve,* and *Regent,* created by Eric Slater for Shelley have become icons among collectors of art deco ceramics. Although their introduction certainly attracted attention with their striking angular shapes and brightly cubist patterns such as *Sunray,* these shapes were not popular in the market. Shelley experimented with adding more traditional floral patterns to the shapes, but the market did not seem to respond favorably. Indeed, *Vogue* lasted a mere three years. What was a costly experiment for Shelley probably helped the company better recognize its customer preferences. The firm went on to become one of the largest producers of more traditional bone china teaware in Staffordshire after World War II.[1]

1. For a lengthy discussion of Shelley Potteries during the 1930s, see Spours 1988, 49–61.

Cat. 88

Casino shape covered vegetable dish with *Athlone* pattern, ca. 1931. Charles Noke, supervising designer; Doulton & Co., Burslem, England, maker; Doulton & Co., New York, importer. Earthenware with printed and painted decoration; h. 4½ in. (11.4 cm), w. 10½ in. (26.7 cm), d. 8½ in. (21.6 cm). Marked: [*lion over crown*] | 10 (year mark for 1937) | MADE IN ENGLAND | ROYAL DOULTON | [*four overlapping Ds*] | ENGLAND | ATHLONE | D. 5552 (pattern number). Dallas Museum of Art, 20th-Century Design Fund, 1998.14.

When it was introduced in 1932, *Casino* came in both earthenware and bone china. A bold, streamlined shape that made use of concentric circles and stepped planes, *Casino* was first

presented with banded patterns.[1] Later a wider range of surface decoration was added to the line, including *Athlone* (1935), which featured stylized maple leaves in rust or green, as pictured. In addition to this earthenware version, *Athlone* was sometimes ordered in more durable whiteware for use in hotels and restaurants.

1. Spours 1988, 122–28.

Cat. 89

All pieces: Clarice Cliff, designer. Earthenware with painted decoration.

Stamford shape covered vegetable bowl, ca. 1930. Newport Pottery Company, Burslem, England, maker; Lawley's China and Glass, London, retailer. h. 7½ in. (19.1 cm), w. 9 in. (22.9 cm), d. 7 in. (17.8 cm). Marked: HAND PAINTED | *Bizarre* | *by* | *Clarice Cliff* | NEWPORT POTTERY | ENGLAND | CHINA GLASS | *Lawleys* | *of* REGENT STREET LONDON, W.1. Dallas Museum of Art, gift of George Roland in memory of Annabelle and Charles Thomas Roland, 1997.52.

Biarritz shape plate and cup and saucer with no. 5948 pattern, ca. 1933. A. J. Wilkinson (Royal Staffordshire Pottery), Burslem, England, maker. All marked: *The Biarritz* | [*crown*] | *Royal Staffordshire* | *England* | *Regd. No. 784849* | 5948 (pattern number). Plate also marked: 12 33 (date mark for 1933). Saucer also marked: N | 10 33 (date mark for 1933). Cup also marked: N. Dallas Museum of Art, 20th-Century Design Fund, 1996.187.1–2.

The high modernist taste for streamlined shapes and spartan decoration was embodied in Clarice Cliff's shapes of the 1930s. Her direct inspiration came from the work of French designer Jean Tetard, from whom Cliff took the idea for the very successful *Stamford* shape around 1930. In 1933 Cliff introduced another Tetard adaptation, the *Biarritz* shape, with its distinctive rectangular plates. Unfortunately, square plates with circular wells were extremely difficult to produce because the sides drooped if the plates were stacked conventionally in the kiln. Cliff devised a method of supporting the ware with sand and special kiln furniture, which solved the warping problem but meant that far fewer pieces could be fired at one time. Consequently, the Bizarre line was expensive to produce and very little of it sold in America; only those pieces with simple, conservative decoration, such as these banded patterns, found a market in the United States, unlike the brightly colored versions inspired by peasant folk art designs that were popular in England.

Cat. 90

Avon shape cake plate and gravy boat with *Desert Star* pattern, 1955. J. Russell Price, shape designer; Cecil Jack Noke, pattern designer; Doulton & Co., Burslem, England, maker; Doulton & Co., New York, importer. Earthenware with printed and painted decoration; cake plate: h. ¾ in. (1.9 cm), diam. 11⅜ in. (28.9 cm). All marked: [lion over crown] / MADE IN ENGLAND / ROYAL DOULTON / [four overlapping D's] / ENGLAND / DESERT STAR / D.6430 / COPYRIGHT / DOULTON & COMPANY LIMITED. Dallas Museum of Art, 20th-Century Design Fund, 1998.49.1–2.

In an effort to appeal to younger American consumers, in 1955 Doulton & Co. launched the *Horizon* line with four china and three earthenware patterns on a new coupe shape designed by the American industrial designer J. Russell Price. Formerly the chief designer of flatware at the Gorham Manufacturing Company, Price was no stranger to tableware design. According to Price, the coupe shape was "designed to carry the eye in a series of harmonious curves . . . and follows the line of the thumb."[1] Doulton's attempt to modernize resulted from the fear that they were losing ground with younger consumers after World War II. Despite the results of a marketing survey among 5,000 American college girls, which revealed that only 40 percent of them liked a modern shape, the company proceeded with plans to revamp its shapes and patterns.

The new shape range was innovative for Doulton. Ample in size to accommodate American entertaining, the serving pieces were a departure from normal English production standards. This cake plate is said to have been the first of its kind to comfortably hold an entire iced layer cake.[2] Yet even with shapes designed by an American to appeal to Americans, success still came down to price. The Doulton patterns were considerably more expensive than their American or Japanese counterparts. Of the seven designs, only *Desert Star* sold well in the United States, and the line was eventually discontinued in 1964.

1. "Doulton Launches New Coupe Shape," *CGJ* 155:7 (Jan. 1955): 59.
2. Ibid.

Cat. 91

***Stonehenge* shape side plate, coffeepot, plate, cup and saucer with *Flowersong* pattern,** ca. 1970. Derek Machin, Sidney Machin, and Roy Midwinter, shape designers; Jessie Tait, pattern designer; W. R. Midwinter, Burslem, England, maker. Earthenware with printed decoration; plate: h. 1 in. (2.5 cm), diam. 10 in. (25.4 cm). Side plate marked: FLOWERSONG / Stonehenge / Midwinter / MADE IN ENGLAND. Coffeepot and cup marked: MIDWINTER / ENGLAND. Plate marked: FLOWERSONG / Stonehenge / OVEN-TO-TABLEWARE. DISH-WASHER SAFE / Midwinter / MEMBER OF THE WEDGWOOD GROUP / MADE IN ENGLAND.

Saucer marked: *Stonehenge* / *Midwinter* / MADE IN ENGLAND / Z. Dallas Museum of Art, gift of George Roland in memory of Annabelle and Charles Thomas Roland, 1997.67.1–4.

Although most books that feature Midwinter pottery cite 1972 as the year of production for the *Stonehenge* shape, ads in *Crockery and Glass Journal* show that the shape was actually on the market as early as 1970.[1] While it was initially imported by Meakin-Midwinter, responsibility for marketing the highly successful shape in America was phased over to Josiah Wedgwood & Sons in New York in 1975, reflecting the earlier takeover of J. & G. Meakin, which had purchased control of W. R. Midwinter in 1968, by the Wedgwood Group in 1970.[2]

The *Stonehenge* shape was popular in America because of the look and texture of its finish.[3] Among the earliest group of patterns developed for the shape, *Flowersong* perfectly captured the fashion for stylized floral decoration, especially daisies, that dominated graphic design in the early years of the 1970s. The pattern was discontinued in 1976.

1. GTR (Dec. 1970): 6; (Aug. 1971): 42.
2. GTR (Apr. 1975): 1, 29.
3. Midwinter interview 1997.

Cat. 92

***Lowestoft* shape creamer, sugar bowl, coffeepot, dish, waste bowl, and teapot with *Gloucester* pattern,** ca. 1925–30. W. T. Copeland & Sons, Stoke-upon-Trent, England, maker; Copeland & Thompson, New York, importer; Tiffany & Co., New York, retailer. Stoneware with printed and gilt decoration; coffeepot: h. 8⅜ in. (21.3 cm), w. 7½ in. (19.1 cm), d. 4¼ in. (10.8 cm). Creamer, coffeepot, dish, and waste bowl marked: COPELAND / SPODE / ENGLAND / New Stone / SPODES GLOUCESTER. Sugar bowl and teapot marked: COPELAND / SPODE / Stone Lowestoft Style / Contemporary / ENGLAND / SPODES GLOUCESTER. Teapot also marked: [within a reserve] TIFFANY & Co. / NEW YORK / Y2649 (pattern number) / F. Dallas Museum of Art, gift of Mrs. Alfred L. Bromberg, 1996.217.1–6.

A series of magazine articles around 1925 featuring Chinese export porcelain prompted Spode's agent in America, Sidney Thompson, to suggest reviving the "Stone China" body.[1] Josiah Spode had developed the ware, with its blue-gray color and Chinese-inspired patterns, around 1800 to compete with genuine China trade porcelains. Thompson recognized the colonial revival trend in America and pushed the Copeland factory to develop the *Lowestoft* shape in both tea- and dinnerware, recalling the porcelain owned by such patriots as Washington and Jefferson. The *Gloucester* pattern was added to the shape around 1930, with subsequent variations available with painted and gilded decoration.[2]

Lowestoft and its patterns remained popular among wealthy consumers who shopped at prestigious shops such as Tiffany & Co., where this set was retailed until the mid-1980s—a testament to the enduring legacy of early American styles.

1. For a thorough discussion of the history of Spode's "Stone China" body, see Copeland 1997, 132–35.
2. The original pattern number was Y2411, with variations including Y2989 (no gold), Y2498 (gold edge finished), Y2649 (gold edge and fine line finished), W118 (black, no gold edge), and W143 (black with gold edge).

Cat. 93

***Coupe Savoy* shape dinner plate with *Partridge* pattern,** 1953. Norman Makinson, designer; Josiah Wedgwood & Sons, Barlaston, England, maker; Josiah Wedgwood & Sons, New York, importer. Bone china with printed and gilded decoration; h. 1 in. (2.5 cm), diam. 10¼ in. (26 cm). Marked: [image of Portland Vase] / WEDGWOOD / BONE CHINA / MADE IN ENGLAND / Z 4 / W 4168 (pattern number). Dallas Museum of Art, gift of George Roland in memory of Annabelle and Charles Thomas Roland, 1997.229.

Originally introduced in bone china as in this example, this stylized holiday pattern was also produced on a gray body earthenware version a year later as *Partridge in a Pear Tree* (no. 489). Both patterns were discontinued in 1961.

***Royal College* shape cup and saucer with *Persia* pattern and coffeepot with *Elizabethan* pattern,** 1958. Neal French and David White, designers; W. T. Copeland & Sons, Stoke-upon-Trent, England, maker; Copeland & Thompson, New York, importer. Cup and saucer marked: 1 / Spode / BONE CHINA / ENGLAND / PERSIA / Y 8018 (pattern number). Coffeepot marked: SPODE / BONE CHINA / ENGLAND / Y 7842 (pattern number). Dallas Museum of Art, 20th-Century Design Fund, T42489, T42478.

Until the emergence of the *Royal College* shape, Spode had produced no new shapes since before World War II. In 1958 Copeland & Sons agreed to manufacture the best design from an exhibition of student work at the Royal College of Art. The tableware shape that resulted won several prizes but failed commercially, especially in the United States, where consumers did not expect contemporary design from established traditional English potteries at formal bone china prices. Well-intentioned but timid efforts such as this one to revitalize the production of Spode and other English manufacturers in the late 1950s and early 1960s contributed to the rash of company closings and mergers during this period.[1]

1. Queensberry interview 1997; Copeland interview 1997; Bryan interview 1997.

Cat. 94

All pieces: Josiah Wedgwood & Sons, Etruria, England, maker; Josiah Wedgwood & Sons, New York, importer.

Beer jug, ca. 1936. Keith Murray, designer. Earthenware; h. 8 in. (20.3 cm), w. 8 in. (20.3 cm), d. 5½ in. (14 cm). Marked: *OF ETRURIA | KM | WEDGWOOD | MADE IN EN-GLAND | & BARLASTON* and *WEDGWOOD* and *MADE IN ENGLAND* and N. Dallas Museum of Art, Barbara and Hensleigh Wedgwood Collection, 20th-Century Design Fund, 1996.249.1.

Demitasse cup and saucer and coffeepot with cm6099 pattern, ca. 1933. Keith Murray, shape designer; Norman Wilson, pattern designer. Stoneware with platinum decoration. Coffeepot marked: *Keith Murray. [underlined] | WEDG-WOOD | MADE IN ENGLAND | MOONSTONE* and *CM 6099 (pattern number) | [illegible]* and *WEDGWOOD* and *ENGLAND* and E. Lid marked: *MOONSTONE* and W. Cup marked: *KM | WEDG-WOOD | MADE IN | ENGLAND* and *CM 6099 (pattern number)* and *WEDGWOOD*. Saucer marked: *KM | WEDGWOOD | MADE IN | EN-GLAND | MOONSTONE* and *WEDGWOOD | MADE IN | ENGLAND | 5Y35 (mark for 1935)* and E. Dallas Museum of Art, anonymous gift by exchange, T42639.

These objects represent the work of two of Wedgwood's most talented twentieth-century designers, Keith Murray and Norman Wilson. Murray was primarily an architect and began to collaborate with the company in 1932 on a number of modernist-inspired shapes for decorative and table wares. The result was an enduring range of clean, simple designs that remained in the Wedgwood catalogue through the 1950s. Although the Murray designs were quite popular in the British home market, only modest sales were recorded in the United States. Murray worked as a freelance designer throughout his association with Wedgwood, and in addition to his prolific career as a ceramic designer he was also the chief architect of the new factory at Barlaston in 1939.[1]

Murray's shapes were well suited to the new glazes produced by Wedgwood in the early 1930s and principally developed by Norman Wilson, who had joined the company in 1927. Wilson's talents were diverse: he oversaw the introduction of important new technology; developed several successful lines of shapes and glazes; and eventually led the company as joint managing director. Equally adept as a designer in modernist and traditional styles, Wilson developed the *Moonstone* glaze, seen on this coffee set, that gave Keith Murray's streamlined shapes a soft modern look. He can also be credited with reintroducing eighteenth-century jasperware,

which appealed to consumers with more traditional taste.

1. For a thorough study of Murray's design for the Barlaston factory, see Gater and Vincent 1988.

Cat. 95

All pieces: Miroslav Havel, designer; Waterford Glass, Waterford, Ireland, maker. Lead glass with cut decoration. All marked: *Waterford*.

No. 604 shape water goblet with *Sheila* pattern, ca. 1955. Waterford Glass, New York, importer; Neiman Marcus, Dallas, retailer. H. 7 in. (17.8 cm), diam. 3⅞ in. (9.8 cm). Mr. and Mrs. William Pasley Collection.

This goblet was given to the owners on the occasion of their wedding in 1967. *Sheila* was one of the most expensive of Waterford's patterns because it featured large panel cuttings, which required almost flawless glass in order to achieve an acceptable standard. Its shape was also the most modern of any by Waterford.

No. 602 shape water goblet with *Colleen* pattern, 1953. Chinacraft, London, England, retailer. Sara Margaret White Collection.

One of Waterford's first commercially available patterns, this goblet has a shape and cut derived from early-nineteenth-century Irish and Czech examples that were adapted to the American taste for large-capacity goblets rather than tumblers for water. This pattern was widely marketed in the United States and was one of a number sold in popular china and glass shops in London to American tourists, who knew the pattern because they had seen it in stores back home.

No. 600 shape water goblet with *Tralee* pattern, 1954. Dallas Museum of Art, gift of Waterford Crystal, Inc., T42341.

Even though it was cut onto a traditional shape, the modern *Tralee* pattern was not a commercial success in the United States.

No. 600 shape tumbler, champagne, and liqueur glasses with *Lismore* pattern, 1952. United States Naval Exchange, United States Naval Station, Argentia, Newfoundland, Canada, retailer. Glenda Lee Harrison Collection.

Among the first group of Waterford patterns produced commercially, *Lismore* was an instant and resounding success. After promising initial sales, the pattern was marketed widely in the United States and soon became the best-selling and most recognizable Waterford pattern. The cutting pattern was inspired by the windows and turrets of

Lismore Castle in County Waterford.[1] Many women purchased sets of the glasses at a substantial savings through Post Exchanges while they and their husbands were stationed abroad in the service. These examples were bought in the PX at the U.S. naval base in Newfoundland in 1961.

All of the illustrated shapes were developed specifically for the American market. Some forms, such as the water goblets, which were called "American goblets" at the factory, were so popular that they helped catapult the company into the forefront of glass sales in America during the late 1950s (fig. 3.3). Others, like the saucer-shaped champagne glass, which was derived from similar glasses in prewar Hollywood movies, were never a commercial success, especially after the vogue for tulip-shaped champagne flutes developed in the 1960s.[2]

1. Havel interview 1998.
2. Murphy interview 1998.

Cat. 96

Back to front:
Cup and saucer, dessert plate, and plate, ca. 1930–35. J. Uffrecht & Co., Neumark, Germany. Earthenware with sprayed and painted decoration; plate: h. 1⅝ in. (4.1 cm), w. 11⅝ in. (29.5 cm), d. 11⅝ in (29.5 cm). All marked: *[upward pointing arrow on perpendicular baseline all in a triangle]*. Dallas Museum of Art, 20th-Century Design Fund, 1997.177.1–3.

Tea set, ca. 1930. Elsterwerda Earthenware Factory, Elsterwerda, Germany. Earthenware with sprayed and painted decoration. Teapot marked: *356/2 | [pentagon shape]* and *MADE IN GERMANY [in a circle]* and *R | 5633B*. Creamer marked: *B* and *MADE IN GERMANY [in a circle]*. Sugar bowl marked: same as creamer except with *5633B | 3*. Plate marked: *5633B | R*. Cup marked: *5633 | 4 B* and *[illegible] TERWERDA [in a circle]*. Saucer marked: *5633B | 4*. Dallas Museum of Art, 20th-Century Design Fund, 1997.168.1–4, 10.

These objects represent the types of German modernist ceramics that were imported into the United States during the 1930s. Progressive in its use of abstract patterns and simplified forms, this tableware nevertheless retains a traditional craft look. The thick handles and knobs on the hollowware, for example, suggest that the pieces were formed by hand in a small art pottery when in reality the Elsterwerda factory employed four hundred workers in 1925. Uffrecht had five hundred employees in the early 1930s.

An identical tea set as well as one of the cups in this set bears a circular mark containing the word *ELSTERWERDA*. That mark was used between 1929 and 1931.[1]

1. For information on these factories, see Zühlsdorff 1988, entries 3-326 and 3-905.

Cat. 97

Covered vegetable dish with *Mahoning* pattern, ca. 1930. Sontag & Söhne, Tettau, Germany, maker; Justin Tharaud, Inc., New York, importer. Porcelain with printed and gilded decoration. Marked: *Royal Bayreuth* / [*T in shield with lion supporters on either side and the date 1794 below*] / *BAVARIA* / *Mahoning*. Dallas Museum of Art, 20th-Century Design Fund, 1997.104.

The so-called Royal Tettau Factory exported two closely related shapes to the United States. This shape, for which the name is not known, was available in the United States with a variety of surface decorations. Most, like *Nurenberg*, were conservative floral patterns.[1] The other shape was called *Iduna* (1928–29). Its conical form and scalloped edges complement the shape featured here, and when suitably decorated, the two shapes could have been used together.[2]

Coffeepot, ca. 1925–30. Thomas & Ens, Marktredwitz, Germany, maker; Rosenthal China Corporation, New York, importer. Porcelain with printed and painted decoration; h. 10⅛ in. (25.7 cm), w. 9½ in. (24.1 cm), d. 5¼ in. (13.3 cm). Marked: *Thomas* [*inside shield*] / *Bavaria* / *1*. Dallas Museum of Art, 20th-Century Design Fund, T42459.

The Thomas factory was acquired by Rosenthal in 1908 and generally used to produce less expensive lines for the company.

***Supremacy* shape cup and saucer, chocolate pot, and sugar bowl,** ca. 1928. Bohemia Keramische Werke, Neurohlau, Czechoslovakia, maker; Fisher, Bruce & Co., New York, importer. Porcelain with painted and printed decoration. Cup marked: *BOHEMIA* / [*rampant lion within B*] / *Made in* / *·Czechoslovakia·* / *···* / *2315* / *7*. Saucer marked: same except without *2315* / *7* and with *Supremacy*. Chocolate pot marked: *BOHEMIA* / [*rampant lion within B*] / *Czecho–Slowakia* / *··* and *2315* / *7*. Sugar bowl marked: same as cup except with *Supremacy*. Dallas Museum of Art, 20th-Century Design Fund, 1996.195.1–3.

When introduced in 1929, the *Supremacy* shape was considered radical because of its square bases and hard angular quality. It was available with many surface patterns, most more conservative than the one pictured. The sugar bowl was also available with tab-shaped handles.[3]

The surface ornament seen on all these vessels, featuring small, abstract flowers and stars, was more avant-garde than most of the patterns accepted by American consumers. While limited quantities of such designs were imported, motifs such as these that owe much to central European and Russian abstraction were more popular in Europe than the United States.

1. *CGJ* 109:8 (Aug. 1931): 46.
2. *CGJ* 112:6 (June 1933): 17; and *Schaulade* 5:2 (Feb. 1929): 78.
3. *Schaulade* 5:2 (Feb. 1929): 77; and Bröhan 1993, v. 2, 447.

Cat. 98

Sugar bowl, creamer, cup and saucer, and plate with *Marlene* pattern, ca. 1930–35. Altrohlauer Porzellanfabriken, Altrohlauer, Czechoslovakia, maker; Marx & Gutherz, Altrohlauer, Czechoslovakia, decorator; Geo. Borgfeldt & Co., New York, importer. Porcelain with painted and gilded decoration; plate: h. 1 in. (2.5 cm), diam. 10 in. (25.4 cm). Sugar bowl marked: *ROYAL* [*in a wreath*] / *EPIAG* / *MADE IN* / *CZECHOSLOVAKIA* / *MARLENE* / *Modèle déposé*. Creamer marked: same as sugar bowl except without *MARLENE* / *Modèle déposé*. Cup marked: *EPIAG* / *Made in Czechoslovakia*. Saucer and plate marked: same as creamer. Anonymous collection.

Cup and saucer, ca. 1935–39. Bohemia Keramische Werke, Neurohlau, Czechoslovakia, maker; Fisher, Bruce & Co., New York, importer. Porcelain with gilded decoration. Both marked: *Bohemia* [*in a shield surmounted by a crown*] / *Royal Ivory* / *Made in* / *Czechoslovakia*. Alice G. Venable Collection.

Crockery and Glass Journal illustrated dessert plates and demitasse cups in this pattern in 1938.[1]

Coffeepot, sugar bowl, and demitasse cup and saucer, ca. 1930–35. Porzellanfabrik Victoria, Altrohlauer, Czechoslovakia. Porcelain with enamel and platinum decoration. Coffeepot marked: [*crown*] / *VICTORIA* / *Czechoslovakia and II*. Coffeepot lid marked: *II*. Sugar bowl and demitasse cup marked: same as coffeepot except without *II* and with *314*. Demitasse saucer marked: same as coffeepot except with *314*. Dallas Museum of Art, 20th-Century Design Fund, 1997.169.1–3.

Czech and German factories began making ivory-colored porcelain for export to the United States in the late 1920s. The illustrated examples are streamlined in shape and have simple ornamental schemes. This look appealed to many Europeans and Americans who wanted modernist tableware. Although not necessarily derived from any particular example, elegant Czech wares such as these are reminiscent of contemporary French tableware.

1. "Right Out of the Kiln," *CGJ* 122:4 (Apr. 1938): 24.

Cat. 99

***Anmut* shape covered vegetable dish,** ca. 1950. Karl Leutner, designer; Heinrich & Co., Selb, Germany, maker. Porcelain with gilded and printed decoration. Dish marked: *52, 17349,* [*crown*] / *H & Co* / *SELB* / *BAVARIA* / *GERMANY* / *Heinrich* / *Anmut* and *C. Hoyng. n.v.* [*imposed over*

a pitcher*] / *Heinrich* / *Bavaria*. Lid marked: *H & Co.* / *52* and *Anmut* / *GOLDEN MEDAILLE* / *IX TRIENNALE* / *MAILAND*. Dallas Museum of Art, 20th-Century Design Fund, 1997.102.

Heinrich & Co. received a gold medal for the *Anmut* shape at the ninth design triennial in Milan in 1951. The shape was heavily promoted on the German market in the 1950s. The fact that the ivory body and conservative oak leaf pattern in this example would have appealed to Americans suggests that this decorative scheme may have been created for the U.S. market. After World War II, Heinrich tableware was imported by Gustave Lap, Inc., in New York; Aristocrat China Company in Atlanta, San Francisco, Dallas, and New York; and Ebeling & Reuss in Philadelphia, New York, Chicago, and Los Angeles.

***Apart* snack plate with cup and coffeepot,** 1957. Hans Achtziger, designer; Lorenz Hutschenreuther, Selb, Germany, maker; Paul A. Straub & Co., New York, importer. Porcelain; coffeepot: h. 8½ in. (21.6 cm), w. 8⅞ in. (22.5 cm), d. 4½ in. (11.4 cm). Pot marked: [*lion over the date 1814 in oval*] / *HUTSCHEN-REUTHER* / *GERMANY* / *Apart*. Cup marked: *LORENZ HUTSCHENREUTHER* / [*lion over JHR in oval*] / *GERMANY* / *Apart* / *2¾*. Plate marked: *Hutschenreuther* / *Selb.* / [*lion over L·H·S in oval*] / *GERMANY* / *Apart*. Dallas Museum of Art, 20th-Century Design Fund, 1997.103.1–2.

The same triangular shape with a plain surface, known as *Diadem*, was designed by Achtziger in 1953 and produced from 1953 until about 1958. Achtziger added relief decoration to the shape in 1957 and released it as *Apart*. Initially only coffee, tea, and chocolate sets were available, but within a year a full line of tableware was in production, as well as matching glass stemware. Straub distributed both versions and the glassware. In 1958 a five-piece place setting of *Apart* cost $8 retail.[1]

1. *CGJ* 163:3 (Sept. 1958): 12; and 165:1 (July 1959): 47.

Cat. 100

All pieces: ca. 1928–30. Attributed to Eva Zeisel, designer; Schramberger Majolikafabrik, Schramberg, Germany, maker; Otto Goetz, Inc., New York, importer. Earthenware with painted and sprayed decoration; plastic (mustard spoon).

Top to bottom:
Cup, saucer, and plate. Plate: h. ⅞ in. (2.2 cm), diam. 7⅝ in. (19.4 cm). All marked: *SMF* / *GERMANY* / *Wheelock* / „*BLACK FOREST*" / *HAND PAINTED* / *POTTERY* / *Underglaze* [*all in a circle*]. Dallas Museum of Art, 20th-Century Design Fund, 1997.178.1–2.

Dessert plate and cup and saucer with *Futura* pattern. Dessert plate marked: *HANDPAINTED* / *SMF* [*in a shield*] / *SCHRAMBERG* / *GERMANY* and

73. Cup marked: same except with 64. Saucer marked: SMF [in a shield] / SCHRAMBERG / Handgemalt. Dallas Museum of Art, 20th-Century Design Fund, 1997.165.1–2.

Mustard pot with spoon. Marked: 3853. and SMF [in a shield] / SCHRAMBERG / Dec. 337 / 31. Dallas Museum of Art, 20th-Century Design Fund, 1997.179.

Eva Zeisel worked in potteries in both Budapest and Hamburg before coming to the Schramberg earthenware factory. While at the pottery in Germany's Black Forest region between 1928 and 1930, she introduced surface patterns and shapes that were heavily influenced by contemporary abstract painting and geometric Bauhaus-style architecture. In 1933 a New York trade observer said, "One of the new ranges at Otto Goetz is their Black Forest art pottery which follows modern tendencies in line and colorings. . . . All the pieces are decorated with a modern arrangement of lines and blocks in two tones of brown, blue, and bright yellow on a yellow glaze. There are open-footed bowls, vases, baskets and a tea pot modeled along 'architectural' lines."[1] Based on comparison with other objects known to have been designed by Zeisel, comments from Zeisel herself, and period trade catalogues, the shapes and decoration of these examples—except the shape of the yellow cup and saucer and plate—can be attributed to the her. The mustard pot shape is not shown in the catalogues, but its decoration is close to that on other items illustrated.[2]

1. CGJ 113:2 (Aug. 1933): 25.
2. For more information, see Montreal 1984, 17–23; Bröhan and Berg 1994, 126, 171; Schramberger 1930; and Schramberger 1931.

Cat. 101

Plate and cup and saucer with Autumn Leaves pattern, ca. 1926–30. C. M. Hutschenreuther, Hohenberg on the Eger, Germany, maker; Graham & Zenger, New York, importer. Porcelain with printed and gilded decoration; plate: h. 1 in. (2.5 cm), diam. 10½ in. (26.7 cm). Plate marked: 1814 [shield surmounted by a crown with the letters CM over HR] / HUTSCHENREUTHER / HOHENBERG / BAVARIA and [knight on horseback] / BLACK / KNIGHT and Registered U.S.A. / Hohenberg Bavaria / Autumnleaves / [Greek cross]. Saucer marked: same except with 760. Cup marked: same except with 794. Dallas Museum of Art, 20th-Century Design Fund, 1997.105.1–2.

Although this pattern was made in Germany, it may have been designed in the United States. Like many of Graham & Zenger's patterns, this one was registered with the U.S. patent office. The vivid colors of the Autumn Leaves pattern reflect the popularity of bold hues in the late 1920s and 1930s. The date of the pattern is based on two facts: the Black Knight

backstamp on these pieces was introduced in 1926 and trademarked the next year, and Autumn Leaves is shown in a trade catalogue of 1930.[1] In the catalogue the pattern sets "a breakfast table in glowing Autumnal tones," in which amethyst glassware and colored linens complement the "tawny yellows, plum, scarlet, and green" of the dishes.

1. "A Trade Mark Symbolizing Fine China," CGJ 104:16 (21 Apr. 1927): 11; and Marshall Field [1930].

Cat. 102

Glass, ca. 1960. Claus Joseph Riedel Tiroler Glashütte, Kufstein, Austria. Lead glass with pressed and cut decoration. Labeled: JR. Dallas Museum of Art, gift of Carole Stupell, Ltd., T42624.11.

Goblet with Brookdale pattern, ca. 1965–75. Justin Tharaud & Son, New York, designer; unknown factory, Germany, glassmaker; unknown factory, Netherlands, decorator. Lead glass with cut decoration. Unmarked. Carole Stupell, Ltd., Collection.

During the late 1960s and 1970s Justin Tharaud & Son imported two notable lines of lead crystal—Royal Netherland and Tharaud Designs. The Brookdale pattern was one of six that made up the Tharaud Designs line and was said to have been derived from "a graceful old china pattern."[1] Except for Bamboo, which consisted of a plain bowl and a stem cut to resemble bamboo, the other patterns also carried opulent cutting and engraving. These other patterns were named Chason, Crown Jewels, Chantilly, and Royal Peacock. Of these, Crown Jewels was said to be "the finest of the fine" and to have taken master engraver Erwin W. Krause "many days to cut and to engrave." The same source noted that "Tharaud Designs full lead crystal is carefully designed in America for American tables."[2] According to Keith Stupell, Justin Tharaud had the glass blanks made in Germany and decorated in the Netherlands, possibly at N. V. Kristalunie Maastrich, which made the Royal Netherland brand for the U.S. importer.[3] In 1976 the suggested retail price for a Brookdale goblet was $50 and that for Crown Jewels, $200.[4] In just three years the prices had climbed to $65 and $300, respectively.[5]

C. '70 wineglass, ca. 1970. Claus Joseph Riedel Tiroler Glashütte, Kufstein, Austria. Lead glass with pressed decoration. Labeled: MADE IN AUSTRIA / JR.24% / PbO / RIEDEL CRYSTAL [all in an oval]. Dallas Museum of Art, gift of Carole Stupell, Ltd., T42624.8.

In addition to selling this design in its plain state, Keith Stupell added color by inserting a plastic sphere in the hole in the stem. Among those who purchased the ornamented version was the Shah of Iran, Mohammed Reza Pahlavi.

Wineglass, ca. 1960. Ludwig Moser & Söhne, Meierhöfen bei Karlsbad, Czechoslovakia. Lead glass with cut decoration; h. 8⅝ in. (21.9 cm), diam. 3½ in. (8.9 cm). Marked: Moser [in an oval]. Labeled: A / carole stupell / SELECTION. Dallas Museum of Art, gift of Carole Stupell, Ltd., T42624.5.

Moser was one of the finest glassmakers in Bohemia. It was especially well known for the purity of its lead glass and the high quality of its panel cutting as seen on the square stem. Having been absent from the U.S. market since World War II, Moser was reintroduced around 1960. In that year the firm advertised panel-cut stemware in Crockery and Glass Journal and distributed a trade catalogue for its Carlsbad Crystal brand.[6] This example is particularly interesting for its use of blue glass cut back to clear.

Alpha old-fashioned glass, ca. 1952. Hans H. Rath, designer; J. & L. Lobmeyr, Vienna, Austria, maker; Liso Makarius Starrett, New York, importer. Glass. Labeled: MADE IN AUSTRIA / L [in a circle] / LOBMEYR. Dallas Museum of Art, gift of Carole Stupell, Ltd., T42624.17.

The designer of the Alpha line, Hans H. Rath, is best known for his lighting designs, which include the immense crystal chandeliers in the auditorium and lobby of the Metropolitan Opera at Lincoln Center in New York. However, Rath also created a series of tableware designs for Lobmeyr that reveal the firm's ability to blow exceptionally thin-walled drinking vessels.[7]

1. "Tharaud Designs" (sales brochure and price list, 1979).
2. Ibid.
3. Keith Stupell, conversation with Charles Venable, 15 Oct. 1999.
4. "Tharaud Designs" (sales brochure and price list, 1976).
5. Ibid.
6. CGJ 166:1 (Jan. 1960): 32; "Bohemian Glass—Witness of History" (Moser trade catalogue, 1960?).
7. For images of Alpha and other Rath designs, see "Lobmeyr: Crystal Giftware" (trade catalogue and price list, 1979), 3, 6.

Cat. 103

Covered punch bowl, ca. 1930–35. Villeroy & Boch, Mettlach, Germany. Earthenware with sprayed decoration; h. 9⅝ in. (24.4 cm), diam. 9⅛ in. (23.2 cm). Marked: [winged Mercury logo] / VILLEROY & BOCH / METTLACH / Made in Saar-Basin. Dallas Museum of Art, 20th-Century Design Fund, T42397.

During the late 1920s and 1930s Villeroy & Boch's factories in Mettlach and Dresden were major producers of earthenware kitchen- and tableware featuring air-brushed decoration.[1] Although the technology for spraying glaze onto ceramics was used at numerous factories in Europe, the United States, and Japan, the Germans were especially adept at exploiting its potential. In this fine example, the decoration works with the austere cylindrical shape to lend the vessel a machinelike quality, the base and lid resembling gears. The medial band of circles resembling bubbles and celestial orbs softens the composition. The covered punch bowl is a traditional central European form known as a *Bolle*.

1. For numerous other examples, see Buddensieg 1984.

Cat. 104

Sanssouci shape plate and cup and saucer with *Chantilly* pattern, 1926. Karl Bayreuther, shape designer; Philipp Rosenthal & Co., Selb, Germany, maker; Rosenthal China Corporation, New York, importer. Porcelain with painted decoration; plate: h. ⅞ in. (2.2 cm), diam. 10⅜ in. (26.4 cm). Plate marked: *Rosen* [X surmounted by a crown] thal / SELB-GERMANY and *Rosen* [X surmounted by a crown] thal / IVORY / GERMANY and *Chantilly*. Cup and saucer also marked: [dot] (date mark for 1938). Dallas Museum of Art, 20th-Century Design Fund, 1997.101.1–2.

Full dinner services in *Sanssouci* were first produced from 1894 until about 1897. In 1926 the shape was adapted and put back into production in both white and ivory-colored porcelain under the direction of modeler Karl Bayreuther, who was active at Rosenthal from 1921 to 1947. The ivory body was made especially for the U.S. market and was decorated with colored backgrounds, as here, or with enamels highlighting the raised ornamentation. Many of these decorative schemes were given eighteenth-century French–sounding names such as *Du Barry* or *Chantilly*. A 1932 review in the *Crockery and Glass Journal* states that "the Sans Souci shape is the big new dinnerware development."¹ The reviewer also noted that the curvilinear shape featuring vine-covered trellises was inspired by Frederick the Great's extraordinary rococo-style summer palace, Sans Souci (built 1745–47), at Potsdam outside Berlin. The *Sanssouci* shape is still in production today as part of Rosenthal's Classic Rose Collection.

1. "Right Out of the Kiln," *CGJ* 110:10 (Oct. 1932): 20.

Cat. 105

Donatello chocolate cup and saucer and pot, ca. 1905. Philipp Rosenthal & Co., Selb, Germany, maker; Rosenthal China Corporation, New York, importer. Porcelain; pot: h. 8⅜ in. (21.3 cm), w. 6¾ in. (17.1 cm), d. 3¾ in. (9.5 cm). All marked: *Rosen* [X surmounted by a crown] thal / SELB BAVARIA / DONATELLO. William Swann and William Leazer Collection.

Donatello was in production between 1905 and 1925 and appears to have been relatively popular in the United States. The shape is a fine example of the German Jugendstil, which was

more restrained and angular than its French counterpart—the curvilinear art nouveau style. In addition to all white, *Donatello* was available in a variety of surface ornament, ranging from solid cobalt blue with gilded accents (ca. 1907) to naturalistic cherries molded in relief and enameled (ca. 1910).¹

1. Hilschenz 1982, 8, 32–33, 234.

Cat. 106

Perlrand shape soup bowl on stand with *Empire* pattern, ca. 1918. Philipp Rosenthal & Co., Selb, Germany, designer; Shenango Pottery Company, New Castle, Pa., maker; Castleton China, New York, distributor. Porcelain with printed and gilded decoration; bowl without stand: h. 1⅞ in. (4.8 cm), w. 6⅝ in. (16.8 cm), d. 4¾ in. (12.1 cm). Both marked: [lyre logo] / CASTLETON CHINA / MADE IN U.S.A. / EMPIRE. Bowl also marked: 12 and 13 and 58. Stand also marked: 3 and 3-0. Dallas Museum of Art, 20th-Century Design Fund, 1996.40.

Perlrand shape soup bowl on stand, ca. 1918. Philipp Rosenthal & Co., Selb, Germany, maker; Rosenthal China Corporation, New York, importer. Porcelain with printed, painted, and gilded decoration. Both marked: *Rosen* [X surmounted by a crown] thal / IVORY / GERMANY. Dallas Museum of Art, 20th-Century Design Fund, 1996.41.

Louis E. Hellmann was the American representative for Rosenthal during the 1920s and 1930s. In 1939 Hellmann arranged for Shenango Pottery to produce a fine china based directly on Rosenthal's *Perlrand* shape that was popular in the United States at the time. This American version was distributed by newly established Castleton China, in which Shenango held a 25 percent financial interest.¹ At present it is unknown whether this line was produced with Rosenthal's permission or if Hellmann simply appropriated the German designs, assuming that the impending war would make it difficult for Rosenthal to take action. However, it is certainly possible that Rosenthal not only sanctioned the American versions but also hoped that they would keep Rosenthal's most profitable patterns alive in the United States during the coming hostilities. Whatever the circumstances, Castleton's versions were indeed very close to the German originals. Not only are the shapes the same, but the white, blue, and gold *Empire* pattern is virtually identical to Rosenthal's pattern of the same name.² Furthermore, the cream-colored body of Castleton China was not dissimilar to Rosenthal's ivory body.

1. Lehner 1988, 420.
2. For an ad for Rosenthal's *Empire*, see *CGJ* 123:6 (Dec. 1938): 8.

Cat. 107

All pieces: Raymond Loewy Associates, New York, designer; Philipp Rosenthal & Co., Selb, Germany, maker; Rosenthal-Block China Corporation, New York, importer.

Model 2000 shape cup and saucer with *Birds on Trees* pattern and coffeepot, sugar bowl, and creamer with *Crystalline* pattern, 1952–53. Porcelain with printed decoration (cup and saucer). Coffeepot: h. 10 in. (25.4 cm), w. 8¾ in. (27.3 cm), d. 4⅞ in. (12.4 cm). Cup and saucer marked: *Rosen* [X surmounted by a crown] thal / SELB–GERMANY / V / DESIGNED BY / Raymond loewy / BIRDS ON TREES. Coffeepot marked: same as cup and saucer except with pattern name CRYSTALLINE and [—•—] and without SELB. Sugar bowl marked: same as cup and saucer except with pattern name CRYSTALLINE and [•V•]. Creamer marked: same as coffeepot except without [—•—]. Dallas Museum of Art: gift of Mr. and Mrs. Duncan E. Boeckman (coffee set), T42526, T42554.1–2; 20th-Century Design Fund (cup and saucer), 1995.181.1.

The *Model 2000* shape appeared in 1954. Unlike *Exquisit*, it is very angular. The shape is closely related to contemporary German designs and was heavily influenced by Hubert Griemert's *Crocus* service (1952–53), which was in production at the Staatliche Porzellanmanufaktur in Berlin while Latham and his colleagues were working on *Model 2000*.¹ The *Crystalline* and *Birds on Trees* patterns were selected by Elizabeth and Duncan Boeckman at Neiman Marcus in Dallas on the occasion of their marriage in 1954.

Exquisit shape plate and cup and saucer with *Coin* pattern and coffeepot with *Bird Cage* pattern from the Continental China line, 1951–52. Porcelain with printed decoration. Coffeepot marked: CONTINENTAL CHINA / [R surmounted by a crown] / DESIGNED BY / Raymond Loewy / GERMANY / Bird Cage. Plate and cup and saucer marked: same except pattern name *Coins*. Dallas Museum of Art, 20th-Century Design Fund, 1995.140, 1995.58.1–2.

During the 1950s the *Exquisit* shape was produced at both Rosenthal's main pottery in Selb and its Johann Haviland factory in Waldershof.² When *Exquisit* was introduced in the United States in 1953 it was available in ten different patterns, including *Bird Cage* and *Coins*. At the time a five-piece place setting retailed for $13.95. *Bird Cage* was called *Papageno* in Europe and was introduced in 1956. *Exquisit* and *Model 2000* are two of the most famous twentieth-century tableware designs. Around 1951 Joseph Block hired Raymond Loewy Associates to create a new dinnerware line to be produced by Rosenthal in Germany for export to the United States. In the end four different shapes were produced. According to contemporary accounts the first three, including *Exquisit*, resulted from "at least half a dozen trips to Europe by Loewy designers."[3] While Loewy certainly had input into the design process, it was Richard S. Latham who is credited for much of the design of these services.

1. Eidelberg 1991, 180–81.
2. *Schaulade* 30:2 (Feb. 1955): 61.
3. "Loewy Designs Modern Dinnerware Patterns for Rosenthal China," *CGJ* 151:1 (July 1952): 71.

Cat. 108

All pieces: Philipp Rosenthal & Co., Bad Soden and Amberg, Germany, maker; Rosenthal China Corporation, New York, importer.

Composition 'G' shape cordial glass with Ice-flower **pattern,** 1963. Richard S. Latham and Claus Josef Riedel, designers. Glass with etched decoration. Marked: *Rosen [X surmounted by a crown] thal.* Dallas Museum of Art, 20th-Century Design Fund, 1997.196.

700 shape water goblet with Tulip Rays **pattern,** ca. 1965. Hans Theodore Baumann, designer. Glass with cut decoration; h. 6⅞ in. (17.5 cm), diam. 2¾ in. (7 cm). Marked: *[crown] / R.* Dallas Museum of Art, 20th-Century Design Fund, 1997.193.

Fortuna sherbet glass, ca. 1956–62. Elsa Fischer-Treyden, designer. Glass. Labeled: *MADE IN / GERMANY* and *Rosen [X surmounted by a crown] thal.* Dallas Museum of Art, 20th-Century Design Fund, 1997.195.

Romance II shape champagne glass with Motif **pattern,** 1962–64. Bjørn Wiinblad, designer. Glass with cut and etched decoration. Marked: *ROSEN [X surmounted by a crown] THAL / STUDIO-LINE.* Dallas Museum of Art, 20th-Century Design Fund, 1997.194.

Rosenthal initiated glass production in 1956 with the aid of Czech workers and introduced the product to Americans in 1962. The first lines sold here were Chicagoan George Butler Jensen's *Linear* stemware and Bjørn Wiinblad's original version of *Romance* (1962). Soon other shapes, including those pictured, were exported to the United States. In keeping with the Studio-Line concept, Rosenthal's stemware often coordinated with matching porcelain tableware and metal flatware. By 1969 glassware sales represented 13 percent of Rosenthal's total U.S. sales.[1]

1. "Rosenthal Price List" (Rosenthal China Canada sales brochure and price list, 1969).

Cat. 109

All pieces: Nippon Toki Kaisha, Nagoya, Japan, maker; Noritake Company, New York, importer. Porcelain with printed and gilded decoration.

Teapot, cup and saucer, and plate with no. 2133 **pattern,** ca. 1955–60. Plate: h. 1 in. (2.5 cm), diam. 10⅝ in. (27 cm). All marked: *Noritake / N [within a wreath] / NIPPON TOKI KAISHA / JAPAN / 2133.* Dallas Museum of Art, 20th-Century Design Fund, 1997.130.1–3.

The mark on this set was first used in 1955. According to Noritake, this pattern was initially made for the Japanese market and later introduced to Americans through the U.S. military Post Exchange.

Normandie shape covered casserole dish with Trent **pattern,** ca. 1955. Marked: *Noritake / Fine / China / japan / TRENT / U.S. DESIGN PAT. / PEND.* Dallas Museum of Art, 20th-Century Design Fund, 1997.129.

Trent was one of six patterns that Noritake introduced in 1955 as part of its new *Fine China* line. These patterns retailed for between $7.95 and $10.95. Noritake advertised *Fine China* as "New throughout! A finer, more beautifully decorated dinnerware than we have offered before! Light, translucent and durable as only the finest china can be."[1] *Trent* (no. 6953) was the most heavily promoted pattern in this line. Although no exact prototype is known, its modernist design appears to have been based on German examples from the early 1950s.[2] It was discontinued in 1960.

1. *CGJ* 157:1 (July 1955): 9, 72; and 157:5 (Nov. 1955): 42.
2. For related examples see *Schaulade* 27 (Oct. 1952): 366.

Cat. 110

Norleans China shape casserole dish with Chatham **pattern,** 1949. Eva Zeisel, shape designer; Meito, Nagoya, Japan, maker; United China & Glass Company, New Orleans, importer. Porcelain with printed, painted, and gilded decoration; h. 5½ in. (14 cm), w. 11¾ in. (30 cm), d. 7¾ in. (19.7 cm). Marked: *MEITO [surmounted by a crown] / NORLEANS / CHINA / CHATHAM* and *Made in / Occupied Japan.* Dallas Museum of Art, 20th-Century Design Fund, 1996.155.

Although the *Norleans* line was designed in 1949 and introduced to the market the following year, Eva Zeisel did not receive design patents for the shapes until 1951 (for example, the creamer is design patent no. 165,042). Initially the line was released with a dozen surface patterns. All of these conservative botanical ornaments may well have been designed by the Meito staff.[1]

1. *CGJ* 145:6 (Dec. 1949): 14–15; and 146:1 (Jan. 1950): 15.

Cat. 111

Cup and saucer and plate with Country Gingham **pattern,** ca. 1974–76. Narumi, Nagoya, Japan, maker; Mikasa, Los Angeles and Secaucus, N.J., designer/importer. Porcelain with printed decoration; plate: h. 1 in.

(2.5 cm), diam. 10⅞ in. (27.6 cm). Cup and saucer marked: © [circular logo] *mikasa* ® / *C7400 / D5400 / OVEN TO TABLE / TO DISHWASHER / JAPAN.* Plate marked: *mikasa / COUNTRY GINGHAM / OTD OVEN TO TABLE / TO DISHWASHER / SAFE IN MICROWAVE OVENS / MINT TAFFY / C7401 / JAPAN [all in a circle featuring a farm scene and a woman churning butter].* Dallas Museum of Art, 20th-Century Design Fund, 1997.201.1–2.

The *Country Gingham* pattern was produced in four colors—*Mint Taffy* (green, illustrated), *Fudge* (brown), *Denim* (blue), *Cotton Candy* (pink), and *Maize* (yellow). Ironically, while its imagery and name linked it with the "back-to-nature" movement of the 1970s, its backstamp reflected increased mechanization in the kitchen. Besides noting this line as "oven to table to dishwasher" safe, Mikasa included the "Safe in Microwave Ovens" mark that was first used in the mid-1970s.

Cat. 112

All pieces: Chunichi Toki Company, Nagoya, Japan, maker; Fitz and Floyd, Dallas, designer and importer.

Set of three graduated dishes, ca. 1983. Porcelain with gilded decoration. Marked: *Fitz and Floyd / Fine Porcelain / LIMITED EDITION.* Dallas Museum of Art, gift of Robert C. Floyd, 1998.129.1–3.

These shell-shaped dishes were made in very limited quantities. Because of the extensive use of high-quality gilding, their cost was too great for commercial production, so they were distributed in a limited edition for use as giftware or tableware.

Plate with Damascene **pattern,** 1982. Porcelain with printed, gilded, and platinum decoration. Marked: *"DAMASCENE" / FITZ AND FLOYD. INC. / ©MCMLXXXII JAPAN / FF / 148.* Dallas Museum of Art, gift of Robert C. Floyd, 1998.68.

Damascene was one of Fitz and Floyd's most elaborate patterns and was difficult to produce. Robert Floyd recalls being inspired by a metal bowl ornamented with an inlay technique known as damascene that he found in Kyoto, Japan. Fitz and Floyd's chief designer, Dale Hodges, remembers that the drafting of the pattern's woven motif was influenced by the square symbols used to denote "ground" on architectural blueprints. According to Floyd, the production of the design was complicated due to the difficulty of using gold and platinum side by side.[1]

Service plate with Grey Renaissance **pattern,** 1981. Porcelain with gilded decoration; h. 1¼ in. (3.2 cm), diam. 12⅛ in. (30.8 cm). Marked: *"Grey Renaissance" / Inglaze / FITZ AND*

FLOYD, INC. | MCMLXXXI | JAPAN | FF | 131. Dallas Museum of Art, gift of Robert C. Floyd, 1998.67.

Grey Renaissance was part of the *Renaissance* line, which featured dinnerware with wide bands in various colors. The line was one of the foundations of Fitz and Floyd's mix-and-match look, as demonstrated here. Colors were carefully chosen so that they would harmonize with other designs made by the Dallas firm.

1. Robert C. Floyd, letter to Charles Venable, 1 June 1999; and Hodges interview 1999.

Cat. 113

Plate with *Starburst* pattern from the Reagan White House service, 1981. Dale Hodges, designer; Chunichi Toki Company, Nagoya, Japan, maker; Fitz and Floyd, Dallas, importer. Porcelain with gilded decoration; h. 1 in. (2.5 cm), diam. 10¼ in. (26 cm). Marked: "Starburst" | *Cobalt Inglaze* | FITZ AND FLOYD, INC. | © MCMLXXXI JAPAN | FF | 16. Dallas Museum of Art, gift of Robert C. Floyd, 1998.128.

Following Ronald Reagan's election as president in 1980, First Lady Nancy Davis Reagan asked Fitz and Floyd to supply dinnerware for use in the private quarters and offices of the White House and on *Air Force One*. Rather than create a totally new design, the *Starburst* pattern was adapted with the addition of the Presidential Seal in raised gold paste work. Dale Hodges, the firm's chief designer, recalls that *Starburst* was inspired by an antique blue and white English plate that featured a similar border.

Cat. 114

Chocolate set with no. 175 pattern, ca. 1918. Nippon Toki Kaisha, Nagoya, Japan, maker; Morimura Brothers., New York, importer. Porcelain with gilded decoration; chocolate pot: h. 6⅝ in. (16.8 cm), w. 6⅜ in. (16.2 cm), d. 4 in. (10.2 cm). Saucers unmarked. Others marked: NORITAKE | M [*within a wreath*] | HAND PAINTED | MADE IN JAPAN | [*five Japanese characters*] | No. 16034. Dallas Museum of Art, gift of Noritake Company, Inc., T42596.1–8.

The no. 175 pattern is one of Noritake's oldest designs. Introduced in 1918, only four years after the pottery began making dinnerware, the design was not taken out of production until 1989.[1] This example has an early mark that may date to the first year of production.

1. Osamu Tsutsui, letter to Charles Venable, 15 Apr. 1999.

Cat. 115

Plate and cup and saucer with *Colonade* pattern, ca. 1931. Nippon Toki Kaisha, Nagoya, Japan, maker; Morimura Brothers, New York, importer. Porcelain with printed, painted, and gilded decoration; plate: h. 1 in. (2.5 cm),

diam. 9⅞ in. (25.1 cm). All marked: M | NORITAKE | IVORY | JAPAN [*all in wreath*] | COLONADE | U.S. DESIGN PAT | APPLIED FOR. Dallas Museum of Art, 20th-Century Design Fund, 1997.128.1–2.

This pattern is typical of the higher-quality dinnerware in the Noritake line made during the 1920s and 1930s. Although the record for *Colonade* has not been found, very similar designs were patented in 1930. The patents for those designs were applied for in 1929 by Urasaburo Tomita of Astoria, New York, who subsequently assigned them to the Morimura Brothers.[1] Although the mark on these examples was first used in 1931, the ivory-colored body was introduced in 1927 for export to the United States.

1. PGBS 41:2 (13 Feb. 1930): 33.

Cat. 116

All pieces: Nippon Toki Kaisha, Nagoya, Japan, maker; Noritake Company, New York, importer. Porcelain with printed and gilded decoration.

New La Salle shape plate with Berkeley pattern, ca. 1957. Shunzo Terano, designer. H. 1 in. (2.5 cm), diam. 10½ in. (26.7 cm). Marked: NORITAKE CHINA | N [*within a wreath tied at bottom with a ribbon*] | R [*within a circular registration mark*] | JAPAN | 5784 | BERKELEY | U.S. DESIGN PAT. | PEND. Dallas Museum of Art, 20th-Century Design Fund, 1997.126.

Pompadour shape salad plate with no. 5548 pattern, ca. 1955. Marked: NORITAKE CHINA | N [*within a wreath tied at bottom with a ribbon*] | JAPAN | 5548. Dallas Museum of Art, 20th-Century Design Fund, 1997.124.

Monterey shape breakfast plate, ca. 1956. Marked: NORITAKE CHINA | N [*within a wreath tied at bottom with a ribbon*] | JAPAN. Dallas Museum of Art, 20th-Century Design Fund, 1997.131.

The *Berkeley* pattern was introduced in 1957 and discontinued in 1961. The no. 5548 pattern was introduced in 1955 and discontinued two years later. Its snowflake design was likely based on the *Snow Star* pattern introduced to the United States in 1955 by the New York importer and distributor Lipper & Mann.[1] Although the *Monterey* coupe shape was available by 1955, the unidentified leaf pattern that is illustrated was apparently introduced in the United States the next year. A 1956 ad for the pattern notes that it was made as a "breakfast-for-two set" that consisted of twelve pieces: two oversize coffee cups and saucers, two large plates, two small plates, two cereal bowls, a creamer, and a sugar bowl.[2]

1. CGJ 155:2 (Feb. 1955): 32.
2. Ibid.; 158:2 (Feb. 1956): 7.

Cat. 117

Plate and cup and saucer, ca. 1893–1917. Brothers Kornilov, Saint Petersburg, Russia, maker; Bailey, Banks & Biddle Co., Philadelphia, retailer. Porcelain with printed, painted, and gilded decoration; plate: h. 1 in. (2.5 cm), diam. 9½ in. (24.1 cm). Plate marked: [*bear holding a teapot and sign reading "J.H.V." logo*] | Made in Russia | by Kornilow Bros. | for Bailey, Banks & Biddle Co. | Philadelphia and 46. Cup and saucer marked: same except with 245. Dallas Museum of Art, 20th-Century Design Fund, 1998.155, 1998.154.

The Kornilov factory was one of the largest and most technically advanced in Russia in the late nineteenth century. A vogue for Kornilov porcelain among wealthy Americans began in the 1890s. Decoration on the export ware is in an overtly Russian folk style. Except for the imperial eagle seen on the plate, the bright colors, geometric patterns, and use of animals are typically Slavic in origin. Kornilov porcelain was sold at Bailey, Banks & Biddle, Tiffany & Co., and other elite china and glass retailers before World War I.[1]

1. Ross 1968, 312–13.

Cat. 118

Avon goblet, ca. 1950. Unknown factory, Sweden, maker; D. Stanley Corcoran, New York, importer. Glass; h. 6⅝ in. (16.8 cm), diam. 3¾ in. (9.5 cm). Unmarked. Dallas Museum of Art, 20th-Century Design Fund, T42502.

Before World War II Sweden exported stemware to the United States, albeit in relatively small amounts. For example, the New York importer J. H. Venon advertised in 1939 that he distributed Kosta's *Ingrid* pattern, which was very similar to *Avon* in shape although it did not have the medial ball.[1] *Avon* was one of the first Swedish designs imported after the war and is representative of much of the Swedish glass bought by Americans. Bold in outline and uncut, Swedish designs influenced glassware that was made both in the United States and abroad at midcentury.[2]

Kungsholm cordial and highball glasses, 1952. Belle Kogan, designer; unknown factory, Sweden, maker; R. F. Brodegaard & Co., New York, importer. Lead glass. All unmarked. Dallas Museum of Art, gift of Belle Kogan, 1998.120.1–2.

Robert F. Brodegaard was among the first to import Swedish glassware after World War II. In 1946 he advertised the pattern *Gothic*, which was said to have been designed exclusively for distribution in America. This was one of several patterns featuring cut ornament that were made for Brodegaard by the Bergdala Glasbruk.[3] The name of the factory that produced *Kungsholm* is unknown. However, a 1953 ad for

Kungsholm notes that Brodegaard's had glass-ware made by the Swedish factories of "Strombergshyttan, Bergdala, and Reisjmyre."[4]

Mirage goblet and sherbet glass, ca. 1973. Joseph Bourne & Son, Denby, England, designer; unknown factory, Sweden, maker; Milnor, Cincinnati, importer. Lead glass. Both labeled: DENBY / MILNOR • SWEDEN. Dallas Museum of Art, gift of George Roland in memory of Annabelle and Charles Thomas Roland, 1997.192.1–2.

These glasses reflect not only the vogue for colored glassware in the 1960s and early 1970s, but also the trend on the part of potteries to have allied stemware lines during the same period. Bourne was a potterymaker but marketed this stemware under its well-known Denby brand name even though the glass actually came from Sweden. Denby's American importer Milnor, formerly Millard Norman, changed its name to Denby Ltd. in late 1973. The fact that the Milnor name is printed on the glasses' labels suggests that the pieces were made prior to that time.

    Mirage stemware was produced in yellow, white, blue, green, brown, and plum. The colors were specifically chosen to coordinate with the stoneware dishes and stoneware-handled stainless flatware that Denby also sold. *Mirage Yellow,* for example, was supposed to be used with the firm's *Minstrel* pattern dinnerware and *Regency Yellow* flatware.[5] The yellow glassware illustrated was selected by Elvis Presley for use in his Memphis home, Graceland.

1. *CGJ* 125:1 (July 1939): 28.
2. For an Avon ad, see *CGJ* 151:1 (July 1952): 53.
3. *CGJ* 138:5 (May 1946): 21.
4. *Gift and Art Buyer* (Jan. 1953): 120.
5. "The Dauntless Stoneware of Denby and England" (trade catalogue, 1980?).

Cat. 119
All pieces: 1933. Thorkild Olsen, designer; Royal Copenhagen Porcelain Manufactory and Faience Manufactory Aluminia, Copenhagen, Denmark, maker. Porcelain with printed and painted decoration. All marked: • ROYAL • / [crown] COPENHAGEN [words encircling the crown] / DENMARK and [three wave symbols].

No. 9586 shape plate with *Fensmark* pattern. H. 1⅛ in. (2.9 cm), diam. 9¾ in. (24.8 cm). Also marked: 1010 (pattern number) / — / 9586 (shape number) and [slash] / 4. Dallas Museum of Art, 20th-Century Design Fund, T42477.

No. 9535 shape demitasse cup and saucer with *Stauder* pattern. Cup also marked: 4 / [slash] / 991 (pattern number) / 9535 (shape number). Saucer also marked: 991 / 9535 and s [indecipherable letters] cf. Dallas Museum of Art, 20th-Century Design Fund, T42480.

No. 9781 shape Demitasse coffeepot with *Quaking Grass* pattern. Coffeepot and lid also marked: 884 (pattern number) / 9781 (shape number). Dallas Museum of Art, 20th-Century Design Fund, T42479.

Along with the shape, Thorkild Olsen designed the three surface patterns pictured. *Quaking Grass* and *Stauder* (named after a herbaceous perennial) date from the early 1930s. The flowers featured in *Stauder* are hand enameled and thus vary from piece to piece. The demitasse cups, for example, each have a different bouquet. The third pattern, *Fensmark,* is named after a Danish town. *Quaking Grass* was the most popular in the United States. The shape was not discontinued by Royal Copenhagen until 1985.[1]

1. Steen Nottelmauer, letter to Charles Venable (11 June 1999).

Cat. 120
Kilta platter and cup and saucer, 1948. Kaj Franck, designer; Arabia AB, Helsinki, Finland, maker; Waertsila Corporation, New York, importer. Stoneware. Cup and saucer marked: [logo of covered dish in semicircle] / [crown] / ARABIA / MADE IN FINLAND. Platter marked: [crown] / ARABIA / WÄRTSILA FINLAND and BA32S. Dallas Museum of Art, 20th-Century Design Fund, 1997.6.1, T42496.

Kaj Franck was chief designer for Arabia from 1946 to 1978. His *Kilta* range of shapes, which was put into production in 1952–53, was originally intended to be inexpensive tableware for Europeans during the austerity of the immediate postwar period. Initially the ware was available in white, black, green, blue, and yellow glazes, which were fired along with the body in a single firing. Not requiring a separate glaze firing greatly reduced production costs. In 1981 Franck reworked *Kilta,* and it was reintroduced as *Teema.*[1]

Model R shape plate with *Tapestry* pattern, ca. 1952. Olga Osol, shape designer; Birger Kaipiainen, pattern designer; Arabia AB, Helsinki, Finland, maker; Waertsila Corporation, New York, importer. Stoneware; h. 1 in. (2.5 cm), diam. 10½ in. (26.7 cm). Marked: [crown] / ARABIA / MADE / IN / FINLAND / 6 / Tapestry and 68 / 1252. Dallas Museum of Art, 20th-Century Design Fund, T42503.1.

In 1947 the Arabia pottery was acquired by the Waertsila conglomerate. This entity jointly marketed the tabletop products of its various subsidiaries. For example, when *Tapestry* was introduced to the American market in early 1953, it was advertised alongside the Notsjoe crystal patterns *Hilkka* and *Valo.*[2] *Tapestry* was in production until 1964.

Blue Fire cup and saucer, teapot, and sugar bowl, 1949. Hertha Bengtson, designer; Rörstrand Porslinsfabrik AB, Lindköping, Sweden, maker. Earthenware. Cup, saucer, and creamer marked: [double crowns] Rörstrand / [crown] MADE IN SWEDEN / © RÖRSTRAND INC / [illegible]. Teapot marked: [double crowns] Rörstrand / [crown] / SWEDEN / [illegible]. Dallas Museum of Art, 20th-Century Design Fund, T42499.1–3.

Although some sources state that *Blue Fire* was in production from 1951 to 1971, it is known to have been available in the United States by the end of 1949.[3] Initially it was imported by Vaco Company, but Rörstrand opened its own showroom in New York in 1950 and took over distribution of the ware. When introduced here, *Blue Fire* was said to be the first pattern offered in the United States by Rörstrand in many years.[4]

1. Opie 1989, 63.
2. *CGJ* 152:3b (16 Mar. 1953): 23.
3. Opie 1989, 112; *CGJ* 145:6 (Dec. 1949): 52; and 147:1 (July 1950): 63.
4. *CGJ* 145:6 (Dec. 1949): 52.

Cat. 121
Fluted Flamestone plate, demitasse cup and saucer, and coffeepot, 1957. Jens H. Quistgaard, designer; Eslau Keramics, Sengeglöse, Denmark, maker; Dansk Designs, Great Neck, N.Y., importer. Stoneware; coffeepot: h. 13½ in. (34.3 cm), w. 7½ in. (19.1 cm), d. 5 in. (12.7 cm). Plate, saucer, and coffeepot marked: DANSK / DESIGNS / DENMARK / IHQ (artist mark) / •. Cup marked: IHQ (artist mark) / DANSK / DANMARK. Dallas Museum of Art, 20th-Century Design Fund (coffeepot), T42495; William Swann and William Leazer Collection (plate, cup, and saucer).

Jens Quistgaard was Dansk's lead designer during the 1950s and 1960s. Danish folk pottery with black glaze inspired him to create *Flamestone.* The original plain version, denoted in trade brochures as "smooth," appeared in 1957. Around 1962 *Fluted Flamestone* was introduced and was the more expensive of the two types. This coffeepot retailed for $19.95 originally, while the plain version was two dollars less. This stoneware line was discontinued in about 1978.[1]

1. "Dansk Designs" (sales brochure, 1963). Dates of introduction and discontinuation provided by Dansk International. Ted Nierenberg identified Eslau as the maker in a conversation with Charles Venable, 15 Sept. 1999.

Cat. 122
Pair of beer mugs, ca. 1954. Gaétan Beaudin, designer; Décor Pottery, Rimouski, Quebec, Canada, maker. Earthenware. Both marked: 56 / [stylized shape of a mug within a circle] / CANADA. Dallas Museum of Art, gift of 20th Century Gallery, T42429.

This design is exceptional for its free-form quality. The art press thought well of it when introduced, and the design was included in the *Studio Year Book* for 1954–55.[1]

Bowl, plate, and cup and saucer with *Agate Pass* pattern, ca. 1971–81. James McBride, designer; Fabrik Inc., Seattle, maker. Stoneware; plate: h. 1⅛ in. (2.9 cm), diam. 10¾ in. (27.3 cm). All marked: *f*. Dallas Museum of Art, 20th-Century Design Fund, 1997.188.1–3.

While very little is currently known about Fabrik Inc., its products were often of very high quality. *Agate Pass* was one of the firm's most successful patterns. Its thick body and hard edge are representative of the somewhat brutal nature of much stoneware in the 1970s.

1. Holme and Frost 1955, 71.

Cat. 123

Goblet, ca. 1950. Barovier & Toso, Murano, Venice, Italy, maker; Carole Stupell, Ltd., New York, importer. Glass. Unmarked. Carole Stupell, Ltd. Collection.

Goblet, ca. 1950. Barovier & Toso, Murano, Venice, Italy, maker; Carole Stupell, Ltd., New York, importer. Glass. Labeled: *Made in Italy*. Carole Stupell, Ltd. Collection.

Goblet, ca. 1923. Salviati & Co., Murano, Venice, Italy. Glass with painted and gilded decoration; h. 10 in. (25.4 cm), diam. 4¼ in. (10.8 cm). Unmarked. Charles A. Robinson Collection.

This goblet is part of a large set of stemware ordered in 1938 by Mary and Jean Baptiste Adoue, who owned the National Bank of Commerce in Dallas. According to the Adoue family papers, this pattern was called *Cawcia*; it features elaborate enamel work depicting hounds running through a field of flowers.[1] Nearly identical examples in the National Design Museum (no. 1979.61.5), New York, are known to have been made by the Salviati Glass Works in 1923.

Bowl, ca. 1945–50. Barovier & Toso, Murano, Venice, Italy, maker; Carole Stupell, Ltd., New York, designer and importer. Glass. Unmarked. Dallas Museum of Art, gift of Carole Stupell, Ltd., T42624.42.

Flower-shaped bowls such as this were conceived by Carole Stupell, who had them produced in numerous colors by several Murano glassworks in the decades following World War II. This example is one of the first versions made.

Plate, bowl on stand, and goblet, ca. 1956. Unknown factories, Murano, Venice, Italy, maker and decorator; Carole Stupell, Ltd.,

importer. Glass with painted and gilded decoration. All unmarked. Carole Stupell, Ltd., Collection.

A service of this design was ordered by the parents of Grace Kelly as a wedding gift on the occasion of her marriage to Prince Rainier of Monaco in 1956. As one of the most prestigious retailers of tableware in the country, Carole Stupell was engaged to provide the service. Using her extensive contacts with Venetian glasshouses, Stupell had the glass made in one factory and decorated in another. Following the royal wedding, the design was executed in other colors and sold to the public by Stupell.[2]

1. Charles Robinson, letter to Stephen Harrison, 25 Sept. 1999.
2. Keith Stupell, conversation with Charles Venable, 15 Oct. 1999.

Cat. 124

Both pieces: ca. 1955. Doccia factory division, Florence; Richard-Ginori Società Ceramica Italiana, Milan, Italy. Porcelain with printed and gilded decoration.

***Vecchio Ginori* shape plate with *Perugia* pattern.** H. 1½ in. (3.8 cm), diam. 10¼ in. (26 cm). Marked: *Richard [surmounted by a crown] | Ginori | MANIFATTURA | DI DOCCIA | FLORENCE | ITALY | PERUGIA*. Dallas Museum of Art, 20th-Century Design Fund, T42485.1.

***Antico Doccia* shape candy dish with *Italian Fruit* pattern.** Marked: *Richard [surmounted by a crown] | Ginori | ITALY | FINEST IN CHINA | SINCE 1735*. Dallas Museum of Art, 20th-Century Design Fund, T42485.2.

Both *Vecchio Ginori* and *Antico Doccia* were adaptations of shapes that had been used at the Doccia factory in the eighteenth century. In keeping with the rococo nature of the originals, Ginori applied simple gilded bands or delicate surface patterns to the shapes. Judging from trade advertisements, both *Perugia* and *Italian Fruit* were available as full dinnerware lines though the importer Fisher, Bruce & Co. in the late 1950s and then through Pasmantier Company after 1960.[1] The *Italian Fruit* pattern was also available on giftware that was evidently not distributed widely in the United States. However, the candy dish, called a *biscottiera* in Italian, is marked in English and is currently being sold on the used dinnerware market as a covered soup bowl.

1. *CGJ* 159:6 (Dec. 1956): 49; 162:5 (May 1958): 37; 167:3 (Sept. 1960): 15.

Cat. 125

All pieces: Ernestine Cannon, designer; Ceramica D'Arte, Salerno, Italy, maker. Earthenware with painted decoration.

Back row:
Tureen, ca. 1947. Marked: *Ernestine | SALERNO ITALY | D19* and *695*. Lid marked *695G*. Labeled: *Ernestine | SALERNO | ITALY*. Dallas Museum of Art, gift of Carole Stupell, Ltd., T42624.36.

Plate, ca. 1947. H. 1 in. (2.5 cm), diam. 10½ in. (26.7 cm). Marked: *Ernestine | SALERNO | ITALY | 720*. Dallas Museum of Art, gift of Carole Stupell, Ltd., T42624.39.

Cup and saucer, ca. 1947. Cup and saucer marked: *E | ITALY | 329 R.N.* Cup also labeled: *CERAMICA D'ARTE | E | SALERNO | ITALY*. Saucer also labeled: *Ernestine | SALERNO | ITALY*. Dallas Museum of Art, gift of Carole Stupell, Ltd., T42624.38.

Bowl and underplate, ca. 1947. Plate marked: *Ernestine | SALERNO | ITALY | 546*. Bowl marked: same except without *SALERNO*. Dallas Museum of Art, gift of Carole Stupell, Ltd., T42624.37.

The objects shown here appear to have been among Ernestine Cannon's earliest shape designs. The coupe plate, rectangular tureen, and cup and saucer with twist handle are all documented in advertising from the late 1940s.[1] The surface decoration, however, may date from the 1950s or early 1960s. Except for the bowl, all of these shapes were still in production in the late 1970s.[2]

Front row:
Plate with *Champignons* pattern, ca. 1975. Marked: *Ernestine | SALERNO | ITALY | 791*. Dallas Museum of Art, 20th-Century Design Fund, T42497.

Cup and saucer with *Red Eva* pattern, ca. 1980. Both labeled: *CERAMICA | D'ARTE | E ® | SALERNO | ITALY*. Dallas Museum of Art, gift of Carole Stupell, Ltd., T42624.29.

The *Red Eva* pattern probably dates from the late 1970s and was originally used on Ernestine Cannon's early plate and cup and saucer shapes. However, around 1980 the pottery introduced the updated shape range from which this cup and saucer comes and applied *Red Eva* to it. Apparently this new shape design was the last introduced by the firm before it ceased production.[3]

1. For examples, see *CGJ* 143:6 (Dec. 1948): 108; and 144:3 (Mar. 1949): 8.
2. "Ernestine" (Ceramar sales brochure and price list, 1979?).
3. For an image of *Red Eva* on the earlier shape, see ibid.

Cat. 126

Tumbler, ca. 1960. CAN factory, Empoli, Italy. Lead glass with pressed and cut decoration. Labeled: *Kristall | CAN* and *MADE IN ITALY*. Dallas Museum of Art, gift of Carole Stupell, Ltd., T42624.6.

This tumbler was part of a large group of glassware ordered by Carole Stupell around 1960. Although the quality of the glass is very fine, having been made using a combination of press molding and cutting, the shipment was poorly packed for transatlantic shipping, resulting in much breakage. As a result Stupell never ordered glass from this factory again.[1]

Venice goblet, ca. 1977. Nason e Moretti, Murano, Venice, Italy, maker; Ceramar, New York, importer. Glass. Unmarked. Dallas Museum of Art, gift of Carole Stupell, Ltd., T42624.26.

Venice was one of several lines of colored glassware produced by the venerable glassworks of Nason e Moretti in the mid-1970s. Available in goblets, wineglasses, and sherbet glasses, *Venice* came in clear glass and seven solid colors—green, cobalt, red, orange, yellow, cranberry, and aqua (illustrated). Combinations of colors were also used to produce two-tone examples with different-colored bowls and feet. In 1977 the suggested retail price of this goblet was $10. The cost of yellow, orange, and red examples was 50 percent higher.[2]

Wineglass, ca. 1960. Nason e Moretti, Murano, Venice, Italy. Glass. Labeled: *Made | in | Italy.* Dallas Museum of Art, gift of Carole Stupell, Ltd., T42624.12.

No. 700 shape champagne glass with no. 255 pattern, ca. 1965. Cristalleria SAVIA, Empoli, Italy. Lead glass with pressed and cut decoration; h. 8⅛ in. (20.6 cm), diam. 2⅞ in. (7.3 cm). Labeled: *A | CAROLE | STUPELL | DESIGN | MADE IN ITALY.* Dallas Museum of Art, gift of Carole Stupell, Ltd., T42624.3.

The no. 700 shape was made in high-quality pressed glass that was then decorated with various cutting patterns. The no. 255 cutting pattern was available on a decanter and pitcher as well as on nine drinking vessel forms. Typically the pattern was produced in colorless glass; however, Stupell had this glass made in two versions featuring cobalt blue or lime green inclusions in the bottom of the bowl.[3]

Goblet, ca. 1975. Carlo Moretti, Murano, Venice, Italy. Glass. Labeled: *moretti | carlo | MC [in a square] | italia | murano.* Dallas Museum of Art, gift of Carole Stupell, Ltd., T42624.2.

This goblet is made of case glass, in which two layers of glass are applied, one atop the other. Here white glass is used for the interior of the bowl and green glass for the exterior, stem, and foot.

1. Keith Stupell, conversation with Charles Venable, 15 Oct. 1999. At present nothing is known about the factory that made this glass.

2. "Hand Blown Colored Murano Glassware, Italy" (Nason e Moretti trade brochure, 1977?); "Hand Blown Murano Stemware by Nason & Moretti-Venice" (Ceramar trade brochure and price list, 1977).
3. "Cristalleria Savia Empoli" (trade catalogue, 1965?).

Cat. 127
All pieces: Gerald Gulotta, shape designer; Block China Company, New York, importer.

España shape tea set with Tierra pattern, 1964. Porcelanas del Bidesoa, Irun, Spain, maker. Porcelain. Teapot marked: *ESPAÑA • TIERRA | BLOCK [with a bee inside the O] | BIDASOA | SPAIN | PATENT DES. 203,855.* Sugar bowl marked: same as teapot except patent design number 203,851. Creamer marked: same as teapot except patent design number 203,853. Cup and saucer marked: same as teapot except patent design number 205,534. Dallas Museum of Art, 20th-Century Design Fund, 1997.161.1–4.

When it was introduced in 1965, *Espana* was one of the most innovative shapes of its generation. Here designer Gerald Gulotta first experimented with combining convex and concave lines, a motif he would develop further in his *Chromatics* shape (1970) for Block China (see cat. 207). *Espana* was also the first shape to use a continuous-line junction of cup to saucer that became a hallmark of Gulotta's later *Up-beat* (1965) and *Transition* (1968) shapes.

Greater freedom to change design details existed at the time, and as a result Gulotta changed the spout of the teapot almost immediately from the indented opening in this example to a straight horizontal one similar to the creamer. Accessories were also added to the line in 1967. Typical of the color palette of the 1960s favoring strong contrasting colors, *España* came in just three solid colors—black, brown, and white. Later a few surface patterns were added before the line was discontinued in the early 1970s.

Transition shape platter, coffeepot, and cup and saucer with Evolution pattern, 1968. Jack Prince, pattern designer; Porzellanfabrik Langenthal, Langenthal, Switzerland, maker. Porcelain with printed decoration; platter: h. 1¼ in. (3.2 cm), w. 9⅞ in. (25.1 cm), d. 13¾ in. (34.9 cm). Platter marked: *BLOCK [with a bee inside the O] | LANGENTHAL | SWITZERLAND [all within a rounded square] | TRANSITION | EVOLUTION © | Pat. Des. 213458/59/61 | 214392 | 215469/70/71 and 3 and 64 40 35 | • and 98.* Coffeepot marked: *BLOCK [with a bee inside the O] | LANGENTHAL | SWITZERLAND [all within a rounded square] | TRANSITION and 88. and [illegible] 0 31 12.* Cup and saucer marked: same as platter except without *3 and 64 40 35 | • and 98.* Dallas Museum of Art, 20th-Century Design Fund, 1997.162.1–3.

Another innovative Gulotta shape was *Transition,* which featured round tops and square bases. Such a form, with its imperceptible "transition" from round to square, was extremely complicated to achieve in porcelain, so many modifications had to be made at the factory before the final result was produced. Though modestly priced at $12.95 to $19.95 for a five-piece place setting in 1968, the line eventually became too expensive to produce and was discontinued in the late 1970s.[1]

While in production the shape was ornamented with at least thirteen surface patterns created by five surface designers: Jack Prince, Pierre Renfre, Howard Treu, Jody Clark, and Bart De Vito. All of the work of these artists was very avant-garde, so much so that sales literature said of the line:

> TRANSITION offers young people a design in china attuned to their constant search for new ways to express themselves. But, instead of rejecting tradition, Transition moves forward with it . . . proving that designs of china can be as truly contemporary as any modern art form.
>
> Transition is a fluid style. In it, classic *circle* flows toward a *square* then returns to circular. The interplay is restful: a slow transition in which the circle never loses its identity, while the square never becomes hard-edge or sharply angular.
>
> It is the interplay of shapes which makes Transition so *recognizable* in the eyes of the young generation as right for today. The patterns selected for Transition complete the feeling of modern art: seem to be more paintings than mere decoration.[2]

1. Gerald Gulotta, conversation with Stephen G. Harrison, 9 Oct. 1999; Prince interview 1997.
2. "Transition" (Block sales brochure, 1968).

Chapter 4
From Warehouse to Your House: Tableware Marketing

Cat. 128
Raymor Modern Stoneware covered casserole dish and pitcher, 1952. Ben Seibel, designer; Roseville Pottery, Zanesville, Ohio, maker; Richards-Morgenthau & Co., New York, distributor. Stoneware; pitcher: h. 10¼ in. (26 cm), w. 8 in. (20.3 cm), d. 6 in. (15.2 cm). Dish marked: *83 | Raymor | by | Roseville | U.S.A. | OVENPROOF | PATENTED.* Pitcher marked: *189 | Raymor | by | Roseville | U.S.A. | OVENPROOF | PAT. PEND. and 5.* Dallas Museum of Art, 20th-Century Design Fund (dish), 1996.32; Andrew Krauss and Ted McDermott Collection (pitcher).

When Roseville Pottery began producing *Raymor* in 1952, the firm hoped that sales would be strong enough to make the pottery profitable. The ware was particularly interesting in terms of both material and design. The use of a stoneware body covered in solid, textured glazes was rather avant-garde for the early 1950s. So too were the bold shapes, especially the diamond-shaped plates. Despite being widely advertised by its distributor and namesake, Richards Morgenthau, the line was probably just too advanced stylistically for the general public. *Raymor* was discontinued, and the pottery closed in 1954. Originally *Raymor* was made in five colors—*Autumn Brown, Avocado Green, Terra Cotta, Beach Gray,* and *Contemporary White*.[1] Later, when the ware was redesigned in part to try to make it more saleable, chartreuse and light blue were introduced.

1. "Richards-Morgenthau Shows New Roseville Pieces," *CGJ* 151:6 (Dec. 1952): 8.

Cat. 129
Platter, bowl, and demitasse cup and saucer with *Metropolis* pattern, ca. 1935. Belle Kogan, shape designer; unknown factory, Germany, maker; Ebeling & Reuss, Philadelphia, importer. Earthenware with printed and painted decoration; platter: h. 1 in. (2.5 cm), diam. 12⅛ in. (30.8 cm). Platter marked: METROPO-LIS | E&R INC. | EST. | 1888 | ERPHILA | MADE IN GERMANY and *Patent Pending* and 6561 / 30. Bowl and demitasse cup and saucer marked: same except without 6561 / 30. Dallas Museum of Art: 20th-Century Design Fund (platter and bowl), 1997.175.1–2; gift of Belle Kogan (cup and saucer), 1998.121.

In November 1936 Belle Kogan received design patent no. 101,958 for the shape of this cup. Two surface patterns were used on the shapes in this range: *Metropolis* was the first, followed by a pattern with sailing scenes called *Regatta*. While Kogan had input into the appearance of the decal designs, the final artwork was created by designers at Commercial Decal in Mt. Vernon, New York. The line sold relatively well and was manufactured in several places. Initially pieces were made in Germany, but by 1938 production had been shifted to Czechoslovakia. Following the German invasion of Czechoslovakia, production was taken over by an unknown East Liverpool, Ohio, pottery. In an unidentified ad Ebeling & Reuss described *Metropolis* as "The spirit of today" and noted that it was available as "Complete open-stock dinnerware, together with occasional pieces for the hostess. Although well-styled and of good quality, Metropolis is moderately priced."[1]

1. Kogan interview 1997; Kogan personal papers; and *CGJ* 122:3 (Mar. 1938): 10.

Cat. 130
Pitcher with *Lilium Ornatum* pattern, ca. 1910. F. Beulet, decorator; Pickard China Company,

Antioch, Ill., pattern designer/decorator/importer; Altrohlau Porzellanfabriken Moritz Zdekauer, Altrohlau, Austria (Bohemia), maker. Porcelain with painted and gilded decoration. Marked: 1190 / 2 and M [crown] Z / [double-headed eagle] | AUSTRIA | Depose and HANDPAINTED | W. PICKARD A. | CHINA [in a circle]. Signed on outside: F. Beulet. Dallas Museum of Art, gift of W. C. and Salley Estes in memory of Mrs. and Mrs. R. E. Risser Jr., 1995.96.

During the early years of its existence, Pickard China imported undecorated blanks from various European factories for use in its own decorating studio.[1]

Plate with no. J7 pattern, 1912. Attributed to Frank G. Holmes, designer; Lenox China, Trenton, maker; Gilman Collamore & Co., New York, retailer. Porcelain with printed, painted, and gilded decoration; h. 1 in. (2.5 cm), diam. 10½ in. (26.7 cm). Marked: L [in a wreath] | LENOX | Gilman Collamore & Co | FIFTH AVENUE & 30TH ST | NEW YORK and X101 / 2 / J7 (pattern number). Dallas Museum of Art, gift of Drs. Sylvia M. and Charles L. Venable, 1998.119.

Cup and saucer and coffeepot, ca. 1907–8. Attributed to Frank G. Holmes, designer; Lenox China, Trenton, maker (coffeepot and saucer); Ceramic Art Company, Trenton, maker (cup). Porcelain with painted and gilded decoration. Coffeepot and saucer marked: L [in a wreath] | LENOX. Cup marked: CAC [in a wreath] | LENOX. Newark Museum, gift of Walter Scott Lenox, 1911, 11.543–544.

The decoration of these pieces was influenced by the contemporary European art nouveau and Arts and Crafts movements. Although other motifs were used, flowers were especially popular decorative devices in both styles.

1. For more information on Pickard, see Reed 1995.

Cat. 131
All pieces: Winslow Anderson, designer; Blenko Glass Company, Milton, W. Va., maker. Glass. Unmarked.

Goblet, ca. 1950. Dallas Museum of Art, gift of Eason Eige, T42318.3.

The Blenko Glass Company received an important commission in 1936 to supply hand-blown reproductions of eighteenth-century glassware to Colonial Williamsburg for sale in its gift shop. The restoration of Williamsburg undertaken by John D. Rockefeller was one of the most talked about and anticipated events of the late 1930s and held the fascination of much of the country. Therefore, the selection of Blenko was an immeasurable boost to that firm's reputation and name rec-

ognition.[1] The stemware blown for Williamsburg was commercially produced only in colorless glass; this goblet is a rare experimental version in blue and green adapted by Anderson based on the no. CW-1G shape goblet designed earlier for Colonial Williamsburg.

No. 600-DOF shape tumbler, no. 943 shape muddler, and no. 939-P shape pitcher, ca. 1947–52. Pitcher: h. 14 in. (35.6 cm), w. 7¼ in. (18.4 cm), d. 6 in. (15.2 cm). Dallas Museum of Art, gift of Eason Eige, T42318.4–6.

Blenko continued to find moderate success in the casual glassware market after the war, particularly with distinctive shapes and colors such as the chartreuse green shown here, created by chief designer Winslow Anderson.[2]

1. "Wedgwood to Produce Ware for Williamsburg Revival; Blenko Glass Company Also Licensed to Make Reproductions," *CGJ* 120: 2 (Feb. 1937): 40.
2. For a comprehensive study of Blenko glass, see Eige and Wilson 1987.

Cat. 132
***Victory* shape sugar bowl and creamer with *Cadet Series* pattern,** 1937. Viktor Schreckengost, shape designer; Salem China Company, Salem, Ohio, maker. Earthenware with painted and platinum decoration. Both marked: VICTORY | by | SALEM | CHINA • CO. | SALEM • OHIO. Sugar bowl also marked: WARRANTED | PLATINUM GOLD | . . . ALLOY . . . |14. Creamer also marked: MADE IN U.S.A. | WARRANTED | PLATINUM GOLD. Dallas Museum of Art, 20th-Century Design Fund, 1996.28.1–2.

***Victory* coffeepot,** 1937. Viktor Schreckengost, shape designer; Salem China Company, Salem, Ohio, maker. Earthenware. Unmarked. Dallas Museum of Art, 20th-Century Design Fund, 1995.175.

Triumph shape cup and saucer, chop plate, coffeepot, and demitasse cup and saucer with *Havana* pattern, 1936. Viktor Schreckengost, shape designer; Limoges China Company, maker, Sebring, Ohio. Earthenware with painted decoration; chop plate: h. 1 in. (2.5 cm), diam. 12⅜ in. (31.4 cm). Cups unmarked. Saucer, chop plate, and coffeepot marked: TRIUMPH [over a laurel branch with two stars] | AMERICAN | LIMOGES | SEBRING • OHIO | HAVANA–T. Demitasse saucer marked: same except without HAVANA–T. Dallas Museum of Art, gift of Mr. and Mrs. Viktor Schreckengost, T42114.

Viktor Schreckengost was a designer for the Sebring family potteries from 1934 to 1943. During that time he created several shape ranges and many surface patterns for both Limoges China and Salem China. *Triumph* and *Victory* are two of his most successful shapes. Highly geometric in their composition, both reflect the impact of French art deco design and American streamlining. According to Schreckengost, the fluting and rings seen on these shapes were intended to give ornament without increasing costs, since those elements were produced during the casting process and did not have to be added by hand.[1] Painted bands like those of the *Havana* and *Cadet Series* patterns served much the same purpose. Simple painted bands were cheaper to apply than decals. Nevertheless, a wide range of printed ornaments were applied on both these modernist shapes. Many of the decorations were highly conservative—applied to the *Victory* shape, for example, were designs called *Doily Petitpoint, Colonial Fireside, Godey Ladies, Minuet,* and *Pioneer* (fig. 5.7).

1. V. Schreckengost interview 1995.

Cat. 133

All pieces: Frank G. Holmes, pattern designer; Lenox China, Trenton, maker. Porcelain with printed and gilded decoration.

Luncheon plate and no. 1125 covered muffin dish with *Ming* pattern, ca. 1905–08. Both marked: L [in a wreath] | LENOX | MING | ©. Dallas Museum of Art, 20th-Century Design Fund, 1995.135.1–2.

Ming was available between 1917 and 1966 on "standard" shape plates and other forms as well as on *Temple* shape plates from 1950 to 1966. The "standard" plate shape and the shape of the muffin dish were both likely designed between 1905 and 1908.

No. 1964 shape dessert plate and no. 1690 shape teapot with *Mandarin* pattern, ca. 1909–19. Marshall Field & Co., Chicago, retailer of teapot. Plate: h. ¾ in. (1.9 cm), w. 8¼ in. (21 cm), d. 8¼ in. (21 cm). Plate marked: L [in a wreath] | LENOX | MANDARIN. Teapot marked: L [in a wreath] | LENOX | MARSHALL FIELD | & COMPANY | CHICAGO. Dallas Museum of Art, 20th-Century Design Fund, T42482.1–2.

Mandarin was available between 1917 and 1965. This teapot shape was designed around 1909, while the plate shape dates to about 1919. *Ming* and *Mandarin* were the earliest of Lenox's full decal patterns. The company had been offering transfer-printed patterns that were filled in with color, but in 1917 they introduced decals to their work as a decorative technique. Perhaps because of their reference to traditional Chinese export motifs rendered with updated colors, *Ming* and *Mandarin* were immediately successful. The original introduction of the patterns coincided with Chinese Chippendale revival style in home furnishings generally, but their popularity extended for fifty years.

Cat. 134

Plaque with sample monograms, ca. 1905–25. Josiah Wedgwood & Sons, Etruria, England. Bone china with painted and gilded decoration; h. 12 in. (30.5 cm), w. 7¾ in. (19.7 cm), d. ¼ in. (0.6 cm). Marked: [image of a Portland vase] | —••— | WEDGWOOD | * | ENGLAND. Dallas Museum of Art, The Barbara and Hensleigh Wedgwood Collection, 20th-Century Design Fund, 1996.251.

Plaques such as these were used as displays in fine jewelry and department stores such as Marshall Field & Co. in Chicago and Tiffany & Co. in New York to show customers the range of customized monograms that could be ordered to embellish a tableware service. Of course, hand-enameled monogramming was extremely expensive and rarely ordered by Americans, but the mere availability of such elaborate custom production gave Wedgwood an air of exclusivity that suited its marketing strategy for less expensive wares. The inclusion of the Great Seal of the United States reminded the customer that Wedgwood had also supplied a large table service to the White House (1903), further enhancing the firm's prestige and reputation in the eyes of the customer.

Cat. 135

The President's House iced tea glass, ca. 1920s. Morgantown Glass Guild, Morgantown, W. Va. Lead glass; h. 6 in. (15.2 cm), diam. 2⅞ in. (7.3 cm). Labeled: [Eagle logo] | THE PRESIDENT'S HOUSE | Handmade Lead Crystal | by | Morgantown. Dallas Museum of Art, 20th-Century Design Fund, 1996.144.1.

This line of glassware was known as no. 7780 before 1961. Most of the pieces were designed in the 1920s and were sold through the years primarily to hotels and restaurants. First Lady Jacqueline Bouvier Kennedy saw examples at the Carlyle Hotel in New York and asked if they could be used in the White House. Morgantown supplied fifty dozen of all twenty-three forms, including an 11-ounce tulip-shaped champagne glass. The White House had been using an imported champagne glass that Mrs. Kennedy wanted to replace with one of America manufacture. Morgantown copied a sample of the imported champagne glass sent from Washington, D.C., and the form became part of the line. Following delivery of the ware to the White House, the firm was given permission to name it *The President's House,* which proved advantageous in subsequent marketing efforts.[1]

1. For a detailed account of these events, see Gallagher 1995, 227.

Cat. 136

All pieces: 1933. Theodore Haviland & Co, Limoges, France, maker; Theodore Haviland & Co., New York, importer.

Shape of 1937 shape demitasse cup and saucer with Nicole pattern. Suzanne Lalique, pattern designer. Porcelain with printed decoration. Both marked: *Theodore Haviland | Limoges | FRANCE | Nicole | Décor de | Suzanne Lalique* and PATE CELADON [in rectangle] | THEODORE | HAVILAND | FRANCE [in shield]. Dallas Museum of Art, 20th-Century Design Fund, T42483.

Shape of 1937 shape demitasse coffeepot. Porcelain; h. 5⅜ in. (13.7 cm), w. 6 in. (15.2 cm), d. 4 in. (10.2 cm) Coffeepot marked: PATE IVOIRE [in rectangle] | THEODORE | HAVILAND | FRANCE [in shield]. Lid marked: T&H. Dallas Museum of Art, 20th-Century Design Fund, T42516.

The *Shape of 1937* shape is part of a significant group of terraced designs made in Europe and the United States in the early 1930s (see cat. 59). It was introduced to the American market in the spring of 1934 and was said to be a "grand modern with all the hard and awkward lines smoothed out."[1] Both ivory- and celadon-colored bodies were available without any decoration. Also initially carried in stock in New York were three surface patterns on each colored body. Among these were *Nicole* and another floral treatment by Suzanne Lalique, as well as a design by Leon V. Solon called *Shanghai Wave.* In 1935 the trade press reported that *Nicole,* among other patterns, had been selected for use on the renowned French ocean liner the S.S. *Normandie.*[2]

1. CGJ 114:4 (Apr. 1934): 27.
2. "S.S. Normandie Carries China and Glass Services for All Travel Classes," CGJ 116:6 (June 1935): 38.

Cat. 137

All pieces: Eric William Ravilious, pattern designer; Josiah Wedgwood & Sons, Barlaston, England, maker; Josiah Wedgwood & Sons, New York, importer. Earthenware with printed and painted decoration.

Queens Ware Concave shape platter with Harvest Festival pattern, ca. 1800–25. H. 1⅜ in. (3.5 cm), w. 16¾ in. (42.5 cm), d. 14 in. (35.6 cm). Marked: HARVEST FESTIVAL | DESIGNED BY | RAVILIOUS | OF ETRURIA | WEDGWOOD | MADE IN | ENGLAND | & BARLASTON | AL9948 (pattern number) | WEDGWOOD | 1 H 53 (date mark for 1953). Dallas Museum of Art, gift of George Roland in memory of Annabelle and Charles Thomas Roland, 1997.220.

Applied to an early-nineteenth-century shape, the *Harvest Festival* pattern was introduced in

1936 but was advertised with the name *Persephone* after 1938 until the war when the name reverted to *Harvest Festival*. The pattern was discontinued in 1961. The central design is closely related to a drawing called *Harvest Festival and Loaves* in the church at Castle Hedingham, Essex, England, where Eric William Ravilious lived. A similar version in bone china with gilded decoration was introduced on the *Lincoln* shape in 1952 as *Coronation Golden Persephone* and adapted for use at the banquet for visiting heads of state given by the British foreign secretary Sir Anthony Eden at the coronation of Queen Elizabeth II in June 1953.[1] The Queen's coronation was the first event of its kind to be broadcast around the world over the new medium of television. As a result, U.S. department stores such as Neiman Marcus in Dallas promoted *Coronation Golden Persephone* as the "Queen's choice," making the pattern a hit in high-end department stores during that period.[2]

Queens Ware Concave shape dinner plate with Garden pattern, ca. 1800–25. H. ⅞ in. (2.2 cm), diam. 10⅛ in. (25.7 cm). Marked: *GARDEN | DESIGNED BY | RAVILIOUS | OF ETRURIA | WEDGWOOD | MADE IN | ENGLAND | & BARLASTON TL259* (pattern number) *| WEDGWOOD | 9 X 53* (date mark for 1953). Dallas Museum of Art, gift of George Roland in memory of Annabelle and Charles Thomas Roland, 1997.226.

The most elaborate of Ravilious's patterns, *Garden* was designed in 1938–39 and consists of a border, ten different vignettes, and many smaller details.[3] It was probably adapted from a watercolor by Ravilious of his wife, Tirzah Garwood, and Charlotte Borden, the wife of illustrator Edward Borden, sitting under a tree in a garden.[4] This pattern and that of the earlier *Harvest Festival* share the same wispy, lithographic quality characteristic of Ravilious's work for Wedgwood in the 1930s.[5]

1. Dennis 1986, 45. For the coronation, the central motif was replaced by the Royal coat of arms.
2. Wedgwood interview 1996.
3. Dennis 1986, 50.
4. Unpublished research notes of Sharon Gater, Wedgwood Museum, Barlaston, England.
5. For more on Ravilious, see Batkin 1982, 171–72.

Cat. 138
Plate with Bacon Rind pattern, saucer with Quanah Parker pattern, and cup with Geronimo pattern, ca. 1955. Acee Blue Eagle, pattern designer; unknown factory, Nagoya, Japan, maker; Knox Refining Company, Enid, Okla., distributor. Porcelain with printed and gilded decoration; plate: h. 1¼ in. (3.2 cm), diam. 10⅛ in. (25.7 cm). Plate marked: (on back) *Fine KNOX China | [teepee] | Bacon Rind | BY ACEE BLUE EAGLE [all in a circle] | JAPAN*; (on front) *Bacon Rind | Osage*. Cup marked: same as plate except pattern name *Geronimo* on bottom. Saucer marked: (on back) same as plate ex-

cept pattern name *Quanah Parker* (on front); *Quanah Parker | Comanche*. Dallas Museum of Art, 20th-Century Design Fund, 1996.178.1–2.

Acee Blue Eagle, who provided the original artwork from which these surface patterns were adapted, was a well-known Creek-Pawnee artist living in Oklahoma. During the mid-1950s the Knox Refining Company, known for operating the first self-service gas station, commissioned Blue Eagle to produce images of eight famous Native American leaders. Featured in the series were Hen-Toh (Wyandot), Ruling His Sun (Pawnee), Geronimo (Apache), Quanah Parker (Comanche), Dull Knife (Cheyenne), Bacon Rind (Osage), Hunting Horse (Kiowa), and Sequoyah (Cherokee). These figures were silk-screened onto glasses to produce "Oklahoma Indian Tumblers"; one tumbler was given away with the purchase of 10 gallons of gas. Weldon Ford, who ran an advertising agency in Enid, originated the idea for the tumblers and coordinated the program for Knox. The giveaway apparently resulted in Knox's sales increasing by 45 percent the first year the tumblers were used.[1]

Following the success of the glass premiums, Knox applied Blue Eagle's designs to Japanese-made porcelain dinnerware that was also given away by the piece at its gas stations. The subject matter of the decoration on these pieces—oil wells, wild horses, jackrabbits, coyotes, and conflicts between Indians and white settlers—reflects the strong Native American heritage of Oklahoma. Evidently the regional character of the porcelain and glassware made them popular gift items, so much so that Knox distributed specially designed mailing cartons so that its customers could ship their premiums to their "family and friends."[2]

1. Robert E. Lee, "Please Call the Glasses 'Tumblers,'" *Daily Oklahoman* (20 Nov. 1995).
2. "Indian Tumblers" (Knox promotional brochure, 1955?).

Chapter 5
Design, Industry, and the Consumer

Cat. 139
Plate with Kew pattern, 1889. Doulton & Co., Burslem, England, maker; Doulton & Co., New York, importer. Earthenware with printed and painted decoration; h. 1 in. (2.5 cm), diam. 10¼ in. (26 cm). Marked: *[lion over crown] | ROYAL DOULTON | [four overlapping Ds] | ENGLAND | KEW | Rd. No. 116918 | Rd. No. 597783 | D 4941* (pattern number) *| XX*. Dallas Museum of Art, gift of George Roland in memory of Annabelle and Charles Thomas Roland, 1997.217.1.

Shown with a facsimile of the design in the original Doulton pattern book.

Cat. 140
Back row:
Goblet, ca. 1880–90. Unknown factory, United States. Glass with pressed decoration. Unmarked. Dallas Museum of Art, Dallas Glass Club Collection, 1992.407.

This piece is decorated with a rabbit, a horse, and a cat.

***Texas* celery vase**, ca. 1900. United States Glass Company, Pittsburgh. Glass with pressed decoration. Unmarked. Dallas Museum of Art, gift of Faith P. Bybee, 1992.B.200.4.

***Dewdrop* pitcher**, ca. 1886–95. Probably Hobbs, Brockunier & Co., Wheeling. Glass with blown-molded decoration. Unmarked. Dallas Museum of Art, Dallas Glass Club Collection, gift of Mrs. Estelle Underwood, 1992.343.

***Wooden Pail* pitcher**, ca. 1880. Bryce, Higbee & Co., Pittsburgh. Glass with pressed decoration. Unmarked. Dallas Museum of Art, gift of Faith P. Bybee, 1992.B.189.

***Jumbo* spoon holder**, ca. 1884. Canton Glass Company, Canton, Ohio. Glass with pressed decoration; h. 11¼ in. (28.6 cm), diam. 6 in. (15.2 cm). Unmarked. Dallas Museum of Art, Dallas Glass Club Collection, 1992.359. Collection of silver turn-of-the-century souvenir spoons, gift of Margaret H. Tremblay, 1992.287.1–5, .7–9, .11–14.

This piece was inspired by the famous circus elephant Jumbo, who died in a train accident in 1883.

***Hob Diamond and Star* celery canoe**, ca. 1886–90. Hobbs, Brockunier & Co., Wheeling. Glass with pressed decoration. Unmarked. Dallas Museum of Art, Dallas Glass Club Collection, gift of Mrs. Russell Remhert in memory of Mrs. Winifred Lawry, 1992.369.3.

Front row:
Covered cheese dish, ca. 1880–90. Unknown factory, United States. Glass with pressed decoration. Unmarked. Dallas Museum of Art, Dallas Glass Club Collection, gift in memory of Mrs. Richard Wilber and Mrs. W. K. Strother, 1992.363.

This dish depicts an owl chasing a cat.

***Pioneer* covered butter dish**, ca. 1879. Gillinder & Sons, Philadelphia. Glass with pressed decoration. Unmarked. Dallas Museum of Art, Dallas Glass Club Collection, gift of Mrs. L. A. Vaughn Jr. in memory of her mother, Mrs. H. J. Harris, 1992.344.

Today collectors call this pattern "Westward Ho."

Hob Diamond and Star berry or ice cream bowl, ca. 1880–90. Hobbs, Brockunier & Co., Wheeling. Glass with pressed decoration. Unmarked. Dallas Museum of Art, Dallas Glass Club Collection, gift of Mrs. Wallis H. Lee, 1992.361.1.

The set from which this bowl comes contains four small individual dishes of the same shape.

Cat. 141
Both pieces: Josiah Wedgwood & Sons, Etruria, England, maker. Earthenware with printed decoration.

Simple Yet Perfect (SYP) shape teapot with Peony pattern, ca. 1905. Lord Dundonald, shape designer; S.Y.P. Teapot Company, Chiswick, London, retailer. Teapot marked: *WEDGWOOD / S. Y. P. / API* (date mark for 1906) and *WEDGWOOD / Peony.* Lid marked: *S.Y.P. Teapot Company / 6 Strand on the Green / Chiswick / London.* Dallas Museum of Art, anonymous gift, 1991.412.75.

Chop plate, 1889. H. 1⅜ in. (3.5 cm), diam. 13 in. (33 cm). Marked: *WEDGWOOD / DEB / A P* (date mark for 1899). Dallas Museum of Art, anonymous gift, 1991.412.56.

Underglaze blue-printed botanical designs were popular with the American consumer in the last decade of the nineteenth century due to the never-ending appeal of Chinese ceramics. Even mistakes such as the frequent bleeding of color into the ground, known popularly as "flow blue," were absorbed by the American market. The allover patterning of the *Simple Yet Perfect* teapot resembles floral designs for wallpaper being produced at the time by English firms such as Morris & Co., which was known to have retailed its Arts and Crafts designs through sophisticated American department stores. The innovative form of a tipping teapot that would allow tea leaves to steep without dispersing into the water was a novelty that survived until 1921, when it was discontinued.[1]

1. Batkin 1982, 124.

Cat. 142
Coffeepot and platter, ca. 1880. Unknown factory, Limoges, France, maker; Alberto Caissellier, Mexico City, Mexico, retailer. Porcelain with printed, gilded, and painted decoration; platter: h. 1¾ in. (4.4 cm), diam. 11¼ in. (28.6 cm). Both marked: *[all in a circle] A LAS TRES BBB / REFUGIO.15. / MEXICO / ALBERTO CAISSELLIER.* Dallas Museum of Art, Faith P. Bybee Memorial Fund, 1997.25.1–2.

Although the maker of these pieces is unknown, the shapes and decorations are very similar to those designed for the Torse service that was made in 1878 by the Pouyat fac-tory in Limoges.[1] This coffeepot and platter were originally part of a large table service. The original retailer of the service was Alberto Caissellier, whose shop in Mexico City was called "At the Sign of the Three BBB." At some point the set was taken to Houston, Texas, where the individual pieces were dispersed.

1. Meslin-Perrier 1994, 94–96.

Cat. 143
All pieces: Doulton & Co., Burslem, England, maker; Wm. S. Pitcairn Corporation, New York, importer. Earthenware with printed and painted decoration.

Corinth shape plate and Octagon shape cup and saucer with Poppy pattern, 1908–10. Leonard Langley, supervising designer. All marked: *[lion over crown] / ROYAL DOULTON / [four overlapping Ds] / ENGLAND / D 3225 (pattern number) /) 8 (date number for 1935).* Cup and saucer also marked: *Rd. No. [illegible] 7,783.* Dallas Museum of Art, gift of Drs. Sylvia M. and Charles L. Venable in honor of George Roland and Stephen G. Harrison, 1997.153.1–2.

This pattern was introduced in 1909, reflecting the art nouveau fashion for naturalistic floral ornament. Available in three colors— pink, yellow, and blue—the pattern remained in production until 1942.

Octagon shape chop plate with Blue Persian pattern, ca. 1910. Leonard Langley, supervising shape designer; Charles Noke, supervising pattern designer. H. 1½ in. (3.8 cm), diam. 12⅝ in. (32.07 cm). Marked: *[lion over crown] / ROYAL DOULTON / [four overlapping Ds] / MADE IN ENGLAND / Rd. No. 597,783 / D 4031 (pattern number) / 25 (date number for 1952).* Dallas Museum of Art, gift of George Roland in memory of Annabelle and Charles Thomas Roland, 1997.216.

This pattern was first introduced in 1912 with a white background and was replaced with the dark blue version in 1917. The dense, colorful patterning was produced through a process developed in the 1840s in which each color was block printed in succession onto transfer paper and then applied to the surface for firing—the forerunner of lithographic decals.

Octagon shape covered vegetable bowl with Woburn pattern, ca. 1910. Leonard Langley, supervising shape designer; Charles Noke, supervising pattern designer. Bowl marked: *Woburn / [lion] / ROYAL DOULTON / [four overlapping Ds] / MADE IN ENGLAND / Rd. No. 597,783 (shape registration) / Rd. No. 723,677 (pattern registration) / U.S. PATENT / APPLIED FOR / D 4654 (pattern number) / 6 (date number for 1933).* Lid marked with same registration marks. Dallas Museum of Art, gift of George

Roland in memory of Annabelle and Charles Thomas Roland, 1997.183.

Although applied to older shapes, this chinoiserie surface design first appeared in 1926. The colonial revival movement in America prompted a revival of Chinese-inspired designs in the 1920s, and many English potteries produced similar patterns, often adapting designs from the early nineteenth century. These elegant but cheerful wares and the fashion for bright colors remained popular throughout the 1930s.

Cat. 144
Angelus shape casserole dish, ca. 1900–09. Homer Laughlin China Company, Newell, W. Va. Earthenware with printed decoration; h. 5⅞ in. (14.9 cm), w. 10¾ in. (27.3 cm), d. 7½ in. (19.1 cm). Marked: *H L [conjoined] / HOMER LAUGHLIN / The Angelus* and *9994* (on lid). William Swann and William Leazer Collection.

The *Angelus* was one of several shape ranges that Homer Laughlin introduced during the first decade of the twentieth century. Featuring delicately molded handles and rims, all these lines were generally modeled on French porcelain from Limoges. Much of the surface ornament designed for these wares was also based on French prototypes. This particular example is decorated with undulating flowers in the art nouveau taste.[1]

1. For an image of the entire *Angelus* range, see Cunningham 1998, 56.

Cat. 145
Champagne glass, ca. 1906–10. Otto Prutscher, designer; Josef Meyr's Neffe, Adolf near Winterberg, Austria (Bohemia), maker. Glass with cut decoration. Unmarked. Dallas Museum of Art, gift of the Friends of the Decorative Arts, 1989.91.

Otto Prutscher produced several variations on this design for stemware that was made in a range of colors.[1] However, the cost of these glasses and the fact that their American distributor, the Wiener Werkstätte, maintained a shop in New York only between 1922 and 1924 meant that such stemware was sold in tiny quantities in the United States.

Platter with Tulip pattern from the Losol Ware line, ca. 1885. Keeling & Co, Burslem, England. Earthenware with printed decoration; h. 1½ in. (3.8 cm), w. 14 in. (35.6 cm), d. 11⅛ in. (28.3 cm). Marked: *Losol Ware / TULIP / [figure of a man kneeling] / EST^ED 1790 [in a rectangle] / K. & C° B / LATE MAYERS / R^d N° 36376 [all in a rectangle] / ENGLAND* and *[undecipherable mark] 168[or 5]6 R.* William Swann and William Leazer Collection.

The registry mark indicates the year 1885, which must apply to this platter's shape. Heavily influenced by the work of the great Scottish architect and designer Charles Rennie Mackintosh, the surface ornament likely dates to the first decade of the twentieth century. Losol Ware was used by Keeling as a trade name from about 1912 to 1936.[2]

Cup and saucer and teapot with *Louise* pattern, ca. 1918–20. Österreichischen Porzellan-Industrie AG (OEPIAG), Pirkenhammer, Austria (Bohemia). Porcelain with painted and gilded decoration. Cup marked: *OEPIAG | [crown over crossed hammers, all in a circle]*. Saucer marked: *OEPIAG | [crown over crossed hammers] | Pirkenhammer | Austria [all in an oval]* and 5849. Teapot marked: *[crown over crossed hammers]* and 5849. Lid marked: 5849. Dallas Museum of Art, 20th-Century Design Fund, 1997.97.1–2.

The Fischer and Mieg factory, which became part of the OEPIAG umbrella of Bohemian porcelain factories in 1918, was known for the high quality of its tableware. In 1920 OEPIAG's name was changed to EPIAG (Erste böhmische Porzellan-Industrie AG) to reflect Bohemia's independence from Austria as part of the new republic of Czechoslovakia. The Fischer and Mieg factory was part of this new holding company as well.[3] Examples of this pattern marked with the name *Louise* are known.

1. For another version, see Fahr-Becker 1995, 121.
2. Godden 1989, 367.
3. Bröhan 1993, vol. 2, 449–57; Zimmerman 1990, 57–58.

Cat. 146

No. 1445 shape service plate with no. A317G pattern, ca. 1909. Frank G. Holmes, pattern designer; Lenox China, Trenton, maker. Porcelain with painted and gilded decoration; h. ⅞ in. (2.2 cm), diam. 10½ in. (26.7 cm). Marked: *L [in a wreath] | LENOX | MADE IN U.S.A.* and 1445 | A317G. Lenox Brands Archives.

Special service plates such as this one were often exhibited by Lenox in the showrooms of its best dealers along with examples of the company's White House china and services made for embassies, foreign heads of state, and U.S. governors' mansions around the country. The retailer informed his best customers about the special exhibit and often advertised it in local newspapers. In some cities, schoolteachers were invited to bring their classes to see "china created for our White House, the home of America's Presidents—china designed by an American artist, made of American clay, burned in American kilns."[1]

Although the no. 1445 shape profile was designed around 1909, Holmes created this specific surface decoration in 1923. The pattern was advertised at a cost of $800 per plate

in the 1930s, which must have made Lenox's stock patterns seem quite reasonable. In 1925, ninety-seven-piece sets of Lenox were priced between $226 and $530 at L. B. King & Co., Detroit, compared with Haviland & Co. sets of similar size priced at $190 to $221 and those by Josiah Wedgwood & Sons priced at $148.[2]

1. From a letter in a Lenox scrapbook (15 Oct. 1931) on the letterhead of Philadelphia retailer J. E. Caldwell. Cited in Denker 1989, 58.
2. Denker 1989, 55.

Cat. 147

All pieces: Frank G. Holmes, pattern designer; Lenox China, Trenton, maker. Porcelain with printed, painted, and gilded decoration.

Plate and no. 1620 shape cup and saucer with *Florida* pattern, ca. 1900–09. Plate: h. ¾ in. (1.9 cm), diam. 10½ in. (26.7 cm). All marked: *L [in a wreath] | LENOX | FLORIDA [in a rectangle] | ©*. Dallas Museum of Art, 20th-Century Design Fund, 1995.134.1–2.

The *Florida* pattern was introduced in 1922 and was applied to over one hundred different shapes. The illustrated cup and saucer shape was likely designed between 1905 and 1908; the plate shape is even earlier.

Plate with *Fountain* pattern, ca. 1900–05. Marked: *L [in a wreath] | LENOX | FOUNTAIN | DESIGN PATENT APPLIED FOR*. Dallas Museum of Art, 20th-Century Design Fund, 1995.132.

Although the *Fountain* pattern was introduced in 1926, this shape was in use by Lenox very early in the century.

No. 1620 shape bouillon cup and saucer with *Pasadena* pattern, ca. 1905–08. Both marked: *L [in a wreath] | LENOX | PASADENA | DESIGN PATENTED*. Dallas Museum of Art, 20th-Century Design Fund, 1997.5.

The *Pasadena* pattern was also introduced in 1926, but the shape of this cup and saucer was probably introduced at least twenty years earlier.
  Frank Holmes began designing exotic, brightly colored stock patterns just after 1920. *Fountain*, with fanciful birds, and *Pasadena*, in the Moorish taste, were designed in 1926 after Holmes's stint as U.S. commissioner to the 1925 Paris exposition; but *Florida*, which features similar motifs and colors, was actually introduced four years earlier. Unlike many Lenox patterns with traditional design references, which remained popular for many years, patterns in this florid style were short-lived and disappeared completely from Lenox's offerings when hundreds of patterns were eliminated after World War II. All three surface patterns were discontinued in 1948.

Cat. 148

Winifred shape covered vegetable dish, 1933. Karl Bayreuther, designer; Philipp Rosenthal & Co., Selb, Germany, maker; Rosenthal China Corporation, New York, importer. Porcelain with painted and gilded decoration. Marked: *Rosen [X surmounted by a crown] thal [word in script] | SELB-GERMANY | WINIFRED* and 2990 | .2. and *[dot]* (date mark for 1937). Dallas Museum of Art, 20th-Century Design Fund, 1997.99.

The *Winifred* shape was named in honor of Winifred Williams Wagner, the daughter-in-law of the nineteenth-century composer Richard Wagner, who directed the Bayreuth Music Festival during the 1930s and early 1940s.[1] The white version of this dish was available for the European market until 1960. The ivory one went out of production during World War II.

Plate with *Eden* pattern, ca. 1930–40. Philipp Rosenthal & Co., Selb, Germany, maker; Rosenthal China Corporation, New York, importer. Porcelain with printed and gilded decoration; h. ⅞ in. (2.2 cm), diam. 10⅛ in. (25.7 cm). Marked: *= | BAVARIA* and *Rosen [X surmounted by a crown] thal | IVORY | GERMANY* and *Eden | U.S. Patent applied for* and 2313 | I 123. Dallas Museum of Art, 20th-Century Design Fund, 1997.100.

The combination of urns, ovals, and garlands seen in the *Eden* pattern is evocative of the work of the eighteenth-century English architect Robert Adam. Although slightly more delicate, the Rosenthal pattern is very close to a 1921 colonial revival pattern (no. V22) by Lenox.

Creamer, coffeepot, and sugar bowl, ca. 1933–40. Oscar Schaller & Co., Schwartzenbach, Germany, maker; Heinrich & Winterling, New York, importer. Porcelain with painted and gilded decoration. All marked: *[S crossed with C within a wreath] | Winterling | BAVARIA*. Teapot marked: 5. Dallas Museum of Art, 20th-Century Design Fund, T42461.

All the pieces here are made of ivory-colored porcelain. While some ware in this body type was sold in Europe, it was developed primarily for the American market. Rosenthal was one of the first foreign firms to make an ivory body, introducing one in 1925.

1. *Schaulade* 9:8 (Aug. 1933): 289.

Cat. 149

Bowl, ca. 1893–1920. Louis Comfort Tiffany, designer; Tiffany Studios, Corona, N.Y., maker. Glass. Marked: *L. C. Tiffany | Favrile*. Dallas Museum of Art, gift of Mr. and Mrs. Nelson Waggener, 1983.26.

Louis Comfort Tiffany perfected his Favrile glassware in 1892, with objects ready for commercial sale a year later. The glowing, iridescent quality of Favrile glass was intended to mimic the same qualities found in ancient glass unearthed in archaeological digs.

No. 138 bonbon dish, ca. 1904. Frederick Carder, designer; Steuben Glass Works, Corning, N.Y., maker. Glass. Marked: STEUBEN AURENE 138. Dallas Museum of Art, Dallas Glass Club Collection, gift of the Dallas Glass Club, 1992.494.

The shimmering, broken gold effect with apparent fractures in the surface is produced by rolling the warm glass in gold leaf before the final cooling.

No. 6333 goblet with *Spanish* pattern, ca. 1920–25. Frederick Carder, designer; Steuben Glass Works, Corning, N.Y., maker. Glass. Unmarked. Newark Museum, Estate of Pearl Gross Lee Fund, 93.110.

The applied decoration on the surface of this goblet was known as "reeding" at the Steuben factory. The color was called *Spanish Green.*

No. 6395 goblet, ca. 1920–25. Frederick Carder, designer; Steuben Glass Works, Corning, N.Y., maker. Glass; h. 10 in. (25.4 cm), diam. 3½ in. (8.9 cm). Unmarked. Dallas Museum of Art, Dallas Glass Club Collection, gift of the Dallas Glass Club, 1992.461.

According to Paul Gardner, who worked as Frederick Carder's assistant for two years, shape numbers beginning with 5000 and above were designed after 1920.[1]

These expensive art-glass tablewares reflect the availability of highly specialized handblown glass during the first quarter of the twentieth century. Tables set with such wares would have been found only in the wealthiest homes in America.

1. Gardner 1971, 136.

Cat. 150

No. 14194 shape covered jug with *Fontaine* pattern, ca. 1923–24. Tiffin Glass Division, United States Glass Company, Tiffin, Ohio. Glass with etched decoration; h. 11⅝ in. (29.5 cm), w. 6¾ in. (17.1 cm), d. 5 in. (12.7 cm). Unmarked. Dallas Museum of Art, 20th-Century Design Fund, 1995.177.

The United States Glass Company advertised pitchers of this shape in 1924 for serving iced tea. Three years later the shape was among five designs advertised as "the newest in beverage sets." In addition to pitchers, these sets included tall tumblers with or without handles, lemon reamers, and ice tubs. Used for the consumption of seasonal drinks like lemonade and iced tea, beverage sets increased in popularity during the 1920s due to the rapid spread of mechanical refrigeration in the home. Commenting on the growing popularity of beverage sets, a 1927 trade magazine noted how "the little tray of sparkling ice cubes makes its welcome appearance at meal times and in between."[1] The *Fontaine* pattern features a fountain and birds, and was probably derived from Frank Holmes's *Fountain* pattern (1926) for Lenox China (cat. 147). The pattern was available on a wide range of glassware including stemware, creamers, and sugar bowls until it was discontinued in 1931.

1. Goshe 1998, 121; and CGJ 104:19 (12 May 1927): 6, 16.

Cat. 151

All pieces: Vernon Kilns, Los Angeles, maker. Earthenware.

Plate, cup and saucer, and coffeepot with *Sierra Madre* pattern, ca. 1937. Gale Turnbull and Jane Bennison, designers. All marked: SIERRA MADRE / TWO-TONE / VERNON KILNS / CALIFORNIA / MADE IN U.S.A. Dallas Museum of Art, 20th-Century Design Fund, 1995.99.1–3.

While Gale Turnbull is credited with designing this shape range, Jane Bennison is the one who suggested the use of upside-down handles on some of the hollowware. Originally the shape was released with solid-colored pastel glazes such as *Ultra California* in 1937. During the late 1930s and 1940s, however, the shape was decorated with several surface patterns. The two-tone *Sierra Madre* and its companion pattern *Rio*, which featured a floral decal ornament in the center, came out around 1939.[1] *Our America* used the same shape as well (see cat. 171).

Montecito shape teapot, cup and saucer, and covered muffin dish with *Modern California* pattern and carafe with *Early California* pattern, ca. 1935. Carafe: h. 8 in. (20.3 cm), w. 8 in. (20.3 cm), d. 6 in. (15.2 cm). Carafe marked: VERNON KILNS / MADE IN / U.S.A. / CALIFORNIA. Others marked: MODERN CALIFORNIA / VERNON / KILNS / LOS ANGELES / AUTHENTIC / CALIFORNIA POTTERY / MADE IN U.S.A. Dallas Museum of Art: anonymous gift in honor of Douglas Hawes (carafe), 1995.86; 20th-Century Design Fund (others), 1995.100.1, 3–4.

The *Montecito* shape appeared in 1935. *Early California* (1936) and *Modern California* (1937) were two of the original decorative schemes used on this shape. *Early California* featured vivid, bright colors, while *Modern California* was offered in pastel shades.

1. For more information, see Nelson 1994, 178–80, 202.

Cat. 152

All pieces: 1939. Morris B. Saunders, shape designer; Franciscan Division, Gladding McBean & Co., Glendale, Calif., maker.

Metropolitan shape teapot and pitcher with *Tiempo* pattern, 1939. Earthenware. Teapot marked: +FRANCISCAN+ / MADE IN CALIFORNIA. Pitcher marked: same with 1. Dallas Museum of Art, 20th-Century Design Fund, 1995.111, 1996.36.

Metropolitan shape demitasse cup and saucer, creamer, and sugar bowl with *Metropolitan* pattern, 1939. Earthenware. Cup and saucer marked: MADE IN / U.S.A. Saucer, creamer, and sugar bowl marked: • FRANCISCAN • / MADE IN / CALIFORNIA / U.S.A. / WARE [all in a circle]. Creamer also marked: 15. Sugar bowl also marked: 18. Dallas Museum of Art: gift of Laguna (cup and saucer), 1996.220; 20th-Century Design Fund (creamer and sugar bowl), 1996.37.1–2.

Metropolitan shape plate with *Trio* pattern, 1939. Esta James, pattern designer. Earthenware with printed decoration, h. 1 in. (2.5 cm), diam. 9¾ in. (24.8 cm). Marked: © FRANCISCAN ® / MADE IN / CALIFORNIA / U.S.A. / Color-Seal / GLADDING, / MCBEAN / & / CO. / OVEN-SAFE [all in a circle]. Dallas Museum of Art, 20th-Century Design Fund, 1996.39.

In 1939 Morris B. Sanders submitted this shape to the Metropolitan Museum of Art's Fifteenth Exhibition of Contemporary American Industrial Art.[1] Gladding, McBean & Co. put the design into production as the *Metropolitan* line the next year. It was available in several two-toned color schemes featuring ivory and gray, turquoise, mauve, and coral. *Metropolitan* was well received by the critics, appearing twice in the London-based *Studio Year Book.*[2]

In 1949 the *Metropolitan* shape was covered with single, high-gloss glazes and sold as *Tiempo.* Among the colors available were *Sprout* (chartreuse), *Stone* (beige), *Copper* (orange), and *Leaf* (dark green). Gray was introduced at some point as well. Five years later, abstract floral decorations were added to the shape and marketed under the name *Trio.*

1. For images of three of the submission pieces with their decal decoration, see CGJ 126:5 (May 1940): 10.
2. Holme 1941, 126; Holme 1943, 94.

Cat. 153

Tricorne shape creamer, sugar bowl, coffeepot, plate, and cup and saucer with *Mandarin* pattern, 1934. Donald Schreckengost, plate designer, Vincent Broomhall and Herbert A. Smith, hollowware designers; Salem China Company, Salem, Ohio, maker. Earthenware with sprayed decoration; coffeepot: h. 7¼ in. (18.4 cm), w. 9 in. (22.9 cm), d. 5½ in. (14 cm). Creamer marked: U.S. PATENT / D. 96445 /

STREAMLINE / BY / SALEM / S 40 HB. Sugar bowl unmarked. Coffeepot marked: [profile of a Puritan woman] / SALEM / MADE IN AMERICA / STREAMLINE PATTERN. Plate and saucer marked: TRICORNE / By Salem / U.S. PATENT / D. 94245. Cup marked: U.S. PATENT / D. 96445 / STREAMLINE / BY / SALEM. Dallas Museum of Art: gift of Drs. Sylvia M. and Charles L. Venable in honor of Karen Zelanka (creamer, sugar bowl), 1996.150.1–2; 20th-Century Design Fund (coffeepot), 1996.52; gift of Kenn Darity and Ed Murchison (plate, cup and saucer), 1995.51.1, 3.

Mandarin was the first brightly colored overall surface decoration created by an Ohio Valley pottery; however, the shape was also produced with numerous decal patterns. Salem China apparently used the names *Tricorne* and *Streamline* interchangeably for this triangular shape, as demonstrated by the fact that both words appear on different pieces of the same set. The double naming stems from the fact that the hollowware was designed and patented after the plates. In October 1934 a trade observer noted upon seeing the plates: "As yet, they have not modeled cups or other pieces for this setup, but the grand Streamline shape which we discussed several months ago is being used. . . . These tricorne sets are being made up in tea and bridge service[s] for the present although they are planning to develop this line for the near future into regular dinner service."[1]

1. "Right Out of the Kiln," *CGJ* 115:4 (Oct. 1934): 20.

Cat. 154

All pieces: J. Paulin Thorley, designer; Taylor, Smith & Taylor, East Liverpool, Ohio, maker.

Clockwise from top:
Laurel shape plate and cup and saucer with Green Wheat pattern, 1932. Earthenware with printed and painted decoration; plate: h. 1 in. (2.5 cm), diam. 10 in. (25.4 cm). Plate and saucer marked: TAYLOR / SMITH / TAYLOR / U.S.A. [all in a wreath]. Plate also marked: 3 36 2 (date mark for 1936). Saucer also marked: 7 36 1 (date mark for 1936). Cup unmarked. Dallas Museum of Art, 20th-Century Design Fund, 1997.30.1–2.

Empire shape creamer and sugar bowl with Green Wheat pattern, 1935. Earthenware with printed decoration. Both marked: TAYLOR / SMITH / TAYLOR / U.S.A. [all in a wreath]. Creamer also marked: 4 36 5 (date mark for 1936) and 1177. Dallas Museum of Art, 20th-Century Design Fund, 1997.30.3–4.

Green Wheat was one of the original patterns offered on the new *Empire* shape introduced to the market in 1936. The *Empire* shape range utilized flatware and cups from the earlier *Laurel* range.

Empire shape covered casserole dish from the Lu-Ray line, 1935. Earthenware. Marked: T.S.&T. / Lu-RAY / PASTELS / U.S.A. Dallas Museum of Art, gift of Greg and Teresa Benkert, T42599.

When the *Lu-Ray* line was announced to the trade in mid-1938, Taylor, Smith & Taylor stated: "Completing the color cycle in modern dinnerware, we offer delightfully delicate pastels on the new Lu-Ray shape."[1] While the use of pastel colors was indeed innovative, the shapes were not. In fact, the pottery did not create new shapes for this line but rather used various forms from the earlier *Laurel* and *Empire* shape ranges and simply covered them in solid mix-and-match glazes. The four original colors were *Windsor Blue*, *Surf Green*, *Persian Cream*, and *Sharon Pink*; *Chatham Gray* was added in 1947. The entire line was discontinued in 1961.[2]

1. "Lu-Ray Pastels" (Taylor, Smith & Taylor sales brochure, 1938), reproduced in Meehan and Meehan 1995, 11.
2. Meehan 1995, 19.

Cat. 155

Lincoln shape plate, Square shape dessert plate, and Peony shape teacup and saucer with Prairie Flowers pattern, ca. 1915. Josiah Wedgwood & Sons, Etruria, England, maker; Josiah Wedgwood & Sons, New York, importer. Bone china with printed and painted decoration; plate: h. ¾ in. (1.9 cm), diam. 10½ in. (26.7 cm). Plate and saucer marked: [image of Portland Vase] / WEDGWOOD / MADE IN / ENGLAND / W 1758 (pattern number) / 4 / PRAIRIE FLOWERS. Cup marked: same except no pattern name. Dallas Museum of Art, gift of Hattie Higginbotham Hartman in memory of Ruth Lindsley Hartman, 1996.154.1–2, .4.

In an early advertisement for this pattern, Wedgwood proudly announced that *Prairie Flowers* was the company's "first design from an entirely American inspiration." The ad went on to say that the artist had "traveled to the West to see one of America's glories— the wild flowers of the plains and prairies in the early Spring."[1] The original version (illustrated) was adapted with minor changes, mostly to edging and center treatments, and was sold through 1932. The pattern was most likely withdrawn along with others when the number of patterns was reduced at the outset of World War II.

1. *CGJ* 107:11 (Nov. 1929): 15.

Cat. 156

Fife shape luncheon plate and cup and saucer with Montrose pattern, 1899. E. E. Franklin, shape designer; attributed to John William Wadsworth, pattern designer; Minton, Ltd., Stoke-upon-Trent, England, maker; Meakin & Ridgway, New York, importer. Bone china with printed, painted, and gilded decoration.

All marked: S 369 (pattern number) / [crown] / MINTONS [within a globe flanked by laurel leaves] / EST. 1793 / MONTROSE [within a ribbon] / ENGLAND. Dallas Museum of Art, gift of George Roland in memory of Annabelle and Charles Thomas Roland, 1997.203.1–2.

This pattern was introduced in 1939.

Boston plate and bouillon cup and saucer with Gobelin pattern, ca. 1924. W. T. Copeland & Sons, Stoke-upon-Trent, England; Copeland & Thompson, New York, importer. Bone china with printed and painted decoration; plate: h. ⅞ in. (2.2 cm), diam. 9⅛ in. (23.2 cm). Plate and saucer marked: "SPODE'S GOBELIN" / Rd. No. 739639 / PATENT APPLIED FOR / USA / SPODE / COPELAND'S CHINA / ENGLAND / R 9641 (pattern number). Cup marked: "SPODE'S GOBELIN" / Rd. No. 77396 / U. S. PATENT / JAN. 8. 1929 / SPODE / COPELAND'S CHINA / ENGLAND / R 9641. Dallas Museum of Art, gift of George Roland in memory of Annabelle and Charles Thomas Roland, 1997.208.1–2.

This pattern was an adaptation of a Gobelin tapestry and was marketed to the most discerning of American consumers. One advertisement for the new surface design in 1931 noted that "families of distinction and discrimination will favor the service both for its charming decoration and for the value of the fine porcelain from which it is made."[1]

1. *CGJ* 109:4 (Apr. 1931): 39.

Cat. 157

Luncheon plate with Festival pattern, ca. 1927. A. G. Richardson & Co., Tunstall, England. Earthenware with printed and painted decoration; h. 9 in. (22.9 cm), w. 9 in. (22.9 cm). Marked: [crown] / CROWN / DUCAL / WARE / ENGLAND / U.S.A. PAT. / 72044 / REG. NO. / 732597. Dallas Museum of Art, 20th-Century Design Fund, 1998.113.

Allover designs for dishes are known as "chintz" patterns because of their resemblance to brightly colored floral textile patterns of the same name. This example, with its delicate depictions of Chinese hanging lanterns, reflects the taste for chinoiserie in the 1920s. Chintz designs were very popular for breakfast wares, lunch wares, and tea-wares at the time and have during the 1980s and 1990s become widely collectible again for their traditional shapes and nostalgic look.

Cat. 158

Soup bowl with Language of Flowers pattern, 1942. Grave V. Neff, pattern designer; Limoges China Company, Sebring, Ohio, maker. Earthenware with printed and painted decoration; h. 1¼ in. (3.2 cm), diam. 8⅛ in. (20.6 cm). Marked: + CANDLE + LIGHT +

[in circle around logo of candle in holder] | MADE IN U.S.A. | LIMOGES [in a shield] | LANGUAGE OF FLOWERS – LC. Dallas Museum of Art, 20th-Century Design Fund, T42490.1.

Goblet and champagne glass with *Language of Flowers* pattern, 1942. Grave V. Neff, pattern designer; Duncan & Miller Glass Company, Washington, Pa., maker. Glass with pressed and etched decoration. Both unmarked. Dallas Museum of Art, 20th-Century Design Fund, T42490.2–3.

In early 1944 when *Crockery and Glass Journal* reported on the *Language of Flowers* collection that had been launched the previous fall, it said that besides china and glass, table linens by Leacock, Inc., were available and that a line of coordinated "wallpaper and other goods [were] to be added."[1] Grave V. Neff, the designer and stylist who was "responsible for this whole idea," noted that she was inspired by the late nineteenth-century children's book illustrator Kate Greenaway. Neff stated: "I visualized her art transformed into livable commodities which I could use. I was sure that what I wanted was the want of many thousands of women—a home with pleasant designs and soft colors. At that time harsh, strident peasant hues were everywhere. Kate Greenaway's pastels were such a contrast and relief from this. It was a completely new trend. Surely, women had always liked dainty colors and feminine designs—and Kate was above all things else, feminine."[2]

According to *Crockery and Glass Journal*, it took Limoges China more than a year to develop the pastel colors that replicated Greenaway's flowers. The trade journal also noted the extensive range of Duncan & Miller's *Language of Flowers* pattern. A 1943 trade catalogue pictures ten stemware shapes and seventeen other forms.[3]

1. "Kate Greenaway—A Promotional Triumvirate," *CGJ* 134:2 (Feb. 1944): 25.
2. Ibid.
3. "Language of Flowers" (Duncan & Miller trade catalogue, 1943), 619–20.

Cat. 159

Lincoln shape plate and covered vegetable dish with *The Granville* pattern, 1929. Charles Noke, supervising designer; Doulton & Co., Burslem, England, maker; Wm. S. Pitcairn Corporation, New York, importer. Earthenware with printed and painted decoration; plate: h. 7⁄8 in. (2.2 cm), diam. 10½ in. (26.7 cm). All marked: [lion over crown] | ROYAL DOULTON | [four overlapping D's] | ENGLAND | THE GRANVILLE | D4948 (pattern number). Dallas Museum of Art, gift of George Roland in memory of Annabelle and Charles Thomas Roland, 1997.215.1–2.

The fashion for dinnerware patterns that recalled earlier designs was especially strong

in the late 1920s after the sesquicentennial of the nation's independence. *The Granville* was marketed as "a charming reproduction of an ancient design which was popular 50 years ago and is equally popular today," instantly making it a symbol of establishment and tradition, particularly in the rich sound of its name.[1] Yet because it was produced in earthenware, it was affordable to middle-class consumers, who helped make it commercially successful for Royal Doulton throughout the 1930s. Among the first group of patterns introduced on the *Lincoln* shape, *The Granville* was discontinued in 1939.

1. *CGJ* 108:3 (Mar. 1930): 20.

Cat. 160

Edme shape covered vegetable dish with *Embossed Grape Vine* pattern, 1908. John Goodwin, designer; Josiah Wedgwood & Sons, Etruria, England, maker; Josiah Wedgwood & Sons, New York, importer. Earthenware with applied decoration; h. 6¾ in. (17.1 cm), w. 9 in. (22.9 cm), d. 7⁄8 in. (20 cm). Marked: WEDGWOOD | MADE IN | ENGLAND | 4 M 13 (date mark for 1913) | U.S.A. PATENT | AUGUST 11, 1922. Dallas Museum of Art, gift of George Roland in memory of Annabelle and Charles Thomas Roland, 1997.222.

Although this pattern is called *Embossed Grape Vine*, it is not actually an embossed pattern but an applied slip-cast decoration thought to have been designed originally in 1775 during the partnership of Josiah Wedgwood and Thomas Bentley.[1] This pattern was one of a number of early applied border designs, including *Laurel*, *Oak*, *Ivy*, *Rose*, *Floral*, and *Trees and Figures*, that were revived around 1900 for the American market to emphasize the eighteenth-century tradition of Wedgwood. These border designs could be ordered on several shapes, including *Queens Ware*, *Patrician*, *Wellesley*, *Corinthian*, *Colonial*, *Shell Edge*, and *Edme*, as in this example.[2]

Patterns with raised decoration such as these were not marketed in Britain or Europe, where the tradition was to place condiments such as salt and mustard on the rim of the plate during a meal. Because of their heavily textured rims, these plates would have been considered awkward to use or even unsanitary. Americans did not share the same tradition, preferring instead to place condiments directly on their food as needed, so the texture of the rim was never an issue in designs for the American market.

The strongly neoclassical *Edme* shape was designed in collaboration with the French retailing firm of Pannier Frères in Paris. It became a best-seller for Wedgwood in America not only in plain white but with the addition of printed and slip-cast decoration and is still in production today. The overglaze-printed U.S.A. patent date on this object may

indicate that the bowl was made and stock-piled in 1913 and later marked with the new patent date before being sold, a common practice with stock shapes and patterns.

1. Wedgwood 1940, U.
2. Ibid., U1–UC.

Cat. 161

Bowl, ca. 1925–30. Nippon Toki Kaisha, Nagoya, Japan. Porcelain with printed, painted, and gilded decoration; h. 2¼ in. (5.7 cm), w. 11½ in. (29.2 cm), d. 8½ in. (21.6 cm). Marked: *Noritaké* | [Komaru symbol in a circle] | MADE IN JAPAN. Drs. Martin and Judith Schwartz Collection.

The Komaru mark (called the double trident mark by collectors) on this bowl was first introduced in 1908 to denote ware exported to "England, etc." Although over time this mark appears to have been used more generally on exported wares, as well as on dishes that remained in Japan's home market, the vast majority of pieces bearing this mark were sold in the United Kingdom.[1]

This Noritake design is among Nippon Toki Kaisha's most dynamic. The angular shape and prismatic decoration featuring faceted gemstones relates to work done in architecture and the decorative arts in Prague in the 1910s and 1920s.[2] Noritake was closely linked with the Czech ceramics industry in the early twentieth century, and therefore samples of Czech ware in the cubist style could have been brought directly from central Europe by representatives of the Japanese firm. Since the Czech-owned firm of Rosenfeld & Lazarus distributed Noritake in London, it is also possible that the firm's staff suggested the design. However, it is just as possible that this cubist design was created by head designer Cyril W. Leigh and his staff in Noritake's American wholesale office, Morimura Brothers. During the interwar period New York merchants imported a variety of avant-garde Czech and German pottery, and thus Leigh could have been inspired by related examples.

1. Noritake 1997, 10.
2. For related examples, see von Vegesack 1992.

Cat. 162

Ruba Rombic plate, salad plate, sherbet glass, and tumbler, 1927. Reuben Haley, designer; Consolidated Lamp and Glass Company, Coraopolis, Pa., maker. Glass with pressed decoration; tumbler: h. 6 in. (15.2 cm), w. 3⅜ in. (8.6 cm), d. 3⅜ in. (8.6 cm). All unmarked. Dallas Museum of Art, 20th-Century Design Fund, 1992.522.1–4.

Ruba Rombic was introduced to the market at the 1928 Pittsburgh glass and china show. Believing that avant-garde cubism would appeal to enough Americans to make the line popular, Consolidated Lamp and Glass produced a relatively large number of pieces in the angular style. In addition to standard tableware, decanters, pitchers, compotes, centerpiece bowls, vases, and lamp bases were also made in the nine colors—*Jungle Green, Jade, Lilac, Sunshine, Honey, Silver, Silver Gray, Silver Cloud,* and *Smokey Topaz* (illustrated). Although the ware was marketed to the trade and to the public using eye-catching print ads and the slogan "Ruba Rombic—An Epic in Modern Art," the line does not seem to have sold well, and the factory closed in 1932.[1]

1. For a lengthy discussion of *Ruba Rombic,* see Wilson 1989, 40–57. For a brief history of Consolidated Lamp and Glass, see Madarasz 1998, 146. The factory reopened in 1936.

Cat. 163

Tea set, ca. 1930. Margarete (Grete) Heymann-Marks, designer; Haël-Werkstätten für künstlerische Keramik, Marwitz, Germany, maker. Earthenware; plate: h. ⅝ in. (1.6 cm), diam. 7⅝ in. (19.4 cm). Teapot, sugar bowl, saucer (yellow), and plate (yellow) marked: *Germany | 181 | 4 | 6 | ⌀L.* Creamer and plate (blue) marked: same except with *181/6/4.* Cup and saucer (blue interior) marked: *181/6 ⌀L.* Cup (yellow interior) marked: *Germany ⌀L.* Dallas Museum of Art, 20th-Century Design Fund, 1997.176.1–3, .5–6, .9–10.

Margarete Heymann-Marks studied at the Bauhaus in 1920–21. Her education there under the tutelage of some of Europe's most progressive artists, designers, and architects is reflected in this tea set. The severe conical form, disk appendages, and vivid two-tone coloration make the design one of the boldest made in Europe during the interwar period. Because of its challenging design, few Americans would have purchased this set. The pieces in this tea set are marked in English *Made in Germany,* and it was acquired by its former owner in a Lancaster, Pennsylvania, antiques mall, suggesting that the set was imported during the 1930s. A variety of decorative schemes were applied to this shape, including plain white and ivory with green and brown abstract motifs. Coffeepots and demitasse cups were also available.[1]

1. For other versions see McCready 1995, 34; and Bröhan and Berg 1994, 150.

Cat. 164

Plate with *Manhattan Skylines* pattern and salad plate, ca. 1929–30. Attributed to Gale Turnbull, designer; Leigh Potters, Alliance, Ohio, maker. Earthenware with printed decoration; plate: h. 1 in. (2.5 cm), diam. 10⅛ in. (25.7 cm). Both marked: *LEIGH | WARE | by | Leigh Potters | inc. | U.S.A. [all in outline of Ohio].* Dallas Museum of Art, 20th-Century Design Fund, 1997.167, T42398.

These plates were probably designed by Gale Turnbull, Leigh Potters' designer in the late 1920s and early 1930s. Turnbull was well traveled and knowledgeable about European modern art. The salad plate was heavily influenced by cubist still lifes by artists such as Pablo Picasso and Georges Braque, in which objects are simultaneously seen from multiple viewpoints. A 1930 advertisement for Stern Brothers department store in New York illustrates two *Manhattan Skylines* service plates, which were available in three colors—black, sepia, and cedar—and cost $20 a dozen. The ad declared the plates "provide striking new freshness for your dinner table," and also noted that "clever hostesses with a flare for the artistic will be quick to appreciate their sophisticated lines and subtle colorings and will use them as rail plates or wall decorations in dining room, grill room or library."[1]

1. *PGBS* 41:10 (10 Apr. 1930): 16.

Cat. 165

The *Aristocrat* shape demitasse cup and saucer, dessert plate, and coffeepot with *Ripple* pattern, ca. 1932. Attributed to Gale Turnbull, designer; Leigh Potters, Alliance, Ohio, maker. Earthenware with printed decoration; coffeepot: h. 7¼ in. (18.4 cm), w. 6 in. (15.2 cm), d. 4 in. (10.2 cm). All marked: *Ripple | green tangerine | grey* and *THE | ARISTO-CRAT | by Leigh Potters | inc. | U.S.A. [within outline of the state of Ohio].* Dallas Museum of Art, 20th-Century Design Fund, 1997.28.1–2, .8.

In 1932 an image of this shape appeared in *Crockery and Glass Journal* with the caption "a novel shape in dinnerware designed by a well-known Parisian artist." In 1934 an ad said that it was "designed by one of the world's famous artists."[1] While it is possible that Charles Sebring commissioned the form from someone like the acclaimed French designer Jean Luce, it is more likely that Gale Turnbull created *The Aristocrat.* Turnbull had traveled widely and studied art in Paris before designing for Leigh and would have been familiar with the work of Luce and other Europeans designing in the art deco style. Furthermore, he continued to travel in Europe while on the Leigh staff.

Charles Sebring had said that he wanted an American designer when he hired Turnbull. In 1929 *Pottery, Glass and Brass Salesman* commented: "Mr. Sebring emphasizes the fact that he feels Mr. Turnbull is much better able to formulate correct ideas of the requirements of the American home than are foreign designers. Being of native extraction, he naturally knows what domestic menage requires in the way of unusual and attractive pottery."[2]

Ultra shape plate, cup, and saucer with *Red Tower* pattern, 1929–30. Gale Turnbull, designer; Leigh Potters, Alliance, Ohio, maker.

Earthenware with printed and painted decoration. All marked: *[within outline of the state of Ohio] LEIGH | WARE | by Leigh Potters | inc. | U.S.A.* and *RED TOWER.* Dallas Museum of Art, 20th-Century Design Fund, 1996.26.1, .3.

The square plate profile was originally designed as part of the *Leigh Ware* line in 1929 (patent no. 80,497). Although the patents were taken out by Charles Sebring, the president of the pottery, Gale Turnbull, who worked for Leigh until 1935, designed the shape and decoration.[3] However, by mid-1930 the shape had been incorporated into an entire new line called *Ultra* in which all the pieces were square. Similarly, *Red Tower* was first used on both round and square plates in the earlier *Leigh Ware* line.[4]

1. *CGJ* 110:4 (Apr. 1932): 23; and 114:2 (Feb. 1934): 7.
2. "Leigh Potters Blaze Modernist Trail," *PGBS* 40 (19 Dec. 1929): 119.
3. Turnbull is noted as the designer in "Leigh Ware," *CGJ* 107:4 (Apr. 1929): 29.
4. *CGJ* 108:5 (May 1930): 2; 107:8 (Aug. 1929): 13.

Cat. 166

Ridgeleigh bread and butter plate and plate, ca. 1934. A. H. Heisey & Co., Newark, Ohio; B. Altman & Co., New York, retailer. Glass with pressed and silvered decoration; dinner plate: h. ¾ in. (1.9 cm), diam. 10 in. (25.4 cm). Both marked: *H [in diamond].* Dallas Museum of Art, gift of Heidi B. Hollomon in memory of her mother, T42293.

Ridgeleigh was an extensive and popular line during the 1930s and was produced in the colors *Sahara* (yellow) and *Zircon* (light green). However, the silver backing found on these examples was probably applied by a specialty decorating firm like the Cape Cod Art Glass Sales Company in Rockland, Massachusetts, or Century Metalcraft Corporation of Chicago.[1] These plates are from a set purchased at B. Altman & Co. in New York and given to Ada Lewis McCarthy of Greenwich, Connecticut, on the occasion of her marriage to Hiram Staunton Brown Jr. in November 1934.

Moderntone plate, underplate, and soup bowl, ca. 1934. Hazel Atlas Glass Company, Wheeling. Glass with pressed decoration. All unmarked. Dallas Museum of Art, 20th-Century Design Fund, 1995.170.1–3.

Moderntone was made in the original colors of cobalt and amethyst from 1934 to 1942. In September 1935 Gimbel Brothers in New York held a sale on *Moderntone* during which one could purchase a forty-four-piece service for eight for just $2.99. The ad for this event claimed that the line was the first example of blue glass dinnerware ever made by machine and that it compared well with a handmade version that the store sold for $12.50 a set.[2] During the late 1940s and 1950s Hazel Atlas reintroduced the line in white glass decorated with sprayed-on pastel colors. The new version was called *Platonite*.[3]

Stanhope cup and saucer, ca. 1935. Walter von Nessen, designer; A. H. Heisey & Co., Newark, Ohio, maker. Glass with pressed and plastic decoration. Both unmarked. Dallas Museum of Art, 20th-Century Design Fund, T42460.

Stanhope was introduced to the market in mid-1936. The line was relatively extensive, and the forms with handles were available with or without the "Plascon" inserts. These plastic rods and discs were produced in several colors, including red, black, blue, yellow, and ivory. Despite the fact that Walter von Nessen was one of America's most famous industrial designers at the time and that the critics praised his designs (*Stanhope* received the 1936 Modern Plastics Competition Award), *Stanhope* did not sell well and was discontinued in 1941.[4]

1. For ads for these firms, see *CGJ* 128:1 (Jan. 1941): 14; and 131:1 (July 1942): 31.
2. *CGJ* 117:3 (Sept. 1935): 43.
3. For examples of the later version, see Florence 1986, 124–25.
4. Bredehoft 1986, 148–55.

Cat. 167
Manhattan compote and plate, ca. 1938. Anchor Hocking Glass Company, Lancaster, Ohio. Glass with pressed decoration; compote: h. 5⅛ in. (13 cm), diam. 5⅜ in. (13.7 cm). Both unmarked. Dallas Museum of Art, 20th-Century Design Fund, 1995.173.1–2.

Manhattan was made in a wide range of tableware and decorative forms while in production between 1938 and 1941.[1]

1. For images of many forms, see Florence 1946, 113–14.

Cat. 168
Goblets with Lust and Sloth patterns from the Seven Deadly Sins series, 1947. Sidney Waugh, designer; Steuben Glass Works, Corning, N.Y., maker. Lead glass with engraved decoration; h. 7½ in. (19.1 cm), diam. 4⅞ in. (12.4 cm). All marked: *Steuben | 1947.* Dallas Museum of Art, gift of Stanley Marcus, 1997.149.1, .4.

These goblets and their five mates (not pictured) are interesting not only for their high-quality engraving in the style of American painter Thomas Hart Benton but also for the gender-specific nature of the ornament. The series depicts men engaged in the sins of lust, gluttony, sloth, avarice, envy, pride, and anger. When retailer Stanley Marcus was given the series in 1947, the "Seven Deadly Sins" theme was considered appropriate for

men only. The goblets were extremely expensive and were likely intended as display items for a man's office or library shelf, or perhaps a bar. However, the form could have been used on the table. Notably, the goblets were featured holding condiments for a dessert course on the cover of the famous chef Helen Corbitt's best-selling 1957 cookbook.[1]

1. Corbitt 1957, paper jacket. For images of the rest of the series, see Madigan 1982, 244.

Cat. 169
Fancy Free shape cup and saucer and teapot with Desert pattern, 1951. Belle Kogan, designer; Red Wing Pottery, Red Wing, Minn., maker. Earthenware with painted decoration. All marked: *RED WING | HANDPAINTED [in the form of a wing].* Teapot also marked: *252.* Dallas Museum of Art, 20th-Century Design Fund, 1997.136.1–2.

According to Belle Kogan, she designed both the *Fancy Free* shape and the *Desert* surface decoration.[1] When introduced to the market in 1952, the design was advertised as suitable for both modern and traditional homes. A sixteen-piece service for four retailed for $12.[2]

Tray and pair of glasses, ca. 1938–50. Unknown factory, United States. Wood and glass with printed decoration. All unmarked. Dallas Museum of Art, 20th-Century Design Fund, 1997.135.1–3.

Although these pieces were not created as a set, they nevertheless have closely related imagery. The glasses depict Central and South American figures in native costume, while the tray features a stereotypical image of a Mexican peasant in sombrero and serape resting against a cactus surrounded by an array of brightly painted pottery.

Century shape plate with Mexicana pattern, 1931. Frederick H. Rhead, shape designer; Homer Laughlin China Company, Newell, W. Va., maker. Earthenware with printed and painted decoration; h. ⅞ in. (2.2 cm), w. 9½ in. (24.1 cm), d. 9½ in. (24.1 cm). Marked: *HLC [conjoined] | HOMER LAUGHLIN | MADE IN U. S. A. | A 39 N 8* (date code for 1939) and *MEXICANA.* Dallas Museum of Art, 20th-Century Design Fund, 1997.134.

Although designed in 1931, the *Century* shape was repeatedly used by Homer Laughlin during the decade as the base for dinnerware of great diversity. The *Mexicana* pattern was introduced to the market in 1937 on both *Century* and Homer Laughlin's *Kitchen Kraft* line. Featuring cactus and Native American pottery, the design was advertised as the one that "started the vogue for the Mexican motif in crockery which has swept the country."[3]

1. Kogan interview 1997.
2. *CGJ* 151:3 (Sept. 1952): 44; *Desert* (Red Wing sales brochure, Jan. 1952).
3. *CGJ* 122:5 (May 1938): 10.

Cat. 170
New Era plate with no. 4045 pattern, ca. 1934. A. H. Heisey & Co., Newark, Ohio. Glass with pressed and cut decoration. Unmarked. Dallas Museum of Art, gift of Kenn Darity and Ed Murchison, T42520.

New Era was one of Heisey's most modern patterns. Introduced in 1934 and made as a full line until 1941, the combination of rectangles and circles was in keeping with art deco taste. Many of the surface patterns applied to this shape, such as the fish (illustrated), were reflective of the style and the love of exotic imagery popular in the 1930s.[1]

Snack plate and mug, ca. 1950. Purinton Pottery Company, Shippenville, Pa. Earthenware with painted decoration. Snack plate marked: *Purinton | SLIP WARE | HANDPAINTED.* Mug unmarked. Dallas Museum of Art, 20th-Century Design Fund, 1995.137.

Montecito shape plate with Tropical Fish pattern, ca. 1935 Harry Bird, pattern designer; Vernon Kilns, Los Angeles, maker. Earthenware with painted decoration; h. ¾ in. (1.9 cm), diam. 10½ in. (26.7 cm). Marked: *BIRD POTTERY | [bird logo] | TROPICAL FISH | VERNON KILNS | CALIFORNIA | PAT. PEND.* Dallas Museum of Art, 20th-Century Design Fund, 1996.171.

Harry Bird worked for Vernon Kilns as a designer during the mid-1930s. During his tenure there he developed a series of patterns that featured enamel glazes that were injected through a syringe into the body of the ware before firing. This patented process, called "inlaid glaze," produced designs that stood in slight relief on the surface. In addition to *Tropical Fish*, Bird also designed *California Flowers*, both of which were made using his inlaid glaze technique. The April 1936 issue of *Crockery and Glass Journal* illustrated these patterns, as well as an image of *Tropical Fish* being displayed for buffet service at James McCreery & Co. in New York.[2]

1. For an image of many *New Era* pieces, see Florence 1995, 140–41. For an illustration of spherical vases by Heisey featuring this cutting pattern, see *CGJ* 114:6 (June 1934): back cover.
2. "Rejuvenation in McCreery's," *CGJ* 118:4 (Apr. 1936): 14, 19. For information on Bird, see Nelson 1994, 122–33.

Cat. 171
Tableware with Our America pattern, ca. 1937. Gale Turnbull and Jane Bennison, shape designers; Rockwell Kent, pattern designer; Vernon Kilns, Vernon, Calif., maker. Earthenware with printed decoration; chop plate: h. ⅞ in. (2.2 cm), diam. 14 in. (35.5 cm). All

marked: "OUR AMERICA" | Designed by | Rockwell Kent | VERNON KILNS | Made in U.S.A. Dallas Museum of Art, 20th-Century Design Fund, 1996.109, 1996.110.1–4, 1997.133, 1997.166.

It is not known whether Vernon Kilns had an official name for this shape, called the "Ultra" shape by collectors. It was introduced around 1937 in a range of pastel colors somewhat subdued for the period (see cat. 151). Around 1939 the well-known artist, illustrator, and author Rockwell Kent was hired to produce some thirty scenes of the American landscape for a pattern to be called *Our America*.[1]

Our America attracted attention on the eve of World War II with its emphasis on patriotic nationalism. This sentiment was further reinforced by Vernon Kilns, whose star-spangled advertisement introducing the pattern in 1940 declared it "Of America . . . by Americans . . . for Americans."[2] Sales were no doubt boosted by an article on American dinnerware production that appeared in *Life* magazine that year featuring the pattern in the lead photograph.[3] The pattern was transfer-printed in four colors—walnut brown, dark blue, maroon, and green—on a cream-colored ground. Each piece, with a few exceptions, displayed a different landscape scene from one of eight geographical regions around the country, all bordered by a ring of stars.

1. For more information on this shape and its patterns, see Nelson 1994, 178–204.
2. CGJ 126:1 (Jan. 1940): 13.
3. "American Dishes: Home Product Fills Gap Made by War and Boycott," Life 9:11 (9 Sept. 1940): 76–79.

Cat. 172
Large chop plate with *Our America* pattern, ca. 1937. Gale Turnbull and Jane Bennison, shape designers; Rockwell Kent, pattern designer; Vernon Kilns, Vernon, Calif., maker. Earthenware with printed decoration; h. 1⅛ in. (2.9 cm), diam. 17 in. (43.2 cm). Marked: "OUR AMERICA" | Designed by | Rockwell Kent | VERNON KILNS | Made in U.S.A. Dallas Museum of Art, 20th-Century Design Fund, T42565.

The large 17-inch chop plate was the centerpiece of Vernon Kilns' *Our America* pattern dinnerware. Featuring a large map of the United States annotated with regional imagery and surmounted by a large bald eagle, this plate presented an appropriately nationalistic tone for the entire dinnerware line (see cat. 171). So impressive an image was it that the chop plate design was featured as the lead illustration in *Life* magazine's 1940 article on American dinnerware production.[1]

1. "American Dishes: Home Product Fills Gap Made by War and Boycott," Life 9:11 (9 Sept. 1940): 76–79.

Cat. 173
***Prestige* juice glass and tumbler,** 1953. Eva Zeisel, designer; Federal Glass Company, Co-lumbus, Ohio, maker. Glass. Both unmarked. Dallas Museum of Art, 20th-Century Design Fund, 1996.169.1–2.

Prestige was introduced to the market in 1954 and came in four glass shapes—cocktail, juice, old fashioned, and highball. Each type of glass was sold by the dozen in prepackaged sets or in a sixteen-piece "tumbler set" that contained four of each variety.[1] In addition to lending stability to the vessels, according to Zeisel, the solid, bulbous bottoms provided the glasses "with extra-ordinary reflections."[2]

Classic Crystal tumbler, 1948. Freda Diamond, designer; Libbey Glass Company, Toledo, maker. Glass. Marked: L. Gift of the estate of Freda Diamond, 1998.158.6.

Accent tumbler, 1967. Freda Diamond, designer; Libbey Glass Company, Toledo maker. Glass. Unmarked. Gift of the estate of Freda Diamond, 1998.158.5.

Mayfair shape plate with *Frosted Leaves* pattern, ca. 1952. Freda Diamond, pattern designer; Edwin M. Knowles China Company, Newell, W. Va., maker. Earthenware with platinum and printed decoration; h. 1 in. (2.5 cm), diam. 9⅜ in. (23.8 cm). Marked: K | KNOWLES | ® [all in an oval] and FROSTED LEAVES | M4039| Designed by FREDA DIAMOND [all in a ribbon]. Anonymous loan.

In 1953 Knowles introduced seven patterns by the well-known designer Freda Diamond. Two—*Platinum Grey* and *Platinum White*—were simple banded patterns on coupe-shaped plates. Also on the coupe shape were three floral patterns called *Paradise*, *Corsage*, and *Silver Spray*. *Frosted Leaves* and *Oslo*, another floral design, were produced on the rim-shaped *Mayfair* blank. While it is probable that the more elaborate patterns were created using printed decals, it is possible that their motifs were mechanically stamped onto the surfaces of the plates.[3]

Old fashioned glass, two tumblers, and juice glass, ca. 1948. Freda Diamond, designer; Libbey Glass Company, Toledo, maker. Glass. All unmarked. Dallas Museum of Art, gift of the estate of Freda Diamond, 1998.158.1–4.

1. CGJ 155:1 (July 1954): 25.
2. Montreal 1984, 77.
3. Unidentified ad dating from 1953.

Cat. 174
***Liberty* shape plate with *Historical America* pattern,** ca. 1928. Frederick Hurten Rhead, shape designer; Homer Laughlin China Company, Newell, W. Va., maker. Earthenware with printed decoration. Marked: [star] | HISTORICAL AMERICA | BETSY ROSS SHOWING | THE FIRST FLAG . . . 1777 | HOMER LAUGHLIN CHINA CO. | MADE IN U.S.A. | PICTURE REPRO-DUCED FROM | ORIGINAL PAINTING BY | JOSEPH BOGGS BEALE | copyright-Modern Enterprises, | Philadelphia, Pa. Anonymous collection.

The *Liberty* shape was an improved version of the *Newell* shape of a year earlier. These were among Frederick Rhead's first designs with Homer Laughlin. The scene in the center of the plate reproduces a painting by Joseph Boggs Beale which depicts Betsy Ross showing the first flag to George Washington.[1]

Americana shape cup and saucer with *Early American Homes* pattern, ca. 1940. Homer Laughlin China Company, Newell, W. Va., maker; J. C. Penney Company, New York, retailer. Earthenware with printed decoration. Saucer marked: EARLY | AMERICAN HOMES | BY | HOMER LAUGHLIN | ARLINGTON | HOME OF ROBT. E. LEE | MADE IN U.S.A. Cup marked: PAUL REVERE'S HOME | MADE IN U.S.A. Anonymous collection.

The *Early American Homes* pattern seems to have been made exclusively for sale at J. C. Penney Company.[2] It featured seven different scenes of colonial and antebellum homes of famous patriots and soldiers as well as Independence Hall.

Gadroon shape platter and plate with *Pink Vista* pattern, ca. 1925. G. L. Ashworth and Brothers, Hanley, England, maker; Hugh C. Edmiston, New York, importer. Earthenware with printed decoration; platter: h. 1⅜ in. (3.5 cm), w. 15¾ in. (40 cm), d. 12¾ in. (32.4 cm). Platter marked: MASON'S | [crown] | PATENT IRONSTONE [within drapery] | VISTA | ENGLAND | GUARANTEED PERMANENT & | ACID RESISTING COLOURS and bVII and HAND | MADE IN [illegible]. Plate marked: same except with PH and without bVII and HAND | MADE IN [illegible]. Glenda Lee Harrison Collection.

G. L. Ashworth and Brothers marketed its dinnerware in the United States as Mason's Patent Ironstone China; however, their product was in fact earthenware, not ironstone (whiteware). It was not until 1968 that the company officially changed its name to Mason's Ironstone China. *Pink Vista* was far and away the firm's most popular pattern throughout the twentieth century. It sold in practically every shop that sold dinnerware, and in the 1950s when the "Early American" style competed with high modernism, it was the biggest-selling pattern for most shops, including such fashionable emporiums as Neiman Marcus in Dallas.[3] It was available in blue, brown, and pink (red), as shown here.

This particular set was purchased in 1949 by Glenda Lee Harrison's mother, Jewel Page Lee, at Rubenstein's in Shreveport, Louisiana. These three patterns show how competitive the market was at midcentury for the traditional consumer—the woman who did not take risks at her table but sought the mantle of respectability by serving her family and guests with colonial revival accessories.

1. For more information on this shape, see Jasper 1993, 50–55.
2. *The Laughlin Eagle* 3:1 (winter/summer 1994), 4.
3. Wedgwood interview 1996.

Cat. 175

Snack plate with *Holiday* shape cup and *Holiday* shape covered casserole dish with *Sea Spray* pattern, ca. 1954–55. Alfred Dube, designer of *Holiday* shape; Stetson China Company, Chicago and Lincoln, Ill., maker; American Commercial, Los Angeles, distributor. Earthenware with painted decoration; casserole dish: h. 6⅛ in. (15.6 cm), diam. 9⅝ in. (24.4 cm). Snack plate marked: *Copyright 1954 | Stetson-China-Co. | Lincoln – ILL.* Cup and casserole dish unmarked. Dallas Museum of Art: gift of Michael E. Pratt (snack set), T42335; 20th-Century Design Fund (casserole dish), T42455.

In 1947 Stetson expanded its factory and increased production of "promotionally-priced, high quality semi-porcelain with smart, attractive under-glaze, hand-painted and over-glaze decorations."[1] "Promotionally-priced" meant that the firm's ware was mainly intended for distribution as part of promotions by grocery, appliance, and other retail stores as inexpensive gifts or sale merchandise. While Stetson made a variety of dishes, including plastic ones, it was best known in the 1950s for its handpainted pottery. This type of abstract surface decoration was made by Stetson primarily in the mid-1950s. Alfred Dube, a highly trained Czech immigrant who had come to the U.S. in 1949, applied for patents on the *Holiday* shape in 1955 and received them in 1957 (for example, design patent number 179,888 for the creamer). Despite the delay, the shape was introduced to the trade in 1955 as "*The* Promotion Line."[2] To decorate the surfaces of his shapes, Dube developed several sophisticated stenciling and stamping techniques that could be used in association with hand painting.[3]

1. *CGJ* 141:6 (Dec. 1947): 33.
2. *CGJ* 156:8 (June 1955): 54.
3. Alfred Dube, conversation with Charles Venable, 11 Oct. 1999.

Cat. 176

All pieces: Eva Zeisel, designer; Hall China Company, East Liverpool, Ohio, maker; Midhurst China Sales Corporation, New York and Los Angeles, distributor. Whiteware with printed decoration.

Tomorrow's Classic shape pitcher with *Fantasy* pattern and sauceboat and ladle with *Dawn* pattern from the Hallcraft line, ca. 1949–50. William Katavolvos, Ross Littell, and Douglas Kelley, designers of *Fantasy* pattern; Charles

Seliger, designer of *Dawn* pattern. Pitcher: h. 8½ in. (21.6 cm), w. 9½ in. (24.1 cm), d. 6½ in. (16.5 cm). All marked: *HALLCRAFT | BY | HC [conjoined] | Eva Zeisel | MADE IN U.S.A. BY HALL CHINA CO.* Dallas Museum of Art: gift of Mr. and Mrs. Robert F. Venable (pitcher), 1991.55; gift of David T. Owsley (sauceboat and ladle), 1994.11.5–6.

Zeisel designed the *Tomorrow's Classic* shape around 1950, following the success of her *Museum* and *Town and Country* dinnerware (see cats. 12, 188). However, the design languished until it finally found a champion in Charles Seliger of Commercial Decal, who was in search of a contemporary tableware design upon which his firm could put decal decorations. Hall China agreed to produce the shape, and from 1951 to about 1960 *Tomorrow's Classic* was made with various glazed and printed decorative schemes (see cat. 189). Zeisel's contract with Hall China stipulated that she supply nine decal designs initially and three additional designs each following year. Some of these patterns, such as *Dawn* and *Arizona*, were created by Seliger, while others like *Frost Flowers* and *Fantasy*, were done by Zeisel's studio assistants and her students at the Pratt Institute, where she taught.[1]

Century shape plate, salad plate, and bread and butter plate with *Sunglow* pattern from the Hallcraft line, ca. 1955–56. All marked: *Eva Zeisel | HC [conjoined] CENTURY | HALLCRAFT | MADE IN U.S.A. BY HALL CHINA CO.* Dallas Museum of Art, gift of David T. Owsley, 1991.11.1–3.

Tomorrow's Classic was very popular, and as a result Zeisel received several other commissions from Hall China. In 1956 her new line of tableware, called *Century*, was released. The line could be used in the refrigerator as well as on the table and was available in solid colors with numerous surface decorations. While all the forms in the line were elegant and beautifully thought out, the plates were especially interesting. In her earlier work Zeisel had experimented with square and oval plates, but here she pulled the form into a teardrop shape, adding extra visual excitement to the tablescape.[2]

1. Eidelberg 1991, 197–98; and Montreal 1984, 48–57.
2. Montreal 1984, 57–58.

Cat. 177

Coupe cup and saucer, teapot, and mug, ca. 1945–47. Edith Kiertener Heath, designer; Heath Ceramics, Sausalito, Calif., maker. Cup and saucer and mug: stoneware. Teapot: stoneware, metal, and plastic. Cup, teapot, and mug marked: *HEATH [vessel logo under T].* Mug also marked: ®. Saucer marked: *HEATH | SAUSALITO | CALIF.* Dallas Museum of Art, 20th-Century Design Fund, 1996.168.1–3.

Heath developed her *Coupe* shapes in the mid-1940s. The prototypes were all developed by hand on a potter's wheel. However, once prestigious retailers including Gump's, Neiman Marcus, and Marshall Field & Co. began placing orders, the designs were modified for mass production. The *Coupe* shapes, as represented here, have remained little changed since 1947.[1] The teapot profile is perhaps Heath's most famous. It, and several other pieces, was selected by the Museum of Modern Art in New York for inclusion in the exhibition *Industry and Handwork Create New Housewares in the United States*, which toured Europe in 1951. The Germans, who had a long tradition of working in stoneware and had produced similar teapots during the 1930s, were particularly impressed by Heath's designs.[2]

Coupe coffeepot, plate, and bowl, ca. 1945–47. Edith Kiertener Heath, designer; Josiah Wedgwood & Sons, Burslem, England, maker. Stoneware; coffeepot: h. 7¾ in. (19.7 cm), w. 9 in. (22.9 cm), d. 5½ in. (14 cm). Coffeepot marked: *HEATH OF CALIFORNIA | WEDGWOOD | MADE IN ENGLAND | OVEN TO TABLE.* Plate and bowl unmarked. Dallas Museum of Art: gift of Edith Heath (plate and bowl), T42560.1, T42558.2; Brian and Edith Heath Collection (coffeepot).

In the early 1960s Edith Heath was approached by Arthur Bryan of Wedgwood, who asked her to come to England and develop prototypes for a new casual line. Edith and her husband, Brian Heath, spent most of 1965 producing around 3,000 pieces at Wedgwood's factory using molds and profiles brought from the United States. The shapes made were the classic *Coupe* range. However, differences in the clay body and firing methods resulted in a glossier, more refined look compared to the ware made in California. Given these problems and the fact that the prototypes did not perform well during market testing in England, Wedgwood ended its efforts to introduce a Heath line in 1966.[3]

1. For an image of hand-thrown examples, see "Complete Dinnerware Sets Thrown on the Wheel," *Ceramic Industry* (May 1946): 86. For early images of the mass-produced line, see *CGJ* 142:4 (Apr. 1948): 49; and 144:6 (June 1948): 23.
2. For images of the work that toured in this exhibit, see "Neues Haurgerät in USA," *Schaulade* 26:6 (June 1951): 193. For images of related German teapots, see *Schaulade* 9:9/10 (Sept.–Oct. 1933): 356.
3. For information on the Heath-Wedgwood effort, see Heath and Ross 1995, 242–51.

Cat. 178

Magnolia bowl, ca. 1940. Dorothy C. Thorpe, designer; Dorothy C. Thorpe, Inc., Glendale, Calif., maker. Glass with etched decoration; h. 2¾ in. (7 cm), w. 15¼ in. (38.7 cm), d. 25¾ in. (65.4 cm). Unmarked. Dallas Museum of Art, gift of the Dallas Antiques and Fine Arts Society, 1997.19.

Following her marriage to George A. Thorpe of Los Angeles in 1923, Dorothy Thorpe (née Carpenter) moved to southern California and began experimenting with glass as a hobby. At first she made tumblers from beer bottles, but it was her use of sandblasting to ornament glass blanks that eventually became a commercial success. In 1932 George Thorpe established a business (incorporated 1939) to manufacture her designs. Dorothy Thorpe succeeded her husband as president following his death, and aided by her son Richard C. Thorpe and A. D. Street (general manager by the 1960s), she expanded her business greatly between 1935 and 1965. In 1958 they acquired the California Bent Glass Company, and in 1962 they moved into larger quarters in Sun Valley, California. In the postwar years Thorpe built an impressive distribution system for her products, which were carried by wholesalers and retailers throughout the country. Among her earliest prestigious clients were Bullock's department store in Los Angeles, Neiman Marcus in Dallas, and Carole Stupell in New York.[1]

This example came from Thorpe's estate and is representative of her finest early work. Such large pieces were expensive when new. This bowl (no. T333), which could be used as a centerpiece for food service, retailed for $29.[2] Etched glass featuring botanical motifs dominated Thorpe's production from the 1930s through the 1950s. It became so popular that other firms, including Tiffin Glass and Duncan & Miller Glass Company, imitated her designs.[3]

1. For general information on Thorpe see Cunningham 1995, 104–5. Detailed business history taken from "Dorothy C. Thorpe, Inc.," Dun & Bradstreet Report, 29 Nov. 1963. Heisey Archives.
2. Thorpe 1941. This copy of the publicity brochure contains a photograph of the *Magnolia* bowl that lists the retail price on the back.
3. CGJ 127:6 (Dec. 1960): 1; and 140:1 (Jan. 1947): cover.

Cat. 179

Jubilee cup and saucer, teapot, and sugar bowl, 1947. Donald Schreckengost, designer; Homer Laughlin China Company, Newell, W. Va., maker. Earthenware; teapot: h. 5 in. (12.7 cm), w. 12 in. (30.5 cm), d. 7 in. (17.8 cm). All marked: *Jubilee* / BY HOMER LAUGHLIN / U.S.A. Dallas Museum of Art, 20th-Century Design Fund, 1995.142.1–3.

Jubilee was designed to celebrate Homer Laughlin's seventy-fifth anniversary and was initially introduced in four colors—*Celadon Green, Dawn Gray, Foam Beige,* and *Shell Pink.* When *Jubilee* was put on the market in 1948, the firm stated: "This new line has the delicacy, the richness, and the personality of fine china. It is jewel-like in its quality, unique in the soft depth and loveliness of its glaze, unmatched in its graceful, flowing lines. It possesses unequalled appeal to the discriminating buyer. It is destined for new records in sales and consumer acceptance."[1] *Jubilee*

proved to be popular and was eventually made in striking two-toned colors featuring a variety of decal decorations.

1. CGJ 142:1 (Jan. 1948): 40.

Cat. 180

Pitcher, sugar bowl, and covered pitcher with Tri-Tone pattern, 1954. Eva Zeisel, designer; Hall China Company, East Liverpool, Ohio, maker. Whiteware with sprayed decoration; pitcher: h. 8⅝ in. (21.9 cm), w. 9 in. (22.9 cm), d. 7 in. (17.8 cm). Pitcher and covered pitcher marked: HALL [*in a circle*] / MADE IN U.S.A. Sugar bowl marked: same except with TRI-TONE / 1567. Dallas Museum of Art, 20th-Century Design Fund, 1995.139.1–3.

Following strong sales of her *Tomorrow's Classic* shape, Hall China commissioned Eva Zeisel to create a twenty-piece line of oven-proof cook- and kitchenware. The designer's efforts resulted in forms that were functional yet beautiful. The covered refrigerator pitcher, for example, was molded to fit the hand without the use of a handle. The line was produced with combinations of several colors and patterns of glazes. *Tri-Tone* is perhaps the most striking. According to Zeisel, the pieces were meant to look as if they had been hand-dipped into blue and pink glaze to produce the tricolor effect. The glazes were actually sprayed on. Because the areas of color had to be perfectly even along their edges, this decoration was particularly difficult to achieve.[1]

1. Zeisel interview 1996.

Cat. 181

White Clover cup and saucer and covered pitcher, 1951. Russel Wright, designer; Harker Pottery, East Liverpool, Ohio, maker. Earthenware; pitcher: h. 8½ in. (21.6 cm), w. 6¾ in. (17.1 cm), d. 5 in. (12.7 cm). All marked: HARKERWARE / Russel Wright. Dallas Museum of Art, 20th-Century Design Fund, 1996.166.1–2.

White Clover was available in four colors: *Golden Spice, Meadow Green, Coral Sand,* and *Charcoal.* Although critically acclaimed when introduced in 1951—the Museum of Modern Art gave it a Good Design award and immediately added the design to its collection—the line's reception on the factory floor and in china departments was different. Harker quickly discovered that the glazes and shapes were more expensive to produce than expected, and that the sizes of the largest plates were nonstandard and required special treatment in the kiln and more costly packaging. Retailers complained that the pottery did not offer the correct assortment of pieces in its starter sets. Russel Wright felt Harker was not aggressive enough about selling to West Coast accounts. *White Clover* was withdrawn in 1955, sales having barely reached 60 percent of their goal.[1]

1. Kerr 1990, 108–12.

Cat. 182

Creamer, sugar bowl, and salt and pepper shakers, ca. 1955. Mary and Russel Wright, designers; Sovereign Potteries, Hamilton, Ontario, Canada, maker. Earthenware. Sugar bowl marked: *Mary & Russel Wright* / BY / SOVEREIGN POTTERS. Others unmarked. Dallas Museum of Art, 20th-Century Design Fund, 1995.164.1–3.

Esquire shape sugar bowl with Grass pattern, plate with Botanica pattern, creamer with Queen Anne's Lace pattern, cup and saucer with Snowflower pattern, and teapot with Seeds pattern, 1955. Russel Wright, designer; Edwin M. Knowles Pottery Company, Newell, W. Va., maker. Earthenware with printed decoration; plate: h. ¾ in. (1.9 cm), diam. 10⅛ in. (25.7 cm). Teapot marked: *Russel Wright* / *by Knowles* / *Seeds* / MADE IN U.S.A. Sugar bowl lid marked: same except pattern name *Grass*. Plate marked: same except pattern name *Botanica*. Creamer and cup unmarked. Saucer marked: same except pattern name *Snowflower*. Dallas Museum of Art, 20th-Century Design Fund, 1995.114.1–2, 1996.167.1–3.

The creation of the *Esquire Collection*, as it was called, was complicated. Because it was to be marketed through discount stores and mail-order firms, the ware needed to be inexpensive to produce, yet appealing. As it turned out, Russel Wright's designs accomplished neither goal. From the beginning there were problems with the sophisticated matte glazes, for example. Retailers also found that the pale ware photographed poorly and thus was hard to sell through catalogues. Shoppers apparently thought it was simply too strange. To improve the situation, Wright suggested new patterns and the restyling of some shapes. But Knowles, which was already under financial stress, discontinued *Esquire* in 1962 and went out of business the next year.

The shape made by Sovereign Potteries apparently originated from Wright's work for Knowles. Although the illustrated forms are more organic, period photographs reveal that the matching teapot was very close to the *Esquire* one. It is possible that this Canadian ware was originally designed as a prototype for *Esquire* or was one of the suggested restylings.[1]

1. For a discussion of both lines, see Kerr 1990, 113–18.

Cat. 183

Chop plate with Colonial Homestead pattern, 1949. Royal China, Sebring, Ohio. Earthenware with printed decoration; h. 1 in. (2.5 cm), diam. 12¼ in. (31.1 cm). Marked: *Colonial Homestead* / *by* / *Royal* [*inside needlework picture*] / PAT. PEND. / *Circa 1750.* Dallas Museum of Art, 20th-Century Design Fund, 1996.128.

Introduced in 1950, this line featured seven forms, each of which was decorated with colonial revival images. The bread and butter plate had a spinning wheel, for example, while the rim soup bowl pictured a seventeenth-century cradle. Royal advertised the chop plate as "the Masterpiece," claiming that it "portrays the interiors of a typical American home of 1750. Each additional item in the service illustrates a portion of the same room in authentic detail—the simple hand made furnishings, the quaint utensils, all the traditional necessities of a hardy pioneer life. A realistic pine wood border distinguishes every piece of the set."[1] A twenty-piece set retailed originally for $4.95.

1. CGJ 146:3 (4 Mar. 1950): 15.

Cat. 184

Both pieces: ca. 1948. Kay Hackett, pattern designer; Stangl Pottery, Trenton, maker. Earthenware with painted and incised decoration.

Plate with *Golden Harvest* pattern. Marked: *Stangl | POTTERY | TRENTON, N.J. [all in an oval] | GOLDEN HARVEST* and *xX* and *o | —*. Dallas Museum of Art, 20th-Century Design Fund, T42500.

Coffee server with *Amber-Glo* pattern. H. 10¾ in. (27.3 cm), w. 5¼ in. (13.3 cm), d. 4¾ in. (12.1 cm). Marked: *Stangl ® | POTTERY | TRENTON, N.J. [all in an oval] | AMBER • GLO* and *STANGL | SEC [in an oval]* (denotes second quality) and *A*. Dallas Museum of Art, 20th-Century Design Fund, 1995.162.

Kay Hackett was one of Stangl's main designers. Concerning *Amber-Glo*, Hackett recalls being influenced by modern Scandinavian pottery and that the pattern was originally designed with a blue flame motif, not the orange and gray eventually produced. However, according to Hackett, Stangl had an arrangement with *House and Garden*—if Stangl would use specific colors that the magazine was promoting, the pottery would receive free advertising in the popular periodical. *House and Garden* requested that gray be used, and so it was incorporated into *Amber-Glo's* color scheme.[1]

Around 1948 Stangl updated its dinnerware shapes. Among the changes was the addition of a coupe-shaped plate. When *Amber-Glo* was introduced in 1954, the pottery explained to consumers that it was designed to be mixed and matched on the table. One ad stated: "This newest Stangl dinnerware pattern was created for casual living. Amber-Glo is a wonderful way for you to express your originality. It can be *mixed* with Stangl Golden Harvest [introduced 1953]. Or it is even more beautiful when *matched* with the distinctive shapes of Amber-Glo itself."[2]

1. Quoted in Duke 1993, 43, 47.
2. CGJ 155:1 (July 1954): 22.

Cat. 185

***Shelledge* plate and cup and saucer with *Flamingo Reeds* pattern,** ca. 1936–49. R. Guy Cowan, shape designer; Onondaga Pottery Company, Syracuse, N.Y., maker. Whiteware with sprayed decoration; plate: h.¾ in. (1.9 cm), diam. 10 in. (25.4 cm). All marked: *Shelledge [in a shell] | SYRACUSE CHINA | PATENTED | Flamingo Reeds*. Dallas Museum of Art, 20th-Century Design Fund, 1996.112.1–2.

In 1936 R. Guy Cowan created the *Shelledge* shape range, which included this plate profile. Although production was interrupted in 1941 by World War II, the pottery added new forms to the range and reintroduced it in 1947 as a complete dinner service. In 1949 Cowan redesigned the hollowware to make it more traditional—for example, the original cup featuring flaring walls and a sweeping handle gave way to the more conservative version that is illustrated. The *Flamingo Reeds* surface pattern was introduced in 1951 and was available until 1959. Whereas *Shelledge* was first ornamented with relief patterns pressed into the wet clay, most postwar patterns like *Flamingo Reeds* relied on the airbrushed glazes at which Onondaga excelled.[1]

1. For information on the *Shelledge* shape range, see Reed and Skoczen 1997, 116–19.

Cat. 186

Plate and tumbler with *Oats* pattern, ca. 1946. Winfield Division, American Ceramics Products, Santa Monica, Calif. Earthenware with painted decoration. Both marked: *WINFIELD | HANDCRAFT | CHINA*. Dallas Museum of Art, 20th-Century Design Fund, 1997.122.1–2.

Originally the *Oats* pattern was one of six produced by the La Mirada Division of American Ceramics Products—the other patterns were *Dawn, Plaid, Wheat, Eucalyptus,* and *Daffodil*. All six patterns were applied to square-shaped plates. Unlike these other patterns, *Oats* was available on three background colors—white, yellow, and sage. In early 1949 American Ceramics Products merged the La Mirada Division with the Winfield Division. Simultaneously, it replaced the porous *La Mirada* body with the more highly vitrified one it had been using for the Winfield line.[1]

Plate, ca. 1945. Glidden Parker, shape designer; Glidden Pottery, Alfred, N.Y., maker. Earthenware with painted decoration; h. ¾ in. (1.9 cm), w. 9¾ in. (24.8 cm), d. 9¾ in. (24.8 cm). Marked: *Glidden | 31*. Dallas Museum of Art, gift of Michael E. Pratt, T42377.

Cup and saucer with *Plume* pattern, ca. 1945. Glidden Parker, shape designer; Ernest Sohn, pattern designer; Glidden Pottery, Alfred, N.Y., maker. Earthenware with incised decoration. Cup marked: *Glidden | 141*. Saucer

marked: *Glidden | 142*. Dallas Museum of Art, 20th-Century Design Fund, T42484.

Glidden's *Plume* pattern, also called *Feather*, appeared on the market in 1946 and was honored the next year by being included in the Twelfth Ceramics National Exhibition held in 1947 by the Syracuse Museum of Fine Arts.[2] Although Glidden Parker is listed as the designer in the catalogue to that exhibition, Ernest Sohn—who worked for Glidden's first distributor, Rubel & Company, in New York from 1945 to 1951—recalls that he designed the surface ornament and Glidden Parker conceived the square-shaped plate.[3]

Fish covered casserole, ca. 1952. Philip Secrest, designer; Glidden Pottery, Alfred, N.Y., maker. Earthenware with painted decoration. Marked: *Glidden | 412*. Dallas Museum of Art, 20th-Century Design Fund, 1997.187.

This design was featured in the Seventeenth Ceramics National Exhibition held in 1953 by the Syracuse Museum of Fine Arts.[4]

1. CGJ 141:1 (July 1947): 8–9; "La Mirada Mandarin Now Called Winfield," 144:2 (Feb. 1949): 65.
2. CGJ 138:6 (June 1946): 47; Syracuse 1947, 6.
3. Ernest Sohn, conversation with Charles Venable, 14 Sept. 1999. For more information on Glidden, see Piña 1994, 97–116.
4. Syracuse 1953, 23.

Cat. 187

***Highlight* bowl,** 1948. Russel Wright, designer; Paden City Pottery, Paden City, W. Va., maker; Justin Tharaud & Son, New York, distributor. Whiteware. Marked: *JUSTIN THARAUD & SON U.S.A. | Russel Wright*. Dallas Museum of Art, gift of Eason Eige, T42318.18.

Highlight was available in five colors: *Black Pepper, Blueberry, Nutmeg, Citron, Dark Green,* and *Snow Glaze*. Russel Wright designed a variety of *Snow Glass* tumblers, lids, saucers, salad plates, and bowls to complement the pottery. These were made at the Paden City Glass Company until 1953, when the glassworks closed. Although *Highlight* won numerous design awards and was included in several important exhibitions that toured the United States and Europe in the early 1950s, its creation and production were plagued by difficulties between designer, distributor, and maker, and the line did not sell well.[1]

***Casual China* cup and saucer, carafe, and salt and pepper shakers,** 1946. Russel Wright, designer; Iroquois China Company, Syracuse, N.Y., maker. Whiteware; carafe: h. 9⅞ in. (25.1 cm), w. 5 in. (12.7 cm), d. 6¾ in. (17.1 cm). Cup marked: *IROQUOIS | CASUAL | CHINA | by | Russel | Wright | U.S.A.* Saucer marked: same as cup except with *[illegible] – 1*. Carafe marked: same as cup except with *O [or Q] – 2*. Salt and pepper shakers unmarked. Dallas Museum of Art: gift of Eason Eige (cup and saucer), T42318.19; gift of the Friends of the Decorative Arts (carafe), 1989.89; gift of David T. Owsley (salt and pepper shakers), 1994.10.1–2.

When *Casual China* was introduced, its original distributor, Garrison Products of New York (1946–48), advertised the line as a "Revolution in China." The ware's tough, thick-walled body was suitable for the oven and icebox and was guaranteed against breakage for one year after purchase. Its elegant, streamlined shapes were designed to stack compactly for ease of storage.[2] *Casual China* was offered in *Cantaloupe*, *Sugar White*, and *Lemon Yellow* (illustrated) and eleven other colors. During the long life of this line various pieces were periodically re-designed, and a major overhaul of most of the shapes occurred in 1951. The cup and saucer is a later version featuring a more curvilinear handle. The line was highly successful and was on the market into the 1960s.[3]

1. Kerr 1990, 103–5.
2. "Revolution in China," *China, Glass and Decorative Accessories* (Aug. 1946): 8–9, 33, 37.
3. Kerr 1990, 85–88.

Cat. 188

Museum **plate, creamer, coffeepot, and cup and saucer**, ca. 1942–43. Eva Zeisel, designer; Shenango Pottery Company, New Castle, Pa., maker; Castleton China, New York, distributor. Porcelain; coffeepot: h. 10 in. (25.4 cm), w. 7 in. (17.8 cm), d. 5½ in. (14 cm). Plate, creamer, and saucer marked: [stylized lyre] / MADE IN U.S.A. / CASTLETON / CHINA / REG. U.S. PAT. OFF. Coffeepot unmarked. Cup marked: [stylized lyre]. Dallas Museum of Art, 20th-Century Design Fund, 1995.97.1–2, 1997.29, 1996.115.

Museum is one of the most important table-wares made in the United States during the twentieth century and, like the country itself, was the product of various foreign and indigenous influences. In 1939 German-born Louis E. Hellmann, formerly president of the Rosenthal China Corporation in New York, founded Castleton China. Hellmann contracted Shenango Pottery to produce porcelain dinnerware for him, and in 1940 introduced adaptations of conservative Rosenthal shapes and patterns (see cat. 106). Shortly thereafter he asked New York's Museum of Modern Art (MoMA) to recommend a designer who could create a modern-style dinnerware line for his new company. Anxious to further modernist aesthetics and thus "improve" taste, MoMA recommended the Hungarian-born and German- and Russian-trained Eva Zeisel, who had come to the United States in 1938.

Reminiscent of the elegant yet functional German services made in white porcelain in the early 1930s, *Museum* was nevertheless highly original. Zeisel's design was not as

severely geometric as its central European counterparts or as white, featuring instead voluptuous curves and a warm, off-white color.[1] Although *Museum* was designed around 1942–43, World War II delayed its introduction until 1946, when it was shown in New York at MoMA; B. Altman's; John Wanamaker's; Black, Starr & Gorham; and Georg Jensen. At the time MoMA officials stated, "This modern dinnerware may well provide a landmark in the American ceramic industry. Heretofore, modern shapes in dinner service have been interpreted only in earthenware."[2] Highly promoted by both Hellmann and MoMA, which included the design in the exhibition *Industry and Handwork Create New Housewares in the United States* that toured Europe in 1951, *Museum* became well known in America and abroad, influencing modern designs in porcelain from California to Germany in the late 1940s and 1950s.[3] Although MoMA championed the dinnerware in its pure white state, it did not sell well unornamented. Decal decorations, usually by other designers, were soon added to Zeisel's shapes to entice consumers.

1. For more information on *Museum*, see Eidelberg 1991, 55–56; and Montreal 1984, 32–37 and 77ff. Zeisel patented the shapes. The coffeepot, for example, was assigned design no. 148,901 on 17 Apr. 1946.
2. "Museum Honors New Castleton Line," *CGJ* 138:5 (May 1946): 39.
3. *Schaulade* 22:6–7 (June–July 1947): 86–87; and "Neues Hausgerät in USA," *Schaulade* 26:6 (June 1951): 192–93.

Cat. 189

Tomorrow's Classic **coffeepot**, 1949. Eva Zeisel, designer; Hall China Company, East Liverpool, Ohio, maker. Whiteware; h. 9 in. (22.9 cm), w. 7½ in. (19.1 cm), d. 4¼ in. (10.8 cm). Unmarked. Dallas Museum of Art, 20th-Century Design Fund, 1995.138.

Fashion **shape teapot with** *Nature Study* **pattern from the Stylecraft line**, ca. 1954. Roy Midwinter, shape designer; Terence Conran, pattern designer; W. R. Midwinter, Burslem, England, maker; Meakin-Midwinter, New York, importer. Earthenware with printed decoration. Marked: NATURE STUDY / [butterfly] / Designed by Terence Conran / A GENUINE HAND ENGRAVING PERMANENT / ACID RESISTING UNDERGLAZE COLOURS / stylecraft / Fashion tableware / by / midwinter / STAFFORDSHIRE / ENGLAND. Anonymous collection.

Fashion **coffeepot from the Stylecraft line**, ca. 1954. Roy Midwinter, designer; W. R. Midwinter, Burslem, England, maker; Meakin-Midwinter, New York, importer. Earthenware. Marked: Midwinter / Stylecraft / STAFFORDSHIRE / ENGLAND / FASHION SHAPE / 6-63 (date mark for 1963). Dallas Museum of Art, 20th-Century Design Fund, T42597.

Inspired by the free-flowing lines and amorphous forms of Russel Wright's *American*

Modern (see cat. 24), Eva Zeisel's *Museum* (see cat. 188), and *Tomorrow's Classic*, Roy Midwinter began work in 1953 on the new *Fashion* shape, first for plates and then in February 1954 for tea- and coffeepots. The surface designs Midwinter left to his talented colleagues, especially Jessie Tait and Terence Conran, the designer of *Nature Study*, one of the first patterns developed for the *Fashion* shape. Here the Midwinter team again drew inspiration from outside sources—in this case, the fashionable line drawings and whimsical black-and-white prints of Italian Piero Fornasetti. Black-and-white compositions in surface designs were a popular draw in the 1950s, whether on ceramics, textiles, or furniture.[1]

1. Jenkins 1997, 12–32.

Cat. 190

Metro **shape cup and saucer and plate with** *Homemaker* **pattern**, ca. 1957. Tom Arnold, shape designer; Enid Seeney, pattern designer; Ridgway Pottery, Cobridge, England, maker. Earthenware with printed decoration; plate: h. 1 in. (2.5 cm), diam. 10 in. (25.4 cm). Cup marked: MADE IN ENGLAND. Saucer and plate marked: RIDGWAY POTTERIES LTD. / [surrounded by image of flowers and cutlery] HOMEMAKER / MADE IN STAFFORDSHIRE ENGLAND / ALL COLOURS GUARANTEED / UNDERGLAZE / AND DETERGENT PROOF. Dallas Museum of Art, 20th-Century Design Fund, 1998.48.1–2.

Bowl, ca. 1958. Homer Laughlin China Company, Newell, W. Va. Earthenware with printed decoration. Marked: Dura-Print / by HOMER LAUGHLIN / MADE IN U.S.A. [all within curved outline]. Dallas Museum of Art, 20th-Century Design Fund, T42375.

The *Metro* shape was adapted for earthenware from the *Sapphire* shape modeled a year earlier for bone china. This adaptation was done at the suggestion of a buyer from B. Altman & Co. in New York who liked the coupe shape of the *Sapphire* plates but thought them too expensive for the store's market—the perennial problem of Americans not wanting to spend much on modern tableware, especially imported versions. The inspiration for the trendy look of *Homemaker* came from ordinary household furniture seen by Enid Seeney at trade fairs and in department store show-rooms. The result was an inexpensive product that had a fresh, new look and a fashion touch. It was the last design for the talented young artist—she left the industry in 1957 to get married and become a "homemaker" herself—but ultimately it became her most successful. A year later the pattern hit the shelves of F. W. Woolworth & Co. and almost immediately inspired an American version by Homer Laughlin.[1]

Both versions were produced using similar techniques. In England the process of machine-printing from an engraved metal plate had appeared in 1955 with the Murray-Curvex machine. About the same time Homer Laughlin introduced its Dura-Print process. Both worked on the principle of a cone-shaped plunger or balloon that received the inked image from the engraved plate and transferred it mechanically to the dish. Greater efficiency was achieved by reducing the time and number of workers needed to accomplish this transfer step.[2]

1. For a thorough discussion of this pattern, see Moss 1997.
2. The Dura-Print process is described in Jasper 1995, 162–65.

Cat. 191

Prototypes for a tea set with demitasse cup and saucer, ca. 1950. Viktor Schreckengost, designer; unknown factory, California, maker. Porcelain; coffeepot: h. 6⅜ in. (16.2 cm), w. 7⅝ in. (19.4 cm), d. 3⅛ in. (7.9 cm). All unmarked. Dallas Museum of Art, gift of Viktor Schreckengost, T42112.

Around 1950 Viktor Schreckengost was commissioned by an unidentified California pottery to create a tea set for mass production. These unique pieces are the final prototypes that were produced from Schreckengost's models and sent to the designer for final approval. Although innovative in shape and made of high-quality porcelain, the set was never put into production.[1]

1. V. Schreckengost interview 1995.

Cat. 192

All pieces: Metlox Potteries, Manhattan Beach, Calif., maker. Earthenware with painted decoration.

Confetti shape butter dish with California Confetti pattern and coffeepot with California Del Rey pattern, 1955. Bob Allen and Mel Shaw, designers. Both unmarked. Dallas Museum of Art, 20th-Century Design Fund, 1996.12, 1996.13.

Freeform shape butter dish and plate with California Aztec pattern, ca. 1954. Frank Irwin, shape designer; Bob Allen, pattern designer. Butter dish unmarked. Plate marked: AZTEC | PoppyTrail | -METLOX | Safe in oven and | dishwasher • durable | Hand-Decorated | Made in Calif. • U.S.A. Dallas Museum of Art, 20th-Century Design Fund, 1996.14, 1996.43.

The *Aztec* pattern was introduced in 1955, a year after the shape.

Freeform shape covered vegetable dish with California Freeform pattern and water pitcher with California Mobile pattern, ca. 1954. Frank Irwin, designer. Pitcher: h. 14½ in. (36.8 cm), w. 5½ in. (14 cm), d. 8 in. (20.3 cm). Both marked: POPPYTRAIL | BY | METLOX | MADE IN

CALIFORNIA. Dallas Museum of Art: gift of the Friends of the Decorative Arts' 1991 Twilight Zone Trip (dish), 1991.89; 20th-Century Design Fund (pitcher), 1996.47.

Freeform's designer, Frank Irwin, appreciated art and was influenced by the work of contemporary sculptors Alexander Calder and Henry Moore. His colleagues Bob Allen and Mel Shaw were animators. Before joining Metlox's staff Allen worked with Metro-Goldwyn-Mayer to found its cartoon studio, while Shaw was employed at Disney Studios working on the movies *Fantasia* and *Bambi*. This fusion of fine art and fantasy was a fertile one. Marketed under Metlox's Poppytrail brand name, these works represent some of the most original tableware made in the United States.[1]

1. For a lengthy discussion of Metlox and these designs, see Gibbs 1995, 7–9, 77–89.

Cat. 193

Encanto shape plate and cup and saucer with Starry Night pattern, 1949. Mary C. Grant, shape designer; Franciscan Division, Gladding, McBean & Co., Glendale, Calif., maker. Porcelain with platinum decoration; plate: h. ⅞ in. (2.2 cm), diam. 10½ in. (26.7 cm). Plate marked: FRANCISCAN Fine CHINA [in an oval surmounted by a Spanish mission] | MADE IN CALIFORNIA | STARRY NIGHT. Saucer marked: Franciscan fine China | MADE IN CALIFORNIA [in an oval surmounted by a Spanish mission] | GLADDING, McBEAN & CO. | STARRY NIGHT. Cup marked: same as saucer except no firm name. Dallas Museum of Art, 20th-Century Design Fund, 1996.129.1–2.

The *Encanto* shape was produced with numerous surface decorations. *Starry Night*, which debuted in 1952, was one of the most unusual. Perhaps because it was rather expensive, selling originally for $17.50 per five-piece place setting, or due to its dark color and contemporary-style ornament, *Starry Night* did not sell well.

Cat. 194

Eclipse shape sugar bowl, chop or cake plate, teapot, and creamer with Starburst pattern, 1953. George T. James, shape designer; Mary C. Brown, pattern designer; Franciscan Division, Gladding, McBean & Co., Glendale, Calif., maker. Earthenware with printed decoration; teapot: h. 5 in. (12.7 cm), w. 8 in. (20.3 cm), d. 6 in. (15.2 cm). Sugar bowl, plate, and creamer marked: © FRANCISCAN ® | MADE IN CALIFORNIA | U.S.A. | Color-Seal | GLADDING, | McBEAN | & CO | OVEN-SAFE [all in the form of a circle]. Plate also has code mark E; sugar bowl and creamer have 4. Teapot marked: GLADDING, McBEAN & CO | ©® | FRANCISCAN | EARTHENWARE | MADE IN U.S.A. [all in the form of an oval]. Dallas Museum of Art: gift of Marie and John Houser Chiles

(plate), 1997.91; 20th-Century Design Fund (others), 1996.179.1–3.

The *Eclipse* shape was part of what Franciscan called its Modern America line, and the *Starburst* pattern was certainly one of its most abstract designs. Nevertheless, George T. James, who applied for patents on the shape in 1953 (for example, patent no. 173,657 for the plate), noted the limits of contemporary design at the pottery in 1954: "Good Design here is not a museum label, nor is it contemporary with a capital 'C,' nor is it the specific ware of any past time or place . . . .Tradition has long been the cornerstone of ceramics. This is especially true of dinnerware. The field is, in a sense, both blessed and cursed because of its deep roots in history and tradition."[1]

1. James 1954, 21.

Cat. 195

True China shape cup and saucer, plate, and teapot with Lute Song pattern, ca. 1958–59. Attributed to Charles Murphy, designer; Red Wing Pottery, Red Wing, Minn., maker. Earthenware with painted decoration; plate: h. ⅞ in. (2.2 cm), diam. 10¼ in. (26 cm). Teapot and cup unmarked. Plate marked: true | china | by | RED | WING | U.S.A. | hand painted | 120. Saucer marked: same except 349 replaces 120. Dallas Museum of Art, 20th-Century Design Fund, 1995.110.1–2, 1996.170.

When *Crockery and Glass Journal* reported the introduction of *Lute Song* in July 1959, it noted that the surface decoration featuring lutes and calligraphy was "suggestive of the Orient." It also commented on how much the bowl profile of the *True China* shape range resembled Asian rice bowls. Originally a five-piece place setting cost $6.50, while a forty-five-piece service for eight cost $64.95.[1] The *True China* shape came in all-white and seven surface patterns, including *Lute Song*.[2]

1. "New Products: A Touch of the Orient," *CGJ* 156:1 (July 1959): 94; "Lute Song" (Red Wing sales brochure, 1963).
2. Reiss 1997, 30–31.

Cat. 196

Tamac tableware, ca. 1946. Tamac, Inc., Perry, Okla. Earthenware; tumbler: h. 2½ in. (6.4 cm), w. 4⅛ in. (10.5 cm), d. 3½ in. (8.9 cm). Salt and pepper shakers unmarked. Others marked: *Tamac* | PERRY, OKLA. | U. S. A. Dallas Museum of Art, General Acquisitions Fund, 1988.46.1–7.

The undulating shapes of *Tamac* were avant-garde in the 1940s. Produced in *Avocado* (green), *Frosty Fudge* (brown), *Frosty Pine* (dark green), *Raspberry* (violet), and cream glazes, this asymmetrical ware was probably accepted by the public because it was intended for casual dining, especially out of doors. Period advertising material notes that several forms were specifically designed for use at barbecues, including the illustrated cup and a large divided plate. Apparently *Tamac* was in production until the pottery closed in 1972.[1]

1. Bess 1995, 73–82; and "Tamac" (sales brochure).

Cat. 197

Conversation shape plate with *Daylily* pattern and salad plate and coffeepot with *Magnolia* pattern, 1949. Walter Dorwin Teague and Doris Coutant, shape designers; Taylor, Smith & Taylor Company, East Liverpool, Ohio, maker. Earthenware with printed decoration; plate: h. ¾ in. (2 cm), w. 11 in. (28 cm), d. 10⅜ in. (26.4 cm). Plate marked: TAYLOR SMITH TAYLOR / U.S.A. / 12-50 (date code for 1950) / CONVERSATION [in a ribbon] / 3 / DESIGNED BY / WALTER DORWIN TEAGUE and DAYLILY / PATTERN. Salad plate marked: same except date code, which is illegible, and number 1 instead of 3. Coffeepot marked: same except date code 10-50 and number 2. Neither the salad plate nor the coffeepot have pattern names. Dallas Museum of Art: gift of Ellen and Bert Denker (plates), 1996.162, 1996.163; 20th-Century Design Fund (coffeepot), 1996.132.

Although the famous industrial designer Walter Dorwin Teague is credited with designing the *Conversation* shape, initial notices state that Taylor, Smith & Taylor's staff designer Doris Coutant "worked closely with the Teague organization in developing the new wares." Initially the shape was released with at least fifteen surface patterns. *Cockerel* and *Oakleaf* were said to be formal, while *Meadowtree*, *Autumn Leaves*, and *Prairie Chicken* were "adaptable to any informal occasion."[1] In an ad for *Daylily*, the decoration of all the patterns was noted as "styled in the 'Teague' manner," suggesting that the motifs were created outside Teague's office.[2] The line received favorable reviews and was featured in the *Studio Year Book* for 1951–52.[3]

1. "Teague Designs New Ware for Taylor Smith & Taylor," *Ceramic Age* (July 1950): 13.
2. *CGJ* 147:6 (Dec. 1950): 70.
3. Holme and Frost 1952, 98, 103.

Cat. 198

Free Form shape tableware with *Primitive* pattern, 1955. Viktor Schreckengost, designer; Salem China Company, Salem, Ohio, maker. Earthenware with decal decoration; platter: h. 1⅝ in. (4.1 cm), w. 14⅛ in. (35.9 cm), d. 11⅜ in. (28.9 cm). Platter, teapot, and gravy boat marked: free·form / by / Salem [in outline of a plate beside a cup] / U.S.A. / Patented / ovenproof / primitive. Cup and creamer marked: Salem [in outline of a plate beside a cup]. Saucer and plate marked: free·form / by / Salem [in outline of a plate beside a cup] / Pat. Pend. / primitive / [two stars] 55U. Salt and pepper shakers unmarked. Dallas Museum of Art, gift of Viktor Schreckengost, T42115.

With its tripod supports and zoomorphic characteristics, *Free Form* was one of the most radical of all twentieth-century tableware shapes. It was available with a wide range of patterns, many rather conservative. According to Viktor Schreckengost, Salem China hoped that *Primitive*, which was based on prehistoric cave paintings, would appeal to men, but the pottery discovered that it was difficult to entice males to purchase tableware no matter how masculine the motif.[1]

1. V. Schreckengost interview 1995.

Cat. 199

All pieces: Josiah Wedgwood & Sons, Barlaston, England, maker; Josiah Wedgwood & Sons, New York, importer.

Globe shape coffeepot and sugar bowl with *Wildflower* pattern, ca. 1932. Norman Wilson, shape designer; Victor Skellern, pattern designer. Bone china with printed and gilded decoration. Both marked: [image of Portland Vase] / WEDGWOOD / BONE CHINA / MADE IN ENGLAND / WILDFLOWER. Coffeepot also marked: W D 3999 (pattern number). Sugar bowl also marked: W D 3998 (pattern number). Dallas Museum of Art, gift of George Roland in memory of Annabelle and Charles Thomas Roland,1997.218.1, .3.

Pear shape cup and saucer and no. 129 shape creamer with *Wildflower* pattern, ca. 1820. Josiah Wedgwood I, shape designer; Victor Skellern, pattern designer. Bone china with printed and gilded decoration. All marked: [image of Portland Vase] / WEDGWOOD / BONE CHINA / MADE IN ENGLAND / WILDFLOWER. Cup and saucer also marked: W D 3997 (pattern number). Creamer also marked: W D 3998 (pattern number). Dallas Museum of Art, gift of George Roland in memory of Annabelle and Charles Thomas Roland, 1997.218.2, .4.

Although marketing efforts in the 1940s placed the origin of the no. 129 shape as early as 1774, it does not appear in the shape books until 1820. The *Wildflower* pattern was introduced in 1945, employing ground colors called *Margaret Rose Pink* (named for H.R.H. Princess Margaret), *Lemon Yellow*, and *Celadon*.

Lincoln shape plate with *Josephine* pattern, ca. 1915. Bone china with printed and gilded decoration; h. 1 in. (2.5 cm), diam. 10⅝ in. (27 cm). Marked: [image of Portland Vase] / WEDGWOOD / BONE CHINA / MADE IN ENGLAND / W 3927 (pattern number). Dallas Museum of Art, gift of George Roland in memory of Annabelle and Charles Thomas Roland, 1997.228.1.

The ivy print for this pattern, introduced in 1943, is the same as that for the *Napoleon Ivy*

pattern, which was originally ordered by the British government in 1815 as a gift to Napoleon for his use in exile on the island of Elba.

These two patterns show the versatility of the Wedgwood design department headed by Victor Skellern (art director, 1934–66) after World War II. Combining old shapes and patterns with new color combinations, the company maintained a fresh but traditional look in the American market. Both the *Pear* and the no. 129 shapes as well as the ivy print for the *Josephine* pattern were among the earliest Wedgwood designs, but the delicate pastel ground colors were newly created during the war to appeal to the American fashion for color-coordinated linens and china, particularly popular on the West Coast.[1] Both patterns were discontinued in 1961.

1. "Report on Visit to America by Victor Skellern" [1949], Wedgwood Archives.

Cat. 200

Contempri shape coffeepot with *Hopscotch* pattern and platter with *Bauble* pattern, 1958. Paul McCobb, designer; unknown factory, Nagoya, Japan, maker; Jackson International, Pelham, N.Y, importer. Porcelain with printed decoration, coffeepot: h. 11¼ in. (28.6 cm), w. 9 in. (22.9 cm), d. 6½ in. (16.5 cm). Coffeepot marked: HOPSCOTCH / CONTEMPRI / designed by Paul McCobb Japan / JACKSON INTERNATIONALE. Platter marked: same except pattern name BAUBLE. Dallas Museum of Art: gift of the Friends of the Decorative Arts' 1991 Twilight Zone Trip (coffeepot), 1991.87; gift of David T. Owsley (platter), 1997.37.

The Jackson Vitrified China Company was founded in Falls Creek, Pennsylvania, in 1917. In 1946 Robert R. Distillator purchased the company and expanded its production, and by the mid-1950s Royal Jackson China was being made at the Falls Creek plant, as well as at a plant in Pelham, New York. A decorating shop was also operated in the Bronx until it was destroyed by fire in 1967. During the 1950s two shape ranges were offered—*Parisienne* and *Prize Design*. The latter was designed by George Ivers.[1]

Jackson International grew out of Jackson Vitrified China Company. Evidently founded as a subsidiary in the late 1950s, Jackson International imported and distributed ceramics and glass from several foreign countries. The *Contempri* line was made exclusively in Japan for Jackson. When introduced to the market in 1959, Paul McCobb's shapes and decorations, with their angular sides and brightly colored geometric patterning, must have seemed very avant-garde. Originally the ware was available in all-white and with seven patterns—*Eclipse*, *Spindle*, *Sticks*, *Sparkler*, *Frost*, *Straws*, and *Hopscotch* (illustrated). A forty-five-piece service for eight in any of these patterns cost $69.95. Following the success of *Contempri*, McCobb created a more formal line for Jackson called *Profile*.[2]

1. "Jackson China Ships New Design," *CGJ* 160:4 (Apr. 1957): 46; "The Fine Art of Dining" (Royal Jackson sales brochure, 1955?); Lehner 1988, 225–26; and McKee 1966, 36.
2. *CGJ* 164:2 (Feb. 1959): 24; 164:5 (May 1959): 2; "Paul McCobb Designs 'Contempri'" (Jackson International sales brochure, ca. 1959); GTR (21 Dec. 1964): 10.

Cat. 201

No. 1382 shape plate with *Butterflies* pattern and coffeepot, ca. 1931. Herman Gretsch, shape designer; Jean Luce, pattern designer; Porzellanfabrik Arzberg, Arzberg, Germany, maker; H. E. Lauffer Company, New York, importer. Porcelain with printed decoration; plate: h. 1 in. (2.5 cm), diam. 10⅛ in. (25.7 cm). Coffeepot marked: *Arzberg | 153 | MADE IN GERMANY*. Plate marked: *Porzellanfabrik Arzberg | Arzberg (Bayern) | JEAN [two conjoined Ls] LUCE [Luce mark within a rectangle] | MADE IN GERMANY*. Dallas Museum of Art, 20th-Century Design Fund, T42498.

Arzberg's no. 1382 is one of the most famous tableware shapes of the twentieth century. Since its introduction in the fall of 1931, it has never been out of production.[1] While its reductionist forms and lack of ornament made it popular in Europe in the prewar years, the same qualities made it unsuitable for the American market, where color and pattern were highly prized.

After World War II some German factories tried to sell their earlier functionalist shapes in the United States. In the early 1950s, for example, Fraser's in California advertised that it was importing from Berlin's Staatliche Porzellanmanufaktur the well-known *Urbino* shape (1931).[2] A few years earlier H. E. Lauffer Company had begun importing Arzberg's no. 1382 shape in classic all-white. By 1952 Lauffer and Arzberg were trying to increase sales in the United States by adding to the line both representational and abstract surface patterns, which were designed by the famous Parisian ceramics designer Jean Luce and "young American designers."[3] Luce designed at least six of the original patterns, including *Butterflies*. By 1955 more patterns had been added, as well as bold two-tone color schemes, on the hollowware.[4]

1. For an extensive discussion of this shape, see Bröhan et al. 1993, vol. 1, 35–47, 50–51.
2. *CGJ* 151:4 (Oct. 1952): 65; and 151:3 (Sept. 1952): 16.
3. *CGJ* 151:1 (July 1952): 33–34.
4. *CGJ* 155:1 (Jan. 1955): 13, 53.

Cat. 202

Both pieces: ca. 1969. Charles Solt and the Lenox Design Department, designers; Lenox China, Trenton, maker. Porcelain with printed and gilded decoration.

Innovation shape plate with *Fantasies* pattern. Marked: *fantasies | © | LENOX | ® | MADE IN U.S.A. [all in a square]*. Dallas Museum of Art, 20th-Century Design Fund, 1995.163.

The *Innovation* shape was designed about 1969. The *Fantasies* pattern was introduced in 1971 and was available for six years.

Innovation shape coffeepot with *Firesong* pattern. H. 11 in. (27.9 cm), w. 9 in. (22.9 cm), d. 4½ in. (11.4 cm). Marked: *firesong | © | LENOX | ® | MADE IN U.S.A. [all in a square]*. Dallas Museum of Art, 20th-Century Design Fund, 1996.125.

The *Firesong* pattern was available from 1970 to 1979. When introduced it retailed for $39.95 for a five-piece place setting.[1]

The *Innovation* shape range, introduced late in 1969, was a major departure from Lenox's trademark traditional style. The line never sold well, and by the late 1970s production of it had virtually ceased except for the creation of replacement pieces. The vibrantly colorful and bold patterns, some reminiscent of the work of artist Peter Max, were remarkably chic for the era, but such profound stylishness did not have a large market, especially in expensive goods that were costly to replace when styles changed. The profile of the plate, with a generous surface and broad outflaring rim, was retained for Lenox's next shape range—*Temperware*.

1. "Tabletoppers' Mood-Molders," GTR (Apr. 1970): 19.

Cat. 203

All pieces: stoneware with painted decoration. Marked: *DENBY | MADE IN | ENGLAND*.

Plate with *Potter's Wheel* pattern, 1973. David Yorath, designer; Denbyware Limited, Denby, England, maker; Denby, Ltd. (formerly Millard-Norman), Cincinnati, importer. Dallas Museum of Art, gift of George Roland in memory of Annabelle and Charles Thomas Roland, 1997.205.

Modeled to look like studio pottery, *Potter's Wheel* appealed to the early 1970s taste for informality and handicraft. The pattern featured earth tones with four color choices for the painted center—rust, blue, green, or yellow, as in this example.

Coffee server with *Arabesque* pattern, 1962–63. Gill Pemberton, designer; Joseph Bourne & Son, Denby, England, maker; Millard-Norman, Cincinnati, importer. H. 12½ in. (31.8 cm), w. 8⅝ in. (22 cm), d. 5⅝ in. (14.3 cm). Dallas Museum of Art, gift of George Roland in memory of Annabelle and Charles Thomas Roland, 1997.206.

Gill Pemberton was the designer most responsible for the bold look of Denby tableware throughout the 1960s. Working closely with potters in the factory and decorator Trish Seal, Pemberton came up with innovative shapes and bold patterns that perfectly suited the vogue for informal but substantial stoneware designs. Her design for *Arabesque*, which was originally called *Samarkand* until Portmeirion Potteries produced a line with that name, was inspired by the traditional gold and red painted decoration Pemberton saw on a visit to the Soviet Union.[1]

1. Hopwood and Hopwood 1997, 72.

Cat. 204

Fine shape coffeepot with *Sienna* pattern, 1962. David Queensberry and Roy Midwinter, shape designers; Jessie Tait, surface designer; W. R. Midwinter, Burslem, England, maker; Meakin-Midwinter, New York, importer. Earthenware with printed decoration. Marked: *Midwinter | FINE TABLEWARES | STAFFORDSHIRE ENGLAND | REGD. 909769*. Dallas Museum of Art, gift of George Roland in memory of Annabelle and Charles Thomas Roland, 1997.66.

The form of this coffeepot was inspired by cylindrical eighteenth-century creamware shapes, which were well suited to applied surface decoration. The shape was also likened to a milk churn. Immediately perceived as fresh and modern by critics, the *Fine* shape represented a rejection of the compound curves of shapes from the 1950s and was among the first designs in what would become a standard form in the 1960s. The *Sienna* pattern, printed in popular earth tones of the period, was probably the best selling of many patterns designed by Jessie Tait for this shape and was in production until 1978.[1]

Coupe Savoy shape plate from the *Variations on a Geometric Theme* series, 1953. Norman Makinson, shape designer; Eduardo Paolozzi and Brian Cour, pattern designers; Josiah Wedgwood & Sons, Barlaston, England, maker. Bone china with printed and gilded decoration; h. ¾ in. (1.9 cm), diam. 10½ in. (26.7 cm). Marked: *[image of a Portland vase] | WEDGWOOD | Bone China | MADE IN ENGLAND | Variations on a Geometric Theme | A Limited Edition of 200 sets of six plates | Eduardo Paolozzi*. Dallas Museum of Art, 20th-Century Design Fund, 1998.55.1.

In 1963 David Queensberry formed a consulting partnership with Martin Hunt, one of his students at the Royal College of Art. Queensberry-Hunt developed into one of the most prolific and well-known industrial design firms in Great Britain during the late 1960s, employing many talented young designers. Queensbury-Hunt championed modern design during this period and was responsible for a number of critically acclaimed but nonetheless commercially doomed projects. One of these projects was a series of six limited-edition plates with designs adapted by Queensbury-Hunt designer Brian Cour from a print by the Scottish artist and sculptor Eduardo Paolozzi titled *Illumination and the Eye* (1966).[2] Drawing from the fascination with optical effects embodied in the Op Art movement, these plates were an expensive venture for Wedgwood, the company that made them. Designed ca. 1968–69, the edition was limited to 200 sets consisting of six designs in a specially produced bright pink acrylic box.

Coffeepot with *Acapulco* pattern, ca. 1969. Villeroy & Boch, Mettlach, Germany, and Septfontaines, Luxembourg, makers; Ceramar, New York, importer. Porcelain with printed decoration. Marked: • ANCIENNE MANUFACTURE IMPERIALE ET ROYALE FONDEE EN 1767 • | VILLEROY & BOCH | SEPTFONTAINES [*within a figural reserve*] | *Vitro–Porcelaine* | »*Acapulco*« | *D'après un dessin original* | *mexicain* | MADE IN LUXEMBOURG. Dallas Museum of Art, 20th-Century Design Fund, T42566.

Brightly colored patterns of Mexican, Spanish, South American, and Middle Eastern motifs saw a resurgence in the 1960s with nearly every manufacturer of casual tableware producing its own version. Villeroy & Boch's *Acapulco*, along with the related patterns *Izmir* and *Cadiz*, was among the boldest of these designs.

The cylindrical shape range with its vibrant surface patterns was especially designed to be stackable. The fact that colorful patterns were some of Villeroy & Boch's best sellers prompted the firm to introduce enameled cookware with matching ornament in the 1970s. That product was produced by the subcontractor ASTA in Austria and also imported into the United States by Ceramar.[3]

1. Jenkins 1997, 32–33.
2. Hanover 1961.
3. "Acapulco" (Villeroy & Boch sales brochure, 1977); "Enameled Steel Cookware" sales brochure and price list (Ceramar, ca. 1977); "Villeroy & Boch: Why the Time Is Now," *GTR* (July 1973): 36.

Cat. 205
Can shape creamer, sugar bowl, and coffeepot with *Hyde Park* pattern, 1959. Susie Cooper, designer; Susie Cooper China, Longton, England, maker; Messrs. Fondeville & Co., New York, importer. Bone china with printed and gilded decoration; coffeepot: h. 8 in. (20.3 cm), w. 8¼ in. (21 cm), d. 4⅜ in. (11.1 cm). All marked: *Susie Cooper* | * | BONE CHINA | ENGLAND | C912 (pattern number) | HYDE PARK. Dallas Museum of Art, gift of George Roland in memory of Annabelle and Charles Thomas Roland, 1997.221.1–3.

The *Can* shape was the most successful of Susie Cooper's postwar shape designs and is still in production today.[1] The simple, linear decoration in brown and black appealed to the modern taste for clean vertical surface patterns in the early 1960s but retained a traditional look with its leaf motif that is both realistic and stylized.

Can shape cup and saucer with *Diablo* pattern, 1959. Susie Cooper, designer; Susie Cooper China for Josiah Wedgwood & Sons, Longton, England, maker; Josiah Wedgwood & Sons, New York, importer. Bone china with printed decoration. Cup marked: FINE BONE CHINA | 'DIABLO' C2150 (pattern number) | *Susie Cooper* | MEMBER OF THE | WEDGWOOD GROUP | ENGLAND. Saucer marked: [*image of Portland Vase*] | WEDGWOOD | *Bone China* | *Made in England* | *Susie Cooper Design*. Dallas Museum of Art, gift of George Roland in memory of Annabelle and Charles Thomas Roland, 1997.227.

The *Diablo* pattern of 1969 owes its inspiration to the Op Art movement of the mid-1960s, which was characterized by optical effects that seem to distort reality. In this example, the superimposed teardrop shapes in different but related colors make the surface appear dynamic.[2] Such fashion-conscious design had little staying power, and the pattern was discontinued in 1976 due to poor sales.

1. Eatwell 1987, 72.
2. For more on the influence of Op Art on industrial design, see Jackson 1998, 83–98.

Cat. 206
Dessert plate with *The Return* pattern from the *Man in Space* series, 1966. Piero Fornasetti, pattern designer; probably Richard-Ginori, Milan, Italy, maker. Porcelain with printed decoration; h. 1 in. (2.5 cm), diam. 9½ in. (24.1 cm). Marked: *Serie* | *de six assiettes* | *specialement dessinees* | *par Fornasetti* | *Pour* | [*within a rectangle*] PARIS MATCH | *Decembre* | *mille neuf cent soixante six* | L'HOMME DANS L'ESPACE | 11 *Le Retour* | © *Copyright Paris Match*. Dallas Museum of Art, gift of Michael L. Rosenberg, 1996.69.3.

Working in Milan, Italy, throughout his career, Piero Fornasetti was essentially a graphic artist whose style grew out of an early rejection of abstract decoration in favor of a kind of hyper-realism better known as surrealism. Fornasetti used repetition in surface patterning and thematic discourse to explore visual realities. Form was subjugated to pattern as Fornasetti cloaked every object imaginable with images from the mundane to the sublime. His decorative themes were drawn from every corner of the world, both the natural and the manmade—including architecture, vegetables, musical instruments, humanity, and science, to name but a few.[1]

In this series of six dessert plates, Fornasetti conveys the awesome images of mankind's venture into space, from liftoff to the return depicted here. Available in black-and-white or with added red-orange tinting to simulate the fire of the rockets, Fornasetti's interpretation of this much-anticipated human event was intended for the fashionable consumer—including even Jacqueline Kennedy Onassis, who owned this plate and its mates in the series.[2]

1. For a comprehensive retrospective of Fornasetti's career, see Mauriès 1991.
2. For images of other plates in the series, see "The Estate of Jacqueline Kennedy Onassis" (Sotheby's, New York, sale catalogue no. 6834), lots 925 and 926. Five black-and-white plates are owned by the Dallas Museum of Art, and five in black and orange are owned by the Sixth Floor Museum in Dallas. Two plates, one from each matched set, were apparently lost or broken before the death of Jacqueline Onassis in 1994.

Cat. 207
Chromatics tableware, 1970. Gerald Gulotta, shape designer; Jack Prince, pattern designer; Porzellanfabrik Arzberg, Arzberg, Germany, maker; Block China Company, New York, importer. Porcelain with printed decoration. Variously marked: BLOCK [*with a bee inside the O*] | BLUE GREEN | CHROMATICS [*all within dish-shaped logos*] | GERMANY | [*various numerical marks*]. Dallas Museum of Art, gift of Gerald Gulotta, T42528.1–23, .25–32.

Chromatics placemat, 1970. Jack Prince, pattern designer; Unknown factory, Finland, maker; Block China Company, New York, importer. Cotton with dyed and woven decoration. Labeled: BLOCK | BLUE GREEN | CHROMATICS [*all within dish-shaped logos*] | 100% LINEN | © | HANDWOVEN•FINLAND | 20 [*within a box*] and BLOCK | CHROMATICS [*all within dish-shaped logos*] | 100% LINEN | 20 [*within a box*] | HANDWOVEN–FINLAND. Dallas Museum of Art, gift of Gerald Gulotta, T42529.1.

Chromatics flatware, 1970. Gerald Gulotta, designer; La Industrial Mondragonesa, Mondragon, Spain, maker; Block China Company, New York, importer. Stainless steel. All marked: BLOCK SPAIN [*image of a griffin and arrow*]. Dallas Museum of Art, gift of Gerald Gulotta, T42545.1–5.

Chromatics goblet, 1970. Gerald Gulotta, shape designer; Jack Prince, color consultant; Cristals de Alcobaca, Alcobaca, Portugal, maker; Block China Company, New York, importer. Glass; h. 4½ in. (11.4 cm), diam. 3¾ in. (9.5 cm). Unmarked. Dallas Museum of Art, gift of Gerald Gulotta, T42553.

The fashion for stackable dishes surfaced in the mid-1960s but was never more fully developed than in Gerald Gulotta and Jack Prince's *Chromatics* tableware for Block China, designed in 1970 and introduced in January

1971. The ceramic and glass components form stacking units of alternating convex and concave shapes. In this way they fit snugly on a shelf not only vertically but side by side as well. Gulotta's use of alternating curves first appeared in his *España* shape of 1968, providing a decorative unifying element to otherwise individual components (see cat. 127). In *Chromatics* he took this element a step further. Individual form is superseded by the overriding need for stackability, so each piece must conform first to a common shape regardless of volume. Alternating convex and concave vertical walls provide the essential means to achieve that concept.

This rational approach was further exploited through Prince's use of alternating colors to demarcate the individual forms in a stack. The result was a veritable symphonic ensemble of color, shape, and size unlike any tableware design that had come before. Ironically, the colors that inspired the name of the line and gave rhythm and life to the shape ultimately led to its demise. Consumer concern over the use of toxic chemicals to produce bright, saturated colors and glazes on porcelain resulted in the perception that *Chromatics* and other brightly colored ceramic tableware were dangerous to use. A law was even passed in California prohibiting the use of chromium and other toxic chemicals in the production of ceramics, although it was never proven that anyone could be harmed from eating off plates decorated with glazes and decals made from these materials.[1] Since perception almost always overrules reality in commercial markets, sales plummeted. Although an attempt was made to add more conventional surface patterns to the line, the effort failed to change public opinion, forcing Block China to discontinue the line in 1973.[2]

1. Block interview 1998.
2. Gerald Gulotta, conversation with Stephen Harrison, 9 Oct. 1999.

Cat. 208
Studio Potter shape chop plate and coffeepot with *Wild Poppy* pattern, ca. 1969–71. John Karresh, shape designer; Elaine Masnick, pattern designer; Metlox Potteries, Manhattan Beach, Calif., maker. Earthenware with printed decoration; coffeepot: h. 14 in. (35.6 cm), w. 7⅞ in. (20 cm), d. 4½ in. (11.4 cm). Chop plate marked: POPPY TRAIL / BY / METLOX / MADE IN CALIFORNIA / 1074. Coffeepot unmarked. Anonymous collection (chop plate); Dallas Museum of Art, 20th-Century Design Fund (coffeepot), 1997.186.

The *Studio Potter* shape was initially introduced as a coupe but was later redesigned with a slight rim around the flatware.[1] Certain shapes were also modified at that time, including this chop plate. Originally an oval shape, the large platter was changed to a

round form in 1971. *Wild Poppy*, with its distinctive bright orange and yellow colors, was introduced on the shape in 1972, and a version with white poppies called *Matilija* came in 1974. A forty-five-piece set originally sold for $169.95.[2]

1. Gibbs 1995, 123–34.
2. GTR (Feb. 1972): 18.

Afterword

Cat. 209
Millennium shape plates with *Red Graphics* and *Black Graphics* patterns, ca. 1983. Helena Uglav, designer; unknown factory, Japan, maker; Mikasa, Secaucus, N.J., importer. Porcelain with printed decoration; left plate: h. ¾ in. (1.8 cm), diam. 10¾ in. (27.3 cm). Left plate marked: *Millennium / VA071 • Red Graphics • Japan / by / Helena Uglav / for Mikasa.* Right plate marked: same except pattern number VA070. Dallas Museum of Art, gift of David T. Owsley, 1997.32, 1997.31.

These plates reflect how fashion-oriented Mikasa had become by 1980. The striking patterns, colors, and superimposed geometric shapes owe much to the Memphis movement founded in Milan in 1981. Led by the architect Ettore Sottsas, Memphis designs were extremely radical when first introduced. A number of tableware producers and their designers, including Mikasa and Uglav, exploited the fashion for Memphis-style design while it was in vogue during the mid-1980s.

Abbreviations for Periodicals

BH&G: *Better Homes and Gardens*

CGJ: *Crockery and Glass Journal*

CGL: *China, Glass, and Lamps*

CI: *Ceramic Industry*

GTR: *Gift and Tableware Reporter*

HB: *House Beautiful*

LHJ: *Ladies' Home Journal*

MP: *Modern Plastics*

PGBS: *Pottery, Glass and Brass Salesman*

Schaulade: *Die Schaulade* (The Showcase; Bamberg, Germany)

Archival Sources

Fostoria Archives: Fostoria Glass Company Archives, Ohio Historical Society, Columbus, Ohio

Heisey Archives: A. H. Heisey & Co. Archives, National Heisey Glass Museum, Newark, Ohio

Lenox Archives: Lenox China Archives, Lenox China, Lawrenceville, N.J.

Minton Archives: Minton, Ltd., Archives, Royal Doulton Limited, Stoke-upon-Trent, England

Spode Archives: Spode Museum, Royal Worcester Spode Limited, Stoke-upon-Trent, England

Waterford Archives: Waterford Crystal Archives, Waterford Crystal Limited, Waterford, Ireland

Wedgwood Archives: Wedgwood Museum Archives, Josiah Wedgwood & Sons, Barlaston, England

Adams 1950
Adams, Charlotte. *Home Entertaining: A Complete Guide.* New York: Crown Publishers, 1950.

Allen 1919
Allen, Lucy G. *Table Service.* 1915. Reprint, Boston: Little, Brown, 1919.

Allen 1941
Allen, Lucy G. *A Book of Hors d'Oeuvre.* Boston: Little, Brown, 1941.

Altman and Altman 1969
Altman, Violet, and Seymour Altman. *The Book of Buffalo Pottery.* New York: Crown Publishers, 1969.

Ames 1992
Ames, Kenneth L. *Death in the Dining Room and Other Tales of Victorian Culture.* Philadelphia: Temple University Press, 1992.

Anderson 1938
Anderson, W. H. Locke. "The History of the U.S. Potters Association, 'The Saga of American Pottery.'" *Pottery, Glass and Brass Salesman* (Dec. 1938): 14–15, 28–29, 33.

Anderson 1997
Anderson, Jean. *The American Century Cookbook: The Most Popular Recipes of the Twentieth Century.* New York: Clarkson Potter, 1997.

Anderson interview 1997
Anderson, Winslow. Interview by Ellen P. Denker, Milton, W. Va., 19 Aug. 1997.

Asbury 1927
Asbury, Herbert. "Professor Jerry Thomas." *The American Mercury* 12:48 (Dec. 1927): 421–30.

Baccarat 1995
Baccarat Glassware. *Baccarat: Stemware Replacement.* Paris, 1995.

Barber 1909
Barber, Edwin Atlee. *The Pottery and Porcelain of the United States: An Historical Review of American Ceramic Art from the Earliest Times to the Present Day.* 3rd ed. New York: G. P. Putnam's Sons, 1909.

Barlow and Kaiser 1983
Barlow, Raymond E., and Joan E. Kaiser. *The Glass Industry in Sandwich.* Vol. 4. Windham, N.H.: Barlow-Kaiser Publishing, 1983.

Batkin 1982
Batkin, Maureen. *Wedgwood Ceramics, 1846–1959: A New Appraisal.* London: Richard Dennis, 1982.

Battersby 1998
Battersby, Martin. *The Decorative Twenties.* New York: Whitney Library of Design, 1998.

Beard and Beard 1928
Beard, Charles A., and Mary R. Beard. *The Rise of American Civilization.* New York: Macmillan, 1928.

Bederman 1995
Bederman, Gail. *Manliness and Civilization: A Cultural History of Gender and Race in the United States, 1880–1917.* Chicago: University of Chicago Press, 1995.

Beecher 1858
Beecher, Catherine. *Miss Beecher's Domestic Receipt Book; Designed as a Supplement to Her Treatise on Domestic Economy.* 3rd ed. New York: Harper and Brothers, 1858.

Berolzheimer 1949
Berolzheimer, Ruth, ed. *500 Snacks.* Chicago: Consolidated Book Publishers, 1949.

Bess and Bess 1995
Bess, Phyllis, and Tom Bess. *Frankoma and Other Oklahoma Potteries.* Atglen, Pa.: Schiffer Publishing, 1995.

Bivins 1972
Bivins, John, Jr. *The Moravian Potters in North Carolina.* Chapel Hill, N.C.: University of North Carolina Press, 1972.

Blaszczyk 1984
Blaszczyk, Regina Lee. "Ceramics and the Sot-Weed Factor: The China Market in a Tobacco Economy." *Winterthur Portfolio* 19:1 (spring 1984): 7–20.

Blaszczyk 1987
Blaszczyk, Regina Lee. "Product Development in the American Tableware Industry, 1920–1945." Master's thesis, George Washington University, 1987.

Blaszczyk 1994
Blaszczyk, Regina Lee. "The Aesthetic Moment: China Decorators, Consumer Demand, and Technological Change in the American Pottery Industry, 1865–1900." *Winterthur Portfolio* 29:2–3 (summer/autumn 1994): 121–53.

Blaszczyk 1995
Blaszczyk, Regina Lee. "Imagining Consumers: Manufacturers and Markets in Ceramics and Glass, 1865–1965." Ph.D. diss., University of Delaware, 1995.

Block interview 1998
Block, Robert, founding partner, Block China Corporation, New York. Interview by Charles L. Venable, New York, 21 Jan. 1998.

Bosker 1996
Bosker, Gideon. *Patio Daddy-O*. San Francisco: Chronicle Books, 1996.

Bracken 1960
Bracken, Peg. *I Hate to Cook Book: More Than 180 Quick and Easy Recipes*. Greenwich, Conn.: Fawcett, 1960.

Brandimarte 1991
Brandimarte, Cynthia A. "Japanese Novelty Stores." *Winterthur Portfolio* 26:1 (spring 1991): 1–16.

Bredehoft 1986
Bredehoft, Neila. *The Collector's Encyclopedia of Heisey Glass, 1925–1938*. Paducah, Ky.: Collector Books, 1986.

Brenner 1998
Brenner, Robert. *Depression Glass for Collectors*. Atglen, Pa.: Schiffer Publishing, 1998.

Bröhan et al. 1993
Bröhan, Karl H., Dieter Högermann, and Reto Niggl. *Porzellan: Kunst und Design, 1889–1939, vom Jugendstil zum Funktionalismus*. 2 vols. Berlin: Bröhan-Museum, 1993.

Bröhan and Berg 1994
Bröhan, Torsten, and Thomas Berg. *Avant-garde Design, 1880–1930*. Cologne: Taschen, 1994.

Bryan interview 1997
Bryan, Sir Arthur, former chairman, Josiah Wedgwood & Sons, Waterford Wedgwood. Interview by Stephen G. Harrison, Barlaston, England, 1 May 1997.

Buckley 1990
Buckley, Cheryl. *Potters and Paintresses: Women Designers in the Pottery Industry, 1870–1955*. London: Women's Press, 1990.

Buddensieg 1984
Buddensieg, Tilmann. *Ceramiche della Repubblica di Weimar*. Milan: Electa Editrice, 1984.

Bushman 1992
Bushman, Richard L. *The Refinement of America: Persons, Houses, Cities*. New York: Alfred A. Knopf, 1992.

Cameron 1986
Cameron, Elisabeth. *Encyclopedia of Pottery and Porcelain, 1800–1960*. New York: Facts on File Publications, 1986.

Campbell Soup 1968
Campbell Soup Company. *Easy Ways to Delicious Meals: 465 Quick-to-Fix Recipes Using Campbell's Convenience Foods*. Camden, N.J., 1968.

Carson 1990
Carson, Barbara G. *Ambitious Appetites: Dining, Behavior, and Patterns of Consumption in Federal Washington*. Washington, D.C.: American Institute of Architects Press, 1990.

Caywood 1955
Caywood, Louis R. *Excavations at Green Spring Plantation*. Yorktown, Va.: Colonial National Historical Park, 1955.

Ceramic 1891
The Ceramic Art Co. . . . Potters and Decorators of Belleek China, Indian China, and Artists' Specialties. Trenton, 1891.

Child 1832
Child, Lydia Maria. *The American Frugal Housewife*. 12th ed. Boston: Applaud Books, 1832.

Chipman 1992
Chipman, Jack. *Collector's Encyclopedia of California Pottery*. Paducah, Ky.: Collector Books, 1992.

Chipman 1998
Chipman, Jack. *Collector's Encyclopedia of Bauer Pottery*. Paducah, Ky.: Collector Books, 1998.

Clark 1986
Clark, Clifford E., Jr. *The American Family Home, 1800–1960*. Chapel Hill, N.C.: University of North Carolina Press, 1986.

Collard 1967
Collard, Elizabeth. *Nineteenth-Century Pottery and Porcelain in Canada*. Montreal: McGill University Press, 1967.

Conti et al. 1995
Conti, Steve, A. DeWayne Bethany, and Bill Seay. *Collector's Encyclopedia of Sascha Brastoff*. Paducah, Ky.: Collector Books, 1995.

Copeland 1989
Copeland, Robert. Unpublished manuscript, 1989.

Copeland 1997
Copeland, Robert. *Spode and Copeland Marks and Other Relevant Intelligence*. 2nd ed. London: Studio Vista, 1997.

Copeland interview 1996
Copeland, Robert, former director, W. T. Copeland & Sons. Interview by Charles L. Venable, Stoke-upon-Trent, England, 8 Oct. 1996.

Copeland interview 1997
Copeland, Robert, former director, W. T. Copeland & Sons. Interview by Stephen G. Harrison and Charles L. Venable, Stoke-upon-Trent, England, 20 Apr. 1997.

Copeland interview 1998
Copeland, Robert, former director, W. T. Copeland & Sons. Interview by Stephen G. Harrison, Stoke-upon-Trent, England, 30 Feb. 1998.

Corbitt 1957
Corbitt, Helen. *Helen Corbitt's Cookbook*. Cambridge, Mass.: Riverside Press, 1957.

Cowan 1997
Cowan, Ruth Schwarz. *A Social History of American Technology*. New York: Oxford University Press, 1997.

CTE [1980?]
Center for Technological Education. *Belle Kogan Design, 1930–1972*. Israel, [1980?].

Cunningham 1982
Cunningham, Jo. *The Collector's Encyclopedia of American Dinnerware*. Paducah, Ky.: Collector Books, 1982.

Cunningham 1995
Cunningham, Jo. *The Best of Collectible Dinnerware*. Atglen, Pa.: Schiffer Publishing, 1995.

Cunningham 1998
Cunningham, Jo. *Homer Laughlin China: A Giant among Dishes, 1873–1939*. Atglen, Pa.: Schiffer Publishing, 1998.

Curtis 1972
Curtis, Phillip H. "The Production of Tucker Porcelain, 1826–1938: A Reevaluation." In *Ceramics in America*, edited by Ian M. G. Quimby, 339–74. Charlottesville, Va.: University Press of Virginia; Wilmington, Del.: Henry Francis du Pont Winterthur Museum, 1972.

d'Albis 1988
d'Albis, Jean. *Haviland*. Paris: Dessain et Tolra, 1988.

d'Albis and Romanet 1980
d'Albis, Jean, and Celeste Romanet. *La Porcelaine de Limoges*. Paris: Editions Sous le Vent, 1980.

Dale 1986
Dale, Sharon. *Frederick Hurten Rhead: An English Potter in America*. Erie, Pa.: Erie Art Museum, 1986.

Dansk 1994
Dansk Designs: 40th Anniversary, 1954–1994. Mount Kisco, N.Y., 1994.

Davies 1983
Davies, Karen. *At Home in Manhattan: Modern Decorative Arts, 1925 to the Depression.* New Haven, Conn.: Yale University Art Gallery, 1983.

Davis 1949
Davis, Pearce. *The Development of the American Glass Industry.* Cambridge, Mass.: Harvard University Press, 1949.

Dawes 1990
Dawes, Nicholas M. *Majolica.* New York: Crown Publishers, 1990.

Denker 1986
Denker, Ellen Paul. "Ceramics at the Crossroads: American Pottery at New York's Gateway, 1750–1900." *Staten Island Historian* 3:3–4 (winter–spring 1986): 21–36.

Denker 1988
Denker, Ellen Paul. "History of Lenox China." Typescript, 1988. Lenox Archives.

Denker 1989
Denker, Ellen Paul. *Lenox China: Celebrating a Century of Quality, 1889–1989.* Trenton, N.J.: Lenox China; New Jersey State Museum, 1989.

Denker and Denker 1984
Denker, Ellen Paul, and Bert R. Denker. "The Staffordshire of America." In *A Capital Place: The Story of Trenton,* edited by Mary Alice Quigley and David Collier, 56–67. Woodland Hills, Calif.: Windsor Publications; Trenton Historical Society, 1984.

Dennis 1995
Dennis, Richard. *Ravilious and Wedgwood: The Complete Designs of Eric Ravilious.* 2nd ed. London: Richard Dennis, 1995.

Detweiler 1982
Detweiler, Susan G. "French Porcelain on Federal Tables." *American Ceramic Circle Journal* 3 (1982): 87–110.

Diamond interview 1997
Diamond, Freda, former Libbey designer. Interview by Ellen Paul Denker, New York, 17 Jan. 1997.

Douglas 1972
Douglas, Mary. "Deciphering a Meal." *Daedalus* 101 (1972): 61–81.

Douglas 1973
Douglas, Mary. *Natural Symbols.* New York: Vintage Books, 1973.

Duke 1993
Duke, Harvey. *Stangl Pottery.* Radnor, Pa.: Wallace-Homestead Book Company, 1993.

Duke 1995
Duke, Harvey. *Official Price Guide to Pottery and Porcelain.* 8th ed. New York: House of Collectibles, 1995.

Eames 1977
Eames, Penelope. "Furniture in England, France, and the Netherlands from the Twelfth to the Fifteenth Century." *Furniture History* 13 (1977): 55–72.

Eatwell 1987
Eatwell, Ann. *Susie Cooper Productions.* London: Victoria and Albert Museum, 1987.

Eichler 1937
Eichler, Lillian. *The New Book of Etiquette.* Garden City, N.Y.: Garden City Publishing, 1937.

Eidelberg 1991
Eidelberg, Martin, ed. *Design 1935–1965: What Modern Was, Selections from the Liliane and David M. Stewart Collection.* New York: Harry N. Abrams, 1991.

Eige and Wilson 1987
Eige, Eason, and Rick Wilson. *Blenko Glass 1930–1953.* Marietta, Ohio: Antique Publications, 1987.

Elias 1978
Elias, Norbert. *The Civilizing Process: The History of Manners.* Translated by Edmund Jephcott. 1939. Reprint, New York: Urizen Books, 1978.

Ewins 1997
Ewins, Neil. "'Supplying the Present Wants of Our Yankee Cousins . . .': Staffordshire Ceramics and the American Market, 1775–1880." *Journal of Ceramic History* 15 (1997): 1–154.

Fahr-Becker 1995
Fahr-Becker, Gabriele. *Wiener Werkstaette, 1903–1932.* Cologne: Taschen, 1995.

Fairfield 1960
Fairfield, E. William. *Fire and Sand: The History of the Libbey-Owens Sheet Glass Company.* Toledo: Libbey-Owens-Ford Glass Company, 1960.

Farrar 1977
Farrar, Estelle Sinclaire. "The Master Engravers of Corning, New York." *Antiques* 107:4 (Oct. 1977): 726–31.

Fauster 1979
Fauster, Carl U. *Libbey Glass Since 1818: Pictorial History and Collector's Guide.* Toledo: Len Beach Press, 1979.

Feller 1988
Feller, John Q. *Dorflinger: American's Finest Glass, 1852–1921.* Marietta, Ohio: Antique Publications, 1988.

Fleming and Honour 1989
Fleming, John, and Hugh Honour. *The Penguin Dictionary of Decorative Arts.* New York: Viking, 1989.

Florence 1986
Florence, Gene. *Collector's Encyclopedia of Depression Glass.* Paducah, Ky.: Collector Books, 1986.

Florence 1995
Florence, Gene. *Elegant Glassware of the Depression Era.* Paducah, Ky.: Collector Books, 1995.

Florence 1996.
Florence, Gene. *Collectible Glassware from the '40s, '50s, '60s.* Paducah, Ky.: Collector Books, 1996.

Floyd interview 1998
Floyd, Robert, founding partner, Fitz and Floyd China. Interview by Stephen G. Harrison and Charles L. Venable, Montecito, Calif., 7 Feb. 1998.

Frelinghuysen 1986
Frelinghuysen, Alice Cooney. "Aesthetic Forms in Ceramics and Glass." In *Pursuit of Beauty,* edited by Amy Horbar, 198–251. New York: Metropolitan Museum of Art, 1986.

Frelinghuysen 1989
Frelinghuysen, Alice Cooney. *American Porcelain, 1770–1920.* New York: Metropolitan Museum of Art, 1989.

Frelinghuysen 1998
Frelinghuysen, Alice Cooney. "Paris Porcelain in America." *Antiques* 153:4 (Apr. 1998): 555–63.

Gallagher 1995
Gallagher, Jerry. *A Handbook of Old Morgantown Glass.* Minneapolis, Minn.: 1995.

Gardner 1971
Gardner, Paul. *The Glass of Frederick Carder.* New York: Crown Publishers, 1971.

Garrett 1990
Garrett, Elizabeth D. *At Home: The American Family 1750–1870.* New York: Harry N. Abrams, 1990.

Gaston 1996
Gaston, Mary Frank. *The Collector's Encyclopedia of Limoges Porcelain.* 2nd ed. Paducah, Ky.: Collector Books, 1996.

Gater and Vincent 1988
Gater, Sharon, and David Vincent. *The Factory in a Garden: Wedgwood from Etruria to Barlaston—the Transitional Years.* Keele, England: Keele Life Histories Centre, University of Keele, 1988.

Gates 1984
Gates, William C., Jr. *The City of Hills and Kilns: Life and Work in East Liverpool, Ohio.* East Liverpool, Ohio: East Liverpool Historical Society, 1984.

Gates and Ormerod 1982
Gates, William C., Jr., and Dana E. Ormerod. "The East Liverpool Pottery District: Identification of Manufacturers and Marks." *Historical Archaeology* 16:1–2 (1982): 1–358.

Giarracco interview 1997
Giarracco, Joseph, former senior china and glass buyer, B. Altman & Co., New York. Interview by Stephen G. Harrison and Charles L. Venable, New York, 13 Mar. 1997.

Gibbs 1995
Gibbs, Carl, Jr. *Collector's Encyclopedia of Metlox Potteries.* Paducah, Ky.: Collector Books, 1995.

Gifford interview 1997
Gifford, Charles, former president, Noritake Company. Interview by Charles L. Venable, Seattle, 25 July 1997.

Godden 1989
Godden, Geoffrey A. *Encyclopaedia of British Pottery and Porcelain Marks.* London: Barrie and Jenkins, 1989.

Goldberg 1983
Goldberg, David J. "Preliminary Notes on the Pioneer Potters and Potteries of Trenton, N.J." Typescript, 1983. New Jersey State Museum, Trenton.

***Good Manners* 1888**
Good Manners. New York: Butterick Publishing, 1888.

Goody 1982
Goody, Jack. *Cooking, Cuisine, and Class.* New York: Cambridge University Press, 1982.

Goshe 1998
Goshe, Ed, Ruth Hemminger, and Leslie Piña. *Depression Era Stems and Tableware: Tiffin.* Atglen, Pa.: Schiffer Publishing, 1998.

Green 1986
Green, Harvey. *Fit for America: Health, Fitness, Sport, and American Society.* New York: Pantheon Books, 1986.

Grehan 1981
Grehan, Ida. *Waterford: An Irish Art.* Huntington, N.Y.: Portfolio Press, 1981.

Grier 1997
Grier, Katherine C. *Culture and Comfort: Parlor Making and Middle-Class Identity, 1850–1930.* Washington, D.C.: Smithsonian Institution Press, 1997.

Grier interview 1998
Grier, Anna, retired business executive. Interview by Katherine C. Grier, Pennington, N.J., 25 June 1999.

Grover 1987
Grover, Kathryn, ed. *Dining in America, 1850–1900.* Amherst, Mass.: University of Massachusetts Press, 1987.

Gulotta interview 1997
Gulotta, Gerald, former shape designer, Block China Corporation. Interview by Charles L. Venable, New York, 26 June 1997.

Gura 1999
Gura, Judith. "Dansk Designs." *Echoes* 8:1 (summer 1999): 105–7.

Hannah 1986
Hannah, Frances. *Ceramics: Twentieth Century Design.* London: Bell and Hyman, 1986.

Hanover 1961
Hanover Gallery. *Eduardo Paolozzi.* London, 1961.

Hartmann 1997
Hartmann, Carolus. *Glasmarken Lexikon, 1600–1945.* Stuttgart: Arnoldsche, 1997.

Havel interview 1998
Havel, Miroslav, former design director, Waterford Crystal. Interview by Stephen G. Harrison, Waterford, Ireland, 16 July 1998.

Heacock and Bickenhouser 1978
Heacock, William, and Fred Bickenhouser. *Encyclopedia of Victorian Colored Pattern Glass.* Book 5, *U.S. Glass from A to Z.* Marietta, Ohio: Antique Publications, 1978.

Heath and Ross 1995
Heath, Edith, and Rosalie Ross. "Edith Heath: Tableware and Tile for the World, Heath Ceramics, 1944–1994." California Craft Artist Oral History Series. Berkeley, Calif.: University of California, 1995.

Hennessey 1985
Hennessey, William J. *Russel Wright, American Designer.* Cambridge, Mass.: MIT Press, 1985.

Hida and Unno 1996
Hida, Toyojiro, and Hiroshi Unno. *Early Noritake.* Nagoya, Japan: Noritake Museum, 1996.

Hilschenz 1982
Hilschenz, Helga. *Rosenthal: Hundert Jahre Porzellan.* Hannover, Germany: Kestner-Museum, 1982.

Hinckley and Ridgway 1954
Hinkley, Hugh, and Bruce Ridgway. "Report to Associated Representatives of Staffordshire Potters on Trip to Washington on December 17, 1954." Manuscript no. 2869. Minton Archives.

Hodges interview 1999
Hodges, Dale, designer, Fitz and Floyd, Inc. Interview by Stephen G. Harrison and Charles L. Venable, Dallas, 20 Apr. 1999.

Hogan 1980
Hogan, Edmund P. *The Elegance of Old Silverplate and Some Personalities.* Exton, Pa.: Schiffer Publishing, 1980.

Holdridge 1950
Holdridge, D. A. *The Fine Ceramics Industry in Germany during the Period 1939–1945.* British Ceramic Research Association Special No. 3. London: B.I.O.S. Surveys, 1950.

Holdway interview 1997
Holdway, Harold, former design director, W. T. Copeland & Sons. Interview by Stephen G. Harrison and Charles L. Venable, Stoke-upon-Trent, England, 22 Apr. 1997.

Holloway 1922
Holloway, Edward Stratton. *The Practical Book of Furnishing the Small House and Apartment.* Philadelphia: J. Lippincott, 1922.

Holme 1940
Holme, C. Geoffrey, ed. *Decorative Art, 1940: The Studio Year Book.* London: Studio Publications, 1940.

Holme 1941
Holme, C. Geoffrey, ed. *Decorative Art, 1941: The Studio Year Book.* London: Studio Publications, 1941.

Holme and Frost 1943
Holme, C. Geoffrey, and Kathleen M. Frost, eds. *Decorative Art, 1943–1948: The Studio Year Book.* London: Studio Publications, 1948.

Holme and Frost 1952
Holme, C. Geoffrey, and Kathleen M. Frost, eds. *Decorative Art, 1951–1952: The Studio Year Book.* London: Studio Publications, 1952.

Holme and Frost 1954
Holme, C. Geoffrey, and Kathleen M. Frost, eds. *Decorative Art,1953–1954: The Studio Year Book.* London: Studio Publications, 1954.

Holme and Frost 1955
Holme, C. Geoffrey, and Kathleen M. Frost, eds. *Decorative Art, 1954–1955: The Studio Year Book.* London: Studio Publications, 1955.

Holmes 1927
Holmes, Frank. "The Advantage of Good Design in Tableware." *Bulletin of the American Ceramic Society* 6:7 (July 1927): 181–83.

Holmes interview 1937
Holmes, Frank, Lenox designer. Interview by Enid Day, Atlanta, Ga., 10 Mar. 1937. Typescript, Lenox Archives.

Hood 1972
Hood, Graham. *Bonnin and Morris of Philadelphia: The First American Porcelain Factory, 1770–1772.* Chapel Hill, N.C.: University of North Carolina Press, 1972.

Hopwood and Hopwood 1997
Hopwood, Irene, and Gordon Hopwood. *Denby Pottery, 1809–1997, Dynasties and Designers.* London: Richard Dennis, 1997.

Horchow interview 1998
Horchow, Roger, former china buyer and head of The Horchow Collection. Interview by Stephen G. Harrison and Charles L. Venable, Dallas, 16 Apr. 1998.

Hume 1970
Hume, Ivor Noel. *A Guide to Artifacts of Colonial America.* New York: Alfred A. Knopf, 1970.

Hume 1987
Hume, Ivor Noel. *Discoveries in Martin's Hundred.* Williamsburg, Va.: Colonial Williamsburg Foundation, 1987.

Internoscia 1982
Internoscia, Aldon K. "Awareness and Usage Study of Crystal, Stemware, and Barware for Fostoria Glass Company and Murray and Chancy Ketchum." Unpublished report, Jan. 1982. Fostoria Archives.

Jackson 1997
Jackson, Lesley. "Automated Table Glass Production in Britain since World War II." *The Journal of the Glass Association* 5 (1997): 69–80.

Jackson 1998
Jackson, Lesley. *The Sixties.* London: Phaidon Press, 1998.

James 1954
James, George T. "Design and Dinnerware." *Pacific Coast Ceramic News* (June 1954): 21.

Jasper 1993
Jasper, Joanne. *The Collector's Encyclopedia of Homer Laughlin China: Reference and Value Guide.* Paducah, Ky.: Collector Books, 1993.

Jenkins 1946
Jenkins, Nancy. *The Perfect Hostess.* New Kensington, Pa.: Westmorland Sterling, 1946.

Jenkins 1997
Jenkins, Steven. *Midwinter Pottery: A Revolution in British Tableware.* London: Richard Dennis, 1997.

Jensen **1980**
George Jensen Silversmithy: 75 Artists, 75 Years. Washington, D.C.: Smithsonian Institution Press, 1980.

Jones 1934
Jones, Joseph M., Jr. *Tariff Retaliation: Repercussions of the Hawley-Smoot Bill.* Philadelphia: University of Pennsylvania Press, 1934.

Jones 1946
Jones, Gladys Beckett. *Manual of Smart Housekeeping.* New York: Chester R. Heck, 1946.

Jones 1993
Jones, Joan. *Minton: The First Two Hundred Years of Design and Production.* Shrewsbury, England: Swan Hill Press, 1993.

Jungeblut 1928
Jungeblut, N. B. "Die keramische Industrie in Deutschland." *Berichte der Deutschen Keramischen Gesellschaft* 9 (1928): 354–80.

Karmason and Stacke 1989
Karmason, Marilyn G., and Joan B. Stacke. *Majolica, A Complete History and Illustrated Survey.* New York: Harry N. Abrams, 1989.

Kasson 1990
Kasson, John F. *Rudeness and Civility: Manners in Nineteenth Century Urban America.* New York: Hill and Wang, 1990.

Keefe 1968
Keefe, John W. *Libbey Glass: A Tradition of 150 Years, 1818–1968.* Toledo: Toledo Museum of Art, 1968.

Kerr 1990
Kerr, Ann. *The Collector's Encyclopedia of Russel Wright Designs.* Paducah, Ky.: Collector Books, 1990.

Klapthor 1975
Klapthor, Margaret. *Official White House China: 1789 to the Present.* Washington: Smithsonian Institution Press, 1975.

Klapthor 1999
Klapthor, Margaret. *Official White House China.* New York: Harry N. Abrams, 1999.

Kogan interview 1997
Kogan, Belle, former contract designer. Telephone interview by Charles L. Venable, 2 Dec. 1997.

Lanmon et al. 1990
Lanmon, Dwight P., Arlene Palmer Schwind, Ivor Noël Hume, Robert H. Brill, and Victor F. Hanson. *John Frederick Amelung: Early American Glassmaker.* Corning, N.Y.: Corning Museum of Glass Press, 1990.

Larrabee 1955
Larrabee, Eric. "Rosebuds on the Silverware." *Industrial Design* 2 (Feb. 1955): 62–63.

Lehner 1988
Lehner, Lois. *Lehner's Encyclopedia of U.S. Marks on Pottery, Porcelain, and Clay.* Paducah, Ky.: Collector Books, 1988.

Lender and Martin 1987
Lender, Mark Edward, and James Kirby Martin. *Drinking in America: A History.* Rev. ed. New York: The Free Press, 1987.

Livingston et al. 1973
Livingston, Jon, Joe Moore, and Felicia Oldfather, eds. *Imperial Japan, 1800–1954.* New York: Pantheon Books, 1973.

Logan 1889
Logan, Mrs. John A., comp. *The Home Manual: Everybody's Guide in Social, Domestic, and Business Use: A Treasury of Useful Information for the Million.* Boston: A. M. Thayer, 1889.

Long and Seate 1995
Long, Milbra, and Emily Seate. *Fostoria Stemware: A Crystal for America.* Paducah, Ky.: Collector Books, 1995.

Lovegren 1995
Lovegren, Sylvia. *Fashionable Food: Seven Decades of Food Fads.* New York: Macmillan, 1995.

Lutes 1937
Lutes, Della Thompson. *Home Grown.* Boston: Little, Brown, 1937.

Lynd and Lynd 1957
Lynd, Robert, and Helen Lynd. *Middletown: A Study in Modern American Culture.* 1927. Reprint, New York: Harcourt, Brace, 1957.

Lystra 1989
Lystra, Karen. *Searching the Heart: Women, Men, and Romantic Love in Nineteenth-Century America.* New York: Oxford University Press, 1989.

Madarasz 1998
Madarasz, Anne. *Glass: Shattering Notions.* Pittsburgh: Historical Society of Western Pennsylvania, 1998.

Madigan 1982
Madigan, Mary Jean. *Steuben Glass: An American Tradition in Crystal.* New York: Harry N. Abrams, 1982.

Malone 1947
Malone, Dorothy. *Cookbook for Brides.* New York: A. A. Wyn, 1947.

Marcus 1993a
Marcus, Stanley. *Minding the Store.* 1974. Reprint, New York: Plume, 1993.

Marcus 1993b
Marcus, Stanley. *Quest for the Best.* 1979. Reprint, New York: Plume, 1993.

Marcus interview 1996
Marcus, Stanley, former president and CEO, Neiman Marcus, Dallas. Interview by Stephen G. Harrison and Charles L. Venable, Dallas, 28 Oct. 1996.

Marling 1994
Marling, Karal Ann. *As Seen on TV: The Visual Culture of Everyday Life in the 1950s.* Cambridge, Mass.: Harvard University Press, 1994.

Marshall Field [1930]
Marshall Field & Co. *Color Follows Color as Course Follows Course: The New Vogue in Dinnerware.* Chicago, [1930].

Matranga 1997
Matranga, Victoria Kasuba. *America at Home: A Celebration of Twentieth-Century Housewares.* Rosemont, Ill.: National Housewares Manufacturers Association, 1997.

Mauriès 1991
Mauriès, Patrick. *Fornasetti, Designer of Dreams.* London: Thames and Hudson, 1991.

May 1988
May, Elaine Tyler. *Homeward Bound: American Families in the Cold War Era.* New York: Basic Books, 1988.

McCready 1995
McCready, Karen. *Art Deco and Modernist Ceramics.* London: Thames and Hudson, 1995.

McCusker 1992
McCusker, John J. *How Much Is That in Real Money? A Historical Price Index for Use as a Deflator of Money Values in the Economy of the United States.* Worcester, Mass.: American Antiquarian Society, 1992.

McIntyre 1990
McIntyre, Douglas W. *The Official Guide to Railroad Dining Car China*. Marceline, Mo.: Walsworth Publishing, 1990.

McKee 1966
McKee, Floyd W. *The Second Oldest Profession: A Century of American Dinnerware Manufacture*. N.p., 1966.

Measell 1987
Measell, James. "The Dalzell, Gilmore and Leighton Company." *Glass Collector's Digest* (June–July 1987): 25–42.

Meehan and Meehan 1995
Meehan, Bill, and Kathy Meehan. *Collector's Guide to Lu-Ray Pastels*. Paducah, Ky.: Collector Books, 1995.

Meikle 1995
Meikle, Jeffrey L. *American Plastic: A Cultural History*. New Brunswick, N.J.: Rutgers University Press, 1995.

Meslin-Perrier 1994
Meslin-Perrier, Chantal. *La manufacture de porcelaine: Pouyat, Limoges-1835–1912*. Limoges, France: Réunion des Musées Nationaux, 1994.

Meslin-Perrier 1996
Meslin-Perrier, Chantal. *Chefs-d'oeuvre de la porcelaine de Limoges*. Paris: Réunion des Musées Nationaux, 1996.

Midwinter interview 1997
Midwinter, Eve, former designer, W. R. Midwinter and Josiah Wedgwood & Sons. Interview by Stephen G. Harrison, Stoke-upon-Trent, England, 25 July 1997.

Miller 1984a
Miller, George L. "George M. Coates, Pottery Merchant of Philadelphia, 1817–1831." *Winterthur Portfolio* 19:1 (spring 1984): 37–50.

Miller 1984b
Miller, George L. "Marketing Ceramics in North America: An Introduction." *Winterthur Portfolio* 19:1 (spring 1984): 1–5.

Mintz 1985
Mintz, Sidney W. *Sweetness and Power: The Place of Sugar in Modern History*. New York: Viking, 1985.

Mintz and Kellogg 1988
Mintz, Steven, and Susan Kellogg. *Domestic Revolutions: A Social History of American Family Life*. New York: Free Press, 1988.

Modern Priscilla 1925
Modern Priscilla Home Furnishing Book. Boston: Priscilla Publishing, 1925.

Montreal 1984
Montreal Museum of Decorative Arts. *Eva Zeisel: Designer for Industry*. Chicago: University of Chicago Press, 1984.

Morris 1994
Morris, Susan. *Purinton Pottery: An Identification and Value Guide*. Paducah, Ky.: Collector Books, 1994.

Morse [1908]
Morse, Sidney. *Household Discoveries: An Encyclopedia of Recipes and Processes*. New York: Success Co., [1908].

Moss 1997
Moss, Simon. *Homemaker: A 1950s Design Classic*. Moffat, Scotland: Cameron and Hollis, 1997.

Mudge 1981
Mudge, Jean McClure. *Chinese Export Porcelain for the American Trade, 1785–1835*. Newark, N.J.: University of Delaware Press, 1981.

Murdock 1998
Murdock, Catherine Gilbert. *Domesticating Drink: Women, Men, and Alcohol in America 1870–1940*. Baltimore: Johns Hopkins University Press, 1998.

Murphy interview 1998
Murphy, Terry, former chief photographer, Waterford Crystal. Interview by Stephen G. Harrison, Waterford, Ireland, 17 July 1998.

Murray 1972
Murray, Melvin L. *History of Fostoria, Ohio, Glass, 1887–1920*. Fostoria, Ohio, 1972.

Myers 1977
Myers, Susan H. "A Survey of Traditional Pottery Manufacture in the Mid-Atlantic and Northeastern United States." *Northeast Historical Archaeology* 6:1–2 (spring 1977): 1–13.

Myers 1984
Myers, Susan H. "The Business of Potting, 1780–1840." In *The Craftsman in Early America*, edited by Ian M. G. Quimby, 190–233. New York: W. W. Norton; Wilmington, Del.: Henry Francis du Pont Winterthur Museum, 1984.

Neil 1916
Neil, Marion H. *Salads, Sandwiches, and Chafing Dish Recipes*. Philadelphia: David McKay, 1916.

Nelson 1994
Nelson, Maxine Feek. *Collectible Vernon Kilns: An Identification and Value Guide*. Paducah, Ky.: Collector Books, 1994

Newbound and Newbound 1989
Newbound, Betty, and Bill Newbound. *Southern Potteries Incorporated Blue Ridge Dinnerware*. 3rd ed. Paducah, Ky.: Collector Books, 1989.

Newell interview 1991
Newell, Jeanne, niece of Louise Allen Holmes, wife of former Lenox designer Frank Holmes. Interview by Ellen P. Denker, McLean, Va., 7 June 1991.

New Jersey 1972
New Jersey State Museum. *New Jersey Pottery to 1840*. Trenton, 1972.

Niblett 1990
Niblett, Kathy. *Dynamic Design: The British Pottery Industry 1940–1990*. Stoke-on-Trent, England: City Museum and Art Gallery, 1990.

Noritake 1997
Noritake Company. *Noritake China: History of the Materials, Development, and Chronology of Backstamps*. Nagoya, Japan, 1997.

O'Leary interview 1998
O'Leary, Jim, design director, Waterford Crystal. Interview by Stephen G. Harrison, Waterford, Ireland, 16 July 1998.

Oliver 1994
Oliver, Suzanne. "Keep It Trendy." *Forbes* 154:2 (18 July 1994): 88–89.

Opie 1989
Opie, Jennifer Hawkins. *Scandinavia: Ceramics and Glass in the Twentieth Century*. London: Victoria and Albert Museum, 1989.

Page and Frederiksen 1995
Page, Bob, and Dale Frederiksen. *Seneca Glass Company, 1891–1983: A Stemware Identification Guide*. Greensboro, N.C.: Page-Frederiksen Publishing, 1995.

Palmer 1976
Palmer, Arlene. "Glass Production in Eighteenth-Century America: The Wistarburgh Enterprise." *Winterthur Portfolio* 11 (1976): 75–101.

Palmer 1989
Palmer, Arlene. "'To the Good of the Province and Country': Henry William Stiegel and American Flint Glass." In *The American Craftsman and the European Tradition, 1620–1820*, edited by Francis Puig and Michael Conforti, 202–39. Minneapolis: Minneapolis Institute of Art, 1989.

Pass and Binns 1930
Pass, Richard, and Charles F. Binns. "Turns of the Potter's Wheel in America." *Transactions of the [British] Ceramic Society* 29 (May 1930): 90.

Pearce 1949
Pearce, Davis. *The Development of the American Glass Industry*. Cambridge, Mass.: Harvard University Press, 1949.

Peat 1992
Peat, Alan. *Midwinter: A Collector's Guide*. Moffat, Scotland: Cameron and Hollis, 1992.

Pfaltzgraff 1989
Pfaltzgraff Company. *Pfaltzgraff: America's Potter*. Foreword by James R. Mitchell. York, Pa., 1989.

Pickle 1980
Pickle, Susan E. *From Kiln to Kitchen: American Design in Tableware*. Springfield: Illinois State Museum, 1980.

Piña 1994
Piña, Leslie. *Pottery: Modern Wares 1920–1960*. Atglen, Pa.: Schiffer Publishing, 1994.

Piña 1996
Piña, Leslie. *Fostoria Designer George Sakier.* Atglen, Pa.: Schiffer Publishing, 1996.

Post 1939
Post, Emily. *The Personality of a House: The Blue Book of Home Design and Decoration.* Rev. ed. New York and London: Funk and Wagnalls, 1939.

Prince interview 1997
Prince, Jack, former pattern designer, Block China. Interview by Stephen G. Harrison and Charles L. Venable, New York, 13 Mar. 1998.

Queensberry interview 1997
Queensberry, David, senior partner of Queensberry, Hunt, Levien. Interview by Stephen G. Harrison, London, 23 July 1997.

Rainwater 1975
Rainwater, Dorothy T. *Encyclopedia of American Silver Manufacturers.* New York: Crown Publishers, 1975.

Reed 1995
Reed, Alan B. *Collector's Encyclopedia of Pickard China.* Paducah, Ky.: Collector Books, 1995.

Reed and Skoczen 1997
Reed, Cleota, and Stan Skoczen. *Syracuse China.* Syracuse, N.Y.: Syracuse University Press, 1997.

Reilly 1989
Reilly, Robin. *Wedgwood Volume II.* New York: Stockton Press, 1989.

Reilly and Savage 1980
Reilly, Robin, and George Savage. *The Dictionary of Wedgwood.* Suffolk, England: Antique Collectors' Club, 1980.

Reiss 1996
Reiss, Ray. *Red Wing Art Pottery.* Chicago: Property Publishing, 1996.

Reiss 1997
Reiss, Ray. *Red Wing Dinnerware.* Chicago: Property Publishing, 1997.

Revi 1965
Revi, Albert C. *American Cut and Engraved Glass.* New York: Thomas Nelson and Sons, 1965.

Rice 1982
Rice, Helen M. "Belle, Who?" Seminar paper, University of Illinois, 1982.

Rice 1994
Rice, Helen M. "Belle Kogan Remembers: A Journey to Design." *Innovation* 13:2 (spring 1994): 33–39.

Rograve and Steinhauer 1993
Rograve, Susan T., and Marcia B. Steinhauer. *PYREX by Corning: A Collector's Guide.* Marietta, Ohio: Antique Publications, 1993.

Rombauer 1946
Rombauer, Irma S. *The Joy of Cooking: A Compilation of Reliable Recipes with an Occasional Culinary Chat.* 1931. Reprint, New York and Indianapolis: Bobbs-Merrill, 1946.

Rorabaugh 1979
Rorabaugh, William J. *The Alcoholic Republic, an American Tradition.* New York: Oxford University Press, 1979.

Rorer 1902
Rorer, Sarah Tyson. *Mrs. Rorer's New Cook Book: A Manual of Housekeeping.* Philadelphia: Arnold and Company, 1902.

Ross 1968
Ross, Marvin C. *Russian Porcelains.* Norman: University of Oklahoma Press, 1968.

Rudin 1997
Rudin, Max. "There Is Something about a Martini." *American Heritage* 48:4 (July–Aug. 1997).

Sautot 1993
Sautot, Dany. *The Story of Baccarat.* Paris: Baccarat Glassware, 1993.

Savoy 1930
The Savoy Cocktail Book. New York: Richard R. Smith, 1930.

Schlereth 1991
Schlereth, Thomas J. *Victorian America: Transformations in Everyday Life.* New York: Harper Collins, 1991.

Schramberger 1930
Schramberger Majolika Handmalerei (trade catalogue). Schramberg, Germany, 1930.

Schramberger 1931
Schramberger Majolikafabrik. (trade catalogue). Schramberg, Germany, 1931.

D. Schreckengost interview 1995
Schreckengost, Donald, designer, Salem China Company, Homer Laughlin China Company, and Hall China Company. Interview by Charles L. Venable and Douglas Hawes, Dallas, 17 Dec. 1995.

V. Schreckengost interview 1995
Schreckengost, Viktor, former designer, Salem China and Limoges China Company. Interview by Charles L. Venable and Douglas Hawes, Dallas, 15 Dec. 1995.

Schreiber 1980
Schreiber, Hermann. *Die Rosenthal Story.* Düsseldorf, Germany: Econ-Verlag, 1980.

Schubert 1926
Schubert, Ethel. *American Etiquette.* Philadelphia: Penn Publishing, 1926.

Schwartz and Schwartz 1991
Schwartz, Martin F., and Judith S. Schwartz. "Designed in America, Sold in America, Made in Japan." *American Ceramics* 9 (spring 1991): 40–47.

Schwind 1984
Schwind, Arlene P. "The Ceramic Imports of Frederick Rhinelander, New York Loyalist and Merchant." *Winterthur Portfolio* 19:1 (spring 1984).

Scribner 1950
Scribner, George K. *A Brief Description of the Commonly Used Plastics and Their Origin.* Boonton, N.J.: Boonton Molding Company, 1950.

Sears 1961
Sears, Roebuck & Co. *Sears, Roebuck Diamond Jubilee Catalogue of 1961.* Chicago, 1961.

Shapiro 1986
Shapiro, Laura. *Perfection Salad: Women and Cooking at the Turn of the Century.* New York: Farrar, Straus, and Giroux, 1986.

Shifman 1998
Shifman, Barry. "Design for Industry: The 'German Applied Arts' Exhibition in the United States, 1912–13." *[Decorative Arts Society] Journal* 22 (1998): 19–30.

Shotliff 1977
Shotliff, Donald A. "The History of the Labor Movement in the American Pottery Industry: The National Brotherhood of Operative Potters—International Brotherhood of Operative Potters, 1890–1970." Ph.D. diss., Kent State University, 1977.

Siemen 1989
Siemen, Wilhelm. *175 Jahre Hutschenreuther: Ein Beitrag zum Firmenjubiläum 1814–1989.* Hohenberg an der Eger, Germany: Museum der Deutschen Porzellan Industrie, 1989.

Snyder 1996
Snyder, Jeffrey B. *Franciscan Dining Services.* Atglen, Pa.: Schiffer Publishing, 1996.

South 1993
South, Stanley A. *The Search for John Bartlam at Cain Hoy: America's First Creamware Potter.* Columbia, S.C.: South Carolina Institute of Archaeology and Anthropology, University of South Carolina, 1993.

Spencer 1983
Spencer, Ethel. *The Spencers of Amberson Avenue: A Turn of the Century Memoir.* Pittsburgh: University of Pittsburgh Press, 1983.

Spigel 1992
Spigel, Lynn. *Make Room for TV: Television and the Family Ideal in Postwar America.* Chicago: University of Chicago Press, 1992.

Spillman 1981
Spillman, Jane Shadel. *American and European Pressed Glass in the Corning Museum of Glass.* Corning, N.Y.: The Corning Museum of Glass, 1981.

Spillman 1986
Spillman, Jane Shadel. *Glass from World's Fairs, 1851–1904*. Corning, N.Y.: Corning Museum of Glass, 1986.

Spillman 1989
Spillman, Jane Shadel. *White House Glassware: Two Centuries of Presidential Entertaining*. Washington, D.C.: White House Historical Association, 1989.

Spillman 1996
Spillman, Jane Shadel. *The American Cut Glass Industry: T. G. Hawkes and His Competitors*. Suffolk England: Antique Collectors' Club; Corning, N.Y.: Corning Museum of Glass, 1996.

Spillman and Farraf 1977
Spillman, Jane Shadel, and Estelle Sinclaire Farraf. *The Cut and Engraved Glass of Corning, 1868–1940*. Corning, N.Y.: Corning Museum of Glass, 1977.

Spillman and Frantz 1990
Spillman, Jane Shadel, and Susanne K. Frantz. *Masterpieces of American Glass*. New York: Crown Publishers, 1990.

Spillman and Frelinghuysen 1990
Spillman, Jane Shadel, and Alice Cooney Frelinghuysen. "The Dummer Glass and Ceramic Factories in Jersey City, New Jersey." *Antiques* 137:3 (Mar. 1990): 706–17.

Spours 1988
Spours, Judy. *Art Deco Tableware*. New York: Rizzoli, 1988.

Sprackling 1941
Sprackling, Helen. *Setting Your Table: Its Art, Etiquette and Service*. New York: M. Barrows, 1941.

Springsted 1985
Springsted, Brenda L. "A Delftware Center in Seventeenth-Century New Jersey." *American Ceramic Circle Journal* 4 (1985): 9–46.

Steck 1942
Steck, Harold Wallis. *Right in Your Own Backyard*. New York: George W. Stewart, 1942.

Stefano 1974
Stefano, Frank, Jr. "James Clews, Nineteenth-Century Potter, Part II: The American Experience." *Antiques* 105:3 (Mar. 1974): 553–55.

Stern interview 1999
Stern, Jewel, historian and hostess. Interview by Stephen G. Harrison and Charles L. Venable, Miami, 24 January 1999.

Stern 1994
Stern, Marc J. *The Pottery Industry of Trenton: A Skilled Trade in Transition, 1850–1929*. New Brunswick, N.J.: Rutgers University Press, 1994.

Stokes 1990
Stokes, Jayne E. *Sumptuous Surrounds: Silver Overlay on Ceramic and Glass*. Milwaukee: Milwaukee Art Museum, 1990.

Stout 1985
Stout, Sandra McPhee. *Heisey on Parade*. Lombard, Ill.: Wallace-Homestead Book Co., 1985.

Stradling 1976
Stradling, J. Garrison. "American Ceramics at the Philadelphia Centennial." *Antiques* 110:1 (July 1976): 146–58.

Stradling 1997
Stradling, J. Garrison. "A Dream of 'Porcellain' in Cincinnati: William S. Merrill's Personal Account of Experiments and Travels, 1824–1828." *American Ceramic Circle Journal* 10 (1997): 73–90.

Stradling and Denker 1997
Stradling, Diana, and Ellen Paul Denker. *Jersey City: Shaping America's Pottery Industry, 1825–1892*. Jersey City, N.J.: Jersey City Museum, 1997.

Strasser 1982
Strasser, Susan. *Never Done: A History of American Housework*. New York: Pantheon Books, 1982.

Streichler 1963
Streichler, Jerry. "The Consultant Industrial Designer in American Industry, 1927–1960." Ph.D. diss., New York University, 1963.

Stupell 1932
Stupell, Carole. "Carole Stupell, Ltd., Scrapbook." Personal papers, 1932–66. Carole Stupell, Ltd., archives, New York.

Syracuse 1947
Syracuse Museum of Fine Arts. *The Twelfth Ceramics National Exhibition*. Syracuse, N.Y., 1947.

Syracuse 1953
Syracuse Museum of Fine Arts. *Contemporary American Ceramics: Selections from the 17th Ceramics National*. Syracuse, N.Y., 1953.

Tamony 1967
Tamony, Peter. "Western Words: Martini Cocktail." *Western Folklore* 26:2 (Apr. 1967): 124.

Thompson interview 1997
Thompson, George, former president, Copeland & Thompson. Interview by Stephen G. Harrison, Peterborough, N.H., 13 Oct. 1997.

Thorpe 1941
Dorothy C. Thorpe, Inc. *Dorothy C. Thorpe, California*. Glendale, Calif., 1941.

Time-Life 1948
Time-Life. *The Market for United Kingdom China, Pottery and Glass in the United States*. New York, 1948.

Tipton 1926
Tipton, Edna Sibley. *Table Service for the Hostess*. New York and London: D. Appleton, 1926.

Travis 1998
Travis, Nora. *Haviland China: The Age of Elegance*. Atglen, Pa.: Schiffer Publishing, 1998.

Tsutsui interview 1997
Tsutsui, Osamu, current vice president for product development, Noritake Company. Interview by Charles L. Venable and Ellen P. Denker, Secaucus, N.J., 22 Oct. 1997.

Tuchman 1995
Tuchman, Mitch. *Bauer: Classic American Pottery*. San Francisco: Chronicle Books, 1995.

USBFDC 1917
U.S. Bureau of Foreign and Domestic Commerce. *The Glass Industry. Report on the Production of Glass in the United States*. Washington, D.C.: Government Printing Office, 1917.

USDC 1915
United States Department of Commerce. *The Pottery Industry: Report on the Cost of Production in the Earthenware and China Industries of the United States, England, Germany, and Austria*. Miscellaneous series no. 21. Government doc. no. C 18.15:21. Washington, D.C.: Government Printing Office, 1915.

USDC 1924
United States Department of Commerce. *Simplified Practice Recommendation No. 5: Hotel Chinaware*. Washington, D.C.: Government Printing Office, 1924.

USDC 1961
United States Department of Commerce. *Household and Commercial Pottery Industry in Japan*. Government doc. no. C 41.100:J27. Washington, D.C.: Government Printing Office, 1961.

USPA 1883–1966
United States Potters' Association. *Proceedings of the Annual Conventions, 1883–1966* (7th–88th conventions) East Liverpool, Ohio.

USTC 1936
United States Tariff Commission. *Pottery: Household Table and Kitchen Articles of Earthenware and of China, Porcelain, and Other Vitrified Wares*. Government doc. no. TC 1.9.102. Report no. 102, 2d s. Washington, D.C.: Government Printing Office, 1936.

Valiere 1992 Valiere, Nathalie. *Un Americain à Limoges: Charles Edward Haviland (1839–1921), Porcelanier*. Tulle, France: Editions Lemouzi, 1992.

Venable 1994
Venable, Charles L. *Silver in America, 1840–1940: A Century of Splendor*. New York: Harry N. Abrams; Dallas: Dallas Museum of Art, 1994.

Villa Terrace 1992
Villa Terrace Decorative Arts Museum. *Celebrating 150 Years of Haviland China, 1842–1992*. Milwaukee, 1992.

Visser 1991
Visser, Margaret. *The Rituals of Dinner: The Origins, Eccentricities, and Meaning of Table Manners*. New York: Grove Weidenfeld, 1991.

von Vegesack 1992
von Vegesack, Alexander. *Czech Cubism: Architecture, Furniture, and Decorative Arts, 1910–1925*. New York: Princeton Architectural Press, 1992.

Walker 1992
Walker, Susannah. *Queensberry Hunt: Creativity and Industry*. London: Fourth Estate, 1992.

Washington 1982
Washington State University. *Noritake Art Deco Porcelain: Collection of Howard Kottler*. Pullman, Wash., 1982.

Watkins 1945
Watkins, Lura W. "Glassmaking in South Boston." *Antiques* 48:4 (Oct. 1945): 216–18.

Watkins 1968
Watkins, Lura W. *Early New England Potters and Their Wares*. 1950. Reprint, Hamden, Conn.: Archon Books, 1968.

Wedgwood 1940
Josiah Wedgwood & Sons. *Catalogue of Bodies, Glazes and Shapes Current for 1940–1950*. Etruria, England, 1940.

Wedgwood interview 1995
Wedgwood, Barbara Boyd, former head buyer, Neiman Marcus, Dallas. Interview by Charles L. Venable and Douglas Hawes, Dallas, 3 Apr. 1995.

Wedgwood interview 1996
Wedgwood, Barbara Boyd. Interview by Stephen G. Harrison and Charles L. Venable, Dallas, 27 Nov. 1996.

Weigley 1980
Weigley, Emma Seifrit. "Mrs. Rorer and New York Foodways," *New York Folklore* 6:3–4 (1980):195–207.

Weisman 1996
Weisman Art Museum. *Serving Art: Rockwell Kent's Salamina Dinnerware*. Minneapolis: University of Minnesota, 1996.

Whipp 1990
Whipp, Richard. *Patterns of Labour: Work and Social Change in the Pottery Industry*. London: Routledge, 1990.

White 1994
White, Carole B. *The Collector's Guide to Made in Japan Ceramics*. Paducah, Ky.: Collector Books, 1994.

Whitmyer and Whitmyer 1994
Whitmyer, Margaret, and Kenn Whitmyer. *The Collector's Encyclopedia of Hall China*. Paducah, Ky.: Collector Books, 1994.

Williams 1985
Williams, Susan. *Savory Suppers and Fashionable Feasts: Dining in Victorian America*. New York: Pantheon Books; Rochester, N.Y.: Strong Museum, 1985.

Wilson 1972
Wilson, Kenneth M. *New England Glass and Glassmaking*. New York: Thomas Y. Crowell, 1972.

Wilson 1989
Wilson, Jack D. *Phoenix and Consolidated Art Glass, 1926–1980*. Marietta, Ohio: Antique Publications, 1989.

Wilson 1994
Wilson, Kenneth M. *American Glass, 1760–1930: The Toledo Museum of Art*. New York: Hudson Hills Press, 1994.

Wilson and Nelson 1996
Wilson, Kenneth M., and Kirk J. Nelson. "The Role of Glass Knobs in Glassmaking and Furniture." *Antiques* 149:5 (May 1996): 753.

Wood interview 1997
Wood, Paul, managing director, W. T. Copeland & Sons. Interview by Stephen G. Harrison and Charles L. Venable, Stoke-upon-Trent, England, 25 Apr. 1997.

Young 1878
Young, Jennie J. *The Ceramic Art: A Compendium of the History and Manufacture of Pottery and Porcelain*. New York: Harper Brothers, 1878.

Younkin 1946
Younkin, Ida Ruth. "All Out for a Barbecue!" *BH&G* 24:10 (June 1946): 46–47.

Zeisel interview 1996
Zeisel, Eva, contract designer. Interview by Charles L. Venable and Ellen P. Denker, New York, 10 Apr. 1996.

Zembo 1976
Zembo Temple Yearbook, 1976. Harrisburg, Penn: R & R Portraits, 1976.

Zimmermann 1990
Zimmermann, Heinrich. *Porzellanfabriken in Böhmen, 1791–1945*. Benediktbeuern, Germany: Riess-Druck und Verlag, 1990.

Zug 1986
Zug, Charles G., III. *Turners and Burners: The Folk Potters of North Carolina*. Chapel Hill, N.C.: University of North Carolina Press, 1986.

Zühlsdorff 1988
Zühlsdorff, Dieter. *Keramik-Marken Lexikon: Porzellan und Keramik Report, 1885–1935 Europa (Festland)*. Stuttgart: Arnoldsche, 1988.

Figure Credits

Chapter 1

Fig 1.1: "Residence of W. Coe, Stratford, Conn.," *Palliser's Model Homes* (Bridgeport, Conn.: Palliser, Palliser & Co., 1878): pl. 9. Courtesy Katherine C. Grier.

Fig. 1.2: Courtesy The Winterthur Library: Decorative Arts Photographic Collection.

Fig. 1.3: Sideboard, ca. 1875, Chicago, walnut, brass, and earthenware, h. 85 in. Dallas Museum of Art, anonymous gift, 1992.308.

Fig. 1.4: Courtesy Heart of Texas Museum and Heritage House, Colorado City, Texas.

Fig. 1.5: Printed by permission of the Norman Rockwell Family Trust. Copyright © 1943 the Norman Rockwell Family Trust.

Fig. 1.6: From a glass plate negative by William Ferris, Jr., Wilmington, Delaware, 29 July 1888. Courtesy Hagley Museum and Library, Pictorial Collections.

Fig. 1.7: "Georgian: A Pattern of Spoons, Forks, and All Other Pieces of Table Flat Ware" (Springfield, Mass.: Towle Mfg. Co., 1906): 63. Courtesy Charles L. Venable.

Fig. 1.8: Fannie Merritt Farmer, *Boston Cooking-School Cook Book* (1896). Courtesy Katherine C. Grier.

Fig. 1.9: *Orfevrerie* (1862): inside cover. Courtesy Orfevrerie Christofle, Paris. Photo by Studio Kollar.

Fig. 1.10: Courtesy Lenox Archives.

Fig. 1.11: "1. Tips back his chair. 2. Eats with his mouth too full. 3. Feeds a dog at the table. 4. Holds his knife improperly. 5. Engages in violent argument at the meal-time. 6. Lounges upon the table. 7. Brings a cross child to the table. 8. Drinks from the saucer, and laps with his tongue the last drop from the plate. 9. Comes to the table in his shirt-sleeves, and puts his feet beside his chair. 10. Picks his teeth with his fingers. 11. Scratches her head and is frequently unnecessarily getting up from the table." Thomas E. Hill, *Hill's Manual of Social and Business Forms* (Chicago: Hill Standard Book Co., 1884). Courtesy Katherine C. Grier.

Fig. 1.12: Hill 1884. Courtesy Katherine C. Grier.

Fig. 1.13: "Breakfast Table, Second Course," Sarah Tyson Rorer, *Mrs. Rorer's New Cook Book* (Philadelphia: Arnold and Company, 1902). Courtesy Katherine C. Grier.

Fig. 1.14: Detail of advertisement of New Process Vapor Range, *Ladies' Home Journal* (May 1893). Courtesy The Winterthur Library: Printed Book and Periodical Collection.

Fig. 1.15: *Montgomery Ward & Co. Catalogue and Buyers' Guide*, no. 57 (spring/summer 1895): 528. Reprint, New York: Dover Publications, 1969.

Fig. 1.16: *Montgomery Ward* 1895, 539.

Fig. 1.17: "Luncheon Cover in Detail," Lucy G. Allen, *Table Service* (Boston: Little, Brown, 1919). Courtesy The Winterthur Library: Printed Book and Periodical Collection.

Fig. 1.18: *Crockery and Glass Journal* 155:2 (Aug. 1954): 54.

Fig. 1.19: Detail of Fostoria Glass Company advertisement, unidentified magazine, [1929?].

Fig. 1.20: "Miroton of Fish and Potato Salad," Janet McKenzie Hill, *Salads, Sandwiches and Chafing-Dish Dainties*, rev. ed. (Boston: Little, Brown, 1907). Courtesy The Winterthur Library: Printed Book and Periodical Collection.

Fig. 1.21: "The Green Teapot Tea Room, 330 Lexington Avenue (1906)," Joseph Byron, *Photographs of New York Interiors at the Turn of the Century* (New York: Dover Publications, 1976).

Fig. 1.22: Tree in home of Mrs. Frederick M. Lege, Jr. (Natalie Mayer Lege), Dallas, 1939. Courtesy Natalie "Schatzie" Lee.

Fig. 1.23: Corning Glass Works advertisement of Pyrex, unidentified magazine, [1950?].

Fig. 1.24: Detail of Hoosier Manufacturing Company advertisement of Tu-Tone Kitchen and Breakfast Group, *The Saturday Evening Post* (27 Sept. 1930).

Fig. 1.25: Alladin Homes advertisement of The Pilgrim home, *23rd Annual Catalog* (Bay City, Mich., 1929). Courtesy Katherine C. Grier.

Fig. 1.26: Chafing dish, ca. 1900–15; Joseph Heinrich, New York and Paris, maker; Cowell & Hubbard Co., Cleveland, retailer; copper, silver, and wood; h. 11¼ in. Marked: COPPER & SILVER / 4; labeled: THE COWELL & HUBBARD CO. Dallas Museum of Art, gift of the Alvin and Lucy Owsley Foundation and memorial funds in memory of Constance Owsley Garrett, 1989.14.a–c.

Fig. 1.27: Oneida Community, Ltd., advertisement, *The Saturday Evening Post* (13 Feb. 1932).

Fig. 1.28: Detail of Frigidaire Corporation advertisment of the Hydrator, *The Saturday Evening Post* (3 May 1930).

Fig. 1.29: *Food Is Fun* (New York: American Gas Association, [1950?]). Courtesy Katherine C. Grier.

Fig. 1.30: Drawing of ranch house, unidentified magazine, [1960?].

Fig. 1.31: Advertisement of Black and White scotch whiskey, unidentified magazine, [1960?].

Fig. 1.32: Ruth Berolzheimer, ed., *500 Snacks* (Chicago: Consolidated Book Publishers, 1949): cover.

Fig. 1.33: "Here's How and When to Serve Cocktails, Wine, and Liqueurs," Fostoria Glass Company sales brochure, [1933?]. Fostoria Archives.

Fig. 1.34: Gideon Bosker et al. *Patio Daddy-O* (San Francisco: Chronicle Books, 1996): 15.

Fig. 1.35: *A Campbell Cookbook*, rev. ed. (Camden, N.J.: Campbell Soup Company, 1968): 136. Courtesy Campbell Soup Company.

Fig. 1.36: *Campbell 1968*, 35. Courtesy Campbell Soup Company.

Fig. 1.37: Unidentified magazine, [1960?].

Fig. 1.38: Corning Glass Company advertisement of *Centura* tableware, unidentified magazine, [1968?].

Fig. 1.39: West Virginia Glass Company advertisement, *Gift and Tableware Reporter* 12 (Dec. 1970): supplement.

Fig. 1.40: Courtesy of Jewel Stern, Miami.

Chapter 2
Fig. 2.1: Plate, ca. 1755, Staffordshire, England, salt-glazed stoneware, d. 10⅜ in. Dallas Museum of Art, gift of Anne J. Stewart, 1989.137.

Fig. 2.2: Bowl, ca. 1640–50, Jingdezhen, China, porcelain, h. 6½ in. Dallas Museum of Art, The Wendy and Emery Reves Collection, 1985.R.953.

Fig. 2.3: Plates, ca. 1815, Paris, porcelain, enamel. Dallas Museum of Art, gift of Ronald S. Kane, T42430.

Fig. 2.4: Pitcher, 1852–58; attributed to Daniel Greatbach, designer/modeler; United States Pottery Company, Bennington, Vermont; parian porcelain. Marked: [diamond-shaped framed lozenge impressed] UNITED STATES/ POTTERY CO./ BENNINGTON, Vt. Dallas Museum of Art, gift of the Friends of Decorative Arts' 1991 Twilight Zone Trip, 1991.86.

Fig. 2.5: Sweetmeat glass, ca. 1740–60, England, lead glass, h. 6⅜ in. Dallas Museum of Art, The Wendy and Emery Reves Collection, 1985.R.275.

Fig. 2.6: (*Left*) Decanter and stopper, ca. 1830, New England, mold-blown glass. Dallas Museum of Art, The Faith P. and Charles L. Bybee Collection, gift of Faith P. Bybee. (*Center*) Decanter and stopper, ca. 1825, United States, mold-blown glass. Dallas Museum of Art, Dallas Glass Club Collection gift, 1941, 1992.380.a–b. (*Right*) Decanter with stopper, ca. 1830–40, Boston and Sand-

wich Glass Company, Sandwich, Massachusetts, mold-blown glass. Dallas Museum of Art, Dallas Glass Club Collection, gift of Mrs. Leonard Brown, 195, 1992.384.

Fig. 2.7: (*Left*) Lafayette salt dish, ca. 1830–35; Boston and Sandwich Glass Company; glass with pressed decoration. Dallas Museum of Art, Dallas Glass Club Collection, 1992.490. (*Center*) California sugar bowl, ca. 1855–75; probably New England Glass Works, East Cambridge, Mass.; glass with pressed decoration. Dallas Museum of Art, Dallas Glass Club Collection, gift in memory of Mrs. Richard Wilber, 1989, 1992.496. (*Right*) Henry Clay cup plate, ca. 1844; unknown factory, New England; glass with pressed decoration. Dallas Museum of Art, Dallas Glass Club Collection, gift in memory of Roy Smith, son of Patt Smith, 1985, 1992.493.

Fig. 2.8: Pitcher, 1875; Karl L. H. Muller, designer; Union Porcelain Works, Brooklyn, N.Y., maker; porcelain, h. 8¼ in. Dallas Museum of Art, gift of the 1990 Dallas Symposium, 1990.90.

Fig. 2.9: Courtesy Library of Congress, LC-USZ62-49803.

Fig. 2.10: "Printing and Transferring Decorations," W. S. Harris, *The Potter's Wheel and How It Goes Around* (Trenton, N.J.: Burroughs and Mountford, 1886): 51. Courtesy Smithsonian Institution Libraries.

Fig. 2.11: William C. Gates, Jr., *The City of Hills and Kilns* (East Liverpool, Ohio: 1984): 421. Printed by permission of the East Liverpool Historical Society. Courtesy Museum of Ceramics at East Liverpool, Ohio.

Fig. 2.12: Gates 1984, 423. Printed by permission of the East Liverpool Historical Society. Courtesy Museum of Ceramics at East Liverpool, Ohio.

Fig. 2.13: Gates 1984, 160. Printed by permission of the East Liverpool Historical Society. Courtesy Museum of Ceramics at East Liverpool, Ohio.

Fig. 2.14: Gates 1984, 93. Printed by permission of the East Liverpool Historical Society. Courtesy Museum of Ceramics at East Liverpool, Ohio.

Fig. 2.15: *Crockery and Glass Journal* 94:6 (9 Feb. 1922): 25.

Fig. 2.16: W. S. George Pottery Company advertisement, *Pottery, Glass, and Brass Salesman* (20 Feb. 1930).

Fig. 2.17: Syracuse China advertisment, unidentified magazine, [1920?].

Fig. 2.18: *Gift and Tableware Reporter* (Jan. 1962): 28.

Fig. 2.19: "The Tableware War," *Modern Plastics* 29:3 (Nov. 1951). Courtesy The McGraw-Hill Companies, Inc., New York.

Fig. 2.20: Melmac dinnerware advertisement, *Crockery and Glass Journal* 145:3 (Sept. 1949): 35.

Fig. 2.21: Carl U. Fauster, *Libbey Glass Since 1818* (Toledo: Len Beach Press, 1979). Courtesy Dallas Public Library. Printed by permission of Libbey Glass Company.

Fig. 2.22: *Scientific American* (28 June 1902): supplement. Courtesy Texas A&M University Library.

Fig. 2.23: Libbey Glass Company advertisement of *Circus* hostess set, unidentified magazine, [1952?].

Chapter 3
Fig. 3.1: *Crockery and Glass Journal* 104:1 (6 Jan. 1927): 44.

Fig. 3.2: *Crockery and Glass Journal* 144:2 (Feb. 1949): 28.

Fig. 3.3: Waterford Archives. Courtesy Waterford Crystal, Ltd.

Fig. 3.4: Geo. Borgfeldt & Co. advertisement, *Crockery and Glass Journal* 108:12 (Dec. 1930): 5.

Fig. 3.5: *Crockery and Glass Journal* 122:1 (Jan. 1938): 11.

Fig. 3.6: *Crockery and Glass Journal* 116:5 (May 1935): 13.

Fig. 3.7: Gates 1984, 322. Printed by permission of the East Liverpool Historical Society, Ohio.

Fig. 3.8: Courtesy Houston Metropolitan Research Center, Houston Public Library.

Fig. 3.9: Morimura Brothers advertisement, *Crockery and Glass Journal* 92:25 (16 Dec. 1920): 232.

Fig. 3.10: Mitteldorfer Straus advertisement, *Crockery and Glass Journal* 115:5 (Nov. 1934): 35.

Chapter 4
Fig. 4.1: *Pottery, Glass and Brass Salesman* (13 Mar. 1930): cover.

Fig. 4.2: Advertisement of Lewis Patent China Sample Trunk, *Crockery and Glass Journal* 67:1 (2 Jan. 1908): 35.

Fig. 4.3: *Crockery and Glass Journal* 93:7 (17 Feb. 1921): 32.

Fig. 4.4: *Crockery and Glass Journal* 112:1 (Jan. 1933): 4.

Fig. 4.5: *Crockery and Glass Journal* 151:4 (Oct. 1952): 40.

Fig. 4.6: Advertisement of Mid-Winter Chicago Gift Show, *Crockery and Glass Journal* 108:1 (Jan. 1930): 10.

Fig. 4.7: *Crockery and Glass Journal* 97:8 (23 Feb. 1922): 30.

Fig. 4.8: *Crockery and Glass Journal* 104:3 (20 Jan. 1927): 21.

Fig. 4.9: Northbrook, Illinois, 1962. Courtesy Crate & Barrel.

Fig. 4.10: Tiffany & Co.'s china selling floor, Union Square, N.Y., ca. 1870–1905. Copyright Tiffany & Co. Archives 1999. Not to be published or reproduced without prior permission. No permission for commercial use will be granted except by written agreement.

Fig. 4.11: *Crockery and Glass Journal* 151:2 (Aug. 1952): 38.

Fig. 4.12: *Crockery and Glass Journal* 151:2 (Aug. 1952): 39.

Fig. 4.13: Marshall Field & Co. advertisement, *Crockery and Glass Journal* 107:6 (June 1929): 44.

Fig. 4.14: *Crockery and Glass Journal* 67:2 (9 Jan. 1908): 35.

Fig. 4.15: *Crockery and Glass Journal* 109:4 (Apr. 1931): 19.

Fig. 4.16: May-D&F department store, Denver, *Gift and Tableware Reporter* 2 (Oct. 1962): 28.

Fig. 4.17: *Crockery and Glass Journal* 108:12 (Dec. 1930): 55.

Fig. 4.18: Slides of Lane family's Thanksgiving table and wedding gifts to Alice G. Lane and Robert F. Venable, Angleton, Texas, 1954. Courtesy Alice Lane Venable.

Fig. 4.19: *Crockery and Glass Journal* 116:6 (June 1935): 38.

Fig. 4.20: Imperial Glass Company advertisement, unidentified magazine, [1950?].

Fig. 4.21: Gladding, McBean & Co. advertisement of Franciscan Fine China, *Crockery and Glass Journal* 146:3 (4 Mar. 1950): 13.

Fig. 4.22: Gates 1984, 427. Printed by permission of the East Liverpool Historical Society. Courtesy Museum of Ceramics at East Liverpool, Ohio.

Fig. 4.23: *Crockery and Glass Journal* 162:1 (Jan. 1958): 39.

Fig. 4.24: Morimura Brothers advertisement, *Crockery and Glass Journal* 93:50 (15 Dec. 1921): cover.

Fig. 4.25: Edwin M. Knowles China Company advertisement, *Crockery and Glass Journal* 101:1 (2 July 1925): 11.

Fig. 4.26: Gladding, McBean & Co. advertisement of Franciscan Pottery, *Crockery and Glass Journal* 117:1 (July 1935): 22.

Fig. 4.27: Lenox China advertisement layout, ca. 1955. Courtesy Lenox Archives.

Chapter 5
Fig. 5.1: Corning Glass Works advertisement of Pyrex custard cups, unidentified magazine, [1924?].

Fig. 5.2: Courtesy Lenox Archives.

Fig. 5.3: Plate design, ca. 1923. Courtesy Lenox Archives.

Fig. 5.4: Courtesy Belle Kogan.

Fig. 5.5: Macbeth American advertisement of Hobnail beverage sets, *Crockery and Glass Journal* 113:1 (July 1933): 2.

Fig. 5.6: Leigh Potters, Inc., advertisement of Leighware, *Crockery and Glass Journal* 107:4 (Apr. 1929): 17.

Fig. 5.7: Salem China Company advertisement, *Crockery and Glass Journal* 124:2 (Feb. 1939): 3.

Fig. 5.8: Castleton China, Inc., advertisement, *Crockery and Glass Journal* 151:6 (Dec. 1952): 32.

Fig. 5.9: Josiah Wedgwood & Sons advertisement, unidentified magazine, [1953?].

Fig. 5.10: A. H. Heisey & Co. advertisement of *Orchid* glassware, page proof, [1950?].

Fig. 5.11: "Creil Reproductions [by Mottehedah]: For Connoisseurs by Connoisseurs" (New York: Carole Stupell Ltd., 1964). Courtesy Carole Stupell, Ltd.

Boldface type indicates illustrations.

A. H. Heisey & Co. (act. 1893–1958), 55, 81, 159, 169, 362, 413; *New Era*, **54**, 55, **168**, **368**, 424, 460; No. 4045 pattern, **368**, 460; *Orchid* pattern, **413**; *Ridgeleigh*, **363**, 460; *Stanhope*, **363**, 460

A. J. Van Dugteren & Sons, 272

A. N. Khouri & Brothers, 191

A. Zen & Figlio, 273

Aaron, Charles (1872–1947), 131

Aaron, Marcus II, 133

Abundance and display, in Victorian dining, 19, 20, 32

Acapulco pattern coffeepot (Villeroy & Boch), 406, **407**, 469

Accent shape snack plate (Knowles), **44**, 45, 423

Achtziger, Hans (b. 1918), 227, 443, 444

Acid-etching, **177**, 438

Acid polishing, 159

Adam, Robert (1728–92), 456

Adams, Charlotte, 91

Adams, W. P. C., 300

Adline Trading Company, 259, 261

Adoue, Mary and Jean Baptiste, 449

Ad valorem taxes, 199

Advertising, 134–35, 141, 159, 183 n. 112, 223, 316, 318

Aeroplane pattern (Onondaga), **126**, 431

Aesthetic style, 327, 430

African Americans, in tableware market, 373

Agate glass (New England Glass), 163

Agate Pass pattern bowl, plate, and cup and saucer (Fabrik), **271**, 449

Agents, 201, 211

Ahrenfeldt, Charles Jules (ca. 1857–1934), 186

Ahrenfeldt & Son. *See* Charles Ahrenfeldt & Son

Airflow teapot (Hall), **75**, 427

Air Force One, 254, 413

Aitken, Harry, 431

Alana pattern (Waterford), 219

Alcoholic beverages, in American home, 83–88

Alfred University, 333, 338

Allen, Bob, 394, 466

Allen, Louise, 341

Allen, Lucy G. (1867–?), 38, 63, 81–82

Allied Chemical and Dye Corporation, 150, 155

Allied English Potteries (act. 1964–72), 210

Alpha old-fashioned glass (Lobmeyr), **232**, 444–45

Alsterfors Glasbruk, 266, 267

Altman's. *See* B. Altman & Co.

Altrohlauer Porzellanfabriken, **226**, 443

Amber-Glo pattern coffee server (Stangl), **383**, 464

Amberina glass (New England), 163

Amelung, John Frederick (1741–98), 110, 114

Americana shape cup and saucer (Homer Laughlin), **372**, 373, 461–62

American belleek, 138, 430

American Ceramics Products Company (act. 1935–67), 385, 464

American Ceramics Society (est. 1898–99), 130, 336

"American China," 124

American China Manufactory (Bonnin and Morris, 1770–72), 107

American China Manufactory (Tucker, 1826–38), 107

American Chinaware Corporation (act. 1929–31), 360

American Commercial (est. 1948), 250, 251

American Contemporary Glass, 171

American Cyanamid Company, 150, 151, 155

American Designers Institute (ADI), 338

"American Dishes: Home Product Fills Gap Made by War and Boycott," 368

American Encaustic Tiling Company (act. ca. 1875–1935), 132

American Etiquette, 48

American Flint Glass Workers Union, 160

American Glass Association, 247

American Homes pattern (Homer Laughlin), **372**, 373, 461–62

American Institute of Architects, 338

American Leipzig Fair Association, 223

American Modern tableware (Steubenville), 64, **65**, 349, 385; table linens, 383

American Potters Association, 186

American Pottery and Glass Reporter, 316

American Pottery Company, 117

American Prestige glasses (Libbey), **172**, 437

American Provincial pattern (Homer Laughlin), 132

American Sweetheart glass (Macbeth-Evans), 427

American System, 112

Anchor Hocking Glass Company (est. 1937), 77, 167, 168, 362, **364**, 460

Anderson, Merry K., 17

Anderson, Winslow, 140, 433, 451, 452

Angelus shape casserole dish (Homer Laughlin), **333**, 454–55

Anmut shape covered vegetable dish (Heinrich & Co.), **227**, 443

Anniversary shape casserole dish (Red Wing Pottery), **58**, 424

Annular shape (Wedgwood), 214

Antico Doccia shape (Richard-Ginori), 276, 413; candy dish, **274**, 275, 276, 413, 449

Apart shape snack plate with cup and coffeepot (Hutschenreuther), **227**, 443–44

Apollinaris, 83

Apple tableware (Franciscan), 217, 383, 412, 428

Arabesque pattern coffee server (Denby), **405**, 468

Arabesque pattern (Northern), 434

Arabia AB, 267, 272; *Kilta* tableware, **269**, 448; Model R shape, **269**, 448

Aratani, George, 250

Argenta ware (Wedgwood), 200, 422

Aristocrat China Company, 226

Aristocrat shape (Leigh), 362; demitasse cup and saucer, dessert plate, and coffeepot, **361**, 459

Arklow Pottery, 263

Army Exchange Service (AES), 231

Arnold, Tom, 389, 466

Art deco, 136, **177**, 189, 195, 257, 356–65, 432, 438

Art glass, 115, 159

Arthur, Chester, 439

Arthur A. Everts Company, 300

Artichoke plate, 81

Artifice, in Victorian food preparation, 20, 32

Art Institute of Chicago, 337

Art Modern shape stem, goblet (Morgantown Glass Works), **169**, 436

Art nouveau, 279 n. 53, 327, **333**, 445, 451, 454, 455

Arts and Crafts style, 13, 327, 332, 451, 454

Art Students League, 342

Artware, 13, 140

Asparagus tongs, 54

Assembly line, 134

Associated Glass and Pottery Manufacturers, 294, 295

ASTA, 469

Astoria pattern covered bowl (Theodore Haviland), **197**, 439

Athlone pattern (Doulton), **205**, 440

Atlanta Merchandise Mart, 289

Atlantic City China and Glass Show, 291

Atlantis Crystal, 470

Austrian Secession, 327

Automation, 179

Autumn Leaf pattern (Jewel), 126

Autumn Leaves pattern plate and cup and saucer (Hutschenreuther), **230**, 231, 444

Autumn Leaves pattern (Taylor), 467

Autumn (Lenox), 140, 339

Autumn Splendor pattern (Taylor, Smith & Taylor), **98**, 99, 429

Avant-garde design, **222**, 362; Rosenthal Studio Line, 239, 242–43

Avon goblet (Unknown factory, Sweden), **266**, 448

Avon shape cake plate and gravy boat (Doulton), **208**, 209–10, 441

Aynsley China (est. 1971), 220

B. Altman & Co., 87, 219, 243, 251, 296, 300

B. F. Drakenfeld & Co., 345

B. J. Brock & Co., **89**, 91, 428

B. Tomby, 226, 227, 281 n. 117

Baccarat. *See* Cristalleries de Baccarat

Bach, Richard F. (1887–1968), 356

Bachhoffner, Charles, 200

Bacik, Charles, 218, 219

Backstamps, 193, 315; Black Knight, 444; Haviland China Company, 193, 195; pseudo-English, 109, 117; Spode, 211

Bacon Rind pattern (Knox), **321**, 453

"Bad Manners at the Table," **32**

Bailey, Banks, & Biddle, 448

Bakelite Corporation, 343

Bakewell, Benjamin, 110

Bakewell, Page & Bakewell, 112

Bakewell & Co. (1809–82), 110, 112, 171

Ballerina tableware (Universal Potteries), 17; coffee pot, **18**, 421

Ball-handled shape, 429

Bamboo pattern (Tharaud), 444

Bangor pattern plate (Buffalo), **128**, 431

Barbara Jean tableware (Sebring), 344

Barbecue tools, 89

Barbier, Georges, 195

Barovier & Toso, **273**, 449

Bartlam, John, 105

Barware, 87–88; *Décor* (Morgantown Glass Works), **168**, 427; *New Era* (Heisey), **54**, 55, **168**, 424

Basket-weave, 424

Bauble pattern (Jackson Internationale), **402**, 468

Bauer. *See* J. A. Bauer Pottery Company

Bauer California Pottery, **102**, 137, 430

Bauhaus, 13, 356, 444, 459

Baumann, Hans Theodor (b. 1924), **403**, 446

Bawo & Dotter, 190, 211, 226

Bayle, 192

Bayreuther, Karl (1891–1953), 445, 455

Beale, Joseph Boggs, 132

Beam, Charles E., 174

Beaudin, Gaétan (b. 1924), 449

Beecher, Catharine (1800–78), 26

Beer, 85

Beer jug (Wedgwood), 214, **215**, 442

Beer mugs (Décor), **271**, 449
Belgian glass, 272
Belgian pottery, 272
Belleek, 140, 327, 344; American, 138, 430; Irish, 430, 433
Belle Kogan Associates (act. 1930–70), 342
Belle shape (Boonton), 151, 343
Belmont Glass Company, 174
Beltane tableware (Lenox), 339
Bengtson, Hetha (b. 1917), 448
Bennett, Edwin (1818–1908), 122, 422
Bennett, James (1812–62), 107, 108, 181 n. 15
Bennett and Chesapeake, 200
Bennison, Jane, 428, 432, 456, 461
Bentley, Thomas (1730–80), 458
Benton, Thomas Hart, 460
Berkeley, William, 104
Berkeley tableware (Ebeling & Reuss), 289, 342
Bernardaud. *See* L. Bernardaud & Cie.
Better Homes and Gardens, 63, 89, 310
Better Homes and Gardens Cookbook, 57
Betty Crocker's Picture Cookbook, 92
Beverage sets, **346**, 347, 456
Biarritz shape plate and cup and saucer (Royal Staffordshire), **206**, 441
Billingsley Rose pattern (Spode), 212, 440
Bing & Grøndahl Porcelaenfabrik, 267
Binney, Amos, 114
Binns, Charles Fergus (1857–1934), 124, 140, 338
Binns, Richard W. (d. 1900), 140
Bird, Harry, 460, 461
Bird and Butterfly pattern, 104
Bird Cage pattern teapot (Rosenthal), **241**, 446
Birds on Trees pattern cup and saucer (Rosenthal), **240–41**, 445–46
Biscayne pattern (Rosenthal), 430
Biscayne sherbet glass (Fostoria), 168, **170**, 436
Bisottiera, 449
Bistro Christianshaven tableware (Dansk), 272
Black, Starr & Frost, 297
Black-and-white designs, 465
Black Graphics pattern (Mikasa), **416**, 417, 470
Black Knight China, 228, **230**, 235, 272, 281 n. 118, 345, 444
Blake, Alfred J., 252
Blanks, 115, 138, 140, 159, 160
Blarney pattern tumbler (Val St. Lambert), **191**, 438–39
Bleininger, Albert V. (1873–1946), 131
Blenko Glass Company (est. 1922): colonial revival ware, 362; Colonial Williamsburg commission, 353; goblet, based on no. CW-IG shape, **301**, 451; Muddler, **301**, 451–52; No. 600-DOF shape tumbler, **301**, 451–52; No. 939-P shape pitcher, **301**, 451–52
Block, Joseph (1895–1977), 239, 242, 446
Block China Company (est. 1963), 228, 231, 239, 242, 281 n. 118; *Chromatics* series, **277**, **410**, 450, 469–70; *Espana* shape, **277**, 405, 450; *Evolution* pattern, **277**, 406, 450; *Tierra* pattern, **277**, 450; *Transition* shape, **277**, 406, 450–51; *Up-Beat* shape, 450
Bloomingdale Flint Glass Works (act. 1820–40), 115
Bloomingdale's, 243, 252, 254
Bloor, William (1821–77), 119
Blown glass, 115
Blue Canton pattern, 278

Blue Fire pattern (Rörstrand), 267, **269**, 448–49
Blue Persian pattern (Doulton), **332**, 454
Blue Ridge Dinnerware (Southern Potteries), **18**, 421
Blue Tulip pattern (Noritake), **96**, 429
Blue Vineyard (Iroquois), 429
Boch, Anthony, 108
Boch, Francis, 108
Boch, Wendelin von (b. 1943), 234
Boch, William, 108
Boda Bruks, 266, 267
Body types, 136, 138, 235, 420, 433, 441
Bohemia Keramische Werke (est. 1921), 235; cup and saucer, **226**, 443
Bohemian glass, 222, 223
Bolle, 445
Bone china, 140, 199, 200, 201, 251, 257, 420
Bonfils, Robert, 195
Bonnin, Gousse (ca. 1741–ca. 1780), 107
A Book of Hors d'Oeuvre (Allen), 82
Boonton Molding Company (act. ca. 1920–after 1962), 151, 343
Boote, Edward, 214
Booth, Thomas, 119
Boraxine, 126
Borden, Charlotte, 453
Borden, Edward, 453
Borosilicate glass (Pyrex), 59, 160, 179, 336, 438
Boston and Sandwich Glass Company (act. 1826–88), 114, 157
Boston Cooking-School Cook Book (Farmer), 27
Boston Crown Glass Manufacturing (act. 1787–1809), 112
Boston Sunday Herald, 67
Boston Tea Party teacups, 119
Botanica pattern (Knowles), **380–81**, 463–64
Botanic Garden (Portmeirion), 210
Bottle kilns, **129**, 134, **134**, 138
Boullemier, Lucien (1876–1949), 140
Bourne, Joseph (1788–1860), 405, 448
Boutique concept, 305
Bracken, Peg, 92
Bracquemond, Joseph-Auguste (Félix) (1833–1914), 193, 439
Branchell Company, 154, 371, 434
Brandt, Edgar, 341
Braque, Georges, 459
Brastoff, Sascha (1918–93), **94**, 428–29
Breakfast sets, 66
Breakfronts, 77
Brearley, Charles, 124
Brewer, John Hart (1844–1900), 117, 119, 123
Brewing Trades Institute, 87
Briard, Georges, 149
Bridal market, 296, 394, 412
Bridal registries, 141, 144, 149, 171, 300, 309, 311–13, 417
Bride's magazine, 143
Bridge sets, 52, **53**, 424
Briggs, Richard, 422
Briggs, William, 193
Brilliant cut glass, 115, **156**, 157–60, **164**, **220**, 327
British Arts and Crafts design, 337
British Board of Trade, 206
British pottery industry, 210; postwar pottery production, 207–10; in U.S. market, 200–217, 279 n. 52., 403–4; World War II pottery production, 206–7
Brodegaard, Robert F. (1915–61), 267
Bromley, William Sr. (d. 1885), 430

Brookdale pattern goblet (Tharaud), **232**, 444
Brooklyn Glass Works (act. 1823–68), 115
Broome, Isaac (1835–1922), 122, 326
Broomhall, Vincent (1906–91), 144
Brothers Kornilov Factory (act. 1835–1918), **265**, 447–48
Brower & Co., 273
Brown, Barbara (b. 1932), 406
Brown, Mary C., 466
Brownfield's Pottery, 336
Brown-Forman, 272
Brunt, William, 119
Brush, Tony, 297
Bryan, Arthur (b. 1923), 210, 216–17, 463
Bryce, James (1812–93), 112, 171
Bryce, John, 112
Bryce, Robert, 112
Bryce Brothers Company (act. 1882–1965), 112, **112–13**, 143, 171, 371, 430
Bryce, McKee and Company. *See* Bryce Brothers Company
Buckingham pattern sherry glass (Baccarat), **191**, 438
Buffalo Pottery (est. 1901), 125, 126, 128, **128**, 149, 430, 431
Buffet (breakfast), 77
Buffet-style dining, 63, 385
Buffet wares, 63, 64
Bullock's, 463
Burley & Tyrell, 211
Burmese glass (Pairpoint), 159
Burroughs, Garret, 119
Butler, Edward (d. 1905), 201
Buttercup pattern (Spode), 211, 412
Butterflies pattern (Arzberg), **402**, 468
"Buy American" movement, 138, 246, 294
Buyers, 296–97

C. M. Hutschenreuther (act. 1814–1969). *See* Lorenz Hutschenreuther
C. Reizenstein Sons, 297, 376
C. '70 wineglass (Claus Joseph Riedel Tiroler Glashütte), **232**, 444
CAD (computer aided design) software, 418
Cadet Series pattern (Salem), **302–3**, 452
Cadiz pattern (Villeroy & Boch), 469
Cadmium, 406
Cains, Thomas, 112
Caissellier, Alberto, 454
Cake mixes, 92
Calder, Alexander (1898–1976), **394**, 466
Caliente line (Paden), 348
California Aztec pattern (Metlox), 394, **395**, 466
California Bent Glass Company, 463
California Chanticleer pattern (Brock), 428
California Confetti shape butter dish and coffeepot (Metlox), **395**, 466
California Del Rey pattern (Metlox), **395**, 466
California Farmhouse pattern (Brock), 428
California Flowers pattern (Vernon Kilns), 461
California Freeform pattern (Metlox), 394, **395**, 466
California Mobile pattern (Metlox), 394, **395**, 466
California potteries, 135–37, 345, 347–48, 385
California Pottery Guild, 137, 415 n. 43
California Pottery tableware (Metlox), 347
Cambridge Glass Company (act. 1901–58), 160, 286, 437
Cambridge pattern (T. Furnival & Sons), 122

Cambridge Square glassware (Cambridge), 160, 437
Cameoware (Harker), 348
Campbell Soup Company, 57, 92
Camp cuisine, 89, 91
Canapés, 81–82
Candescent tableware (Boonton), 151
CAN factory, Empoli, Italian lead glass tumbler, **276**, 450
Canned soups, 92
Cannon, Ernestine, 276
Canova pattern pearlware, 107
Canova pattern (Ridgway), 181 n. 13
Can shape: creamer, sugar bowl, and coffeepot (Susie Cooper), **408**, 469; cup and saucer (Wedgwood), **408**, 469
Canton China, 104
Canton Glass Company (act. 1883–99), 453
Cape Cod Art Glass Sales Company, 460
Cape Cod Glass Works (act. 1858–69), 114
Capistrano pattern (Red Wing Pottery), **58**, 383, 424
Caprice pattern (Red Wing), 343
Capri goblet (Baccarat), **191**, 438
Capri plate, sherbet glass, and iced tea glass (Fostoria), **170**, 436
Carbon Corporation, 150
Carborundum Company, 210, 212, 214
Carder, Frederick (1863–1963), 435, 456
Carder, Timothy (act. at Lenox China since 1980), 140
Card parties, 48, 52, 54
Caribbean punch set (Duncan & Miller), **45**, 423
Carlsbad Crystal brand (Moser), 444
Carlton ware, 201; jug (Haynes), **24**, 421–22
Carnegie Institute of Technology, 333
Carnival pattern (Homer Laughlin), 131
Carnot pattern, 35
Carole Stupell, Ltd. (est. 1934), 278, 297, 371, 449, 450; plate, bowl on stand, and goblet, **273**, 449
Carr, James (1820–1904), 117–18, 123, 181 n. 57
Carrara Modern cup and saucer (Iroquois), **18**, 421
Carson, Barbara G., 100 n. 16
Carson, Edward L., 131
Carson Pirie Scott & Co., 160
Carter, Jimmy, 413
Carter, Rosalynn, 413
Cartlidge, Charles (1800–60), 108, 109
Cascade pitcher (United States Pottery), **107**
Case, Clinton P., 131
Cased glass, 163
Case glass goblet (Carlo Moretti), **276**, 450
Casino bridge sets (Limoges), 52, **53**, 424
Casino shape covered vegetable dish (Doulton), **205**, 440
Casseday, Samuel, 107
Casserole dishes, 57, **58**, 59
Cassidy's of Canada, 226
Castleton China (act. 1939–76), 144, 239, 429; *Bourbon* pattern, **145**, 433; club marketing plans, 314–15; *Empire* pattern, **238**, 445; market testing, 371; *Museum*, 385, **388–89**, 465; *Pilgrim* shape, **145**, 433
Casual China (Iroquois China), 385; cup and saucer, carafe, and salt and pepper shakers (Iroquois China), **387**, 465
Casual dining, 48, 52
Catalina Clay Products (act. 1927–37), 103, 136, 345; *Coupe* shape, **102**, 103, 430

Caterer jug, covered (Wedgwood), **24**, 421
Cauldon Pottery (act. ca. 1920–58), 210
Cauliflower plate and teapot (Griffen Smith & Co.), **24**, 422
Cawcia pattern goblet (Salviati), **273**, 449
CCC Royal Bohemian, 235
Central Glass Works (act. 1863–91), 160
Centura glass (Corning), 94, **95**, 150, 179–80
Centurion shape (Spode), 203, 211; covered vegetable dish, **203**, 440
Century Metalcraft Corporation, 460
Century shape (Hall), 389; plate, salad plate, and bread and butter plate, **373**, 462
Century shape (Homer Laughlin), 132, 348, 460; plate, **366–67**, 460; soup bowl, **68–69**, 426
Century Vellum (Homer Laughlin), 348
Cerabati-Holding, 198
Ceramar, 227, 234, 281 n. 117, 469
Ceramica D'Arte Ernestine Cannon D'Agostino, 273, 276–77, 449–50; bowl and underplate, **275**, 450; cup and saucer with *Red Eva* pattern, **275**, 450; plate, **275**, 449; plate and *Champignons* pattern, **275**, 450; tureen, **275**, 449
The Ceramic Art: A Compendium of the History and Manufacture of Pottery and Porcelain (Young), 109
Ceramic Art Company (act. 1889–1906), **139**, 327, 432–33
The Ceramic Art (Young), 118, 124
Ceramic Industry, 336
Ceramics. *See* Pottery
Ceramics: Twentieth Century Design (Hannah), 14
Ceramics and Glass Journal, 66
Chafing dishes, 64, **66**
Chain stores, 126
Chairs, dining, 22
Challinor, Edward, 138
Challinor, Taylor & Co., **158**, 435
Chambrun, René de, 192
Champagne glass (Josef Meyr's Neffe), **334**, 455
Champagne goblet (attrib. Hawkes), **156**, 435
Champagne or sherbet glass (attrib. Morgantown Glass Works), **168**, 436
Champagne pitcher, **84**, 85, 427
Champignons pattern (Ernestine Cannon), **275**, 408, 450
Chance Brothers, 179
Chanou, Nicholas, 108
Chantilly pattern glass (Tharaud), 444
Chantilly pattern highball tumbler (attrib. Steuben), **156**, 435
Chantilly pattern (Rosenthal), 235, **236**, 445
Chantilly pattern plate (Worcester), **202**, 440
Charles Ahrenfeldt & Son, 186, 195, 279 n. 10; *Chateaux de France*, 189; *Ivoire de France*, 189
Charm magazine, 91
Chason pattern (Tharaud), 444
Chateaux de France pattern (Ahrenfeldt), 189
Chelsea Wicker shape (Spode), 203
Chesapeake Pottery (act. 1880–82), 321
Chess Men glasses (Block), 470
Chevron pattern (Denby), 405
Chicago Merchandise Mart, 289, 291
Chicago Molded Products, 152
Chicago Winter Gift Show, 291, 294
Child, Julia (b. 1912), 94–95
Child labor, 127, **130**

Child's plate and mug (Warwick China), **127**, 431
China: bone, 140, 199, 200, 201, 251, 257, 420; defined, in American usage, 124; fine, 138–43, 394–400; institutional, 125, 131, 149, 332; reproduction, 413
China blanks, 138, 140
China cabinets, 23–24
China closet, 22
China, Glass and Lamps, 316
China, Glass, and Pottery Association of New York, 370
China, Glass and Tablewares, 418
Chinastone line (Lenox), 141, 171
Chinese Chippendale pattern (Worcester), **202**, 439–40
Chinese Chippendale revival, 452
Chinese Garden pattern (Flintridge), 434
Chinese tableware, 278, 440, 454
Chinoiserie, 458
Chintzware, 289, 350, 458
Chip-and-dip sets, 81
Chocolate cup and saucer and pot (Willets Manufacturing Company), 433
Chocolate pot, shape no. 47 (Ceramic Art Company), **139**, 432–33
Christmas Tree pattern (Spode), **55**–56, 212, 424
Chromatics series (Block), 406, 450; dinnerware, **410**, 469–70; flatware, **410**, 470; goblet, **410**, 470; placemats, **410**, 470
Chromium, 470
Chromolithographic prints, 23
Chunichi Toki Company, 252, 447
Circus pattern (Libbey), **162**
Clark, Clifford E. Jr., 22
Clark, Decius, 107
Clark, George W. (d. 1913), 131
Clark, Jody, 451
Classic Crystal tumbler (Libbey), **370**, 461
Claus Joseph Riedel Tiroler Glashütte, **232**, 444
Clay, Henry, 103, 112
Clermont pattern (Tirschenreuth), 227
Cleveland, Grover, 439
Clews, James (1790–1861), 107
Cliff, Clarice (1899–1972), 203, 206, 360, 362, 424, 440, 441
Clifton ware (Haynes), 422
Cloudburst pattern (Cavitt-Shaw), **44**, 423
Coal, 222
Coalport Pottery (est. ca. 1796), 210
Cobalt, 167
Cockerel pattern (Taylor), 467
Cocktail Hour series (Vernon Kilns), **88**, 428
Cocktail party, 54, **81**, 81–82
Cocktail plates, **88**, 428
Cocktails and drinking, in the American home, 83–88
Cocktail snacks, 81–82
Coffee mugs, 252
Coffeepot and demitasse cup and saucer (Wedgwood), 214, **215**, 442
Coin pattern (Rosenthal), **241**, 446
Collamore's. *See* Gilman Collamore & Co.
Collector's book, 14
Colleen pattern (Waterford Glass), 218, **220**, 442
Colonade pattern (Noritake), 261, **262**, 447
Colonial Fireside pattern, 452
Colonial Homestead pattern chop platter (Royal China), **382**, 464
Colonial Kitchen pattern (Homer Laughlin), **60**, 61

Colonial pattern (Wedgwood), 458
Colonial revival, 65, 218, 349–53, 383, 426, 441, 454
Colonial Williamsburg: muddler, **301**, 451–52; No. 600-DOF shape tumbler, **301**, 451–52; 939-P shape pitcher, **301**, 451–52
Colony pattern (Salem), 362
Colorado pattern (Baccarat), 192
Colored slip, 433
Color-Flyte line (Branchell), 154; sugar bowl and creamer, **152**, 434
Color Follows Color as Course Follows Course: The New Vogue in Dinnerware, 345
Comcor glass, 179
Comelera, Paul, 421
Commemorative items, 431
Commercial Decal (est. 1938), 326, 394, 451, 462
Composition 'G' shape cordial glass (Rosenthal), **242**, 446
Condon, Phyllis, 316
Conran, Terence (b. 1931), 210, 465
Consolidated Lamp & Glass Company, 357, 362, 459
Constellation shape creamer, sugar bowl, plate, salad plate, and covered pitcher (Salem), **79**, 427
Consumer-focus groups, 418
Consumer Reports, 150
Contempri shape coffeepot (Jackson Internationale), **402**, 468
Continental Ceramics Corporation, 235
Continental line (Rosenthal), 239, **240**, 446
Continuous-melt tank, 169
Convenience foods, 92, 97
Conversation shape plate (Taylor), **399**, 467
Cookbook for Brides, 92
Cooking: revival, 1960–80, 94–99; in the 1880s, 20
Cookout tableware, 81, **89**, **90**, 91
Cooley, Cornelius (d. 1994), 309
Cooper, Audrey Denness, 309
Cooper, Susie (1902–95), 203, 252, 403, 406, 469
Cooperative Emploese Vetrai, 275
Co-Operative Flint Glass Company (act. 1869–1937), 293
Cooper Union, 333
Cooper-Willis, Euan, 210
Copeland, John, 217
Copeland, Robert (b. 1925), 209, 211, 217
Copeland, Ronald (1884–1958), 209
Copeland, Sidney, 217
Copeland, Spencer (b. 1923), 217
Copeland & Duncan (act. 1922–66), 211
Copeland & Thompson (act. 1923–66), 56, 211, 212
Copper-wheel engraving, 115
Coralitos line (Pacific Clay), 347
Coral pattern (Montgomery Ward), 35, 37
Corbitt, Helen, 460
Cordial glasses (Block), **410**, 470
Corelle glass (Corning), 179
Corinthian pattern (Wedgwood), 458
Corinth shape plate and cup and saucer (Doulton), **332**, 454
Corning Glass Works (est. 1868), 59, 94, 150, 156, 159, 163, 179–80; development and promotion of Pyrex, 336, **337**; laboratory, 160; shock-resistant glass, **179**; Steuben Division, 165
Corningware, 179, 180
Corn-on-the-cob sets, 55, **80**, 81, 427

Coronado tableware (Franciscan), 347; demitasse cup and saucer and coffeepot, **137**, 432
Coronado pattern (Lenox), 140, 339, 341
Coronation Golden Persephone pattern (Wedgwood), 453
Corsage pattern (Knowles), 461
Coster, Dominique de, 198
Cotswold (Schumann), 280 n. 108
Country Casual pattern (Pfaltzgraff), 149
Country Garden pattern (Red Wing), 343
Country Gingham pattern (Mikasa), 252, **253**, 446
Country Lane pattern (Brock), 428
Country Modern pattern snack plate and cup (Brock), **89**, 91, 428
Country-Time pattern (Pfaltzgraff), 149
Coupe Savoy shape (Wedgwood): dinner plate, 212, **213**, 441–42; plate, *Variations on a Geometric Theme* series, **407**, 469
Coupe Savoy shape, **262–63**, 385, 394, 441, 447, 462, 463; coffeepot, plate, and bowl (Wedgwood), **374**, 462–63; coffeepot (Lenox), **142**, 433; cup and saucer, teapot, and mug (Heath), **374**, 462; plate (Catalina Clay Products), **102**, 103, 430; plates, 64, 136, 347, 349, 394, 428, 450, 461; Stangl, 464
Cour, Brian, 469
Courtney shape stem, champagne glass (Morgantown Glass Works), **168**, 436
Coutant, Doris, 467
Cowan, R. Guy (1884–1957), 138, 431, 464
Cox & Co., 287
Coxe-DeWilde Pottery (act. 1688–92), 104
Coxon, Jonathan, 140
Crackle glazes, 327
Craft aesthetic, 385, 443
Craftone line (Noritake), 261
Crate & Barrel, 297, **299**, 322
Creamer, coffeepot, and sugar bowl (Heinrich & Winterling), **344**, 456
Creamware, 103, 105
Crescent China Company. *See* Leigh Potters
Crimmel, Henry, 174
Crimmel, Jacob, 174
Cristal de France, 192
Cristalleries de Baccarat (est. 1764), 190, **191**, 191–92, 297, 438
Criterion shape cup (Knowles), **44**, 45, 423
Crockery and Glass Journal, 124, 223, 227, 259, 273, 316, 428, 467; Belle Kogan on design, 343; Carr's autobiography, 181 n. 57; on china and glass sales in jewelry stores, 297; on demand for color, 347; on demand for "short sets," 65; on Glasgow Pottery, 118–19; "Is Main Street Moving?", 320; "Is There a Place for Japanese-Made Ceramics and Glass in Our Country?", 249; on the *Language of Flowers*, 458; on Maddock & Miller, 201; "Manufacturers Certain Ivory Body Has Come to Stay for Long Time," 344; on repeal of Prohibition, 87; "Using Bridge Sessions to Stimulate Sales," 52
Crockery Journal, 118
Crocus service, 446
Croquettes, 57
Crown Ducal Ware, 201
Crownford China Company, 190
Crown Jewels pattern (Tharaud), 444
Crystal D'Arques glass (Durand), 191
Crystal Glass Company, 435

Crystalline pattern (Rosenthal), **240–41**, 445–46

Cubist designs, **356**; salad plate (Leigh Potters), **360**, 459

Cup board, 22

Cuspidors, 108, 118

Cut glass. See Brilliant cut glass

Czecho Peasant Art Company (act. 1918–31/32), 228; cup and saucer, covered bowl with underplate, coffeepot, and mug, **49**, 423–24

Czechoslovak Ceramics, 232

Czechoslovak Glass Export Company (Glassexport), 232

Czech tableware, 48, **49**; glass, 222, 223; promotion and distribution, 223–28; trade fairs, 223; U.S. imports of, 223, 228; wartime and postwar, 228–33

D. G. & D. Haviland. See Haviland China Company

D. Stanley Corcoran, 267

Dainty food, 41, **48**

Dallas Crystal Stemware (Plastics Manufacturing Company), 152

Dallas Trade Mart, 252, 289

Dalzell, David B., 174

Dalzell, W. A. B., 160, 174

Damascene pattern plate (Fitz and Floyd), **254**, 447

Dammouse, Albert-Louis (1848–1926), 193, 439

Danish Modern, 385, 404

Dansk Designs (est. 1954), 252, 267, 272; *Bistro Christianshaven* tableware, 272; *Fjord* flatware, 272; *Flamestone* shape, 267, **270**, 272, 404, 449; *Fluted* pattern, **270**, 449; *Generation* tableware, 272; niche marketing, 373, 376; outlet stores, 321

D'Arcy, 316

Daum, 192

Davis, Theodore R., 439

Davison-Paxon, 339

Dawn pattern (Hall), **373**, 462

Day, Enid, 339

Daylily pattern (Taylor), **399**, 467

Dayton Hudson Corporation, 305, 322

Dealer exclusives, 141

Deanna shape (Knowles), 349

Debonaire creamer (Kenro), **152**, 434

Decalcomania (decals), 120, 122, 129, 140, 151, 452

DeCasse, Henri, 107

DeCasse, Louis François (1790–after 1850), 108

Decorating departments, 119–20

Décor line (Morgantown Glass Works), **86**, 427

Décor Pottery, Quebec, 267, 449; beer mugs, **271**, 449

Dedham Pottery (act. 1895–1943), 327

Deep Sea Fish pattern (Onondaga), **127**, 431

Deldare line (Buffalo Pottery), 126

Delfino, Matthew, 234

Della Robbia pattern (Homer Laughlin), **133**, 353, 432

Deluxe serving bowl and divided vegetable bowl (Boonton), **152**, 434

Denby, Ltd., 448

Denby Pottery, 210, 448; *Arabesque* pattern, **405**, 468; *Chevron* pattern, 405; *Minstrel* pattern, 448; *Mirage* glassware, **266**, 448; *Mirage Yellow* glass, **266**, 448; *Ode* pattern, 405; *Potter's Wheel* pattern, **405**, 468; *Regency Yellow* flatware, 448; *Samarkand/ Arabesque* pattern, **405**; stoneware

lines, 405. See also Joseph Bourne & Son

Denker, Ellen Paul (b. 1947), 17

Denman, John Rufus (1877–1956), 165

Department stores, 126, 300–307, 418

Depression glass, **73**, 167

Derby pattern (Tirschenreuth), 227

Desert pattern (Red Wing), 343, **366**, 385, 460

Desert Rose (Franciscan), 217, 383, 412; plate and coffeepot, **94**, 428

Desert Star pattern (Doulton), **208**, 209, 441

Designers, 135, 325, 333–43, 368, 370, 412

Design exhibitions, 337

Design for the Machine, 337

Detroit Institute of Arts, 337

De Sphinx, 272

DeVilbiss, 138

De Vito, Bart, 451

Dewdrop pitcher (Hobbs, Brockunier), **328**, 454

Diablo pattern (Wedgwood), 406, **408**, 469

Diadem tableware (Hutschenreuther), 444

Diamond, Freda (1905–98), 166, 233, 365, 370, 371, 437, 461

Diamond Jubilee Sears, Roebuck Catalog, 77

Dingley Act, 199

Dining: casual, 48, 52; chairs, 22; implements, 26; informality as a style, 61, 63–64; nooks, 59; as social gatekeeping, 19; tables, 22. See also Formal dinner party

Dining rooms, **22**; pictures, 23; in 1920s, 59; in the 1920s, **61**; Victorian, 22–23

Discontinued patterns, 418–19

Discount distributors, 320–21

Discount stores, 418

Dishes, politics of, 228

Dishwashers, 376, 429

Distillator, Robert R., 468

Doccia porcelain factory, 276, 449

Dogwood glassware (Macbeth-Evans), 167, 427

Doily Petitpoint pattern, 452

Domestic Receipt Book (Beecher), 26

Domestic science, 38, 57

Dominick and Haff, 338–39

Donatello chocolate cup and saucer and pot (Rosenthal), 235, **237**, 445

Donatello shape (Rosenthal), 235, **237**

Dooley, Cornelius "Con" (d. 1994), 219

Doorknobs, 118

Doremus, Frederick H., 281 n. 117

Dorflinger, Christian (1828–1915), 115

Dorflinger Glass Works (act. 1865–1921), 157, 159, 162, 326

Dorn, Marion V. (1896–1964), 400

Dorothy C. Thorpe, Inc. (act. 1932–80s?), 297, 463

Dose, Frederic (d. 1908), 186

Double trident (Komaru mark), 458–59

Dougherty, George, 436

Doulton & Co. (est. 1854), 200, 201, 203, 289; Arts and Crafts–influenced tableware, 327; *Athlone* pattern, **205**, 440; *Avon* pattern, **208**, 209–10, 441; *Blue Persian* pattern, **332**, 454; *Casino* shape, **205**, 440; *Corinth* shape, **332**, 454; *Desert Star* pattern, **208**, 209, 441; experiments in modernism, 210; *The Granville* pattern, 203, **354**, 458; Horizon line, 441; *Kew* pattern, **324**, 453; *Lincoln* shape, **354**, 458; *Octagon* shape,

332, 454; *Poppy* pattern, **332**, 454; *Woburn* pattern, **332**, 454

Down the Hatch pattern cocktail plate, **88**, 428

Drapeau pattern plate (F. Winkle & Co.), **121**, 431

Drésa, 195

Dresdner Art China, 280 n. 108

Drexel Institute of Technology, 92

Drop-leaf table, 22

Dube, Alfred (b. 1923), 462

Dufrêne, Maurice (1876–1955), 189

Duhrssen, Alfred, 394

Dummer, George, 108, 115

Dumond, Frank, 338

Duncan & Miller Glass Company (act. 1865–1955), 45, 336, 362, 376, 436, 463; *Caribbean* punch set, **45**, 423; *Language of Flowers*, **358**, 458; *Terrace*, **43**, 423

Dundonald, Lord, 454

Dunlevy, S. C, 293

Durand Art Glass Company (1924–31), 165, 180

Durand International (est. late 1960s), 191

Dura-Print process, 466

Dutch glass and pottery, 272

Dymaxion House, 337

E. I. du Pont de Nemours & Co., 150, 345

Early California pattern (Vernon Kilns), 347, **347**, 456

East Liverpool, Ohio, 108–10

East Liverpool Porcelain Works, 119

Ebb Tide pattern (Theodore Haviland), **196**, 439

Ebeling, Frederick W. (1856–1927), 289

Ebeling, Henry, 289

Ebeling, Robert W., 289

Ebeling & Reuss (est. 1886), 227, 289–90, 342; *Berkeley* tableware, 289, 342; *Metropolis* pattern, 289, **290**, 342, 451

Eclipse shape sugar bowl, chop or cake plate, teapot, and creamer (Franciscan), **397**, 466

Econorim shape (Onondaga), 431

Eden pattern, plate (Rosenthal), **344**, 456

Edge, W. H., 122

Edith Heath Ceramics (est. 1944), **374**, 405

Edme shape (Wedgwood), 203, 458; covered vegetable dish, **355**, 458

Edwin M. Knowles China Company (act. 1900–63), 130, 349; *Accent* shape, **44**, 45, 423; *Ballerina* tableware, 421; *Botanica* pattern, **380–81**, 463–64; *Corsage* pattern, 461; *Criterion* shape, **44**, 45, 423; *Deanna* tableware, 349; *Esquire* collection, **380**, **381**, 463–64; *Frosted leaves* pattern, **370**, 461; *Grass* pattern, **380**, **381**, 463–64; *Mayfair* shape, **370**, 461; *Oslo* pattern, 461; *Paradise* pattern, 461; *Platinum Grey* pattern, 461; *Platinum White* pattern, 461; *Queen Anne's Lace* pattern, **380**, **381**, 463–64; *Seeds* pattern, **380**, **381**, 463–64; *Silver spray* pattern, 461; *Snowflower* pattern, **380**, **381**, 463–64; *Williamsburg* shape (Knowles), 353

Egg plates, 55, 81

Eggshell ware (Homer Laughlin), **133**, 314, 426, 432

Eichler, Lillian, 61

Elbert H. Gary service, goblet (Stevens & Williams), **156**, 434–35

Elephant shape tureen (Worcester), **118**, 430

Elite shape (Paden), 348–49

Elizabethan pattern (Spode), 212, **213**, 442

Ellis, William, 105

El Patio shape chop plate and teapot (Franciscan), 432

El Rancho pattern cup and saucer and luncheon plate (Wallace China), **89**, 428

Elsinore pattern (Franciscan), 433

Elsterwerda Earthenware Factory, tea set, **222**, 443

Embassy glassware (Libbey), 165; water, cordial, and Sherbet glasses, **172**, 437

Embossed Grape Vine pattern (Wedgwood), **355**, 458

Embossed Queens Ware (Wedgwood), 203, 412

Emerald Flair glassware (Libbey), 167

Emerson, Walter H. (1902–47), 132

Empire pattern (Rosenthal), 239; soup bowl on stand, **238**, 445

Empire pattern (Taylor, Smith & Taylor), 349; covered casserole dish, **350**, 457; creamer and sugar bowl, **350**, 457

Encanto Nuevo shape (Franciscan), 423

Encanto shape (Franciscan): coffee and tea set, 41, **42–43**, 423; plate and cup and saucer, **396**, 397, 466

English pottery. See British pottery industry

Engraving, 160, 165

Enright Le-Carboulec, 267

Entertaining, in the post-1920 period, 61–64

Epicure tableware (Homer Laughlin), 132; coffeepot, **148**, 149, 434

Erie pattern plate (Thomas Till & Sons), **121**, 430–31

Ernestine Cannon. See Ceramica D'Arte Ernestine Cannon D'Agostino

ERPHILA. See Ebeling & Reuss

España shape (Block), 405, 470; teapot, sugar bowl, creamer, and cup and saucer, **277**, 450

Esquire shape (Knowles), 385; sugar bowl, **380**, **381**, 463–64

Etching, 166; acid, **177**, 438

Etiquette, 25

Etruria Works. See Ott & Brewer

European Common Market, 233

Everywoman's Guide to Harmonizing Patterns: Crystal, China, Silver, 376

Eve pattern (Shelley Potteries), 440

Evolution pattern (Block), **277**, 406, 450

Exclusive distribution rights, 318

Expansion table, 22

Exposition of Modern French Decorative Arts, 337

Exquisit shape (Rosenthal), 239, 391, 394; coffeepot, **241**, 446

F. Winkle & Co., **121**, 431

F. W. Woolworth & Co., 66, 126, 131, 321, 322, 371, 426, 466

Fabrik Inc. (act. 1973–86), 267; *Agate Pass*, **271**, 449

Factory outlet concept, 252

Fairwin pattern goblet (Morgantown Glass Works), **177**, 437

Family meals, 33–34

Fancy Free shape (Red Wing), 343; cup and saucer and teapot, **366**, 460

Fannie Farmer's School of Cookery, 38

Fantasies pattern (Lenox), **404**, 406, 468

Fantasy pattern (Hall), **373**, 394, 462

Farmer, Fannie Merritt (1857–1915), 27, 38

Farmhouse Provincial pattern (Brock), 428

Farwell, Field & Co. *See* Marshall Field & Co.

Fashionable Foods: Seven Decades of Food Fads (Lovegren), 41

Fashion shape (Midwinter), 389; coffeepot and teapot, **390**, 465

"Fast Fire" kiln, 149

Fauster, Carl, 165, 166

Favier, Henri, 341

Favrile glassware (Tiffany), **345**, 456

Feather pattern. *See Plume* pattern

Federal Glass Company (act. 1901–80), 343, **370**, 461

Federated Department Stores, 322

Feldspar, 222

Fensmark pattern plate (Royal Copenhagen), **268**, 448

Fenton Art Glass Company (est. 1906), 287

Fenton, Christopher Webber, 107

Festival pattern luncheon plate (Richardson), **352**, 458

Festoon pattern goblet (Fostoria), **170**, 436

Field, Leiter & Co. *See* Marshall Field & Co.

Fiesta Ironstone tableware (Homer Laughlin), 426

Fiesta ware (Homer Laughlin), 66, 69, **72**, 73, 131, 132, 133, 149, 348, 368, 426

Fife shape luncheon plate and cup and saucer (Minton), 350, **351**, 457

Fifth Avenue Building, 286, **287**

Filament stem, 436

Filled patterns, 140

"Fillers-in," 127

Fine china, 138–43, 394–400

Fine China line (Noritake), 261

Fine China shape teapot (Sascha Brastoff), **94**, 428–29

Fine shape (Midwinter), 403; coffeepot, **406**, 468–69

Finland Ceramics & Glass Corporation, 267

Finnish pottery, 267

Firesong pattern coffeepot (Lenox), **404**, 406, 468

Fischer-Treyden, Elsa (1901–95), 446

Fish and game services, 54

Fish covered casserole (Glidden), **386**, 464–65

Fisher, Bruce & Co., 54, 227, 249, 267, 276, 281 n. 117, 449

Fisher, John, 114

Fisher, Richard, 114

Fish pattern platter (Johnson Brothers), **28**, 29, 422

Fitz and Floyd China (est. 1960), 250, 252, 254, **254**, **255**, 408, 413, 447

Fitzhugh pattern (Spode), 203

Fitzpatrick, Bernard J., 218, 219

Fitz-Patrick, Patrick (1933–70), 252

500 Snacks, 82

Five-Step tableware (Lenox), **141**, 433

Fjord flatware (Dansk), 272

Flair shape (Northern), 385; platter, **153**, 434

Flamestone shape (Dansk), 267, 272, 404; plate, demitasse cup and saucer, **270**, 449

Flamingo Reeds pattern (Syracuse China), **384**, 385, 464

Flash Frisco pattern (Rosenthal), 430

Flash Marking pattern (Rosenthal), 430

Flash One pattern (Rosenthal), **99**, 429–30

Flash shape (Rosenthal), 97, 99, **99**; covered bowl and platter, **99**, 429–30

Flatiron Building, 286

Flatware, 26, 272, **410**, 448, 470

Flintkote Company, 315

Flintridge China Company. *See* Gorham Manufacturing Company

Floral pattern (Wedgwood), 458

Florida pattern (Lenox), 339; plate and cup and saucer, **340**, **341**, 455

"Flow blue," 327, **330**, 331, 454

Flowersong pattern (Midwinter), 209, **209**, 405, 406, 441

Floyd, Robert (b. 1931), 252, 408, 447

Fluted pattern coffeepot (Dansk), **279**, 449

Fly, Anthony, 18

Fly, Mary Anna, 18

Foley's, 296

Folkstone line (Noritake), 261

Follot, Paul (1877–1941), 279 n. 53

Fondoso line (Red Wing), 342

Fontaine pattern covered jug (Tiffin), **346**, 347, 456

Food: fads, 30; fashion system, 92; social meaning of, 24–25

Ford, Weldon, 453

Fordney-McCumber Tariff of 1922, 195, 199

Foreign Advisory Corporation, 272

Forest Green (Anchor Hocking), 168

Formaldehyde, 152

Formal dinner party, 19–20, 25, 26; in 1960–80, 94–99; contradictory messages, 30; menus, 26–**27**

Fornasetti, Piero (1913–88), 406, 409, 465, 469

Fort Pitt Hotel, Pittsburgh, 293, **294**

Fortuna sherbet glass (Rosenthal), **242**, 446

Fostoria Glass Company (act. 1887–1986), 160, 174–78, 220, 287; automation, 169; *Biscayne* glassware, 168, **170**, 436; *Capri* glassware, **170**, 436; colored glass in modern shapes, 394; decanter set, 177, **178**; design program, 174; *Festoon* pattern, **170**, 436; *Frosted Artichoke* pattern, 174; introduction of colored glassware, 345; *Knickerbocker* pattern, **170**, 436–37; magazine advertisements, 316; *Mayfair* glassware, 174, **175**, 437; No. 4020 shape, **167**, 177, 437; *Onyx* colored glass, 436; *Oriental ruby* color, 436; *Precedence* glassware, 168, **170**, 436; showroom, **287**; stemware, **170**; table-setting slides, 310; *Victoria* pattern, 174; *Vision* pattern, 178; *Westchester* shape, **170**, 174, 436

Fostoria Melamine Dinnerware, 152, 155

Fountain pattern (Lenox), 339, 456; plate, **340**, **341**, 455

Fowler, Orson, 38

Franciscan Division, Gladding, McBean & Co., 41, 394, 405; *Apple*, 217, 383, 412, 428; *Coronado* line, **137**, 347, 432; *Desert Rose* line, **94**, 383, 412, 428; *Eclipse* shape, **397**, 466; *El Patio* shape, 432; *Elsinore* pattern, 433; *Encanto Nuevo* line, 423; *Encanto* shape, 41, **42–43**, **396**, 397, 423, 466; Franciscan Cosmopolitan China, 261; Franciscan Procelain, 261; Franciscan Ware, **94**, **96**, 135, 136, **137**; *Geranium* pattern, **137**, 432; *Ivy* pattern, 383, 428; *Madrigal* pattern, 429; *Mandalay* pattern, 429; *Masterpiece* china, 146, 376; *Masterpiece* line, 433; *Merced* shape, 433; *Metropolitan* shape, **348**, 456–57; *Minaret* pattern, 429; *Modern America* line, 466; *Montecito* shape saucer, **137**, 432; *Ondine* pattern, 429; *Ovide*

(Redondo) shape, **146**, 433; *Padua* pattern, 432; *Rancho* shape cup, **137**, 432; *Sandalwood* pattern, 41, **42–43**, 423; *Shalimar* pattern, **96**, 429; *Shasta* pattern, 433; *Starburst* pattern, 394, **397**, 466; *Starry Night* pattern, 394, **396**, 397, 466; *Tiempo* pattern, **348**, 456, 457; *Trio* pattern, **348**, 457; *Westwood* pattern, **146**, 267, 433–34; *Woodside* pattern, 17

Franck, Kaj (b. 1911), 448

Frankfurter crown casserole, 92, **93**

Franklin, E. E., 457

Franklin Flint Glass Works. *See* Gillinder & Sons

Franklin Institute, 108, 109, 119

Frankoma Pottery (est. 1933), **89**, 428

Fraser's, 227, 281 n. 117

Fred C. Reimer Company, 227, 281 n. 117

Frederick & Nelson, 305

Frederik Lunning, Inc. (act. ca. 1946–ca. 1965), 267, 272

Free-blown blanks, 159

Freedom from Want (Rockwell), **25**

Free Form shape (Salem), **400**, 467

French, Neal, 442

French art deco, 452

French glass, 190–92

French porcelain, 327

French pottery, 25, 42, 279 n. 4

Friedman, Ephraim, 150

Fritchie, Hieronimus William (Hawkes) (ca. 1857–1940), 434, 435

Fritsche, William (Thomas Webb & Co.), 435

From Kiln to Kitchen: American Design in Tableware (Pickel), 14

Frontier Days pattern (Vernon Kilns), 428

Frosted Artichoke pattern (Fostoria), 174

Frosted Leaves pattern plate (Knowles), **370**, 461

Frost Flowers pattern (Hall), 462

Fry Glass, 162

"Fuddling cup," 87

Fuerst, Edward E. (b. 1903), 165, 437

Fuller, Buckminster, 337

Funabashi, Alfred, 250

Furniture casters, 108

Furniture knobs, 114

Futura pattern dessert plate and cup and saucer (Schramberger), 228, **229**, 444

Future shape casserole dish (Red Wing Pottery), **58**, 424

G. L. Ashworth and Brothers, 462

G. Torlotting, 266

Gabriel, René, 195

Gadroon shape platter and plate (Mason's), **372**, 373, 462

Gaertner, Rudolph (act. 1901–ca. 1938), 326

Gallimore, William Wood, 432

Game and hunting imagery, **29**, 100 n. 10

Game sets, 27

Gang wheels, 159

Garden pattern plate (Wedgwood), **318**, 453

Gardner, Paul, 456

Garwood, Tirzah, 453

Gary, E. H., 434

Gas appliances, **75**

Gefle, 267

Gelatin salads, 92–93

General Agreement on Tariffs and Trade (GATT), 149, 180, 192, 199

General covered leftover dish and covered butter dish (Hall), **75**, 426

General Electric, 160

General Federation of Women's Clubs, 40

Generation tableware (Dansk), 272

Gentility, 21–24

"Gentility in the Dining-Room," **32**

Geo. Borgfeldt Corporation, 219, 227, 228, 249, 272, 281 n. 117

George F. Bassett & Co., 190, 227, 231, 266, 281 n. 117

George Gatchell & Co., 218

George Jones & Sons (act. 1861–1907), 200

Georgetown tableware (Iroquois), 429

Georgian pattern (Bryce Brothers), 171

Georgian shape (Homer Laughlin), 132

Georg Jensen Silversmithy, 267, 272

Geranium pattern plate, cup, and saucer (Franciscan), **137**, 432

German Applied Arts, 327

German tableware, 207, 222–44, 391

Geronimo pattern cup and saucer (Knox), **321**, 453

Geyer, Bruno, 140

Giarrocco, Joseph (b. 1919), 251, 296

Gifford, Charles (b. 1929), 261, 263–64, 296

Gift and Tableware Reporter, 94, 155, 171, 267, 278, 297, 316

Gilding, 231

Gilkes, John J. (1923–85), 429

Gilliland, John, 115

Gillinder, William, 115

Gillinder & Sons, 156, 159, 454

Gilman Collamore & Co. (act. 1861–1930), 298, 451

Gimbel Brothers, 131, 309, **310**

Ginori family, 276

Gladding, McBean & Co. (act. 1875–1984), 135, 136–37, 149, 217, 261, 267, 316, 347, 429, 457. *See also* Franciscan Division, Gladding, McBean & Co.

Glasbake, 160

Glasgow Pottery (act. ?–1807), 117, 118–19

Glass, in America: before 1880, 110–17; after 1880, 156–63; barware, 54, 55, 87–88, **168**, 424, 427; colored, 167, 345; French imports, 190–92; German imports, 190–92, 222; glass plates, 41, **48**; imports, 179–80, 185–86; industry mechanization, 167; industry struggle for survival after World War II, 168–72; utilitarian ware, 110, 160

Glasscutters, 159, 160

Glazing, **129**

Glendale pattern cup and saucer (Lenox), **142**, 433

Glidden Pottery (act. 1940–57), 385, **386**, 464–65

Globe shape coffeepot and sugar bowl (Wedgwood), **401**, 467

Gloucester pattern tea set (Spode), 203, **212**, 441

Gobelin pattern plate and bouillon cup and saucer (Salem), 350, **351**, 457–58

Goddess of Liberty pattern compote (Challinor, Taylor & Co.), **158**, 435

Godey Ladies pattern (Salem), 362, 452

Goetz, Otto, 228

Golden Bouquet pattern (Northern), 434

Golden Foliage pattern (Libbey), 166, 172; pilsner, tumbler, and beverage glasses, **173**, 437

Golden Harvest pattern plate (Stangl), **383**, 464

Golden Wheat pattern (Homer Laughlin), 132

Gold Medallion pattern Chinese ware, 278

Gold stamping, 134

"Good from kiln" pieces, 127

Good Housekeeping Institute, 336

Good Manners, 37

Goodwin, John (1867–1949), 214, 458

Gorham Manufacturing Company (est. 1831), 147, 149, 209, 441

Gorham Silversmiths, 272

Gothic pattern (Bergdala Glasbruk), 448

Gouda, 272

Goupy, Marcel (1886–1980), 189, 279 n. 53

Gourmet, 95

Gourmet culture, 95

Graham, Sylvester, 38

Graham, William P., 281 n. 118

Graham & Zenger (act. 1906–ca. 1936). See Black Knight China

Grand Prize pattern punch bowl and stand (Libbey), 164, 436

Graniteware, 109, 200, 420

Grant, Mary K., 432

The Granville pattern plate and vegetable dish (Doulton), 203, 354, 458

Grass pattern sugarbowl (Knowles), 380, 381, 463–64

Great Atlantic and Pacific Tea Company, 57

Greatbach, Daniel (act. in America after 1839–d. after 1866), 107

Great Britain. See British pottery industry

Great Depression, 187, 195

The Greatest Show on Earth (Libbey), 162

Great Northern Railroad, 431

"The Great Wall of China," 308–9, 309

Gredelue, A., 191

Greenaway, Kate (1846–1901), 353, 383, 458

Green Wheat pattern (Taylor, Smith & Taylor), 350, 457

Greenwood Pottery Company (act. 1868–ca. 1933), 124, 125

Gretsch, Herman (1895–1950), 468

Grey Renaissance pattern (Fitz and Floyd), 254, 447

Griemert, Hubert, 446

Grier, Anna Foster, 81, 91, 92

Grier, Katherine "Kasey" (b. 1953), 17, 81, 96, 97

Griffen, Smith & Co. (act. 1877–92), 24, 422

Griffen, Smith, and Hill, 200

Griffin, Joseph, 218

Guérin, William (1838–1912), 190

Guérin-Pouyat-Elite (act. 1921–33), 190, 191

Gulotta, Gerald (b. 1921), 405, 406, 450, 469, 470

Gump's, 297, 309–10

Gunthel, Alfred B., 272

Gustave Lap, 226

Gustavsberg, 267, 272

H. C. Fry Glass Company (act. 1901–35), 160

H. E. Lauffer Company, 468

H. J. Heinz Company, 57, 59

H. Naito Company, 249

H. P. Sinclaire & Co. (act. 1904–29), 162

Hackett, Kay, 464

Hackney, Frederick, 421

Hadley, James, 430

Hafner, Dorothy (b. 1952), 99, 429, 430

Hagueneau glassware, 436

Haley, Reuben (1872–1933), 356, 459

Hall China Company (est. 1903), 126, 143, 149, 254, 348, 389; Airflow teapot, 75, 427; Dawn pattern, 373, 462; Fantasy pattern, 373, 394, 462; Frost Flowers pattern, 462; General leftover dish, 75, 426; Hercules pitcher, 75, 426; Nora pitcher, 75, 426; Plain leftover dish, 75, 427; Sundial casserole, 75, 426; Sunglow pattern, 373, 462; Tomorrow's Classic shape, 373, 389, 390, 462, 465; Tri-Tone pattern, 378, 389, 463

Hallcraft line, 462

Hall's Department Store, 97

Hamill, Virginia (1898–1980), 166, 370

Hand decorating, 129

Hand painting, 462

Hannah, Frances, 14

Hanover pattern (Tirschenreuth), 227

Hard cider, 83

Hard-paste porcelain, 104

Harker Pottery Company (act. 1840–1972), 348, 379, 463

Harlequin tableware (Homer Laughlin), 66, 131, 348; plate, cup and saucer, jug, salt and pepper shakers, 68–69, 426

Harlequin sets, 305, 412

Harmony House (Sears), 77, 79, 126, 427

Harrison, Caroline Scott, 186, 189, 438

Harrison, Stephen (b. 1965), 18

Harrison White House service, plate (Tressemans & Vogt), 187, 188, 438

Harthill, John (1910–95), 209

Harumitsu Katch Pottery, 257

Haruta & Co., 249

Harvest Festival pattern plate (Wedgwood), 318, 453

Harvest pattern (Homer Laughlin), 131

Harvest pattern (Lenox), 341

Harvest Time pattern pitcher (Iroquois), 98, 99, 429

Hassell, Thomas, 56

Hassinger, Alice, 17, 18

Hassinger, Milton, 18

Hastings, Daniel, 114

Hattersley, Charles, 109

Hauser, Victor F.

Havanna tableware (Limoges), 303, 452

Havel, Miroslav, 218, 219, 442

Haviland, Charles (1839–1921), 193

Haviland, Daniel, 193

Haviland, David (1814–79), 186, 193

Haviland, Edmond, 193

Haviland, Georges (1870–after 1931), 193, 195

Haviland, Robert (1897–?), 193

Haviland, Theodore (1842–1919), 193, 195

Haviland & Company (act. 1864–before 1941), 193

Haviland Brothers & Co. (act. 1838–65), 193

Haviland China Company (act. 1925–31), 35, 104, 186, 187, 189, 190, 193–98, 327

Hawaiian Flowers pattern (Vernon Kilns), 365

Hawaiian styles, 365, 368, 460–61

Hawe, W. Frank M., 336

Hawkes, Thomas (1846–1913), 159

Hawkes & Co. See T. G. Hawkes & Co.

Hawley-Smoot Tariff, 199, 246

Hayes White House service, oyster plate (Haviland), 194, 439

Haynes, B. D., 421, 422

Haynes, David Francis, 421

Hazel Atlas Glass Company (act. 1902–56), 167, 362, 363, 460

Heath, Brian, 463

Heath, Edith K. (b. 1911), 210, 233, 373, 374, 385, 462, 463

Heath & Rose pattern plate (Spode), 202, 440

Heat-resistant reinforced porcelain, 261

Heinrich & Winterling, 223, 226, 227, 234, 344, 443, 456

Heisey. See A. H. Heisey & Co.

Held, John Jr., 428

Heller Designs, 94

Hellmann, Louis E. (1886–1964), 235, 239, 385, 445, 465

Hellmich Manufacturing Company, 154

Helps for the Hostess, 57

Hemphill, Joseph (1770–1842), 107

Henderson, David (d. 1845), 105, 107

Henderson, James, 105, 107

Henjes, Herman, 187

Henk, Ernest, 433

Henri, Robert, 338

Hercules covered pitcher (Hall), 75, 426

Heritage (Pfaltzgraff), 149

Herman C. Kupper, Inc., 186, 189, 190

Hewitt, Jean, 95–96

Heymann-Marks, Margarete (1899–ca. 1988), 357, 358–59, 459

Higgins & Seiter Company, 32, 39

High-fired earthenware, 376

Highlight bowl (Paden City), 385, 387, 465

Hilkka glassware (Notsjoe), 448

Hill, Janet McKenzie, 41

Hill, William, 422

Hill's Manual of Social and Business Forms, 32

Hilson, C., 117

Hinode Company, 257

Historical America pattern (Homer Laughlin), 132, 372, 373, 461

Hoare, John (1822–96), 159

Hobbs, Brockunier & Co. (act. 1863–90), 163, 174, 328, 453, 454

Hob Diamond glassware (Hobbs, Brockunier): berry or ice cream bowl, 328, 454; celery yacht, 329, 453

Hodges, Dale (b. 1937), 252, 447

Hoening, Louis, 320

Hogan, Nan, 434

Hogan, Thomas, 434

Holdway, Harold (b. 1913), 56, 424

Holiday shape cup and covered casserole dish (Stetson), 372, 373, 462

Holloway, Edward Stratton, 59

Holmegaards (est. 1825), 267

Holmes, Frank Graham (1878–1954), 135, 140, 336, 338–41, 350, 356, 433, 451, 452, 456; A317 pattern, 340–41; Florida pattern, 340; Fountain pattern, 340; Ming pattern, 306; Pasadena pattern, 340; Tenare pattern, 141; The Virginian pattern, 67

Home economics, 57

Home Grown (Lutes), 22, 32–33

Homemaker bowl (Homer Laughlin version), 391, 466

Homemaker pattern bowl (Ridgway), 391, 466

The Home Manual: Everybody's Guide in Social, Domestic, and Business Life (Logan), 27

Homer Laughlin China Company (est. 1873), 61, 66, 69, 70, 109, 122, 123, 126, 131–33, 136, 149, 167, 254, 286; "Add-A-Place," 314; Adobe pattern, 365; Americana pattern, 372, 373, 461–62; American Homes pattern, 372, 373, 461–62; American Provincial pattern, 132; Angelus shape, 333, 454–55; Carnival pattern, 131; Century shape, 68–69, 132, 348, 366–67, 426, 460; Century Vellum glaze, 348; colored dinnerware, 348; copy of Homemaker pattern, 391, 466; Della Robbia pattern, 133, 353, 432; Eggshell ware, 132, 133, 314, 315, 426, 432; Epicure tableware, 132, 148, 149, 434; Fiesta Ironstone, 426; Fiesta ware, 66, 69, 72, 73, 131, 132, 133, 149, 348, 368, 426; and Frederick Rhead, 336; Georgian shape, 132; Golden Wheat pattern, 66, 68–69, 131, 348, 426; Harlequin tableware, 66, 68–69, 131, 348, 426; Harvest pattern, 131; Historical America pattern, 132, 372, 373, 461; Jubilee tableware, 132, 377, 463; Kitchen Kraft line, 132, 460; Liberty shape, 372, 373, 461; Mexicana pattern, 365, 366–67, 460; mix-and-match colored dishes, 430; Nautilus shape, 132, 133, 432; Navajo pattern, 365; Newell shape, 461; No. C22 pattern, 68–69, 426; Old Mexico pattern, 365; Pastoral pattern, 131; Pink Organdy pattern, 70–71, 426; Rhythm line, 131, 132; Rhythm Rose pattern, 132; Riviera tableware, 69, 132, 189, 348, 429; Skytone pattern, 132; Suntone pattern, 132; Swing pattern, 70–71, 70–71, 362, 426; Tango shape, 426; Tea Rose pattern, 131; Theme pattern, 132; Tudor Rose pattern, 131; Wells Art shape, 132; White Flower, 131, 132; Wild Rose body, 131; Yellowstone body, 131

Hoover, Herbert, 338, 349

Hopscotch pattern platter (Jackson Internationale), 402, 468

Horace C. Gray Company, 219, 287

Horchow, Roger (b. 1928), 252, 296, 321

Horchow Collection catalogue, 321

Horizon line (Doulton), 441

Hors d'oeuvres, 81–82, 82

Hostess casserole dish (Corning), 179, 438

Hostess Sets, 166

Hotel ware, 125, 332, 420

Hot Toddy pattern cocktail plate (Vernon Kilns), 88, 428

House and Garden, 95, 464

Household appliances, 21

Household Discoveries (Morse), 23

House of Dior, 418

Houser, Victor F., 136

Hovmantrops Glasbruk, 267

Howard Sterling Company (act. 1878–1901), 338

How to Cook in Casserole Dishes (Neil), 57

How to Mix Drinks, or, The Bon Vivant's Companion (Thomas), 85

How to Set a Table, 39

Hummel figurines, 289

Hunt, Martin (b. 1942), 469

Hunting and game imagery, 23, 29, 100 n. 10

Hutschenreuther USA (est. 1972), 226. See also Lorenz Hutschenreuther

Huxtable, Garth, 171

Hyde Park pattern coffee set (Susie Cooper), 408, 469

Iceflower pattern glass (Rosenthal), 242, 446

Iduna shape (Sontag & Söhne), 443

The I Hate to Cook Book (Bracken), 92

Ile de France (Theodore Haviland), 195

Illumination and the Eye, 469

Imoto Brothers, 249
Imperial Bohemia China Corporation, 223, 280 n. 108
Imperial Chess pattern (Flintridge), 434
Imperial Crest pattern (Fitz and Floyd), 252
Imperial Geddo pattern, 124
Imperial Glass Company (act. 1901–84), 159; advertising, **182;** "trousseau treasures," **313**
Impero shape (Richard-Ginori), 276, 413
Imported tableware, 123–24, 179–80; British, 200–217; Czech, 223, 228; French, 186–92; German, 190–92, 222–44; Japanese, 245–54; from 1950s through 1970s, 400–405
Independence shape (Noritake), 408; coffeepot, cup and saucer and plate, salad plate, water goblet and sherbet glass, **96,** 429
Indiana Glass Company (est. 1907), 362; *Norse* line, 385; *Pyramid,* **50,** 424; *Tea Room,* 50, **51,** 424
Indiana Pottery Company (act. 1837–early 1870s), 107
Indonesian tableware, 278
Industrial designers, 135, 325, 368, 370, 412; contract, 342; innovation, 412; interwar years, 333–43
Industry of All Nations, 108
Informal shape coffeepot (Iroquois), **98,** 99, 429
Ingrid pattern (Kosta), 448
Inkstands, 108
Inlaid glaze, 461
Innovation shape coffeepot and plate (Lenox), **404,** 468
An Inquiry into the Effects of Ardent Spirits on the Human Mind and Body (Rush), 83
Institutional ware, 125, **127,** 131, 132, 149, 185, 332, 420, 431
International Exhibition of Modern Architecture, Museum of Modern Art, 356
International Exhibition of Modern Art (Armory Show), 356
International Exposition of Modern Decorative and Industrial Arts, Paris, 338, 349–50
International Molded Plastics, 151
International tableware. *See* Imported tableware
International trade fairs, 223
Interpace Corporation, **96,** 429
Ipsen, Louis (d. 1946), 136
Irish and Scottish Linen Guild, 309
Irish Belleek, 430, 433
Irish Glass Bottle Company, 218
Iris pattern (Red Wing), 343
Iron Mountain Stoneware (est. 1965), 405
Ironstone, 200
Iroquois China Company (1905–70), 125, 310
Irwin, Frank, 394, 466
Irwin, Rodney C., 424
Isinglass, 92
"Is There a Place for Japanese-Made Ceramics and Glass in Our Country?" (Miller), 249
Italian ceramics, 272–73, 275
Italian Fruit pattern dish (Richard-Ginori), **274,** 275, 276, 449
Italian glass, 272, **273,** 273–75, **276,** 406, 449, 450
Ivers, George, 468
Ivoire de France body (Ahrenfeldt), 189
Ivory-bodied ware, 138, **226,** 235, 344, **344,** 394, 433, 443, 445, 456

Ivrene, 427
Ivy pattern (Franciscan), 383, 428
Ivy pattern (Wedgwood), 458
Izmir (Villeroy & Boch), 469

J. A. Bauer Pottery Company (act. 1909–62), 103, 135–36, 167; Bauer California Pottery, 137, 430; *Plain* line, 345–46; *Ring* ware, **102,** 345, 430
J. & G. Meakin (act. 1851–1970), 201, 441
J. & I. Block. *See* Block China Company
J. & L. Lobmeyr (est. 1823), 444–45
J. A. service, 214
J. Clingenberg, 226
J. C. Penney Company, 126, 131, 302, 371, 373, 461
J. G. Durand & Cie. (est. 1815), 179, 190–91
J. Hoare & Co. (act. 1868–1921), 156, 159
J. H. Venon, 266
J. H. Weatherby & Sons, 35
J. J. Newberry & Co., 126, 131
J. L. Hudson & Co., 300, 305
J. M. Gilbert Company, 272
J. Uffrecht & Co., cup and saucer, dessert plate, and plate (est. 1845), **222,** 442–43
Jackson, C. D., 207
Jackson Internationale (Jackson Vitrified China Company) (act. late 1950s–67), 272, 402, 468
Jackstraw pattern (Salem), 427
Jacob Meyer Brothers, 235
Jade pattern (Flintridge), 434
Jadeite, 77
James, George T., 466
James Kent, Ltd. (est. 1897), 289
James McCreery & Co., 52
James W. Tufts, Inc. (act. ca. 1875–1915), 422
Japan Ceramics and Industrial Federation, 249
Japanese Art Store, 249, 250
Japanese-style motifs, 120, **121,** 430, 431, 433, 439
Japanese tableware, 245–64; domination of U.S. market, 254; higher grades, 247–48; innovations, 250–54; porcelain exports, 199, 400; postwar expansion, 207, 247–48; problem of image, 248–50; trade surplus with U.S., 246; U.S. imports before World War II, 246–47
Japan Pottery Design Center, 248–49
Japan Pottery Export Association, 249
Japan Pottery Inspection Association, 249
Japan Pottery Manufacturers' Federation, 249
Japonisme, 439
Jarves, Deming (1790–1869), 114
Jasperware, 442
Jaulmes, G. L., 195
Jeannette Glass Company (est. 1898), 73, 167, 171
Jenny Lind. *See Goddess of Liberty* pattern
Jensen, George Butler, 446
Jersey Glass Co. (1824–62), 105, 115
Jersey Porcelain and Earthenware Company (act. 1824–29), 105, 107
Jewel pattern cup and saucer (Lenox), **142,** 433
Jewelry stores, 297–300
Jewel shape (Spode), 203, 211, 412; plate, **202,** 440
Jewel Tea Company, 126
Jobbers, 287
Jobling, James A., 179

Johannsfors Broakula (est. 1891), 266
John Aynsley & Sons (act. 1864–1971), 220
John Maddock & Sons, 195, 201
Johnson, Robert L., 201
Johnson Brothers (est. 1883), 201, 210; fish platter, **28**
John Wanamaker's, New York, **308**
Jones, George Bartlett (1848–1927), 114, 201
Jones, McDuffee & Stratton Corporation (est. 1871), 207, 314
Jordan Marsh, 297
Josée, 192
Josef Meyr's Neffe, 455
Joseph Bourne & Son (est. 1812). *See* Denby Pottery
Josephine pattern plate (Wedgwood), **401,** 467
Josiah Wedgwood & Sons (est. 1759), 103–4, 143, 201, 207, 209, 220; acquisitions, 210, 217; American branch, 214; *Annular* shape, 214; *Argenta* ware, 200, 422; beer jug, 214, **215,** 442; border designs, 458; branch house in America, 211; *Caterer* jug, **24,** 421; chop plate, **330,** 454; coffee pot and demitasse cup and saucer, 214, **215,** 442; *Colonial* pattern, 458; Colonial Williamsburg commission, 353; *Corinthian,* 458; *Coronation Golden Persephone,* 453; *Coupe Savoy* shape, 212, **213, 407,** 441–42, 469; *Coupe* shape, **374,** 462–63; *Diablo* pattern, 406, **408,** 469; *Edme* shape, 203, **355,** 458; *Embossed Grape Vine* pattern, **355,** 458; *Embossed Queens Ware,* 203, 412; experiments in modernism, 210; *Floral* pattern, 458; "Flow-Blue" chop plate, **330,** 454; *Garden* pattern, **318,** 453; *Globe* shape, **401,** 467; *Harvest Festival* pattern, **318,** 453; *Ivy* pattern, 458; *Josephine* pattern, **401,** 467; *Laurel* pattern, 458; *Lincoln* shape, **401,** 453, 467; *Lincoln Square* shape, 350, **351,** 457; *Matte Green* glaze, 214; *Matte Straw* glaze, 214; modernist wares, 214, **215;** *Moonstone* glaze, 214, 442; new factory, 214, 216; No. 12 shape, **401,** 467; *Oak* shape, 458; *Partridge in a Pear Tree* pattern, 442; *Partridge* pattern, 212, **213,** 441–42; *Patrician* shape, 203, 458; *Pear* shape, **401,** 467; *Peony* pattern, **330,** 454; *Peony* shape, **330,** 350, **351,** 454, 457; *Persephone* pattern, **318,** 453; plaque with sample monograms, **316,** 452; *Prairie Flowers* pattern, 350, **351,** 457; *Queens Ware Concave* shape, 214, **318,** 430, 453, 458; *Rose* pattern, 458; *Shell Edge* shape, 458; showroom, **216;** *Simple Yet Perfect* (SYP) shape, **330,** 454; *Trees and Figures* pattern, 458; *Variations on a Geometric Theme* series, **407,** 469; *Wellesley* shape, 203, 458; *Wildflower* pattern, **401,** 467; wine cooler, **118,** 430
The Joy of Cooking (Rombauer), 57
Jubilee tableware (Homer Laughlin), 132; cup and saucer, teapot, and sugar bowl, **377,** 463
Jugeat, Jacques, 279 n. 35
Jugendstil, 327, 445
Juillerat, Marcel (act. at Lenox China since 1973), 140
Jumbo spoon holder (Canton Glass), **329,** 453
Justin Tharaud & Son, 227, **232,** 272, 281 n. 117, 444

Kahla, 234
Kähler Ceramics (est. 1839), 267
Kailess shape (Spode), 424
Kaiser, Charles (ca. 1877–after 1948), 257, 259
Kaolin, 104, 107, 124, 231, 257
Karhula-Iittala Glassworks (est. 1881), 267, 272
Karresh, John, 470
Kasson, John, 25, 33
Kaufmann Brothers, **308**
Keeling & Co. (act. 1886–1936): Tulip pattern platter, Losol Ware Line, **334–35,** 455
Kellogg Toasted Corn Flake Company, 57
Keltcraft line (Noritake), 261
Kendall, C., 300
Kennedy, John F., 413
Kennedy Round Agreements, 192, 199
Kent, Rockwell (1882–1971), 368, 369, 432, 461
Kenton Mail Order, 321
Kenwood Electronics, 250
Kerry pattern dish (Spode), **203,** 440
Kew pattern plate (Doulton), **342,** 453
Keyhole escutcheons, 108, 118
Keystone Show, 294
Kilns: bottle, **129, 134,** 138; "fast fire," 149; tunnel, 131–32, 133, 134, 259
Kilta shape platter, cup, and saucer (Arabia), **269,** 448
Kingsley pattern (Lenox), 93, 140; plate, **142,** 433
Kitchenaid, 376
Kitchen cabinets, **61**
Kitchen Kraft line (Homer Laughlin), 132, 460
Kmart, 321, 322, 418
Knickerbocker glasses (Libbey), 160, **172**
Knickerbocker tumbler and sherbet glass (Fostoria), **170,** 436–37
Knowles, Edward M., 353
Knowles, Taylor and Knowles (act. 1854–1931), 109
Knox Refining Company, 321, 453
Kny, William, 435
Kogan, Belle (b. 1902), **342**–43, 376; and Boonton Molding Company, 151; design philosophy, 325, 343, 371; design training, 336; and Ebeling & Reuss, 289; *Fancy Free* shape and *Desert* surface decoration, 460
Komaru mark (double trident), 458–59
Kondo, Ken (b. 1949), 252
Koor Corporation, 343
Koscherak Brothers, 227, 231, 281 n. 117
Kosta-Boda-Afors (merged 1946), 267
Kosta Glasbruk (est. 1742), 266, 267
Krause, Erwin W., 444
Krautheim Procelain Factory (est. 1884), 232
Kresge. *See* S. S. Kresge Company
Kristalunie Maastricht, (est. 1834), **191,** 439
Kroger Company, 57
Kungsholm cordial and highball glasses, **266,** 448
Kupittaan Savi, 267
Kyoto, Japan, 245

L. Bernardaud & Cie. (est. 1919), 187, **189,** 190, 438
L. Straus & Sons (act. ca. 1888–1907), 300
LaBelle Glass Company, 293
Labor relations, 127–30
Ladies' Home Journal, 30, 39, 59, 73, 74

Ladies' luncheons, 39–47, 48, 54

Lager beer, 85

Laguna pattern plate and cup and saucer (Thorpe), **94**, 429

Lalique, 192, 279 n. 35

Lalique, René (1860–1945), 341, 436, 437

Lalique, Suzanne (b. 1899), 195, **317**, 452, 453

Lamberton China (act. 1869–92), 125

Lamson Rheinfrench, 165–66

Lancaster Colony Glass (est. 1962), 178

Langley, Leonard, 454

Language of Flowers, 383; goblet and champagne glass (Duncan & Miller), **358**, 458; soup bowl (Limoges), **353**, 458

Lanterns pattern (Red Wing), 343

Larkin, John D., 126, 128

Larkin Soap Company, 126, 431

Latham, Richard S. (b. 1920–?), 243, 446

Latham, Tyler, and Jensen, 152

Laughlin, Matthew (1799–1876), 131

Laughlin, Shakespeare (1847–81), 122, 131

Laughlin Brothers. *See* Homer Laughlin China Company

Laureline (Boonton), 152

Laurel Potteries, 126

Laurel pattern (Wedgwood), 458

Laurel shape (Taylor, Smith & Taylor), 349, 457; plate and cup and saucer, **350**, 457

Lauren, Ralph (b. 1939), 418

Laveno Italian Ceramics, 278

Lawley Group (act. 1948–64), 210

Lazarus & Rosenfeld (act. 1898–1934), 257

Leacock, Inc., 458

Lead, 129, 406

Lead crystal, 110, 157, 191

Lefoulon, Michel, 107

Legacy shape stem goblet (Morgantown Glass Works), **177**, 438

Leger, M. A., 279 n. 53

Leiderdrop, 272

Leigh, Cyril W. (1890–1967), 257, 459

Leigh Potters (act. 1926–ca. 1934), 360, 459

Leighton, Clare (b. 1900–?), 210

Leigh Ware, 360, 361–62, 459

Leipzig fair, 223, 235

Leiter, Levi Z., 304

Lemon squeezers, 118

Lenox, Walter Scott (1859–1920), 119, 138, 140, 181 n. 63, 325, 326, 338, 430, 432, 433

Lenox China (est. 1906), 39, 93, 140–43, 149, 286, 326, 327; acquisition of Bryce Brothers, 171; advertising, 143, 144, 316, 319; A317G pattern, **340**, **341**, 455; *Autumn* pattern, 140, 339; *Beltane* line, 141; *Chinastone* line, 141, 171; *Coronado* pattern, 140, 339, 341; *Coupe* shape, **142**, 433; *Fantasies* pattern, **404**, 406, 468; fine china, 138; *Firesong* pattern, **404**, 406, 468; *Five-Step* line, 433; *Florida* pattern, 339, **340**, 341, 455; *Fountain* pattern, 339, **340**, 341, 455; and Frank Graham Holmes, 135, 338–41; *Glendale* pattern, **142**, 433; *Harvest* pattern, 341; *Innovation* shape, **404**, 468; ivory-colored dinnerware, 131, 344; *Jewel* pattern, 433; *Kingsley* pattern, 93, **142**, 433; *Lenox Rose*, 341; *Mandarin* pattern, **306**, 339, 452; manufacturing and marketing between 1945 and 1948, 144, 149;

Maryland pattern, 339; *Ming* pattern, 140, **306**, 339, 452; *Moderne* pattern, **161**, 435–36; No. J7 pattern, **298**, 451; No. 1445 shape service plate, **340**, **341**, 455; *Oxford* line, 141; *Pasadena* pattern, **340**, 341, 455; A 391 pattern, 341; reduction of active patterns, 371; *Rhodora* pattern, 341; *Rutledge* shape, 93, 341; *Starlight* pattern, 341; success during 1950s, 254; *Temperware* line, 141, 171, 405, 468; *Temple* shape, 452; *Terrace* line, **141**, 339, 433; *Three-Step* line, **141**, 339, 433; *The Virginian* pattern, **67**, 140, 339; *Washington Wakefield* line, **67**, 339, 353; *Westwind* pattern, 339; White House service, 339

Lenox Crystal (est. 1965), 143, 171, 178, 220, 371

Lenox Plastics (act. 1958–ca. 1980), 152, 154

Lenox Rose pattern (Lenox), 341

Lenoxware, 154, 155, 371

Le Retour pattern, from the *L'Homme dans l'Espace* series (Piero Fornasetti), **409**, 469

Leutner, Karl, 443

Lewis, Jacob, 107

Lexington shape stem, goblet (Morgantown Glass Works), **177**, 437

Libbey, Edward D. (1854–1925), 114, 162, 163, 165

Libbey, William L. (d. 1883), 114, 162, 163

Libbey Glass Company (est. 1888), 159, 162, 163–68, 326, 343, 362–65; *Accent* pattern, **370**, 461; *American Prestige* line, **172**, 437; *Circus* pattern, **162**; *Classic Crystal* shape, **370**, 461; design development department, 165–66, 370; *Embassy* line, 165, **172**, 437; *Emerald Flair* line, 167; glass-pressing technology, 163; *Golden Foliage* pattern, 166, **172**, **173**, 437; *Grand Prize* pattern, **164**, 436; *Knickerbocker* line, 160; Libbey-Nash series, 165; *Light Ware*, 160; machine-made bottles and tablewares, 160, 162, 165; *Malmaison* pattern, **172**, 437; *Modern American* line, 165, 437; No. 300 claret jug, **156**, 435; No. 285 ice cream tray, 435; No. K13 shape, **172**, 437; punch bowl, **164**; as subsidiary of Owens-Illinois Glass Company, 171–72

Libbey Glass Works, **157**

Libbey-Owens-Ford Company, 165

Liberty, James H., 195

Liberty shape plate (Homer Laughlin), **372**, 373, 461

Lickhard, Karl (1880–?), 226

Lightbulbs, 160, 163

Lightner, T. G., 171

Light Ware (Libbey), 160

Lilium Ornatum pattern, pitcher (Pickard), **298**, 451

Limoges China Company (act. 1900–ca. 1955), 19, 104, 186; *Casino* bridge sets, 52, **53**, 424; *Havanna* pattern, **303**, 451; *Language of Flowers*, **353**, 458; *Triumph* shape, **303**, 362, 452

Lincoln shape plate and covered vegetable dish (Doulton), **354**, 458

Lincoln shape (Wedgwood), 453; plate, **401**, 467

Lincoln Square shape dessert plate (Wedgwood), 350, **351**, 457

Linconite (Stetson), 155

Lindeneher, Edouard (d. 1910), 193, 438

Linear annealing lehrs, 157

Linear stemware, 446

Linköping, 267

Linton, George, 309

Lipper & Mann, 447

Lismore pattern glass (Waterford), 218, 219, **221**, 442

Lithographic decorations, 326

Locke, Joseph (1846–1936), 163

Loewy, Raymond (1893–1986), 239, 336

Logan, John A., 27

Longton Government Art School, 336

Lord & Taylor, 337

Lorenz Hutschenreuther (est. 1857), 223, 226, 227, 234; *Apart* line, **227**, 443–44; *Autumn Leaves* pattern, **230**, 231, 444; *Diadem* line, 444; *Richelieu* pattern, 227

Lorne pattern covered butter dish (Bryce Brothers), **112–13**, 430

Losol Ware, **334–35**, 455

Louise pattern cup and saucer and teapot (Fischer and Mieg), **335**, 455

Louisiana Purchase Exposition of 1904, 165

Lovegren, Sylvia, 41

Lowestoft shape (Spode), 211, 413; creamer, sugar bowl, coffeepot, dish, waste bowl, and teapot, **212**, 441

Luce, Jean (1895–1964), 189, 402, 424, 432, 459, 468

Ludlow, J. W., 160

Luncheon sets, 66

Lunning, Frederik (1881–1952), 267

Lunning, Just, 272

Lunning Lily pattern, 272

Lu-Ray line (Taylor, Smith & Taylor), 349, **350**, 457

Lure, Jean (1895–1964)

Lust pattern goblet (Steuben), **365**, 460

Lutes, Della Thompson (d. 1942), 22, 32–33, 41

Lute Song pattern teapot, plate, cup, and saucer (Red Wing), **398**, 399, 467

Lynd, Helen Merrill, 48, 66

Lynd, Robert S, 48, 66

M. W. Beveridge, 438

Macbeth-Evans Glass Company (act. 1899–1936), 77, **78**, 167, 353, 362, 427

Machin, Derek, 441

Machin, Sidney, 441

Machine Art, 337

Machine-blown stemware, 272

Mackintosh, Charles Rennie (1868–1928), 455

Mackintosh School, 327

Macomber Associates Audit Reports, 144

Macy, Rowland H. (1822–77), 300

Macy's. *See* R. H. Macy & Co.

Maddock, John, 122, 201

Maddock, Mildred, 336

Maddock & Miller, 201, 428

Maddock Pottery Company (act. 1892–1922). *See* Thomas Maddock's Sons Company

Madel Brothers, 356

Madelon pattern (Straus), 187

Madrigal pattern (Franciscan), 429

Magnolia bowl (Thorpe), **375**, 463

Magnolia pattern salad plate and coffeepot (Taylor, Smith & Taylor), **399**, 467

Magnor Crystal, 267

Mah-jongg ware, 52, 53, 54

Mahoning pattern covered vegetable dish (Sontag & Söhne), 223, **224**, 443

Mail-order sales, 35, 126, 321

Maize glass (New England), 163

Majolica, **24**, 55, 103, 118, 200, 326, 422

Majolikafabrik, Schramberger, **229–30**

Makers' marks, 109

Makinson, Norman, 441, 469

Malaysian tableware, 278

Malinite body, 136

Malinovsky, Andrew, 136

Malmaison pattern champagne glass (Baccarat), **191**, 438

Malmaison pattern goblet (Libbey), **172**, 437

Malzan, Traugott, 234

Manchester Pheasant pattern glass (Morgantown Glass Works), **29**, 422

Mandalay pattern (Franciscan), 429

Mandarin pattern coffee set (Lenox), 339; dessert plate and teapot, **306**, 452

Mandarin pattern (Salem), **349**, 457

Mandel Brothers, 160

Manhattan compote and plate (Anchor Hocking), **364**, 460

Manhattan Skylines pattern plate (Leigh Potters), **369**, 459

Man in Space series (Pieto Fornasetti), **409**, 469

Mansard pattern (Spode), 211

Manufacturers' Export Association, 246

Marbella pattern teapot (Southern Potteries), **18**, 421

Marcus, Edward (1909–77), 278

Marcus, Stanley, 300, 311, 318, 320, 460

Mardi Gras pattern plate (Salem), **44**, 423

Marenoes pattern tumbler (Baccarat), **191**, 438

"The Market for United Kingdom China, Pottery and Glass in the United States," 207

Market research and testing, 144, 371–76

Marks & Rosenfeld, 227, 281 n. 177

Marlene pattern sugar bowl, creamer, cup and saucer, and plate (Altrohlauer Porzellanfabriken), **226**, 443

Marseille bowl (Theodore Haviland), **187**, 438

Marshall, H. A., 160

Marshall Field & Co., 141, 160, 201, 300, 304–7, **305**, 452; bridal registry, 305; Bride's House, 312; Dymaxion House, 337; introduction of solid colored tableware, 430; and Lenox China, 304–5; open stock concept, 314; Rosenthal Room, 238

Martha Washington Tea, 40

Martin, Robert F., 151

Martin, William, 438

Martini, 87–88

Marty, André, 195

Maryland pattern (Lenox), 339

Masnick, Elaine, 470

Mason, Milton, 203, 434

Mason's Ironstone China, **372**, 373, 462

Mass-market glass, 162, 417

Mastering the Art of French Cooking, 94–95

Masterpiece line (Franciscan), **146**, 433

Masterpiece pattern (Taylor, Smith & Taylor), 429

"Matchmakers Colors," 434

Matilija pattern (Metlox), 470

Matranga, Victoria, 417

Matsushita, Riutaro "Reo" (1908–69), 261

Matte Green glaze (Wedgwood), 214

Matte Straw glaze (Wedgwood), 214

Max, Peter (b. 1937), 406, 468

May, Robert A., 336, 423

May-D & F, 309

May Department Stores Company, 322

Mayer China (est. 1881), 125, 149

Mayfair compote (Fostoria), 174, **175,** 437

Mayfair shape plate (Knowles), **370,** 461

McBride, James, 449

McBurney, W. Craig, 429

McCartney, W. C., 160

McCobb, Paul (1917–69), 402, 468

McCoy, Thomas T. (1841–93), 326

McCrory's, Baton Rouge, Louisiana, **315**

McDonald, Philip, 157

McDonald's, 150

McGrath, Joseph, 218

McKee, Frederick, 112

McKee, H. Sellers, 162

McKee, James, 112

McKee & Brothers (act. 1854–1901), 159, 160, 162

McKinley, William, 165

McKinley Tariff, 199

Mead, Henry (1774/5–1843), 107–8

Meadow Lace pattern plate (Theodore Haviland), **196,** 439

Meadowtree pattern (Taylor), 467

Meakin & Ridgway, 201, 210

Meikle, Jeffrey, 150

Meito, 250, 446

Melamine tableware, 91, 94, 150–55, 155, 434

Melmac, 151

Melody Series plate, **63**

Memphis movement, 418, 470

Menzies, Alex G., 286, 322 n. 2

Merced shape (Franciscan), 433

Mercer Pottery, **122,** 431

Merchandise Mart, Chicago, 304

Merchandise marts, 249, 287, 289, 291, 304

Mermod & Jaccard, 165

Metasco, 259, 261

Metlox Potteries (act. 1927–89), 136, 137, 347, 394; *California Aztec* pattern, 394, **395,** 466; *California Confetti* shape butter dish and coffeepot, **395,** 466; *California Del Rey* pattern, **395,** 466; *California Freeform* pattern, 394, **395,** 466; *California Mobile* pattern, 394, **395,** 466; *California Pottery,* 347; *Confetti* pattern, 394; *Freeform* shape, 394, **395,** 466; *Matilija* pattern, 470; *Mission Bell* pattern, 347; *Navajo* pattern, 385; *Pintoria* tableware, 347; luncheon plate, **136,** 432; Poppytrail brand, 466; *Studio Potter* shape, 404; chop plate and coffeepot, **411,** 470; *"200" Series* tableware, 347; *Wild Poppy* pattern, 408, **411,** 470

Metropolis pattern (Ebeling & Reuss), 289, 342; platter, bowl, and demitasse cup and saucer, **290,** 451

Metropolitan Museum of Art, New York, 337, 338

Metropolitan shape (Franciscan): demitasse cup and saucer, creamer, and sugar bowl, **348,** 456–57; plate, **348,** 457; teapot, **348,** 456

Metro shape cup and saucer and plate (Ridgway), **391,** 466

Mexicana pattern (Homer Laughlin), 365, **366–67,** 460

Mexican glass, 278

Mexican styles, 365, **366–67,** 460

Meyercord Company, 326

Meyers, Willard, 165, 166

Microwave ovens, 21, 94, 417

Middle-class cuisine, 19, 21

Middletown (Lynd and Lynd), 48, 57

Midwinter. *See* W. R. Midwinter

Midwinter, Eve (b. 1927), 210, 403

Midwinter, Roy (1923–90), 209, 210, 389, 403, 441, 465, 468

Mikasa (est. 1948): *Black Graphics* pattern, **416,** 417, 470; *Country Gingham* pattern, 246, 252, **253;** Mikasa Dinnerware, 250–52; *Millennium* shape, **416,** 417, 470; outlet stores, 321; *Red Graphics* pattern, **416,** 417, 470

Milk churn shape, 403, 469

Millard Norman. *See* Denby, Ltd.

Millennium shape plates (Mikasa), **416,** 417, 470

Miller, Gladys, 249

Miller, H. Garver, 370

Miller, John J., 201

Millionaire Line (Tupperware), 150; set of six cups and saucers, **152,** 434

Mills Act, 199

Milnor. *See* Denby, Ltd.

Minard, G. E., 316

Minaret pattern (Franciscan), 429

Ming Lace pattern (Northern Industrial), 151, **153,** 434

Ming pattern (Lenox), 140, 339; luncheon plate and covered muffin dish, **306,** 452

Minkin, Robert (b. 1928), 210, 404

Minstrel pattern (Denby), 448

Mint julep, 88 n. 2

Minton Ltd. (est. 1793), 200, 203, 206, 210, 350, **351, 457**

Minuet pattern, 452

Miracle-glass, 77

Mirage goblet and sherbet glass (Denby), **266,** 448

Mission Bell tableware (Metlox), 347

Mix-and-match dinnerware, 252, **254,** 347, 408, 412, 447

Mizuno, J. T., 248

Moby Dick (Vernon Kilns), 432

Modelmakers, 325–26

Model 2000 shape (Rosenthal), 239, 391, 394; cup and saucer and coffeepot, sugar bowl, and creamer, **240–41,** 445–46

Mode pattern (Shelley Potteries), 440

Modern America line (Franciscan), 466

Modern American line (Libbey), 165, **172,** 437

Modern California pattern (Vernon Kilns), **347,** 456

Modern (casual) tableware, 66–67

Moderne carafe (Inland Glass), **64,** 394

Moderne pattern demitasse cup and saucer and coffeepot (Lenox & Rockwell Silver), **161,** 435–36

Moderne pattern no. 476 goblet (Seneca), **172,** 437

Modernist tableware, 13–14, 66, 174, **206, 224–25,** 239, 276, 356–65; 443; European, **334–35,** 455

Modern Line. See New Era

Modern Plastics, 150, 152

Modern Priscilla Home Furnishing Book, 59

Moderntone plate, underplate, and soup bowl (Hazel Atlas), **363,** 460

Mogi, Momonoi & Co., 249

Mold-blown glass, 114, **328–29,** 453–54

Molded pottery, **119**

Molded salads, 92–93

MoMA, *New Housewares in the USA,* 465

Monogramming, 452

Monroe, James, 110

Monsanto Chemical Company, 150

Montecito shape saucer (Franciscan), **137,** 432

Montecito shape (Vernon Kilns): carafe, **347,** 456; plate, **368,** 460–61; plate

and covered casserole, **89,** 428; teapot, cup and saucer, and covered muffin dish, **347,** 456

Monterey shape (Noritake), **262–63,** 447

Monterrey pattern sugar and creamer (Thorpe), **94,** 429

Montgomery Ward & Co., 32, 35, 131, 302, 321, 432; *Catalogue No. 57, Spring and Summer 1895,* 35–37, **36,** 65; *Coral* pattern, 35, 37; *New Art China,* 66

Montrose pattern (Minton), 350, **351,** 457

Moon, L. W., 300

Moonstone glaze (Wedgwood), 214, **215,** 442

Moore, Henry, 466

Moretti, Carlo, **276,** 450

Morgan, Mary, 163

Morgantown Glassware Guild (act. 1939–71), 87, 177–78; avant-garde work, 362; *The President's House,* **317,** 452

Morgantown Glass Works (act. 1899–1937), 168, 177, 437; *Art Modern* shape, **169,** 436; *Courtney* shape, **168,** 436; *Décor* line, **168,** 427; *Fairwin* pattern, **177,** 437; *Legacy* shape, **177,** 438; *Lexington* shape, **177,** 437; *Manchester Pheasant* shape, **29,** 422; *Nasreen* pattern, **177,** 438; *Normandie,* 87, **88,** 427; *Palazzo,* 436; *Paragon* shape, **168,** 436; *The President's House,* **317,** 413, 452; *Queen Anne* shape, **29,** 422; *Superba* pattern, **177,** 438; *Walpole,* **169,** 436; *Yale* shape, **169,** 436

Morimura, Ichizaemon (1839–1919), 257

Morimura, Toyo (1854–99), 257

Morimura Brothers. *See* Noritake China, Inc.

Morimura Gumi (Morimura Group) (est. 1876), 257, 259

Morley, George (act. at Lenox China 1895–1900), 140

Morley, William (1865/6–1935), 140

Morley & Co., 200

Morris, George, 107

Morris & Co. (act. 1875–1940), 454

Morrison, Alexander, 118

Morse, Sidney, 23

Morwel shape plate (Onondaga), **127,** 431

Mosa and Fris, 272

Moses, John (1832–1902), 117, 118–19, 122

Motif pattern glass (Rosenthal), **242,** 446

Mottehedah, Inc. (est. 1962), 413

Mount Clemens Pottery Company (act. 1914–87), 126, 132

Mountford, Arthur, 131

Mount Washington Glass Company (est. 1837–94), 112, 114, 156

Mrazek, Joseph (1889–1959), 423, 424

Mrs. Rorer's New Cook Book, 34

The Mt. Vernon pattern (Lenox), **67**

Muddler (Blenko), **301,** 451–52

Mueller, William G., 223, 226

Mugs, 404; beer, **271,** 449; coffee, 252; shaving, 118

Müller, Karl L. H. (1820–87), 122

Müller-Munk, Peter (1904–67), 333, 336

Multilingual trade catalogues, 223

Munroe, Edmund, 114

Murai, Yasukata (1854–1936), 259

Murano glass, **273,** 449

Murphy, Charles (1909–94), 58, 343, 424, 467

Murphy, J. Allen, 418

Murphy, Terry, 221 n. 12

Murray, Keith (1892–1981), 214, **215,** 362, 442

Murray-Curvex machine, 466

Museum (Castleton), 64, 385, 394, 462; plate, creamer, coffeepot, and cup and saucer, **388–89,** 465

Museum of Modern Art, New York, 13, 337, 465; Good Design Award, 434; Good Design exhibitions, 376; *Industry and Handwork Create New Housewares in the United States,* 462; *The Responsive Eye,* 406

Nagoya potteries, 245, 246, 447

Nagoya Seitosho, 249

Nagoya Shokai, 250

Napoleon Ivy pattern, 467

Narumi, 250, 251

Nash, A. Douglas (1885–1940), 165, 436

Nasreen pattern water or iced tea glass (Morgantown Glass Works), **177,** 438

Nathan Straus & Sons, 187, 189

National Alliance of Art and Industry, 338, 433

National Association of Colored Women, 40

National Brotherhood of Operative Potters (NBOP), 129

National Glass Budget, 316

National Industrial Recovery Act, 246

National Table Setting Contest, **142,** 143, 310

Natural gas, 117

Nature Study pattern teapot (Midwinter), **390,** 465

Nautilus shape covered casserole dish (Homer Laughlin), 132, **133,** 432

Navajo pattern (Homer Laughlin), 365

Navajo pattern (Metlox), 385

Neff, Grave V., 458

Neil, Marion Harris, 57

Neiman Marcus, 243, 244 n. 35, 252, 278, 296, 371, 453; china and glass promotions, 300; L'Hexagone Room, 310; wedding business, 311

The Netherlands, 272

Netherlands pattern finger bowl (Kristalunie Maastricht), **191,** 439

Newark Museum, 337

New Art China (Montgomery Ward), 66

"New Art" styles, 327

New Bedford Glass Company (1818–88), 114

The New Book of Etiquette (Eichler), 61

New Decade line, 261

Newell shape (Homer Laughlin), 461

New England Glass Company, 115, 157, 159, 163

New Era (Heisey): plate, **368,** 460; saucer champagne glass, rye bottle, and wine glass, **54,** 55, 424

New La Salle shape (Noritake), **262,** 447

New York City Pottery, 118, 122, 123

New York Gift Show, 291

New York Glass and China Show, 291

New York Housewares Manufacturers' Association, 291

New York Merchandise Mart, 287

New York Times Heritage Cookbook, 95–96

Niche markets, 373, 417

Nicole pattern cup and saucer (Theodore Haviland), **136,** 195, 453

Nierenberg, Martha (b. 1924), 272

Nierenberg, Ted (b. 1923), 272

Nippon Toki Kaisha (Nippon Porcelain Company) (est. 1904), 257, 259, 261, 446, 447, 458–59

Nitto line (Noritake), 261, 405

No. 129 shape creamer (Wedgwood), **401**, 467

No. 138 bonbon dish (Steuben), **345, 456**

No. 255 pattern (Carole Stupell), **276**, 450

No. 285 ice cream tray (attrib. Libbey Glass), 435

No. 300 claret jug (attrib. Libbey Glass), **156**, 435

No. 467 goblet (Seneca), **172**, 437

No. 600-DOF shape tumbler (Blenko), **301**, 451–52

No. 600 shape tumbler, water goblet, champagne, and liqueur glasses (Waterford Glass), **221**, 442

No. 602 shape water goblet (Waterford Glass), **220**, 442

No. 604 shape water goblet (Waterford Glass), **220**, 442

No. 700 shape champagne glass (Carole Stupell), **276**, 450

No. 939-P shape pitcher (Blenko), **301**, 451–52

No. 1382 shape plate and coffeepot (Arzberg), **402**, 468

No. 1445 shape service plate (Lenox), **340, 341**, 455

No. 2133 pattern (Noritake), **248**

No. 4020 shape decanter with four glasses (Fostoria), **167**, 177, 437

No. 4045 pattern (Heisey), **368**, 460

No. 5948 pattern (Royal Staffordshire), **206**, 441

No. 6333 goblet (Steuben), **345**, 456

No. 6395 goblet (Steuben), **345**, 456

No. 7780 (Morgantown Glass Works). *See The President's House*

No. 8675 pattern (Stevens & Williams), **156**, 434–35

No. 14194 shape covered jug (Tiffin), **346**, 347, 456

No. 15,039 shape liqueur glass (Tiffin), **177**, 437–38

No. C22 pattern (Homer Laughlin), **68–69**, 426

No. J7 pattern plate (Lenox), **298**, 451

No. K13 shape goblet (Libbey), **172**, 437

Noke, Cecil Jack (d. 1954), 441

Noke, Charles (1858–1941), 440, 454, 458

Nora pitcher (Hall), **75**, 426

Noritake China (Inc., U.S., est. 1946; Ltd., Japan, est. 1981), 143, 180, 245, 246, 247, 249, 250, 259, 261–64, 287, 296; *Colonade* line, 261, **262**, 447; *Craftone* line, 261; Fine China Inc., 261, 446; fine china sales in U.S., 400; *Folkstone* line, 261; *Keltcraft* line, 261; mah-jongg ware, 52, 53; modernist decoration, **262**, 263, 447; *Monterey* shape, **262–63**, 447; *New Decade* line, 261; *Nitto* line, 261, 405; No. 2133 pattern, **248**; Noritake No. 175, **258**, 447; *Noritake Progression China*, 261; *Normandie* shape, **248**, 446; *Pompadour* shape, **262–63**, 447; *Primachina* line, 261; *Primastone* line, 261; *Royal Bone China* line, 257; snack sets, 52, **53**, 424; stoneware, 405; *Stoneware* line, 261; *Trent* pattern, **248**

Noritake factory, **256**

Norleans China (Meito), 250, **251**, 446

Normandie martini mixer with rod (Morgantown Glass Works), 87, **88**, 427

Normandie shape covered dish (Noritake), **248**, 446

Norse line (Indiana Glass Company), 385

Northern Industrial Chemical Company, 151, 152, 434

Nosek, Hans (act. at Lenox China 1903–05, 1939–54), 138, 140

Notsjoe, 267, 272, 448

Nu-cut glass, 159

Number plates, 108

Nurenberg pattern, 443

Oakleaf pattern (Taylor, Smith & Taylor), 467

Oak pattern (Wedgwood), 458

Oats pattern plate and tumbler (Winfield), **386**, 464

Octagon shape chop plate, covered vegetable bowl (Doulton), **332**, 454

Ode shape (Denby), 405

Oesterlig, John (1824–83), 326

Ohaza Noritake (Noritake-cho), 257

Ohio pattern (Baccarat), 192

Ohio gas boom, 174

Ohio State University, 333

Ohio Valley Potteries, 347–48

"Oklahoma Indian Tumblers," 453

Old Mexico pattern (Homer Laughlin), 365

Old Orchard pattern (Iroquois), 429

Olsen, Thorkild (1890–1973), 448

Onassis, Jacqueline Kennedy, 177, 412–13, 429, 452, 469

Ondine pattern (Franciscan), 429

Onondaga Pottery (est. 1871, renamed Syracuse China in 1966), 124, 125, 135, 138

Onyx colored glass (Fostoria), 436

Op Art movement, 406, 469

Open House tableware (Flintridge), 434

Open stock, 35, 37, 207, 314

Orchid pattern (Heisey), **413**

Oriental Ruby color (Fostoria), 436

Orrefors Glasbruk, 267, 281 n. 117

Oslo pattern (Knowles), 461

Osol, Olga (b. 1905), 448

Otagiri, 252, 283 n. 200, 404

Ott, Joseph (1827–96), 119

Ott & Brewer (act. 1871–93), 119, 122, 326, 327, 338; dessert plates and compote, **120**

Otto Goetz, Inc., 227, 249, 281 n. 117, 444

Our America pattern (Vernon Kilns), 432, 456; coffeepot, dessert bowl, bread plate, cup and saucer, small chop plate, luncheon plate, and plate, **369**, 461

Outlet store concept, 272, 321

Oval tableware (Rosenthal), 239

Oven-to-table ware, 63, 98, 99, 376, 429

Overseas Mercantile Company, 223, 280 n. 108

Overshot glass, **84**, 427

Ovide glassware (Hazel Atlas), 167

Ovide (Redondo) shape cup and saucer, teapot, creamer, and sugar bowl (Franciscan), **146**, 433–34

Ovington Brothers, 297, 308

Owens, Michael J. (1859–1923), 160, 162, 163, 165, 171

Owens-Corning Fiberglass Corporation, 165

Owens-Illinois Glass Company (est. 1929), 165

Oxford line (Lenox), 141

Oxford pattern (Tirschenreuth), 227

Oyster plates, **31**, 54, **194**, 422

Oyster supper, 32–33

P. Palmer & Co. *See* Marshall Field & Co.

Pacific Clay Products (act. 1881–1950s?), 136, 137, 347

Pacific Rim, 278

Paden City Glass Company (act. 1916–52), 465

Paden City Pottery Company (act. 1914–63), 348–49, 385, **387**, 465

Padua pattern chop plate and teapot (Franciscan), 432

Page, Bob (b. 1945), 419

Pagoda Lantern pattern cup, saucer, and coffeepot (Flintridge), **147**, 434

Pairpoint Manufacturing Company (act. 1880–1937), 159, 162

Palazzo glass (Morgantown Glass Works), 436

Palm, Fechteler & Co., 326

Palm Brothers Company, 326

Palmer, Potter (1826–1902), 304

Pannier Frères, 458

Pantries, 23

Paolozzi, Eduardo (b. 1924), 406, 469

Paper tableware, 91, 101 n. 101

Paperweights, 108, 156

Paradise pattern (Knowles), 461

Paragon shape stem, wineglass (Morgantown Glass Works), **168**, 436

Parfumerie Française, 341

Parian ware, 107, 118, 119

Paris Art Centre line (Haviland), 189, 195

Parisienne line (Jackson), 468

Paris International Exposition of Modern Decorative and Industrial Arts, 337, 339, 341, 356

Parker, Glidden M. Jr. (1913–80), 233, 464

Parlors, 22

Partridge pattern plate (Wedgwood), 212, **213**, 441–42

Pasadena pattern bouillon cup and saucer (Lenox), **340**, 341, 455

PASCO, 227

Pasmantier Company, 276, 449

Pass, James (1856–1913), 124, 138

Pass, Richard, 124

Pastoral pattern (Homer Laughlin), 131

Patent infringement, 160

Patios, 89

Patrician shape (Boonton), 151, 343

Patrician shape (Wedgwood), 203, 458

Pattern-matching services, 418

Patterns of the Past, 418

Paul A. Straub & Co., 226–27

Payne-Aldrich Tariff, 199

Peachblow glass (Hobbs), 163

Pearlware (pearl white), 103, 104, 107

Pear shape cup and saucer (Wedgwood), **401**, 467

Peasant folk art designs, 267, 383, **383**, 441, 464

Pemberton, Gill, 468

Penney's. *See* J. C. Penney Company

Peony shape (Wedgwood), **330**, 454; teacup and saucer, 350, **351**, 457

Perfection Salad (Shapiro), 38

Persephone pattern. *See Harvest Festival*

Persia pattern teacup and saucer (Spode), 212, **213**, 442

Perugia pattern plate (Richard-Ginori), **274**, 275, 276, 449

Pesin, Harry, 221 n. 12

Petal pattern (Kresge), 126

Petalware glass (Macbeth-Evans), **78**, 167, 427

Petri, Trude, 428

Pfaltzgraff Pottery (est. 1811), 149, 183 n. 100

Pforzheim, Germany, 342

Phenix, Newton J., 24

Philadelphia Centennial Exposition of 1876, 122–23, 131, 156–57, 163, 200

Philadelphia Cooking School, 38, 336

Philadelphia Museum of Art, 337

Philipp Rosenthal & Co. (est. 1879/80). *See* Rosenthal China Corporation

Phoenix Glass Works (1820–70), 112

Picasso, Pablo, 459

Piccoli, Carlo, 281 n. 117

Pickard China Company (est. 1898), 138, 178; *Lillium Ornatum* pattern, **298**, 451

Pickard Studios (est. 1898), 144

Pickel, Susan E., 14

Pickle jar, covered, on stand with tongs, **31**, 422

Picnics, 26

Picture Cook Book, 95

Piece rates, 129

Pilgrim shape plate (Onondaga), **126**, 431

Pilgrim shape (Theodore Haviland), 195; coffeepot and demitasse cup and saucer, **145**, 433

Pillow Talk pattern plate (Noritake), **96**, 429

Pinch glassware (Russel Wright), 385

Pincio pattern (Richard-Ginori), 276

Pink Organdy pattern cup and saucer (Homer Laughlin), **70–71**, 426

Pink Vista pattern platter, plate (Mason), 203, **372**, 373, 462

Pintoria line (Metlox), 347; luncheon plate, **136**, 432

Pioneer covered butter dish (Gillinder), **328–29**, 452, 454

Piracy, 160

Pitcairn, William S., 201

Pittsburgh glass and pottery trade show, 235, 250, 286, 291, 293

Place settings, 25, 314, 417–18

Plain line (Catalina), **102**, 136

Plain covered casserole dish teapot (Hall), **75**, 427

Plain line (Bauer), 345–46

"Plascon" inserts, 460

Plastics Manufacturing Company, 151

Plastic tableware, 150–55, **152, 153, 154**, 343

"Plastic Tableware and Public Health," 151–52

Platinum Grey pattern (Knowles), 461

Platinum trim, 394

Platinum White pattern (Knowles), 461

Platonite line (Hazel Atlas), 460

Plaza Accord, 264 n. 30

Pleat and Panel pattern bread tray (Bryce Brothers), **112–13**, 430

Plum Blossom pattern (Red Wing), 343

Plume pattern cup and saucer (Glidden), **386**, 464

Plunger-cut glass, 159

Pollock, Jackson, 421

Pomona (New England), 163

Pompadour shape (Noritake), **262–63**, 447

Pompeii pattern (Richard-Ginori), 276

Ponti, Giovanni "Gio" (1891–1979), 276

Poppy pattern plate, cup and saucer (Doulton), **332**, 454

Poppytrail brand (Metlox), 466

Porcelain buttons, 108

Porcelaine G.D.A., 195, 198

Porcelain Masterpiece Series (Rosenthal), 243

Portmeirion Pottery (est. 1962), 210, 405, 468

Portugese tableware, 278

Porzellanfabrik Arzberg, 234, 402, 468

Porzellanfabriken Victoria, coffeepot, sugar bowl, and demitasse cup and saucer, **226**, 443

Porzellanfabrik F. Thomas, 235
Porzellanfabrik Langenthal, 450
Porzellanfabrik Victoria, 257
Post, Emily (1873–1960), 61
Post Exchange (PX) system, 231, 247, 248, 259, 442
Potters' National Union (PNU), 129
Potter's Wheel pattern plate (Denby), **405**, 468
Pottery, in America: 1880–1900, 117–23; before 1880, 103–10; anti-Japanese sentiment, 246–47; early fine china, 138–43; interwar years, 134–35; potter's strike, 123; 1900 to World War I, 123–30
Pottery Barn, 297, 322, 322 n. 23
Pottery, Glass, and Brass Salesman, 316, 332, 459; cover, **284**
Pottery, Glass, and Brass Salesmen's Association, 286
Pouyat factory, 454
The Practical Book of Furnishing the Small House and Apartment (Holloway), 59, 61
Prague trade fair, 232
Prairie Chicken pattern (Taylor), 467
Prairie Flowers pattern plates, cup and saucer (Wedgwood), 350, **351**, 457
Pratt Institute, 333, 342, 385, 427
Precedence champagne glass and plate (Fostoria), 168, **170**, 436
Premiums, 126, 129, 131, 167
Prepackaged food, 417
Prescut glass, 159
Presentation, 20, 32, 48
The President's House (Morgantown Glass Works), 413; iced tea glass, **317**, 452
Presley, Elvis, 266, 448
Pressed blanks, 159, 160
Pressed glass, **36**, **112–13**, 114, **116**, **158**, 327, **328–29**, 453–54; lead-crystal tableware, 178; nonlead, 115; patterned, 115
Press molding, 107
Prestige shape (Hellmich), 154, 389
Prestige shape juice glass and tumbler (Federal), **370**, 461
Price, J. Russell, 209, 441
Price Brothers teapots, 201
Price fixing, 127
Primachina line (Noritake), 261
Primastone line (Noritake), 261
Primavera shape cup and saucer and plate (Theodore Haviland), 195, **196**, 439
Primitive pattern tableware (Salem), 394, **400**, 467
Primrose pattern teapot, plate, cup and saucer (Theodore Haviland), **196–97**, 439
Prince, Jack (b. 1926), 406, 450, 451, 469, 470
Prince shape plate (Worcester), **202**, 440
Princess Grace of Monaco, 273, 438
Printed-and-filled patterns, 339
Priscilla shape (Theodore Haviland), 195, 439
Prize Design line (Jackson), 468
Processed foods, 57, 59
"Product Design—The Answer to Price Advance" (Hawe), 336
Profile line (Jackson), 468
Progressive designs, **233**
Progressive dinners, 67, 73, 81
Prohibition, 81, 83, 85, 87
Prototypes for a tea set with demitasse cup and saucer, **391–92**, 466
Prouty, Willis O., 136
Prutscher, Otto (1880–1949), 455
Public Health and Melamine Tableware, 152
Pukeberg Glasbruk (est. 1871), 266

Pull-downs, 129
Punch sets, 41, 45, **45**, 423, 436
Purinton Pottery Company (act. 1941–59), 368, 460; palm tree pattern, 385
Putzki, Paul (1858–1936), 189, 438
Pyramid pitcher (Indiana Glass Company), **50**, 424
Pyrex (borosilicate glass), **22**, 59, **78**, 160, 179, 336, 438
Pyroceram body, 150, 179

Quaker City Cut Glass Company (1902–26), 165
Quaker Oats Company, 131
Quaker Silver Company, 342
Quaking Grass pattern (Royal Copenhagen), 267, **268**, 448
Quant, Mary (b. 1934), 406
Quartz, 222
Queen Anne shape champagne glass (Morgantown Glass Works), **29**, 422
Queen Anne's Lace pattern creamer (Knowles), **380**, **381**, 463–64
Queen Elizabeth II, 318, 453
Queensberry, David (b. 1929), 210, 403, 468, 469
Queens Ware (Wedgwood), 214, 430, 458; *Concave* shape dinner plate and platter, **318**, 453
Quezal Art Glass and Decorating Company, 165
Quistgaard, Jens (b. 1919), **270**, 272, 449

R. F. Brodegaard & Co., 343
R. H. Macy & Co., 150, 300; *Art in Trade*, 337
R. Wallace and Sons (est. 1834), 39
Raby, Edward (b. 1863), 430
Raguenet and Maillard, 341
Railroad plate (Sterling), **127**, 431
Ranchero shape teapot and plate, cup and saucer (W. S. George), **44**, 423
Ranch house, 74, **77**
Rancho shape cup (Franciscan), **137**, 432
Random Harvest pattern casserole dish (Red Wing Pottery), **58**, 424
Ranney, William B., 293
Rapelje, Ronald D., 289
Raritan Formation, 105
Rath, Hans H., 444, 445
Ravenna pattern (Weatherby), 35
Ravilious, Eric William (1903–42), **318**, 453
Raymond Loewy Associates (act. 1944–61), 239, **240–41**, 242, 243, 391, 394, 402, 445, 446
Raymor Modern Stoneware covered casserole dish and pitcher (Roseville), 287, **288**, 451
Reagan, Nancy, 140, 413
Reagan, Ronald, 140, 339, 413
Reagan White House service plate (Fitz and Floyd), 144, 254, **255**, 447
Red Eva pattern cup and saucer (Ceramica), **275**, 450
Red Graphics pattern plate (Mikasa), **416**, 417, 470
Red Tower pattern plate, cup and saucer (Leigh), **361**, 459
Redware, 104
Red Wing Pottery (act. 1936–67), 46, 58, 342; *Anniversary* shape, **58**, 424; *Capistrano* pattern, **58**, 383, 424; *Caprice* pattern, 343; *Country Garden* pattern, 343; *Cylinder* shape, 404; *Desert* pattern, 343, **366**, 385, 460; *Fancy Free* shape,

343, **366**, 460; *Fondoso* line, 342; *Future* shape, **58**, 424; *Iris* pattern, 343; *Lanterns* pattern, 343; *Lute Song* pattern, **398**, 399, 467; *Plum Blossom* pattern, 343; *Random Harvest* pattern, **58**, 424; *Town and Country* line, **46–47**, 423; *True China* shape, **398**, 399, 467; *Tweed-Tex* pattern, 424; *Zinnia* pattern, 343
Reed & Barton (est. 1824), 342
Reeding, 456
Refgaard, Niels, 272
Refrigeration, 74
Refrigerator ware, **75**, 463
Regatta pattern, 289, 451
Regency Yellow flatware (Denby), 448
Regent shape (Shelley Potteries), 440
Regimental Oak shape plate (Spode), **55**, 55–56, 424
Regional cooking, 95–96
Reijmyre, 267
Reizenstein, Louis (1856–1947), 297
Relief-molded rims, 339
Renfre, Pierre, 451
Replacements, Ltd. (est. 1981), 419
Reproduction china, 413
Residential line (Northern), 385; covered vegetable and soup bowls, **153**, 434
Restaurant dining, 21
Retail tableware sales: buyers, 296–97; department stores, 300–307; open stock, place setting, and packaging, 314–22; specialty and jewelry stores, 297–300; store displays and selling techniques, 308–14
Reuss, Theodore, 289
Reuss, Theodore Jr., 289
Rhead, Frederick Hurten (1880–1942), 131, 132, 144, 149, 336, 348, 426, 460, 461; on American industrial design, 368, 370, 376, 385; *Century* shape, **68–69**; *Fiesta* ware, **72**, 424; *Riviera* line, **69**; *Swing* line, **70–71**
Rhinelander, Frederick, 103
Rhode Island School of Design, 333, 342
Rhodora pattern (Lenox), 341
Rhythm line (Homer Laughlin), 131, 132
Rhythm Rose pattern (Homer Laughlin), 132
Rhythm pattern (Seneca Glass), **172**, 437
Rice, Helen, 343
Richard-Ginori Società Ceramica Italiana (est. 1896), 273, **274**, 275–78, 413, 449
Richard, Giulio, 275–76
Richards, Harper, 287
Richards-Morgenthau & Co., 287
Richardson, H. H., 304
Rich cut glass. *See* Brilliant cut glass
Richelieu pattern (Hutschenreuther), 227
Ridgeleigh bread and butter plate and dinner plate (Heisey), **363**, 460
Ridgway, William (1788–1864), 108, 181 n. 13
Ridgway Potteries (act. 1955–73), 201, 389
Riedel, Claus Joseph (b. 1925), 446
Right in Your Own Backyard (Steck), 89
Riley, Armin, 297
Riley, Bridget, 406
Ringware (Bauer), 345; salad and bread and butter plates, **102**, 430
Rio pattern (Vernon Kilns), 456
Ripple pattern coffeepot, plate, cup and saucer (Leigh), **361**, 459
Riviera line (Homer Laughlin), 132, 189, 348; luncheon plate and covered casserole dish, **69**, 429

Robert F. Brodegaard & Co., 448
Robinson, Enoch, 114
Rochester Tumbler, 162
Rock crystal, 159, 327, 435
Rockingham ware, 108–9, 118, 119, 124, 326
Rockwell, Norman, **25**
Rockwell Silver Company (act. 1905–78), 160
Roe, Carl B., 160, 174
Roessler & Hasslacher Chemical Company, 345
Romance shape (Rosenthal), 405
Romance II shape champagne glass (Rosenthal), **242**, 446
Roman Coin pattern plate, cup and saucer (Sascha Brastoff), **94**, 428–29
Rombauer, Irma S. (1877–1962), 57
Romesnil, 192
Rondelet line (Fitz and Floyd), 252
Rondo pattern goblet (Kristalunie Maastricht), **191**, 439
Roosevelt, Franklin D., 140, 339
Rorer, Sarah Tyson (1849–1937), 38, 39, 336
Rörstrand Porslins Fabriker AB (est. 1726): *Blue Fire* pattern teapot, cup and saucer, 267, **269**, 448–49
Rose Amber glass (Pairpoint), 159
Rose China, 259
Rose Mandarin pattern, Chinese porcelain, 104
Rosemary pattern (Iroquois), 429
Rose Medallion pattern, Chinese porcelain, 104
Rosenfeld, Abraham, 257
Rosenfeld, Benedikt, 257
Rosenfeld, Louis, 257
Rosenfeld & Lazarus, 459
Rosenfeld family, 257, 264 n. 3
Rosenthal, Philip (b. 1916), 239, 242–43
Rosenthal, Philipp (1855–1937), 235–44, 445
Rosenthal-Block China Corporation, 239, 391
Rosenthal China Corporation, 223, 226, 235–44, 344, 355–56; *Bird Cage* pattern, **241**, 446; *Birds on Trees* pattern, **240–41**, 445–46; *Biscayne* pattern, 430; *Chantilly* pattern, 235, **236**, 445; *Classic Rose Collection*, 445; *Coin* pattern, **241**, 446; *Composition 'G'* shape, **242**, 446; *Continental* line, 239, **240**, 446; *Crystalline* pattern, **240–41**, 445–46; *Donatello* shape, 235, **237**, 445; *Eden* pattern, plate, **344**, 456; *Empire* pattern, **238**, 239, 445; *Exquisit* shape, 239, **241**, 391, 394, 446; *Flash Frisco* pattern, 430; *Flash Marking* pattern, 430; *Flash One* pattern, **99**, 429–30; *Flash* shape, 97, 99, **99**, 429–30; *Fortuna* shape, **242**, 446; *Iceflower* pattern, **242**, 446; *Model 2000* shape, 239, **240–41**, 391, 394, 445–46; *Motif* pattern, **242**, 446; niche marketing, 373, 376; *Oval* shape, 239; *Porcelain Masterpiece Series*, 243; *Romance* shape, 405; *Romance II* shape, **242**, 446; *Rosenthal Ivory* body, 235; *Royal Ivory* body, 235; *Sanssouci* shape, 235, **236**, 445; *700* shape, **242**, 446; *Spectra* line, 243; *Studio-One* concept, 446; *Thomas Ivory* body, 235; *Tulip Rays* pattern, **242**, 446; *Winifred* shape covered vegetable dish, **344**, 455
Rosenthal Ivory body (Rosenthal), 235
Rosenthal Porzellan, 97, 99
Rosenthal Studio concept, 239, 242–43
Rosenthal USA, 243

Rose Quartz pattern (Flintridge), 434

Rose Sachet pattern (Taylor, Smith & Taylor), 429

Roseville Pottery (act. 1892–1954), 287, **288**, 451

Rose (Wedgwood), 458

Rotary glass press, 167

Rougher, 159

Royal Bone China line (Noritake), 257

Royal College shape (Spode), 210, 404; coffeepot and cup and saucer, 212, **213**, 442

Royal Copenhagen Porcelain Factory (est. 1755), 267, **268**, 272, 448

Royal Crown Derby Company (act. 1890–1964), 210

Royal Doulton. *See* Doulton & Co.

Royal Dresden Porcelain Corporation, 281 n. 117

Royale line (Branchell), 154

Royal Ivory body (Rosenthal), 235

Royal Jackson China, 468

Royal Krona, 267

Royal Leerdam, 272

Royal Netherland lead crystal, **191**, 272, 439, 444

Royal Peacock pattern (Tharaud), 444

Royal Ruby color (Anchor Hocking), 167

Royal Tettau Factory. *See* Sontag & Söhne

Royal Winton, 289

Royal Worcester, 201

Royal Worcester Spode, 210

Ruba Rombic plate, salad plate, sherbet glass, and tumbler (Consolidated Lamp and Glass Company), 356, **357**, 459

Rubel & Company, 464

Rush, Benjamin, 83

Russel, Frederick Bret, 421

Russian pattern (Hawkes), 157, 159

Russian service. *See Service à la russe*

Rutgers University, 333

Rutledge pattern (Lenox), 93, 341

S. Pearson and Son, 210

S. S. Kresge Company, 126, 321, 322

Saarinen, Eliel (1873–1950), 338

Safedge, 165, 172

Saggers, 134

Sainte-Anne Glassworks. *See* Cristalleries de Baccarat

Saint-Louis, 192

Saint Raphael shape teapot, demitasse cup and saucer and luncheon plate (Theodore Haviland), 195, **196–97**, 439

Sakier, George (1897–1988), 174, 177, 336, 345, 436, 437, 452

Salads, Sandwiches and Chafing-Dish Dainties (Hill), 41

Salamander Works, 107

Salamina pattern chop plate (Vernon Kilns), **138**, 432

Salem China Company (est. 1898), 79, 126, 348, 349, 457; *Cadet Series* pattern, **302–3**, 452; *Victory* shape, **302–3**, 452

Salem Pottery Company, 131

Salesmen, 285–86

Salt-glazed stoneware, 103, **104**

Salviati Glass Works (est. 1877), **273**, 449

Samarkand/Arabesque pattern (Denby), **405**

Sandalwood pattern tea and coffee set (Franciscan), 41, **42–43**, 423

Sandblasting, **375**, 385, 436, 463

Sande, Rhoda, 310

Sanders, Morris B., 457

Sandwich glass, 114

Sandwich Manufacturing Company. *See* Boston and Sandwich Glass Company

Sanssouci shape plate and cup and saucer (Rosenthal), 235, **236**, 445

Sapphire pattern (Flintridge), 434

Sapphire shape plate, cup and saucer (Ridgway), 389, **391**, 466

Sascha Brastoff Inc. (act. 1948–73), **94**, 428–29

Savliati & Co. (est. 1877), **273**, 449

The Savoy Cocktail Book, 85, 87

Scammell China Company (est. 1923), 125

Scandinavian tableware, 385; glass, 167; pottery, 265–72; stoneware, **271**, 449

Schneider, 192

Schramberger Majolikafabrik (est. 1912), 228, **229**, 444

Schreckengost, Donald (b. 1911), 132, 149, 349, 376, 377, 434, 457, 463

Schreckengost, Viktor (b. 1906), 394; *Free Form* shape and *Primitive* pattern, **400**, 467

Schuck, Charles, 167

Schumann Bavaria, 280 n. 108

Schumann China Corporation, 223, 280 n. 108

Schwartz, Judith, 264 n. 3

Sculptural work, 122

Seal, Trish, 468

Sears, Roebuck & Co., 35, 79, 131, 302, 321, 385, 427, 432

Sea Spray pattern casserole dish (Stetson), **372**, 462

Sebring, Charles Leigh (1885–1970), 360, 459

Sebring, Frank A. (1865–1936), 360

Sebring Brothers, 183 n. 74

Sebring Pottery Company (act. 1887–1940s?), 344, 360–62, 362

Secrest, Philip, 464

Sedan pattern (Morimura), 257

Seeds pattern teapot (Knowles), **380**, **381**, 463–64

Seeney, Enid, 466

Segal, Carole, 297

Segal, Gordon, 297

Seger Institute for Ceramic Research, 257

Seibel, Ben (1918–85), 149, 427, 429

Seiler, 192

Seliger, Charles, 462

Semiautomatic feeder, 167

Seneca Glass Company (act. 1891–1983), 169, 172, 362; *Moderne* pattern, **162**, 437; No. 467 goblet, **172**, 437; *Rhythm* pattern, 437

Service à la russe, 27, 30, **30**, 38

Service plates, 408

Serving cart, 61, 63

Seto, Japan, 245

Seven Deadly Sins series (Steuben), **365**, 460

700 shape water goblet (Rosenthal), **242**, 446

Seventeen magazine, 142, 143, 310

Sèvres, 192

Sgraffito ware, 103

Shadowtone (Onondaga), **127**, 431

Shaker sets, 54

Shalimar pattern plate and cup and saucer (Franciscan), **96**, 429

Shanghai Wave pattern (Theodore Haviland), 453

Shape of 1937 shape (Theodore Haviland), 195; demitasse coffeepot, cup and saucer, **317**, 452–53

Shapiro, Laura, 38

Shasta pattern (Franciscan), 433

Shaving mugs, 118

Shaw, Mel, 394, 466

Shawl pins, 108

Sheila pattern glass (Waterford Glass), 218, **220**, 442

Shell and Seaweed jug (Griffen Smith & Co.), **24**, 422

Shelledge plate and cup and saucer (Onondaga), **384**, 464

Shell Edge shape (Wedgwood), 458

Shelley Potteries (act. 1925–66), 201, **203**, **204**, 205, 210, 440

Shenango China (act. 1901–92), 125, 144, 149, 195, 198, 239, 429, 433, 445, 465

Shirley, Frederick, 112

Shirley, William, 108

Shoemaker & Co., 272

Shopping malls, 320

"Short sets," 65

Showrooms and warehouses, 286–90

Sideboards, 22, 23, **23**; in the postwar era, 77; in the 1920s, 59, 61

Sienna pattern coffeepot (Midwinter), **406**, 468–69

Sierra bowl (Jeannette Glass Company), **73**, 365, 426

Sierra Madre pattern plate, cup and saucer, and coffeepot (Vernon Kilns), **347**, 456

Silhouette glassware (Bryce), 171

Silkscreening, 134, 166, 376, 422

Silvered glass (mercury glass), 114

Silver overlay, 140, 435–36

Silver-plated flatware, 26

Silver Spray pattern (Knowles), 461

Silver Wheat pattern (Taylor, Smith & Taylor), 429

Simms, Basil, 117

Simple Yet Perfect (SYP) shape teapot (Wedgwood), **330**, 454

Skellern, Victor (1909–66), 209, 216, 467

Skyline shape teapot (Southern Potteries), **18**, 421

Skytone pattern (Homer Laughlin), 132

Slater, Eric (1902–84), 440

Slip-casting, 433, 458

Slobodkin, Simon H. (1892–1956), 423

Sloth pattern goblet (Steuben), **365**, 460

Small beer, 83, 362

Smith, Thomas Carll (1815–1901), 118

Snack sets, 40, 41, **44**, 45, **46**, 52, **53**, 54, **89**, **368**, 423, 424, 428, 460

Snowflower pattern cup and saucer (Knowles), **380**, **381**, 463–64

Snow Glass (Paden City Glass), 465

Snow Star pattern (Lipper & Mann), 447

Snuff jars, 107

"Social body," 25

Social drinking, 81, 83–88

Socialized kitchen, 74

Società Ceramica Laveno, 276

Société Céramique, 272

Society of the Plastics Industry, 152

Soda-lime glass, 157, 163, 167

Soft drinks, 85

Sohn, Ernest, 464

Sol A. Stolaroff, 250

Solid-color bodies, 134, 136, 376, 394

Solon, Léon Victor (1872–1957), 279 n. 53, 336, 453

Solt, Charles, 140, 468

Sontag & Söhne, *Mahoning* pattern covered vegetable dish, 223, **224**, 443

Sottsas, Ettore (b. 1917), 470

Soup bowl on stand (Rosenthal), **238**, 445

South Boston Flint Glass Works (act. 1813–27), 112

Southern Potteries (act. 1917–57), **18**, 267, 368, 427

Sovereign Potteries, 463, 464

Soy Kee & Co., 278

Spaghetti sets, 54–55

Spanish goblet (Steuben), **345**, 456

Spanish tableware, 278

Specialty retailers, 297, 418

Specialty tableware, 54–56

Spectra line (Rosenthal), 243

Speeler, Henry, 109

Spencer, Ethel, 23, 33, 41, 94

Spode, 55–56, 56, 200, 201, 203; American import partners, 211–12, 214; backstamp, 211; *Billingsley Rose* pattern, 212, 440; *Buttercup*, 211, 412; *Centurion* shape, **203**, 211, 440; *Chelsea Wicker* shape, 203; *Christmas Tree* pattern, **55–56**, 212, 424; *Elizabethan* pattern, 212, **213**, 442; experiments in modernism, 210; *Fitzhugh* pattern, 203; *Gloucester* pattern, 203, **212**, 441; *Heath & Rose* pattern, **202**, 440; *Jewel* shape, **202**, 203, 211, 412, 440; *Kailess* shape, 424; *Kerry* pattern, **203**, 440; *Lowestoft* shape, 211, **212**, 413, 441; *Mansard* shape, 211; niche marketing, 373, 376; *Persia* pattern, 212, **213**, 442; *Regimental Oak* shape, **55**, 55–56, 424; *Royal College* shape, 210, 212, **213**, 404, 442; "Stone China" body, 441; *Walpole* shape, 440

Sprackling, Helen (b. 1896), 63

Spray painting, 134

Spring Garden pattern (Northern), 434

S.S. Normandie, 432, 453

Stackable dishes, **410**, 412, 470

Staffordshire, 420

Staffordshire potteries, 108, 210, 214

Stamford shape, 441; covered vegetable bowl (Newport Pottery Company), **206**, 440

Stangl Pottery (est. 1805/14), 136, 167, 267, **383**, 464

Stanhope cup and saucer (Heisey), **363**, 460

Starburst pattern plate (Fitz and Floyd), **254**, 447

Starburst pattern tea set, platter (Franciscan), 394, **397**, 466

Starlight pattern (Lenox), 341

Starry Night pattern plate, cup and saucer (Franciscan), 394, **396**, 397, 466

Star shape (Federal), 343

Starter sets, 77, 315

Stauder pattern cup and saucer (Royal Copenhagen), **268**, 448

Steak knives, 100 n. 19

Steck, Harold Wallis, 89

Stemware, 87; annealed, 191; filament stem, 436; machine-blown, 272

Stephens, James P., 124

Stephens, Tams & Co. *See* Greenwood Pottery Company

Stepped Edge Service (Lenox), **141**, 433

Sterling China (est. 1917), 125

Stern, Jewel, 95, 97

Stern Brothers, 316

Stetson, Joseph W. (1898–1977), 154

Stetson, L. B. (c. 1890–1931), 154

Stetson, Philip R. (b. 1936), 155

Stetson Chemical, 155

Stetson China Company (act. 1919–66), 154–55, **372**, 373, 462

Steuben Glass Works (est. 1903), 162, 165, 345, 362; *Chantilly* pattern, **156**, 435; *Lust* pattern, **365**, 460; No. 138 bonbon dish, **345**, 456; No. 6333

goblet, **345**, 456; No. 6395 goblet, **345**, 456; overhaul of marketing strategy, 265, 362; *Seven Deadly Sins* series, **365**, 460; *Sloth* pattern, **365**, 460; *Spanish* goblet, **345**, 456
Steubenville Pottery Company (act. 1879–1959), **65**, 349
Stevens & Williams, **156**, 434–35
Stiegel, William Henry (1729–85), 110
Stoke-on-Trent Government Science and Art School, 336
Stoke-upon-Trent, 211, 420
"Stone China" body (Spode), 441
Stonehenge shape (Midwinter), 210, 405; side plate, coffeepot, plate, cup and saucer, **209**, 441
Stoneware, 105, **118**, 210, 420; factory-produced, 404–5; salt-glazed, 103, **104**; Scandinavian, **271**, 449
Stoneware line (Noritake), 261
Stratford shape chop plate (Worcester), **202**, 439–40
Stratoware (Universal Potteries), **76**, 77, 385, 427
Straub, Paul (1865–1959), 226–27
Straub, Walter J. (1874–1953), 226
Streamline shape (Salem), **349**, 457
Street, A. D., 463
St. Regis American Porcelain (Ebeling & Reuss), 289
Studio concept, 239, 242, 243, 404
Studio-Haus, 243
Studio-Line (Rosenthal), 239, 242, 243, 430
Studio-One concept (Rosenthal), 446
Studio Potter shape (Metlox), 404; chop plate and coffeepot, **411**, 470
Studio Year Book, 423, 437, 449, 457
Stupell, Carole (1905–97), 40, **40**, 191, 297, 310, 432, 449
Stupell, Keith, 444
Stylecraft brand (Midwinter), 389, **390**
Suburban life, 73–81, 89
Sugihara, Kyuichi, 261
Sugihara, Tomiyasu, 251
Sullivan, Louis (1856–1924), 165
Sundial covered casserole dish (Hall), **75**, 426
Sunglow pattern plates (Hall), **373**, 462
Sunray pattern tea set (Shelley Potteries), **204**, 440
Suntone pattern (Homer Laughlin), 132
Superba pattern goblet (Morgantown Glass Works), **177**, 438
Suppers, 63
Supremacy shape cup and saucer, chocolate pot, and sugar bowl (Bohemia Keramische Werke), **225**, 443
Surrealism, 469
Susie Cooper Pottery (act. 1929–80), 210, **408**, 469
Süssmuth, 272
Swanson & Sons, 92
Swedish glass, 265–67, **266**, 448
Swedish movement, 385
Sweet Home Soap, 126
Swing line (Homer Laughlin), 132, 362; coffeepot, creamer, and sugar bowl, cup and saucer, **70–71**, 426
Symmetry shape platter (Johnson Brothers), **28**, 29, 422
Syracuse China (est. 1966), 124, 125, 138, 166. *See also* Onondaga Pottery
Syracuse Museum of Fine Arts, Ceramics National Exhibition, 464, 465

T. Furnival & Sons (act. 1851–1968), 122
T. G. Hawkes & Co. (act. 1880–1962), 157, 327, 434

Tables, dining, 22
Table Service (Allen), 38–39, 81
Table Service for the Hostess (Tipton), 41
Table setting, 20; displays, 309–10; scientific, 38–39; simplification of, 144
Tabletop style books, 39
Tableware: American style, 376–85; brand awareness and the rise of advertising, 315–22; casual trend, 404; colonial revival designs, 349–53; color craze, 344–49; craft aesthetic, 385; demand for traditional design, 412–14; design in the 1960s, 400–402; effect of dishwashers on, 376; exotica, 365–68; as fashion, 418; fine china, 394–400; the gilded age, 325–31; increased consumer awareness, 400–414; industrially produced, 13–14; influence of clothing fashions in 1960s and 1970s, 406; innovation in 1940s and 1950s, 385–94; interwar years, 64–65, 332–68; matching sets, 25–26; at midcentury, 93–94; new approaches to surface decoration, 405–12; Nordic lines, 385; novelties, 37, 41; packing and shipping, 315; retail selling, 296–322; specialty, 30, **31**, 54–56; western theme, 385; wholesale trade, 285–95; World War II and beyond, 77–81, 368–400
Tahiti pattern plate, cup and saucer (Cavitt-Shaw), **44**, 423
Tait, Jessie (b. 1928), 210, 441, 465, 468
Taiyo Trading Company, 249
Tajimi Company, 249
Takahito Mikasa, Prince, 250
Takito, Ogawa & Co., 249
Talc clay body, 136
Tamac salt and pepper shakers, plate, soup bowl, tumbler, barbecue cup and saucer (Tamac), **398**, 399, 467
Tams, James (1845–1910), 125
Tams, William (1822–66), 124
T & V brand (Vogt & Dose), 190
Tango shape (Homer Laughlin), 426
Tanjeloff, Julio, 243
Tankard sets, 431
Tank furnaces, 157
Target, 322, 418
Tariff Act of 1824, 110, 112
Tariffs, 117, 123, 180, 185–86, 199, 200, 207
Tassie, John M. (b. 1917, act. at Lenox China 1942–76), 141, 144, 267, 289, 325, 336, **342–43**, 371
Tatman's, 297
Tatman's, 297
Taylor, James, 109
Taylor, Smith & Taylor (act. 1899–1982), 349, 370
Taylor and Speeler, 119
Taylorism, 39
Taylorton shape bread tray (Taylor, Smith & Taylor), **98**, 99, 429
Tea and coffee services, 41, **42–43**, 66
Teacups, 40
Tea dances, 86
Teague, Walter Dorwin (1883–1960), 233, 336, 362, 437, 467
Tea parties, 40
Tea Room goblet and pitcher (Indiana Glass Company), 50, **51**, 424
Tea Rose pattern (Homer Laughlin), 131
Tea set, Margarete (Grete) Heymann-Marks, 357, **358–59**, 459
Technological improvements, 127, 129, 134
Teema line (Arabia), 448
Television, 21, 91–92, 376

Television parties, 91
Temperance movement, 83
Tempered glass, 191
Tempest, M., 117
Temperware (Lenox), 141, 171, 405, 468
Temple shape (Lenox), 452
Terano, Shunzo, 447
Terrace cup and saucer plate, goblet, champagne glass, tumbler, and juice glass (Duncan & Miller), **43**, 423
Terrace line (Lenox), 339; covered casserole dish, **141**, 433
Tetard, Jean, 441
Texas pattern (Baccarat), 192
Texas celery vase (United States Glass), **328**, 454
Textiles, 383
Textured surfaces, 276
Thanksgiving dinners, 25
Tharaud & Son. *See* Justin Tharaud & Son
Tharaud Designs, 444
Theme shape (Homer Laughlin), 132
Theodore Haviland & Co. (est. 1893), 190, 193, 195, 198; *Astoria* pattern, **197**, 439; and Castleton China, 144, 145; *Ebb Tide* pattern, **196**, 439; *Ile de France* body, 195; ivory-colored body, 195; *Marseille* bowl, **187**, 438; *Meadow Lace* pattern, **196**, 439; *Nicole* pattern, 195, 453; 1937, 195; *Pilgrim* shape, **145**, 195, 433; *Primavera* shape, 195, **196**, 439; *Primrose* pattern, **196–97**, 439; *Priscilla* shape, 195, 439; *Saint Raphael* shape, 195, **196–97**, 439; *Shanghai Wave* pattern, 453; *Shape of 1937* shape, **317**, 452–53; U.S. sales, 186, 187, 327
Theresienthal Glassworks, 281 n. 117
Third Reich, 231
Thomas, Anna, 96
Thomas, Jerry, 85, 87
Thomas and Ens. *See* Rosenthal China Corporation
Thomas Ivory body (Rosenthal), 235
Thomas Maddock's Sons Company, 124, 125, 431
Thomas Till & Sons, **121**, 430–31
Thomas Webb & Co. (est. ca. 1835), 435
Thompson, George E., 211, 217, 233
Thompson, Harry, 211
Thompson, John F., 117
Thompson, Sidney E. (1881–1958), 56, 211–12, 440, 441
Thorley, Joseph Palin (1892–1987), 336, 360
Thorpe, Dorothy C. (1901–89), 373, 385, 429, 436
Thorpe, George A., 463
Thorpe, Richard C., 463
Three-Step line (Lenox), 339; plate and cup and saucer, **141**, 433
Tiempo pattern pitcher, teapot (Franciscan), **348**, 456, 457
Tierra pattern tea set (Block), **277**, 405, 450
Tiffany, Louis Comfort (1848–1943), 456
Tiffany & Co. (est. 1837), 39, 141, 159, 163, 297, **299**, 435, 448, 452
Tiffany Studios (act. 1892–1938), 162, 165, 345, 362
Tiffin Glass (act. 1888–1984), 169, **177**, **346**, 463
Time-Life International, 207
Tipton, Edna Sibley, 41
Tirschenreuth & Co. (est. 1838), 226–27, 234
Toddy sticks, 118
Toilet articles, 122
"Tom and Jerry" sets, 37, 87
Tomita, Urasaburo, 264 n. 8, 447

Tomorrow's Classic shape (Hall), 389; coffeepot, **390**, 465; pitcher, sauceboat, and ladle, **373**, 462
Topaz pattern (Flintridge), 434
Torse service, 454
Towle Manufacturing Company (est. 1882), 27, 342
Town and Country line (Red Wing Pottery), 41, 389, 462; teapot, creamer, cruet, salt and pepper shakers and syrup jug, **46–47**, 423
Town & Country shape coffeepot and cup and saucer (Flintridge), **147**, 434
Trade Expansion Act, 199
Trademarks, 183 n. 111, 190, 195
Trade shows, 291–95
Trade unions, 129, 200
Tralee pattern glass (Waterford), 219, **221**, 442
Transfer printing, 107, 119, 120, 140, 326
Transition shape (Block), 406; platter, coffeepot, and cup and saucer, **277**, 450
Tray and pair of glasses, wood and glass, Hispanic motifs, **366–67**, 460
Treasures of Tutankhamen, 408
Trees and Figures pattern (Wedgwood), 458
Trenton, New Jersey, 108–10
Trenton China Company (act. 1859–91), 125
Trenton School of Industrial Art, 333
Trent pattern (Noritake), **248**
Tressemanes, Emilien, 186
Tressemanes & Vogt (act. 1891–1919), 438
Treu, Howard, 451
Tricorne shape creamer, sugar bowl, coffeepot, plate, and cup and saucer (Salem), 348, **349**, 457
Trio pattern plate (Franciscan), **348**, 457
Tri-Tone pattern (Hall), 389; pitcher, sugar bowl, and covered pitcher, **378**, 463
Triumph shape (Limoges), **303**, 362, 452; cup and saucer, chop plate, coffeepot, and demitasse cup and saucer, **303**, 452
Trophy images, **23**
Tropical Fish pattern plate (Vernon Kilns), **368**, 460–61
True China shape cup and saucer, plate, and teapot (Red Wing), **398**, 399, 467
Truman, Harry S., 140, 339
Tsutsui, Osamu (b. 1938), 261
Tucker, Thomas (1812–90), 107
Tucker, William Ellis (1800–32), 107
Tudor Rose pattern (Homer Laughlin), 131
Tulip pattern platter, *Losol Ware* line (Keeling & Co.), **334–35**, 454–55
Tulip Rays pattern (Rosenthal), **242**, 446
Tunnel kilns, 131–32, 133, 134, 259
Tupper, Earl S. (1907–83), 150, 434
Tupperware Corporation, 150
Turnbull, Gale (b. 1889–?), 336, 360, 361, 428, 432, 456, 459, 461
Tuscan China, 289
Tuska, M. B., 249
Tuska Merchandise Company, 249
Tutankhamun pattern (Fitz and Floyd), 254
TV dinner, **91–92**
TV trays, 21
TV-tray tables, 91, 92
Tweed-Tex pattern (Red Wing Pottery), 424
"200" Series line (Metlox), 347

Uglav, Helena, **416**, 470
Ulrich, Charles, 119, 181 n. 63

Ultra California line (Vernon Kilns), 456
Ultra shape plate, cup, and saucer (Leigh), **361**, 362, 459
"Ultra" shape (Vernon Kilns), **369**, 461
Umbertone body (Leigh), 360
Underglaze blue, 454
Underglaze decorations, 327
Underwood-Sherman Tariff, 199
Uniform wage scale, 129
Union Carbide, 150
Union Flint Glass Company (act. 1826–44), 115
Union Glass Works (act. 1854–1924), 162
Union Porcelain Works (act. 1863–ca. 1922), **31**, 118, 122
United China & Glass Company (act. 1850–after 1950), 250, 446
United Glass Bottle Manufacturers, 179
United States Glass Company (act. 1891–1938), 295, **328**, 343, 430, 454, 456
United States Porcelain Works, 119
United States Potters' Association (est. 1875), 109, 117, 122, 127, 129, 135, 149, 246, 365; Art and Design Committee, 144; First National Dinnerware Exhibit, 376
United States Pottery Company (act. 1899–ca. 1903), **107**
Universal Potteries (act. 1934–76), 17, **18**, 63, **63**, **76**, 126
Up-beat shape (Block), 450
Upholstery fabric, 383
Urban, Josef (1872–1933), 280 n. 108, 338
Urbino shape (Fraser's), **428**, 468
U.S. Commercial Company (USCC), 231, 232, 247
Utilitarian glass, 110, 160

Vaco Company, 267, 449
Vallerysthal et Portieux, 192
Valo glassware (Notsjoe), 448
Val St. Lambert, 272
Vannes-le-Chatel, 192
Variations on a Geometric Theme series (Wedgwood), **407**, 469
Varney, Hubert Haddon, 423
Vaupel, Louis (c. 1812–1903), 114, 163
Vebo, 266
Vecchio Ginori shape (Richard-Ginori), 276, 413; plate, **274**, 275, 449
Vedder, Katherine (Kay) L., 310
The Vegetarian Epicure (Thomas), 96
Venable, Charles (b. 1960), 17
Venetian glass, 273
Venice goblet (Nason e Moretti), **276**, 450
Vernon Kilns (1916–60), 136, 137, 347, 368, 394
Vetreria Artistica Valdesana, 275
Vianne, 192
Victoria pattern (Fostoria), 174
Victorian America: dining implements, 26; dining in, 20; gentility, 21–24; social meaning of food, 24–25; theatrical social life, 21
Victory Factory, Bohemia, **234**
Victory shape (Salem), 362; coffeepot, sugar bowl and creamer, **302–3**, 452
Vienna pattern plate (Buffalo), **128**, 431
Villeroy & Boch (est. 1836), 233, 234, 445
Vintage silverplated flatware, 26
The Virginian plate (Lenox), **67**, 140, 339
Virtual tableware, 418
Vision line (Fostoria), 178
Visser, Margaret, 21
Vista pattern (Mason), 203, 412

Vitreous tableware, 149
Vitrified China Manufacturers Association, 151–52, 332
Vogt, Charles (d. 1886), 186
Vogt, Charly, 186
Vogt, Gustav (1849?–1937?), 186
Vogt, John (1815–1906), 186
Vogt, Klaus, 243
Vogt & Dose (act. 1840–1931), 186, 187, 190, 226
Vogue pattern glass (Tiffin), **177**, 437–38
Vogue shape tea set (Shelley Potteries), **204**, 205, 440
Von Nessen, Walter (1889–1943), **363**, 460

W. H. Grindley & Co. (est. 1880), 203
W. R. Midwinter (act. 1910–87), 209, 210, 389, 403; *Fashion* shape, 389, **390**, 465; *Fine* shape, 403, **406**, 468–69; *Flowersong* pattern, **209**, 405, 406, 441; *Nature Study* pattern, **390**, 465; *Sienna* pattern, **406**, 468–69; *Stonehenge* shape, **209**, 210, 405, 441; *Stylecraft* brand, 389
W. S. George Pottery Company (act. ca. 1900–ca. 1960), **44**, 356, 423
W. T. Copeland & Sons (est. 1770). *See* Spode
W. T. Grant Company, 131
Wadsworth, John William (1879–1955), 457
Waertsila Corporation, 272, 448
Wagner, Winifred Williams (1897–1980), 455
Wagon Wheel plate and dessert bowl and underplate (Frankoma Pottery), **89**, 91, 428
Waldorf-Astoria Hotel, 64
Wallace China Company, **89**, 428
Wal-Mart, 418
Walpole cocktail glass (Morgantown Glass Works), **169**, 436
Walpole shape (Spode), 440
Walters, William T., 163
Waltersperger, 192
Walton, Sam, 418
Wanamaker's, 160
Wanamaker's, New York, **308**
Wardle Art Pottery, 336
Washington Wakefield plate (Lenox), **67**, 339, 353
Waterford Flint Glass Works (act. 1784–1851), 218
Waterford Glass, 207, 218–21, **220**, 413, 442
Waterford Glass Group (est. 1948), 210
Watertown Manufacturing Company, 151
Watkin, Bertram, 431
Waugh, Sidney (1904–63), 362
Wedding-gift giving, 30, 32, 97, 311–13
Wedgwood. *See* Josiah Wedgwood & Sons
Wedgwood, Barbara Boyd (b. 1929), 203, 278, 295, 296, 300
Wedgwood, Clement Tom (1907–60), 214
Wedgwood, Hensleigh (1908–91), 216, 300
Wedgwood, Josiah I (1730–95), 422, 467
Wedgwood, Kennard (1873–1950), 214, 216
Weil, Max, 385
Wellesley shape (Wedgwood), 203, 458
Wells, J. M. Jr., 149
Wells, Joseph M., 246
Wells, Joseph III, 133

Wells, W. Edwin (1863–1931), 123, 131
Wells Art Glazes, 348
Wells Art shape (Homer Laughlin), 132
Werner, Lewis R., 280 n. 108
Wesp, George, 244 n. 13
Westchester shape (Fostoria), 174; cordial glass and wineglass, **170**, 436
Western theme, 385
Westerwald Prize, 430
Westinghouse, 138
"Westward Ho" pattern. *See* Pioneer
Westwind pattern (Lenox), 339
Westwood pattern tea set (Franciscan), **146**, 267, 433–34
Wheaton Industries, 179
Whieldon, Thomas (1719–95), 422
White, David, 442
White Clover line (Harker), 385; cup and saucer and covered pitcher, **379**, 463
White Flower pattern (Homer Laughlin), 131, 132
White House service, 140, 144, 186, 189; Harrison, 187, **188**, 438; Haviland, 193; Hayes, **194**, 439; Kennedy, 177, 412–13, 429, 452, 469; Lenox China, 339; Reagan, 144, 254, **255**, 447; table glass, 177
White ironstone, 109
White kaolin clay, 222
Whiteware, 109–10, **118**, 119, **122**, 124, 257, 326, 327
Whitney, Henry, 114
Whole foods cooking, 96–97
Wholesale tableware trade: salesmen, 285–86; showrooms and warehouses, 286–90; trade shows, 291–95
Wiener Werkstätte (act. 1903–32), 223, 455
Wiinblad, Bjørn (b. 1918), **242**, 405, 446
Wildflower pattern coffee set (Wedgwood), **401**, 469
Wild Poppy pattern coffeepot and chop plate (Metlox), 408, **411**, 470
Wild Rose glass (New England Glass), 163
Wild Rose pattern (Homer Laughlin), 131
Willets Manufacturing Company (act. 1879–1908), **139**, 327, 338
William Adams & Sons, 201, 210
William Adams, Inc., 190, 272
William Boch and Brothers, 108
William Guérin & Co. (act. 1903–21), 190
William H. Plummer & Co., 297
Williamsburg shape (Knowles), 353
Williams-Ellis, Susan, 431
Williams Sonoma, 322 n. 23
William Young and Company, 124
Wilson, Norman (1902–85), 442, 467
Wilson, Woodrow, 140, 144, 339
Wilson-Gorman Tariff Act, 123, 199
Wilton pattern (Tirschenreuth), 227
Winans, Mary Jane, 428
Winchester '73 pattern plate, casserole (Vernon Kilns), **89**, 91, 385, 428
Window dressing, 309
Wine, 83, 85, 95
Winfield Pottery (act. 1929–62), 385, **386**, 464
Winifred shape covered vegetable dish (Philipp Rosenthal), **344**, 455
Winquest, Robert, 251
Winsor Blue pattern, 457
Wirkkala, Tapio (1915–85), 403
Wirkner, Sigmund (act. at Lenox China 1900–10), 140
Wistar, Caspar (1696–1752), 110
Wm. S. Pitcairn Corporation, 201

Woburn pattern vegetable dish (Doulton), **332**, 454
Women: clubs, 40, 48, 52; magazines, 57; white urban, as arbiters of taste, 337
Women's Christian Temperance Union, 40
Women's Home Companion, 63
Woodland Rose (Northern), 434
Woodside pattern (Franciscan), 17
Woolworth's. *See* F. W. Woolworth & Co.
Worcester Royal Porcelain Company (est. 1751), 2–3, 94, 140, 200, 201; *Chantilly* pattern, **202**, 440; *Chinese Chippendale* pattern, **202**, 439–40; *Elephant* shape tureen, **118**, 430; *Prince* shape plate, **202**, 440; *Stratford* shape chop plate, **202**, 439–40
Workshop system, 127
World's Columbian Exposition of 1893, 159, 163, 165
Wormley, Edward J. (1907–95), 287
Wright, Mary (1905–52), 349, 379, 385, 463
Wright, Russel (1904–76), 14, 233, 336, 385; *American Modern*, 64, **65**, 349, 383, 423, 465; *Esquire Collection*, **380–81**, 465; *Highlight* line, **387**, 465; melamine, 150–51, **153**; *White Clover*, **379**, 463
Wrigley, William, 430

Yale shape stem, champagne glass (Morgantown Glass Works), **169**, 436
Yamato, 250
Yankee Doodle pattern (Noritake), **96**, 429
Yellowstone (Homer Laughlin), 131
Yellowware, 108, 109, 118, 124
Yorath, David, 468
Yorktowne pattern (Pfaltzgraff), 149
Young, Jennie J., 109, 118, 124
Young, William, 109

Zeh & Schenck, 289
Zeh, Ebeling & Reuss. *See* Ebeling & Reuss
Zeisel, Eva (b. 1906), 14, 41, 64, 171, **229**, 233, 444; Museum, 385, **388–89**, 389, 465; *Norleans*, 250, **251**, 446; *Prestige* glassware, **370**, 461; *Silhouette* glassware, 171; *Stratoware*, **76**, **77**, 427; *Tomorrow's Classic* line, **373**, 390, 462; *Town and Country* line, **46–47**, 423; *Tri-Tone* line, **376**, 463
Zembo Temple pattern plate (Thomas Maddock's Sons), 124, **125**, 431
Zinnia pattern (Red Wing), 343